VOLUME I

Islands of the Mid-M

Penobscot Bay

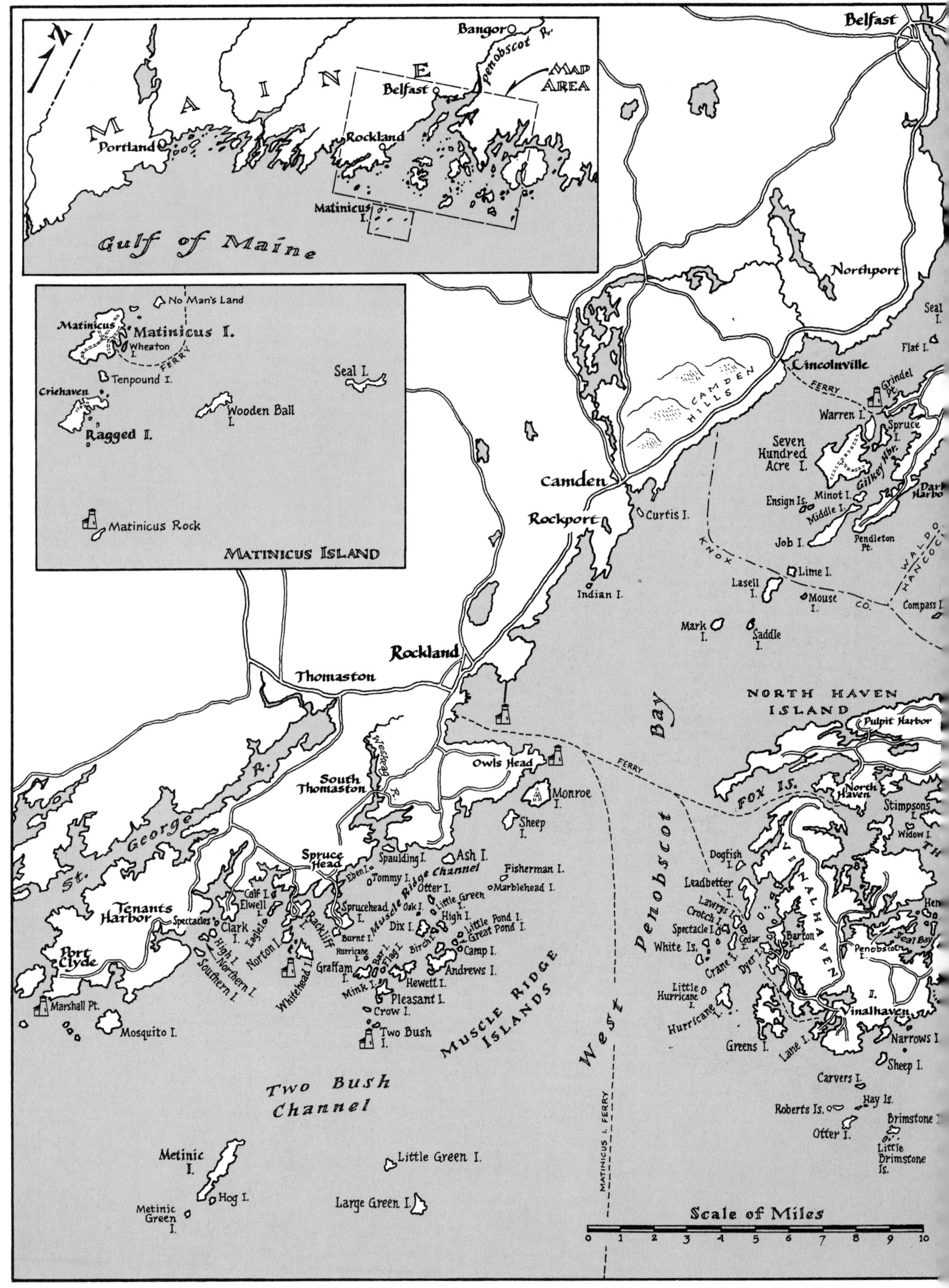

Belfast
Bangor
Penobscot R.
MAINE
Map Area
Portland
Rockland
Matinicus I.
Gulf of Maine
No Man's Land
Matinicus
Matinicus I.
Wheaton I.
Ferry
Tenpound I.
Criehaven
Ragged I.
Wooden Ball I.
Seal I.
Matinicus Rock
MATINICUS ISLAND
Northport
Lincolnville
Camden Hills
Camden
Rockport
Curtis I.
Indian I.
Rockland
Thomaston
St. George R.
South Thomaston
Weskeag R.
Owls Head
Monroe I.
Sheep I.
Spruce Head
Spaulding I.
Ash I.
Muscle Ridge Channel
Fisherman I.
Marblehead I.
Tenants Harbor
Port Clyde
Marshall Pt.
Mosquito I.
Two Bush I.
Muscle Ridge Islands
Two Bush Channel
Metinic I.
Hog I.
Metinic Green I.
Little Green I.
Large Green I.
West Penobscot Bay
Matinicus I. Ferry
Knox Co.
Waldo
Hancock
Warren I.
Seven Hundred Acre I.
Spruce I.
Gilkey Hbr.
Ensign Is.
Minot I.
Middle I.
Job I.
Pendleton Pt.
Lime I.
Lasell I.
Mouse I.
Mark I.
Saddle I.
Compass I.
North Haven Island
Pulpit Harbor
Fox Is.
North Haven
Stimpsons I.
Widow I.
Dogfish I.
Leadbetter I.
Lawrys I.
Crotch I.
Spectacle I.
White Is.
Cedar I.
Barton I.
Crane I.
Dyer I.
Little Hurricane I.
Hurricane I.
Vinalhaven I.
Vinalhaven
Penobscot I.
Seal Bay
Greens I.
Lane I.
Narrows I.
Sheep I.
Carvers I.
Hay Is.
Roberts Is.
Otter I.
Brimstone I.
Little Brimstone Is.
Scale of Miles
0 1 2 3 4 5 6 7 8 9 10

Islands of
Penobscot Bay
Searsport
Sears Island
Cape Jellison
Penobscot River
Penobscot
Ellsworth
Turtle Head
Castine
Bagaduce R.
Nautilus I.
Holbrook I.
Hutchins I.
Rogers I.
Hospital I.
ISLESBORO
Islesboro
ISLAND
Cape Rosier
Blue Hill
Brooksville
Blue Hill Falls
Union River
Harbor I.
Eggemoggin Reach
Western I.
Pond I.
Pumpkin I.
Birch I.
Barred Is.
Hog I.
LITTLE DEER ISLE
Beach I.
Scott Is.
Great Spruce Head I.
Sheep I.
Pickering I.
Eaton I.
Stave I.
Long I.
Bartlett I.
Scrag I.
Barred Is.
Butter I.
Carney I.
Sedgewick
Bear I.
Bradbury I.
Crow I.
Heart I.
Fling I.
Hardhead I.
Eagle I.
Brooklin
Blue Hill Bay
The Porcupines
Dagger I.
Bald I.
Chatto I.
Torrey Is.
DEER ISLE
Deer Isle
Sheepshead I.
Sheep I.
Little Babson I.
Campbell I.
Conary I.
Babson I.
Naskeag Pt.
MOUNT DESERT ISLAND
Burnt I.
Calderwood I.
Babbidge I.
Southeast Hbr.
Bear I.
Hog I.
Freese I.
Sunshine
White I.
Sheep I.
Harbor I.
Smutty Nose I.
South-west Harbor
Fort I.
Second I.
Andrews I.
Stonington
Mahoney I.
Pond I.
Crow I.
Sheep I.
Moose I.
Mark I.
Scott I.
Russ I.
Grog I.
Eastern Mark I.
Lazygut Is.
Opechee I.
Sheep I.
Eagle I.
Bass Harbor
Crotch I.
Green I.
Camp I.
Bold I.
Johns I.
Black I.
Scraggy I.
Farrel I.
John I.
St. Helena I.
Coombs Is.
Devil I.
Shingle I.
Shabby I.
Millet I.
Sparrow I.
George Head I.
Bare I.
Saddleback I.
Buckle I.
Orono I.
Phinney I.
FERRY
Phoebe I.
Ewe I.
Wreck I.
Spruce I.
Enchanted I.
Jericho Bay
Round I.
Hardwood I.
Ram I.
Round I.
Harbor I.
McGlathery I.
Merchant I.
HANCOCK CO.
KNOX CO.
Bills I.
Southern Mark I.
Hat I.
Nathan I.
Pell I.
Swans Island
SWANS I.
Burnt I.
Burntcoat Hbr.
Ringtown I.
East Penobscot Bay
Kimball I.
Isle au Haut
ISLE AU HAUT
Fog I.
Harbor I.
York I.
Marshall I.
Green I.
Baker Is.
Sister Is.
Heron I.
Scrag I.
Harbor I.
Crow I.
Duck Harbor
John I.
Frenchboro
LONG ISLAND
Great Duck I.
Little Spoon I.
Great Spoon I.
Western Head
Western Ear
Head Hbr.
Eastern Hd.
Eastern Ear
COUNTY
J. Luoma 97

For Paul, Cynthia, and Charlie

VOLUME I

Islands of the Mid-Maine Coast

(Revised Edition)

Penobscot Bay

CHARLES B. McLANE
CAROL EVARTS McLANE

Tilbury House, Publishers
Gardiner, Maine

The Island Institute
Rockland, Maine

First printing, revised edition: May, 1997.

10 9 8 7 6 5 4 3 2 1

Library of Congress Cataloging-in-Publication Data:

McLane, Charles B. and Carol Evarts
Islands of the mid-Maine coast / Charles B. McLane and Carol Evarts McLane.
p. cm
Originally published: Woolwich, Me. : Kennebec River Press, 1982.
Includes bibliographical references and index.
Contents: v. 1. Penobscot Bay
ISBN 0-88448-184-0 (alk. paper). — ISBN 0-88448-185-9 (obk. : alk paper)
1. Islands—Maine..Atlantic Coast—History. 2. Islands—Maine—Atlantic Coast—Description and travel.
3. Atlantic Coast (Me.)—History. 4. Atlantic Coast (Me.)—Description and travel.
I. McLane, Carol Evarts. II. Title
F27.A75.M39 1997
974—dc21 96-53524

Designed on Crummet Mountain by Edith Allard, Somerville, Maine
Editing and production: Jennifer Elliott, Jane Crosen, Ruth LaChance, Barbara Diamond
Layout: Nina Medina, Basil Hill Grapics, Somerville, Maine
Cover Separations and Film: Graphic Color, Fairfield, Maine
Printing (text) and binding: Maple Vail, Binghampton, NY
Printing (cover and jacket): The John P. Pow Company, South Boston, MA

Co-published by:
Tilbury House, Publishers
132 Water Street
Gardiner, ME 04345

The Island Institute
410 Main Street
Rockland, ME 04841

Contents

Illustrations

Maps and Plans

Preface to the Original Edition (1982)

The present study began innocently enough, as most things do, with wondering: wondering who lived on the smaller islands of Penobscot and Blue Hill bays as one sailed idly past them on summer days; or, in anchoring to explore a shoreline, found a cellar hole choked with alder. Why did they first settle there? What did they do? Why did they leave (or "remove," as the expression goes)? Who came later? This was an unpretentious exercise at the start. It costs nothing to wonder and little to ask. And when the asking led to some rudimentary records, in local historical societies and libraries, it was still a modest pastime for a foggy day. If there was ever to be a serious effort put into this endeavor, it would be at some future date. A preoccupation for retirement.

At a certain point the idea of piecing together the history of these islands acquired an urgency. Perhaps it was the challenge of the federal census in the Augusta archives where my wife and I found settlers recorded on islands we never suspected had been inhabited. Perhaps it was when, in a single week, telephone calls I made to three former islanders I hoped to interview brought forth the news that they had died within the month. The study would not wait until the illusory "retirement." It had to be done *now*. I still had to fit the undertaking into other commitments, but at least the project began gradually to take concrete shape. And the shape—such is the crippling mania for macro-study that afflicts some in my profession—emerged as nothing less than an inventory of all the once-inhabited, or habitable, islands in our normal cruising range: seaward and inward from Port Clyde to Bass Harbor Bar. I excluded from the start the five larger islands inhabited since Revolutionary times: Islesboro, Deer Isle, Vinalhaven, North Haven, and Swans Island; each of these has been the subject of historical research and all have had one or two volumes published about their early settlement. Under pressure of time I reluctantly weaned three other islands of intermediate size from my list: Matinicus, Isle au Haut, and Verona. Even with these eliminations the list is formidably long. Excluding ledges and outcroppings that could hardly qualify as "habitable," even by the standards of William Golding's Pincher Martin, there are some 275 islands in the area covered in this study, 123 of which were settled at one time or another and the rest used by settlers for haymaking, grazing, timber, weirs, offshore fishing "rights," and so forth. I note in passing, lest it be imagined I am padding my inventory, that the Maine Island Registry identifies for this same region approximately a thousand separate "islands."

I could understandably be charged with being greedy. Why didn't I concentrate on fewer islands where I had adequate information and leave the rest for future inquiry? I justify the fuller listing in this way: precisely by showing where information is meager and historical records inadequate, I hope to persuade others to improve on my history by exploring local sources at their command, especially that richest source of all—the dwindling number of elder citizens along the coast who know these islands from firsthand experience. It is immaterial whether new findings are immediately published or deposited in some safe place such as a local historical society; the important thing is that they be available to future students of the islands. I would, of course, welcome any corrections or supplementary information myself, for I hope to carry this study further, at a later date. (A communication will always reach me at P.O. Box 237, Brooklin, ME 04616).

In this spirit of pooling information, let me share with any who may be interested a catalog of the sources used in the preparation of the present study. I began with a questionnaire to island owners seeking all relevant information they had concerning the history of their respective islands, including the names of those who might know more. The response was encouraging—about sixty percent (only two explicitly declined to cooperate, in the interests of their privacy)—and many provided ownership data that led me to the county registries of deeds. The secondary questionnaires to non-owners, meanwhile, provided much information about residence on the islands at the turn of the century and promoted subsequent interviews that yielded additional detail. My debt to these senior Maine citizens, many of whom spent their childhood on the islands, is very great; a list of these informants is included in the Bibliography.

Apart from the firsthand testimony of former island residents, the next most helpful sources of information proved to be the federal census and the title record. The decennial census—though doubtless with some inaccuracies and with quite incomplete data before 1850, when only heads of families were listed—is the surest record of residence at a given time. Not all islands were listed separately, for many are counted as part of other communities and their residents undifferentiated from those of the township to which they belonged. Much work, therefore, remains to be done with the federal census to separate the island inhabitants from their fellow townsmen. The federal census, to the date of this publication, covers the period 1790 to 1900, excluding 1890 when all census records in Washington, D.C., were destroyed by fire; Maine census schedules are in the State Archives in Augusta. As far as title record is concerned, the deeds that make up this record are not of paramount importance in themselves, for recorded ownership does not necessarily signify residence, but where a deed explicitly refers to a settler or a farm, this can be taken as certain proof of habitation at a given date; many early deeds identify an island by referring to the person or family living on it at the time. The deeds for the Penobscot Bay–Blue Hill Bay region are recorded in the registries in Ellsworth, Belfast, and Rockland, and for the very early years in Wiscasset. I need hardly mention that it would require an army of researchers to exhaust the historical information contained in these voluminous records.

Other sources of information used in the present study include the following: maps and charts dating from pre-Revolutionary times to this century (a separate list of maps is included in the Bibliography, together with an indication of where the rarest of them may be found); items collected by local historical societies, often fragmentary but providing leads to additional data; genealogical material, such as the multi-volume compilation of unpublished notes by Dr. Benjamin Lake Noyes at the Maine and Deer Isle historical societies; private letters and records of former island residents (altogether too few of these, I fear, and I wish future island researchers better luck). My own visits to the islands have also helped to round out the story, especially where gravestones are still standing or cellar holes can be located. In time even an amateur learns to distinguish between a farm cellar, indicating year-round residence, and a mere foundation on the shore, suggesting seasonal residence by fishermen; one can even date a stone wall by the depth of deposit around it and the extent to which it has sunk into a low-lying glade between granite outcroppings. Finally, there are the published materials, ranging from scholarly articles in learned journals of the Massachusetts or Maine historical societies to items in back files of newspapers like the Rockland *Courier-Gazette.* These publications constitute the bulk of the annotated Bibliography at the end of this volume, and I single out here only one category of monograph, which should be the starting point for anyone concerned with Maine island history: the township studies of the region that touch on early island settlement—Cyrus Eaton's *History of Thomaston, Rockland, and South Thomaston*; John Pendleton Farrow's *History of Islesborough*; H. W. Small's *History of Swans Island*; George L. Hosmer's *Historical Sketch of the Town of Deer Isle*; O. P. Lyons' *A Brief Historical Sketch of the Town of Vinalhaven*; Charles A. E. Long's *Matinicus Isle: Its Story and Its People*; and Samuel Eliot Morison's *The Story of Mount Desert Island.*

A few remarks concerning the format of this study: (1) I have grouped the 275 islands, for the convenience of those interested in a particular cluster, in ten divisions and within each division have attempted to treat the islands in some logical sequence. The Index lists the islands alphabetically so that any reader may readily find the one he or she is seeking. (2) The name given the island is as it appears on current charts of the United States Coast and Geodetic Survey, whether or not this is the name in popular use or preferred by the current owner. (3) The island histories intentionally do not cover contemporary developments in any detail—they rarely go beyond the last recorded year-round residence—and the names of present owners are not indicated except where to omit them would be an injustice to history itself. (4) A tenderness for readers who may be resistant to footnotes, the usual baggage for research scholars, has prompted me to devise another method of showing sources: a parenthetical notation in the text, giving in short form the proper reference, which is readily identified in the Bibliography beside the full entry. At the same time an awareness, born of years of research, that nothing is more frustrating to scholars than the passing on of doubtful or unauthenticated "facts" has led me to cite these sources meticulously and to qualify with appropriate demurrer claims whose accuracy admits of some doubt.

A final word, and caution, concerning the islands and their owners—and I bring up the matter here not solely out of a sense of debt to the latter for their cooperation but because I am aware that a study like this, no matter how far it immerses itself in the past, will inevitably attract attention to the islands today and so jeopardize the privacy that island owners, like property owners anywhere, deserve. In my initial questionnaire I asked the owners whether they wished me to include some statement concerning visits to their islands. The answers were so varied that I quickly concluded no possible service would be accomplished by my attempting to instruct prospective visitors. A book in print is fixed; island owners change, or change their minds, so that an instruction good for today is not necessarily valid for tomorrow. Accordingly I make this general observation to readers in behalf of all island owners—and I make it in boldface type so that there can be no misunderstanding:

The islands are with few exceptions the private property of individuals, and no one should take for granted a right to disembark on any island (above high-water mark) without the explicit invitation or permission of the owner.

—Charles B. McLane
Brooklin, Maine

Preface to the Second Edition (1997)

The Preface to the original edition is left as written fifteen years ago. It explains the reasons for undertaking this enterprise of island histories (the initial volume has been followed by three others),[1] and it adequately indicates the sources consulted at that time.

A new edition of the original volume has been projected for some years. Its editor, Thea Wheelwright (who launched the Kennebec River Press in part to publish these volumes), is long retired; the volume is out of print and the facilities to reproduce it as it was written are dispersed. Beyond this, the capabilities my wife and I developed over two decades of island research have, I hope, matured to a point where we could provide keener insights into the past than when we were preparing the original volume. We have traveled farther; we have probed town records more zealously; we have searched more thoroughly the materials in the historical societies; we have interacted with other scholars in the field of Maine's maritime history.

The new edition, then, is a significantly enlarged version of the original. The format is much the same: an Introduction covering the Penobscot Bay islands[2] in the perspective of Maine's maritime history, followed by individual studies of some 250 islands, organized in nine geographic divisions: Matinicus and the outer islands; the western shore;

[1] They are, under the overall title *Islands of the Mid-Maine Coast*, as follows: Vol. II, *Mount Desert to Machias Bay*, 1989; Vol. III, *Muscongus Bay and Monhegan Island*, 1992; Vol. IV, *Pemaquid Point to the Kennebec River*, 1994. Vol. II, like the original volume, was published by Kennebec River Press; Vol III and IV were jointly published by The Island Institute of Rockland, Maine, and Tilbury House of Gardiner.

[2] The original volume covered the islands of Blue Hill Bay as well, some two dozen of them; these are omitted in the present edition since they were covered in a separate volume published in 1985 as *Blue Hill Bay* (Kennebec River Press)—in effect, a second edition of that portion of the original study.

Fox Islands—Vinalhaven, North Haven and surrounding islands; Islesboro and its islands; mid-Penobscot Bay islands; the Deer Isle division; Isle au Haut and neighbors; islands of the eastern shore; and the Swans Island division. New material has been introduced into nearly all notices, with many new residence, valuation, and genealogical tables, which, it is hoped, will engage the attention of those seeking more minute detail without inconveniencing less fastidious readers. The greatest dimensional change in the new edition is the coverage given to the larger islands which were omitted in the original volume, whose stated objective was coverage of only "the medium-sized and smaller islands." Isle au Haut and Matinicus, then, two critical islands all but ignored in the original volume, are treated here in some detail; the five macro-islands in the Bay—Deer Isle, Vinalhaven, North Haven, Islesboro, and Swans Island—are noted with, I hope, appropriate essays. (Among the larger islands in the Penobscot Bay region, only Verona, formerly Orphan Island, bridged twice to the mainland for many years, is omitted in this volume.)

I add a few remarks to the pointers set forth in the last two paragraphs of the original Preface. Regarding Point 3 (coverage of the islands only through the period of indigenous settlement), I am less fussy today on this point than previously; the principal *focus* of the volume continues to be local year-round settlement on or usage of these islands, but I do not now sign off peremptorily whenever a rusticator comes on the scene. Second, the source that gave such zest to the writing of the original volume (and perhaps to the reading of it as well) is now silenced: the aging community of individuals who grew up on the Penobscot Bay islands and so generously shared their memories. I have in any case kept from the first edition the fruit of those memories and left intact the identity of those informants from the 1970s. Finally, the caution in the final paragraph about the need to respect the privacy of island owners is no less relevant in the 1990s than it was fifteen or twenty years ago—perhaps even more so.[3]

This will be the last island history my wife and I compose together, for Carol died while we were on a vacation in Europe soon after this edition was completed.

—Charles B. McLane
Brooklin, Maine

[3] Many of the islands covered in this volume are now included—with their owner's permission—in the Maine Island Trail Association. Visits to these islands, and in some cases overnight stopovers, are permitted to members of MITA. Membership and the association's guidebook are available from the Maine Island Trail Association, P.O. Box C, Rockland, ME 04841.

Acknowledgments

My principal informants for the original edition of this volume, interviewed in the 1970s, are listed with brief identifications in Section 3 of the Bibliography; the listing is the same I used in the first edition, and I hope this is appropriate acknowledgment of their very considerable contribution to this volume.

I list below the persons who have provided me particular assistance in the preparation of the present revision:

On *Matinicus*—Clayton Young
In *Spruce Head*—C. William Colby
At *Owls Head*—Edward Coffin, Malcolm Jackson, and Luella Post
On *Vinalhaven*—Roy and Esther Heisler
On *North Haven* —Samuel and Eleanor Beverage
On *Islesboro*—Ruth M. Hartley, Ilene Boardman, and Ralph Gray
On *Deer Isle*—Clayton Gross, Genise Welcome, and Neville Hardy
On *Isle au Haut*—Lynne Mattingly and Harold VanDoren
On *Swans Island*—Dexter Lee
On *Long Island (Frenchboro)*—Vivian Lunt

VOLUME I

Islands of the Mid-Maine Coast

Penobscot Bay

Islands of Penobscot Bay in the Perspective of Local Maritime History

The object of this introductory essay is to focus attention on the role islands in the region under inspection played in the unfolding of local history. It is not the history of the region itself that concerns us, but rather the ways in which the islands were affected by, and sometimes influenced, the course of history in the Penobscot Bay area.

I pass quickly over the era of Indian habitation, not because it was unimportant—it lasted at least five thousand years, probably longer—but because our knowledge of it is still too fragmentary to allow anything more than preliminary hypotheses on Indian movements and behavior. There are periods in these millennia when even the middens are silent, suggesting there was migration away from the coast. But throughout most of this era, seasonal residence on the islands, as well as on the coastal shores and riverbanks, appears to have been the norm. The Indians came in the summer to fish because the harvest was abundant; in the winter months they left the coast and returned to the more benign interior to hunt. There is little evidence of warfare between these Indian nations or tribes. Resources were so plentiful that competition was unknown before the arrival of the European. Bruce Bourque writes: "Without agriculture, which did not extend into the Penobscot Bay area in prehistoric times, a band of Indians might not consider even their campsite worth defending in the unlikely event that another band should want it. Another suitable location was probably always available just around the next island, and movement was easy" (Bourque, "Bear Island").

European Discovery of the Penobscot Bay Region

The first Europeans to visit the region were the Italian, Spanish, French, Portuguese, and English explorers who followed Christopher Columbus and until the seventeenth century were still seeking the elusive "northwest" passage to the Orient. The Florentine Verrazano, sailing under the French flag, passed Penobscot Bay in 1524 and, according to Samuel Eliot Morison, named the three highest islands he saw—presumably Monhegan, Isle au Haut, and Mount Desert—after three teenage princesses of Navarre: Anne, Isabeau, and Catherine. In 1525 the Portuguese Estevan Gomez, sailing for Spain, rounded Mount Desert from the east, crossed Blue Hill Bay, and possibly sailed up Eggemoggin Reach and into the Penobscot River before leaving the bay via *Cap de Muchas islas*, now Owls Head (Morison, *Northern Voyages*, 311, 329). Other such voyages were made into the region during the sixteenth century, but not many, and few mariners kept accurate enough record of their observations to give us any clue to life on the islands beyond an occasional Indian encampment.

A resurgence of interest in European exploration along the shores of North America in the last decades of the sixteenth century led to several remarkable expeditions in our area in the first two decades of the seventeenth. The most famous was that of Samuel de Champlain, geographer for the de Monts expedition, which sought to establish a French foothold on the North Atlantic coast. Late in the summer of 1604, he explored the coast westward from the St. Croix River, where de Monts was to spend the winter. Champlain stopped at Mount Desert Island, which he named *l'Isle des Mont-déserts*. He continued outside Isle au Haut, which he named *Isle Haulte*, around the Fox Islands and into West Penobscot Bay past Owls Head and Islesboro and up the Penobscot River. He was now in the vicinity of the legendary jeweled city Norumbega that for half a century or more had been rumored to be—and had been even so described by overly imaginative mariners—up the Pentagoët (or Penobscot) River.

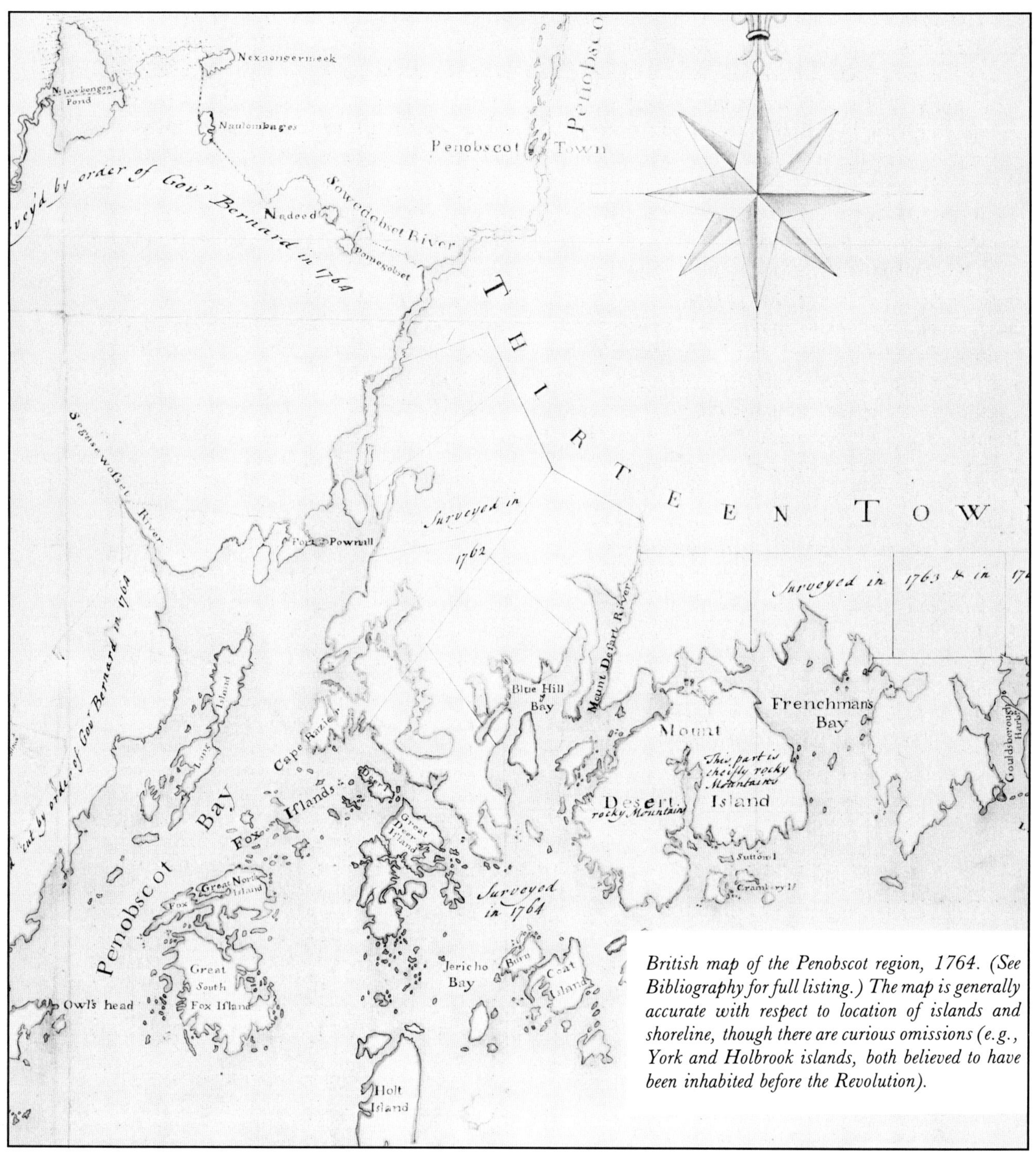

British map of the Penobscot region, 1764. (See Bibliography for full listing.) The map is generally accurate with respect to location of islands and shoreline, though there are curious omissions (e.g., York and Holbrook islands, both believed to have been inhabited before the Revolution).

Champlain sailed as far as the falls above modern Bangor, found nothing of Norumbega, needless to say, but did parley with friendly Indians before returning to the bay and continuing his explorations westward to the Kennebec. He did not mention settlements in his meticulous account of this expedition, but he did leave maps that show a number of the larger islands clearly and hint at many more (Morison, *Champlain*, 47–53).

Champlain was followed by other explorers, both English and French, during this era of intensifying rivalry between the two nations for control of the region. In 1605, when Champlain was making another westward probe along the coast in search of a more satisfactory site for a French settlement after a disastrous winter on an island in the St. Croix River, the Englishman George Waymouth spent several weeks in the Muscongus Bay region. He explored Monhegan Island, which he named St. George Island; the group farther toward shore presently called the St. George Islands, which he called Pentecost Harbor; and the St. George River up as far as the present site of Thomaston. The Waymouth expedition enjoyed cordial relations with local Indians during its first days in the region, but, in taking five Indian braves captive before it departed, left a legacy of ill will that was to plague English voyagers in the area for many decades to come. However, in London the information provided by the Indian captives stimulated interest in further exploration. An English settlement known as the Popham colony was attempted at the mouth of the Kennebec two years later, but it lasted no longer than its French predecessor at St. Croix.

Another short-lived settlement in the region was planted in 1613 by a French Jesuit named Father Biard, then living at Port Royal in Nova Scotia. The original intent was to establish a colony at Pentagoët (that is, at Castine—for Pentagoët was the Indian name of both the Penobscot River and the historic peninsula at the mouth of the Bagaduce). The party landed first on Mount Desert Island and was persuaded by friendly Indians, who knew Father Biard from an earlier visit, to settle there. An encampment was accordingly built and called St. Sauveur.[1] Within a few weeks of the Jesuits' arrival, Captain Samuel Argall of the Virginia colony, under orders to destroy any French settlements in territory claimed by England (which included Mount Desert), discovered the colony and dispersed or captured the hapless settlers. This may have been the first direct Anglo-French encounter in North America.

In 1614 Captain John Smith led another expedition from the Virginia colony to the New England coast, affirming English jurisdiction as far as possible in that era before the Plymouth colony. He stopped for some weeks at Monhegan, looking for gold and copper, but turned his men to fishing when he discovered the fisheries so much more extraordinary than the minerals. He, too, went as far as Pentagoët but found no encampment there. He did, however, mention "Indians fishing among the isles."[2] John Smith's description of the Penobscot Bay islands is worth repeating here, for it gives us an idea of how they must have appeared in the virgin days before the first settler's axe:

> But all this coast to Penobscot, and as farre as I could see Eastward of it is nothing but such high craggy Cliffy rocks and stony Iles, that I wondered such great trees could growe upon so hard foundation. It is a countrie rather to affright, than delight one. And how to describe more plaine spectacle of desolation or more barren I knowe not. Yet the sea there is the stangest fish-pond I ever saw; and those barren Iles so furnished with good woods, springs, fruits, fish and foule, that it makes mee thinke though the Coast be rockie, and thus affrightable; the Vallies, Plaines, and interior parts, may well (notwithstanding) be verie fertile. But there is no Kingdom so fertile hath not some part barren: and New England is great enough to make many Kingdoms and Countries, were it all inhabited
> (Smith, *New England*, 43).

The close of his panegyric makes clear Captain Smith's object: to bestir his Majesty's

[1] The location of St. Sauveur has been in dispute. Some say it was on the west side of Somes Sound at what is now called Fernalds Point; others maintain it was at Lamoine, north of Mount Desert Island.

[2] Bruce Bourque argues that for five thousand years or more Indians fished on the coast of Maine, their most ambitious catches, indeed, occurring some forty-five hundred years ago (the late Moorehead phase) when they harvested swordfish and other large species. When the first Europeans reached the shores of Maine in the sixteenth and seventeenth centuries, they were struck by the sophistication of Indian fishing gear—for example, weirs; scholars have been similarly impressed by the proliferation of fishing terms in Indian place-names (Bourque, "Fishing in the Gulf of Maine").

government in London to encourage settlement in New England. To prepare the way and to make the hoped-for settlers feel at home, the famous map Smith prepared during his expedition substitutes good English names for those he found locally in use along the coast: *Pembrocks* for Penobscot Bay, for example, *Lowmounds* for Nusket (Naskeag), *Hoghton's Iles* for Metinic and the Green Islands, and so forth (see Map 1614 Smith, in Bibliography, Part II). In a later volume Captain Smith amplified his nomenclature along the New England coast:

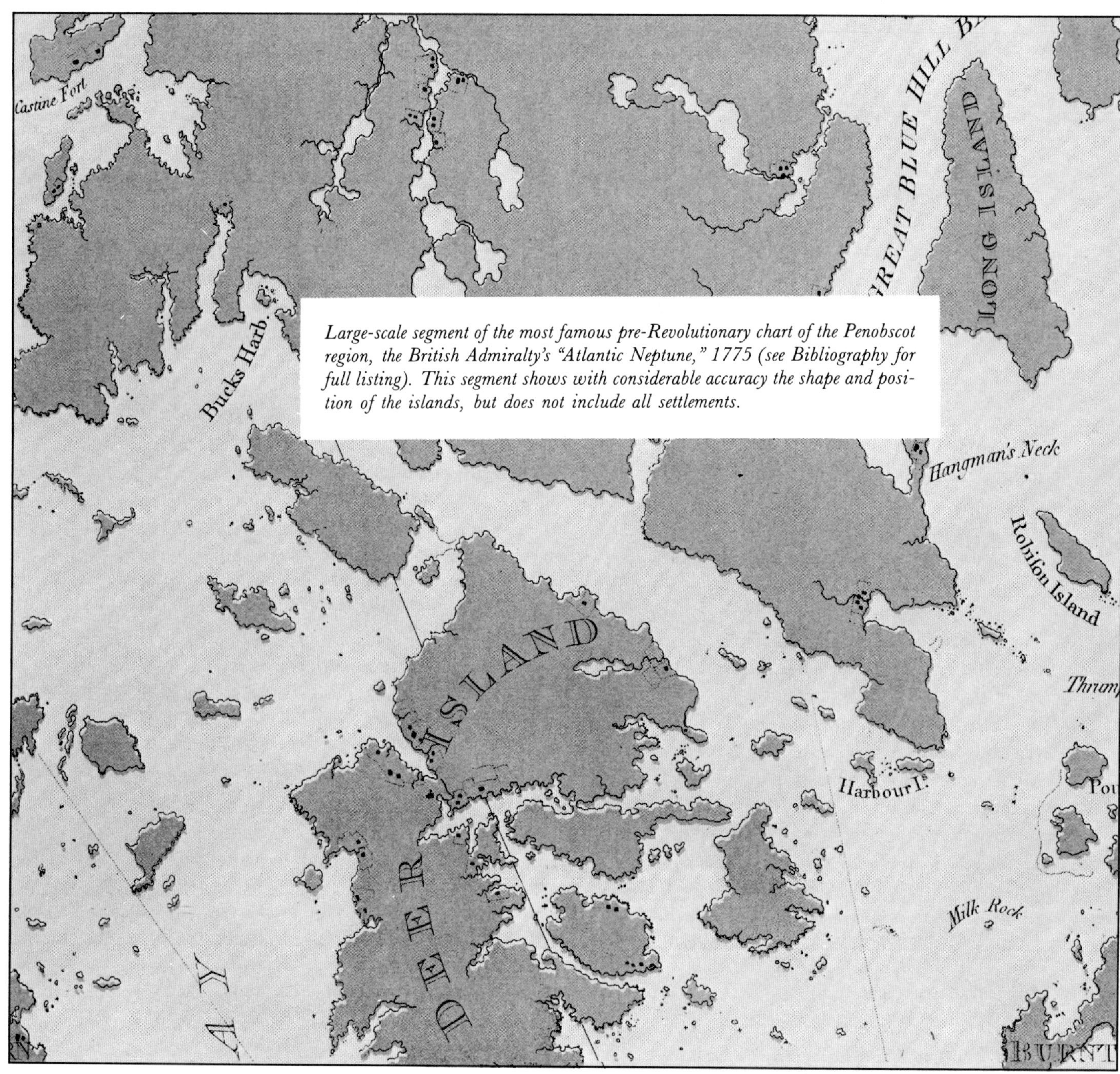

Large-scale segment of the most famous pre-Revolutionary chart of the Penobscot region, the British Admiralty's "Atlantic Neptune," 1775 (see Bibliography for full listing). This segment shows with considerable accuracy the shape and position of the islands, but does not include all settlements.

> Malicious mindes amongst sailers and others, drowned that name [New England] with the echo of Muscongus, Canady and Pemaquid; till at my humble sute, our most gracious King Charles, then Prince of Wales, was pleased to confirme it by that title, and did change the barbarous names of their principall Harbours and habitations for such English, that posterity may say, King Charles was their Godfather; and in my opinion it should seeme unmannerly presumption in any that doth alter them without his leave (Smith, *Advertisements*, 25).

None cared for Charles I as "godfather," as matters turned out, and most of John Smith's ingenious nomenclature became no more than an historical footnote—except, of course, for *New England* itself, which thanks in part to John Smith came into general use about this time.[3]

Early Settlement

The explorations of Smith, Argall, Waymouth, Champlain, and others are richly described in maritime histories of Maine and are part of the recorded opening of this region. They do not, however, shed much light beyond random nomenclature on the islands we are discussing. As far as any evidence of European settlement is concerned, most voyagers explicitly stated that they found none. "There were no settlements on the New England coast up to 1620," one author--ity on the matter bluntly stated some years later.[4]

This judgment is only partly true. There were no *permanent* settlements like the Plymouth colony to come, but there were attempted settlements like Popham's and St. Sauveur and, more important, seasonal fishing stations on the outer islands. Crude stone structures still in evidence on Matinicus in post-Revolutionary times are believed to date from the sixteenth century, when Portuguese and English fishermen, driven westward from the Grand Banks by storms or coming in search of fresh water and to dry their fish, remained long enough to build shelters. Father Biard found no residents on Matinicus in 1611, but he did note discarded English fishing boats on the shore. John Smith's enthusiastic account of the offshore fisheries in 1616 led to several temporary summer settlements on Monhegan in the following years (Rowe, *Maritime History of Maine*, 21). There were also residents and a fishing station at Damariscove Island off Boothbay before 1620. The earliest habitation then was on the outer islands; the coast itself was the "meyne," as Smith called it, and eventually Maine.[5]

No comparable settlement existed on islands closer to shore, and there were good reasons for this. For one, the outer islands remained ice free in winter; not so the islands nearer the coast, where huge ice floes tied up navigation for months at a time. Champlain, following the disastrous winter at St. Croix in 1604–05, wrote that no one should presume to understand the North Atlantic coast until he had wintered there, for "winter in this country lasts six months" (Morison, *Champlain*, 55). It was hardly true, as a regular thing, then or now, but the bitter St. Croix experience was much recounted in the century following and discouraged settlements near shore. Small wonder that, apart from Port Royal on the west shore of Nova Scotia, the French made their most enduring settlements in the New World in the comparatively benign St. Lawrence region, far from the ruthless winters of New England and the relentless tides of the Bay of Fundy. Meanwhile, we should remember that the early visitors to these shores were fishermen and when they discovered that cod was as plentiful around the outer islands in winter as in summer, they naturally tarried there, venturing among the shoreward islands only in the warmer months.

Another barrier to settlement of the shoreward islands was the hazard of encounters with local Indians. Although the Tarratines, who seasonally occupied many of the Penobscot Bay

[3] In addition to the anglicized names in our area noted above, John Smith proposed the following on his 1614 map and later versions of it. The original name, if shown on Smith's map, is in parentheses:

Matinicus group (Matinnack)—Willowby Island
Castine (Penobscot)—Aborden
Camden area (Mecadacut)—Dunbarton
Brigadier Island—Gunnells Island
Swans—Fines Island
Pemaquid (Pemmadquidd)—St. John's Towne
Manana (Monanis)—Manana
Note: This "barbarous" name somehow survived.
Isle au Haut—Sorico, later Martius Ile
Muscle Ridges—Gerrards Island
Owls Head—Point Travers

[4] Reverend Henry Thayer, Maine Historical Society, *Collections*, III: 2, 384.

[5] Williamson notes (*History of Maine*, I: 277) that although the name Maine (or Meyne) was generally in use by the early seventeenth century, the formal designation of the district was probably in honor of the English queen who had recently inherited the province of Maine in France.

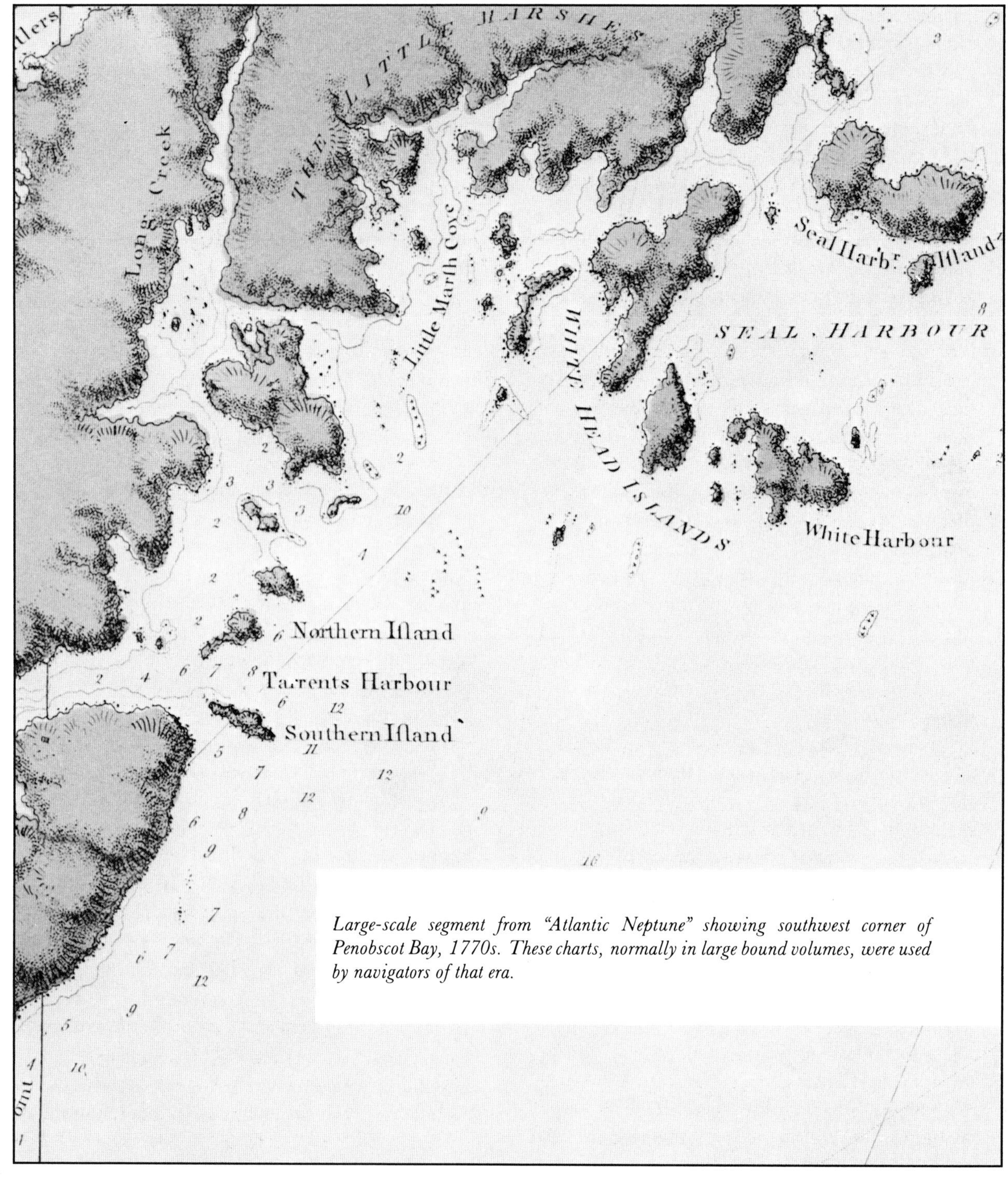

Large-scale segment from "Atlantic Neptune" showing southwest corner of Penobscot Bay, 1770s. These charts, normally in large bound volumes, were used by navigators of that era.

islands, were among the more peaceable of the North American "savages," their behavior was unpredictable enough to give pause to any Englishmen who thought to settle near them—Englishmen especially, it should be noted, for memories of Waymouth's capture of five braves in Muscongus Bay lingered. The French, it is true, cohabited more tranquilly with the Tarratines: John Smith acknowledged this as early as 1614—more than half a century before Baron de Castin arrived on the scene—in noting that the French "live with those people as one nation or family" (Smith, *New England*, 42). But for the English the inner islands were unsafe for settlement until the long arms of their government could protect them from Indian raids and reprisals. Nor were the outer islands always safe from Indian attack: one of the most famous island massacres took place on Matinicus as late as 1757—not without provocation, it should be said. Ebenezer Hall, the first "permanent" settler there, was murdered and his wife and children carried off after he persisted in burning over the nearby Green Islands to improve the hay, despite several formal protests by Indians who collected birds' eggs and grass on these islands.[6]

Henry S. Burrage (*Beginnings of Colonial Maine*, 393) has suggested another reason for the slow development of permanent settlements along the Maine coast (he was speaking of the entire coast, not simply the offshore islands). The leaders in Maine, he wrote, were "on the wrong side"—by which he meant that they were loyalists, not republicans—and this had a negative effect on the stability of the communities they sought to establish. "Neither they nor their promoters in England were inspired by the high ideals with reference to freedom, religion and governmental interests that drew to the shores of Massachusetts bay the Pilgrims and the Puritans." Noble sentiments by this nineteenth-century state historian—and, of course, he is quick to point out that later leaders in Maine gave proper expression to their democratic feelings—but barely germane to the purposes of this volume, since so little settlement was seriously attempted in our region before the eve of the American Revolution.

The principal reason for the absence of early settlement of the Penobscot Bay islands and the adjoining shores as well, except in a few fortified places like Pentagoët, was not primarily weather, Indians, or leaders being "on the wrong side," but the incessant rivalry between England and France for sovereignty over this sector of the New England coast. British and French claims, based on Crown grants, early explorations, and alleged "settlement," were invariably overlapping. French claims extended at one time as far south and west as the Hudson River; English claims included all of Acadia, that is, modern New Brunswick and Nova Scotia. As the overlap narrowed to a more plausible region of dispute, the islands with which we are concerned proved to be in the center of the disputed territory: the "ambulatory" boundary between French and English possessions along the New England coast normally fell between the Kennebec and St. Croix rivers. It was constant fighting over this boundary between the French and their Indian allies on one side, and the English and Bay Colony settlers on the other, that made safe settlement on the Penobscot Bay islands impossible. Thus permanent settlements are found in York, Casco Bay, and the Damariscotta region by the 1650s, and intermittent settlement is found even in the Muscongus Bay region by 1740; but no settlements of any significance, except at Pentagoët, reached Penobscot Bay until the 1760s after the French and Indian War.[7]

Anglo-French Rivalry in Eastern Maine

From the 1670s, when the first Indian war (King Philip's) broke out, to the 1760s, when the sixth Indian war ended, recurrent warfare between the colonists and local Indians in Maine, often linked to hostilities between England and France in Europe, blocked further eastward settlement into our area. Pentagoët, or Castine, was the only site

[6] The children were never recovered, but the widow was ransomed in due course and returned to Windham, Maine, according to an account in *Historical Sketch of Windham, Maine*, 1897 (called to my attention by Clayton Young of Matinicus). The episode, which is well documented, is also described in *Bangor Historical Magazine*, VII: 114/1658.

[7] Early-eighteenth-century maps suggest settlement only at a few places in Penobscot Bay: e.g., Castine; a trading station on the Weskeag River managed by Thomas Lefebvre (shown on some maps as "La Farver House"); and unspecified "French inhabitants" on Deer Isle (Map 1721 Coasting Pilot).

more or less permanently occupied during this hundred-year period, and the forts there inevitably became strongholds to bolster successive British and French claims—mainly the latter, for, thanks to the efforts of settlers like Baron de Castin, the French were able to control this strategic outpost the greater part of this troubled time. A census ordered in 1688 by Governor Edmund Andros of the Bay Colony, during one of the periods when Castine was brought temporarily under British rule, shows the effect these prolonged rivalries were having on settlement in the region: in the entire area from the Penobscot to the St. Croix the census-taker found "perhaps forty-five souls," that is, Europeans. They were distributed as follows: Baron de Castin, his Indian wife (daughter of a chieftain) and household at Pentagoët; Charles St. Robin and a Frenchman, with their families, at Naskeag; one French and one English family under the names Lowry and Hinds on Great Gott Island (called *Petit Plaisants*); the Baron de Cadillac and his family on the east side of Mount Desert; and scattered other families farther east. The total poplation in the Province of Maine at this time was probably something over six thousand (Williamson, I: 447, 588).[8]

The critical Anglo-French confrontation for our purposes was the French and Indian War of the 1750s, which ended in an unambiguous victory for the English. Not only was the disputed boundary between the Massachusetts Bay Colony and Acadia now resolved in England's favor, but in the fall of Quebec the French for all practical purposes lost Canada as well. Maine Indians, decimated by six wars with Massachusetts colonists in the preceding century and ravaged by disease, also made their peace with the victors and were no longer a serious threat to settlement. Fort Pownall, constructed in 1759 at the mouth of the Penobscot River, underscored British control of the region.

[8] The accuracy of the Andros census admits of some doubt: he himself went as far east as Castine only once—in April 1688, the date when the census was ordered; meanwhile the severe Indian uprisings during this period, caused in part by the seizure of Castin's property, must have hampered his census-takers. Andros was officially named Governor of New England after his return from the 1688 visit; he retained the title less than a year, however—until his arrest following the abdication of James II (see "Andros Tracts," Vol. I).

Now island settlement began in earnest. In 1764 the Bay Colony ordered a survey of "all islands belonging to the Province of Penobscot Bay...with their Distance and Bearings from each other and from the Continent," the cost of the survey to be covered by the sale of islands (Massachusetts Archives, 118: 24). In 1768 a broadside was issued by a claimant of vast lands east of Penobscot Bay in which reference was made to "islands in the neighborhood admirably well situated for carrying on the Cod-Fishery"; this claimant hoped to settle two hundred families on his lands within two years (Sawtelle, "Sir Francis Bernard and Mount Desert," 239). The claimant, the Earl of Stirling, was successfully challenged in court by Sir Francis Bernard, Governor of the Bay Colony, for possession of the lands in question—but such efforts to attract settlers to the area were characteristic of the ten to fifteen years preceding the Revolution. Thirteen townships were created in the area between the Penobscot and St. Croix, their incorporation to take place as soon as settlers in them could establish their credentials and organize themselves. A census taken in 1772 reported settlers in our region as follows:

Area (west to east)	No. of Families
Tallent's (Tenant's) Harbor	6
Camden	16
Penobscot River and islands	105
Bagaduce, including Castine	90
Naskeag	56
Blue Hill Bay	39
Fox Islands (Vinalhaven and North Haven)	36
Long Island (Islesborough)	14
Deer Isle and islands	59

(Maine Historical Society, Miscellaneous Box 39/1).

If one counts five to a family—probably a modest estimate—one finds some 2,290 residents in the Penobscot Bay–Blue Hill Bay region on the eve of the Revolution; approximately half of these settlers were living on islands.

The removal of French and Indian threats to settlement in the region did not, of course, eliminate conflicts among the settlers themselves. This area was settled at a time when hostility between the American colonists and the home government was growing daily in Boston, New York, Philadelphia, and Jamestown. Inevitably, sentiment for independence spread into this northeastern frontier. There were mixed views on the issue, as there were elsewhere, and it would be an error to argue that patriotism in Maine was especially advanced by the mid-1770s. Indeed, on the islands it could be said to have developed reluctantly. In the rigorous preoccupation with clearing land, raising crops, filling their crude cellars against the severe winters, and simply maintaining their marginal existence, islanders had little time for thoughts of revolution.

The American Revolution

When the Revolution did break out, no immediate rush of volunteers followed. Committees of Correspondence were created in the leading centers—at Blue Hill, on Mount Desert, on Deer Isle, and so forth—but the settlers were not markedly enthusiastic for the American cause. The early reverses of George Washington's tattered armies encouraged the expression of openly Tory sentiment, especially on those islands dependent on Castine, where loyalist feelings were dominant. Meanwhile, the money paid by the captain of a passing British war sloop for a suckling pig or a lamb was as good as—indeed better than—Continental tender; any islander could, and did, ask, if his loyalty was challenged, how he could be expected to turn away a British sloop. Cordwood for the British still entrenched in Boston was sold off a number of islands during the greater part of the war, though this was generally acknowledged to be disloyal.

It would be a mistake, however, to imagine that all islanders were selfishly oriented and unconcerned with the outcome of the Revolution. Conscription quotas were usually filled in time, and as the war progressed there were volunteers. There were also privateers and their supporters. John Robinson on Robinson's (now Tinker) Island, in Blue Hill Bay, piloted American privateers to safe anchorages away from British war sloops. The razing of the community at Naskeag in 1778 was brought on by a patriot's musket fired on a British vessel from Harbor Island (Hutchinson, *When Revolution Came*, Chapter V). British reprisals and depredations took place on a number of islands as the war dragged on and the position of the English grew more desperate; even the British naval victory at Castine in 1779 could not alter the growing isolation of the Royalist forces and the rising solidarity of the settlers.

The colonists' approaching victory did not immediately dislodge the British from the Penobscot Bay region; they remained for several years in occupation of Castine. And now there arose a new version of the old dispute over the eastern boundary. The British, playing the role of their former French adversaries, sought to press the boundary between the new nation and British Canada as far west as they could and so argued for the Penobscot River, which would have left half the Penobscot islands under the Crown. In the region between the Penobscot and St. Croix rivers it was contemplated that a new colony to be called New Ireland would be established as a haven for loyalists; had it come into existence, it would, of course, have been a thorn in the side of the United States—no less than Northern Ireland (Ulster) has been a thorn in the side of the modern Irish Republic. John Adams, negotiating with the British in Paris, said that his main problems were the question of the eastern boundary and the Tories. He remained unyielding in his demands, and in the end the English gave up their idea of a New Ireland; the St. Croix was eventually acknowledged as the frontier, as it is today.[9]

Land Grants and Speculation After the Revolution

This uncertainty over Maine's eastern boundary probably accelerated plans to settle lands east of the Penobscot, including the islands. As early as 1783 the Massachusetts Land Commission, created in 1781, appointed a special committee for Lincoln County, which embraced the eastern lands, and this committee promptly named Rufus Putnam its surveyor, with instructions to survey all the islands lying between the Penobscot and St. Croix rivers. These surveys were completed early in 1785, and with them Putnam submitted a brief report listing the island settlers he discovered in the area. Leaving aside the outer islands (Matinicus group) and those on the western shore (including Islesborough), which are not included

[9] Maine Historical Society, *Collections*, Series II, I: 389-400.

in Putnam's survey, he identified approximately two hundred households on some three dozen islands from mid-Penobscot Bay to Machias Bay (see Appendix A, page xxx). All but eighteen of these households were in Penobscot Bay, the greater percentage of them on Deer Isle and the Fox Islands. But the smaller and medium-sized islands are also represented: more than a dozen in Penobscot Bay were occupied.

The object of Rufus Putnam's census was to allow the Commonwealth Land Commission to "quiet" settlers who had been in constructive residence on islands for some years—before January 1, 1783, according to a resolve of the General Court. And indeed in the following years, as unappropriated lands were sold, early settlers who remained in residence were given settler's deeds, usually of one hundred acres.

The distinction between "unappropriated" and "alienated" lands with which the Land Commission wrestled was sometimes relatively uncomplicated and at other times extremely vexing. In theory, all titles proceeded from the Crown, and, after the Revolution, from the Commonwea!th of Massachusetts. Thus the vast Waldo (or Muscongus) Patent, once its boundaries were established, was not particularly difficult to unravel. Initially this grant of some thirty square miles between the Penobscot and Muscongus rivers had been made by the Plymouth Council, which had a Crown grant to all New England lands, to John Beauchamp of London and Thomas Leverett of Boston; subsequently it was acquired by Samuel Waldo, a vigorous promoter of settlement in this region from the 1730s to 1750s; and after the Revolution by his son-in-law General Henry Knox, who served for five years as Washington's Secretary of War before resigning his post and moving to Thomaston to supervise his vast holdings. Settlers in this region—including island settlers—accordingly secured their deeds from the Waldo and later Knox interests. Mount Desert, by contrast, together with some of its adjacent islands, was the subject of rival claims: the descendants of Sieur de la Motte Cadillac, the de Gregoires, based theirs on a grant from Louis XIV in 1689; while the heirs of Sir Francis Bernard, former Governor of the Massachusetts Bay Colony, claimed on the basis of a grant from the Bay Colony in 1762 after Mount Desert Island had passed from French to British control. In this case the Massachusetts General Court resolved the dispute in 1787 by awarding the eastern half of the island to the Cadillac descendants and the western half, together with most of the surrounding islands, to the Bernards.

Where there were no such recognized grants, the settlers themselves sometimes petitioned collectively for possession of the lands they occupied, often seeking incorporation as a township at the same time—as on Deer Isle, the Fox Islands, and Islesborough. And if there was neither prior grant nor action by the General Gourt to guide it, the Land Commission simply sold off the unappropriated lands as opportunities arose. In the mid-Penobscot Bay region, for example, numbers of islands were sold in a bloc to single absentee purchasers, some of them with suspiciously close ties to the Land Commission. Governor James Bowdoin of Massachusetts came into possession through one of these land speculators of an island dominion of more than three thousand acres that included Little Deer Isle, Long Island in Blue Hill Bay, Pickering Island, Bradbury, and Great Spruce Head.[10] In 1786 Colonel James Swan, Adjutant General of Massachusetts and an intimate friend of General Knox, bought Burnt Coat (now Swans) Island and twenty-four adjacent islands—a domain of nearly ten thousand acres—for £18,000.

An English traveler to the United States during this era remarked that one could not expect to understand the fledgling nation if one did not understand land speculation—(Allis, "William Bingham's Maine Lands," Colonial Society of Massachusetts, *Publications*, Vol. 36, p. 32)—and surely land speculation was rampant in the Penobscot Bay region. I cannot refrain from noting that there is something unseemly, especially so soon after the American Revolution, in this land scramble among the great and powerful, while humble settlers on the islands eked out a precarious living. What, after all, had the Revolutionary War gained them if instead of a

[10] The Bowdoins were descended from a French settler in the Casco Bay region, Pierre Baudoin, who received a 100-acre grant from Governor Andros in 1687 ("Andros Tracts," III: 79).

rare British tax collector or occasional war sloop demanding modest tribute, they now had to deal with the ubiquitous land agents of wealthy politicians and bankers? The kindest thing that can perhaps be said of this era is that in the end many of the great land investments failed. Colonel Swan spent his last years in a debtors' prison in Paris, and few of his island tenants who took mortgages bothered to pay up; the mighty Henry Knox teetered for a time on the brink of bankruptcy because of his overextended dominions; the Bowdoin holdings were divided after his death and soon passed out of the family; the smaller speculators eventually disposed of their island holdings at marginal profit. Where islands, often unnamed, escaped the speculator's net, a squatting father would deed to a squatting son, the transaction duly recorded in the county registry and the Land Commission none the wiser. In a word, ownership of the islands during the nineteenth century passed in one way or another to those who worked them.

Speculation in islands did not obstruct settlement, and this of course is the heart of our discussion. By 1790, according to the first federal census, eighteen households and sixty-six inhabitants were on the smaller islands in Hancock County—that is, on islands not yet associated with any township. In 1800, the total was 84; in 1810 it was 214, and in 1820 it was 481 (Greenleaf, *Statistical View of District of Maine*, 148). This was only in Hancock County. In the Lincoln County sectors of Penobscot Bay there were as many again.[11] By the 1830s I estimate that no fewer than seventy-five medium-sized and smaller

[11] Hancock County, created in 1789, embraced all the coastal islands east of Vinalhaven. The outer islands (Matinicus group), the Muscle Ridges, and other islands on the western shore were initially in Lincoln County and after 1860 in Knox—along with Vinalhaven. The Islesborough group as far south as Lime Island was included in Waldo County after its incorporation in 1827.

Schooner loading cordwood on the Bagaduce, 1890s; such scenes were enacted on most Penobscot Bay islands throughout the nineteenth century. (Courtesy of Deer Isle Historical Society.)

islands in the Penobscot Bay–Blue Hill Bay area were inhabited year-round, the great majority of them by single families. Nathaniel Hawthorne, traveling through the region in 1837, remarked on this single-family tenancy on the islands:

> ...the sole family being lords and rulers of all the land which the seas gird. The owner of such an island must have a peculiar sense of property and lordship; he must feel more like his own master and his own man, than other people can
> (*American Notebooks*, entry for August 12, 1837).

Perhaps indeed it was this sense of privacy and sovereignty that attracted the early settlers, much as today's visitors—both local and rusticator—are lured to the most remote islands. Or it may have been the prospects of economic advantage compared to opportunities on the more crowded main.

Occupations of Penobscot Bay Islanders

The occupations of the islanders paralleled those on the mainland. Lumbering inevitably came first, not only to clear the land but to feed Boston and other markets along the coast with timber for building, then cordwood for domestic hearths, and eventually kilnwood for the lime industry in Thomaston and Rockland. The coastal forests along the New England seaboard had been leveled eastward during the seventeenth and eighteenth centuries, and by the Revolution the standing timber in the Penobscot Bay region had become a source of some significance. Since logs from the islands were easily rafted to nearby mills or loaded onto coasters, islands were stripped as promptly as the coast itself—and often sooner. The outer islands, which grew no forests because of the acid soil left by generations of nesting seabirds, yielded hay for the coastal markets; the Green Islands and Metinic, for instance, were harvested regularly from pre-Revolutionary times, usually for Boston's Haymarket.

Lumbermen and haymakers were transients as a rule. The first serious settlers on the smaller islands were farmers, and they remained dominant through most of the nineteenth century. Farming was a more rewarding occupation than fishing for an isolated islander. Man cannot live on fish alone, but a farmer can clothe himself with wool from his sheep and feed himself with a variety of produce from his fields and livestock. If he had excess produce, he could sell it to a passing coaster for cash to buy the few necessities he could not produce. The root cellars, dug wells, and miles of stone walls crisscrossing the islands are testimony to the husbandry of these early settlers.

But I should not leave the impression that fishing was a neglected occupation. All islanders fished to some extent; their children, meanwhile, scoured the rocky shores and mud flats for shellfish. Fishing was a seasonal occupation on most of the smaller islands. A summer fisherman could easily survive on an island, alone or with his family, and was closer to the fisheries than his brother on the main, but when cold weather came he had to retreat to more established communities, for protection if not conviviality. This is why so few early year-round residents of the smaller islands were fishermen; the evidence of their passage is rarely more than a crude foundation near the shore, on which some successor's fish shack probably stands today, plus a shallow summer well for surface runoff.

When, however, one speaks of the larger islands (Deer Isle, Swans, Isle au Haut, Matinicus, the Fox Islands) and, of course, the mainland communities in Penobscot Bay (Belfast, Bucksport, Camden, Castine), there is a different story to tell. Fishing was paramount in the regional economy during the decades before the Civil War. From 1850 to 1865 Maine's share of the entire United States catch in the cod and mackerel fisheries rose from thirty-five percent to fifty-two percent; fishermen in Penobscot Bay accounted for about a third of Maine's catch in the same years.[12] The fish, of course, came mainly from distant fisheries like the Grand Banks and the Gulf of St. Lawrence, on expeditions sometimes lasting three or four months; the fishermen and vessels, however, came from Penobscot Bay ports. Residents of the smaller islands were normally excluded from this activity by their distance from the fishing ports: crews on the bankers and mackerel schooners came naturally from the estab-

[12] These percentages are taken from Wayne M. O'Leary's "The Maine Sea Fisheries, 1830–1890," one of the most authoritative of many studies of Maine's pre-eminence in the industry in the nineteenth century (see Bibliography for full details of this study).

lished centers, and increasingly by mid-century from mainland townships.

There were a number of reasons for the surge in Penobscot Bay fishing in the mid-nineteenth century. The most important single factor was probably favorable market conditions. The ever-rising demand for fish, especially in the southern states and the Caribbean (expanding slavery and single-product economies like Cuba's), meant that the vast reserves in the North Atlantic fisheries could be profitably exploited. Meanwhile, federal bounties encouraged larger vessels and longer expeditions—and ultimately more fish.[13] The steady increase in Maine's population meant that there were more men available for crews.

The boom was not to last. The Civil War created problems for Maine fishermen: not necessarily manpower shortages (enlistment was not high in Maine), but inflation. The cost of fishing gear and especially of salt rose so sharply during and after the war that the proceeds of the catch were insufficient to cover them. Meanwhile, the federal bounties, which had always been subject to regional politicking, were repealed in 1868, never again to be reenacted; this effectively ended Maine fishing at the Grand Banks, with a consequent decline of cod brought to market. There was also a technological revolution in fishing after the Civil War to which Maine fishermen on balance were slow to adjust, according to Wayne O'Leary (Chapter VI, "The Maine Sea Fisheries"): the shift from hand-line fishing to trawl and seines. Finally, a change in the tastes of consumers affected the industry in Maine. Customers in New York, Philadelphia, Washington, and throughout the south wanted *fresh* fish, which put Maine fishermen at a disadvantage beside local fishermen with quick access to markets. These considerations led to a steep decline in Maine's share of the East Coast fishing industry in the decades after the Civil War. A Congressional survey in 1880 reflects the decline. The Deer Isle fleet, for instance, which in mid-century had numbered more than eighty fishing vessels (thirty-five Bankers and mackerel schooners, and fifty boats in the local fishery), was called, in 1880, "the poorest class of vessels of any town on the entire coast"; Isle au Haut, which had forty vessels in the offshore and Banks fisheries in the 1820s, had only three in 1880 (Goode, *Fishery Industries of the United States*, 40, 42).

The number of fishermen in the Penobscot Bay region inevitably declined: on Vinalhaven, for instance, the number dropped from 282 to 160 during the twenty years between 1860 and 1880; on Deer Isle, from 502 to 293.[14] On both islands many shifted occupation to quarrying. But on a medium-sized island, the decline in certain fisheries did not mean a significant drop in population. Islanders diversified their skills and became more resourceful. The fish oil and guano industry, for example, preoccupied many islanders after the Civil War, before the menhaden abruptly disappeared in 1879. The so-called "pogy factories," presses that extracted the fish oil and left the residue for fertilizer, were not unique to islands, but many were established on islands, closer to the fishing grounds, and brought seasonal employment to local residents. Weir fishing in Maine dates from the 1870s (leaving aside the primitive weirs constructed by Indians). In its heyday early in the twentieth century weir fishing engaged many hundreds of islanders throughout the region. Lobstering, which began on a small scale as early as the 1850s, was to become the major occupation of Maine fishermen by the end of the century. New attention was focused on the islands, not so much for seasonal residence—though there was that, too—but for the "privilege." State laws acknowledged no fishing rights attached to shore ownership, but the fishermen themselves did, and the multiple conveyances and leases of offshore islands recorded in the last decades of the century reflected the anxious competition among fishermen: lobstermen needing assurance of a rocky shore off which they could put their traps (with no competition shoreward of them); weirmen needing a stretch of shore from which they could extend their weirs; purse-seiners requiring a convenient location to stow their gear for instant use when schools of

[13] The bounties, initiated as early as 1792 but standardized for Maine only in 1819, were paid to the owners of vessels greater than five tons that fished for cod at least four months of any given season (February to November).

[14] The figures are from O'Leary and Goode.

mackerel or herring were located.

Of far greater importance to life on the islands than these new developments in the fishing industry was quarrying. The restless demand after the Civil War for granite—for construction, for paving blocks and curbstones, and for ornamental facing for public buildings—triggered a boom that influenced island life more profoundly than any other single development since the Revolution. The transportation of Maine granite by schooner to Boston and New York gave a special advantage to the immediate coast, and in particular to the islands, where loading was easier. No fewer than thirty-five islands treated in the present study were quarried, a dozen of them extensively. The duration of the operations varied: on some, leaving aside those with merely exploratory motions, an entire operation—including the importation and housing of foreign workers—might last no more than a decade; on others, like Crotch Island off Stonington, the granite age lasted over a century from beginning to end. The stonecutters were transients as a rule, living in temporary housing (and rarely counted in the decennial census), but they came in such numbers—there were said to be as many as two thousand quarry workers at one time on Dix Island alone—and with a lifestyle so distinctively their own that few island communities could revert to their normal ways after the quarrymen departed.[15] Other minerals were also probed in the post-Civil War years—silver, gold, and copper in particular—but few ventures proceeded beyond the planning stage, and I am not aware of any island ventures that proved profitable.

As to other trades on the medium-sized and smaller islands, there were few, of course, compared to those in larger mainland communities. I know of no island cobblers, for example, no tinkers, no coopers, and only a few island blacksmiths; services of this sort were normally provided by itinerant specialists who, like occasional peddlers, sailed from island to island in season in whatever vessels they could keep afloat. Boatyards existed on a few islands. On Eagle Island, for instance, there were at one time as many as four boatshops that specialized in small vessels and peapods. From the 1880s on, meanwhile, there was a rudimentary vacation trade: by 1900 eight or ten Penobscot islands had boardinghouses that catered to summer rusticators.

I would note finally, with respect to all these occupations and enterprises, that so long as trade and communication were by sea, island communities were at no disadvantage compared to those on the mainland—and indeed were sometimes favored. However, as basic transportation shifted to rail, all island activities suffered. Farmers had greater difficulty marketing their crops; island granite could no longer compete commercially with Vermont marble close to Barre's railheads. If island fishermen for a time suffered less, since in the days of sail the closer they lived to the fisheries the better, they too felt the inconvenience when the gasoline engine shortened the distance from well-stocked, protected harbors to the fishing grounds. In short, there came a time when the disadvantages of island living so far outweighed the advantages that removal could no longer be postponed.

Political Organization in the Penobscot Bay Region

Something should be noted here of the political organization of the islands. The great majority of them attached naturally to the nearest incorporated township and were an integral part of these communities. School districts were established as they were needed; tax rates were fixed; the indigent were cared for; and even roads were maintained at the town's expense on some islands. Where incorporated townships overlooked nearby islands—as Deer Isle overlooked the inhabited islands of Deer Island Thorofare in its initial incorporation in 1789—misunderstandings and resentment arose.[16] After the Civil War, when Deer Isle taxes rose steeply to cover the bounties

[15] I use the term "quarrymen" to embrace all associated with the industry, but of course there were many distinctions: the entrepreneur was spoken of as quarryman no less than his superintendent or the boss of a particular crew. Stone and paving cutters, sharpeners, polishers, apprentices, and unskilled quarry workers were also known as quarrymen. Of all categories, the stonecutter was normally the most skilled. (See Smalley, *St. George*, 209ff.)

[16] The islands south of Merchant Row were always considered as attached to Isle au Haut and eventually separated from Deer Isle with Isle au Haut; the islands north of Merchant Row, called the Thorofare islands, were in limbo—neither formally part of the township of Deer Isle nor of any other.

paid in lieu of recruits (comparatively few Penobscot Bay islanders answered the call during the Civil War, persuading townships to underwrite substitutes instead), the Thorofare islanders refused payment of the new taxes on the well-grounded principle of "no taxation without representation." Deer Islanders resolved the issue finally by successfully petitioning the Legislature in 1868 for the formal adoption of the Thorofare islands (Hosmer, *Sketch of Deer Isle*, 37). In other situations the residents of smaller islands resisted inclusion in larger townships and sought to create their own township or plantation. Matinicus, for instance, separated from Vinalhaven in 1840, and Ragged Island (or Criehaven) broke away from Matinicus in 1897. Isle au Haut and its outlying islands left Deer Isle in 1874. Residents of the Muscle Ridge Islands established themselves briefly as a separate plantation at the turn of the century.

One group of islands—most lie in the middle of Penobscot Bay between Islesboro, North Haven, and Deer Isle—never belonged to any township. Although several of these islands have been settled since Revolutionary times, they have remained "unorganized lands"; except for occasional specific purposes such as dealing with the recruitment issue during the Civil War, the residents on these islands were never moved to organize themselves as a community, though they have often shared facilities, such as schools. These islands were wards of the state, one might say, and owners paid—and still pay—taxes to Augusta.[17]

The Maine Forestry Commission had jurisdiction over the state's offshore islands when Maine was separated from Massachusetts in 1820. The medium-sized and smaller islands were divided between the two states—as equally as possible in value, but according to no discernible logic as to location—and the land agents of each state proceeded to validate existing claims or to sell off the islands where claims were disallowed. This gave rise to another era of speculation, evident in the large number of sales of Penobscot Bay islands in the 1820s and 1830s; the Massachusetts agents were more active in this regard than Maine agents, and most of the islands assigned to Massachusetts had been sold before those remaining were formally transferred to Maine in 1853. The Maine Forestry Commission periodically issued lists of islands conveyed and advertised those still available for purchase. In 1874, for example, sixteen islands that state authorities said had never been properly conveyed by Maine or Massachusetts were auctioned—to the dismay of owners who believed they held good title (Maine Archives, "1874 sales"). As late as 1914, the Commission listed some twenty-five islands in Penobscot Bay never properly conveyed—including York Island off Isle au Haut, which had been inhabited and deeds for which had been duly recorded for more than a century.[18]

Social Life, Education, and Religion in the Islands

Social life among the islands was necessarily seasonal and, perhaps because of this, intense and imaginative while it lasted. I know of no evidence that suggests islanders were less sociable than mainlanders and much that suggests the opposite. Berrying parties, picnics, outings on neighboring islands form a pattern of social life that, as nearly as we can tell, stretches back to post-Revolution-

[17] The islands under state jurisdiction listed in the 1976 Coastal Island survey prepared by the Maine State Planning Office (Maine LURC, 1976) include the following—excluding minor islets and ledges:

Hancock County

Bald	Horsehead
Barred and Chain Links	Little Spruce Head
Beach and Barred	Marshall
Bear	Pickering
Birch (off Little Deer Isle)	Porcupines
Butter	Pumpkin
Compass	Resolution
Eagle	Scott Islands
Eaton	Scrag
Fling	Great Spruce Head
Hardhead	Western
Hog (opposite Cape Rosier)	

Knox County

Andrews	Graffam
Bar	Hewett
Birch	High
Camp and Pond	Mink
Crow	Otter
Dix	Oak
Fisherman	Pleasant
Flag	

Note: The above Knox County islands were formerly in the Muscle Ridge Plantation

Green Islands	Ragged (Criehaven)
Lasell	Saddle
Metinic	

[18] For a detailed report on the status of the islands and the history of these procedures, see Maine, Forestry Commission, *Report*, 1914, 99–165.

ary times. By the latter decades of the nineteenth century, dancing was a favorite pastime. Saturday night dances in the loft over the old lobster factory on Isle au Haut were a regular occurrence in the 1870s, and residents came from nearby islands to attend them (Wasson, *Sailing Days on the Penobscot*, 129). Eagle Island had its "dance-hall" over a boatshop early in this century; and if there was no formal facility, any parlor would do.

Drinking was inevitably a periodic problem on the islands. Rum addiction was apparently strong in Revolutionary times: the stores for the Penobscot Expedition of 1779—perhaps one reason for its disastrous outcome—included twelve hundred gallons of rum and molasses "in equal quantities" (Howard, *History of New England*, II: 9). On Deer Isle a riot occurred as late as 1831, when warrants were issued for the arrest of two merchants for the illegal sale of "ardent spirits" to known drunkards whom local authorities had "posted," according to the practice of the times (Hosmer, *Sketch of Deer Isle*, 23). In brief, the imbibing of strong spirits was endemic among the male population of these frontier communities until the 1830s, and it naturally reached to the smaller islands; several of those in Deer Island Thorofare gained a hoary reputation for rioting and debauchery. During the late 1830s and 1840s temperance societies made significant headway, and by the 1850s the state was legally dry. As the quarrying era began, laws were rigorously enforced on most granite islands; for example, on Hurricane, Clark, and Dix, where grog shops could undermine the efficiency of immigrant workers and lead to accidents. This did not mean, of course, that liquor was unavailable in ports like Rockland and Stonington, and Saturday nights in such towns, we can imagine, resembled the shanty barroom towns of the West in Gold Rush times. As far as the indigenous island fishermen were concerned, state Prohibition probably caused little inconvenience; there were few traders or itinerant peddlers who did not keep a supply of liquor cached among their bait barrels and other stores; indeed, it is so today.

Islanders intermarried extensively—not necessarily within families, though there were many marriages between second and third cousins and some between first,but from island to island. It was normal to find several siblings in one island family marrying siblings on another island: no fewer than five of Peter Hardy Eaton's children on McGlathery, for instance, married Harveys on Russ Island in the 1850s. I think there was both a natural attraction of islander for islander, because of a common experience, and a shared instinct to build a barrier against the unknown and troubling "modernization" of the mainland communities. More islanders removed than remained, of course—it could hardly be otherwise among the large families reared on the islands in the nineteenth century—but it is interesting that those who left retained their identity as islanders long after they removed, often longer than it took a new arrival to establish his or hers.

Schools were a natural focus of community life on the islands. On the larger islands, of course, they existed from the time of incorporation in the late eighteenth century, but by the mid-nineteenth century there were also schools on many of the smaller and medium-sized islands: in 1842, according to Clayton Gross, six of the thirty schools carried on the records of Deer Isle were located on the islands lying between Deer Isle itself and Isle au Haut (*Island Ad-Vantages*, May 14, 1976); a school was operating on Seven Hundred Acre Island in 1847 (Dakin, *Monterey*, Appendix). There were potentially four ten-week terms a year—in fall, winter, spring, and summer—and island schools would operate in terms when a teacher was available and enough pupils were enrolled. Smaller islands rarely had more than one term a year before the 1890s, and even larger islands often had only two. Five scholars was normally the lower limit for enrollment; if the number fell below this figure, pupils were transported to a neighboring school or boarded out. No smaller or intermediate islands had high schools, and when secondary education became obligatory at the end of the nineteenth century, teenage islanders were sent to the nearest community that had a high school, often boarding with relatives. The beginning of high school education for island children in many cases precipitated a family's decision to remove altogether.

Formal religion appears to have played a less critical part in our island communities than in communities elsewhere. Few could afford churches—of the smaller and medium-sized islands covered in this volume, only three had churches (Isle au Haut, Matinicus, Criehaven), and even these functioned irregularly. The principal reason why religious life was erratic on islands was that there was usually neither a regular clergyman nor a fixed place of worship. Services were held periodically wherever it was suitable to hold them, sometimes with a visiting preacher in attendance; at other times, depending on the denomination, with a lay reader. Meanwhile the Maine Seacoast Mission, established in 1902 as a nondenominational organization ministering to the islands, made periodic visits to the communities, initially in its sloop HOPE and later in the motorized SUNBEAM; SUNBEAM IV came into service in 1964 and SUNBEAM V in 1994. For those still left on the islands, and especially for lightkeepers and their families before the lights were automated, these visits by the Maine Seacoast Mission were undoubtedly a strong stimulus to religious life, but the Mission was organized, it should be noted, about the time most of the islands were being evacuated.

Islanders were overwhelmingly Protestant, at least until the arrival of the Irish and Italian quarrymen in the granite era. Most islanders considered themselves Methodist or Baptist, the two prevailing denominations in the region in the nineteenth century, but I do not gain the impression that these Protestants held particularly to denominational distinctions. Mormonism was made of sterner stuff; where converts of the Church of Jesus Christ of Latter Day Saints settled, religious faith was more intense. Mormon missionaries arrived on North Haven as early as 1837 and converted as many as a hundred residents, a number of whom went west the next year;[19] membership in the Baptist Church on North Haven, according to church records, fell from 134 to 54 in the following years—apparently in consequence of Mormon conversions (Beveridge, *North Island*, 43). Conversions were also reported on Deer Isle in 1843 (Hosmer, 191).

The greatest surge in Latter Day Saints activity was after the Reorganized Church was created in 1860—following the assassination of Joseph Smith in 1844 and the emergence of doctrinal diferences, notably concerning polygamy, between the followers of Brigham Young in Utah and those who professed allegiance to the teachings of the martyred Joseph Smith. The latter faction, the Reorganized Church (or RLDS), was particularly active along the coast of Maine in the 1860s. McGlathery and Bear islands off Deer Isle, for example, the home of one branch of the Eatons, were early centers of Latter Day strength. Still, on balance, I do not find that religion of any persuasion played a dynamic role in the history of the islands.

From the 1880s on, as the population figures show, the medium-sized and smaller islands one by one lost their permanent communities. I have already suggested an economic reason for depopulation, the replacement of coastal transportation: first sail and later steam, by rail; and a social reason: the desire of families to keep together when teen-age children went ashore to high school. But there are so many reasons for removal, and so many combinations and variations of them, that it would be idle to attempt a generalization here on *why* the islands were abandoned. This is part of the history of the individual islands themselves, the central focus of this study, and I put off discussion of the matter to the separate entries which follow.

[19] The missionaries were Elders Jonathan Hall and Wilford Woodruff, who later became head of his church in Salt Lake City. An account of the Hall-Woodruff mission in the Fox Islands is given in Richard Shelton Williams, *The Missionary Movements of the LDS Church in New England, 1830–1850* (MA thesis in Brigham Young University, 1969), 120ff.

The Outer Islands

The outer islands of the Maine coast, those standing ten miles or more off the main, have always exercised a fascination over mariners past and present. Relics of some geologic barrier eons ago, they stand—or rather lie, for none of them are high—in magnificent isolation. Here was the first landfall of Europeans in the sixteenth century. On a few there were fishing stations before the arrival of the MAYFLOWER at Plymouth.

Matinicus dominates the outer islands of Penobscot Bay and so is the first to be discussed in this inventory. It was not noticed in any detail in the first edition of this volume—chiefly because there had already been full coverage of its history in a monograph published in the 1920s.[1] I turn to Matinicus in the present volume with a particular pleasure, also with some trepidation. It was the first island on the Maine coast I ever visited, on a maiden adventure at sea in 1932 under no less a master than Samuel Eliot Morison, a family friend.[2]

Matinicus

The name appears to derive from an Indian (probably Micmac) term for an island well out to sea (Eckstorm, *Indian Place-names*, 97). It thus joins the company of other coastal islands with names of similar etymological origin: Metinic, Manana, Petit Manan. The spelling, needless to say, varied recklessly in the early years: *Mantinicus*, *Montenecus*, *Matinnie*, *Metynacus*, and even *Martinique*. There were inevitably other names given by early cartographers: e.g., *Willowby Isles*, by Capt. John Smith (who anglicized all names along the coast after his 1614 expedition in an effort to please King James I—see pages 6–7). But the original Indian name persisted.

Settlement

The earliest landings on Matinicus by Europeans are lost in time. It would be satisfying to imagine Vikings blown from Greenland or probing southward from *L'Anse aux Meadows* in Newfoundland, coming onto the island, but there is no certain evidence of it. The earliest dwellings, now obliterated, were thought to be those of "French or Dutch fishermen" (Williamson, I: 64)—presumably French (that is, Norman or Basque) known to have fished regularly on the Grand Banks during most of the sixteenth century. By the early seventeenth century there was surely periodic settlement on Matinicus and perhaps a fishing

[1] The 1926 history, long out of print, is Charles A. E. Long, *Matinicus Isle: Its Story and Its People* (see Bibliography for details). Long's volume relies on, in addition to extensive interviews conducted on the island in the early twentieth century (when he summered there), a few previously published studies: Williamson, *History of Maine*, I: 63; *Bangor Historical Magazine*, VII: 113/1657; O. P. Lyons, *Town of Vinalhaven*, 56–58; Johnson, *History of Bristol*, 306; and Maine Historical Society, *Collections*, I: 551. None of these sources are in marked conflict on details. There is also a short pamphlet by Celia Philbrook Emmons. "Highlights of Life on Matinicus Island" (1960), and a "visitors' guide" entitled "Tales of Matinicus Island" by Donna K. Rogers (1990), both drawn from the above materials.

[2] If I may pursue reminiscence of that voyage to Matinicus on the Morisons' yawl IDLER, we were a crew of three: Mr. Morison, his son Peter, and I. Samuel Eliot Morison, to a boy of thirteen, was not the formidable figure I knew him to be some years later, but he was a meticulous and exacting skipper. Peter and I spent long hours polishing brass and more than once suffered our captain's contumely for unseamanlike performance. But there were light moments, too, as when Peter and I were judges of a flapjack competition between Mr. Morison in our galley and two gentlemen on a neighboring schooner in Matinicus Harbor in theirs—Dr. Putnam, then Librarian of Congress, and Eliot O'Hara, a well-known watercolorist. Pancakes with more distinguished credentials never left a skillet, and Peter and I were hard put to declare a winner. The voyage ended, I recall, with my receiving my first degree, presented ceremoniously by Mr. Morison when my parents arrived to pick me up at Pretty Marsh: an A. B., for "able-bodied seaman," neatly inscribed on a piece of driftwood. I wish I could say I had it still.

station, as on Monhegan and Damariscove islands. In 1611 the Jesuit explorer Father Pierre Biard found the remains of English vessels on Matinicus, though no settlers were there at the time.

Records of habitation on Matinicus or any of the neighboring islands in the first half of the seventeenth century are nonexistent, but there is a reasonably reliable estimate of the number of vessels there during the thirty years preceding the first Indian war (1676–78): twenty, according to Sylvanus Davis, a knowledgeable settler in eastern Maine.[3] If one assumes that each boatowner was a head of household (as appears to be the case for other fishermen in the Davis tally), then there could have been a settlement of about one hundred on Matinicus, using the modest calculation of five to a household.[4] A voyager in 1693 noted that Matinicus, as well as Pemaquid and Monhegan, "are all filled with dwelling houses and stages for fishermen, and have plenty of cattle, arable lands and marshes" (Joselyn, *Account of Two Voyages to New England*). In 1686 an English official in the Duke of York's County Devon (Pemaquid) warned the French Baron de Castin at Pentagoët (Castine) not to threaten "the subjects of the English King...among others those living on Martinique [sic]" (cited in Long, 19). Clearly, then, there was settlement on Matinicus during the seventeenth century, though we cannot put names to the settlers.

The first identifiable community on Matinicus was in the 1720s when William Vaughn of the Damariscotta trading family, a recent graduate of Harvard, opened a fishing station there. He employed numerous vessels and built dwellings for his men around what is called "Old Wharf Cove," north of the present Matinicus Harbor. It was during Vaughn's stay that Captain John Gyles, commander of the fort on the St. George River, reported to Governor Dummer of the Massachusetts Bay Colony that Indians, while seal hunting on Matinicus, were overtaken by bad weather and to avoid starvation had killed a cow and several hogs. The governor wrote back in some dudgeon that such "violence and robbery" were not to be tolerated and that proper restitution to William Vaughn should be

[3] Sylvanus Davis's deposition was made in 1702 and may be found in numerous sources: e.g., Sullivan, *History of Maine*, 39 and Johnson, *History of Bristol*, 97. His figures for the thirty-year period have been interpreted in various ways, but are not in question for Matinicus.

[4] Clayton Young of Matinicus has called to my attention a report that a force of seven hundred men went to Matinicus during the first Indian war (King Philip's), apparently for defense purposes; his source is Francis Parkman, *A Century of Conflict: France and England in North America*, Boston: Little, Brown & Co., Vol. I, 1892.

Matinicus Harbor, with Wheaton Island on right. The "Gut" between the two is used by local fishermen, but is not easily passable at low tide. (Courtesy of Mrs. Kenneth Ives.)

Matinicus matrons preparing lobster feed, 1887.
(Photo from Courier-Gazette, *courtesy of Clayton Young.)*

promptly made.[5] There is no report as to whether restitution was made, but it does not appear that this episode or other difficulties with Indians led to the closing of the station a few years later; it was rather the destruction of his facilities in winter storms that led Vaughn to abandon the enterprise. Penobscot Indians continued to use Matinicus as they had for generations, to hunt seals and fowl and to gather birds' eggs. It was the tense relations between the Indians and the next known European settler, Ebenezer Hall, that led to the 1757 massacre of Hall and the abduction of his family noted in the Introduction (page 9).

Ebenezer Hall, Jr., to whom Ebenezer, Sr. had deeded the island together with its buildings and twenty-five head of cattle, was not on the island at the time of the massacre, but returned in the early 1760s to take up his inheritance. He was joined in 1765 by his brother-in-law Abraham Young of York (Ebenezer, Jr. had married Susannah Young a few years before). From this time on Matinicus was never without habitation.

In the 1780s, some twenty years after Ebenezer Hall, Jr. and Abraham Young came to Matinicus, Alexander Nichols, Jr. of Bristol took up residence on the north end of the island on land deeded him by his father, who had it from Ebenezer Hall, Jr. (Lincoln 17/225). John Crie, a Scot, also came onto the island in the 1780s, married Mary Hall, daughter of Ebenezer and Susannah, and settled on land given him by his father-in-law. The next settler was Isaiah Tolman, who bought out Alexander Nichols, Jr. in 1790 (Lincoln 25/255). All five households are in the 1790 federal census, plus those of two sons of Abraham Young (Joseph and Benjamin) and of three others about whom nothing is known since they did not remain (see census table, page 32). In 1794, according to Vinalhaven records,[6] the first five householders in the 1790 census schedule for Matinicus are included in the tax schedule, plus Ebenezer Hall III; Alexander Nichols had left the island, as well as the unidentified householders in the 1790 schedule. The census table below continues the story of expanding residence and family proliferation.

[5] The text of the correspondence is in "Documentary History," X: 363; see also Long, 21.

[6] Matinicus was at the time part of Vinalhaven.

Summer sunrise over Matinicus Harbor before the breakwater, c. 1900; most of the fishing fleet is already out. (Courtesy of Clayton Young.)

The Matinicus community, to judge from this census table, shows remarkable stability and continuity compared to other island settlements in the Penobscot region. Few of the early householders appear to have left the island, and most of those that did (that is, the ones shown in only one census schedule) were descendants of island families. It was not uncommon in the case of other island communities (e.g., Isle au Haut, Swans Island, Long Island/Frenchboro) for nearly all the early settlers to leave.

Occupations on Matinicus

The earliest settlers on Matinicus mixed their farming and fishing. The historian Williamson, writing about the island in the 1820s, said of its residents (page 64):

> They are a very industrious, humane and moral people; the men are engaged in fishing and farming; and the women manufacture the principal part of the family clothing. The Islanders own six fishing craft from ten to fifty tons each, and raise annually about 400 bushels of wheat and abundance of vegetables; living together in prosperity, quietude and happiness, without law and without rulers.

The description may be too idyllic to be believed, yet in some respects is not far from the truth: the residents until well into the nineteenth century continued to be both farmers and fishermen. The six fishing vessels Williamson reported were large enough for expeditions into the Bay of Fundy and even into the Gulf of St. Lawrence; trips to the Grand Banks have also been reported—though the numbers were probably not significant. Agricultural and animal husbandry, meanwhile, continued through the century, as the 1867 and 1891 tax records at the end of this notice make clear. Most householders, fishermen or not, built homes on the central ridge of the island, surrounded by pastures and orchards; a few of their ample farms still stand.

But the economy of the island was based on the fisheries, not on agriculture. Although the earliest forays were for cod, as elsewhere on the Maine coast, the herring fishery became increasingly important: in 1840, according to a congressional report some years later, there were no fewer than seven smokehouses on Matinicus curing 10,000 boxes annually for the Boston market (Goode, *Fishing Industries of the United States*, 57). The smoked herring enterprise had subsided by 1880, but herring were still caught off the island for bait, both by local residents and fishermen from as far away as Gloucester and Cape Cod. The mackerel fishery was also important in mid-century; haul-seines were in use by 1840, followed by purse-seines and later trawls. Lobstering began in the 1860s and by the early twentieth century had become the major source of income on Matinicus. The congressional report of 1880 noted forty Matinicans then in the "shore fisheries"—that is, fishing off the island in small boats—and eleven sailing vessels totaling about 250 tons (an average of 22.7 tons each). Such vessels would have engaged another fifty or more fishermen for an estimated total of ninety to a hundred. This is too high an estimate for Matinicus alone, whose total population in 1880 was only 243; some of the crew members of the vessels presumably came from other communities. The figures dramatize, however, the extent to which fishing had become the dominant occupation and preoccupation on the island.[7]

[7] The breakdown of occupations, as shown in the 1880 census schedule for Matinicus, was as follows (see also the table of island occupations on page 278):

Fisherman	49	Stonemason	3	Wheelwright	1
Farmer	9	Net mender	2	Domestic	1
Shipwright	2	Dressmaker	1	Teacher	1
Trader	2	Mailman	2	"Scholars"	38

Matinicus Harbor from Mount Ararat with schooner at wharf, about World War I: store and Post Office in near building; Wheaton Island right, Black Ledges seaward. (Courtesy of Clayton Young.)

Other enterprises and occupations on Matinicus were associated with the fishing industry. The Matinicus Fish Company of the 1800s, for instance, bought, processed, and marketed the fish brought in from the fisheries. A Vinalhaven concern, the W. B. Kittredge Company, also did business on Matinicus. These enterprises were the precursors of twentieth-century lobster buyers who kept their floating "cars" in the harbor to buy and process the catch as well as to sell the lobsterman bait, gasoline—and, *sub rosa*, spirits (the island was officially dry).

Boatbuilding was another activity on the island, especially in the winter when cold weather and gale winds often made fishing difficult, if not impossible. The 1880 congressional report notes the excellent qualities of the open, sloop-rigged boats built on Matinicus by part-time shipwrights in their backyards: more than 150 such vessels, as well as 20 dories, were built during the 15 years after the Civil War (Goode, 57).

The author of the congressional report concluded that if Matinicus had a more protected harbor it might develop into a major fishing port. Winter storms continued to maul the harbor, and loss of boats and gear was high: e.g., nine vessels

Matinicus housewives washing, 1890s; note the cultivated fields before the island was overgrown with spruce.
(Courtesy of Maine Historic Preservation Commission.)

in a gale in 1841.[8] Although the plantation requested help as early as 1847, a breakwater was built, at state expense, only in 1911.

Matinicus: The Municipality

Matinicus was considered part of the township of Vinalhaven after the latter's organization in 1789, although not mentioned in the act of incorporation. Relations between the two communities are obscure: in 1801 Vinalhaven voted *not* to allow Matinicus to pay a tax and in 1819 *levied* such a tax—but beyond these entries in Vinalhaven town records I find no other references to Matinicus, even to its incorporation as a separate plantation in 1840 (Lyons, *Brief Historical Sketch*, 56).

Matinicans began to hold regular town meetings in 1840, and a record of the meetings survives. Here are some entries during the first quarter century of the plantation:

1841 Ezekiel Burgess found in the woods with his throat cut; jurors ruled his death a suicide.

1843 Benjamin Condon, Jr. died "accidentally" by hanging in Robert Marshall's house.
Note: The plantation was off to a rocky start.

1844 The total vote for presidential electors was 33—"all Democrats here," the town clerk wrote.

1847 Mark Quincy selected "to try for assistance to build a Breakwater to our Harbour."
Note: It would be sixty-four years before the assistance arrived.

1850 Voted to build a "good and substantial" stone wall around the burying ground...and all agreed to work on it, as well as on a road from Freeman Hall's to the wharf at the harbor.
Note: This was a stone pier, known in modern times as the "Steamboat Wharf," built between 1830 and 1850; Freeman Hall probably lived on Harbor Point, opposite Wheaton Island.

1852 Voted to lay out one-third of the school fund in a summer term, two-thirds in a winter term.
Note: The school budget in 1858 was $132; that is, 50 cents from every resident according to the last federal census.

1859 Assessors to decide whether the plantation was obliged to support John Piper and family.
Note: Piper had come from another community and normally, as a pauper, would have been supported by his place of origin; Matinicus presumably was unable to collect the charge.

1860 A March meeting was adjourned to the next day, when—in quick succession—Isaac Tolman refused to serve as treasurer; Ezekiel Ames, Mark Young, and Rufus Young "positively" declined to serve as assessors; and Otis Abbott resigned as moderator and "left the stand and meeting unorganized."
Note: So went plantation democracy for that meeting; a slate of Philbrooks, Condons, and another Ames resurrected the plantation in due course.

1864 *Voted:* to "hire" (borrow) $300 for volunteers to fill the island quota (for service in the Civil War).

1866 *Voted:* to set off Racketash (Ragged) Island as a separate school district and to "pay them their proportion according to what they paid in."
Note: The Ragged Island school had been an issue raised repeatedly in plantation meetings (see further discussion under Criehaven, page 50).

Schools, as in most communities, were the perennial issue in Matinicus plantation meetings: how much to levy for building repairs, firewood, salaries, and other expenses. The first schoolhouse was probably built around 1800, opposite the present location of the church on the high road. A new schoolhouse was under discussion in planta-

[8] Donna K. Rogers, in her pamphlet on Matinicus (page 56), makes interesting observations about the hold weather and tide have on Matinicans:

> "...for most mainlanders the weather is merely a passing thought or topic of polite conversation, to the islander it is as important as the food he eats...the fisherman is never quite sure of what he is doing next. If it's calm enough he hauls traps, if it blows too hard he works in the shop, if it's too cold and windy for either he stays home and knits heads.... He sets traps when the tide is high, whatever time of day that is, because it allows him to get to the wharf. He cleans, repairs, or paints his boat, not the first thing in the morning as he would like, but when the tide is low enough to allow him access. He plans shopping days to the mainland when the tides are right for loading and off-loading and the wind isn't blowing too hard and counts himself fortunate if he manages both at the same time...."

tion meetings in the 1850s, and the September meeting in 1860 was held in the completed building. A new school deserved new "Back Houses," and two were presently ordered, "the agent to exercise his own judgment as to construction." The number of scholars was quite constant from the Civil War to the end of the nineteenth century, ranging from twenty-five to thirty-five.[9] By the 1890s school was normally taught in three terms, out of an option of four: winter term, twelve to fourteen weeks; spring, six to eight weeks; summer, eight weeks; and fall, ten

[9] Attendance was not mandatory until late in the century, and many teenage males chose the fisheries. In 1848, for instance, *enrollment* in one term was fifty-two, but only thirty-seven attended (that is, seventy-one percent).

Will Norton's fish house on Matinicus, 1880. The Matinicans in the photo are identified as follows on the back of the stereopticon slide: Will Norton and Henry Young (sitting) at left; Fred Norton and David Babson (seated) to their right; Aunt Nancy and May Norton (on walkway); and Wes Ames at far right. Others are not identified.
(Courtesy of Maine Historic Preservation Commission.)

Year	Term, Length	Teacher	Salary	No. of Pupils
1896	W, 13 weeks	Henrietta Hall	$7.50	33
1897	W, 14 weeks	Henrietta Hall	7.50	33
1897	Sp, 8 weeks	Henrietta Hall	6.00	27
1897	Su, 8 weeks	Henrietta Hall	6.00	25
1898	W, 12 weeks	Herbert S. Palmer	?	31
1898	Sp, 6 weeks	H. Emma Gordon	5.50	27
1899	W, 12 weeks	George C. Purrington	10.00	27
1899	Su, 8 weeks	Helen R. Stubbs	?	30
1899	F, 10 weeks	Mertie B. Whitehouse	5.50	24

weeks. Teachers' salaries were low, but not more so than on other islands. (Listed above are the teachers and their weekly salaries on Matinicus in the last years of the century.)

Only Henrietta Hall appears to be a Matinican; the others came from the mainland (to judge from their surnames), and their room and board were covered by the plantation (about $2.50 a week). The subjects Henrietta Hall taught her thirty-three students in the winter of 1896 are worth noting: to all of them, arithmetic, penmanship, reading, and spelling; to thirteen, geography; to twelve, grammar; to five, algebra; to four, composition; to eight, history; and to four, physiology.[10]

The Matinicus school has continued through the twentieth century with periodic renovations and a completely new building in 1990 (built beside its predecessor), but with a declining number of students: rarely above a dozen in the last decades of the twentieth century. In the 1990s, thanks to an imaginative, award-winning teacher who stayed for five years, the school flourished. Most graduates of the island school go on to high school in Rockland or to private schools partially funded by the plantation.

Church, Post Office, and Store: Mortar of a Community

What else beyond a school binds a community together? A church sometimes. Matinicus has had several. The earliest denomination were Baptists in 1805, a branch of the Rockland congregation. Williamson noted that they had twenty-two members in the 1820s, but this group never had a church building. In 1850 a Methodist preacher, Abraham Plummer, settled on the island and he, followed by his son John, conducted services for some years—but again without a parish house. It was not until 1905, following evangelical work by the Advent Christian Church and the Christian Endeavor Society, that a Congregational Church was built and dedicated. The building still stands—but whether it has served as a force in binding the island community together may be questioned. There has rarely been a settled minister; summer preachers have occasionally been provided by the Maine Sea Coast Mission, whose monthly visits on the diesel-powered SUNBEAM from November to April may be said to offer the strongest bonding provided by a religious organization.[11]

The post office is another institution capable of unifying island communities: it is public, it is regular (usually), it is neutral. Mail was first brought to or from Rockland by anyone sailing to the mainland. It was not until 1874 that mail delivery was managed on any kind of schedule: three times a week. The mailboat (originally Henry Philbrook's schooner EVERETT and after 1888 Hiram Smith's vessels) was also the first regular public transportation to and from the island. In 1897 the steamer BUTMAN began its seventeen-year service under Captain William G. Butman. The BUTMAN sank off the island on a calm day in 1915, for reasons unknown; there

[10] The data in the foregoing paragraphs are taken from materials preserved in the old schoolhouse.

[11] The Maine Sea Coast Mission is ecumenical, with a mission to undertake, in the words of its by-laws, "religious and benevolent work in the neglected communities...along the coast and on the islands of Maine." See page 343, below, for a typical discussion at a social hour in January 1973 between islanders and the SUNBEAM staff.

were no losses, not even the mail. The carrier after W. G. Butman was not so fortunate: his vessel, the BEATRICE, was lost with all aboard (Captain Burton Wallace and two passengers) on a winter night in 1920. From the 1920s to the 1960s Stuart Ames and Stuart Ames, Jr. were skippers of the mailboat, which during most of these years was the 65-foot MARY A., a diesel-powered packet that beguiled generations of Matinicans and others who visited the island. Since the 1980s mail has come by air (twelve to fifteen minutes from Owls Head), and sea transport is irregular: a state ferry makes a trip a month to bring and take off vehicles, and a converted lobster boat makes a round trip to Rockland several times a week in season.

The post office itself, meanwhile, went hand in glove with the general store, and the history of this institution goes back at least to the 1830s: records show that Freeman Hall ran a facility on the harbor about that time, for which he built his first stone wharf. In the 1850s a general store emerged in Henry Young's homestead on the high road, which was the headquarters of his far-flung enterprises: Henry Young and Co. It was here that the first post office was installed. In 1884 both store and post office were moved to the harbor, where they remained for more than a century. The post office is *still* there; the store was closed in 1990.

And this raises a large question. "How," asks Clayton Young, Henry Young's great-grandson who ran the Matinicus store for a quarter of a century, "do you keep an island community together without a general store?" How, indeed? If there appears to some recent visitors to Matinicus to be a touch of *fin de siècle* malaise about the island, it is in large measure due to the loss of this facility. To be sure, the loss of the store works little hardship on island larders: lobstermen need only run over to Vinalhaven to stock up; or, since most of them are reasonably prosperous today,

Schooner JULIA FAIRBANKS, *mail and passenger ferry between Matinicus and Rockland, 1879–1908. (Courtesy of Clayton Young.)*

This 1874 bill to Henry Young from a Rockland grocer suggests what products were available in the Matinicus store in that era. The quantity "Bbes" is obscure—probably boxes or barrels. "Atlas," "Everett," and "Horsford's" were trade names, according to Clayton Young (a later storekeeper). "Pork back" was salt pork. "Plate beef" was the cut, used salted for corn beef. "Locks" was probably padlocks. The "lead" item could have been red lead in powder form, mixed with oil to put on the bottom of boats to kill sea life such as kelp and barnacles—no longer legal.
(Courtesy of Clayton Young.)

ESTABLISHED 1832
INCORPORATED 1891
John Bird Company
WHOLESALE GROCERS, COFFEE ROASTERS AND MANUFACTURERS.
BIRD BLOCK, SEA ST.
TERMS: ON DEMAND INTEREST AFTER 30 DAYS
Rockland, Maine April 13 1874
Sold to Henry Young

they can send their wives by Penobscot Air to Rockland ($35 each way); or they simply telephone an order to a mainland grocer and drive out to the airstrip to pick it up when they hear the next plane circling to land.[12] The loss of the island store is more visceral than material. Where do they meet their fellow islanders? Where do they hear and pass on gossip? At the post office, perhaps—but the post office alone is a poor substitute for the cracker barrel at the general store; it was never more than an extension of the store.

[12] Penobscot Air has no fixed schedule; it carries six to eight passengers and flies on demand in clear weather.

Let me extend the discussion: Why should off-islanders care about the closing of the store? Matinicus, it should be observed, is an island that for reasons obscure to outsiders and barely grasped by islanders themselves generates powerful attachments. (My father, after first going out to Matinicus on legal business in the 1940s, rarely missed a year without spending a week on the island until he was incapacitated by a stroke. On Vinalhaven I once met a young woman who had been married for some years to a Matinicus Ames, then divorced; she returned to Vinalhaven and remarried, but every evening when it was clear she would drive to the lower end of Carvers Harbor and gaze fondly southward at the low profile of Matinicus on the horizon.) Off-island aficionadoes may blanch at certain occurrences on Matinicus: teenagers shooting gulls in the harbor; abandoned jalopies pushed into Cato Cove; rusticators buying up large parts of the island; broken marriages; the lobster wars of yore—and the closing of the island store. But to put matters in proper perspective, outsiders need to remember that the residents of Matinicus have been coping with their problems for some four hundred years—not always successfully, to be sure (as Ebenezer Hall in the 1750s), but meeting and resolving crises. The life of the island continued. Against this background it would be premature to consider the closing of the island store in the 1990s a final catastrophe.

Residence on Matinicus, 1790–1880

Note: The following households are shown on Matinicus or nearby islands (excluding Criehaven) between 1790 and 1880, according to federal census records. Age is at first appearance (excluding 1790). Wives, shown in census schedules from 1850, are indicated in parentheses. Numbers left of the slash in the decennial columns are male, those to the right female. All males may be presumed fishermen, primarily, unless otherwise noted: Fa, farmer; or spelled out. Dollar sums after certain householders represent the census-taker's estimate of combined real estate and personal valuations (over $1,000) in 1860 or 1870, whichever is highest.

Head of Household	**1790**	**1800**	**1810**	**1820**	**1830**	**1840**	**1850**	**1860**	**1870**	**1880**
Hall, Ebenezer, 45+	12	4/3	1/2							
Young, Abraham, 45+	10	3/1	1/1							
Young, Joseph, -45	1	3/2	4/3							
Crie, John, -45, Fa	3	3/4	3/4	3/4	1/2					
Tolman, Isaiah, 45+	6	2/2	2/2							
Allen, Jonathan	6									
Nickells, Alexander	5									
McDaniel, James	5									
Andrews, Amos	5									
Young, Benjamin	6									
Hall, Ebenezer, Jr., -45		2/2	4/2							
Young, Abraham, Jr., -26, Fa		2/2	5/3	5/3	2/3					
Tolman, Luther, -26, Fa		2/1	4/1	6/3						
Hall, James, -26		2/2	4/5	7/4						
Young, Timothy, 45+		1/0								
Fernald, Nathaniel, -45		4/3	7/4							
Young, Timothy, Jr., -26		1/1								
Hall, John, -45, Fa			4/4	5/2						
Hall, George, -45			4/3							
Hall, David, 24 (Susan), Fa			3/2	5/5[13]						
Young, Ebenezer, -26			2/1							
Tolman, Isaac, 32 (Eunice)			6	6/7	5/6	4/7	1/3			
Young, Alexander, -45			1/3							
Allen, John				1/2						
Crie, Ebenezer, 30s				2/4	5/4					
Condon, Benjamin, 70s, Fa				1/3	2/2	1/1				
Condon, Joseph W., 30s				1/2	4/6					
Condon, Benjamin, Jr., 23 (Hannah)				1/3	5/3	8/4	4/4			
Hall, Susanah				0/1						
Smith, Jacob				4/2						
Young, William, 20 (Ruth) $1,400				1/2	3/4	6/7	6/6[14]	3/3		
Young, Rufus, 28 (Sally), Fa				4/5	5/4	3/6	6/4			
Burgess, Ezekiel, 60s					3/2					
	1790	**1800**	**1810**	**1820**	**1830**	**1840**	**1850**	**1860**	**1870**	**1880**

[13] David Hall moved to Criehaven before 1830.

[14] William Young was keeper of Matinicus Rock Light in 1850.

Head of Household	1790	1800	1810	1820	1830	1840	1850	1860	1870	1880
Philbrook, Alex., 35 (Matilda), Fa $2,000					2/3	3/3	4/3	3/2		
Burgess, Benjamin, 30 (Lavina)					2/5	5/7	6/5	4/3	3/2	
Crie, John, Jr., 43 (Sarah)					5/5	7/4	2/1			
Ames, Joseph, 40s					7/3	4/4				
Burgess, Ezekiel, Jr., 30s					3/3	2/2				
Allen, Charles, 50s					3/3					
Shaw, John A. 60s					3/1[15]					
Condon, James, 37 (Mary), Fa					6/3	8/3	6/3	4/2	4/2	
Brown, Albert, 30 (Sarah)					2/2					
Spear, John B. 30s					2/1					
Burgess, Samuel, 29 (Thankful)[16]					1/2	2/5	2/6	3/5		
Hall, Freeman, 30 (Patience), Fa $1,800					2/3	7/7	4/6	3/3	1/2	1/1
Condon, Seth, 22 (Phebe/Sally)					2/1	3/3	4/3	4/2	1/2	1/2
Tolman, Luther II, 26 (Sarah/Ellen) [17]					3/3	5/5	9/5	7/2	3/4	2/1
Marshall, Robert, 56 (Lydia)					2/5[18]	2/3	2/3	-	0/1	
Young, Mark, 31 (Susannah), Fa $2,700						2/1	4/1	4/2	3/3	
Burgess, John						3/4				
Burgess, Thomas, 34 (Mary)						5/4	5/5			
Young, Tollman, 30 (Almira), Fa						2/4	3/6			
Young, Lydia, 60s						2/2				
Tolman, Isaac, Jr., 21 (Susan), Fa $1,000						3/4	1/2	1/4	5/4	1/1
Ames, Lewis, 27 (Sarah) $1,500						1/1	1/1	3/3	3/2	2/2
Abbott, Samuel S., 59 (Abigail)[19] $2,000						5/5	5/5	2/1		
Condon, Joseph II, 23 (Sarah)							1/3			
Condon, Thomas, 29 (Eliza/Louise), Fa							3/3	5/5		
Ames, Ezekiel, 28 (Antonette) $3,200							2/1	1/3	5/3	5/2
Smith, Freeman, 37 (Rhoda) $1,300							4/2	8/2		
Crie, William, 30 (Mercy), grocer							4/3	4/2	1/4	1/2
Plummer, Abraham, 41 (Betsey)							6/1			
Condon, Seth II, 28 (Elcy)							2/2	4/3	4/5	1/3
Derry, John, 42 (Abigail)							2/2	1/1	1/1	
Abbott, Otis, 26 (Hannah) $1,400							3/5	3/6	2/2	3/1
Abbott, Hiram, 28 (Hannah) $1,100							1/3	2/4	3/3	
Piper, John S. , 32 (Mary)							1/2	2/3	0/3[20]	0/2
Norton, Jonathan, Jr., 29 (Harriet)							3/1	3/4	2/2	2/5
Marshall, Augustus, 21 (Georgianna)							1/1	1/4		
	1790	**1800**	**1810**	**1820**	**1830**	**1840**	**1850**	**1860**	**1870**	**1880**

[15] John Shaw was keeper of Matinicus Rock Light from 1824 to the 1830s.
[16] Samuel Burgess was keeper of Matinicus Rock Light from 1853 to 1861.
[17] Luther Tolman normally boarded up to five single fishermen.
[18] Robert Marshall had been on Criehaven in 1830 and may have continued residence there in 1840 and 1850.
[19] Samuel Abbott was keeper of Matinicus Rock Light in 1840; in 1850 he appears first in the census and was living, it is believed, on Wooden Ball Island.
[20] Mary Piper is a widow in 1870.

Head of Household	1790	1800	1810	1820	1830	1840	1850	1860	1870	1880
Ames, Joseph, 40 (Peggy), Fa $1,900								3/1	3/2	1/3[21]
Smith, Frances, 29 (widow)								2/2		
Tolman, Luther III, 38 (Sarah) $1,000								1/1	1/2	
Young, Henry, 37 (Julia) $3,500								2/8	4/8	8/8[22]
Philbrook, Hanson, 32 (Sarah), Fa								3/1	3/2	3/2
Eldridge, Jonathan, 34 (Hannah)								2/3		
Lucas, John, 20 (Rhoda/Helen)								1/2	1/4	
Tracy, William C., 32 (Margaret)								2/2		
Coombs, Ephraim, 43 (Lavidia), carpenter								1/4		
Condon, O., 31 (Elsie)								2/2		
Condon, Seth III, 24 (Sarah)								2/1		
Noyes, Martha, 30 (widow)								0/2		
Tolman, Jefferson, 31 (Sally)								2/3	2/1	
Young, John, 33 (Susan)								3/2	5/4	8/3
Hammond, John, 23 (Margaret), Methodist minister								2/1		
Young, William, Jr., 31 (Mary A./Lizzie), Fa $1,200								1/3	2/4	3/2
Burgess, Ezekiel III, 33 (Ruth)								1/3	2/3	
Vinal, Charles B., 37 (Nancy)								2/1	3/1	
Gregory, William, 28 (Laura)[23]								1/1		
Fall, Randolph, 30 (Eliza)								1/1		
Pratt, George, 42 (Margaret), Fa								4/4		
Foster, John, 40 (Caroline), Fa								4/4		
Rackliff, Job, 60 (Lydia), Fa								3/3		
Andrews, George, 35 (Rebecca), Fa								1/3		
Rackliff, Job, Jr., 25 (Eliza)								2/2		
Young, Rufus II, 31 (Margaret)									2/1	
Tolman, Charles, 23 (Cora)									1/7	
Young, Mark II, 23 (Ruth)									1/3	
McFarland, William, 78 (Ann)									1/1	
Young, Hiram, 41, (Abby)									3/2	
Norton, William, 42 (Nancy)									2/2	1/3
Abbott, Jacob, 35 (Emily)									2/3	3/3
Howard, Charles, 44, Fa (Amanda)									1/1	1/1
Philbrook, Henry 32 (Esther), mail carrier									3/4	2/3
Burgess, Lewis, 30 (Ginny)									2/2	3/1
Perry, William C., 42 (Margaret)									3/2	3/2
Tolman, H. P., 23 (Mary)									2/1	
Philbrook, William, 32 (Lydia)									4/3	4/5
Hall, Walter, 40 (Eliza)									1/1	
	1790	1800	1810	1820	1830	1840	1850	1860	1870	1880

[21] Peggy Ames is a widow in 1880.

[22] Henry Young normally had a half-dozen or more retainers or boarders in his household.

[23] William Gregory and the next six householders may have been living on islands around Matinicus in 1860 (e.g., Criehaven, Green Islands); I do not recognize any of them as residents of Matinicus.

Head of Household	1790	1800	1810	1820	1830	1840	1850	1860	1870	1880
Condon, Alden 34 (Clara)									1/1	2/2
Young, Timothy, 35 (Harriet)									2/1	2/1
Burgess, John II, 35 (Clara)									1/1	1/3
Dyer, Melzie, 27 (Alzada)									3/2	4/3
Young, Mark III, 44										1/1
Young, Piri? B., 34 (Lud?)										2/2
Tolman, Iddo?, 59 (Sally), Fa										1/2
Abbott, Otis II, 30 (Emeline)										1/1
Jeston, Aldavead, 30 (Rosilland)										1/5
Ames, Wilmer, 26 (Isabell)										2/3
Lufkin, Zebelon, 38 (Sarah)										3/1
Norton, Freeman, 32 (Lisetta)										4/1
Condon, Henry, 55										3/3[24]
Condon, Chris, 52 (Betsy)										2/3
Smith, Hiram, 23 (Ava)										1/1
Smith, George, 17 (Everline)										2/1
Ring, Eben, 53 (Sarah)										1/1
Robbins, William, 29 (Louise)										1/1
Orn, John, 59 (Lucy)										1/1
Clark, Charles, 36										1/0
Abbott, Thomas, 32 (Adavilla)										3/2
Wallace, William, 45										1/0
Hall, Harris?, 37 (Permilia)										3/3
Totals	**1790**	**1800**	**1810**	**1820**	**1830**	**1840**	**1850**	**1860**	**1870**	**1880**
Households	10	12	16	16	24	24	32	49	45	47
Persons	59	52	95	104	152	191	209	257	210	203

[24] Household includes James Condon, 89, and family of Widow Sarah Brown, 32: one male, three females.

Matinicus Valuations, 1867

Note: The following data are taken from tax records of Matinicus Plantation. The key is as follows:

Taxpayer	Normally head of family unit; NR means "non-resident"
RE	Dollar value of real estate: land and buildings in residence lot
Pers	Personal valuation: value of livestock, vessels; cash on hand, etc.
Boat	Dollar value of vessels owned; % of ownership, if partial, in parentheses
Ox	Number of oxen (value of an ox: $20)
Cow	Number of cattle, all ages (value of a cow: $15; yearlings: $10)
Shep	Number of sheep (value of a sheep: $1.50)
Other	Other holdings, dollar value, (interest in parentheses);[25] other islands owned

Taxpayer	RE	Pers	Boat	Ox	Cow	Shep	Other
Ames, Lewis	335	324		1	6		
Ames, Ezekiel	500	367	300	1/2	2	16	
Ames, Joseph	500	202	150	1/2	1	16	
Abbott, Otis	300	454	300	2	2	16	HP (2/15), 50
Abbott, Hiram	187	102			1	45	Wooden Ball, 234
Condon, James	567	93		1	4	12	Wheaton, 50
Condon, Seth	177	19			1	2	Tenpound, 80
Condon, Seth L.	200	1.50				1	
Crie, William	660	77		1	2	15	Ragged (3/64), 66
Crie, Robert F. [26]	570	94		2	2	26	Ragged (11/64), 570
Denny, John	225						
Burgess, Benjamin	233	53			3	12	HP(1/15), 25
Burgess, Ezekiel	185	3				2	
Hall, Freeman	500	70		2	2	12	HP(9/25), 100
Lucas, John O.		67					
Abbott, Samuel		25					
Norton, Jane	200	108	100 (1/2)			5	
Norton, William	233	43			3	5	
Philbrook, H. T.	300	224	100 (1/4); 70 (3/16)	1	1	6	HP(1/10), 50
Philbrook, H. A.	250	274	150 (3/8); 75 (3/16)	1	1	6	HP(1/10), 50
Philbrook, William P.		50					
Perry, W. C.	200	15					
McFarland, W. A.	208		208 (1/8)				
Condon, Oliver	134						
Tolman, F. K.	467	111	50 (1/4)	1	1	14	HP(1/10), 50
Tolman, Isaac	467	111	50 (1/4)	1	1	14	HP(1/10), 50
Tolman, Luther	300	52			1	25	
Tolman, Luther S.			55 (1/3)				
Tolman, William			55 (1/3)				
Tolman, Jefferson	150	30				2	

[25] HP signifies land on Harbor Point (fraction owned).

[26] Robert Crie lived on Ragged Island, which was part of Matinicus Plantation. He eventually owned the entire island.

Taxpayer	RE	Pers	Boat	Ox	Cow	Shep	Other
Tolman, William			55 (1/3)				
Smith, Freeman	267	158	134 (1/2)		1	6	
Smith, Warren			55 (1/3)				
Wilson, Robert	250	39			2	6	
Young, William	300	60			1	30	
Young, Mark	467	367	300	1	1	18	No Mans Land, 50
Young, Timothy	267	40		1	1		
Young, Hiram	100						
Young, John	185						
Young, Mark II	517	869	300; 417 (1/4)		2	3	
Young, Henry	1,300	667		2	5	28	500, stock in trade
Hall, Ezra (NR)						22	Ragged (1/8), 267
Brookman, Henry (NR)						128	Ragged (11/16), 1000
Taxpayer	**RE**	**Pers**	**Boat**	**Ox**	**Cow**	**Shep**	**Other**

Totals:

Total valuation, 1867	$19,284.50	No. of boats	9
No. of taxpayers	43[27]	No. of boat owners	16
State tax	$105.78	No. of oxen	17
County tax	$23.19	No. of cows	44
Plantation expenses	$217.00	No. of sheep	507

[27] An additional nineteen adult males on Matinicus in 1867 paid the poll tax only.

Matinicus Valuations, 1891

Note: The following data are taken from tax records of Matinicus Plantation. The key is as follows:

Taxpayer	Normally head of family; NR means "non-resident"
RE	Land and buildings, dollar value
Pers	Personal valuation: value of vessels, livestock; cash on hand, etc.
Boat	Dollar value of vessels owned; % of ownership, if partial, in parentheses
FH	Fish house at harbor, dollar value
Ox	Number of oxen (value of an ox: $20)
Cow	Number of cattle, all ages (value of a cow: $15; yearlings: $10)
Shep	Number of sheep (value a sheep: $1.50)
Other	Other holdings, dollar value (HP, Harbor Point); store, wharf; etc.

Taxpayer	RE	Pers	Boat	FH	Ox	Cow	Shep	Other
Ames, E. B.	600	72	12			3	10	
Ames, Edward	525	120			2	1	40	
Ames, P. E.		100	50 (1/2)					
Ames, Mrs. P. F.	500	104	85			1	3	
Ames, Miss H. H.		43	43 (1/16)					
Ames, E. E. heirs	125	43	43 (1/16)					
Ames, H. J.	150	106	85 (1/8)			1	4	
Ames, W. L.	150	238	50; 165 (1/4)			1	5	
Abbott, Otis H.	270	137					1	
Abbott, Otis	250	101	7; 50(2/15)	6	2	2	16	Store, 50
Burgess, L. A.	222	56	15; 25(1/15)			2	7	
Dyer, Frank		35	35					
Crie, Robert F.[28]	2,200	598	25 150		4	2	175	Stock in trade, 50
Condon, A. B.	25	10	5			2		Tenpound (1/22), 3
Condon, Seth J.	250	85	42 (7/11)		2	3		Tenpound (10/22), 30
Condon, Oliver	150	16	10	4			2	
Condon, Seth E.	75	173	93				3	
Condon, H. J.			15					Wheaton, 100
Crie, William heirs	325							
Hall, James E.			70					Parlor organ, 20
Howard, Charles	400	71	50 (1/5)		2	1	14	
Miller, Rufus			15	20				
Norton, Jonathan	150							
Norton, Mrs. N. J.	250	71		25		3	4	Parlor organ, 20
Norton, F. A.	250	38	5				3	Boat stock, 30
Norton, A. A.			5				2	
Perry, W. C.	175		30	20				
Perry, A. L.		10	10					
Philbrook, H. A.	425	250	115 (1/4)	35	1	1		HP (1/10), 38
Philbrook, H. T.	375	85	50 (1/8)	35	1	1		HP (1/10), 38

[28] Robert Crie lived on Ragged Island (Criehaven).

Taxpayer	RE	Pers	Boat	FH	Ox	Cow	Shep	Other
Philbrook, W. J.	50	50	50					
Rhodes, F. S. [29]	275	20						Wilson lot, 200; parlor organ, 20
Robbins, W. T.	85	18	3			1		
Smith, Hiram	225	85	50 (1/8)	15				Parlor organ, 20
Tolman, Grace	600	57		15		2	18	HP (1/10), 38
Tolman, O. K.	600	83	7	15	2	2	4	HP (1/10), 38; camp, 10
Young, John	200	15	10	5				
Young, Mark	275	118	75 (3/4)			2	15	HP bldgs., 100; No Mans, 60
Condon, Seth	75	24				16		Tenpound (1/2), 33
Young, Fred L.	200		35					
Young, Mark heirs	400			25				
Young, E. A.		288	7; 25 (1/16)		2	4	17	Boatshop, 66; horses, 55
Young, Henry	2,000	2,205	700; 450; 50 (1/8); 125 (1/16); 100 (1/32)					4 other lots, 580; piano, 30; Wharf, 500; stock in trade, 750
Young, W. B.					1	1	2	Boatshop, 125; boat stock,10
Philbrook, O. E.	40		5					
Harbridge, Harry			5					
Thompson, James			10					
Clark, Charles			20					
Young, L. H.	4							
Crie, John E. (NR)		125						
Abbott, Hiram (NR)							60	Wooden Ball, 250
Young, William,	285	131	25(1/4)		1	3	22	
Ring, Charles H.			30					
Ames, W. G.	75		50 (1/2)					
Robert Crie & Co. (NR)								HP bldgs., 75
Young, Timothy	225	48	3			2	10	Condon lot (2/10), 12
Tolman, Charles J.			25					

Totals:

No. of taxpayers	46[30]			No. of vessels	38
Total valuation, 1891	$22,235.00			No. of vessel owners	28
Total to be collected	$387.56			No. of oxen, horses	20
Appropriations: Schools	200	County tax	17.74	No. of cows	40
Plantation	30	State tax	64.82	No. of sheep	220

[29] Rhodes lived on Ragged Island.

[30] An additional twenty-four adult males paid only the poll tax ($1.00).

Youngs of Matinicus Island

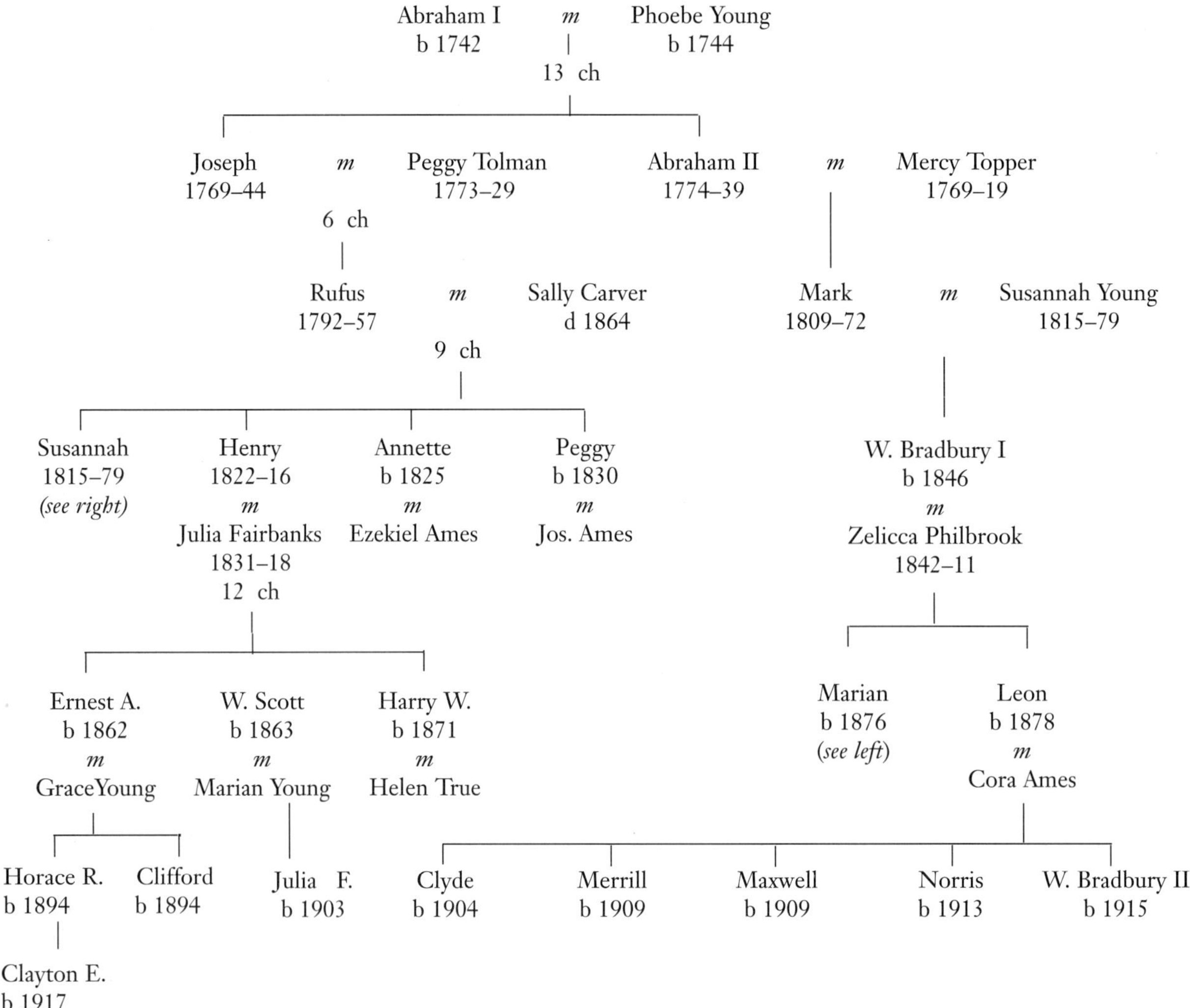

Note: I include as an example of continuity of residence on Matinicus an abbreviated six-generation genealogy of part of the Young family. The table does not include all Young households on Matinicus in the nineteenth century (there are a dozen reflected in the table versus about two dozen in census schedules), but it suggests the pattern of intermarriage on the island.

Metinic

The early habitation on Metinic is evidence of the greater safety settlers felt on the outer islands compared to those closer to shore. The winters were milder, Indian war parties less frequent, and the sight of passing vessels was comforting. I have no record of the earliest transients on this island, but in 1750, according to Cyrus Eaton (*History of Thomaston*, I: 62), Ebenezer Thorndike of Beverly, Massachusetts, "took from the tribe (Abnaki) a lease for ninety-nine years of Metinic Island,[31] which he cultivated as a farm and of which he maintained possession uninterrupted except by the British toward the close of the Revolution." According to a deposition in 1823 by Ebenezer's son Robert, the latter was present when Ebenezer "took possession of the Island of Metinic and broke the soil."[32] That was in 1753; by 1758 Ebenezer had cattle on the island and was regularly cutting hay; in the 1760s he had a year-round tenant to supervise and improve his husbandry. This dwelling is shown on the eastern shore near the narrows on British Admiralty charts surveyed before the Revolution (Map 1776 "Atlantic Neptune"). At about the same time he acquired the Metinic lease from the Abnaki, Ebenezer bought six hundred acres between South Thomaston and St. George, where he manufactured salt, caught salmon, and engaged in trade with the Indians. He lived on the island only at the end of his life; after his wife died (1802), he went to Metinic to live with his son Benjamin who had moved onto the island after the Revolutionary War.

During the Revolutionary War, Ebenezer, identifying himself as a Cape Elizabeth mariner, gave to his eldest son Joshua "in consideration of love and good will" the northern portion of the island (Knox Lands 9/292). The "condition" of the grant, according to Cyrus Eaton, was Joshua's residence on the island and supervision of "the cattle and sheep with which it was well stocked." Joshua remained only a short time; robbed three times by Tories and British marauders, and faced with the crowning humiliation, as Eaton describes it, of having his teakettle smashed and his feather bed shredded to the winds, he removed to the mainland in 1780 (*Thomaston*, I: 154).[33]

Ebenezer had twelve children, including several sons who may have lived on the island at one time or another. Benjamin Thorndike, the fifth son, is the only one (apart from Joshua) we know for certain to have settled there: he is shown with a family of seven in the 1800 census, along with two other families—the Henry Dyers (six) and the Samuel Martins (seven), a total of twenty. Ebenezer Thorndike lived to a very old age (family records say one hundred), and in his declining years business ventures apparently failed. He contracted debts—both to his descendants and to others—that were satisfied in part by seizure of his Metinic holdings. In 1813, for example, Robert Thorndike, Jr. and two other creditors won a suit against Ebenezer and took from the island four cows, six tons of hay, and thirteen sheep. They also seized a seventy-acre lot in the center of the island (Knox Lands 17/387). Soon thereafter Ebenezer's son Benjamin also recovered judgment against his father and took a seventy-eight-acre lot at the south end of the island (Knox Lands 17/414). Joshua Thorndike apparently held title to the northern end of the island, despite his failure to fulfill his father's "conditions," for we find several mortgage conveyances from him to a Thomas McLelan around 1800 (Knox Lands 9/290 and 13/30). Thomas McLelan is Thomas McKellar, whom Robert Thorndike notes as a titleholder in his 1823 deposition mentioned above; he married Ruth Thorndike, a daughter of Benjamin, and settled for several years on Metinic before moving to Sprucehead Island (see page 111).

A "Plan of the Island at Matinec" surveyed in 1813, in possession of one of the present

[31] There are many different spellings of the island name—Montinick, Mantinic, Metincok, Metinick—all meant to render the Indian term for "far-out island," the same name given Matinicus (Rutherford, *Dictionary of Maine Place-names*, 108 and Eckstorm, *Indian Place-names*, 97).

[32] The depostion, apparently made in connection with the division of offshore islands between Maine and Massachusetts, is in the possession of one of the present owners.

[33] Eaton goes on to say that while serving with the colonists Joshua was captured by the British and held in irons for nine months aboard HMS ALBANY. The loss of the ship on the Triangles off Metinic after the war, Eaton writes, was "one of the gratifying incidents" of Joshua's life.

owners, shows the holdings on the 301-acre island as of that date: the northern half by Joshua Thorndike, Jr. with a house and barn shown on the western shore; a four-acre strip across the island below this lot set off to Benjamin Thorndike; the seventy-acre lot set off to Robert Thorndike, Jr. and others; and the seventy-eight-acre lot at the southern end of the island by Benjamin Thorndike "on execution" against Ebenezer. It is uncertain what validity these various conveyances and executions within and outside the family had at the time of the separation of Maine from Massachusetts in the 1820s. It was Joshua Thorndike, Jr. who evidently acquired formal title to the *entire* island in 1824; he paid $240 to the state of Massachusetts for his title (Knox Lands 24/418).

Joshua Thorndike died in the 1820s, and this occasioned another partition of Metinic Island. Joshua's son Charles inherited the south end of the island with half of the buildings, valued at $1000, a generous figure for the era. No other Thorndikes were mentioned, but several in-laws were named: in addition to the McKellars (wife Ruth), there were Snows (wife Lucy) and Snowdeals (wife Hannah)—all surnames which figured prominently in the subsequent life of the island (Knox Lands 35/548, recorded 1846).

I take for granted more or less continuous habitation on Metinic Island during these years of shifting ownership, even though explicit references to residence are meager. Benjamin Thorndike quit the island in 1816, according to an article in the *Courier-Gazette* (December 26, 1922), and returned to a farm on the mainland. Williamson, in his history of Maine completed during the 1820s, noted that Metinic Island was owned by the Thorndikes of St. George and South Thomaston, and stated: "There are two families on the Island, who cultivate the land with considerable success, though fishing is their principal employment" (I: 62). Reference to a "salt works on Joshua's land" (that is, the northern sector) is in a deed conveying interest in the island to Ebenezer, Jr.'s heirs following Joshua's death in 1826 (Knox Lands 35/436). The farm-

Aerial photo of Metinic Island, looking northwesterly toward the mainland; the Snow-Post farm buildings are in the middle of the island at the waist. (Courtesy of Luella Snow Post.)

house, which was still standing near the narrows in the late twentieth century, was said to have been built in 1813—and the date was "confirmed" in the much-told legend of the builders watching the battle of the BOXER and the ENTERPRISE from the scaffolding. (Watching the *smoke* from the battle would be more accurate, since the famous battle was fought between Monhegan and Pemaquid Point, ten or a dozen miles away).

Residence evidently continued through the nineteenth century, although census-takers were casual in taking notice of it. A special census in 1837 showed sixteen persons on "Montinick" Island, under the names John Allen and George Snowdel (Snowdeal). Both surnames are well known in the area. Another resident in the 1830s, according to the *Courier-Gazette* article cited above, was George Shuman, who in 1834 left the island to take up the mainland farm where Benjamin Thorndike spent his last years. The 1840 census shows John Allen still in residence on Metinic, along with Charles Thorndike (presumably Charles W., oldest son of Benjamin). There were nineteen persons on the island that year. I find no further census schedule until 1870. In 1861 the old Thorndike farm at the narrows was reportedly sold to Winslow Waterman of North Haven (*Courier-Gazette* article). It is not known whether he himself settled there or, if so, for how long. He is not shown in the 1870 census, which lists Samuel C. Denison (possibly Parsons—the name is unclear), thirty-six, laborer, with his wife Olivia and four minor children, and Ira Pool, forty-one, farmhand, with wife Nancy and five minor children—a total of thirteen. The census-taker enters the following rather dismal observation: "The inhabitants catch some fish in the summer, shoot sea fowls in Fall and Winter months...resources small." I have no further census data for Metinic, but maps printed at the end of the 1870s show a more prosperous community on the island than the 1870 census count suggests. An 1880 chart, for example, shows a cluster of four buildings at the narrows: the 1813 farm and outbuildings, and two others a mile away at the north end; there is fencing, and most of the island is cleared (Map 1880 CGS 4). These same buildings, and even a few more, are still

The Snow family of Metinic Island in the early twentieth century, descendants of Ebenezer Thorndike who acquired the island from Indians before the American Revolution. (Courtesy of Luella Snow Post.)

shown—indicating residence and upkeep—in the topographical surveys of the early 1900s (e.g., Map 1904–06 Tenants Harbor quad). The northern cluster was for some years the residence of the Pools, or Pooles, and eventually passed to the Withams of Rockland; the buildings at the north end were abandoned by the mid-twentieth century, and most had fallen in by the 1990s. The southern half of the island passed eventually from the Thorndikes to the Snows and Posts of Rockland. Most of the buildings here have been kept up and have been regularly in use through the twentieth century. Willis Snow farmed the island for some years early in the twentieth century, then sold to his brother Woodbury. Woodbury Snow, a retired lobsterman in his nineties when I interviewed him in the 1970s, lived year-round on Metinic Island until 1940, though his wife Eleanor and daughter Luella returned to Rockland each September for the school year. The experiences of the Snows of Metinic Island—the grueling winter of 1932, which Woodbury Snow survived alone, the cooperative venture in "fishing on halves" after World War II, and so forth—would fill volumes and go far beyond the account intended here.

After Woodbury's death in 1980 (he died a year short of his hundredth birthday), the island passed to his daughter Luella Post and to her sons. For more than two centuries, then, this has been a working island, worked and owned by local men and women. Its rigors were too severe to attract out-of-state vacationers, its easterly anchorage too precarious for cruising yachtsmen. The island has accordingly been untouched by tourism and gentrification. It is appropriate that the residents today are descendants of Ebenezer Thorndike, who negotiated the initial lease of the island from Abnaki Indians nearly two-and-a-half centuries ago.

Thorndikes, Snows, and Posts of Metinic Island

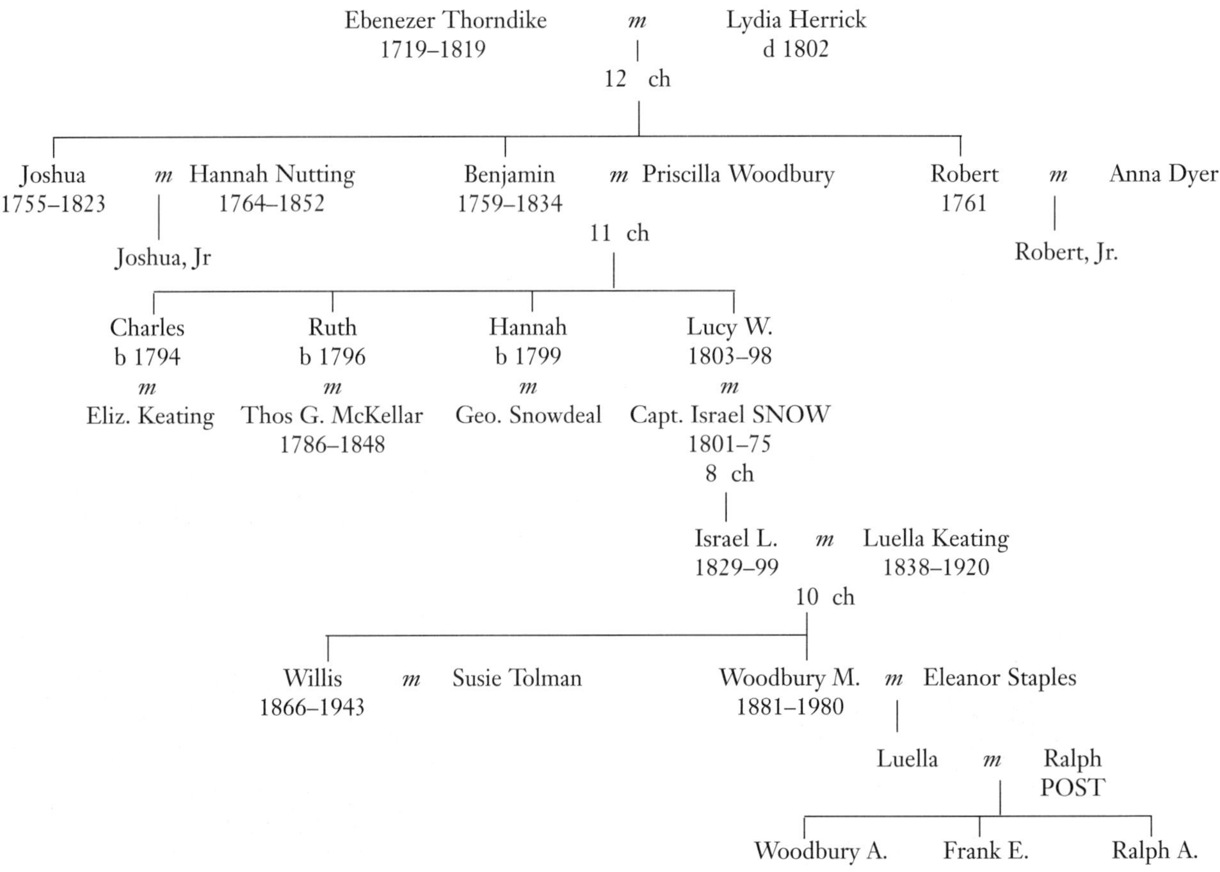

Metinic Green and Hog

These satellites of Metinic Island have had no independent "history." Metinic Green is called *Metinic Rock* on pre-Revolutionary charts (Map 1776 "Atlantic Neptune"), but appears under its present name in maps and deeds of the nineteenth century. *Hog Island* is shown under this name in an 1813 survey in the present owner's possession. Williamson (I: 64) confused the two in his 1832 history and identified Hog Island as lying half a mile southwest of Metinic, "containing two acres of miserable barren land." The island in question—Metinic Green—has in fact had little use beyond providing the fishing privilege to its owners, usually residents of Metinic itself. Hog Island had a dug well and a building on it around 1900: the structure shows in maps early in this century (e.g., Map 1904–06 Tenants Harbor quad). It is doubtful that this building was used for year-round residence, but Hog Island has served as an occasional summer residence for many generations of fishermen who frequent these grounds.

Green Islands (Large and Little Green)

These two islands, each with its own history, have one common characteristic: a deep acid soil, which made them from the earliest times ideal for hay and pasturage, but little else. No tree of any significance ever grew on either. A coastal map of 1691 names Green Island—only one, to be sure, but it could stand for either (Map 1691 New England). British Admiralty charts surveyed before the Revolution labeled them the Green Islands, and no subsequent cartographer thought of a better name, except to distinguish them as Large and Little. The same Admiralty charts, in one edition, show two buildings on the north end of the larger island. These could indicate residence, but it is more likely they were barns; a voyager in 1770 notes on Large Green Island "a temporary shed for the convenience of the haymakers" (Owen, "Narrative of American

Storehouse at top of landing on Big Green—or Large Green—Island. (Courtesy of Randolph Hopkins.)

Voyages," 738). I expect the "hay-makers," at that early date, came from Matinicus or Metinic, both inhabited at the time, and the crop was probably shipped on coasters direct to the Boston Haymarket. Williamson (I: 64), though he errs in their bearing and their size, notes that together the Green Islands yielded a hundred tons of hay a year in the 1820s; neither was then inhabited.

Although neither island appears to have had steady habitation until the latter half of the nineteenth century, there was considerable interest in both, to judge from the numerous conveyances recorded in the Rockland Registry of Deeds. Little Green, for example, beginning in 1770, was divided into halves, then quarters, then eighths before 1802, and thereafter parcels were regularly exchanged between haymakers of St. George and Thomaston—Linnekins, MacFarlands, Allens, Otises, Thorndikes (of Metinic Island), and others. Large Green was for many years in the dominion of the Halls and Cries of Matinicus and Ragged Arse.

I have seen no record of the earliest regular settlement on Large Green Island, but the federal censuses of 1870 and 1880 show the following residents:

1870	**1880**
Nelson Andrews, 35, farmer Rebecca, 29, wife 4 minor children	James Andrews, 54, fisherman Melissa, 47, wife 1 adult son, fisherman 1 son, 5 daughters
James Andrews, 44, farmer Melissa, 37, wife 2 sons, 4 daughters	Robert Hurd [Heard], 59, farmer 1 daughter 2 servants, fishermen
Total: 14	**Total: 13**

The Andrewses were probably from Andrews Island in the Muscle Ridge Islands; James eventually removed to Norton Island (see page 109). Robert Hurd, or Heard, was doubtless from St. George. The 1870 census gives some indication of Nelson's and James's worth: each had a real estate valuation of $800, which indicates they owned parcels of the island, and a personal valuation of $300. The agricultural census shows they each had the same improved land and livestock: fifteen acres of improved land, nineteen unimproved, four to five cows, and about thirty sheep. The census-taker adds this note: "The above

Duck hunters on Big Green Island in front of "Nate's Camp"—that is, Nathan Witham's—1930s. The hunters are identified as follows, from left to right: Maynard Dean, Murray Hopkins, a guest, Sumner Hopkins, Ed Hopkins, Mont Hanley, and Roy McConchis. (Courtesy of Randolph Hopkins.)

families make a small crop of hay and vegetables, catch and cure some fish in summer, pick up driftwood for fuel and shoot sea fowls in fall and winter months." This is undoubtedly what the Andrewses *did* do, but there are ways of saying it that sound less censorious; the census-taker, who reported in the same vein on Metinic Island, had a low opinion of life offshore.

We know from charts where these families lived on the island: one prepared in the 1870s shows five buildings at the north end, facing the cove, and some fencing (Map 1880 CGS 4). Farming gave way to fishing in due course, for it was fishing surely that brought the Withams to the island early in the twentieth century. Edwin Witham of Rockland bought the eastern half of the island, which was divided roughly on a north-south axis, and descendants of Robert Heard owned the western half. They shared the "Boghole"—that is, the north cove—and fixed a complex rig for launching and landing boats in foul weather; the pilings from this device are still visible in the cove today. The families sharing the island before the Withams' time, according to Edwin Witham's grandson, often feuded with each other.[34] Though responsive in emergencies and quick to lend a hand in hauling up a boat in danger, the families sometimes passed months without speaking to one another. The present Edwin Witham provides other interesting details of life on Large Green Island, or Big Green Island as he calls it, both before and after the Withams' arrival. Though fishing had become the main occupation of the settlers, the two large farms were kept up for some years. The nesting seabirds severely limited the garden crop: potatoes grew, but little else—the squash ran wild but yielded no harvest. The grass, by contrast, stood shoulder high except where sheep and cattle kept it down. Even when farming on the island ceased and the livestock was sold, hay was still harvested. Farmer Dodge, for example, from Dodge Mountain behind Rockland, used to take hay regularly off Large Green Island in the early years of the twentieth century. The children went ashore to school—Edwin Witham's three boys to Ash Point, which the family could see through the Muscle Ridge islands with a powerful British Admiralty telescope left on the island many years before. The telescope was also used to track the course of islanders returning from the mainland over the eight or ten miles of open water; in the early years they moved in dories, later in Friendship sloops.

The Withams gave up their year-round residence in about 1920—the Heard farm had been abandoned some years earlier—and thereafter used the island only in season. The well-built farmhouses and barns collapsed in due course, and the summering lobstermen built small camps for their families. A few such camps, still clustered around the Boghole, were in seasonal use late in the twentieth century. Withams have not often been in residence in recent years since most are engaged in the fish company founded in Rockland by Edwin's sons in the 1920s—a company in which Franklin D. Roosevelt once had an interest, it is said.

Little Green Island never had year-round residents, though lobstermen have summered here; a fish shack was still standing on the east end in the 1970s, though not in use for some years. There is an old well, now stoned up. Until the 1950s, according to a recent owner, this island was the northernmost nesting ground for laughing gulls. Leach's petrels also nest here, as do the usual varieties of gulls, eider, and other seabirds. Audubon expeditions have often stopped at the island, and Louis Darling gathered material here for his book *Gull's Way* (Wm. Morrow, 1965).

[34] These would be the families of James Andrews and Robert Heard, shown in the 1880 census above: according to Bernard Rackliff of Sprucehead Island, a bitter lawsuit between the two over title to the island dragged on for some years and was finally won by Heard.

Ragged (Criehaven)

Ragged Island appears on charts surveyed before the American Revolution as *Ragged Arse* (Maps 1754 Johnson and 1776 "Atlantic Neptune"), and one assumes—unless this was the name given by some gusty English seaman—that it was the surveyor's attempt to render *Racketash*, Abnaki for "island rocks." An early survey in 1819 continues to name the island Ragged-arse (Knox Plan Book); a census-taker in 1830, mincing no words, called it Ragged Ass; his successors in 1840 and 1850 returned to the Abnaki, but misspelled it *Hacketash*, while conveyances during this era call it *Ragger-task*; the first American coastal charts gave up on the Abnaki and named it simply *Ragged*, which is still the official name. *Criehaven* (after settler Robert Crie) was the name of the plantation incorporated there in 1896 and inevitably extended to the island itself; those close

Aerial view at low tide of Ragged Island with village of Criehaven, October 1974. Tenpound Island in near background, left center; Wheaton Island beyond (at mouth of Matinicus Harbor, not visible); No Mans Land beyond. (Photo by Robert Hylander.)

to the island still prefer this name. Matinicus lobstermen—out of perversity—continue to call it Ragged Arse, as it was in the beginning. So much for nomenclature.

The first conveyance I find is in the 1799 will of a Bristol land speculator, Alexander Nickles, who leaves to his son John, Ragged Arse as well as Fisherman Island off Pemaquid (Lincoln 8/169). Assuming the Nickles claim to Ragged Arse to have been valid, John Nickles must have conveyed very quickly to Ebenezer Hall of Matinicus, for in 1802 the latter sold to Benjamin Lain (Lane) of Vinalhaven; the sale price was $250 (Knox Lands 1/178). I then lose sight of conveyances until after the separation of Maine from Massachusetts in 1820 and the division of coastal islands between them. Ragged Arse falling to Masschusetts, the island was reconveyed by the Commonwealth in 1831 to Henry Brockman, a Swedish land investor of Bucksport, and David Hall, then living in Belfast (Knox Lands 3/78).

By this time—if not earlier—settlers were on the island. According to the federal census of 1830, two families were in residence, totaling fourteen persons: David Hall himself, then in his fifties, with a wife in her forties, one son in his twenties, and six children under twenty; and Robert Marshall in his thirties, a wife in her twenties, and three minor children (see census table below). I do not identify Robert Marshall, but David Hall was presumably a grandson of the original Ebenezer Hall of Matinicus; he gives his occupation as fisherman in a mortgage deed of this period to a Portland merchant (Knox Lands 3/148). Washington and Ezra Hall, shown in the 1840 census with households totaling eighteen persons, were probably sons of David. In 1835 David sold an undivided eighth of the island and its sheep, as well as a quarter interest in all buildings and the wharf, to Washington (Knox Lands 3/232), who apparently quit the island before 1850, since he is not shown in the census of that year. In 1857 Washington sold all his interest in the island to Willard F. Hall of Belfast (Knox Lands 54/385). Ezra Hall, meanwhile, appears to have quit the island as early as 1845 when he sold his three-sixteenths of the island and sheep to Henry Brockman (Knox Lands 44/448). Brockman remained an absentee owner of the island until sometime after mid-century.

From this fragmentary title record, it appears that the Hall interest in Ragged Island had virtually come to an end by mid-century. David Hall is still there in 1850, but at sixty-four it is unlikely he played a large part in the the island's development. Of the new arrivals from Matinicus, Robert F. Crie, in his mid-twenties in 1850, was to become the dominant figure in the island community during the next half century.

Robert was a grandson of John Crie, who settled on Matinicus after his discharge from the British Army in 1783. He married a daughter of Washington Hall (*not* the Hall of this name in the 1840 census). Robert and his eighteen-year-old bride Harriet moved onto Ragged Island in 1848. They lived first in a log cabin, according to Charles Long (page 101), then in 1849 moved into a newly built frame homestead overlooking both the harbor and Sea Cove on the southeast shore; this building served the Cries for more than three-quarters of a century and, with several additions, serves the present owner today.

The history of Ragged Island is so intimately related to the rise of Robert Crie that a recitation of his accomplishments will serve our purpose here. He was primarily a farmer in his early years on the island. The agricultural census of 1850 exaggerates in showing him with 350 acres under cultivation—the entire acreage of the island is not this much—but the listing of 300 sheep may be accurate; his activities were considerably more ambitious, according to this census, than those of anyone then farming on Matinicus. In 1880, when the agricultural census-takers were more exacting, Robert Crie is still shown with a larger farming operation than any of the dozen or so farmers indicated on Matinicus: 220 acres of meadowland, nearly as much as the *total* on Matinicus, more than 12 tons of hay, and 110 sheep—not counting spring lambs headed for the market. He was also engaged periodically in lumbering operations as wooded sectors of the island were cut over. From the 1870s or 1880s on he extended his operations into the fish business and maintained salting and packing facilities in the harbor as well as a supply store for fishermen. Warehouses were built along the shores of the harbor, with quarters for the packers above; the salted cod and other fish were shipped to the Boston market in the fall.

By 1879 Robert Crie had bought up all parcels of Ragged Island and ran it as a private fiefdom. There was inevitably rivalry with Matinicus, of which Ragged had always been a part. In 1896 the community was incorporated separately as Criehaven. It established its own schools (schools had been a source of continuous friction with Matinicus); it opened its own post office; and separate ferry service was provided soon after incorporation, the BUTMAN calling at Criehaven as well as at Matinicus. This was the community Robert Crie had created before his death in 1901.[35]

The residence table (page 54) indicates some of the members of this community. Most, to judge from their surnames, came from Matinicus and their stay was brief—brief because Robert Crie would not sell them land. Unless it was in his interest to do so. One such case was that of Andrew Anderson in the 1900 census: Andrew (he should be Carl Anton Anderson, according to his granddaughter Dorothy Simpson) was persuaded by a small grant of Crie acreage to move from Matinicus to Ragged Island with his wife and five young children to make up the statutory number of pupils in the Criehaven school. Another exception was Frederick S. Rhodes, who came initially as a schoolteacher, married Charlotte Crie (Robert's daughter), and through her acquired land north of the neck. Although Rhodes's normal residence was in Boston (the reason why his household appears only in the 1870 census), he maintained a large farm on Ragged Island and played a significant role in the community there, especially in the last decade of Robert Crie's life when he was crippled by a stroke. The *Maine Register* for 1900 lists "Hillside Farm," the Rhodes's residence, as a "hotel" catering to summer guests.

The principal business of Ragged Island, in 1900, however, was not hospitality but fishing. Of the twenty-four adult males on the island in the 1900 census, all but two are fishermen or connected with the fishing industry (only Eben Crie is shown as a farmer). The facilities around the harbor were taken over after Robert Crie's death by a new generation of islanders. Herbert McClure, for instance, a Scot who came onto the island in the 1890s as a weirman, remained for forty years running the fish-packing industry, as well as a general store and the post office. The Simpsons—Alfred, Fred, and Herman—reportedly rowed to Ragged Island in a dory in the 1890s and established residence; their descendants were still fishing the shores of the island a century later. One descendant, the island's principal historian Dorothy Simpson (she was a step-daughter of Herman and married Alfred's son), has passed on to me information about several of these turn-of-the-century islanders: Calvin Higgins in the 1900 census (called Ed Higgins) disappeared without a trace when fishing one day in his dory; Albert Hall, probably a descendant of the early Halls, drowned while sailing his sloop to Tenants Harbor (date unknown); Simon White was a French Canadian, his name anglicized from Le Blanc; Peter Mitchell was Danish, a model boatbuilder as well as a fisherman. Dorothy Simpson also mentions others not shown in the census: Harry "Harbridge," for example, whose only known surname came from the fact of his residing in a cottage called "Harboredge." He apparently came from Matinicus late in the nineteenth century and was returned there for burial after his death—under a stone reading "Honest Harry."

An article in a Boston newspaper in 1908 provided further scraps of information. There were fourteen adult males in the plantation, according to the article: John (probably Joseph) Alves is noted as the oldest resident, an inhabitant for thirty years after stopping off from an expedition to the Grand Banks; "Ed" Higgins is said to be the only bachelor; John Ericson, a six-foot three-inch Swede, newly arrived, is called the "Pooh Bah" of the island; Herman Simpson was constable.[36] Hatton Wilson, meanwhile, came

[35] Word of Robert Crie's death, according to his granddaughter Olive Wilson, was sent by carrier pigeon to the consulting doctor in Rockland, Dr. Gould, who alerted members of the family in Boston in time for the burial in the island cemetery. Details of the Robert Crie era are given in Long, *Matinicus Isle*, 101–05, and are supplemented by additional material in Dorothy Simpson, *Maine Islands*, 152–56 (see Bibliography). Olive Rhodes Wilson, who spent many seasons on the island, has also provided me with many details of life there at the end of the Robert Crie era.

[36] *Boston Sunday Globe*, September 13, 1908, courtesy of Mrs. Kenneth Ives of Owls Head.

onto the island in 1912 from Port Clyde; he was originally a fisherman but later took over the store run by Eben Crie. Hatton's son Leslie married Olive Rhodes, daughter of Frederick and Charlotte.

With some probing one could discover dozens of other residents on Criehaven early in this century. Census figures given in the *Maine Register* show forty-six residents in 1910, sixty-three in 1920, and sixty-seven in 1930. A study of the island in 1930, prepared in connection with a request for federal assistance in building a breakwater, notes twenty families living there.[37]

The population of Criehaven held up in the early decades of the twentieth century, as the above figures show, but the vigor of the community was gradually drained by natural disasters and changing times after Robert Crie's death. A severe northwest gale destroyed the steamboat wharf in 1908; soon after it was replaced, fire destroyed most of the warehouses on the harbor (Long, *Matinicus Isle*, 104). More important than these mishaps was the slackening interest of the Cries themselves in devoting their lives to the island. One son, Frank, who was asthmatic, moved west. John (whose children, if he had any, quit the island before 1900) removed before 1920. Eben died in 1922. Horatio (Rache), who was the son chiefly responsible for carrying on the family business after his father's death, was the last to leave. He continued for some years to take an interest in island affairs.[38] It was evidently Horatio, when he was living in Rockland as State Commissioner for Sea and Shore Fisheries, who persuaded Ragged Islanders to dissolve the Criehaven plantation as constituted in 1896. The Cries and Rhodeses, who as the principal landowners paid most of the taxes for the plantation, were finding the levy increasingly burdensome and in consequence sought a "wild land" category for Criehaven that would allow the school and post office to continue but would obviate the need for town meetings and further taxation. The State Legislature approved the dissolution of the plantation in 1925, placing the island under the jurisdiction of the state. The school, in fact, continued to the eve of World War II, though with fewer and fewer pupils. The Maine Seacoast Mission

[37] A copy of this study is at the Maine Seacoast Mission in Bar Harbor.

[38] He died in San Diego in 1948 at the age of seventy-seven; his remains were returned to the island for burial.

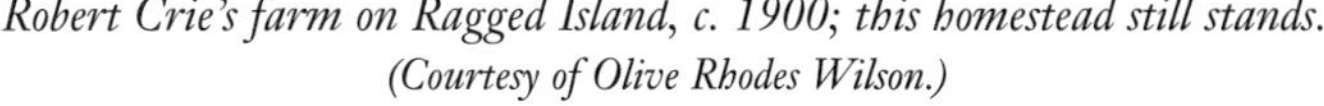

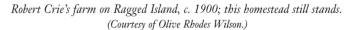

Robert Crie's farm on Ragged Island, c. 1900; this homestead still stands.
(Courtesy of Olive Rhodes Wilson.)

took over title to the school building and held several services there when the SUNBEAM visited the island, allowing its use for classes and as a general meeting place at other times. The post office continued intermittent operation as late as the 1960s, when the postmistress retired and there was no one to replace her. Ferry service also lasted, though on a reduced schedule, to about this time. The demise of the Criehaven community, then, was a great deal more leisurely than Charles Long, writing in the mid-1920s, had implied: he believed Criehaven was already extinct as a year-round community (page 103).

In the 1940s the Hogstrom brothers—Ragged Island appears over the years to have attracted a steady flow of Northern Europeans: Scots, Swedes, Danes, and Norwegians—bought up the remaining Crie interests and lived for some time on the island year round. They were also in the fish business and, among other things, provided clams to Snow's canning industry in Portland. They removed with their wives when they reached retirement age and in the 1960s sold the island—or the ninety percent of it they had acquired—to an energetic New Jersey jeweler. Ragged Island continues to have a lively summer community of fishermen and vacationers, some of them descended from former residents, but there has rarely been year-round habitation in recent years: Neil and Oscar Simpson (sons of Herman) spent several winters on the island with their wives in the mid-1970s.

Ragged Island and Matinicus, lying as they do in close proximity well out to sea—with Monhegan, they are the most remote island communities off the coast of Maine—naturally invite comparison. One wonders, in particular, why Matinicus has remained to this day a vigorous and prosperous year-round community while Criehaven foundered. The physical characteristics of each are, of course, relevant. It is no slight, I hope, to Matinicus to call Criehaven one of the fairest islands imaginable, with its graceful contours, its stretches of still open if uncut meadows, its cluster of tidy homesteads in the "city" by the harbor, and its dramatic coves and headlands; but it is half the size of its neighbor. When living space was critical to support a viable community, especially in early eras of settlement when much depended on farming, the advantage of Matinicus over Ragged is clear to see. Both harbors, I am sure, have been more cursed than praised by mariners; it is a moot point whether easterly gales are more benevolent than northerly, and both com-

Fishing community of Criehaven on Ragged Island, c. 1900; school house and chapel are at far left, Robert Crie farm is in center, and fish curing sheds are at right. (Courtesy of Olive Rhodes Wilson.)

munities have suffered heavily over the years. But Matinicus Harbor has been protected by a breakwater since 1911, at a time when its construction was perhaps critical to the survival of the island's increasingly motorized fishing fleet; the Criehaven breakwater, although requested at the same time, was completed only in 1937—after years of frustration and government procrastination. Matinicus succeeded in tying in to the telephone cable laid to Matinicus Rock Light as early as 1929; Criehaven did not have telephone communication until many years later.

The success of Matinicus Islanders in gaining benefits Ragged Islanders were denied, however, is no more than a reflection of the greater vitality of the Matinicus community in the first place—and I would like to suggest why this may have been so. It was not due so much to the greater size or any other physical advantage of Matinicus, or to its earlier established settlement, or to the bad luck of the Ragged Islanders in natural disaster, but rather to the sequence of personalities who invigorated each community. Ragged Island was dominated by a single figure during the last half of the nineteenth century—"King Crie" he was called—and when he died there was no provision for succession; no one person could fill his shoes. Leadership in the community was diffused among his sons while they remained on the island and among recent arrivals, most of whom had come—it should be recalled—more as Robert Crie's tenants (or peons, if you will) than as settlers in their own right. On Matinicus, by contrast, there was never from the time of Ebenezer Hall a single family, let alone a single personality, who dominated the affairs of the island. Charles Long (page 30) tells a nice tale of an elderly Hall and an elderly Young who challenged each other as to who should be "King" and agreed to resolve the issue in a hollering match from the top of Mount Ararat, overlooking the harbor; the senior Young won the match, and Hall, in a sportsmanlike manner, "acknowledged for all time the supremacy of the Young blood—in all matters pertaining to hollering." But no further, and that is the way it has been on Matinicus. Halls, Youngs, Tolmans, Ameses, Philbrooks, and in the twentieth century Bunkers have shared a balanced leadership in the island's affairs—not without their own rivalries, to be sure.

Speaking of rivalry, it would be idle to ignore as a possible factor in contrasting the fortunes of the two communities the so-called "feud" that has been carried on since the time when the Ragged Islanders broke away from Matinicus in 1896 and took the island's "fishing grounds" with them. The persistent crossing of the invisible lines has exacerbated the feud, and hostility naturally passed from the fishermen themselves to the other residents on each island. (Ragged Islanders, more fastidious about the character and appearance of their island, disdain the alleged "fast" living on Matinicus and the abandoned jalopies along its byways. A summer visitor on Matinicus, hearing gunfire one day on Criehaven, asked a Young what they were shooting over there and received the laconic reply, "Each other.") To suggest, however, that the feud—which is not unlike territorial rivalries between fishermen along the entire coast and even among the fishing families on Matinicus itself—was responsible for the eclipse of Criehaven would be a distortion of reality. Dorothy Simpson cites Herbert McClure for a more compelling reason for evacuation: the loss of the school, when the children had to be sent to the mainland for education, meant that mothers went with them; husbands, out of ennui, soon followed (correspondence with the author). She adds two reasons of her own—the surrender of the community's sovereignty to the State of Maine in 1925 and "a lot of rugged individualism misplaced." Dorothy Simpson concludes, "More and more it seemed better to just leave the island alone for the worst months." But on any day in the summer season, no one would guess Ragged Island had ever been abandoned.

I close by reminding readers that while the three early novels of Elizabeth Ogilvie—*Storm Tide*, *Ebb Tide*, and *High Tide at Noon*—do not pretend to be history, the Bennett's Island she portrays is a fine fictionalized treatment of Criehaven in this century.

Residents of Ragged Island (Criehaven), 1830–1900

Note: The following householders are believed to have resided on Ragged Island between 1830 and 1900. Age of householder is at first appearance. Spouses, if known, are in parentheses. In the decennial columns males are to left of slash, females to right. See also Matinicus census, especially for 1860.

Householder	**1830**	**1840**	**1850**	**1860**	**1870**	**1880**	**1900**
Hall, David, 44 (Susan)	4/5	?	1/1				
Marshall, Robert, 30s (Lydia)	2/3	?					
Hall, Washington, 30s		4/4					
Bramhall, Joshua, 30s		2/3					
Hall, Ezra, 30s		3/2					
Wilson, Robert, 38 (Olive/Fanny)			1/1	1/1	1/1	1/1	
Crie, Robert F., 24 (Harriet), trader			1/1	3/3	4/2	5/1	3/1
Leighton, Joseph, 34 (Susan)			4/2	6/3			
Abbott, Samuel, Jr., 21 (Eliza)				1/1	1/1		
Rhodes, Frederick, 44 (Cynthia)[39]					1/2		
Stinson, Nathan, 25 (Arvilla)					3/1		
Leighton, Willard, 21 (Adeline)					1/1		
Schrader, Frederick, 25 (Lottie)						1/1	
Hutchins, Robert, 41 (Eliza)						1/2	
Hall, James E., 29 (Ida)						1/2	
Wallace, James R., 32						1/2	
Stinson, William, 35 (Abbie)						3/1	
Crie, John, 49 (Nancy)							1/1
Crie, Horatio, 29 (Mabel), trader							3/2
McClure, Herbert, 33 (Annie)							2/1
Anderson, Andrew, 45							4/0
Davis, Almonius, 43 (Ella)							3/2
Jones, Samuel, 39							1/1
Simpson, Alfred, 42 (Lena)							3/1
Simpson, Frederick, 39 (Lizzie)							3/2
Totals:	**1830**	**1840**	**1850**	**1860**	**1870**	**1880**	**1900**
Number of households	2	4?	4?	4	6	7	9
Number of persons	14	18?	12?	19	19	23	44

Note: The following fishermen were living on Ragged Island in 1900 without families:

Thomas Ames, 79	*Calvin Higgins, 38*
Albert Hall, 69	*Edward Johnson, 71 (living w. Higgins)*
Joseph Alves, 52 (Portugal)	*Simon White, 22*
Peter Mitchell, 28	*Lewis Wardsworth, 70*
H. Hutchins, 19	*Jeremiah Wardsworth, 70*

[39] This should be Charlotte, daughter of Robert Crie.

Tenpound

The origins of this island's name, which appears on charts surveyed before the American Revolution, are too remote to determine with any certitude. One can choose between the fee in His Majesty's legal tenure that once changed hands with title, or a ten-pound cannonball that according to local legend was once discovered on the island. Tenpound was never inhabited, except by the usual nesting eider and herring gulls; for a time, early in this century, a pair of ravens nested there, but they removed after their eggs were broken. Wild strawberries abound, which makes the island a favorite berrying-ground for Matinicus housewives. And sheep were regularly pastured on Tenpound for as long as farming persisted on Matinicus. (I slept for many years under a blanket made of Tenpound wool.) The island was given to the National Audubon Society by the last owner and the last farmer on Matinicus, Clifford Young.

Wheaton

The Matinicus community owes its existence in part to this island, for during the many years before the breakwater was constructed in 1911, the only protection for Matinicus Harbor and the growing fleet there was provided by Wheaton Island. (Early mariners used the cove to the west—Old Cove—but the losses there were so severe in southeast gales that it was abandoned two centuries ago.) Wheaton is separated from Matinicus itself by a narrow channel, nearly bare at low tide.

The name, according to a recent owner (whose information comes from a Thomaston historian), is after a Colonel Wheaton who received a royal grant before the Revolution "to [lands in] Thomaston and several offshore Islands." There is indeed a Mason Wheaton who in 1777 received title to Sheep Island south of Owls Head—not from George III but from Nathaniel Crockett (Knox Lands 10/127)—and this could be the "colonel" in question. What use he made of his island off Matinicus I do not know, nor do I find a conveyance to David Peirce who acquired title sometime before 1814. In the latter year, Peirce, who was presumably of the Thomaston family of that name but then living in Belfast, sold to George Hall and John Crie of Matinicus; the sale price was $65 (Knox Lands 1/348). Seven years later the island was sold to James Condon for $100 (Knox Lands 1/546), and this began almost ninety years of Condon tenure. The island is named *Wheaton's* in both the 1814 and 1821 deeds but is called *Brimstone* in the 1822 division of islands between Maine and Massachusetts at the time of separation (*Bangor Historical Magazine*, III: 207/685); I have no idea why the name was changed, nor do I know why Brimstone was left to Massachusetts while Matinicus was assigned to Maine. In 1874 Wheaton, having reverted to Maine, was included in an auction of offshore islands the State of Maine felt had not been properly deeded. James Condon claimed "peaceful possession" for over fifty years and noted the construction of a home and fish house; he cited the 1821 deed for his claim. The state concurred and assigned the island to Henry, James's son, for $50 (Maine Archives, "1874 Island Sales").

James Condon opened a general supply store on Wheaton Island around 1830, and it ran intermittently under Condon control into the twentieth century. A store ledger covering the period 1839 to 1843, now in the possession of a descendant, Vesta Condon, shows a wide variety of products and services, all neatly listed in the aboriginal spelling of that era. I give a few samples—but the specialist is referred to Vesta Condon's 1941 article about her great-grandfather's store (see Bibliography); prices are in dollars and cents:

1 oz. gumberwhack	.10
1 pare shoes	1.66
2 lb shoger	.25
7 lb Caffe	.10
$^{1}/_{2}$ lb Cian peper	.05
for mending orgen	.20
for mending hankar	.42
12 lb nales	.90
1 gal molases	.57
1 lb chocklet	.16
2 pare oil trouses	2.25
$42^{1}/_{2}$ lb of mennilar	6.95
Dublin (doubling?) & twisting of 33B of worpe	8.25

And then, of course, there was liquor. A glass of rum, gin, brandy, or wine cost three cents, with varying prices for larger quantities; wine with two eggs in it (for hangovers, one presumes) cost five cents. Sales of these beverages were brisk in 1839 but fell off in 1843—possibly, Vesta Condon suggests, because a Temperance Society was organized on Matinicus about this time. Charles Long, historian of Matinicus, reports a melancholy tale of several islanders crawling under James Condon's store one night and boring into his rum barrel above, only to discover too late they had thought of no way to stop the flow of the precious liquid when their buckets were full.

Henry Condon sold the northern half of the island to John Matelock in 1905 and the southern half, where the store was, in 1909. The Matelocks were already on the island in 1900, according to the federal census: John Matelock, forty-one; his wife, Lizzie, twenty-four; her son by a previous marriage, Thomas Walker, six; and Horatio Flagg, thirty-nine, a boarder. Matelock, according to a recent owner, was a German seaman who before moving onto Wheaton Island had worked as a blacksmith in the Panama Canal Zone. On Wheaton he was both blacksmith and boatbuilder, after constructing his shop there from lumber he took from abandoned granite sheds on other

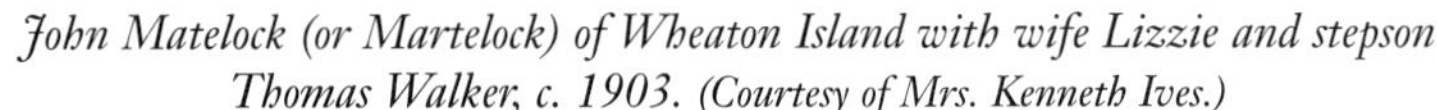

John Matelock (or Martelock) of Wheaton Island with wife Lizzie and stepson Thomas Walker, c. 1903. (Courtesy of Mrs. Kenneth Ives.)

islands and transporting it on his sloop. He lived in two rooms over the shop and was married there. Later the house was expanded so that the original structure became the "el" of the new building, which was still standing in the 1980s. Thomas Walker, John's stepson, was lost from his dory off Matinicus Rock in March 1916, according to a news clipping in the possession of Mrs. Kenneth Ives of Owls Head; he was said to have been paying court to the lighthouse keeper's daughter there at this time.

John Matelock died in the 1930s and his widow removed to Rockland; she sold Wheaton Island in 1951.

No Mans Land

This name appeared on maps at the end of the seventeenth century and designated the islands east of Matinicus (Map 1691 New England). Matinicus itself was not named on this map though the Rock was, as *Mentinicus*. The name *No Mans Land* probably reflected some uneasy compromise between English and other European fishermen who visited the area periodically long before the earliest Halls and Youngs. By the American Revolution the name was limited to the single island that bears it still (Map 1776 "Atlantic Neptune").

The earliest deed I discover for No Mans Land was in 1803 when Ebenezer Hall sold to George Hall for $20; in 1812 George sold to James Hall for $10; and in 1827 James sold for the same price to Benjamin and Ezekiel Burgess of Camden (Knox Lands 1/208, 1/300, and 3/14). These conveyances were apparently not honored by Maine State officials: at an island sale in 1874 the state conveyed the island to Samuel Lovejoy of Rockland, and claims to No Mans Land put to the State of Maine by the heirs of William Young, who had acquired the island from Benjamin Burgess in 1844, were set aside (Maine Archives, "1874 Island Sales").

No Mans Land surely never had regular habitation—though there are the remains of a crude foundation and pieces of an iron stove that betoken at least temporary residence. Bird life, on the other hand, has been more or less constant and figures prominently in what little history of the island there is. Early in this century (according to Clayton Young of Matinicus, who has his information from past officials of the National Audubon Society), the then owner of the island, Mark Young, was hired by a New York bird lover, William Dutcher, to protect the herring gulls during their nesting period on No Mans Land. This bird lover later founded the Association of Audubon Societies that eventually became the National Audubon Society—so the island, it could be said, played a part in the origins of this famous organization.[40] In 1911, according to Charles Long (*Matinicus Isle*, 13), a new owner of No Mans Land put two foxes on the island—a pair, he thought—to feed on the gulls and reproduce. The gulls left, however, and the foxes turned instead to the owner's small flock of sheep; when the foxes proved to be of the same sex, they were shot and the venture was abandoned.

The gulls in due course returned, followed by cormorants, but the most distinctive species that now breeds on the island is the eider duck. According to Maine state officials, a thousand pair of eider breed on No Mans Land—which is twice as many as on any other island along the Maine coast. It is this that caused the conflict between a recent owner and state officials. The former, himself a conservationist, bought the island with the idea of putting up a small summer cottage. He planned to use rainwater, designed his sewage disposal system ingeniously through a rock cleft, and was in all respects conscientiously ecological—yet his building permit was denied by state officials on the grounds that his human presence would disturb the eider duck. He countered with the proposal that if he could not build on No Mans Land, the state should allow him to find another island site along the coast by paying for

[48] Clayton Young has in his possession the diary of an early visit to Maine by William Dutcher in 1901, including a day-long visit to the gull colony on No Mans Land.

this one. There, over price, the negotiations foundered.[41]

I do not know whether the state's prohibition extended to an unruly ram that a Matinicus resident once banished to No Mans Land (with the owner's permission) when it became apparent that the safety of Matinicus schoolchildren was being threatened.

[41] The dispute has been written up in various newspapers, including the *Maine Times*, clippings of which the owner has provided me.

Matinicus Rock

The only alternate name this outermost fortress off the coast of Maine has had is *Wooden Ball Rock*—a name that appears on several editions of the 1776 "Atlantic Neptune" and is mentioned in the deed transferring the island to the United States Government in 1826. The purchase price of the island was $25, shared equally by Maine and Massachusetts (Knox Lands 1/564). The first lighthouse was built in 1827, twin wooden towers with a cobblestone dwelling joining them. The "castle" was built in 1834, an all-weather storehouse and sanctuary for the keeper and his family in severe storms. In 1846 the towers and dwelling were rebuilt with granite—and none too soon, for

Matinicus Rock Light and Coast Guard installations, October 1974; the Coast Guard buildings are now used seasonally by the National Audubon Society. (Photo by Robert Hylander.)

in November 1849, a storm destroyed the breakwater, much of the machinery and part of the house, and extinguished the light; the keeper and his family retreated on this occasion to the castle. There was rebuilding in 1857 after another severe storm, and thereafter the installations remained intact until 1923 when the north tower was taken down for reasons of economy. In the 1860s a fog signal was installed and the crew increased from one to four members (Sterling, *Lighthouses of the Maine Coast*, 144).

A list of the keepers of Matinicus Rock Light follows this entry, with their dates of service and other pertinent details. Most keepers, like their peers in the lighthouse service, were on the Rock for an average of five to eight years before moving on to their next posting. A number, however, became fixtures in the region and played important roles in Matinicus Plantation. Samuel Abbott, for instance, settled on Matinicus with his large family after his tour of duty on the Rock; he owned land and raised sheep on Wooden Ball and other grazing islands in the vicinity. His progeny appear in census schedules for Matinicus and Ragged islands through the nineteenth century (see pages 33–35 and 54). Keepers with surnames like Young, Hall, and Tolman were, of course, native Matinicans. Samuel Burgess, meanwhile, was living on Matinicus when he was appointed keeper in 1853; the 1860 census shows a son

Twin towers of Matinicus Rock Light, 1880s; those on the rocks in foreground—at least one with a rifle for shooting seabirds (including puffins)—are the family and friends of Keeper John H. Grant.
(Courtesy of Maine Historic Preservation Commission.)

Benjamin, twenty-three, with wife Eliza, in his household, as well as a daughter Abby—heroine of the great storm of January 1856. Her father had sailed to Matinicus for supplies and was there when the storm broke, leaving behind an invalid wife, four small daughters, and Abby, then seventeen; an adult son was also off the island. The family was obliged to retreat to the towers for protection from the storm, since the windows of the keeper's dwelling were shattered, one by one, and the Rock was awash. Abby Burgess kept the lights burning, both during the storm and for the four long, hungry weeks following before the seas subsided enough for Samuel Burgess to return. As Dorothy Simpson observes (*Maine Islands*, 151), for many years there was not a young girl along the coast—and well inland, too—who did not know of Abby's heroism. She married the son and assistant of the successor keeper, Captain John Grant (1861–1890), and after several more years on the Rock moved with her husband to Whitehead Island Light, where she served as assistant keeper (see page 106).

The lives of successive keepers of Matinicus Rock Light have been sufficiently chronicled (e.g., Sterling, *Lighthouses of the Maine Coast*; see Bibliography), and I will not prolong this entry except to note that the relationship between the families on the Rock and the residents of both Matinicus and Criehaven remained cordial through the years of the Lighthouse Service. In the 1940s the keepers were replaced by Coast Guardsmen, who manned the light until it was automated in 1983.

The only other activity on Matinicus Rock has been birdwatching, for this is a rare breeding ground for the Atlantic Puffin, the Razorbill Auk, and the Arctic Tern; indeed, Matinicus Rock has the largest tern population of any United States island (Deborah Davis, "New Light from Old Towers," *Island Journal*, VII:71). The association between the National Audubon Society and the Matinicus Rock Light Station is a century old. It began in 1900, when the society hired the keeper as a wildlife warden. Since then, Audubon staff and volunteers have monitored bird life on the island in the summer months. After automation, the Audubon Society leased the Coast Guard facilities and established a permanent summer station maintained by four field staff from May through August. Visitors today are restricted to the waters around the Rock, but whenever possible staff members row out to the watchboats to give lectures on bird life.

Keepers of Matinicus Rock Light, 1827–1920s

*Note: Ranks are shown as **K**, keeper; **1AK**, etc. as assistant keepers. Dates of service are shown. "Other remarks" include census information, as follows: year of census, age at time, name of spouse (if known), males/females in household.*

Name	Service	Other Remarks
John Shaw **K**	1827–30s	1830C: 60s; 3/1
Samuel Abbott **K**	1830s–40s	1840C: 40s; 6/4
William Young **K**	1840s–53	1850C: 50 (Ruth); 6/6
Samuel Burgess **K**	1853–61	1860C: 59 (Thankful); 3/5
John H. Grant **K**	1861–90	Longest serving keeper; resigned. 1870C: 68[42]; 1880C: 75; 3/1
Wm. G. Grant **1AK, K**	1875–1900	Promoted **K**, 1890; died 1900. 1880C: 38 (in John H. Grant house)
John F. Grant **2AK**	1876–87	1880C: 43 (Samantha); 3/1
Knott C. Perry **3AK**	1877–81	Transferred
Jacob T. Abbott **3AK**	1881–86	Position abolished
Jarvis H. Grant **2AK**	1887–88	Resigned
Wm. F. Stanley **2AK**	1888–91	Promoted and transferred
Thad. Wallace **3AK**	1888–91	Promoted, 1890
Aldiverd Norton **3AK**	1890–97	Promoted twice and transferred
Llewell. Norwood **3AK**	1891–95	Promoted and transferred
Fred. Hodgkins **3AK**	1892	Resigned
George A. Lewis **3AK**	1892–98	Promoted and transferred
James E. Hall **3AK, K**	1896–1908	Promoted **2AK**, then **K**, 1900
Merton Tolman **3AK, K**	1900–11	Promoted **K**, 1908
Chas. Burgess **3AK**	1897–1900	Promoted to **2AK**, then **1AK**
Elmer Holbrook **3AK**	1898–08	Promoted to **2AK**, then
Chas. Dyer **3AK, K**	1905–16	Promoted all ranks; **K**, 1911
Harold Hutchins **3AK**	1909–12	Promoted to **2AK**, then **1AK**
Art. Mitchell **3AK, K**	1912–19	Promoted to **2AK**, then **K**, 1916
George Studley **3AK**	1912	
J. H. Upton **2AK**	1912	
Frank O. Hilt **K**	1919–1920s	

Note: United States Coast Guard personnel manned the station from the 1920s to 1983.

[42] John H. Grant is shown in the household of another keeper in 1870: Christopher Chase, 68, wife Caroline. I find no such keeper listed in the

Wooden Ball

This island is shown with its present name on the 1776 "Atlantic Neptune," the inference being that the island was once forested. The earliest conveyance I find for Wooden Ball is a quitclaim deed in 1767 from "John Allin of Misquits [Mosquito] Harbor" to Ebenezer Hall, fisherman of Matinicus; the deed covers two-thirds of the island together with "eight sheep and a half" (Knox Lands 6/66). The island was used for pasturage, then, in pre-Revolutionary times, and I assume it continued to be used for sheepgrazing and perhaps farming into the nineteenth century. In 1837, for instance, in conveying a quarter interest in the island to Ebenezer Crie of Matinicus, John Emery of Thomaston reserved to his wife Margaret the right to pasture six sheep there during her lifetime (Knox Lands 3/334). In 1840 the federal census shows nine persons on the island: Ezekiel Hall, with his family, and Joseph Sweetland. In 1850 Samuel Abbott, aged sixty-nine, formerly keeper of Matinicus Rock Light, may have lived on Wooden Ball for a few years before moving to Matinicus.[43] I find no other year-round residents until 1900, when the federal census shows the following: Jeremiah Hamilton, seventy-three; A. Hamilton, forty-two; and the latter's wife Nellie, thirty-seven. It is also known that George Bunker, who later settled on Matinicus, spent two winters with his family on Wooden Ball Island around World War I (Clifford Young interview, 1975).

Ownership of Wooden Ball shifted between the Halls, Cries, and Youngs of Matinicus, the Rankins and Emerys of Thomaston, and Samuel Abbott. Abbott farmed the island after he left the Lighthouse Service, but I suspect most of the other owners held interest there for the fishing privilege, whether they summered on the island or not. The Abbott interest lasted through the century: according to the late Frank Dyer of Lincolnville, his father leased a fish camp on the island from Julie Abbott for several seasons in the 1890s. Such camps are shown at the narrow part of the island on maps of Wooden Ball in the 1880s (e.g., Map 1880 CGS 4) and must have existed for many decades before this.

Abbott descendants eventually sold to the Withams of Rockland, from whom title passed in 1955 to an Owls Head fisherman.

[43] His position at the beginning of the 1850 census schedule, followed by William Young on Matinicus Rock, suggests he may not have been living on Matinicus proper. There were ten in his household (five males and five females).

Seal (off Matinicus)

A map of the 1750s names this island, together with its neighbor to the west, the *Seal Islands* (Map 1754 Johnson). The 1776 "Atlantic Neptune" calls it *Seal Rock*; the surname has survived to the present.

Farther from Matinicus than Wooden Ball, Seal Island appears to have been used less by early settlers for pasturage or hay—which could have been because of the difficulty of landing on the island as much as its remoteness. Indians visited it regularly, even into the twentieth century, to gather eggs; the island is a breeding ground for a wide variety of seabirds, including Arctic terns, Leach's petrels, guillemots, and Mother Carey's chickens (Long, *Matinicus Isle*, 12). Fishermen have fished the shores of Seal Island for at least two centuries and many have summered there over the years. According to Erland Quinn, who used to visit the island frequently when he was yacht captain for the Porters of Great Spruce Head, four camps were on the island in the 1930s—and so many rabbits descended from the few brought out by the fishermen's children that they had to be liquidated to save the sparse vegetation (Enk, *Family Island in Penobscot Bay*, 329).

After World War II, during which Seal Island was closed to fishing and used as a bombing range, the fishing grounds around it were in some dispute between Matinicus and Vinalhaven lobstermen. The latter appear to have won the privilege and since 1948 up to a half a dozen Vinalhaven families have summered on the island to protect it. This seems appropriate, to judge from early deeds which show Seal Island being transferred from one Vinal to another as early as the 1840s (e.g., Knox Lands 44/333, an 1848 conveyance from William to David Vinal). Taxes are paid to Vinalhaven by the present owners.

In July 1978 a fire of unknown origin burned over the island for one foggy week, destroying the vegetation and many nesting birds. Efforts by Outward Bound volunteers, the Maine Forest Service, and state prison trusties to contain the blaze were frustrated by exploding shells left from World War II bombing runs; it was more prudent to let the fire burn itself out. The aspect of the island when the fog and haze finally lifted was desolate: ashes and the charred bodies of seabirds. Yet within a few years a sardine fisherman who visits the area regularly observed that the grasses and birds had returned—"seemingly in greater abundance and variety than ever before."[44]

[44] Joe Upton, "Fire in the Fog," *Island Journal*, III: 28. For a contemporaneous account, see also *Island Ad-Vantages*, July 28, 1978.

Islands of the Western Shore

The islands of the western shore, from Mosquito at the entrance to Penobscot Bay to Curtis off Camden, stretch some twenty miles over six townships and so admit of no common denominator. The grouping with the most distinctive unity is surely the Muscle Ridge Islands—and I signal this in a short entry for this cluster (pages 73–75).

Islands treated in Division II are arranged as follows: Group 1, from Mosquito Island northeasterly to Clark Island; Group 2, the Muscle Ridges, again northeasterly as nearly as possible from Two Bush to Otter; Group 3, the islands inward from the preceding, what has been called the "Whitehead group," from Calf Island northeasterly to Sprucehead; and Group 4, the rest of the widely spaced islands from South Thomaston (The Gig) to Camden.

Group 1: Mosquito Island to Clark Island

Mosquito

The early spellings of this island's name are varied: *Muskeito* or *Musketo* on British Admiralty charts, *Mesquito* and *Moschetto* on the earliest surveys of the town of Cushing (Map 1785 Knox County), and *Musqueto* in the first recorded deeds. Whether this was simply careless orthography by surveyors attempting to spell the ubiquitous insect of the family *Culchidae* that may have infested the island or a more sophisticated effort to render the Abnaki for muskrat, *musquaro*, we may never know. Albert Smalley on his map of St. George (Map 1970), citing an Indian chieftain, leans to the latter thesis; Philip Rutherford (*Dictionary of Maine Place Names*, 108), to the former.

The island was used for many years and seasons by Indians, as evidenced by the sizable middens in which arrowheads and other artifacts have been discovered. It also served as a landmark to countless European navigators from the time of Champlain; all who entered Penobscot Bay from the west or left it from the east passed close to the island—though they may not always have recognized it as such since it is easily confused at a distance with the headland behind it.

It is uncertain when the first white settlers came onto Mosquito Island. Some have argued (recent owners, for instance) that the stone house still standing near the northwest corner of the

Stone homestead built on Mosquito Island in the early 1800s. (Courtesy of Commander Albert J. Smalley).

island was built before the American Revolution, but I believe this is unlikely. If it were so, eighteenth-century mariners would not have failed to mention so prominent a feature. Nor is residence indicated in the early charts, including the very reliable 1776 "Atlantic Neptune."[1]

By the 1780s residence on the island is probable. A 1788 list of island residents in the Waldo Patent indicates Richard Martin on Island No. 19, called *Marshalls Island*—but its position in the list makes it clear this is Mosquito. Was he actually in residence and was his dwelling the stone house? Richard Martin's *residence* on the island may be questioned: an 1808 instrument after his death—a quitclaim from most of his heirs to one heir, Thomas Martin—explicitly notes that Richard Martin was living on a mainland farm, not the island, at the time of his death (Knox Lands 13/302); this farm, on Mosquito Harbor, had been deeded to Richard Martin "of Bristol" by Stephen Vickery of St. George in 1785 (Knox Lands 7/136). The stone house on the island could certainly have been built for a tenant or a dependent—even for Richard Martin himself in his younger years. The precise date of its construction may never be discovered. Here is what a recent owner says about the house's construction (in a questionnaire returned to the author):

> It is 45" thick at the base—rising 3 stories where the eaves are huge triangular blocks 6 inches thick. The outside of the house is straight and the taper is in the inside. The beams are *island* spruce keyed into the plates. The granite was cut on the island and the holes showing how it was split is a method that has not been used in 200 years. The granite was cut with a tonguing iron and kiln dried wooden pegs driven in and then boiling water poured on and the swelling caused the rock to split. The panelling is hand planed wide spruce boards that are slipped into each other and built in before the floors were laid. The bricks are hand made and the mortar in the granite rocks is roasted shells when it would have been a short trip to go to Thomaston and get lime at the time of General Knox. Some of the boards in the floor and roof are 35¾"—which may mean that 36 inch boards were cut down so as not to come within the King's Pines. The plaster in the walls has ox hair and sheep wool as insulation and binder.

Mosquito Island, despite its size, apparently remained a single-family island through the nineteenth century. A reliable chart in the 1870s shows no other buildings there except the stone house, with a wagon track along the inner shore to a landing in the southwest cove; there is also fencing (Map 1873 CGS 5). On a topographical map early in the 1900s two structures are shown in the northwest corner, one apparently a barn associated with the farm (Maps 1904–06 Tenants Harbor quad). The descendants of Richard and Thomas Martin retained title to the island to World War II, and many of them lived there.[2] From scattered records we know something of their activity. In 1857, for example, the granite for the twin light towers on Matinicus Rock as well as for the foundations of the lighthouse on Southern Island off Tenants Harbor came from Mosquito Island (Smalley, *St. George*, 184). How long granite was quarried on Mosquito Island is unknown; quarrying appears in any case to have been intermittent, for the scars left by the stonecutters are superficial compared to those on other quarry islands. Another enterprise on the island was a "pogy" factory, where menhaden were processed for oil and fertilizer; a communication in 1868 between Fred O. Martin of Mosquito Island and C. O. Wilcox of Tiverton, Rhode Island, relates to this activity (Smalley, 119). The remains of the pogy house are still visible on the northeast shore. There was, meanwhile, sheepherding, which continues today; periodic logging for cordwood and pulp; fishing from Mosquito Harbor (called Lobster Fare on one early chart: Map 1754 Johnson); and limited farming—since the soil is shallow.

A few residents may be identified from St. George tax and school records. David Griffin is

[1] Southhack's "New England Coasting Pilot" (Map 1721) shows a dwelling called "La farver house" on the mainland near the island, but the island itself is unnamed and uninhabited. Thomas La farver (or LeFebvre) certainly existed—a French trader in the region in the early eighteenth century—but the base of his operations was the Wessaweskeag River (present South Thomaston), not Mosquito Island. See "Thomas LeFebvre et le Fief Kouesanouskek," a paper prepared in Quebec by Father Honorius Provost (full listing in Bibliography).

[2] I have no exact count of Mosquito Island residents since the federal census does not distinguish them from Martins and other residents at Martinsville (a district of St. George). The island is now in the township of St. George, but previously it was part of Cushing and before that of Wiscasset.

shown on the island in 1864—probably as a tenant; he has eight cows, ninety-seven sheep, and his valuation is $1,000. The next year Fred O. Martin is taxed for the island, with the same valuation. In 1877 the tax schedule makes clear the two Fred O. Martin properties: island and mainland farm. Valuations cover the following:

> F. O. Martin, island: 1 house, 1 barn, 2 cows, 2 oxen, 120 sheep
>
> F. O. Martin, farm: 1 house, 1 barn, 2 cows, 2 horses, carriage, piano

School records for the island are fragmentary since there was no regular school there. In 1884 Sarah Jones taught a ten-week term on Mosquito Island. In 1888 there were two pupils on the island: Lewis and Lucy Clark, aged sixteen and nine. I know nothing of a Clark family, presumably tenants.

Martin descendants, tenants, and/or caretakers appear to have given up residence before the first World War. A buyer from the Martins in 1941 said that the stone house had at that time been vacant for about a quarter of a century. Since World War II the island has been used as a seasonal residence by owners from away.

If the history of this commodious and strategically placed island seems singularly barren, it is perhaps because it was always, from the eighteenth century, an extension of the mainland farm. The island had no identity of its own. Doubtless there was drama among the few people living there, but no report of it ever filtered down to sources accessible to historians—at least this one.

A word finally on Mosquito Island wrecks. The seas that often build up before the prevailing southerlies over open water, the treacherous shoals to be avoided eastward (Roaring Bull and Metinic Ledge), the fog that frequently blankets Port Clyde, and the promise of shelter behind the island conspire to make the southwest shore of Mosquito a mariner's graveyard. I hesitate to estimate the number of ships that have foundered on this shore, but if a report of three in three successive winter seasons in the 1890s can be credited,[3] then the total must be in the hundreds.

[3] Martha P. Emery, "Dan Carter of Port Clyde," *Maine Life*, October 1973. Dan's father Wilson Carter lived three years on Mosquito Island in the 1890s.

Northern and Southern

Both of these islands, flanking the entrance to what was once called *Tarrent's Harbor*,[4] were known by their present names in Revolutionary times. They appear as Northern and Southern islands, for example, on the 1776 "Atlantic Neptune." In 1793 Avery Hart conveyed both islands to John Hart, "he being now in possession of same" (Knox Lands 7/476). The phrase did not necessarily mean that John was living on one island or the other. Avery's title must be considered insecure inasmuch as the "larboard" island (that is, Southern) was conveyed a year later from Clark Linneken to Thomas Henderson and Patrick Wall for the handsome price of twelve shillings (Knox Lands 7/572). A number of conflicting deeds, in fact, are recorded during this period, conveying parcels of one island or both to and from Harts, Hendersons, Ripleys, and Linnekens, all of St. George (e.g., Knox Lands 9/415, 9/436, and 15/74); none of these deeds give further clues to early habitation on either island.

It is unlikely that either Northern or Southern island was settled before 1850, but we know both to have been lived on during the last half of the century. An 1873 map (CGS 105) shows a building on the southwest shore of Northern Island, just above the neck. This was presumably the home of John Allen, Jr., who is said to have moved from the Muscle Ridge Islands to Northern Island in the 1860s; his son John is also believed to have lived on this island in

[4] The harbor is variously spelled on pre-Revolutionary maps: *Tarance*, *Terrence*, *Talant's*, etc. (Maps 1754, 1764, 1776). It was given its modern spelling, *Tenants Harbor*, only after 1800; I do not know the origin of the name or the reason, if any, for the shift of consonants. Although settlers were in the area from the late eighteenth century, apparently no established community existed at Tenants Harbor until the 1830s (Smalley, "St. George," 57).

the later decades of the century, though the Allens apparently never owned it (correspondence with Stephen Sullivan, genealogist of St. George families). A building shows on Northern Island on maps of the early 1900s (Maps 1904–06 Tenants Harbor quad).

Southern Island was inhabited continuously from 1857, when the lighthouse was built there and Levi Smalley became the first keeper, until 1933 when the light was discontinued. A cluster of buildings was associated with the installation: the light tower itself, the keeper's home and outlying sheds, a boathouse, a stone structure for the storage of combustible materials, and a barn. The daughter of the last keeper, Captain Predley, says that the family tended a small garden and kept a cow and a pig. Southern Island was famous for its berries—especially strawberries, whose fragrance was so potent (it is said) that it was easily caught by mariners passing in and out of Tenants Harbor.

After the light was shut down in 1933—replaced by a lighted bell buoy off the eastern tip—Southern Island was sold to private individuals. Half of it, the gift of a benefactor, was owned for a time by the Knox County General Hospital in Rockland. In the latter decades of the twentieth century the island has been owned and extensively used by painter Andrew Wyeth and his son Jamie. Several of the old light station buildings still stand, preserving the stark and pristine character of the island. Spruce, however, have begun to overrun the fields kept open by a succession of light keepers and their families, spanning more than three-quarters of a century.[5] The eider, it is said, are no longer nesting. And the strawberries are gone.

There is rumor—but I give it no more credence than this, for it crops up in varying versions throughout our area—that the crews of German submarines landed on both islands during World War II, the proof being German newspapers, cigarette stubs, and containers negligently left there and later discovered by vigilant civil defense personnel. Our careless enemies!

[5] I do not have the names of all keepers, but here are some of them (from the National Archives):

1872–80	David C. King *Note: He is shown in the 1880 census, fifty-four years old, with wife Martha, and one son.*
1880	Thomas H. Bibber (served only one month)
1880–90	Eben D. Carlton
1890–92	William H. M. Weyman (died in service)
1892–98	Thaddeus A. Wallace (died in service)
1898	Mrs. T. A. Wallace (temporary appointment)
1898–1912	Joseph N. Jellison
1923–33	Captain Predley

High and Spectacles

High Island is No. 39 on the Great Plan of the Waldo Patent, and its first proper conveyance was in 1812 from Joseph Peirce of Boston, representing the owners of the patent, to Robert Henderson of St. George, a mariner (Knox Lands 16/538). Spectacles Island was sold in 1800, along with facing shore property, by Ellis Dowlf to Enoch Ripley (Knox Lands 9/414). Both Henderson and Ripley were landowners in the area in the early nineteenth century, but I have not followed the disposition of these two properties. Some quarrying was carried out on High Island in the latter half of the century, and elder residents are reasonably certain that there were year-round settlers after the quarrying era. I have not, however, discovered who they were, how long they stayed, or what they did. Spectacles, which Philip Rutherford (*Dictionary of Maine Place Names*, 111) says is named for its "eyeglass shape" (as seen by early crows, no doubt), has been used primarily for grazing sheep.

Clark

This island, *No. 41* of the Great Plan of the Waldo Patent, was named *Smith's Island* on the earliest post-Revolutionary surveys (e.g., Map 1785 Knox County). I do not identify Smith, there being no settler of this name known to me in the vicinity, but the island goes by this name in the first record of possession by Peter and Isaac Hall in 1788. In 1799 Peter and Isaac conveyed three-quarters of the island, undivided, to John Clark of Cushing for $280 (Knox Lands 9/390). In 1804 a different Hall, Caleb, with a nice disdain for fractions, conveyed a one-third portion to still another Hall, Elijah, and this was specified as the southeast end of the island (Knox Lands 12/130). In 1809 Elijah sold the same piece to Nathaniel Sevey (or Seavey) for $300, noting his boundary with John Clark's land (Knox Lands 15/76). These conveyances were, of course, without validity until authorized by the owners of the Waldo Patent, who by the early 1800s were Thorndike, Sears & Prescott; this trio in due course transferred nine-sixteenths of the island to John Clark and Nathaniel Seavey. How the remaining seven-sixteenths were formally conveyed is uncertain, but a Seavey descendant states that John Clark already held title to the island when he came from England—having presumably bought from the Patent holders there (Smalley, "St. George," 201).

John Clark settled on the north end of the

Oxen and quarrymen at loading wharf on Clark Island, 1870s.
(Courtesy of Commander Albert J. Smalley.)

island and had a sizable farm. Nathaniel Seavey, who married Clark's daughter Miriam, remained in possession of his portion of the island for several decades and may also have settled there: a mortgage deed in 1824 makes reference to *Clark and Sevey's Island*, a designation normally reserved for residents (Knox Lands 27/294). As early as 1807 the town of St. George voted to maintain a road from the head of Long Cove (present Route 73) to the bar that connected the island to the mainland, presumably so that the island's produce could be taken off by land; a passable road, however, was not put in before the 1870s (Smalley, 92, 205).

Quarrying began on Clark Island in the 1830s. In 1833 Nathaniel Seavey, having avoided foreclosure of the 1824 mortgage, leased granite rights for nine years to two stonecutters, Paul R. Weeks and Freeman Barker; the rent was $225 plus taxes (Knox Lands 32/170 and 171). The operations of these two contractors are not known, but maps surveyed in the 1850s show a road from the bar across John Clark's land to a cluster of buildings and a wharf near the easternmost tip of the island; the largest of the abandoned quarries are in this locality (Map 1864 CGS 312). Granite was apparently loaded aboard coasters at this location and at another pier on the island's most southerly nub; this pier and a road running the length of the island to it are shown in a map surveyed a few years later (Map 1873 CGS 105). Open fields and stone walls still show on this map, on the northern two-thirds of Clark Island, and there were still relatively few residents on the island proper. Evidently the quarrymen lived initially on the mainland across the bar—a community still known as Clark Island. (Indeed, the island proper and the mainland community often appear to be confused in records of the area.)

The Fogg family—Isaiah, Lucius, and Alvin in particular[6]—figure in island conveyances during the 1850s and 1860s. They held the controlling interest in Clark Island before and after the Civil War. A mortgage deed in 1859 makes reference, *inter alia*, to paving block and "fort stone" quarried at Clark Island—the latter product apparently for fortifications at Portland, Boston, and New York harbors. Photographs of quarrymen posing before a sign that reads "Clarks Island Granite Works, 1873" show several dozen workers; other photographs from the same era show many pair of oxen, rails, heavy lifting equipment, sizable cutting sheds under construction, a two-and-a-half story boardinghouse, a three-masted schooner loading at the wharf, and miscellaneous other details testifying to an already extensive operation. (A larger selection of these photographs is in Smalley, 156ff.) When Isaiah and Alvin Fogg sold the island in the 1870s to George Mark and Milton St. John of New York and New Jersey, respectively, they included polishing machines, steam boilers, and other sophisticated equipment in addition to the oxen (Knox Lands 27/366 and 40/162). St. George tax records for 1876 indicate some two dozen taxpayers under "Clark Island"—though

Stonecutter at work on Clark Island, c. 1900.
(Courtesy of Maine Historic Preservation Commission.)

[6] I find the following Foggs in St. George census schedules (to show their ages, spouses, and occupations), but I do not identify their precise residence: 1850, Isaiah Fogg, 44 (Charlotte), trader; 1870, Albion Fogg, 34 (Maria), quarryman, and Josiah Fogg, 46, farmer.

without indication of whether they were on the island proper or the mainland.[7]

Mark and St. John expanded quarrying operations on the island. With contracts for a post office and customs house in Hartford, the Standard Oil building in New York, the mausoleum at Woodlawn Cemetery, and various other installations, they employed about one hundred stonecutters plus supporting crews of quarrymen, jobbers, sculptors, and so forth. By 1880 almost as many quarry workers were living on the island as across the bar, to judge from the count of schoolchildren that year: fifty-one on the island, sixty-six on the facing mainland, according to Albert J. Smalley (page 56).

George Mark sold his interest to the St. Johns in 1882. Milton St. John died in 1886 and his widow carried on operations for another dozen years, apparently winning the respect of the community while piloting the enterprise through a slack period. In 1888–89 there were only fourteen

[7] These were the 1876 taxpayers for "Clark Island," with their livestock and with indication of home ownership (x):
Clark Island Granite Company: 13 small houses, 1 large; 8 oxen; 2 horses

Ellis Pierson (x)
William Ulmer (x)
Robert Kirkpatrick (x)
Philip Ulmer
George Watts (x)
E. L. George (1 cow)
Frank Kane (x)
L. B. Scribner (1 cow)
James Rowan (x)
? Weever
Geo. & Wm. Monarch (x)
Robert Ashworth (1 horse)
A. D. Drake (x)
Martin Hopkins II
J. E. Dunn (1/2 x)
Christopher Collett (x)
Martin Hopkins
Hiram Peavey (x)
Lyman Scribner (x)
J. S. White (3 cows)
Alexander Humphries
James McDougal (2 horses)
Joseph Cassabelli (x)
A. A. Keen & Co. (2 horses)
Elisha Henansen
Hills & Doe Co. (x)

Schooners loading granite at Clark Island. (Courtesy of Maine Historic Preservation Commission.)

stonecutters, but there were seventy paving-cutters and sixty quarrymen—"indicating," as Smalley (page 204) explains, "that a good deal of pier stone and random stock was being shipped together with a fair amount of monumental stone, both cut and uncut." The population may have dropped somewhat during this era; a "census" in 1892—actually those said to be receiving mail at the island post office—lists a total of fifty-five (*St. George Chronicles*, 50).[8] The same year, however, Mrs. St. John was successful in persuading the town of St. George to raise $1,500 for a stone causeway across the bar, and this appears to have brought more residents onto the island: a map surveyed around 1900 shows more than thirty buildings on Clark Island, the majority of them dwellings (Maps 1904–06 Tenants Harbor quad). Mrs. St. John sold the quarries in 1898 (Knox 110/586). The new owners incorporated under the name Clark Island Granite Works and continued operations.

A paving cutter born on Clark Island in 1902, Everett Baum, himself the son of a paving cutter (Charles Baum), has left vivid evidence of the quarryman's life early in the twentieth century.[9] The work was harsh and the rewards meager. To make extra money for his large household (his wife Georgina McConchie, her two brothers, and eight children), Charles Baum worked nights at the Clark Island cutting shed: $1.50 for a ten-hour shift. Dollar bills rarely passed through his hands since he was paid in credit at the company store, where it was virtually obligatory to buy supplies if one expected to hold one's job. The married quarrymen lived in identical company dwellings, a story and a half, three rooms downstairs, an open attic for sleeping, no bathroom. Single quarrymen lived in the company-owned boardinghouse, called the White House. Everett Baum estimated that there were about four hundred workers in the Clark Island quarries in the peak years, three hundred of them stonecutters. The quality workers, Baum said, were the Swedes—among some fifteen nationalities who made up the Clark Island work force; the next most capable were the English stonecutters.

Baum made a distinction between stonecutters and paving cutters, based on his career as one of the latter after he had served his apprenticeship (with his father) and become a paving cutter in his own right: the paving cutter was paid by the piece and so had full independence as to when and where he worked; the stonecutter was salaried and compelled to work, especially in the winter, in dust-clogged sheds where the risk of contracting lung diseases was very real. But paving cutters were not free of danger, especially to the eyes: paving cutters became practiced surgeons in removing slivers of granite with magnets from their companions' retinas.

Everett Baum stated that for all practical purposes the Clark Island quarries ceased to operate after the strike of 1897–98—that is, a few years before he was born (*Island Journal*, II: 19). The date is premature. There was indeed a bitter strike—the Clark Island paving cutters were the oldest and most respected quarrymen's union on the coast of Maine—and there were lean times in the first decade of the twentieth century.[10] The strike, however, did not cripple the new Clark Island Granite Works. By the 1920s work was back to normal and in 1930 the number of quarrymen on the island was over 300, comparable to the peak years of the 1890s (Grindle, *Tombstones and Paving Blocks*, 218).

The granite industry in the end could not survive the decline in the demand for ornamental stone and the replacement of granite by reinforced concrete and brick in the construction business. The quarries on Clark Island, which was always considered—along with Dix, Hurricane, and Crotch—one of the four great "quarry islands" in the region (leaving aside the mega-islands like Vinalhaven and Deer Isle), were

[8] I list the householders below, though I know little about any of them:
Christopher Collett, wife, and fourteen children (on the 1876 tax list)
Samuel Cummings
William J. Fogg and wife
James Harrison, wife, and one child
Abiatha R. Leighton and wife
James McConchie, wife, and five children
four McLeod children (no parents)
John Snow, wife, and two children (a contractor in early 1900s)
Thomas Vennor, wife, and four children
Thomas Williams, wife, and eight children

[9] Everett Baum was interviewed by John Van Sorosin for a piece in *Island Journal*, II: 18 (1985).

[10] The Clark Island union had only fifteen members in 1907, for instance, compared to 107 in the neighboring union at Long Cove (Maine Bureau of Labor Statistics, *Report*, 1907).

worked less and less after World War I and closed down completely before World War II, about one hundred years after operations began. A few quarrymen continued to live on the island, and two of them were still there when prospective cottagers bought the island from the Deer Isle Granite Corporation in 1957: Carl Swanson (with wife Betsy) and Gustav Johnson, both of Swedish extraction. These tenants soon departed, and the cottagers remained the sole occupation of Clark Island during the following decades.

Group 2: Muscle Ridge Islands

It is often assumed that some casual cartographer simply misspelled *mussel* in his charting, for the intent must surely have been to name the bivalve mollusk that abounds in the area, not local brawn. But the bivalve itself, it should be remembered, has been subjected to varied spellings: *muscala* in Latin, *muscelle* in Old English, and indeed *muscle* in Middle English. Our cartographer then was not in error but following a hallowed tradition; his successors have not thought it worthwhile to improve on his spelling.

The Muscle Ridges comprise fifteen to twenty islands (depending on one's method of counting them) and have always been considered an extended island community. A list of voters in the "Muscle Ridge Plantation" in 1844 has been preserved, though it is not clear that such a plantation existed at that date. The voters were:[11]

John Allen	Peter Gibson
Noah Andrews	Amos Gregary
James Child (son-in-law of Job Rackliff)	Thomas Horn
Israel Elwell	Job Rackliff
Israel Gregary	David Tomsin (Thompson)

Assessors: Job Rackliff, Israel Gregary, Thomas Decker
Clerk: Noah Andrews

In 1852, according to records in the Maine State Archives, six residents of the Muscle Ridge Islands (the residents are unnamed) petitioned for incorporation and asked that an organizational meeting be held at Moses Shaw's home to elect officers. I find no further record in Augusta of this petition, but a quarter century later, in 1878, another petition was prepared. This one named the islands to be included, seven in all (Dix, Andrews, Hewett, Grafton, Pleasant, Crow, and High), and called for a meeting in March at "the hall on Dix Island." Meanwhile, a few calls to meetings have been preserved, and some of the officers elected are named: in 1869, for instance, O. A. Crockett, clerk; David H. Smith, John Foster, and John Odiorne, assessors. A few years later D. H. Smith was plantation clerk; H. B. Simmons and J. B. Pratt were assessors. In 1878, a more complete list of officers suggests a plantation was in full sway. They were as follows:

George Cutler, Moderator
C. P. Dixon, Jr., Treasurer and Collector
J. B. Pratt, H. B. Simmons, O. B. Spear, 1st, 2nd, and 3rd Assessors
D. H. Smith, Clerk
H. B. Simmons and Michael Tracy, Constables
E. S. Montgomery, Surveyor of wood and lumber
D. H. Smith, E. S. Montgomery, A. N. Johnson, School Committee
H. B. Simmons, Surveyor of weights and measures

It was voted that there would be a single school district for the plantation, with the school located on Dix Island. A sum of $125 was voted for plantation expenses. H. B. Simmons followed D. H. Smith as plantation clerk and held the post from 1879 to 1881.

It is clear that the plantation in 1878 was the creation of the Dix Island Granite Company. David Smith, its clerk, was agent for the company; C. P. Dixon, Jr., plantation treasurer, was also an officer of the granite company. The corporation, already in full control of the economic, cultural, and social life of the extended community, wished merely to tie up loose ends by controlling the municipality as well. It was a short-lived munici-

[11] The list was uncovered by Malcolm Jackson, founder of the Muscle Ridge Historical Association in Owls Head.

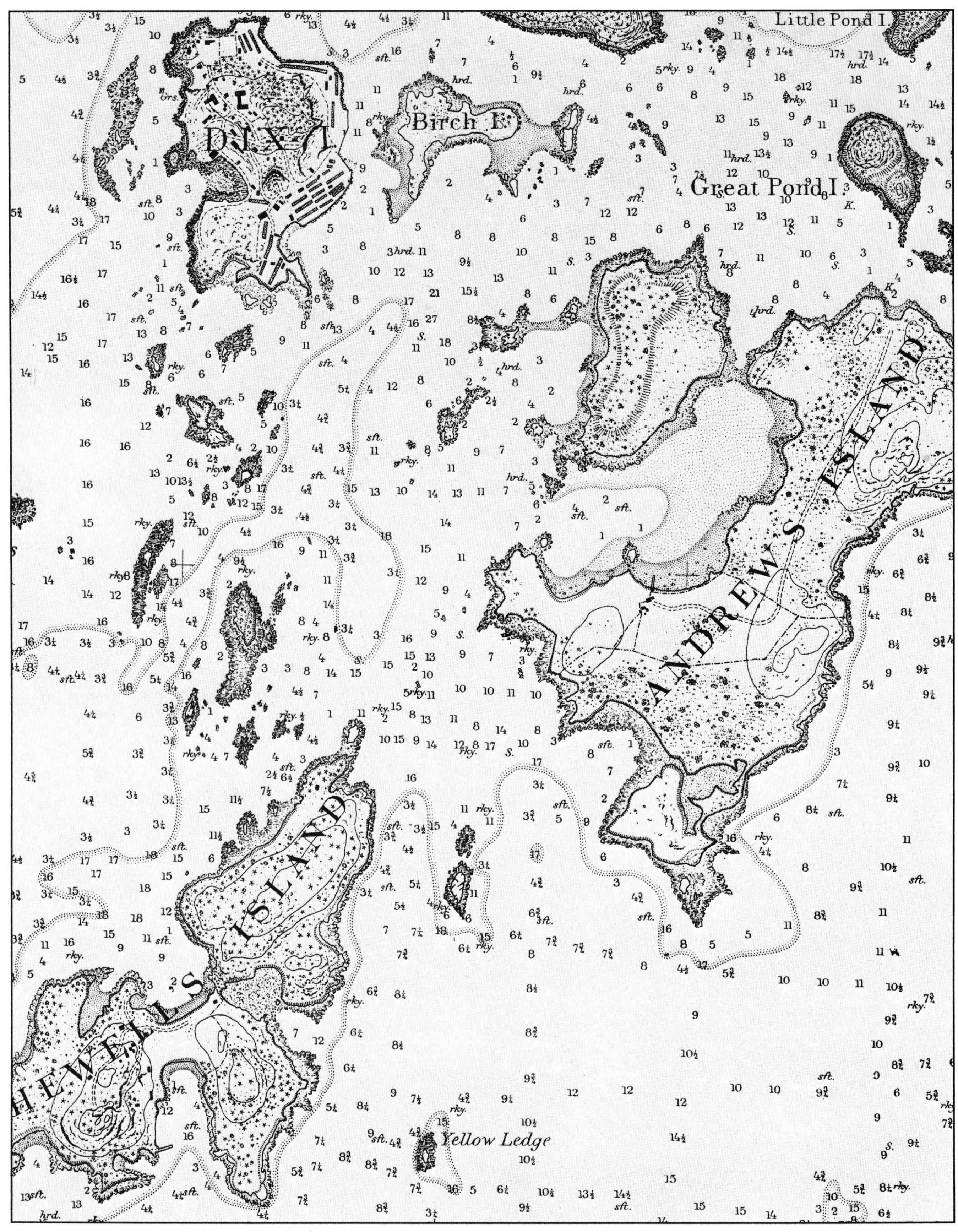
Little Pond I.
Birch I.
DIX I.
Great Pond I.
ANDREWS'S ISLAND
HEWETT'S ISLAND
Yellow Ledge

pality. The plantation of 1878 ended with the abrupt collapse of the Dix Island Granite Company, as we shall see, in the early 1880s. A note in the Maine State Archives, written by a former assessor of the plantation later in the 1880s, reported "no organization at Muscle Ridge for the past two years. The Postmaster gave me this [the form to certify the holding of an annual meeting, required by law] as I was one of the last assessors at Muscle Ridge and I do not know the address of the last clerk...."

Opposite page: *Dix Island and surrounding islands in the Muscle Ridges, as surveyed in 1860s for a chart printed in 1874 (see Bibliography for full listing). Note the number of buildings on Dix Island: cutting sheds, boardinghouses, private dwellings, etc. Hewett (Hewell) has more modest quarrying, and the quarries on High Island are not yet opened.*

The Muscle Ridge Plantation was reactivated in 1905 and lasted a decade—with town meetings, budgets, a school (at times), and the usual activities of small municipalities. Federal census schedules show about two dozen households in the Muscle Ridges during this decade, with some forty to fifty residents. Frank Crockett, caretaker of the abandoned holdings of the Dix Island Granite Company and still resident in the agent's dwelling, was the architect of the plantation and its factotum, assisted by his son R. H. Crockett. Muscle Ridge Plantation, in its second incarnation, ended early in World War I—in more dignified fashion than its predecessor in the 1880s.

It is appropriate to open this segment with a listing of all those we know from federal census schedules to have lived in the Muscle Ridges from 1820 to 1910.

Residence in the Muscle Ridge Islands, 1820–1920

Note: This table lists those who, according to federal census schedules, lived in the Muscle Ridge islands from 1820 to 1920. Age, if shown, is at first appearance in census. Spouses, if known, are in parentheses. Occupations are shown as follows: B, blacksmith; C, carpenter; Fi, fisherman; Fa, farmer; L, laborer; Q, quarryman or stonecutter; T, teamster; other occupations are spelled out. Real estate valuations for 1850 and real estate/personal valuations for 1860 (over $500) are also shown. Males in a household are to left of slash, females to right.

The islands on which residents lived are indicated in the census schedules from 1880 on, and are often known (or suspected) for earlier years. Some households moved from one island to another. Symbols for the islands, where they can be identified, are used as follows (used rarely in 1860 and 1870 when virtually all residence is assumed to have been on Dix Island):

Andrews, ***A***	Andrews Neck, ***AN***	Birch, ***B***	Camp, ***C***	Dix, ***D***
Flag, ***F***	Graffam, ***G***	Graffam Bar, ***GB***	Hewett, ***He***	High, ***Hi***
Mink, ***M***	Otter, ***O***	Pleasant, ***Pt***	Pond, ***Pd***	Two Bush, ***TB***

Head of household	**1820**	**1830**	**1840**	**1850**	**1860**	**1870**	**1880**	**1900**	**1910**	**1920**
Andrews, Amos ***A***	1/2									
Andrews, Jonathan, 23 (Sarah), Fi, $800 ***A***	1/3	5/3	5/3	2/3						
Raleigh, Michael	3/1	5/2								
Allen, Samuel ***He***	4/3	3/4								
Peabody, Solomon ***He***	5/4									
Anderson, Jonathan	1/2									
Neef, William ***He***	1/5									
Allen, Jonathan D?	3/2									
Perkins, William F?	1/1									
Patten, Ebenezer ***He***	1/2									
Cole, Edward, 40s		2/2								
Gregory, Israel, 35 (Sophia), Fa, $3000 ***He***		4/6	4/4	5/2						

Head of household **1820** **1830** **1840** **1850** **1860** **1870** **1880** **1900** **1910** **1920**

Head of household	1820	1830	1840	1850	1860	1870	1880	1900	1910	1920
Thompson, William, 50s		2/1								
Maker, Joshua, 30s, ***He***		4/2								
Horn, Thomas, 40s		2/4								
Metcalf, Patrick, 30s		3/4								
Andrews, Noah, 20s ***A***			4/3							
Allen, John, 42 (Anna), Fi, ***He***			4/3	2/4						
Allen, Andrew, 20s ***Pt***			3/2							
Allen, Daniel, 20s ***He***			2/1							
Jackson, John, 50s			5/4							
Rivers, Thomas, 31 (Emelia), Fi ***He***			1/2	6/2						
Johnson, James, 25 (Polly), S ***A***				2/3						
Shaw, Moses, 26, Q D				4/0						
Rackliff, Job, 45 (Lydia), Fa, $600 ***A***				6/4						
Childs, James, 33 (Mary), S ***A***				1/1	1/2					
Andrews, Theodore, 25 (Sarah) ***A***				1/1						
Gyer (Geer), Daniel, 30 (Elizabeth), Q ***D***?				4/3						
Note: Six single quarrymen were boarding in Muscle Ridge households in 1850, presumably on Dix Island.										
Brannan, Joanne, 33 (widow) ***He***?					1/4					
Russell, Edward, 25 (Margaret), Q					2/1					
Odiorne, John, 34 (Clarissa), Q					3/4	6/3	5/5			
Donahue, Bartholomew, 35 (Catharine), Q					2/3					
Sewell, Zolmony, 36 (Elizabeth), Q/L					4/3	5/2				
Sweeney, Owen, 32 (Mary), Q					2/2					
Limeburner, Thomas, 45 (Hannah), Q					2/2					
Clark, Jonathan, 34 (Mary), B					3/3					
McCrackey, James (Mary), Q $0/1,500					1/1					
Palmer, John, 36 (Hannah), Q $8,000/1,000					1/1					
Quigley, Patrick, 34 (Bridget), Q					2/2					
Hamlen, Charles, 27 (Mary), Q					1/1					
Spear, James, 44 (Sarah), teamster $1,000/300					2/2					
James, Andrew, 30 (Jane), Q $0/1,000					1/3					
Sweeney, Patrick, 24 (Jane), Q					1/1					
Brannan, James, 30 (Marilla), Q ***He***					3/1	4/1				
Carlin, Michael, 30 (Catherine), Q					2/4					
Shean (Sheehan), Cornelius, 28 (Bridget/Sarah), Q/grocer					1/2	1/3	1/0			
Frye, Alphonso, 26 (Sarah), B					2/1					
Sanborn, Gilman, 47 (Mary), teamster					2/5					
Donahue, Florance, 35 (Mary), B $0/5,000					3/3	4/3				
Sleeper, Brainard, 34 (Mary), Q $0/1,000					1/1					
Butler, John, 31 (Louise), Q					3/1					
Henrick, Patrick, 27 (Ellen), Q					4/3					

Head of household 1820 1830 1840 1850 1860 1870 1880 1900 1910 1920

Head of household	1820	1830	1840	1850	1860	1870	1880	1900	1910	1920
Carter, Daniel, 29 (Mary), Q					3/1					
Waite, John, 45 (Mary), C					6/1					
Walsh, John, 36 (Mary), Q					3/1					
Mulligan, James, 35, Q					1/1					
Stafford, Patrick, 42 (Martha), Q[12]					5/3					
Gray, James, 35 (Mary), B $1,000/500					2/1					
Crockett, William, 35 (Harriet), F $1,500/600					3/4					
Beals, Lewis, 27, (Elizabeth), merchant					2/4					
Meservy, Washington, 41 (Mary), teamster					5/2					
Note: Twenty-three single quarrymen were boarders on Dix Island in 1860.										
Crockett, Oscar A., 24 (Eliza), packetmaster						2/2				
Smith, David H., 43 (Alvira), agent Dix I. Granite Co. $3,000/10,000						1/2				
Foster, John H., 27 (Emely Jane), Q						2/2				
Rackliff, Cyrus, 34 (Emely), Q						3/2				
Martin, William J., 34 (Elizabeth), teamster						1/3				
Cannon, James, 50 (Bridget), Q						2/4				
Martin, Andrew, J., 40 (Sarah), Q						3/1				
Ivy, Henry, 40 (Eliza), Q						1/1				
Burns, Thomas F., 35 (Mary), Q						1/1				
McDonald, Michael, 35 (Mary), L						2/3				
Carleton, Asa, 28 (Frances), Q						1/1				
Auspland, Jacob, 49 (Emeline), Q						3/3				
McManus, Peter, 40 (Sarah), Q						1/1				
Brainard, James, 45 (Marzella), Q						4/1				
McCormack, Peter, 26 (Elizabeth), Q						1/1				
Dyer, Timothy, 22 (Mary), Q						2/1				
Eldridge, Reuben, 60, Fi						1/0				
Foster, John, 50 (Caroline), Fi						3/4				
Simmons, Hanson B., 27 (Victoria), Q						2/1	3/3			
Note: One hundred and six single quarrymen and workers lived in boardinghouses on Dix Island in 1870; there were also a few female domestics.										
Fogg, Rodney L., 40 (Mary), Sup't, Dix I. Granite Co. ***D***							2/2			
Wall, William, 28 (Lucy), Q ***D***							2/1			
Cavanagh, Patrick, 33 (Eliza), Q ***D***							2/4			
Duncan, Peter, 45 (Margariett), Q ***D***							4/4			
Thomson, Joseph, 30 (Fanny), Q ***D***							1/3			
Cairns, John, 40 (Agnes), B ***D***							4/4			
Doull, Daniel, 22 (Ella), caulker ***D***							2/1			
Geddes, Daniel, 33 (Ellen), Q ***D***							1/5			
Gould, John, 30 (Jane), Q ***D***							3/3			
Head of household	**1820**	**1830**	**1840**	**1850**	**1860**	**1870**	**1880**	**1900**	**1910**	**1920**

[12] Patrick Stafford was a single boarder in 1850.

Head of household	1820	1830	1840	1850	1860	1870	1880	1900	1910
Montgomery, Stanley, 31 (Elena), clerk ***D***							2/1		
Crocket, A. F., 33 (Maggie), S ***D***							1/2		
Hall, Samuel E., 46 (Julia), C ***D***							1/1		
Stanley, Joseph, 34 (Mary), machinist ***D***							1/1		
Daily, John, 41 (Almena), C ***D***							1/1		
Crocket, Frank A., 26 (Florence), Q ***D***							1/1		
Killman, William, 28 (Elsie), Q ***D***							1/1		
Auspland, Webber, 26 (Ada), B ***D***							2/3		
Kelley, William, 28 (Helen), Q ***D***							2/4		
Tracy, Michael, 37 (Amy), watchman ***D***							1/4		
Cutler, George O., 30 (Elsie), Q ***D***							3/4		
Thompson, Daniel K., 45 (Abby), Q ***D***							1/1		
McKeele, Daniel, 32 (Ann), Q ***D***							1/4		
Chase, Otley, 22 (Sadie), Q ***D***							3/1		
Chase, William W., 65 (Susan), L ***D***							2/4		
Shakespear, Robert, 34 (Elizabeth), Q ***D***							1/3		
Johnson, Abraham, 50 (Emily), Fi ***A***							3/2		
Odiorne, Elisha, 32 (Alis) ***A***							1/3		
Herrington, Elias, 44 (Catherine), Fi ***He***							1/2		
Spear, Oliver B., 40 (Lizzie), Fi ***G***							2/4		
Meservy, Herbert, 26 ***G***							1/0		
Wentworth, Charles, 49 (Eliza), Fi ***Hi***							1/1		
Chase, Steven, 31 (Flora), Fi ***Hi***							2/2		
Merchant, George, 21 (Fanny), Fi ***Hi***							1/1		

Note: Eighty quarrymen and laborers were in boardinghouses on Dix Island in 1880.

Head of household	1820	1830	1840	1850	1860	1870	1880	1900	1910
Norton, Alteverd, 50 (Rosilla), lightkeeper ***TB***								1/2	
Pruett, Joseph, 35 (May), assistant keeper ***TB***								2/3	
Elwell, Eben, Fi ***Pt***								1/0	
Nason, John (Eliza), Fi ***He***								2/1	
Smith, Charles, 33 (Susie), Fi ***He***								1/2	
Hurd, Charles, 67, Fi ***He***								1/0	
Wallace, Albert, 32, Fi ***He***								1/0	
McDaniel, John, 63 (Maria) ***He***								1/1	
Burke, Charles, 30 (Mamie) ***He***								1/1	
Jennings, Edward, 44, Fi ***A***								1/0	
Hart, Alexander, 37, Fi ***A***								1/0	1/0
Granza, John, 32, Fi ***A***								1/0	
Hopkins, Edward, 32 (Ada) ***G***								3/2	
Perry, Cortland, 37 (Winifred) ***G***								2/1	
Carr, Charles, 32 (Temperance), Fi ***GB***								4/2	

Head of household	1820	1830	1840	1850	1860	1870	1880	1900	1910	1920

Head of household	**1820**	**1830**	**1840**	**1850**	**1860**	**1870**	**1880**	**1900**	**1910**	**1920**
Elwell, Llewellyn, 19; in 1910 with wife Maggie and family ***F***								1/0	3/2	
Robbins, Albert, 50 (Mattie) ***AN***								2/2		
Porter, Fred, 26, Fi and Edward Stover, 50, 48, Fi: partners ***C***								2/0		
Brown, Edward, 40 (Addie), Fi ***Pd***								3/3		
Drinkwater, Leroy, 28, Fi ***Pd***								1/0		
Smith, Albert, 35 (Lizzie), Fi ***B***								2/2		
Wentworth, James, 64, Fi and John Woodward, 49, Fi ***Hi***								2/0		
Nason, James, 59 (Roxana), Fi O								2/1		
Carlson, Angus, 39 (Amie), Fi; boarder, Holman McCusick, 52, Fi ***D***								2/3		
Crockett, Frank, 46 (Florence), Superintendentt Dix Island Granite Co. ***D***								2/2	2/1	1/2
Wood, John, 56 and son Seaman L., 33, Fi ***F***									2/0	
Colby, William W., 29 and boarder Oscar Winchenbaugh, 34, Fi ***M***									2/0	
Brawn, Jerome C., 35 (Mirala), lightkeeper ***TB***									1/1	
Dolliver, Lewis, 39 (Edith), assistant keeper ***TB***									1/1	
Perkins, Edward H., 28, Fi ***He***									1/0	
York, Henry F., 35 (Grace), Fi ***He***									2/2	
Rackliff, Alvin T., 25 (Julia), Fi ***AN***									2/1	1/1
Atkinson, Albert, 42 (Lydia), Fi ***A, D***									2/1	1/2
Douchell, John F., 44, Fi ***A***									1/0	
Michelson, Michael, 45, Fi ***A,***									1/0	1/0
Williams, Fred A., 26 (Leona), Fi ***B***									2/2	
Frazer, Charles A., 30 (Lena), Fi ***B***									1/1	
Allen, Walter R., 36, L ***D***									1/0	
Brown, George A., 62 (Lizzie), grocer salesman ***D***									1/1	
Brown, Sidney, 37 (Nina), Q ***D***									1/1	
Rines, John, 58, Fi ***D***										1/0
Elwell, Leroy, 43 (Annie), Fi ***AN***										1/1
Dyer, Randall, 28 (Inez), Fi ***AN***										2/1
Harvey, Charles, 23 (Marion), Fi ***AN***										3/1
Maddocks, Fred, 63 (Albina), Fi ***AN***										1/2
Drinkwater, Jasper, 42 (Bessie), caretaker ***G***										6/2
Head of household	**1820**	**1830**	**1840**	**1850**	**1860**	**1870**	**1880**	**1900**	**1910**	**1920**
Totals:										
No. of households	10	9	8	10	34	27	35	25	22	10
No. of persons	46	58	50	59	186	260	157	70	41	30
No. of men	21	30	28	35	112	218	70	42	29	18
No. of women	25	28	22	24	74	42	87	28	12	12

Two Bush and Crow

British Admiralty charts surveyed before the American Revolution show the *Two Bush Islands* as including Two Bush Island itself and surrounding ledges (Map 1776 "Atlantic Neptune"). Williamson (I: 63) notes Two Bush in 1820, "so called because it has exhibited two bushes conspicuous to the passing mariner," but he adds a cautionary note to future mariners that only one remained standing. Early coasting manuals warned inbound mariners to keep the island "a pistol shot off the port bow" to be clear of the ledges. *Crow Island* is named in deeds as early as 1808 and never had another name. Since both islands were without fresh water, neither was settled until the lighthouse was put on Two Bush at the end of the nineteenth century. A Rackliff, it is reported, spent a summer in residence on Crow island many years ago, but quit because of thirst after one season.

Both islands were sold by the State of Maine to Alden Shea in 1884 for $10 (Knox 67/124)—a price that was to appear absurdly low in a few years' time. There are several versions of how the United States government acquired Two Bush for a light station in the 1890s. According to Alden Shea's descendants, he was hoodwinked by an individual posing as an agent for the federal government and sold the island a few weeks before a *bona fide* representative appeared; a court case ensued, which negated the previous sale—but Shea's legal costs canceled out any profit (Simmons interview). Records in Rockland tell a different story. Alden Shea clearly conveyed the island in 1892 for $100 to Charles F. Guptill of South Thomaston, presumably not the *poseur* in question; Charles conveyed to Emily Guptill in 1895, and the court proceedings involved *her* possession of the island, not Alden Shea's. There appear to have been two issues: her title, contested by an administrator of the will of William McLoon, and the price she was attempting to exact from the United States government. Emily Guptill's title was upheld, but I am uncertain from the record whether she got her price (Knox 82/377, 100/591, and 102/424).

The early keepers of Two Bush Light were as follows, according to records in the National Archives, with additional data from census schedules: age, (spouse), males/females in household (see table below).

There were two keepers manning the light until the reorganization of the service in 1912, compensated as follows: $540 monthly for the captain, $450 for his assistant. The keepers' children boarded on Whitehead Island during the school months, one of the mothers accompanying them.

Marine disasters were frequent off this hazardous landfall at the entrance to the inner bay, but probably not as numerous as the legends that have grown up around them. Where fact shades into legend is impossible to say, but two mishaps are worth recording. One involved the schooner JENNIE J. PILLSBURY, which struck a ledge off Two Bush and was safely "moored" there, so the skipper thought, before the crew rowed ashore to await the next high tide; but when they returned, the schooner had slipped its moorings and disappeared into the fog—whether rediscovered or not the legend neglects to say (NEAFOH, Robert B. Applebee interview, November 1964). The second tale (which we may entitle "Man's Best Friend...") is told of a fishing schooner CLARABELLA that, caught in a thick

Keepers, Assistant Keepers	**Dates**	**Census Data**
Alteverd A. Norton, K	1897–1909	1900: 50 (Rosilla), 1/2
Joseph A. Pruett, AK	1897–1901	1900: 35 (May), 2/3
Roscoe L. Dobbin, AK	1901–1902	
William G. Thompson, AK	1903–1905	
Benjamin F. Wakefield, AK	1906–1908	
Lewis W. Dolliver, AK	1908–1910	1910: 39 (Edith), 1/1
Jerome C. Brawne, K	1909–1912	1910: 35 (Mirala), 1/1
Leroy S. Elwell, K	? – ?	1920: 43 (Annie), 1/1

northwest gale off the Green Islands, ran for cover in the Muscle Ridges but lost her way and foundered off Two Bush. The captain and his companion put off in a dory and, guided by the barking of the keeper's dog, found the island; the dog meanwhile roused the keeper who hauled the two fishermen ashore when their dory capsized (Sterling, *Lighthouses of the Maine Coast*, 147).

Two Bush Light was automated in 1964. Hapless mariners off its shores today must make do for themselves.

Pleasant

The earliest reference I find to this island in deeds at the Rockland Registry is in an 1808 mortgage from Stephen Peabody—said to be of Lincoln, Massachusetts, though his residence is given in most deeds as the Muscle Ridge Islands—to John Ulmer of Thomaston (Knox Lands 14/137). The mortgage was apparently paid up, for in 1811 Stephen Peabody conveyed Pleasant Island, together with Crow and Two Bush, to Jacob Ulmer for the same price shown in the 1808 mortgage: $210. No reference is made in these deeds to residence; nor does Williamson (I: 63) note any habitation on the island in the 1820s, though he considers it "a site worthy its name." Philip Ulmer conveyed to Enoch Ripley of St. George in 1818 for $100 (Knox Lands 19/632), and thereafter I lose sight of title transfers until a mortgage deed in 1856 from Daniel S. Hall to Urial Patton (Knox Lands 35/89). But the Peabodys were tenacious, for in 1860 Pleasant Island was among the Muscle Ridge islands that a later Stephen Peabody sold to Joseph Hewitt for $500 (Knox lands 5/43).

This brief and admittedly incomplete recital of early title transfers of Pleasant Island gives us little clue as to who farmed it in the first half of the nineteenth century. The cellar hole still visible on the western slope of the island, facing Mink Island; the dug well near the shore below it, still used by the present owners; and the stone walls crossing the island clearly date from this era. There are candidates among those listed in the decennial censuses from 1820 on as living on the Muscle Ridge Islands but not identified with a particular one: Michael Raleigh and William Perkins in 1820; Michael Raleigh, again, Edward Cole, Jeremiah Safford, and others in 1830—and so forth. It is also possible that one of the Peabodys, Stephen or Solomon, resided on Pleasant Island for a time. The records are too distant and too imprecise for me to identify this energetic early settler, though it is to be hoped that some future researcher will find a clue.

The McLoons of Rockland were associated with ownership of Pleasant Island during the last four decades of the nineteenth century, during which it was used for offshore fishing rights and eventually weirs. The island was never quarried. For a time, early in the twentieth century, Pleasant was owned by the Jordan family of New York, who had acquired title when a McLoon mortgage was foreclosed (Knox 2/444). Jordan heirs still owned the island in 1921, valued at $1,000 (see Appendix 4B.) In due course the island was acquired by Maude I. Shea; she passed title through relatives to a descendant who in the 1970s (when I last visited Pleasant Island) lobstered from the island in the summer and wintered in Florida. Like its neighbor Hewett, Pleasant Island has been the summer home of a colony of lobstermen and their families since the early 1900s. In 1900 a solitary fisherman was living on Pleasant Island year-round: Ebenezer Elwell, aged twenty-nine (see census table, page 78). The owner in the 1970s recalled that in his youth as many as eighteen or twenty children were on the island every season. Many of the families were, of course, Sheas and their relations, but there were others: John Wood and his son Seaman, for example, who spent summers in a camp at the southern tip of the island for a quarter of a century.[13] Another seasonal resident lived in a cabin above the cliffs on the western

[13] This was probably after 1910, when John and Seaman Wood are shown on Flag Island (see census table, page 79).

shore close to where a ship, missing Two Bush Light in a southeast storm, ran ashore, nearly putting its bow through his bedroom window; and, of course, there were many others, too numerous to list even if I could.

The summer colony had shrunk by the 1970s. Apart from the owner and his immediate family, one other family from Belfast had recently bought the southern peninsula beyond the neck. The diminished population had perhaps encouraged the osprey to return in strength, for no fewer than eight pairs were nesting on the island in 1975.

Mink

This tiny island, I believe the smallest in this study, has the distinction of having been at one time the most densely populated. No fewer then half a dozen fish camps were still standing in the 1970s, remnants of a bustling colony earlier in the century. A dug well with an excellent supply of water is still there. The summer fishermen, however, have abandoned the island, and the buildings stood empty the last time I saw the island.[14]

[14] Marion Arey's recollections of her life on Mink Island as a child are in *Island Journal*, IV: 63.

Graffam, Bar, and Hurricane

A careless misspelling of Graffam by an early cartographer was eventually corrected: the island is properly shown on current charts, though it appeared on most maps in the nineteenth and early twentieth centuries as *Grafton.* It is curious, given the island's closeness to shore, generous size, and aspect, that it never sustained long habitation—at least as far as I have been able to discover. There is no reference to residence in the early deeds; Williamson (I: 63), naming it correctly in his 1832 description and calling it "a pleasant one, well swarded into grass," notes that there are no inhabitants; and the federal census lists no one we can surely identify with the island before 1880. There are no ancient cellar holes.

The title deeds being reasonably clear and complete in the Rockland Registry, it is perhaps useful to review ownership for any clues to possible habitation or to other uses the island may have had. The earliest deed I have seen is dated 1793: it is from William Heard of Thomaston, an important trader in island and shore properties during this era, to Joseph and Daniel Mathews, yeomen respectively of Thomaston and Cushing, and conveys to them for £3 a two-thirds interest in the two most westerly islands of the Muscle Ridge group, totaling about fifty acres—unmistakably Bar and Graffam islands; the remaining third interest, according to the deed, is "believed" to be owned by Stephen Peabody (Knox Lands 7/472). There may, however, be a conflicting claim on the island, for Malcolm Jackson, in his chart of early lots in South Thomaston, notes Prince (or possibly Pierce) Graffam as the first owner and his earliest conveyance—to Solomon Peabody (Map 1991, Jackson). Graffam, in any event, never lived there. In an 1811 conveyance to William Rackliff, Jr., "of St. George or alias Musriges," Graffam is said to be a yeoman of Lincolnville; the island, for which the purchase price was $275, is called "Weston Musrige or Graffam's Island" (Knox Lands 15/359). William Rackliff was the eldest son of William Rackliff, Sr., then living on Rackliff Island; it is certainly possible that the son lived for a time on Graffam, but if so it was not a long settlement.

The deeds through the next decades are not instructive for our purposes. They involve mortgages to the land brokers Thorndike, Sears & Prescott; foreclosures and sale to off-island speculators like John Gleason, a storekeeper in Thomaston; return of title to Graffam's heirs, more mortgages, and so on. None of these owners apparently were interested in the island

Oliver B. Spear, 1860s; Civil war veteran who later lived on Graffam Island. (Courtesy of Joy Jordan, a descendant.)

from the viewpoint of settlement. In 1857, it was bought by Horace Beals of Dix Island, surely with the intention of working it into the granite empire he was on the point of creating. But this never occurred. Beals's death and the preoccupation elsewhere of the Dix Island Granite Company organized by his heirs left Graffam Island untouched by the quarry boom. An 1874 map of the Muscle Ridge Islands at the height of the granite era shows Graffam, almost alone among the larger islands of this group, with no signs of habitation or other activity. A family was, however, living there in 1880, according to the census of that year: Oliver B. Spear, a fisherman aged forty, with a household of six. Spear was a Civil War veteran.[15] He evidently remained on the island only a few years, or shared the island with another household, for Horace Norton of the Whitehead Lifesaving Station noted in his journal in January 1884 that he borrowed from a Mrs. Pool "on Grafton Island" her copy of *King's Family Physician* (George Carey, "Family Island," *Island Journal*, V: 38). In 1900, federal census schedules show two families on the island: those of Edward Hopkins and Cortland Perry, both fishermen (see residence table, page 78).

Early in this century Graffam Island was acquired by an energetic weirman from South Thomaston named Edwin V. Shea, who had extensive interests in the area and whose operations proved profitable. He sold Graffam in 1919 to the Underwood Company, which was the major fishing concern in the Muscle Ridges for the next thirty years or more. During the 1920s local lobstermen summered on the island, and a few probably spent occasional winters as well, but a fishing community comparable to those on Hewett, Pleasant, and other islands in the Muscle Ridges never developed on Graffam.

In 1929 a cottager with a considerable domain in Tenants Harbor bought Graffam Island for $5,000. At the time there were two fish camps on the island, a barn, and a rickety wharf. The new owner soon built a log cottage of five rooms facing west, a dwelling that still stands.

There was also a Portuguese fisherman from the Madeira Islands on Graffam named Maurice Escorcio, and he was retained as caretaker. He had a wife and two children. He drowned four years later in a freak accident off the northeast corner of the island: his eleven-year-old son was dragged off the stern of their boat when a spear he was trolling overboard struck a large bottom fish, and the father leapt in to save the boy. Both were dragged under in the fast currents of Muscle Ridge Channel, as mother and another child watched from the shore.[16]

Walter Drinkwater, descendant of Sprucehead and Muscle Ridge fishermen (his father fished on High Island), was the next caretaker on Graffam Island and lived there, off and on, for nearly fifty years (1934 to his death in 1982). He was a lifelong bachelor (after an ill-considered early marriage) and, while enjoying company, preferred the solitude of a hermit-like existence. He interspersed his duties as caretaker

[15] According to a descendant (Joy Jordan of Birch Harbor), Oliver Boynton Spear was born in Thomaston in 1842; he lived there, on Graffam Island, in South Bristol, and in Sheepscot, where he died in 1925. He married Sarah Elizabeth Butler of Union. His father, James Reed Spear, is quite possibly the James Spear shown as a teamster on Dix Island in the 1860 federal census (see page 76).

[16] I am indebted to George Carey, a descendant of the Tenants Harbor owner, for this and other details of twentieth-century life on Graffam Island in his article "Family Island," cited above.

with lobster fishing and miscellaneous other occupations, and was a warm counselor to fresh generations of Tenants Harbor heirs.

The owners of Graffam have usually owned Bar Island as well, though there are separate owners today. In 1900, according to federal census schedules, a Scottish fisherman named Charles Carr, thirty-two, was living there with his wife Temperance and four minor children, but it is not likely that many families lived on the island year-round. Seasonal residence, on the other hand, both in this century and the last, was normal. A story-and-a-half, cellarless, clapboarded dwelling was used into the 1930s; there is a dug well and a wharf on the island. Albert Burton of Sprucehead told me that his family used Bar Island around 1900—presumably on a lease, or as squatters, since the Burtons do not appear in the title record—but I do not know who the other fisherman-residents were. It is also possible that quarrymen working on Dix or Hewett in the 1880s lived on Bar Island: a deed dating from this era included a ban on the sale or consumption of intoxicating beverages, the object presumably being, as the present owner remarks, "to maintain the morale—or at least the efficiency—of the stone workers."

Hurricane Island, about an acre in size, has normally gone along with Graffam and Bar as far as ownership is concerned, but today it is owned by a Sprucehead fisherman for the lobstering privilege. It has obviously never had habitation, and I have no knowledge of the origin of its name but suspect it derives from its lying in the path of prevailing southwesterlies sweeping up Muscle Ridge Channel.

Flag

This small island was the seasonal residence for many years of Alden G. Shea, an energetic fisherman in the Muscle Ridges during the heyday of weiring. In the 1880s a Robert Snow claimed the island and indeed collected rent from Alden Shea; Snow passed word that his father had been given the island by an earlier resident named Perkins, no date specified. In 1884 Shea, after living some years on the island, bought it from John F. Day for $30; Day had acquired the island from the State of Maine for $10 the same year (Knox Lands 64/165 and 67/86). Shea henceforth refused to pay Snow rent, and there the matter rested. A lawyer for a subsequent owner searched the records and found no evidence that either Robert Snow or Perkins ever owned the island.[17]

[17] I am indebted to C. William Colby of Sprucehead Island for the information about the Snow-Perkins claim and its refutation.

There were already buildings on Flag Island when Alden Shea acquired title: two are shown on a map printed a decade earlier (Map 1874 Dix Island). Three buildings are shown there on maps from early in this century (e.g., Maps 1904–06 Tenants Harbor quad). One of these was surely the home of Llewellyn C. Elwell, aged nineteen, shown there alone in the 1900 census; in 1910 he had a family—wife Maggie (she was his second wife) and three children. John Wood and his son Seaman were also in residence on the island, both of them lobstermen like Elwell (see census table, page 79).

In 1918 Alden Shea sold Flag Island to the Underwood Company, whose lawyer made the title search referred to above. Tax records in Augusta, however, still show the island owned by Shea as late as 1921, valued at $200 (see Appendix 4B).

Hewett (or Hewell)

Why the name of this island was persistently misspelled as Hewell on charts over the years is a mystery, for as anyone in the area will tell you the name is Hewett, or Hewitt, and has been for over a century. The island had previous names, *Long Island* appearing most frequently on the earliest deeds. The earliest reference to a conveyance I have seen is to one dated 1767 from Joshuway Alley to Stephen Peabody and Thomas Keef; this is mentioned in an 1822 deed from William Keef to Abel Patten, which notes the conveyance of the island "fifty-five years before...it being the same that was took up and since settled" (Knox Lands 25/377). The settler was in all likelihood Stephen Peabody himself, for he appears in several deeds of the era as "of Long Island." But Stephen at one time or another owned other islands in the Muscle Ridges—Pleasant, Crow, and Two Bush, for sure, and probably Graffam—so we must admit to some uncertainty as to which he actually lived on. Possibly he moved from one to another, and equally possible, there may have been *two* Stephen Peabodys—father and son.

Another deed, dated 1778, appears in conflict with the 1767 conveyance: in this, James Rantine, a yeoman "of Musoilriges" (and therefore another early settler in the area), sells to Jonathan Nutting of St. George for £100 "*Long Mussilridg Island* lying southwest from Snow's and Martha's Island" (Knox Lands 6/272); the latter island is believed to be Andrews. Since Andrews Island lies northeast of Hewett, the identity of Hewett Island in this conveyance would appear to be beyond doubt. In 1784, according to a later conveyance—once again to the peripatetic Stephen Peabody—George Ulmer, Esq., of Ducktrap, claims to have bought Long Island from the estate of Captain Nutting and to have deeded it promptly to our man Peabody; but Stephen lost the deed, which was the reason for the new conveyance in 1805 containing the foregoing information (Knox Lands 11/525). Stephen, meanwhile, not waiting for his new deed, had sold Long Island to Solomon Peabody, both of them said to be "of Muscle Ridge Island"; this was in 1803, though the deed was not recorded until 1811. The price was $300, a figure large enough in those days to suggest that improvements had been carried out on Hewett. Another resident associated with these improvements was Samuel Allen, mentioned in an 1816 warranty deed from Solomon Peabody to David Seavey: the deed refers explicitly to a "dwelling house and barn" on Long Island, "the same island now improved by Samuel Allen" (Knox Lands 17/169). In none of the conveyances through 1811, be it noted, is there reference to a division of the island; all deeds appear to treat it as a whole.

Leaving title aside, there was undeniably residence on the island during most of the nineteenth century. The 1820 census, the first that notes inhabitants on the Muscle Ridge Islands, lists four settlers who could have lived on Long Island: Samuel Allen, noted above; Solomon Peabody, who acquired title from his father Stephen[18]; William Neef, who could be the William *Keef* in the 1822 deed noted above; and Eben Patten, who could be related to the *Abel* Patten to whom William Keef deeded the northern third of the island in this same deed. It is unlikely that as many as four families resided on the island at the same time, but each of the above is a *possible* settler in 1820. Williamson (I: 63) does not mention residents on what he calls *Peabody's Island* in his survey of the Muscle Ridge group about this time; indeed, he describes the island as "poor land," but the census data, I believe, belie his judgment.

The only family in the Muscle Ridges that we recognize for a certainty as resident on Long Island in the next four censuses—1830, 1837, 1840, and 1850—is that of Israel Gregory, and we know this from his present-day descendants among the Elwells and Rackliffs whose family genealogies place him there. Moreover, the grave of his first wife, Ruth Maker Gregory (1793–1849), may still be seen in the center sector of the island, beside that of her fourteen-year-old son Israel, who was drowned on a Christmas excur-

[18] Solomon Peabody was married to Lydia Alley, who, according to Cyrus Eaton (*Tales of Warren*, 600), died in the Muscle Ridges; this may explain the family's removal—to judge from census data—before 1830.

sion to the main a few years earlier, a fact not mentioned on the gravestone but noted in a Gregory genealogy in the possession of Herbert Elwell. Doubtless other gravestones are in the Gregory family burial ground on Hewett, but they are too far covered by earth to discover easily. Israel, the father, married again immediately— precipitously, it would seem, to judge from the scant few months between the burial of Ruth and his marriage to Sophia—and remained for a few more years on Long Island. He is shown in the 1850 census with a household of seven and a real estate valuation, though we have no record of his ever owning the island, of $3,000—the largest, by a considerable margin, of those listed in the Muscle Ridge Islands. (Israel outlived his second wife, married again, and died at the age of 104).

Joseph Hewett, who gave his name to the island, acquired title before 1856 when he mortgaged to William McLoon (Knox lands 26/12 East Lincoln records). I am not aware of a Hewett residence on the island, but it is possible that Joseph lived there a few years—if so, probably in the old Gregory farm, which is shown (with no tenant named) on the 1857 map of Lincoln County, near the tidal bar on the northwest cove. No Hewett is named in the 1860 census for the Muscle Ridge Islands. All I know of Joseph Hewett is contained in the few conveyances where he is named: in the 1856 mortgage to William McLoon, noted above; in an 1860 conveyance of ten Muscle Ridge islands, including "Hewitt's, or Peabody's Island," from Stephen Peabody to Joseph Hewett (Knox 5/43)—a puzzling conveyance in light of the 1856 mortgage; and in William McLoon's foreclosure of the latter in 1858 (Knox 1/85).[19] The island remained under McLoon ownership for more than a century.

By the early 1870s quarrying activity, already established on Dix Island, had extended to Hewett. An 1874 map of the Muscle Ridge Islands (page 174) shows, in addition to the old Gregory farm, a building near the northeast tip and ten or a dozen in the southwest sector of "Hewell's Island" connected by a network of wagon tracks that led to the cove facing south into Home Harbor, where there was a granite pier; this pier still stands today as a breakwater for the fishing fleet moored in the inner harbor. Quarrying was confined to the southern third of the island, below the bar, but I do not know whether this was initially an extension of the Dix Island Company's operations or another venture; nor do I have knowledge of the destination of the stone, the contracts that kept the activity going, or the length of time the quarries were open. From my not particularly expert investigation of the cuts, I would think quarrying continued intermittently for some twenty-five or thirty years, that is, to about 1900, and this squares with recollections of elderly residents of the area. The 1880 federal census shows two families living on Hewett Island (which is shown, incidentally, under ownership of the McLoon interests): James Brannen, a farmer,[20] with his wife and three sons, all fishermen; and Elias Herrington, a fisherman, with wife and child. No quarrymen are shown, but this was probably because they were considered transients; most small quarries like this one operated only in the summer months. Herbert Elwell, who spent some years on Hewett Island early in the twentieth century, identifies Jim Brannen as keeper of a boardinghouse for the Scottish and Irish stonecutters who worked the quarries; the operator, Herbert Elwell recalls, was William Gray of Philadelphia. To judge from the number of well-laid granite foundations still to be seen among the spruce groves on the south end of the island, there must have been some fifty or seventy-five seasonal residents in the heyday of the granite boom. In 1900 there were five homesteads on the island, and all adult males were fishermen.

After the end of the quarrying, Hewett Island became the base for a summer fishing community that has continued to the present day. Weirs surrounded the island during the era of weir fishing, and lobstering has been the principal occupation of the seasonal residents. The McLoon Fish Company maintained two lobster pounds on

[19] I am indebted to one of the present owners for details on the 1856 mortgage and subsequent foreclosure. Another Hewett—James H. H., of Thomaston—bought Crane Island in Hurricane Sound in the 1870s, and the object of the purchase was clearly quarrying. Joseph Hewett may have been of this family and may have had the same object in buying his Muscle Ridge island; if so, it is not likely that he retained title long enough to start significant motions.

[20] Brannen's productivity is given in the 1880 agricultural census: eight acres under tillage; sixty in meadow; twenty unimproved; and six tons of hay harvested (see Appendix 3).

the island during most of the twentieth century, and this kept a small crew on Hewett during the winter. The earliest of the pounds (I do not have the date of its construction) was built on the easterly side of the bar that nearly cuts the island in two at the northwest cove. Seas making in from the open ocean have necessitated frequent repairs to an outside breakwater; a derelict brig was deliberately beached some years ago in the northwest cove to provide a breakwater for seas from the west—until the ancient timbers rotted away, leaving only the bow and stern pieces protruding above the tides. The second pound is in the southwesterly sector of the island, facing north.

Hewett was a fisherman's island during this long era, and the experiences shared by the families of St. George and Sprucehead lobstermen are too numerous and too varied to review here.[21] In recent years the island has been owned by a corporation of summer residents, who have built small vacation cottages. Fewer lobstermen are on the island than previously, but the pounds have been operating. Meanwhile, the fact that several of the new owners are descended from McLoons gives continuity to the island's ownership.

[21] For the half-dozen households still resident on Hewett Island in 1910, see the Muscle Ridge Islands residence table, page 79; in 1920 there were only two households on the island.

Andrews

The earliest identifiable resident in the Muscle Ridge Islands appears to have been Benjamin Hamblin (or Hamblen), who settled on the northern half of Andrews Island a decade before the American Revolution. Two recorded deeds give testimony to the place and time of this residence: a 1792 conveyance of the northern half of *great Muscle Ridge island* (unmistakably Andrews) refers to it as "that part of said island on which one Benjamin Hamblin formerly lived" (Knox Lands 7/283); in 1767 Benjamin, already removed to the Fox Islands, sold the entire Muscle Ridge group to William Simonton, Jr. of Cape Elizabeth (Knox Lands 6/168). The 1792 conveyance was from Robert Snow of Pownalborough to Amos Andrews, and there is some likelihood that Snow had also settled for a time on his sector of the island: a 1788 deed identifies what we take to be Hewett Island as "lying southwest from *Snows and Martha's Island* "—that is, Andrews (Knox Lands 6/272). I do not identify "Martha," but it is a reasonable asumption, given the habit of naming islands after residents, that both Robert Snow and Martha lived there—Snow on the northern half, Martha (Mathews?) on the southern. A span of some twenty-five years is covered by these deeds, and no one would argue on the basis of this fragmentary evidence that we have a sure grip on the early settlement of Andrews Island.

Amos Andrews, grantee in the 1792 conveyance, is described as a fisherman of "Mountenceous island in Hancock County." This is probably Matinicus, which at the time was considered to be in Hancock. In another deed, relating to the conveyance of High Island in 1805, Amos Andrews is said to be "of Welch's Island" (Knox Lands 12/72)—an island I do not identify. Amos Andrews was a restless fisherman, associated with many islands, but he was probably the progenitor of the family that was most closely associated with Andrews Island during the first half of the nineteenth century and gave the island its name. It was not, however, known by that name for some years. Williamson (I: 63) calls it *Andersons Island* in the 1820s—presumably after Jonathan Anderson who appears in the 1820 census of the Muscle Ridges and probably lived on the island. The deeds, meanwhile, continue to refer to it as *great Muscle Ridge island*, e.g., an 1828 mortgage deed from John Andrews of St. George to the land brokers Thorndike, Sears & Prescott (Knox Lands 33/395). But the federal censuses from 1820 to 1850 list a succession of Andrews residents in the Muscle Ridges, and while we cannot be certain all of them lived on Andrews Island, there is a strong probability of it. An Andrews descendant, Albert Burton of Spruce Head, believes that his forebears owned the entire island by the mid-nineteenth century, and thinks that a number of them were buried there (though recent owners do not know where the burying ground was located). The Andrewses appear to have been farmers as well as fishermen, to judge from the number of stone walls, cleared fields, and wagon tracks that are shown on maps surveyed after 1850. An 1880 map, for example (CGS 4), surveyed between 1863 and 1875, shows a wagon track running the length of the island from the Northeast Cove, called the Thunderhole, to a cluster of five or six buildings and landing on the south shore of the great cove below the Neck (the barred sector of the island). To the west two more buildings show on the south shore of the Neck itself, and another in open land just east of the Neck, a total of eight or nine buildings. The present owner adds that there are at least one ancient cellar hole and two dug wells at the northern end of the island, which may have been the site of still another Andrews residence—since this was the sector Amos Andrews initially bought from Robert Snow.

In the absence of a reliable genealogy of the Andrews family, I am unable to identify the various members of the family that farmed the island prior to the quarrying era. The census after 1850 does not show any local Andrewses living in the Muscle Ridges,[22] and we must assume that they had removed from the area, leaving ample evidence of their tenure behind them.

Quarrying as such touched Andrews Island only lightly, on the western arm, but the presence of many hundreds of quarrymen on neighboring islands undoubtedly affected life on Andrews. Perhaps not during the great boom on Dix Island—for a map of the area at the peak of this boom in 1874 shows no additional growth on Andrews Island—but later activity on High and Hewett islands appears to have stimulated construction on the Neck. Half a dozen buildings are shown here on the western shore on topographical maps from the turn of the century when no farm buildings are left standing on Andrews Island itself, farming having apparently been abandoned by this time (Maps 1904, Rockland quad, and 1908 Rockland folio). The 1880 federal census, the first to list the Muscle Ridge islands separately, shows two households on *"Stapler's Island,"* which in the absence of other contenders, I take to be Andrews. The 1900 census shows three fishermen on Andrews Island, all single, and one family on Andrews Neck. In 1910 there were five households on Andrews and in 1920 three. These decennial residents are listed in a table on pages 78–79, but it should not be imagined that they were the *only* settlers on the island and the Neck during these decades.[23]

The Neck continued to be the most active sector of Andrews Island during the early years of this century. During the decade in which the Muscle Ridge Islands were organized as a plantation, from 1904 to 1914, the school was apparently located on the Neck. Allie (Alvin) Rackliff also maintained a store there for some forty years or more, the only store in the Muscle Ridges after the end of quarrying on Dix and High islands. Senior residents in the area recall sailing or rowing to Allie Rackliff's store on the Neck for ice cream. Dances were occasionally held there, to which summer visitors came from Ash Point and elsewhere. The store was regularly stocked in the early years by a smack out of Rockland that came through the islands once or twice a week with fresh supplies. In later years it was stocked by Allie Rackliff himself on periodic visits to the mainland. It was still functioning, though on a limited basis, after World War II.

In 1930 Andrews Island was acquired from Thomas Dwyer, "the sole shareholder of the [defunct] Dix Island Granite Company," by the William Underwood Company (Knox 223/555). Weir fishing was by then in full swing, and Andrews became part of the extended Under-wood holdings in the region. Weirs were fixed between most of the islands of the Muscle Ridge group, the lobstermen setting their traps where there was space in between. Fishermen had by this time returned to Andrews Island in growing numbers, some summering with their families, a few living year-round to be nearer the fisheries. No accurate report exists of the number of fishermen living summers or year round among the Muscle Ridges in the 1930s, but a reasonable estimate for An-

[22] James Andrews in the 1860 census is shown as from Connecticut.

[23] According to tax records in Augusta, in 1921 Andrews Island was valued at $1,500 and Andrews Neck at $1,200—the two highest valuations in the Muscle Ridges (see Appendix 4B).

drews Island, including the Neck, might be between thirty and fifty.

The owner of Andrews Island in the 1970s, a retired lobsterman, acquired the island from the Underwood Company in 1952 and used it with his family for summer residence; their cottage was located at the southwest end of the island near the sites of the Andrews farm buildings more than a century before. The Neck, owned separately, was still the site of a summer fishing community not much smaller than that of fifty years before—although without the benefit of Allie Rackliff's icecream cones. I have not visited the island in twenty years, yet I imagine it to be much the same.

Great Pond, Little Pond, and Camp

There is no pond on any island in this cluster, but they were called the "two Pond Islands" in a deed as early as 1833, according to the present owner; the "pond," it is speculated, was a spring on the largest of the three. Since the island now called Camp is attached to Great Pond at low water, it was presumably considered part of it. Little Pond has also appeared as *Woodsey Island* in some deeds, and Camp has sometimes been called *Sheep*.

There is no record of early settlement on these islands, though Great Pond and Camp were surely used seasonally by local fishermen. Residence on Great Pond and Camp in 1900 and 1910 (four fishermen in 1900, one in 1910) is shown in the census table on pages 78 and 79. Two buildings appear on the southwest shore of Great Pond and one on the west shore of Camp in a 1908 survey (Maps 1907–08 Rockland folio). Residence on Great Pond has been the most constant, since this is the only island of the three with reliable water, supplemented by a dug well. According to a former owner, Louis W. Bosse, three camps were on Great Pond in the 1920s, one owned by a Massachusetts man named Hart who accommodated "boarders," mostly relatives, in tents. Local fishermen, however, have been the normal seasonal inhabitants of Great Pond Island in this century, their summer quarters perched on ancient Indian middens. Weirs surrounded the island before World War I, and since the weir-fishing era the residents have been lobstermen. It is evidently a close community, assembling each season as other island communities in the Muscle Ridges do, to harvest its particular "territory."

Dix

The early history of Dix Island, one of the most famous and in its day certainly the most heavily populated of the "quarry islands," is obscure. One item of prehistory is mystifying but worth recording here: early in the 1860s, an ancient burying ground was discovered on Dix Island in which, according to an account at the time, "many skeletons, much decayed, seem to have been buried in a circle, with their feet pointing inwards towards the centre"; one leg bone was said to have been some inches longer than the same bone in the tallest people of the modern era (Eaton, *History of Thomaston*, I: 11). I have seen no comment and surely venture none of my own on these prehistoric giants on Dix Island and the symbolism of their interment. (The bones, according to Cyrus Eaton, were presented to the Natural History Museum of Thomaston).

Nor are we much more enlightened by what scant evidence there is of early European habitation of the island. It is not named in early deeds, apart from the general designation Muscle Ridges, and where the name "Dix" came from is unclear. Rutherford (page 103) says, "possibly for Dr. Elijah Dix of Boston," but I am unaware of any connection between the island and the doctor, who did indeed come to the Penobscot Bay region where he died in the early 1800s—in Dixmont, a town that bears his name.

The first recorded deed that *probably* refers to Dix Island was in 1778, conveying *Carr's Island* and three small islands to the north and east, from John Adams to Jonathan Crockit and William Heard, all three described as yeomen of

Thomaston; the price was £10 (Lincoln 13/58). The chief argument for this cluster being Dix, Oak, Little Green, and Birch, rather than Graffam, Hurricane, Bar, and Flag—which also fit the above description—is that "Carr's Island" is said to lie "in or near to Thomaston," an identification better suiting the former cluster than the latter. As to who Carr may have been, there is no clue.

Since deeds executed before and during the Revolution often lacked validity in the post-Revolutionary era, it is not surprising to find the island deeded by a different claimant a few years later. In 1811 Joseph Pierce, whose title derived from the owners of the Waldo Patent, sold the island for $75.16 to William Heard, Jr. (Knox Lands 16/30); the island now goes by its number in the Great Plan of the Waldo Patent—No. 65—but its location and size (two-and-a-half miles from William Heard's "mansion" at Ash Point and forty acres "more or less") leave no doubt that this is Dix Island. There is still no mention in the deeds of residence there. Williamson (I: 63), writing in the 1820s, appears to call this island *Allen's Island*, "the residence of one family until expelled by poverty." Allens, Samuel and Jonathan, are in the 1820 census for the Muscle Ridges, but it is unclear which of them lived so unprofitably on Allen's Island, assuming Williamson's identification of the island is accurate; Samuel we know to have been living on Hewett Island prior to 1816.

The first resident on Dix Island we can unambigously identify is Job Rackliff, son of William Rackliff, Sr. of Rackliff Island. In 1839 he bought from William Heard an undivided half interest in Dix Island, now so named for the first time (Lincoln 3/365), and in 1848 he bought the rest of the island, "the same on which Job Rackliff now resides" (Lincoln 13/189). In 1850, he is listed in the Muscle Ridge census: aged forty-five, profession not given but with a real estate valua-

The Horace Beals mansion on Dix Island with guests, c. 1870; from a stereopticon slide. (Courtesy of William Butman.)

tion of $600 and a household of ten, including a sailor named James Childs and his wife (Job's daughter); Job's wife was Lydia Elwell. Rackliff descendants on Sprucehead Island, meanwhile, confirm from family records that Job lived for some years on Dix Island. Whether he was more fisherman or farmer we do not know; subsequent quarrying obliterated all signs of his home and endeavors.

Job sold the island, "together with all buildings thereon," to Horace Beals and Alexander Lawrence of New York immediately after acquiring the second half in 1848 (Lincoln 13/190)—that is, a few years before he himself quit the island, if census records are correct. The initial object of the Beals purchase is not clear; according to one historian, Beals accepted the island—presumably Lawrence's share in it—for a bad debt and considered it a useless place, except perhaps as a setting for suicide.[24] But it is likely that the energetic Mr. Beals had more creative plans from the outset. According to another student of Dix Island history, Norman Drinkwater, Horace Beals was involved in other Maine properties in the 1850s: in the Commercial House in Rockland, for example, and in a mineral springs resort near Augusta—which closed after three seasons and became known as "Beal's Folly." By the mid-1850s, according to a Lincoln County map of 1857, Beals had opened a quarry near the southwest corner of Dix Island and apparently started his famous "mansion" on the northwest tip that was a landmark in the area for many years; this stone structure, which was to have rivaled General Knox's home in Thomaston, was small in comparison to the "cottages" subsequently built at Bar Harbor and Islesboro, but it was elegantly appointed with marble fireplaces in every room, vaulted ceilings, and a walled ornamental garden setting the mansion apart from the rest of the granite-strewed island. A coach house accommodated the horses and carriage that, it is said, bore Mrs. Beals the few hundred yards to the landing. A large boulder still visible today near the house was chiseled flat to make a platform where Mrs. Beals could rock away August afternoons watch-

[24] Dick Bowring, *Maine Coast Fisherman*, March 1949, page 25.

One of the boardinghouses and other cottages on Dix Island, from a stereopticon slide of the 1870s; these buildings were dismantled before 1900. (Courtesy of William Butman.)

ing the traffic move up and down Muscle Ridge Channel.[25]

Many legends have arisen concerning Mrs. Horace Beals, enriched inevitably with the passage of time. That she was beautiful and vain can perhaps be taken for granted; that she was a Russian princess is patently false; and that she was heartless toward the husband who did so much to please her is at best debatable. According to Norman Drinkwater's account, after Horace Beals died, during or just before the Civil War, his widow successfully disposed of his Rockland and Augusta properties, and anticipating the postwar boom in the construction of post offices and other public buildings, put the remainder of her inheritance to good use. Using her connections in her native Philadelphia and in Washington, she secured lucrative contracts for Dix Island granite and so launched an enterprise that altered the character of the Muscle Ridge Islands for some decades. The Dix Island Granite Company, with Horace Beals's heirs controlling a third of the stock, was the agency that supervised the formidable operations on the island. Mrs. Beals did, it is true, eventually quit the island—apparently unnerved by the monster she had created—and in due course married an English peer (the source, apparently, of rumors concerning her royal origins).

The largest single contract negotiated by the Dix Island Granite Company, awarded a few years after the Civil War, was the New York City Post Office, and it brought as many as two thousand workers to the island by the early 1870s. Many of these were imported from Ireland and later Scotland—the latter, as a Southern lady who visited the island in 1875 bluntly put it, "to supersede the uncertain Irishmen, who could be depended on for nothing but getting drunk."[26] A four-and-a-half story boardinghouse called the Shamrock House was built to accommodate four to five hundred Irish workers; the United States government subsequently built and sold to the Dix Island company the Aberdeen House to accommodate as many Scots. Other quarrymen and stonecutters lived in additional boardinghouses that crowded the island. Drinkwater states that there were as many as 150 buildings on Dix at the peak of the boom—and if the estimate is high, it is not astronomically so. An 1874 map of Dix Island shows some 80 or more structures, about half of them cutting sheds aligned in rows on an extension of the island to the west built up by grout. At the peak of operations eight quarries were worked on the island and fifty-two oxen hauled the stone from quarries to sheds. The pay was high for the era—between $2.50 and $6 a day, depending on the type of work—and the weekly payroll, according to Drinkwater, sometimes surpassed $100,000.

It was a predominantly male society on Dix Island, boys doing the work of maids and waitresses at the boardinghouses. The island was indeed so unaccustomed to female company, according to the Southern lady cited above, that at the appearance of her party a pair of oxen hauling a cart of granite from the quarries very nearly panicked. Still, this account cannot be wholly true, for the census figures of 1860 and 1870 show a number of families living on Dix—not merely families associated with management (like the Lewis Beals in 1860, Daniel H. Smith in 1870, and the Crocketts, who were to preside over the final years of the Dix Island operation), but stonecutters' families as well. The census lists only a small percentage of the quarrymen actually residing on Dix Island, and we accordingly have a very imperfect estimate of the total number of them at a given time. The 1870 figure of 260 for all of the Muscle Ridge Islands, for example, must be considered a fraction of the number of persons actually living in the area during this period (see census summary, page 79).

Dix Island was not without social life. An opera house, seating 450, said to be the best of its size in Knox County (which in those days may not have been an extravagant claim), was built on the western side of the island and featured concerts and performances by traveling companies, sometimes from Broadway. During a winter shutdown in 1879, because of deep snow, the quarrymen put on an amateur production of "Ten Nights in a Bar Room"—which was as close as the workers could legally come to liquor since the

[25] Norman Drinkwater, Jr., "The Stone Age of Dix Island," *Downeast Magazine*, September, 1963, pages 43–47.

[26] Ella Rodman Church, "A Visit to Dix Island," *Southern Magazine* (Baltimore), Vol. 16 (1875), pp. 615–18.

island was dry. The proceeds from this production went into the local union treasury, and spectators came from as far away as Hurricane Island (Grindle, *Tombstones and Paving Blocks*, 29). The strict prohibition of liquor sales on this island did not, of course, apply to shore communities, and it is reported that a large share of the weekly payroll wound up in tavern cash registers in Rockland on Saturday nights (Bowring). The FIREFLY, the company steamer that made daily runs between Rockland and Dix Island (its captain was Oscar Crockett, later the founder of the Crockett Steamship Line that crisscrossed Penobscot Bay in the 1890s), could carry some seventy-five passengers for these weekend safaris; others would make their way to shore on Saturday afternoons in whatever conveyances they could find.

The driving force behind the Dix Island Granite Company after Mrs. Beals, according to Roger L. Grindle, was Deacon Corland P. Dixon of Brooklyn, New York, identified along with General Davis Tillson of Hurricane Island, Milton St. John of Clark Island, and J. R. Bodwell of Vinalhaven as one of the "Granite Ring" (Grindle, 4, 27).[27] After completion of the New York City Post Office, new contracts were slow in coming—contracts, for instance, for an extension of the Treasury Building in Washington, the trim for the Metropolitan Museum in New York, and the Philadelphia Post Office (the latter contracted floor by floor as government appropriations became available). C. P. Dixon stretched out these contracts as well as he could, but there were lean years after 1875. Pay fell to between $1.75 and $2.50 for a ten-hour day. Since the Dix Island Granite Company had been created for high-quality finished work, not simply for quarrying rough construction and paving block, the skilled stonecutters—irrepressible Irishmen and dour Scots alike—gradually dispersed. Operations continued fitfully through the last years of the decade. The 1880 census lists some 150 persons still on Dix Island—again, a low estimate insofar as quarrymen were concerned. Rodney Fogg, superintendent from the early 1870s, was still on hand; Frank Crockett, who was to succeed him, is shown as quarryman. The exodus apparently took place soon after 1880 and was so precipitous, according to Drinkwater, that "table places were left set at the boardinghouses." Some of the equipment was undoubtedly disposed of in orderly fashion, but most of it was removed by scavengers. An abortive attempt to revive quarrying was made in the 1890s, when on the initiative of new owners many of the older buildings, including the Aberdeen House, were taken down and others, like the Shamrock House, repaired. Rumors of fresh orders for finished stone for the cathedral of St. John the Divine and for new buildings at Columbia University circulated freely, but in the end came to nothing (Grindle, 144). In 1900 two households were on the island, according to the federal census: Frank Crockett, his wife Florence, and two children; and Angus Carlson, a Swedish fisherman with a household of five.

Frank ("Governor") Crockett remained on the island for some years after the exodus, as caretaker for the defunct Dix Island Granite Company. He lived in the superintendent's house above the northeast cove and kept a varied menagerie of cows, geese, hens, and sheep—the latter, led by a ram named Obie, quartered in the Beals's mansion before it was sold and torn down. The other buildings still standing were sold off one by one, many of them to the Rockland Lime Company for lumber; the Shamrock House was dismantled and sold to the descendants of Job Rackliff for a barn in the Makertown sector of Spruce Head. Frank Crockett, meanwhile, was instrumental in the belated reincarnation of Muscle Ridge Plantation in 1905 (see above, page 75). A few fishermen also lived on Dix Island, most of them seasonally, but several year round. According to one of the latter, the prohibition of liquor sales was so far relaxed—or ignored—that a saloon operated for the benefit of local and transient fishermen.[28] The Crocketts removed in the 1920s, and their home was dismantled like the others, leaving none of the original buildings from the quarry boom standing by 1930. State of Maine tax records for 1921 show Thomas Dwyer as owner of the island, then valued at $1,200 (see Appendix 4B).

[27] Grindle may confuse C. A. Dixon, who apparently remained in New York arranging orders, with his son C. P. Dixon, described as the company agent in charge of operations on the island.

[28] Interview with Harland Hurd; whether this was a reality or a thirsty lobsterman's fantasy, I will not venture to say.

In 1930 the William Underwood Company acquired Dix Island, as it did many others in the Muscle Ridges, for weir rights. Fishermen continued to use it, living in small cottages they built and maintained for their families during the summer months. Four such lobstermen from Spruce Head and Rockland owned the island for half a dozen years after World War II and used it with great regularity and enjoyment: Ralph Billings, Arthur Arenson, Russell Stewart, and William Butman. They sold the island in the 1950s. Summer residence during the following decades grew more irregular, although a few cottages still stood in fair to good repair. When I last visited Dix in the 1970s, before it was sold to a more energetic group of summer cottagers, it had the deserted atmosphere unique to old quarry islands—the haunting stillness of the lily pools, the muffled echoes of grout-built shores extending beyond the island proper, and the silent testimony of granite cellar holes choked with young spruce. The only living thing on the island at this time, apart from birds and vegetation, was a friendly young ram who guided me about—descendant, perhaps, of "Governor" Crockett's Obie.

Clam, Nettle, Birch, Little Green, and Oak

These small islands surrounding Dix, several of them awash in storms, have no independent history but were accessory to their formidable neighbor. Birch and Little Green were surely used for pasturage by the early Allens and later by Job Rackliff; all five were undoubtedly used as a spill-over for quarrymen and equipment during the granite era. In the twentieth century most of them have been used for seasonal residence by local fishermen, but I find record of year-round residence on only one: the 1900 federal census shows a Canadian fisherman named Albert Smith, with wife and two children, on Birch Island.

High (Muscle Ridges)

It is doubtful that there was early residence on High Island, with so many other islands in the Muscle Ridges providing better anchorages and more fertile soil for planting. No early cellar holes are on the island, no sign of stone walls or ancient wells. The name, which has been attached to it from the early 1800s (from its greater elevation as compared to other islands in the area), has stayed with it to the present day.

The first recorded deed I have seen is dated 1805, when Amos Andrews conveyed to Joseph Coombs of Thomaston for $65 (Knox Lands 12/72). In 1835 Asa Coombs sold an undivided half interest in High Island for $400 to Stephen Titcomb of Boston (Knox Lands 33/373). The price seems high for an island that as far as we know had had no improvement to that date, and the conveyance may have been part of a larger purchase including property in Thomaston; the following year the same undivided half of High Island, together with a parcel in Thomaston, was conveyed for an even higher price, $1,200, by Stephen Titcomb to Joseph Hastings, also of Boston. What these land speculators had in mind is unclear, but the cycle of life on High Island appears to have remained undisturbed. An occasional squatter undoubtedly lived there, and the island was surely cut over once or twice in the first half of the nineteenth century, as most islands in the area were, but maps surveyed after 1850 show no habitation and no activity of any sort; in the 1870s, for example, when the Dix Island Granite Company was at the peak of its activity, a map shows High Island heavily wooded and without a sign of residence (Map 1874 Dix Island).

Residence was soon to follow, however, if indeed there were not already settlers. The 1880 census shows three fishermen on High Island, with their families: Charles Wentworth, Steven Chase, and George Merchant (see page 78); the island was owned at that time by George

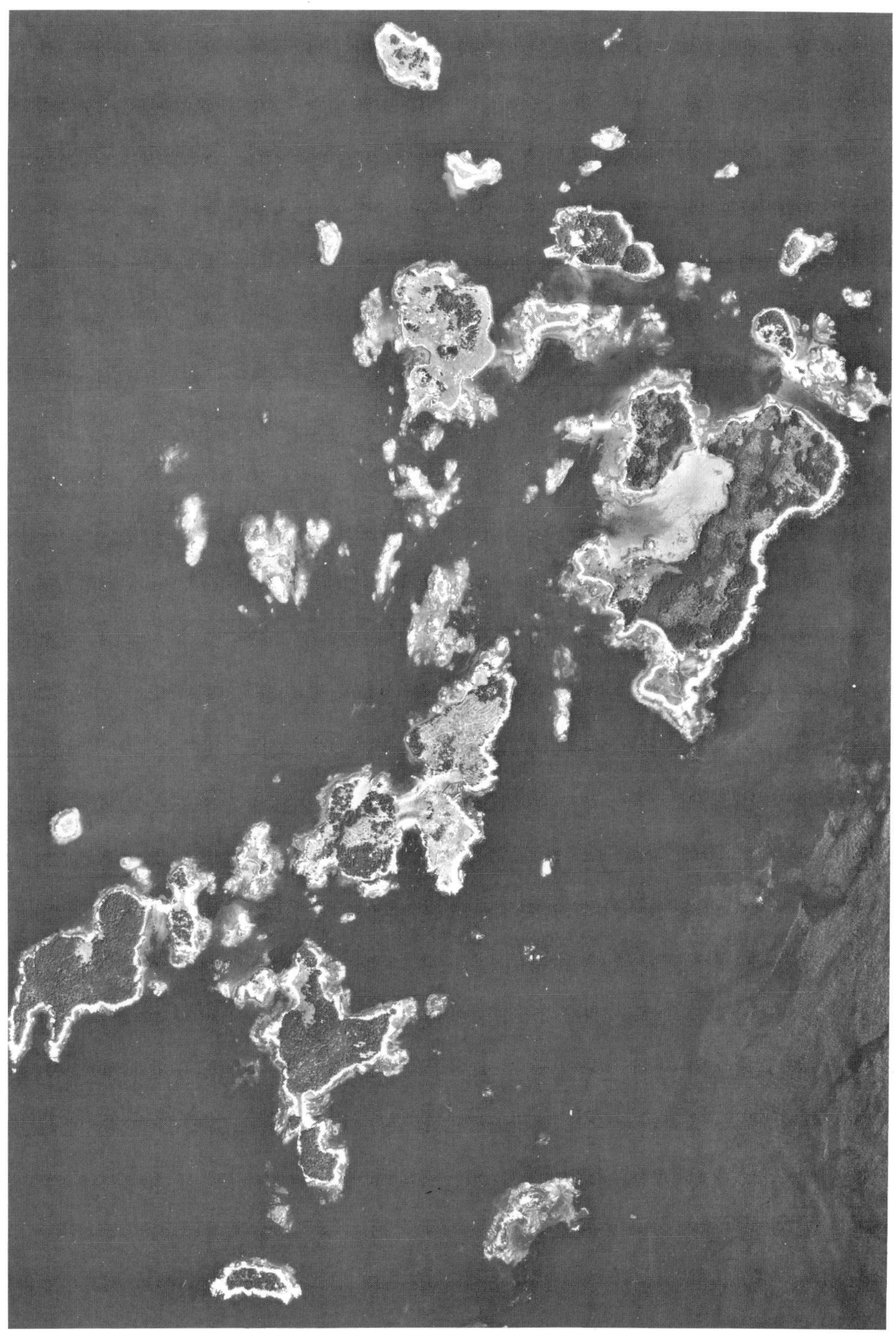

Aerial view of Muscle Ridges, August 1963—from Two Bush Light at bottom to Otter Island at top; fishermen's cottages show on most of these islands with use of magnifying glass.
(Photo by U.S. Air Force.)

Coombs. Some years later, Samuel Dyer, a peripatetic fisherman from Islesboro, also lived on High Island. His son Frank—a retired lobsterman in Lincolnville in the 1970s—was born on the northwest corner of the island in 1896 (Frank Dyer interview).

In 1894, a decade or more after quarrying had been suspended on Dix Island, quarries were opened on the southwest end of High. The original company, which acquired title from weirman William McLoon, was the High Island Granite Company; this company was succeeded by the Consolidated High Island Granite Company, which leased the quarries to William Gray and Sons of Philadelphia. It was the latter company that apparently conducted the most extensive operations on High Island, early in the twentieth century, and most of the pink granite from the quarries was used in Philadelphia: in the new Wanamaker store, the Pennsylvania Railway Station, and the Philadelphia Public Library (Dale, *Commercial Granite of New England*, 237). Two wharves for loading the stone were built on the shores below the quarries; the stone was transported from quarries to shore by rail. A Rockland company contracted to build cutting sheds on the island, as well as two boardinghouses to accommodate some two hundred quarrymen, many of them imported Italians.

Conditions on High Island were not easy. The scarcity of water meant that it had to be pumped from two inoperative quarries on Dix Island, through a pipe running across Birch Island (Harland Hurd interview). The fare in the boardinghouses was execrable—"hard-boiled eggs like golf balls or doughnuts that would make good links for a stone chain."[29] Local liquor laws led to periodic raids by the county sheriff and confiscation of the red wine necessary to the morale of the luckless Italians. There was also periodic inactivity through want of orders—for example, for twelve months or more during 1907 and 1908. A branch of the Granite Cutters Union was organized on the island in 1903 and successfully negotiated some improvements in living and working conditions in 1905. This union had 60 members in 1904; in 1906 membership was 135 in two unions, and in 1908 it was 118 in three unions (Maine Bureau of Labor Statistics, *Report*, 1905, 1907, 1909). The census-taker apparently considered quarrymen as transients, whether resident on the island or not, for the 1900 schedule—the only schedule we have for High Island during its quarrying era—shows but two residents, both fishermen (page 79).

Quarrying ended on High Island before World War I, and the evacuation was apparently as abrupt as on Dix Island thirty-five or forty years earlier—without the saving dignity of a "Governor" Crockett to preside over the exodus. The frame buildings quickly disappeared (who could say where?), the rails were removed, the equipment was sold or left to rust away in the alder groves that soon claimed the quarry area. All that remained by the end of the twentieth century, besides the waterlogged excavations, were the magnificent granite wharves, the envy of lobstermen "unlucky" enough to be living on other islands in the Muscle Ridges that escaped quarrying.

The post-quarry years are quickly covered. In 1921 the island was still owned by the Consolidated High Island Granite Company, assessed at $1,000, but was sold soon thereafter to a realty company in Philadelphia. This company conveyed the island to a Massachusetts owner in 1972. A few lobstermen continued to summer on the island, and infrequently there were one or two year-round resident fishermen (e.g., Jim Skeynes and Albert Atkins in the 1930s). In recent years an occasional "solo" from the Outward Bound School (see page 63) has tested his (or her) endurance on High Island.

[29] Grindle, *Tombstones and Paving Blocks*, 179, citing reports published in the *Granite Cutters International Journal* in 1905.

Otter (off Dix)

This is Island No. 67 in the Great Plan of the Waldo Patent, and its first known conveyance by that designation is from Thorndike, Sears & Prescott to William Heard of Ash Point in 1812 (Knox Lands 17/51). The name Otter appears on maps only in the last half of the nineteenth century (e.g., Map 1874 Dix Island).

Otter was never settled, although there must have been transient squatters on it during the quarrying era on nearby Dix and High islands—and there is report (unverified) of a dance hall there during that era. In 1900, according to the federal census, a fisherman named James Nason was living on Otter with his wife and one child. Year-round residence, however, was surely the exception on Otter Island, seasonal residence the norm. Like most of the other Muscle Ridge islands, this was a fisherman's haven through most of the twentieth century, before becoming the summer retreat of a family from Texas.

There was a brief period when Otter Island stood at the threshold of prominence: in 1906 it was considered as a site for a much-needed light and signal station at the north end of Muscle Ridge Channel. It was estimated that 20,000 vessels a year were using the passage, and there were frequent accidents, including the loss of the CITY OF ROCKLAND two years before; steamship companies since that accident had maintained their own bell on Otter Island, the Department of Commerce wrote the Treasury. The estimated cost of the facility, according to a report in 1908, was $19,000. In 1910, $14,000 was actually appropriated for the station, though believed insufficient; a minimum of $17,000 was requested—and that was the last heard of the project (United States Lighthouse records, Otter Island file). Existing lights—Whitehead, Two Bush, and Owls Head—were evidently deemed sufficient for Muscle Ridge Channel.

GROUP 3: Whitehead Islands

Residence in Whitehead Area of St. George, 1850–1900

Note: The following lived in the Whitehead sector of St. George between 1850 and 1900, according to my reading of the federal census (with the help of C. William Colby of Sprucehead Island). Age is at first appearance in census; spouse is shown in parentheses. Householders may be assumed fishermen unless another occupation is shown: C, carpenter; S, sailor; Fa, farmer; M, master mariner; Q, quarryman; B, blacksmith; AK and K, assistant keeper and keeper. Males in a household are to left of slash; females to right. Islands where these residents are believed to have lived are shown as follows: ***Wh****, Whitehead;* ***No****, Norton;* ***El****, Elwell;* ***Ra****, Rackliff. The dollar figure after some householders represents their highest valuation in 1860 or 1870 (over $1,000), according to the census-taker.*

Householder	1850	1860	1870	1880	1900
Elwell, Robert, 50 (Hannah) ***El***	2/5	5/7	5/4		
Bartlett, Joshua, 69 (Marian), K ***Wh***	2/1				
Norton, Joseph, 49 (Mary), S/M ***Wh***	5/6	5/6			
Norton, Amos, 31 (Hannah) ***No***	5/2				
Norton, Jon., 60 (Deborah), $1,250 ***No***	3/4	1/2[30]			
Stanton, Nathan, 29 (Adeline), Q ***No***	3/1[31]				
Allen, John P., 35 (Elvina) ***No***	4/3				
O'Larry, Dennis, 29, Q ***Ra***	7/4[32]				
Maker, Benj. C., 23 (Marian/Mary) ***Ra***	1/1	2/4			

[30] Deborah was head of household in 1860.
[31] Nathan Stanton and John P. Allen were sons-in-law of Jonathan Norton and may have been living in his household on Norton Island.
[32] Seven Irish stonecutters and three wives were boarders in this household.

Householder	1850	1860	1870	1880	1900
Maker, Joshua T., 50 (Rebecca) ***Ra***	4/4	2/2	1/1		
Maker, James R., 26 (Susan) ***Ra***	2/2				
Rackliff, William, 68 (Elinor), Fa ***Ra***	1/2				
Canfield, John M., 36 (Margaret), B ***Ra***		3/3			
Maker, William M., 27 (Lucinda) ***Ra***		2/3			
Maker, Israel G., 30 (Eunice), Q ***Ra***		4/1	5/2		
Rackliff, Freeman, 28 (Hanna) ***Ra***		3/1			
Mays, Chas, 30 (Mary), b'dinghouse k'per ***Ra***		7/3[33]			
Stearns, Lucy, 53 ***Wh***		3/2[34]			
Rackliff, Almira, 42 ***Ra***			0/2		
Herrick, Patrick, 37 (Ellen), Q, $1700 ***Ra?***			5/3[35]		
Rackliff, Job, 65 (Lydia), S ***No***			3/1		
Norton, Horace, 24 (Asenath/Cynthia), S /K ***Wh***			3/3	4/4[36]	
Long, Hezekiah, 45 (Sarah), K ***Wh***			4/4		
Fogg, Isaiah, 46, Fa ***Ra?***			2/0[37]		
Fogg, Alvin, 39 (Maria), Q ***Ra?***			4/1		
Zenner, Ennoch, 35 (Sophronia) ***Ra?***			2/2[38]		
Grant, Isaac K., 45 (Abbie), K ***Wh***				5/2[39]	
Smalley, Eli, 26 (Eunice), Q				1/2	
Metcalf, Lizzie, 48 ***Wh***				2/2[40]	
Snow, Forrest A., 41 (Catherine), surfman ***Wh***					6/3
Wiley, Andrew E., 54 (Cora) ***Wh***					2/1
Jelleson, Frank, 48 (Mattie), K ***Wh***					5/2
Hodgkins, Walter B., 51 (Lizzie), C ***Wh***					4/4
Connors, George, 39 (Addie), AK ***Wh***					1/1
Andrews, James, 74 (Hannah) ***No***					1/2
Andrews, Hiram, 21 (Avies) ***No***					1/2

The foregoing give the following totals, including those for neighboring Sprucehead Island (these totals should not be taken as definitive):

	1850	1860	1870	1880	1900
Whitehead	14	16	14	19	29
Norton	25	3	4	-	6
Elwell	7	12	9	-	-
Rackliff	28	40	30	?	?
Sprucehead	12	39	119	50	49

[33] Six Scotch-Irish quarrymen lived in the boardinghouse, also two domestics.
[34] Lucy Stearns was the widow of Keeper Isaac Stearns, who died in 1860. A temporary keeper and assistant keeper were in her household.
[35] Three quarrymen and a teamster were boarding with Patrick Herrick.
[36] Horace Norton was keeper of the lifesaving station in 1880.
[37] Isaiah and Alvin Fogg were in Spruce Head village in 1850 and frequently on Clark Island in the 1860s, but apparently living on Rackliff Island in 1870.
[38] The Zenners had nineteen seamen boarding in their home.
[39] The Grants had three boarders: son Francis Grant, surfman, and two carpenters, aged fifty-four and forty-nine—probably on the island for some building project.
[40] Her son Forrest Snow, twenty, surfman, was living in this household.

Calf

Calf is locally called *Makers Island*, after Ellis Maker, who bought it in 1884 from Thurston Daggett and lived there for some years (Knox Lands 68/241). Daggett acquired it from William Rackliff, who had bought it from James Elwell for $30 in 1839 (Lincoln 3/4); all these owners were native to the area. Ellis Maker's wife, Alice, was a daughter of James Andrews of Norton Island. Their home—two dwellings were on Calf Island at one time—is said to have been made out of timber from the Aberdeen House on Dix Island after it was torn down; this homestead was still standing in the 1970s.

Ellis Maker, aged forty-seven, appears in the 1900 federal census, head of a household of six including sons Bert, Lawrence, and Sanford, and his mother-in-law Melissa Andrews. He is still there in 1910, this time with a household of four (three males and one female). There was another family on the island in 1910, according to the federal census: Charles H. Wall, thirty-nine, with wife Helen, two daughters and a son. No Maker children were of school age at this time, but the Walls would have been rowed across the bay daily to school in Makertown.

Ellis Maker died in 1916, his wife Alice the next year. The island, appraised at $300, was left to their son Sanford, who fished the waters of Wheeler Bay until mid-century. His widow, Jeanette, evidently continued to use the island, at least intermittently, until the 1960s. She sold a decade later, and the new owners built a summer cottage on the site of the original dwelling.[41]

[41] I am indebted to the present owner for census and probate data relating to the Makers.

Elwell

This was the most westerly of the "White Head islands," according to the authoritative "Atlantic Neptune" (1776). Indeed, in a 1796 conveyance it is called "formerly...inner white head and now known by the name of Elwell's Island" (Knox Lands 9/223). The deed in question conveyed two-thirds of the island, No. 44 in the Waldo Patent, from Andrew Elwell and Andrew, Jr. to Robert Elwell for $200; the language of the instrument indicates that it was a legitimate transaction, involving proper compensation to the Peirces, then part-owners of the famous patent. Robert Elwell married a widow from the Muscle Ridges, Hannah Gregory Allen, and settled on his island; this was probably in the 1840s (see table, page 97). In addition to Hannah's two children, the couple raised ten more, according to descendants (Bernard Rackliff and the late Ralph Cline). Robert was a coastal trader, as well as a modest farmer and fisherman, and sustained a moderately prosperous husbandry. He quit the island in due course—probably because of the difficulty of educating his many children there—and settled in the Makertown district north of Wheeler Bay, where he built the school his children attended. After Robert Elwell's death in 1875, his heirs allowed taxes on the island to lapse, and it was eventually acquired by Eugene Rackliff, whose descendants owned it into the 1980s.

It is curious that no indication of habitation on Elwell Island is on maps printed in the last century; even the name of the island is omitted in many. Yet the family of Robert Elwell was surely settled there for several decades, and the cellar hole of their homestead, as well as the remnants of the wharf, are there to prove it.

Eagle (Wheeler Bay)

This small island of five acres has had more history than its size would suggest. In 1836 it was conveyed for $160 from Stephen Varney, who owned a considerable amount of real estate in the area, to the Maine Atlantic Granite Company (Knox Lands 34/300). Local report varies as to whether quarrying began at that time or some years later. Albert Smalley has suggested that a scowload of stone was quarried then ("St. George," 183). Others state that quarrying was undertaken only in the 1890s by Ashel and Joshua Norton, two brothers who owned the island. Working with hand tools, they built a stone wharf, erected a derrick, laid rails to their "quarry," and eventually accumulated enough stone to load a vessel (interviews with Ralph Cline and Bernard Rackliff, both of whom remembered the Norton brothers). Here the two versions of the operation come together: a single consignment, it is said, left Eagle Island, but the vessel (or scow) carrying it foundered and sank in a gap between Norton and Rackliff islands. The granite can still be seen there at low tide. According to the Cline-Rackliff version, the loss was too much for the uninsured brothers and they suspended operations.

There were undoubtedly other residents on Eagle Island, but given the absence of a cellar hole they were probably not there year round. There is, however, a stone-lined well and other evidence of seasonal habitation, and a building is shown on Eagle Island on topographical maps printed early in the twentieth century (e.g., Maps 1904–06 Tenants Harbor quad).

Whitehead

Whitehead Island was one of the earliest landmarks for mariners entering Penobscot Bay from the west, its white cliffs and bold easterly tip guiding vessels into Muscle Ridge Channel or to safe anchorage in Seal Harbor. The open Atlantic and Penobscot Bay, it is said, meet at Whitehead. It is not surprising, then, that the island shows on the earliest charts and was used as a reference point in the earliest navigators' manuals. Nor is there any wonder that Whitehead was the location of the United States government's first light station in the Penobscot Bay region.

There is some difficulty in identifying a *single* Whitehead Island in early documentation since the name was attached to the cluster of islands forming the southern and western perimeter of Seal Harbor (modern Norton, Rackliff, Elwell, as well as Whitehead). The "Atlantic Neptune" (1776), for instance, so names this cluster; a description of the Waldo Patent in 1788 also refers to the "Whitehead Islands; being one large and two small" (*Bangor Historical Magazine*, II: 61/291). As late as the mid-nineteenth century, the name "Whitehead Islands" was still attached to the entire cluster (Map 1857 Lincoln County). Locally, the true Whitehead Island was surely recognized, but in deeds the name was easily confused.

We cannot positively identify the earliest full-time residents of Whitehead, but a temporary settler in 1782, according to an early visitor, was a Captain York.[42] Another may have been Richard Chapell, who claimed ownership in the 1780s: Malcolm Jackson, veteran charter of the Waldo lands in the Owls Head-St. George region, numbers our island fifty-seven in the Waldo Patent and calls it *Chapell's* after this French survivor from the French and Indian wars (Smalley, *St. George*, 72).[43] When Chapell in 1799 conveyed—or *sought* to convey—the island to Joseph Coombs, reference was made to two dwellings on "Whitehead or Chapell's Island" (Knox Lands 9/25). But Richard Chapell's claim may not have been valid, for nothing is heard further of either Richard Chapell or Joseph

[42] The visitor was John Fairbanks; his journal is in Maine Historical Society *Collections*, II: 6, page 139.

[43] Richard Chapell (or Chaple) claimed ownership of a number of islands in the region; there is better evidence that he resided for a time on modern Hupper Island off Port Clyde rather than on Whitehead (see, in this island series, III: 86).

Coombs in connection with Whitehead Island. Meanwhile, in 1796 another claimant, Thomas Kiff (or Kief) "of Whitehead," sold the island for $150 to Stephen Peabody "of Musselridge Island"—that is, Hewett Island (Knox Lands 8/409)—and Stephen Peabody in 1805 sold to his son-in-law Stephen Norton; this was the earliest Norton association with the island. In 1820 Stephen Norton lost the island through indebtedness—it was sold to Joseph Peirce in a sheriff's sale (Knox Lands 21/493)—but four years later Norton bought it back, and thereafter the island remained in the Norton family for more than a century. In 1828 Stephen Norton sold to his son Joseph, who was probably already in residence.

Residence on Whitehead became more certain with the establishment of the light station there in 1805 (see below). In 1810 Hezekiah Prince, a local magistrate, noted in his diary that he married John Foster on Whitehead (*Remarks of My Life*, 66). In 1820 the historian William D. Williamson (I: 62) noted a single family on Whitehead; this family might have been the lightkeeper's, or it could have been one of the several Norton families noted in the 1820 federal census as living in the "St. George Islands" (that is, islands within the township of St. George).

Nortons prevailed on Whitehead Island through most of the nineteenth century. In 1841, according to St. George tax records, Joseph Norton's acreage on Whitehead was valued at $200 and his tax ($5.31) was equal to Jonathan Norton's on Norton Island (in the sector, only Thomas McKellar on Sprucehead paid more). In 1850 his tax was less but his relative position among taxpayers in the Whitehead sector was about the same. [44] In 1865 Horace Norton, successor to Joseph, cultivated thirty acres on the island and, for livestock, had two cows, two calves, and four sheep. This was not, of course, remarkable husbandry, and one hopes that Horace Norton did better with his fishing—before he became keeper of the lifesaving station. Whitehead did not share, as Rackliff and Sprucehead did, in the quarrying boom.

How many lived on Whitehead Island? Until the lifesaving station was opened in the 1870s, it is reasonable to imagine only the lightkeeper and his family, together with one Norton family, at the most two. A chart surveyed in the 1860s shows three buildings on the island in addition to the lighthouse: one just north of it (the keeper's dwelling) and two at the northern end of the island, with fencing and wagon tracks (Map 1874 Dix Island). With the establishment of the lifesaving station, several surfmen moved onto the island with their families, swelling the community considerably. Census figures for 1900 show some thirty permanent residents on the island, and there were surely more in season. In mapping of the early 1900s seven buildings are shown on Whitehead, most of them at the northern end.

Before turning to the light and lifesaving stations on Whitehead, a word should be said of the area schools in the nineteenth century. School District No. 16 (St. George) was established in 1836 for Whitehead, Jonathan Norton's, and Rackliff islands. Registration for the early years is lost entirely and is erratic for all years, but a few statistics for mid-century are of some interest. During the quarrying era Rackliff and Sprucehead islands had large school populations: Albert Smalley ("St. George," 54) states there were as many as sixty pupils on Rackliff in the 1870s; Sprucehead, it is said, had thirty.[45] Whitehead and Norton islands, where there was no quarrying, did not experience significant fluctuation in school enrollment. The enrollment for the two islands in 1884, for instance, was twelve. With the growth of the service stations on Whitehead in the twentieth century, however, school registration grew: Robert Sterling, for instance (*Lighthouses of the Maine Coast*, 151), notes a school of thirty-five on the island in the 1920s.

The figures in the table below, from St. George records, are fragmentary, but at least offer a segment of school enrollment in the Whitehead District over a decade in the middle of the nineteenth century.

[44] Joseph Norton was listed as a "pauper" in the 1860 census schedule, but that presumably did not reflect the status of his entire large household—eleven persons.

[45] Smalley's figure of sixty on Rackliff Island may be high, given the estimated number of residents on the island; the figure of thirty for Sprucehead, however, seems accurate.

School Registration, Whitehead District, 1846–1856

Note: The data below, showing the number of pupils per household in the Whitehead district, come from incomplete St. George school records. The school for Whitehead and Norton islands—surely combined in most years—did not change size appreciably during the granite era since no quarrymen with large families came onto either island. The Rackliff Island school, by contrast, grew significantly in the 1860s and 1870s—see Albert Smalley's estimate above—but had dropped to seven by 1884. School enrollment on Elwell Island in 1884 was also seven. The Sprucehead Island school, we have seen, grew in the peak quarrying years and declined thereafter (page 114).

Householder	Island	1846	1847	1848	1849	1850	1851	1852	1853	1854	1855
Joseph Norton	Whitehead				7	8	9	8	8	8	6
Jonathan Norton	Norton				4	3	4	4		2	3
Amos Norton	Norton					1	2	2			
Robert Elwell	Elwell	2			4	3					
William Rackliff, Jr.	Rackliff	1									
John McKellar	Sprucehead[46]							5	5	5	6
Mrs. Thos. McKellar	Sprucehead							5	5	6	

[46] Sprucehead Island was transferred from St. George township to South Thomaston in the 1860s.

Light and Lifesaving Stations

Whitehead is the only island on the Maine coast to have hosted both a light and a lifesaving station, and it is testimony to the maritime importance of the area that the two installations were there. Muscle Ridge Channel between the mainland and the Muscle Ridge Islands was the preferred route of entry into Penobscot Bay from the west and the exit from it. It was the shortest route to and from Rockland and gave shelter from the often turbulent seas of the outer bay.

In 1803 Henry Knox himself, owner of the Waldo Patent, conveyed ten acres on Whitehead to the United States government for a lighthouse. It was built on the southeast headland in 1804 at a cost of $2,200; the station was officially established in 1807, the fourth in Maine (after Portland Head, Seguin, and Franklin Island in Muscongus Bay).[47] By the late 1800s the light and accompanying bell were maintained by a crew of three keepers. In 1933 the station acquired the capability of producing its own electricity, but the full three-man crew was still needed to operate the air compressors and generators. During these decades in mid-century Whitehead served as a relay station for the lights at Two Bush Island and Matinicus Rock. In the 1950s electricity was provided from the mainland and the station could now become fully automated. Automation came finally in 1982, after 175 years of manned service. With automation, year-round residence on Whitehead Island ended.

Some idea of the pace of life at a major light station can be gained through extracts from the maintenance record of the station on file at the National Archives (the extracts cover a fifty-year period from the 1850s to the early 1900s):

1853 Keeper complains that the fog bell (installed in 1840) is not working.
Note: The bell was an ingenious device, powered by the sea and tides, that drove a wooden beam in such a way that a hammer was activated against the bell four times a minute.

1855 A third-order Fresnel lens is substituted for reflectors around the light.

1860 The fog bell is repaired.
Note: It was presumably operated by hand during the preceding seven years.

1867 The keeper's house is repaired and the woodwork repainted.

[47] A student of the station and a longtime seasonal resident of the island notes that although the lamps were lit as early as 1805, they were not "proven" before 1807 (correspondence with David A. Gamage—grandson of the last civilian keeper of the light station, Arthur Beal).

1868 Illuminating apparatus is checked and repaired; new cistern pump installed; stove overhauled; new boat and equipment acquired.

1869 A new steam fog signal (whistle) is under construction in a new building to replace bell; a new well is dug.

1870 A cistern is built for the steam fog signal, now completed.
Note: The station records do not discuss a problem that arose with this cistern, but David Gamage does: moose evidently were attracted to the reservoir and occasionally stirred up the muddy bottom, thus fouling the water for the boilers; "the keepers," Gamage writes laconically, "were obliged to chase, lure, or otherwise induce the beasts to vacate the reservoir which was no easy task and somewhat outside normal lightkeeping duties."

1871 Road graded from landing to fog signal building; coal shed and new wharf are built.

1872 Extensive repairs this year to keeper's house.

1875 Duplicate fog signal established.
Note: David Gamage writes: "It was the practice to provide duplicate fog signals, one for backup because of numerous breakdowns and boiler failures, poor water quality, inferior construction, and salt air."

1877 Rain shed and brick storage tank are built.

1880 House floors repaired; covered way between house and tower rebuilt; woodwork repaired; fog signals repaired; boathouse rebuilt, with winch; landing stage repaired.

1882 Cellar floor to house is cemented; road repaired.

1883 Mineral oil substituted for lard oil; new lamps installed.

1885 New steam boiler and smokepipe installed for north signal.

1890 Reservoir for fresh water, 28' x 36' x 6', is excavated and connected with cistern in boiler house.

1891 Keeper's house (rubble-stone) is demolished and new frame house built.

1897 New fog signal boiler. Complaints about inadequate accommodations: "This is an important station, having a third order light and steam fog signal. There are three keepers...." An appropriation of $3,400 is recommended for new housing.

1899 Temporary dwelling is converted to permanent; land surveyed and recorded.

1902 Fog signal boiler and automatic clocks are installed; arrangement made for supplying boilers with salt water, if necessary.
Note: An "automatic clock," according to David Gamage, is a device to activate the fog signal on a time cycle.

1904 Another new fog signal boiler.
Note: This appears to have been the third boiler in seven years. (The moose must have been getting the upper hand.)

The light station surely averted many mishaps in Muscle Ridge Channel, but it could not eliminate them, as shipping increased geometrically in this waterway. Ships hauling pulpwood for the lime kilns, then lime for the markets to the westward, granite from the Dix Island and other quarries, and passengers from Boston to the growing number of Penobscot Bay resorts after the Civil War, numbered two hundred a day in season. Inevitably there were shipwrecks. Accordingly, a lifesaving station was authorized on Whitehead Island and inaugurated in 1874, the first in the Penobscot Bay region. Horace Norton, though an indifferent seaman according to local report, stipulated in conveying the land to the United States government that he be named to head the station. And he was in fact the first keeper, with a complement of local lads as surfmen: Freeman Shea, Herbert Elwell, James Elwell, Charles Allen, Forrest Snow, and Eben Maker (Smalley, 176). The crew was on full duty six months of the year, from November to April; the captain, or keeper, was on duty year round, and was authorized to put together what crew he could in the off-season months. Records of the first years of the station (recently discovered in the walls of the original boathouse) include this 1887 account of a typical rescue:

> The vessel was seen at half past 5 oclock in the morning. She was laying on the rocks badly busted to leeward and to the starberd side. The stern was aground but the bow was afloat. The crew had ran a kedger to windward and taken

the line to the fore-halyards. This was done to keep her from rooling over on her side. But as the stern was aground it held her bow up to windward and kept her on the rocks. I got a surfman and alternate and went to her as soon as possible. We had the halyards cast off and cleared from the line. That let her bow swing round before the wind when she came off the rocks. Instructs were left at the Island for the surfmen to haul the colors down that were flying on the station and come directly to the wreck. Five of the men were there in about an hour. We were obliged to throw part of the deckload overboard to keep the vessel from rooling over on her side as half of the deckload was set on one side and consequently very heavy and the vessel filling up fast though the pumps were kept going. A boat was sent out to the schooner Lucy J. Warren of Swans Island. Capt M. Stinson who came up and took her in tow and carried her into lobster cove where she ran on the flats. The Keeper and two surfmen went out in a small boat and got her kedge and line which was left on the rock when the Lucy J. Warren took her in tow. At low water (5 oclock PM) holes were bored in her bottom and the water ran out after which the boat returned to stations. The surfmen who were present were J. F. McKello [McKellar], J Elwell, F. Shea Alternate for E. Meservey, F. Grant alternate for F. Snow and M Elwell alternate for S. Cummings.

H. Y. Norton Keeper[48]

With the creation of the United States Coast Guard in 1915, the lifesaving station became the Whitehead Life Boat Station. More men were assigned to the station—seventeen in 1941—and motorized patrol craft were increasingly used. The station became a base for search-and-rescue operations, and during Prohibition and World War II for coastal patrols. No fewer than five of the six year-round dwellings on the island were occupied during these years by Coast Guard personnel, whose children filled the one-room schoolhouse at the light station. In 1954 the Whitehead Life Boat Station was closed, replaced by a new Coast Guard station in Rockland.

[48] Another reported episode of the early years of the lifesaving station—told by the writer Wilbert Snow, himself a native of Whitehead Island—has understandably irritated David Gamage. The episode concerns the alleged oversight, in a rescue during the 1870s, of two Negro seamen who froze to death in the abandoned wreck. The story, Gamage feels, demeans the surfmen who manned the station: it is highly unlikely, Gamage argues—and surely not reported in any station records—that surfmen would leave two seamen, of whatever color, aboard a doomed vessel.

Old lifesaving station on southwest shore of Whitehead Island, built in 1873; a new station replacing this one on the northeast shore functioned until the mid-1950s. (Courtesy of Commander Albert J. Smalley.)

Valuations in the Whitehead District of St. George, 1875 and 1888

Note: The following persons were assessed in District 15 of St George (the "Whitehead" district) in 1875 and 1888. If residents are identified with certainty, they are located as follows: ***C****, Calf Island;* ***N****, Norton Island;* ***W****, Whitehead Island. Those not located were probably resident on Whitehead. The district is believed to have also included Elwell Island, which was vacant at these dates. The categories of ownership are shown as follows:*

Acre	Acreage owned	**Ox**	Number of oxen
Hom	Homestead owned	**Cow**	Cattle, all ages
Barn	Barn owned	**Sheep**	Number of sheep

1875

Name	Acre	Hom	Barn	Ox	Cow	Sheep	Other
Norton, Horace **W**	30	1	1		4	4	
Rackliff, Job **N**	12	1	1	2	2	26	
Fleming, John							
Long, Hezekiah							
Grant, Oscher E. **W?**[49]							
Man, Oliver P. **W?**	1/4	1					
Shuman, George	1/2	1	1			1	
Elwell, Bertha	1/4	1					
McKellar, Albert						1	

1888

Name	Acre	Hom	Barn	Ox	Cow	Sheep	Other
Fogg, Isiah		1	1			1	
Shea, Freeman **W**	1/4	1	1			1	
Elwell, Fred							
Grant, Isaac H.							Vessel valued at $672
Maker, Ellis, **C**	7	1					
Maker, Israel M.		15	1	1			
Shea, Charles **W**							
Snow, Forrest A. **W**							
Andrews, James **N**	12	1	1				
Elwell, Herbert **W**							

[49] This person is not identified, but given his surname he may be related to Keeper Isaac H. Grant, who took up his duties on Whitehead in 1875.

Lightkeepers, Whitehead Island, 1805–1950

*Note: The following list, made up from data in the National Archives and from material gathered by David A. Gamage and C. William Colby, includes known lightkeepers on Whitehead Island from 1805 to 1950. Keepers are designated by **K**, assistant keepers by **AK1** and **AK2**.*

Name	Term	Remarks
Dolph, Ellis **K**	1805–07	
Otis, Ebenezer **K**	1813–16	Died in service
Haskell, Charles **K**	1816–21	
Davis, Samuel **K**	1821–40	
Perry, William, Jr. **K**	1840–41; 1845–49	Lost his position, then reinstated[50]
Bartlett, Joshua **K**	1849	
Pillsbury, Dennis **K**	1853	
Stackpole, Samuel B. **K**	1853–58	
Thomas, Albert **AK**	1854	
Stackpole, Edwin R. **AK**	1856	
Stackpole, Eugene **AK**	1857	Removed
Snow, Elisha **AK**	1857–59	Resigned
Stearns, Isaac **K**	1858–60	Died in service
Shoutts, Thomas **AK**	1859–60	Resigned
Ludwig, Samuel **AK**	1860	Resigned
Spear, William **K**	1860–61	Resigned
Spear, William, Jr. **AK**	1860–61	Resigned
Quinn, Ephraim **K**	1861–62	Removed[51]
Perry, William **AK**	1861–62	Resigned after Quinn dispute
McKellar, Archibald **K**	1862	
McKellar, James **AK**	1862	
Spaulding, Edward **K**	1862–65	Resigned
Spaulding, E. Cooper **AK**	1862–66	
Long, Hezekiah **K**	1865–75	Removed
Norton, Horace **AK**	1866–74	Served intermittently
Long, Abbie B. **AK**	1867–75	Daughter of Hezekiah Long
Grant, Isaac N. **K**	1875–90	Resigned
Grant, Abby B. **AK**[52]	1875–90	Resigned
Perry, Knot **AK**	1876	Temporary[53]
Upton, George L. **K**	1890–92	Resigned
Jellison, Frank N. **AK1, K**	1890–05	Appointed **K** in 1892
Stevens, Daniel **K**	1892	Acting app't cancelled; trans.
Matthews, George **AK1**	1892–98	Transferred
Jellison, Joseph W. **AK2**	1895–98	Promoted **AK1**; transferred
Hodgkins, Walden B. **AK2**	1899–02	Promoted **AK1**; transferred
Wilson, Otto A. **AK2**	1899	Transferred
Connors, George S. **AK2**	1899–02	
Merrit, Edward T. **AK2**	1902–03	
Reed, Elmer **AK1, K**	1902–12	Appointed **K** in 1905; trans
Joyce, George M. **AK2**	1903–05	
Faulkingham, A. **AK1, AK2**	1905–09	Promoted 1907
Flood, Stephen F. **AK1**	1905–07	

[50] David Gamage notes that Perry lost his position because of politics. Until 1896, when keepers were included in the Civil Service, appointments and removals were politically motivated.

[51] Dismissed following dispute with Assistant Keeper Perry.

[52] This was the former Abby Burgess, who at seventeen managed the Matinicus Rock station during a prolonged storm in 1856 when her father, the keeper, was absent (see page 60). She married Isaac N. Grant.

[53] Knot Perry served a few months during Abby Grant's confinement.

Name	Term	Remarks
Ingalls, Frank B. **AK2**	1907–09	Transferred
Moore, Fairfield H. **AK1**	1909–11	Transferred
Purrington, John E. **AK2**	1909–11	Transferred
Leighton, Lester **AK2**	1911–13	Transferred
Robinson, Charles **AK**	1913–?	Transferred
Wass, Hervey H. **AK1**	1913–19	Transferred[54]
Mitchell, Arthur B. **K**	1919–32	Transferred
Beal, Arthur J. **K**	1932–50	Retired
Alley, Frank **AK1**	?	Transferred to Coast Guard
Alley, G. Lester **AK2**	?	Retired

[54] Hervey Wass was keeper of Libby Island Light in Machias Bay from 1919 to 1941. His son Philmore B. Wass wrote about this station in his *Lighthouse in My Life* (Down East Books, 1987).

Lifesaving Station Personnel, Whitehead Island, 1874–1913

Note: The men below served at the Lifesaving Station on Whitehead Island between 1874, when the station opened, and 1913 when the service was absorbed in the United States Coast Guard. Keepers are designated with the letter **K**; *the others are surfmen (not identified until the 1880s).*[55] *Age shown is at start of service. "Other" information includes the normal occupation of the surfmen and exceptional reasons for retirement (most left the service for "other business").*

Name	Age	Term	Other
Norton, Horace F. **K**	28	1874–82	
Shea, Freeman **K**	38	1882–1911	Surfman from 1878; died in service
Snow, Forrest A.	22	1880–1913	Fisherman
Elwell, Albert	23	1882–87	Fisherman; illness in family
Rackliff, Henry E.	25	1882–87	Seaman
Clark, William W.	19	1883–85	Fisherman; failed exam
Meservey, Ernest	34	1884–87	Seaman
Shea, Charles	19	1885–96	Fisherman
Maker, Alonzo **K**	32	1885–1913	Fisherman; surfman until 1911
Robinson, Sylvanus	44	1887–89	Seaman
Kinney, James E.	30	1887–1913	Seaman
Harrington, Clarence E.	21	1887–88	Seaman
Mann, Leland	18	1889–91; 1896–1907	Coaster; failed physical; negligence
Thomas, James W.	37	1888–89	Seaman; sick
Clark, Winfield S.	25	1891–1904	
Elwell, David H.	32	1891–1902	Fisherman
Smalley, John S. (temp)	35	1896–96	Seaman
Larrabee, Eugene N.	33	1902–07	
Phillips, William H.	31	1904–05	Transferred
Johnson, Willard A.	25	1905–07	
Dunn, Lee R.		1905–13	
Ramsell, Clifford R.	35	1907–13	
Davis, Daniel E.		1907–09	
Wass, Hervey H.	32	1907–13	Trans. to light station
Beal, Thomas W.	33	1909–13	
Smith, Howell P.	31	1911–13	Troublesome, negligent
Tabbutt, Winfred	43	1912–13	
Foss, Willard	25	1913–13	Steamboat worker

[55] See page 103 for the names of the first surfmen at Whitehead.

Norton

Norton Island, if not exactly the twin of Whitehead, was intimately linked with it in the early years. First, the two are geologically linked inasmuch as they are barred to each other over two small islands known locally as the Brown Islands. They also shared names: both were part of the *Whitehead* cluster on early charts, and both bore the supplementary name *Chapell's* (or *Chaple's*) for many years; Richard Chapell was an eighteenth-century transient who lived briefly on Whitehead proper, but claimed both islands.

In 1799 Chapell, in a conveyance that appears to include both islands, sold to a Joseph Coombs of Thomaston, who in 1814 sold to Ebenezer Otis of St. George "Chaples Island, eighty acres..." together with two small islands "between said Chaples and Whitehead Island, three acres each" (Lincoln 88/175; also Knox Lands 17/560 or 570). The phrasing of the deed seems clearly to indicate that "Chaples" is the modern Norton, the two small islands being the Brown Islands. In 1818 there is an indication that the island had its first settler: Thomas and Rebecca Sylvester for $50 sold to Jonathan Norton "the island commonly called Chaples Island on which the said Jonathan now lives" (Knox Lands 20/254; I have not discovered how the Sylvesters acquired title). Jonathan Norton evidently remained on the island into the 1850s, his widow Deborah succeeding him (see residence table, page 97). Jonathan on Norton Island and Joseph on Whitehead were brothers, Jonathan about ten years senior. Their husbandry, to judge from St. George tax records, was comparable—and modest. Jonathan left Deborah an estate valued at $1,250 in the 1860 census schedule.

In 1833 Jonathan Norton had lost a suit brought against him by several Gloucester merchants and was obliged to surrender title to the island to meet his debts (Knox Lands 30/277). Title for several years passed back and forth among Boston and Portland businessmen, with indentures and "rock rights" quoted at startling figures for a Maine island in that era: $25,000 and $140,000 (Lincoln, East 1/14 and 1/15; Knox Lands 34/425). There was no quarrying in the end and title returned in due course to Norton heirs. Jonathan was still living on the island in 1850, together with a son and two sons-in-law: Amos Norton, Nathan Stanton, and John P. Allen.

After Jonathan's death the island was sold in 1860 for $500 to John Foster, then living on the north end of Metinic Island. Jonathan's widow Deborah moved off the island to live with a daughter in the Keag district of South Thomaston (also known as The Gig), where she died in 1884. John Foster lived with his family on Norton Island for several years before removing in 1864 to Andrews Island.[56] The next tenant was Job Rackliff, a peripatetic islander who moved from island to island all his life (Rackliff, Dix, Andrews, Large Green, and so forth). He farmed Norton Island in the 1870s. He is shown in an 1875 valuation table for St. George with twelve acres under cultivation, a yoke of oxen, two cows, and twenty-six sheep—which was better farming than his Norton predecessors could claim.[57] Job Rackliff removed before 1880 (he is not in the St. George census for that year). A few years later James Andrews came onto the island with his family, including a son Hiram; James Andrews had been living on Large Green Island (see page 46). James and his third wife Hannah died on Norton Island, leaving Hiram, who was the last resident farmer there. Hiram's fame in the area, according to local legend, arose from the three or four beautiful daughters he reared (only one of the daughters had been born by 1900, to judge from the federal census—page 98—but the rest were apparently born in time to beguile the lobstermen who sang their praises in interviews with me in the 1970s).

Norton Island was cut over for pulp in the 1920s. There was seasonal residence after this, initially by local lobstermen and later by out-of-state vacationers. The buildings on the island have long since disappeared, the last of them burned as a hazard in the 1950s. A cellar hole and one dug well, together with tumbled stone walls, are all that remain to testify to more than a century of residence and farming on Norton Island.

[56] Correpondence with C. William Colby of Sprucehead Island.

[57] Job's wife Lydia held title to the island, which was conveyed to her by John Foster in 1871 (Knox 1/529).

Rackliff

William Rackliff, who quite possibly was born in England, was the first settler on this island and it has borne his name ever since. He is listed in the 1790 census with five children, according to a descendant, Bernard Rackliff, and is believed to have been living at that time on a farm near the middle of the barred island, on what is now called Balm of Gilead Hill. Family legend identifies his first wife as an Indian princess, which may be fanciful; his second, it is known, was a daughter of Job Philbrook of Islesborough. A survey made of *Rackly's Island* in 1801 for Benjamin Rackliff—his relationship to William is unclear—indicates the farm in an eighty-five-acre plot in the central sector of the island; the eastern and western plots are shown respectively as fifty and forty-one acres, without homesteads (Knox Lands 9/615). In 1816 a mortgage deed from William Rackliff to Thorndike, Sears & Prescott, owners of the Waldo Patent, refers to the island as "the same now occupied by said Rackliff" (Knox Lands 19/150). William had a large family, and late in his life, in the 1830s, we find numerous conveyances between members of his family and even outside the family (e.g., Knox Lands 33/574, 33/507, 33/727, and 34/103). An 1837 deed made clear the rather complex ownership of the island at this time: in this instrument, William deeded the island to the Overseers of the Poor in the town of St. George in return for $400 and maintenance for himself and his wife during the remainder of their lives, *excepting* fifty acres already deeded to his son John, forty to his son Job, and fifteen each to another son James and to Jonathan Tenant Maker (a son-in-law apparently): the town's parcel was thus about forty-six acres (Knox Lands 34/353).

By this time, Rackliffs had been joined on the island by Makers and Elwells, and no layman at all familiar with the complex genealogies of these three families in the St. George-Spruce Head region would lightly attempt to sort out those of them who settled and intermarried on Rackliff Island (see residence table, pages 98–98). By the 1860s half a dozen farms are shown along a road that ran southeasterly from the bar over Balm of Gilead Hill and down to the opposite shore (Map 1864 CGS 312). Albert Smalley's map of St. George shows a schoolhouse in the center of the island as early as 1835; in the 1870s, according to Smalley (*St. George*, 54), the school had sixty pupils, presumably from neighboring islands and the Makertown sector on the mainland, as well as Rackliff itself. (See pages 101–02 for further discussion of schools in the region.)

Farming was apparently the main occupation of these settlers, but two wharves shown in the 1863 charts, flanking the nub on the southeast shore, indicate that quarrying activity was also in progress. In fact, we know quarrying to have begun at least two decades earlier from a deed in 1846 that explicitly refers to it. The deed is from one Massachusetts contractor to another, involving $500 for a one-eighth interest in a fifteen-acre parcel, which Joshua Maker had previously conveyed to the grantor, and on which there was already a "stone quarry" (Knox Lands 35/40). Albert Smalley (interview) believed that William Rackliff sold quarrying rights on the island to the Gaults, or Galts, as early as 1831.

Quarrying was intermittent on Rackliff Island. Activity in the 1830s and 1840s was doubtless spasmodic, but in the 1860s and 1870s, according to local sources (Ralph Cline and Bernard Rackliff), two companies were working the island: one under William Hendricks, which opened a quarry on the northeast slope in 1865,[58] and the Dix Island Granite Company, which opened on the southeast slope. The stone cut was mostly for construction rather than for ornamental purposes; numerous individual motions for paving block were also started, chiefly at the lower end of the island near what has always been called the "Barley Field." As many as two hundred quarrymen were said to be working on Rackliff at the height of the boom, although it is believed that the majority of them lived off the island. There was at least one small boardinghouse on the island, run by Charles Mays, and several residents took in boarders (see residence table).

[58] An 1888 tax valuation for Rackliff Island shows the Atlantic Granite Company with sixty acres valued at $3,100; this may have been Hendricks's company.

The Dix Island Granite Company outlasted its competitor, and "Governor" Frank Crockett, the last superintendent of the company, was said to have been influential on Rackliff Island in the final decades of the nineteenth century. According to Ralph Cline, Rackliff Island spruce, cut under the aegis of Frank Crockett, was hauled away by his brother Oscar, who ran the Crockett Steamship Company, and was used in the construction of piers up and down Eggemoggin Reach—a fraternal enterprise that spanned Penobscot Bay.

I have an imperfect picture of the last years of year-round residents on Rackliff Island. With the end of the quarrying era and the disappearance of the Crocketts, the island, by now too scarred for profitable farming, became the residence of itinerant fishermen, and the turnover in population was probably rapid. The school had long since closed. The cattle were taken off the island, leaving for a time only a small flock of sheep. No Rackliffs, Makers, or Elwells, to my knowledge, lived on Rackliff in the twentieth century. The last year-round native inhabitants, Chester Wall, a lobsterman, and the widow of Joseph Lowe, another lobsterman, quit the island in the 1920s, according to Ralph Cline.

Rackliff has been developed by a New Hampshire realtor in recent years. The shallow bar linking the island to the mainland, over which oxen could always be driven at half tide, was easily transformed into a causeway onto the island; now a motor road encircles it, with a dozen or more freshly built summer homes spewing off toward the shores. William Rackliff of Balm of Gilead Hill could walk his island today from one end to the other and not know where he was.

Sprucehead

Author's Note: No effort was made in the first edition to present a comprehensive treatment of Sprucehead Island, on the perhaps specious grounds that it had been too long linked to the mainland (since 1898) to be considered a proper island; other coastal islands were excluded for similar reasons—though the real reason undoubtedly was to save the author time and trouble. Sprucehead is indeed an island, moreover one with a rich history. C. William Colby, a lifelong resident of the island and a lobster fisherman away from his research, has gathered an impressive volume of information about Sprucehead's past: genealogies of the principal settlers on the island, especially the McKellars; land and title records; the development and flowering of the granite industry, which began on the island in the 1820s and ended only in 1913; federal census schedules; school reports; and the long struggle of the islanders for the bridge linking the island to the mainland at Elwell Point. He has kindly consented to my incorporating his findings in this edition, and readers will be grateful for his generosity. What follows, then, is in large part the fruit of C. William Colby's research—or a portion of it, for his material is extensive—set forth in my words.

If the island now called *Sprucehead*[59] was settled in Revolutionary times, we do not know the names of the settlers. The island was, in any case well known to residents of the area: it made the north-easterly arm of Seal Harbor, and was indeed called *Seal Harbor Island* in charting of the 1770s (e.g., "Atlantic Neptune," 1776). Later, when Seal Harbor was known as Lobster Cove, the island became *Lobster Cove Island*, and still later *Elwell Island* after the numerous Elwells who settled there. Andrew Elwell, who came from Gloucester, Massachusetts, was the first known settler on the island; the date of his coming is uncertain, but it is believed that he found evidence of settlers who had preceded him. In 1793, according to deeds, Andrew Elwell quitclaimed the island to Finlay Kalloch, and the same year Elwell and Kalloch, for £50, quitclaimed the western third of the island to James Matthews. The eastern two-thirds, which contained the future quarry sites, was acquired by

[59] NOAA charts today name the island *Sprucehead*—one word—though the township is *Spruce Head*. I will follow my custom of using the NOAA spellings, although I am aware that local preference is for two words, for both township and island. A further note on nomenclature: The mainland village, originally called Seal Harbor, was changed to Spruce Head in the 1890s when the post office was opened—to distinguish it from Seal Harbor on Mount Desert Island.

Robert Elwell in 1801: two hundred acres for $200.[60]

It is doubtful whether these early deeds had any validity since Sprucehead was surely within the Waldo or Muscongus Patent, which by the end of the century belonged to General Henry Knox and was sold by him in 1806 to Thorndike, Sears & Prescott, Massachusetts investors. The latter conveyed the western third of Sprucehead properly to William Bryant, who settled there for a decade or more (he appears in St. George tax records regularly between 1803 to 1815). In 1817 Bryant sold to Thomas G. McKellar; this marked the beginning of the McKellar ascendancy on the island. Thorndike, Sears & Prescott sold the remaining two-thirds of the island to John Gleason of Thomaston, an associate of General Knox, and Gleason in 1830 sold this parcel to McKellar.

Thomas McKellar was reared in the Wylie Corner sector of St. George, where his father John was active in municipal affairs. In 1800 Thomas acquired land on Metinic Island, and in 1811 he moved there for several years; in 1813 he married Ruth Thorndike, who was living on the island, and their first child was born there. The McKellars moved to the Sprucehead sector of St. George after the 1817 purchase of the western third of the island, along with Elwell Point on the facing shore. The sale price of the two lots, $500 for each, suggests that both were by this date developed farmland. The McKellars settled for two years on Elwell Point, but by 1819 moved to the island where they lived in what came to be known as Century House, a domicile believed to date from the early nineteenth century and still standing at the end of the twentieth.

From 1819 until his death in 1848, Thomas McKellar devoted his considerable energies to the development of his island. He opened up additional meadow and pasture land. He multiplied his livestock. Above all, he launched quarrying on Sprucehead Island, some years before quarrying became general in the region. He opened the first quarries in the 1820s, C. William Colby tells us, on the strength of contracts with New Orleans builders. After acquiring the eastern two-thirds of the island in 1830, he leased rights to various contractors, as detailed below. At his death in 1848 Thomas McKellar left, beside his wife Ruth Thorndike, eight of his eleven children, several of whom continued to live on the island and manage its affairs. The eldest son John—after Ruth herself—played the leading role in the island's husbandry; he had begun to accumulate property of his own even before his father's death (Burnt Island, for instance) and inherited a sixth of Sprucehead proper. He continued, for several years after his marriage to Lucy Condon, to live in Century House, along with his mother, younger siblings, and orphaned nephews.[61] In due course he built his own home on the island. John died in 1863, and his younger brother Joseph (known as "J. T.") took on his mantle.

The farm was undoubtedly the principal occupation of the McKellars. J. T. was the guiding force of the operation; the orphaned nephews were his principal helpers: Hannah Fales's sons Benjamin T. and Fred W., Mary Kellars's son Charles,[62] and in due course John's son Thomas E. (see genealogical table, page 117). Others were also surely engaged on the farm for it appears to have been a large enterprise. One account estimated that during the Civil War there were as many as a thousand sheep on the island farm, which yielded "a considerable revenue in wool and lamb."[63]

It was not the farm, however, that brought substantial wealth to the McKellars, but the sale of granite rights on the island. The island was well positioned to profit from the mushrooming growth of the industry after the Civil War. Quarries had been opened as early as the 1820s, possibly by Thomas G. McKellar himself; from the 1830s to the 1860s, after Thomas acquired the rest of the island, more than a dozen contractors from New York and Pennsylvania as well as from Rockland, Belfast, and Portland leased granite

[60] I omit deed references in this notice, but they are easily located in the Knox County Registry of Deeds in Rockland with relevant dates and the names of the parties.

[61] Thomas and Ruth McKellar's progeny were not blessed with long lives: five died before they were thirty (three of these, plus one son-in-law, on sea voyages), and three others before they were fifty; only three of the eleven children lived beyond sixty.

[62] The spelling Kellach and Kellar are alternate for the same surname; they are not normally interchangeable with McKellar.

[63] The estimate, according to C. William Colby, was given by Joseph McKellar's nephew, Charles G. Hoyt, in an interview with a Florida newspaper (date unspecified).

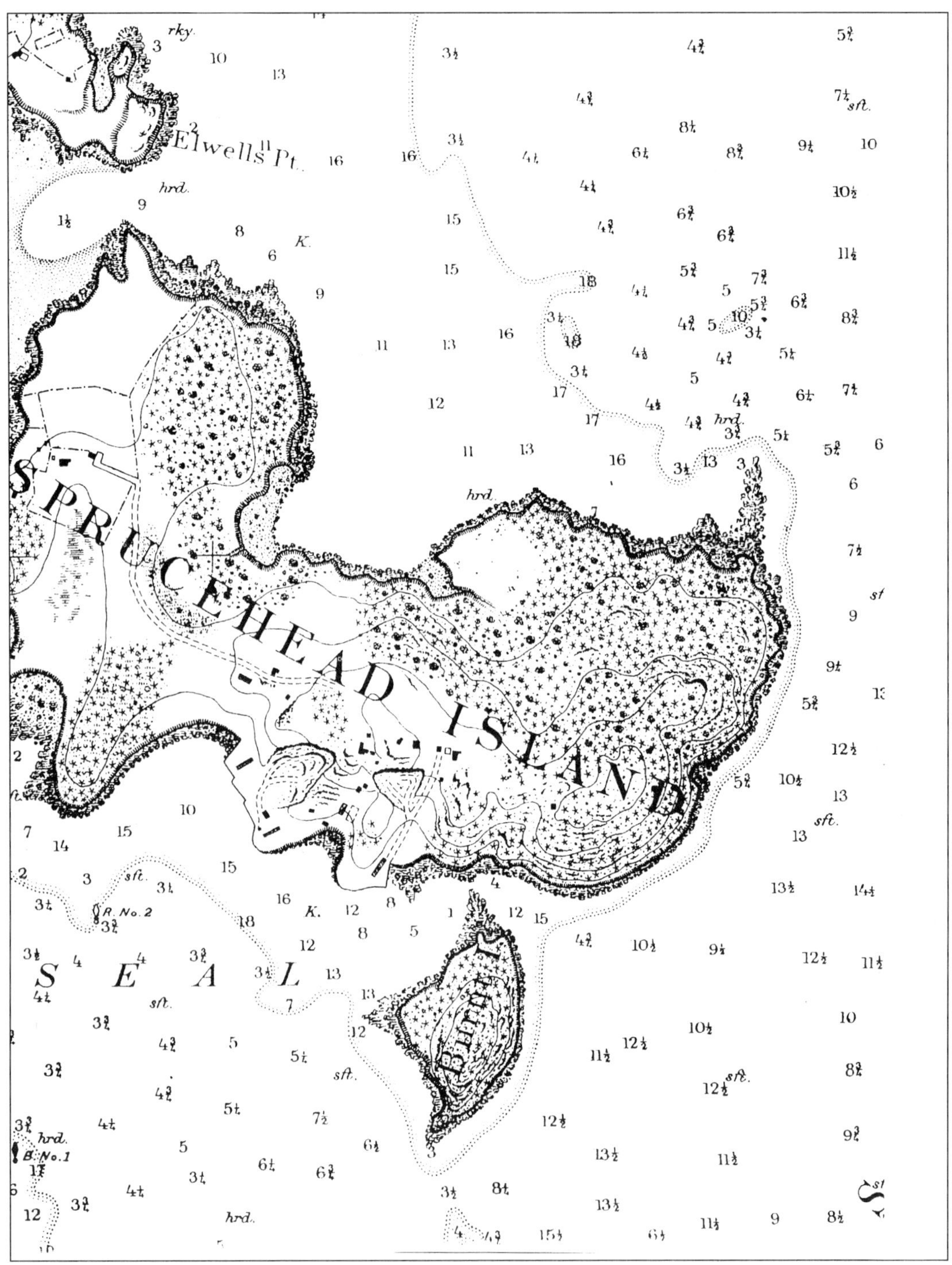

Sprucehead Island in about 1870, with roads, farms, and quarry installations; segment of Map 1874 "Approaches to Dix Island," surveyed between 1868 and 1871.

rights from the McKellars; moreover, these leaseholds were on the southern shores of the island facing a deepwater harbor where vessels could easily remove the stone. The most ambitious of the early companies on Sprucehead was Cobb, Wight & Case of Rockland, long pre-eminent in the lime industry and eager to diversify its activities into granite. Early in the 1860s this company bought out the interests of a New York operator, E. B. Peet, and at the same time acquired from the widow of John McKellar her undivided one-sixth interest in the island.

At about the time Cobb, Wight & Case established itself on Sprucehead, Merrick Sawyer, a fifty-year-old quarryman from Portland, bought two small lots from McKellar heirs and opened a quarry. He moved onto Sprucehead with his family in 1863 and for three decades played a significant role in the life of the community. He served often as school agent for the island. He built a boardinghouse for his twenty-five to thirty workers and, since he was of a religious disposition, encouraged prayer meetings and church services there. He played an active role in the matter of a bridge to the mainland (discussed below). In his personal finances Merrick Sawyer was less successful. "Sawyer, unlike his competion of Cobb, Wight and Case and later the Bodwell Granite Company," William Colby notes, "never appeared to get very rich in the business. In fact, he always seemed to have cash-flow problems."[64] Sawyer died in 1893, much respected by his fellow islanders and his workers—regardless of cash flow problems.

The principal contractor on Sprucehead Island was the prestigious Bodwell Granite Company, founded in 1871 by a consortium of well-known operators including Joseph R. Bodwell of Hallowell (later governor of Maine), Moses Webster, and Edmund Walker of Vinalhaven, as well as the principals of Cobb, Wight & Case, noted above. The new Bodwell company promptly absorbed Bodwell & Webster, the original enterprise founded by these two entrepreneurs on Vinalhaven, and for $23,000 acquired the Sprucehead holdings of Cobb, Wight & Case. This was a tidy figure for granite rights at that date and indicates the ascendancy of the industry in Maine. The Bodwell Granite Company was undoubtedly one of the giants in the field and for some years received contracts across the country to provide stone for bridges, post offices, libraries, and other public buildings. As late as the 1890s the Bodwell company was described as "the largest capitalized granite company in the United States...or the world" (cited from a contemporary quarrying journal in Grindle, *Tombstones and Paving Blocks*, 94).

No doubt the Sprucehead quarries gained some fame through association with the name Bodwell, but it would be a mistake to equate the company's operations on Sprucehead with those on Vinalhaven. None of the principal stockholders or officers of the company took up residence on Sprucehead. The number of workers there, though the company built two boardinghouses and numerous small camps to accommodate them, was a fraction of those employed on Vinalhaven in peak periods. Moreover, the granite produced on Sprucehead was chiefly construction block; there were not the facilities to produce the more valuable ornamental stone that was cut and polished on Vinalhaven—or for that matter, on neighboring islands like Dix or Clark. An inventory of the Bodwell holdings on Sprucehead in 1894, presented to the assessors of South Thomaston for tax purposes, will put the company's activities in a more modest perspective.

[64] Sawyer's 1886 valuations were as follows, according to C. William Colby: boardinghouse, $600; ox barn, $65; two stores, $100; quarry and wharves, $1,700. His tax was $59.20.

Rockland, Me, April 6, 1894

To the Assessors of Taxes, South Thomaston, Maine

The Bodwell Granite Company submits below a list of its property Real and Personal located at Spruce Head Island, owned by said company on the first (1st) day of April, 1894, and subject to taxation by the town of South Thomaston, viz:

Real Estate	**Personal Property**	
Granite Quarry and wharf:	1 Steam drill	
20 acres, opened & unopened	6 Horses (4 good, 2 poor)	
Clark Granite Quarry so-called	1 Steam hoisting engine	
4 Houses	3 Derricks	
1 Store	Quarry Tools	$85
1 Barn	Cutters Tools	125
3 Stone sheds (2 good, 1 poor)	Carts & Wheels	115
2 Carpenter shops	1,500 cubic feet Granite	
1 Blacksmith shop	Stock in Trade in Store:	
	20 Barrels flour	80
	Dry goods & clothing	80
	Hardware	12
	Boots & shoes	60
	Groceries, West India goods	75
	Crockery	12
	50 tons Coal	275
		$594

Very Respectfully
Bodwell Granite Company
By E. H. Lawry, Treas.

Note: Most of this inventory is self-explanatory, but a few remarks may be helpful. There is no explanation for the name of the Bodwell quarry, the "Clark Granite Quarry so-called"; it is not in any case related to the Clark Island quarries. The "4 houses" are presumably residences of company officials (e.g., Superintendent Blethen), and possibly some workers. The boardinghouses are not listed and may have been removed. The "store" is the company's all-purpose store, a fixture on all quarry islands. And so forth.

Sprucehead's ranking as a quarrying island is not, in any case, the focus of this notice; rather, the impact of quarrying on the island community. It was a formidable impact. The majority of residents were there, after mid-century, because of the quarries. Even McKellar descendants and their in-laws, who continued to own most of the island and kept the family farm solvent, worked in the quarries or in close association with them. The only stores on the island were company stores. The school, started in 1852 to provide education for the children of quarrymen coming onto the island in growing numbers, continued to depend on the industry for its pupils and its teachers. The peak enrollment in the "McKellar Island School, No. 14" came in the 1870s: thirty pupils.[65]

[65] William Colby lists the teachers in the District 14 school from the 1870s to 1913. There is no significant information about any of them beyond a few salaries: $17.50 for a female teacher in 1871; $38 for another in 1886. The names, however, are worth recording here for those seeking to close genealogical gaps:

1870s
Mary D. Putnam
Lizzie Marsh
Etta Philbrook
Lucy Philbrook
Alice W. Hall
Lottie E. French
Etta B. Jackson
Ida D. Rowell

1880s
Minnie W. Babb
Louisa L. Merriner
J. N. Sawyer
Blanche L. Wilson
Adella F. Veasi
Madie A. Kalloch
Grace E. Hoyt

1890s
Alice S. Graves
Susie Littlefield
Maggie A. Godfrey
Teresa Hamlin
Minnie Andrews
Susie M. Post
Ella L. Maddocks

1900-13
Helen W. Adams
Maerita Adams
Scott Rackliff
Olive J. Magune
S. Mertice Gott
Florence M. Smalley
Cora Harrington
Edith Porter
Edward A. Smalley
Delia Butler
Flora Jackson

The bridge from Sprucehead to the mainland also owed its existence to the quarries—indirectly. In early years Thomas McKellar's sheep had been a reason for *not* proposing a bridge from Elwell Point, but with the passage of time the convenience to quarrymen unable to find quarters on the island and so boarding in Seal Harbor (the mainland village now called Spruce Head) outweighed the inconvenience of straying sheep, and the idea of a bridge was broached. But it was many years between the broaching and the building. The majority of residents in South Thomaston, which separated from St. George in 1865, lived in the Keag[66] sector of the township and vigorously resisted sharing in the cost of a bridge that benefited only the residents of Seal Harbor and Sprucehead; petitions for the bridge were accordingly voted down routinely in town meetings. In 1880 Merrick Sawyer, Bodwell officials, and some fifty residents of Sprucehead Island petitioned the state legislature, and the latter in due course considered the petition, along with a passionate counter-petition from The Keag. This counter-petition is of interest to us because it casts some doubt on the profitability of the quarrying operations at this time; it read in part:

> whereas...the principal granite quarries upon Sprucehead Island have proved comparatively worthless by reason of impurities and black knots preventing further profitable working of them forcing the proprietors to the serious contemplation of abandoning the same...Therefore, be it resolved...that the public convenience and necessity do *not* require that such way and bridge should be established.... And furthermore be it resolved that the petitioners are unreasonable in their demands in asking for an expansion bridge to accommodate those quarries which the proprietors are about to abandon....

The quarries were not, in fact, abandoned at this time and the bridge petition, under the guidance of J. T. McKellar (who was then serving in the state legislature), was accepted. However, the Keag faction succeeded in stalling construction of the bridge for another dozen years. It was inaugurated finally in 1896, nearly twenty years after the first petition.

When the Bodwell Granite Company ceased operations in 1913, the island virtually closed down. The boardinghouses emptied. The single remaining store closed. The school was boarded up. As C. William Colby writes (in a rare moment of introspection in his otherwise no-nonsense record):

> ...a strange silence settled over Spruce Head Island. An eerie sound that hadn't been heard for over 80 years—no more drilling, blasting, or grinding of machinery to break the stillness of the morning air.

It was not, of course, the end of life on Sprucehead Island. (Rum-running during Prohibition, for instance, preoccupied an unspecified portion of the citizenry.) In due course and after lengthy legal wrangles among the McKellar heirs, the island was resettled, principally by fishermen. There was an effort in the 1930s to turn the island into a vacation colony, or a bedroom community. A number of cottages were built, and Merrick Sawyer's boardinghouse was converted to the Rockledge Inn for tourists. Gentrification did not succeed entirely. Fishermen, past and present, still predominate on the island proper, but of the seventy-five vessels in the harbor, only a few are owned by island residents—a circumstance that has caused some islanders to wonder (a century too late) whether that bridge should ever have been built.

[66] Or "The Gig"; the spellings are interchangeable locally.

Residence on Sprucehead Island 1850–1900

Note: The following lived on Sprucehead Island from 1850 to 1900, according to the federal census. Age is shown at first appearance. Spouses are in parentheses. Occupations are indicated as follows: B, blacksmith; C, carpenter; Fa, farmer; Fi; fisherman; S, sailor; Q, quarryman. In the decennial columns, males are to left of slash, females to right.

Householder	**1850**	**1860**	**1870**	**1880**	**1900**
McKellar, Ruth, 54	2/4	5/4[67]	3/3	2/2	
McKellar, John, 36 (Lucy), Fa	2/1	6/5[68]			
Fales, Hannah, 30 (widow)	2/1				
Fosgate, Francis, 28 (Cynthia), clerk		5/4[69]			
Robinson, Edward, 25 (Nancy), Q		2/1			
Blasedell [Blaisdel], Thomas J., 42 (Mary), Q		1/2	1/2		
Kelly, Greenwood, 30 (Cordelia), Q		3/1			
Kaler, Timothy, 40 (Catherine),Q			2/2		
Savage, James, 37 (Sarah), Q			1/1		
Savage, Mark, 25 (Elenora), Q			2/4	3/4	
Perry, Seth, 33 (Mary), Q			3/1		
McLaughlin, William, 31 (Ellen), Q			6/2		
Monks, James, 40 (Hanna), Q			1/1		
Herson, Patrick, 38, Q			1/1		
Cain, Patric, 35 (Mary), Q			2/2		
Ryard, James (Edna), B			3/1		
Elwell, Frederic, 25, Q			1/0		
Gallagher, Thomas, 48 (Margaret), Q			20/3[70]	3/1	
Robinson, Erastus, Jr., 26 (Elozia), B			2/3		
Morse, Nelson, 29 (Martha/Ellen), Q			2/1	2/2	
Taylor, Edward, 31 (Mahala), Q			1/1	1/1	1/1
Sawyer, Merrick, 60 (Laura), contractor			7/5[71]	3/1	
Grant, David, 33 (Emeline), Q			20/5[72]		
Hall, Silas, 42 (Nancy), Q/C			1/2	2/2	
Tibbetts, Woodbury, 29 (Cynthia), Q				4/2	
Blethen, John, 35 (Mary), Q				5/3[73]	
Waldron, William, 37 (Catherine), Q				4/1	
Burns, George, 41 (Lucinda), laborer				4/3	
Johnson, Henry, 34 (Cora), Q				4/1	
Heal, Arthur, 37 (Aramenta), Q				1/2	

[67] Joseph McKellar, thirty-one, is head of household in 1860 with a valuation of $1,145; the household includes several orphaned grandchildren of Ruth McKellar.

[68] The John McKellar household in 1860 included, besides sundry McKellars, two boarders: quarryman James Christian, twenty-four, and his wife (Elizabeth); and Tronas Snowdeal, twenty-nine, a carpenter.

[69] The Fosgate household in 1860 included several quarrymen as boarders, among them William Brainard, aged twenty-one (later head of the Bodwell Company).

[70] Gallagher ran a boardinghouse with seventeen quarrymen, mostly Scots and Irish.

[71] The Sawyers took in eight boarders: five males, three females.

[72] The Grants ran a boardinghouse, accommodating nineteen males (mostly quarrymen and teamsters) and two females.

[73] The Blethen household included five boarders: three males, two females.

Householder	1850	1860	1870	1880	1900
Clark, Horace W., 40 (Azora), Q				1/2	
Taylor, Robert, 64 (Abigail), Fa				2/2	
Smith, Charles, 31 (Susan), S					1/2
Williamson, John, 52 (Priscilla), Q					2/1[74]
Fales, Frederick, 54, S, and brother Benjamin T. (bachelors)					2/1
Harrington, George, 29 (Dellma), Q					3/1
Adams, Willis, 42 (Mary), sup't, Bodwell Granite Works					4/3
Elwell, Andrew, 26 (Lucy), Q					1/1
Graves, Frank, 48, Q					1/0
Philbrook, Warren, 35 (Fannie), Q					4/3
Meservey, Herbert, 48 (Nancy), Q					1/4
Harrington, Clarence, 34 (Rosey), Q					1/1
Mann, Oliver, 56 (Sophronia), Q					2/1
Williamson, William, 59 (Mary Ann), Q					3/3
Totals					
No. of households	3	6	17[75]	15	13
No. of males	6	22	79	41	27
No. of females	9	17	40	29	22
Total persons	12	39	119	50	49

[74] This household inluded Joseph T. McKellar, seventy-one, who had normally lived with his mother, Ruth McKellar.
[75] And two boardinghouses.

McKellars of Sprucehead Island

Note: Those in italics lived on Sprucehead Island as adults.[76]

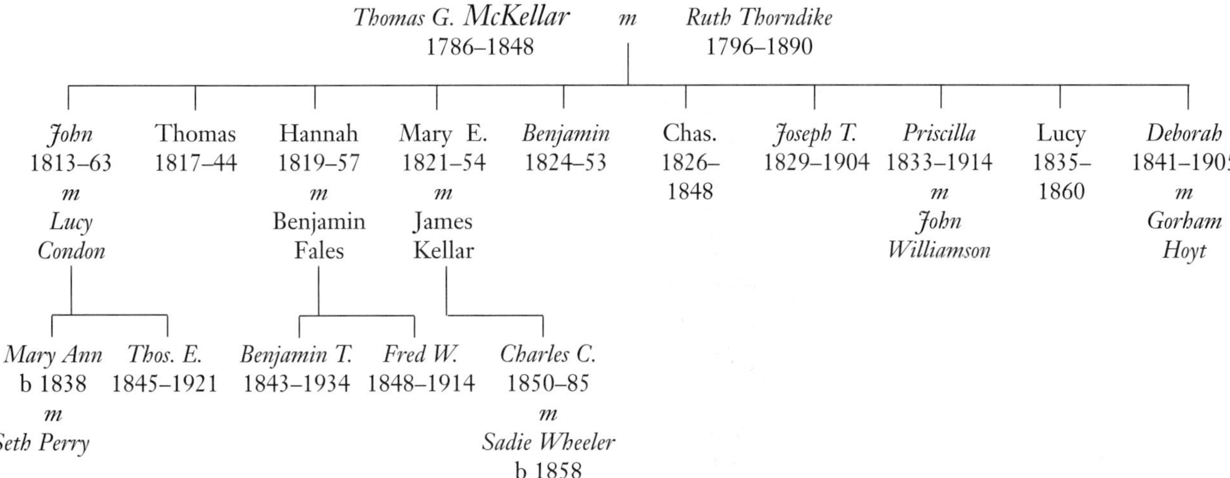

[76]Thomas and Ruth McKellar's short-lived tenth child—Frederick (1937–39)—is not shown in the table.

Burnt (off Sprucehead)

An early name for this island was False Sprucehead, but it often bore both names: e.g., in a conveyance from Andrew Elwell to John McKellar in 1835 for $5: "Burnt or False Spruce-head" (Knox Lands 33/238). The island was never settled, but it must have had squatters during the long quarrying era on Sprucehead proper. It was often used for pasturage. In the twentieth century the island has been linked to Sprucehead by a private bridge serving cottagers who own it.

Group 4: Islands North of Sprucehead

Tommy and Eben

These two small islands near the mouth of the Weskeag River north of Sprucehead Island are named for two Thorndikes—either father and son or two brothers. Cyrus Eaton (*History of Thomaston*, I: 62) writes of Ebenezer Thorndike, a settler in the area as early as 1750: "...he took up, as the phrase is, 600 acres of land on both sides of the line between the present towns of South Thomaston and St. George. Here he put up some rude buildings, manufactured salt; carried on the fishery—catching salmon in the mouth of the Wessaweskeag and drying his nets on the small island, still called, from him, Eben's Island." Malcolm Jackson suggests that the islands may have been named for Ebenezer's two sons—Ebenezer, Jr. and Thomas—who inherited from him. The islands have been used during the last two centuries for pulp, pasturage, weir fishing, fishing rights, and, irregularly, seasonal residence. A small fish works operated on Tommy in the last decades of the twentieth century.

Spaulding

"...if island it may be called," Cyrus Eaton writes of Spaulding (*History of Thomaston*, I: 1), referring to its mid-tide bar to the mainland. Taking my cue from Eaton, I give this island brief notice.

It is named *Adom* (or *Adam*) *Island* in a 1785 deed, which may be its earliest recorded conveyance; this is from Pierce Grafton (or Graffam) to Israel Lovett, both of Thomaston, and the island was included with a 110-acre lot facing on the Wessaweskeag River (Knox Lands 6/473). It is unlikely that Israel Lovett settled either on the island or on his lot; subsequent deeds referring to his numerous transactions show him living on the St. George River—that is, on the other side of the peninsula. I find no record of his conveyance of the island to Timothy Spaulding, but in 1801 Henry Knox, who as owner of the Waldo Patent had better title to this property than Lovett, sold the shore lot to Spaulding for $75.70, and I take it for granted that the island was included with it (Knox Lands 11/224). The island was thus named after this early-nineteenth-century settler. There my research ends: I do not know whether he lived on the island or merely used it for farming and timber.

Ash

This is shown as *Birch Island* in the 1776 "Atlantic Neptune," but soon took the name of the promontory off which it is located—Ash Point. The name comes from the ash groves that, according to Cyrus Eaton (*History of Thomaston*, I: 8), once abounded in the area. *Ash Point Island*—No. 58 in the Muscongus or Waldo Patent—was conveyed to William Heard, a yeoman of Thomaston, by the Boston land brokers Sears & Thorndike in 1807 (Knox Lands 17/51). This is the first conveyance I have discovered, though Malcolm Jackson suggests the island may have belonged formerly to the Crocketts, the first settlers on Ash Point, and later to Stephen Peabody, who acquired it from John Crockett in 1770.

When Ash Island was settled is unclear, though it evidently was, since an ancient cellar hole and well exist there according to a recent owner. Williamson (I: 63), normally quite precise about island residence, says that Ash island was not inhabited in 1820. The maps in the latter half of the century, which normally showed habitation if there was any, give no sign of it in the case of Ash—though fencing is shown on a map of the 1860s (Map 1864 CGS 312). I conclude, therefore, that someone lived on the island, and probably farmed it, sometime between 1820 and 1860—but not for many years; a long residence would have attracted more attention. According to a recent owner, the northwest sector of Ash was still treeless in the 1920s. Other early uses of the island may have included lime burning—the same owner reports a small kiln there—and perhaps cutting timber for the Ash Point boatyards; at the very least the island must have served as a convenient breakwater for these famous yards.[77]

In 1889 an enterprising Boston realtor, John Mattson, persuaded that the day of the summer cottager had arrived, laid out a plan for 212 lots in a summer colony at the south end of the island; there was to be a hotel at the tip, and the streets led to terraces named Idaho, Iroquois, Samoset, and so forth (Knox Plan Book I: 87). I am not aware that any cottages were built, but some lots may have been sold, for the father of a recent owner was obliged to buy up the island piecemeal as individual parcels became available.

The remains of a tripod are on the eastern point of the island where there was a beacon to guide vessels through Muscle Ridge Channel. It was on Grindstone Ledge, half a mile south of Ash Island, that the steamer CITY OF ROCKLAND struck in the fog on July 26, 1904; the passengers were safely removed but the vessel was lost.

[77] See "Boats of Ash Point, Maine," *American Neptune*, October 1942.

Fisherman and Marblehead

Marblehead is called *Remarkable Rock* on one edition of the "Atlantic Neptune" (Map 1776)—one of two islands so designated in Penobscot Bay, the other being Brimstone off Vinalhaven. Its neighbor, meanwhile, was called alternatively *Fishermen's* or *Mark Island* (Williamson I: 64). Both, then, were used as navigational aids for mariners entering or leaving the inner bay. This must have been what recommended Fisherman as a rendezvous for British war vessels in the War of 1812, according to Cyrus Eaton (*History of Thomaston*, I: 288); surely the British captains did not imagine they could conceal their vessels behind so small an island.

I have no history to record of Marblehead, and little of Fisherman. In 1807 the latter was sold to William Heard of Ash Point, along with several other islands in the vicinity (Knox Lands 17/51). William Heard willed the island to a widow, Sally Crockett—presumably his daughter—in 1843 (Knox Lands 35/542). I know nothing of other conveyances during the nineteenth century, but around 1900, according to a recent owner, hay was regularly cut and removed for livestock ashore. In the first decades of the twentieth century the island was used seasonally by fishermen, and a camp was erected, of which remains still stand. Birds, however, eventually prevailed over fishermen, a reversal of the usual order: in 1944 a colony of cormorants estimated at 1,500 nested on Fisherman Island, was driven off by resident fishermen with clubs, but soon returned.[78] Today the cormorants, eider, and other nesting birds have rendered the island effectively unusable by man.

[78] *Maine Coast Fisherman*, October 1946, 25.

Sheep (off Owls Head)

This is Island No. 77 in the Great Plan of the Waldo Patent and was first claimed by Nathaniel Crockit (or Crockett), a settler at Owls Head. In 1777 he conveyed the island—called *Crockit's Island*—together with a shore plot opposite Monroe Island to Mason Wheaton and Benjamin and Micah Packard, all of Thomaston; the price was £76 (Knox Lands 10/227). It is doubtful that the conveyance was valid. Nothing further is heard of Mason Wheaton and the Packards in connection with the island. In 1798 Isaac Barnard quitclaimed Sheep Island to John Ulmer, gentleman, for $200 (Knox Lands 8/599). Whether Barnard's title was any better than Crockett's is debatable, but in 1812 the owners of the Waldo Patent properly conveyed Sheep Island to Andrew Ulmer for $100—"the same island which s'd Ulmer has Improved upon" (Knox Lands 19/592). Andrew Ulmer himself surely never lived there, but William Williamson (I: 64), writing in the 1820s, mentioned a house and barn as well as "very good land." There is also evidence that the island was inhabited in 1822: according to Cyrus Eaton (*History of Thomaston*, I: 326), a summons was delivered there at that date.[79] Residence, at least by farmers, appears to have ended by the 1860s, if not earlier. Eaton (*History of Thomaston*, I: 8) writes of Sheep Island, as of its neighbor Monroe, "at present if not generally uninhabited." A map of the Rockland area about the same time shows two fish shacks on the east shore (Map 1863 Rockland Harbor), but it does not appear that the island was regularly settled after this date. As for ownership, Andrew Ulmer died in 1857 without having deeded Sheep Island in his lifetime, and it is not mentioned in his will. According to Owls Head historian Malcolm Jackson, the island was deeded to successive owners along with the facing shore property at Owls Head—Lot No. 44.

[79] Eaton mentions the episode because the constable, a Lieutenant O. Robbins, Jr., was drowned while returning to Rockland; Eaton does not give the name of the resident.

In 1910 the United States government, seeking to establish a signal at the northern tip of the island for a measured mile in connection with naval trials, petitioned for condemnation and in due course compensated the owners as ordered: they were at that date Lewis F. Starret and Mary C. and Lucy C. Farnsworth (Knox Lands 152/187).

It may seem curious that so substantial an island close to the mainland never attracted more year-round settlers. A glance at any chart of the region suggests a reason: the water on all sides of it festers with shoals and ledges. The hazards of approach may have kept permanent settlers away, but not campers and fishermen in season. Summer squatters have been a regular feature of Sheep Island into recent times.

Monroe

This strategically located island off Owls Head, a landmark to navigators from Champlain's time forward, has more history than can possibly be uncovered. It would be a rash historian who tried to estimate the number of pinnaces, brigs, war sloops, and other sail that have found shelter in the lee of this island, or the number of mariners who swarmed over its shores looking for distraction. Owls Head Harbor may well have been the most frequented transient anchorage in the entire

Penobscot region until well into the nineteenth century. "Five hundred sail have been seen passing Owl's Head in one day," a mariner writes in the 1850s (Carter, "Coast of New England," 227).

But for all this activity *around* the island, we are generally ignorant of what happened *on* it. British Admiralty charts surveyed before the American Revolution call Monroe and Sheep the *Owl's Head Islands*, with the famous harbor marked abreast of the northerly of the two. I have not discovered a record of the island's inhabitants during the last decades of the eighteenth century and first of the nineteenth, but there may have been a More (or Moore)—for *More's Island* is one name Williamson gives it in the 1820s (*History of Maine*, I: 64); the other name he gives is *Munroe's Island*, after the occupant at that time. Hugh Munroe (or Munrow) was living there when he purchased the island in 1816 on a $175 mortgage from the brokers Thorndike, Sears & Prescott (Knox Lands 18/562). It is not known how long he lived there with his family, but Cyrus Eaton (*History of Thomaston*, I: 8) states that Hugh Munroe "early settled and lived out his days there." He gave the island his name (slightly altered), and it never thereafter had another. We know from local records that a granddaughter, Sarah Antoinette Monroe, was born on the island in 1834; her father, Captain William Monroe, is said to have been born there as well, in about 1796 (correspondence with Malcolm Jackson).

The Monroes probably quit the island in the mid-1830s. In 1835 the estate of John Gleason, to whom Hugh Munroe's unpaid mortgage had been assigned by Thorndike, Sears & Prescott, conveyed the island to another brokerage firm, Robinson, Robbins & Robbins of Thomaston (Knox Lands 34/115); in 1847 this firm sold the island to Mark L. and Joseph B. Ingraham, and this began the Ingrahams' tenure. The 1857 map of Lincoln County shows an "I. Ingraham" and an "N. Ingraham" in residence on the island.[80] In 1874 Eleanor Ingraham, who had been deeded the island by Mark L. and Joseph B. Ingraham, sold to her mother, Sarah C. Hewett, from whom it passed before the end of the century to Ellen W. Duryea (Knox 37/212, 84/49).

[80] Malcolm Jackson does not identify "N. Ingraham" but believes "I. Ingraham" was Isaac Thomas Ingraham, whose wife was Sophia Pillsbury.

Owls Head Light off Rockland, c. 1900.
(Courtesy of Maine Sea Coast Mission.)

Tillson's Wharf in Rockland, c. 1890: steam ferries PENOBSCOT *(Boston-Bangor run) and* MOUNT DESERT *(Rockland-Bar Harbor) are arriving.*

Beached finback whale in Rockland Harbor, 1938. The wharf in background belonged to the Maine Central Railway and was once used for loading coal onto the steam ferries. (Courtesy of Edward W. Coffin.)

Ellen Duryea was the owner of the island in 1910 when the United States government sought to complete its trial naval course by placing a signal on Monroe Island comparable to the one already negotiated with the owners of Sheep; Ellen Duryea demurred, and the government went to court for a condemnation order. From Ellen Duryea the island passed through her heirs to the present owner.

This recitation of title record does not help to identify the residents of Monroe Island after the Ingrahams. Cyrus Eaton, writing in the mid-1860s, describes Monroe Island as uninhabited, although maps of this era show buildings and wagon tracks on the island (e.g., Map 1863 Rockland Harbor). In an 1880 chart three buildings are shown on the west shore, whether these were settled farms or the homes of fishermen it is not easy to guess (Map 1880 CGS 4). In 1907 two structures are shown, on the south end near the western shore (Map 1907 Rockland quad). The cellar holes of these buildings are still visible, but I have discovered no record of who lived on the island after the Ingrahams—until the census of 1920, which shows an octogenarian fisherman from Nova Scotia, Joseph A. Cohoon, with his son John, forty-three, and an elderly single woman, Constantine Carter, sixty-five.

In the absence of a more substantial record of residence, it may be permissible to pass on a popular legend about Monroe Island. It is a gentle legend concerning a lady of the 1880s living on the island who, seeing an advertisement for a parlor organ, immediately wanted one—a status symbol, I assume. She ordered the organ and it was in due course delivered from Rockland, but proved too large for the humble dwelling where she lived. Undaunted, she had the rear of the cabin cut away and when the instrument was installed, covered the open area with the packing box in which the organ had arrived. She then sat down with her neighbors to admire her possession—for none of them knew how to play (Beryl Borgerson questionnaire). Not all legends are so benign. Others concern poaching, rum-running, and on occasion heavy offshore drinking bouts (see Dorothy Simpson, *Maine Islands*, 58).

Monroe Island has come into quieter days in the twentieth century. After it was cut over for pulp in the 1930s, the island became a game preserve. A conservation easement has been added to keep it "forever wild"—not in the spirit of the wayward mariners and fishermen who gave the island its hoary reputation, but of the mink, waterfowl, migratory birds, deer, and occasional moose who alone frequent Monroe Island today.

Indian

This island at the entrance to Rockport Harbor received its name, according to local historians, from the Indians who took refuge there during the French and Indian War (Robinson, *History of Camden*, 36). The island has never had another name. It was claimed by the Twenty Associates, a group of a well-to-do late-eighteenth-century landowners along this sector of the western shore, and apparently leased by them for one year in 1804 to Robert Thorndike; Thorndike refused to vacate the premises, and in 1810 the Associates instructed their agent, Joseph Pierce of Boston, to evict him and re-lease the island (Knox Lands 15/201).

The seven-acre island was sold to the United States government by Silas Piper in 1849 for a light station; the purchase price was $25, which does not suggest the island had significant value. Congress appropriated $3,500 for the construction of the original lighthouse, which began operation in 1850. In 1859 the Indian Island (sometimes called Beauchamp Point) light was discontinued on the argument it was too close to Negro Island Light off Camden. In 1875, however, it was re-established with a $9,000 appropriation. The normal repairs and improvements of the station are recorded in the National Archives (United States Lighthouse records: Indian Island file) until the light was abandoned in 1932. The island was subsequently sold by the government as a summer residence. I have the names of only three keepers during the sixty-five years the station was in operation:

Date	Name	Remarks
1882–1894	Knot C. Perry	Died in service
1894–1902	David S. Arey	Resigned
1902–1912	Edmund Coffin	

Curtis

Note: This island, with its lighthouse, is pictured in Fitz Hugh Lane's painting on the jacket of this volume.

Curtis Island was known as *Negro Island* from Revolutionary times to the 1930s, but I do not know the origin of the latter name. It was part of the land claimed by the Twenty Associates and called *Mark Island* by them. In 1806 the Associates gave the island, together with other properties in Camden, to their agent Joseph Pierce in appreciation of his services (Knox Lands 16/6). A conveyance of the island the year before from Joseph Pierce, in behalf of the Associates, to John Door was evidently canceled (Knox Lands 15/213). In 1811 Pierce sold to John Dow of Boston—quite possibly the John Door of the 1805 transaction—and Dow sold the island for $400 to the United States government for the light station in 1835 (Knox Lands 39/12). There was another claimant of Negro Island: depositions submitted in 1832 argued that Abraham Ogier, a settler on the facing shore as early as 1773, had pastured hogs and planted potatoes on the island before the Revolution, had been driven away by the British in 1779, and had repossessed it after the war; Lewis Ogier, Abraham's son, had grazed sheep there for forty years and, it was claimed, "had never been interrupted in his possession." These depositions by Lewis and a relative, Abram Ogier, were duly recorded (Knox Lands 37/485), but apparently ignored.

Negro Island Light was established in 1836 on an appropriation of $4,500. It was improved in 1856 and again in 1889 when the keeper's dwelling was replaced and a new barn and boathouse constructed. The light was automated in 1972. These were some of the keepers (from National Archive records):

Dates	Name	Remarks
1836-?	M. K. M. Bowers	First keeper
1879-1882	Fred D. Aldus	Resigned
1882-1896	Henry Wiley	Died in service
1896-1909	Howard M. Gilley	
1909-1920s	Aldiverd A. Norton	Served previously on Matinicus Rock and Two Bush Island

Negro Island, meanwhile, was renamed *Curtis Island* in 1934, after Cyrus H. K. Curtis, publisher of the *Saturday Evening Post*, a long-time summer resident and benefactor of Camden.

The Fox Islands (Vinalhaven and North Haven)

The Fox Islands are said to have been named by an English explorer, Martin Pring, who sailed into Penobscot Bay in 1603. He chose that name, according to legend, because of the large number of silver foxes he found, or saw (it is not known whether he went ashore). Mapmakers subsequently mislocated the islands—or silver foxes appeared in profusion throughout the bay—for maps as late as the 1750s give the name to nearly all islands in the mid-Penobscot Bay region, including Deer Isle (e.g., Map 1754 Johnson). The two main islands of the original group are rarely separated in early charting, nor are the outlying islands shown, until Governor Bernard of the Bay Colony ordered a plan of the bay in the 1760s: this plan, surveyed with some care, distinguishes between the Great North and Great South Fox Islands and indicates most of the surrounding ones, though without names; the mid-Penobscot Bay Eagle Island cluster still went by the name of the Fox Islands (Map 1764 Penobscot).

To judge from the erratic charting of the Fox Islands in early years, most navigators evidently bypassed the shoal waters surrounding them (especially the South Island[1]) and ignored the Thorofare. English fishermen reportedly were fishing around the islands from the early eighteenth century—there is an account of an Indian attack on a fishing vessel in the Thorofare in 1722, said to have been the cause of Governor Dummer's War (Beveridge, *North Island*, 14), but no permanent settlement on the Fox Islands is reported before the 1760s, following the French and Indian War (1755–1763). On the eve of the American Revolution approximately two dozen families had settled, two-thirds of them on the North Island (Map 1776 "Atlantic Neptune").

[1] The preference of residents of both islands (which I respect here) is that North Island and South Island be capitalized.

The Revolution led to new hardships for the settlers, especially those on the North Island who were more accessible to British war sloops and therefore subject to the quartering of troops, to the commandeering of livestock and food supplies, and, in the event of resistance, to reprisals. The settlers were also compelled to pledge allegiance to the Crown. Many left during the war, but they returned after the peace and were joined by new settlers. In June 1785 sixty-four settlers on the two islands, including certain male minors, petitioned the new Commonwealth of Massachusetts for a grant of the islands they had settled for twenty years or more. The petition was granted, subject to the usual conditions that two hundred acres be set aside for the ministry and another two hundred for the grammar school. The two main islands, together with their forty or more satellite islands, henceforth belonged to John Calderwood and his fellow petitioners.[2]

The naming of the township after John Vinall was not initially popular on the two islands. Benjamin Bevarage (normally Beverage or Beveridge), a leading citizen of the North Island, wrote some years later that the choice of the name was "not by the request of the inhabitants nor has the name ever been agreeable to them"[3]; John Vinall (normally Vinal) was merely the petitioners' agent who presented the petition to the General Court and did not live on either island. The name Vinalhaven, however, persisted—for both

[2] A photostat of this petition is in Beveridge, pp. 22–25. Not all of the sixty-four signatories could claim twenty years' residence by themselves or their forebears—as a 1786 census by Rufus Putnam makes clear (see page 473)—but the Commonwealth acknowledged title on the basis of settlement prior to January 1, 1784. Putnam's census, signed on March 18, 1786, shows seventy-four settlers, including certain male children, fifty-five of whom are signatories of the petition. The remaining nineteen were new arrivals or had not lived on the islands long enough to qualify as petitioners. Half a dozen signers are missing from the census, presumably because of death or removal in the intervening months.

[3] From a statement discussed in the next paragraph.

View of Carvers Harbor, south from Harbor Quarry Hill, early 1900s; Lane Island is in near background, across harbor; Roberts Island is left rear.
(Courtesy of Vinalhaven Historical Society.)

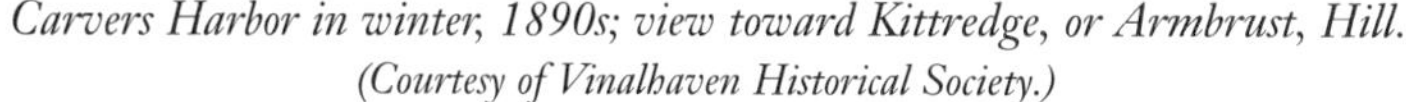

Carvers Harbor in winter, 1890s; view toward Kittredge, or Armbrust, Hill.
(Courtesy of Vinalhaven Historical Society.)

islands until 1846, then for the southern island after North Haven became a separate township.[4]

Responses by two settlers to a 1819 questionnaire by the historian William D. Williamson shed light on the profile of the township early in the nineteenth century; the responses are by Benjamin Bevarage (noted above) and Thomas Waterman, both of the North Island (copies of their replies, dated respectively in 1819 and 1821, are at the North Haven Historical Society). The township had 190 voters and 230 rateable polls. There were 300–400 pupils in eight school districts, four on each island; the town raised $400 annually for the schools. There were three stores, also three sawmills and two gristmills (most of the mills on the South Island). The Baptist Church, according to Waterman, claimed 121 members, the Methodist eighty, and the Congregationalist five (Bevarage's figures here are 125 Baptists, thirty Methodists, and no Congregationalists). There was no regular preacher on either island in 1819.

As for the productivity of the township, improved land was said to be 2,860 acres, unimproved 13,667. Land was held by grant from the General Court of the Commonwealth of Massachusetts at an initial price of one to twenty dollars an acre. The North Island was predominantly agricultural. "No part of the state," Bevarage wrote, "produces better beef, pork, mutton, butter, and cheese." North Island farmers also grew wheat, corn, barley, oats, and vegetables in abundance. The South Island, though "mountainous and barren," was rewarded in its fine harbors. This was above all a fishing island, with ten vessels over fifty tons and many over five; total tonnage in the fisheries was about seven hundred. Spruce on the South Island, meanwhile, was made into spars to ship to the Southern states. The town in 1819 supported twenty-five paupers, but only sixteen in 1820. "The inhabitants of this town," Waterman concluded, "are noted for their humanity and benevolence, particularly to strangers."

An appropriate way to see how the township behaved and reacted to different crises is to excerpt segments from the town records (which are preserved in full in the Vinalhaven Town Office and summarized conveniently in "Brief Historical Sketch of the Town of Vinalhaven"—see Bibliography). Town meetings were held alternately on the North and South islands until 1846.

1790 School teachers were to be hired for both islands; Michael Bowen was teacher on the North Island at £4 18s (the next year his salary was raised to £16—that is, for a term).

1792 A minister (denomination unspecified) was hired for four months at £16; meetings were to be held in parishioners' homes on both islands.

1793 *Voted:* £36 for John Vinal's "past services" as agent.

1794 *Voted:* To hire Michael Bowen as schoolmaster for twelve months on the North Island at £46 10s. An article for hiring a minister was passed over.

1795 *Voted:* £6 for a transcription of Rufus Putnam's plan of the islands (see footnote xxx, above).

1796 *Voted:* To hire a minister at £40.
Note: Thomas Waterman reported in 1821 that the town still made no provision for a settled minister, but the practice of hiring term preachers was apparently in place by 1800.

1799 *Voted:* Not to raise money for preaching.
Note: This was the first year accounting shifted from the pound to the dollar; the two denominations appear to have been at parity.

1800 The town was divided into eight districts, four on each island. Each island was to draw its own share of money from the town treasury and maintain its own roads.
Note: This early move toward "devolution" did not endure.

1801 *Voted:* Not to allow Matinicus Isle to pay taxes to the township.
Note: This was because Vinalhaven did not wish to provide services to Matinicus—which was never formally part of the township.

1805 *Voted:* Not to have any school on the North Island...$230 voted for support of schools on the South Island.
Note: On the face of it there would appear to be a stand-off between the residents of the two islands on the school issue, but I believe there was no crisis: the

[4] If John Vinall's role in the founding of the new township was incidental, that of his son William, who served as the township's first representative at the General Court and for many years was counted as a town father, perhaps vindicated the use of the surname.

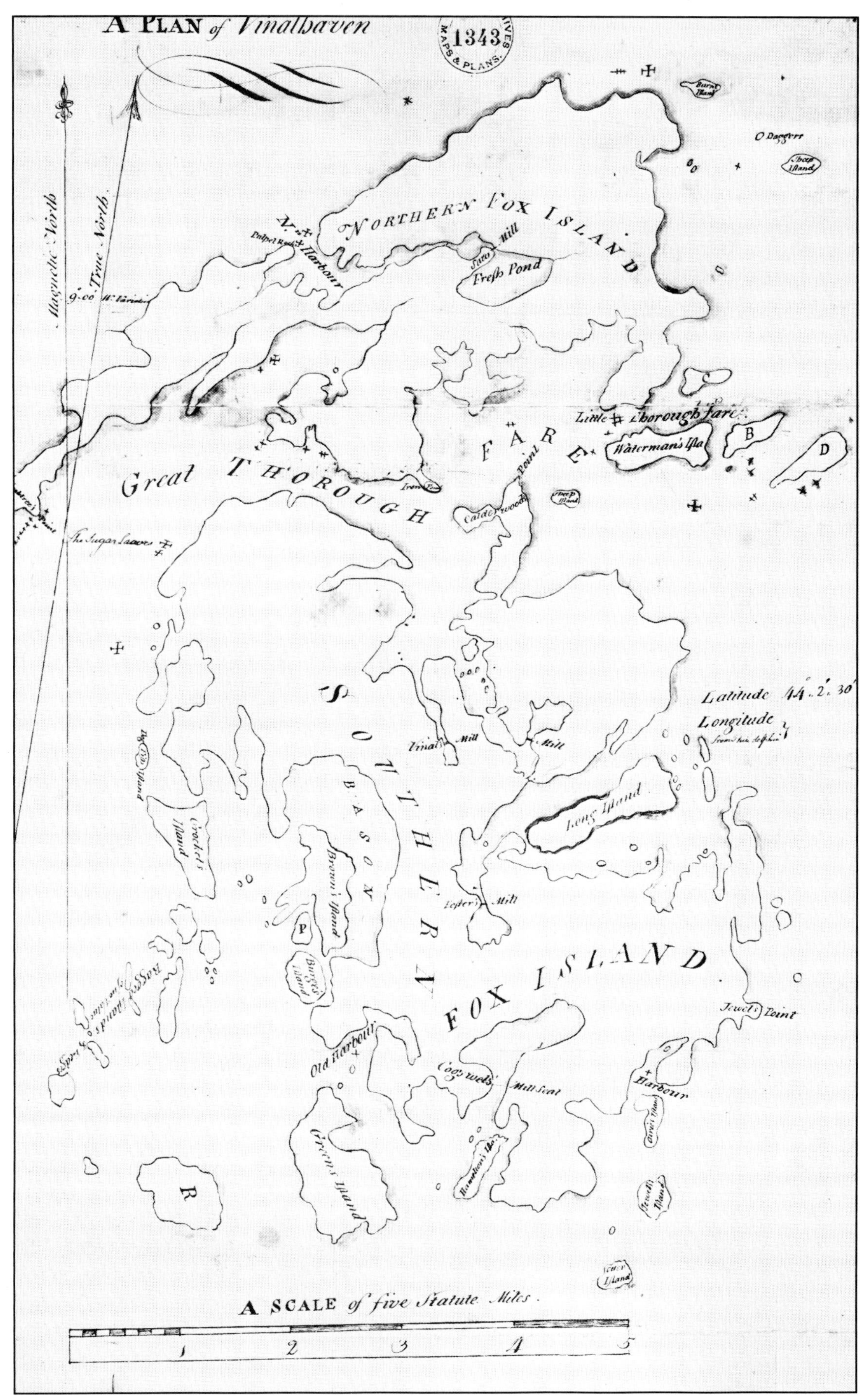
A PLAN of Vinalhaven
1343
MAPS & PLANS
Magnetic North
True North
NORTHERN FOX ISLAND
Fresh Pond
Harbour
Little Thorough fare
Waterman's Isla
B
D
Great THOROUGH FARE
The Sugar Loaves
Calderwoods Point
Latitude 44. 2. 30
Longitude
Long Island
SOUTHERN FOX ISLAND
BASON
Brown's Island
Crockets Island
P
Burgess Island
Vinal Mill
Mill
Foster's Mill
Jewels Point
Old Harbour
Cogswels' Mill Seat
Harbour
Greens Island
R
A SCALE of five Statute Miles
1
2
3
4
5

North Island simply had a balance from the previous year and so needed no funds. The town clerk's phrasing of the minutes was obscure.

1806 *Voted:* To pay a bounty of 10 cents on crows and blue jays and 20 cents a head on eagles.
Note: A black day for conservationsists.

1807 On the question of Maine's separation from Massachusetts, voters against were 84; none were for separation.

1811 For labor on town roads, the rates were: 12 cents per hour for men; 12 cents for a yoke of oxen; 12 cents each for a plough; 6 cents for a cart

1813 Voted: To form a militia to protect the township from British attacks, which escalated as the war with England (War of 1812) went into its second year.
Note: The episode of the schooner FLY, noted in the town records, is discussed under the White Islands, pages 153–54

1815 The new pay schedule for labor on town roads was: 25 cents an hour for men; 25 cents for a plough; 121/2 cents for oxen.

1818 Road work was paid as follows this year: 4 cents an hour for men; 4 cents for oxen and for ploughs; 2 cents for a cart.
Note: There is no explanation for these see-saw reimbursements for road work—unless it was Whigs and Tories in City Hall.

1819 *Voted:* To assess a tax on Matinicus, John Green to be collector.
Note: It was evidently decided elsewhere that Vinalhaven must accept Matinicus for the time being; John Green was presumably chosen collector because he had many relatives on Matinicus.

Benjamin Bevarage represented the township at a convention in Portland to draft a state constitution, which was adopted by Vinalhaven: 32 to 2.
Note: Opposition to statehood for Maine had come principally from maritime interests troubled by the federal "Coasting Law" of 1789: coastal vessels from one state were obliged to stop in the first noncontiguous state—which meant that vessels from Maine, if independent, could skip New Hampshire but must stop in Massachusetts before proceeding to their principal destinations further south. In 1819 the law was repealed, removing a chief obstacle to statehood.

1822 A committee was chosen to consider the feasibility of an alewife fishery on the North Island, to be run for the benefit of the township.

1825 A reward of $20 was offered for the apprehension of the persons who destroyed the dam at the outlet of the freshwater pond (on the North Island).

1829 The town voted to grant licenses to sell spirituous liquors.
Benjamin Crabtree (North Island) was elected representative to the state legislature by two votes; the election was protested, but the protest was defeated, 89 to 21.

1830 *Voted:* To allow tax collectors two percent of what they collected, *if* they collected within one year all taxes assigned them—otherwise, no reimbursement.
Note: The normal procedure—before and after this vote—was to allow tax collectors a fixed amount (usually $20–$40) whether they collected all taxes due or not.

1831 After many years of fluctuation, budget allotments leveled off in this era as follows:
Roads and bridges, $600 (in 1790s, averaged $500)
Schools, $625 (in 1790s, averaged $400)
Support of indigents, $650 (in 1790s, averaged $250)

1836 The vote for shire town—that is, of Hancock County—was as follows: Castine, 153; Ellsworth, 1.
Note: The Vinalhaven inhabitants lost, of course, but did not remain long in Hancock County: both islands were included in Knox County at its incorporation in 1860. The year 1836 was the year of the ROYAL TAR episode, described in the town records—and reviewed under Bluff Head Island, pages 164–65.

1841 A number of voters on the South Island having petitioned the state legislature for a town way over the tidewaters of "Carver's mill stream," a special meeting was called by other voters to protest the petition and to instruct the town's representative to the legislature (William Thomas) to "remonstrate" against the petition.

Opposite page: *Earliest map of the Fox Islands, by John Vinal, 1786. (See Bibliography for listing.)*

Fish-drying flakes at Carvers Harbor, 1890s; the photo is a reminder that fishing continued to be a major business in Vinalhaven in the midst of the quarrying boom. (Courtesy of Maine Historic Preservation Commision.)

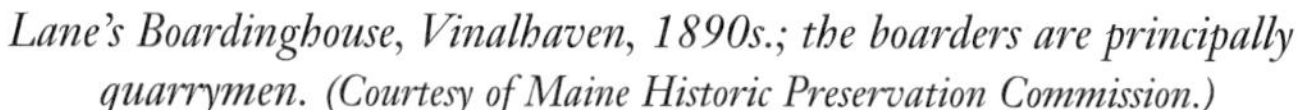

Lane's Boardinghouse, Vinalhaven, 1890s.; the boarders are principally quarrymen. (Courtesy of Maine Historic Preservation Commission.)

Downtown Vinalhaven, c.1890.
(Courtesy of Maine Historic Preservation Commission.)

Cutting shed at Vinalhaven quarries, 1890s.
(Courtesy of Maine Historic Preservation Commission.)

1842 An article relative to the licensing of retail dealers of spirituous liquors was postponed "indefinitely."
Note: The licensing issue, while a major political topic in Augusta, appears not to have galvanized residents of either island; the ultimate vote in Vinalhaven in 1858—both communities voted "dry"—attracted only thirty voters, no more than ten percent of the number eligible.

1843 On the first vote for separation of the North Island from Vinalhaven, the vote was 62 in favor, 83 opposed.

1846 A second article on separation of the North Island, in response to a petition by 179 residents, was passed over at the town meeting but passed by the legislature; the town of Fox Isle (the name lasted a year) was incorporated in June.

Town records do not reveal the reasons for separation, but they are obvious enough and extend beyond mere geography: the inconvenience to settlers on both islands of crossing the Thorofare for frequent meetings or to transact business. The divergent occupations on the two islands increasingly drove the communities apart. By mid-century a hundred vessels were owned by Vinalhaven fishermen, more than three times as many as were owned on North Haven (Goode, "Fishery Industries of the United States," 51). Farming on North Haven, meanwhile, bred settlers with a different outlook.

If such differences were already evident at the time of separation, lifestyles and patterns diverged even further in the last half of the century as the great quarries were opened on Vinalhaven and rusticators arrived on North Haven. Let us consider, then, quarrying and rusticators, for the evolution of the two islands in the later decades of the nineteenth century owes more to these two forces than to any others.

Quarrying began on the South Island as early as the 1820s, but erratically—in Areys Cove on the eastern shore and on Leadbetter and Dyer islands on the western. There were motions again on Leadbetter in the 1840s, but it was not until after mid-century that the large granite companies were organized. Moses Webster came to Vinalhaven from New Hampshire in 1851 and soon joined Joseph R. Bodwell (a future Maine governor) in a firm named Bodwell and Webster

Children's party at Carvers Harbor, c. 1900; children are at Dodge Point, near present ferry landing, Vinalhaven village in background.
(Courtesy of Vinalhaven Historical Society.)

Village at Pulpit Harbor on North Haven, looking southwest across Flye Point; there were as many dwellings behind the photographer as shown here. Before 1900 the homesteads belonged to Witherspoons (Edward, James C., John, and Sands), Thurstons (David and James), Isaac Leadbetter, and Elisha Calderwood;three of the buildings in the village are still standing. The Pulpit Harbor schoolhouse is nearest the camera.
(From Sands Witherspoon glass slides at North Haven Historical Society, courtesy of Samuel H. Beverage.)

Road machine and villagers at Pulpit Harbor on North Haven, c. 1900; a new road is under construction to bypass the earlier one running in front of the dwellings; the closest belonged to Xenophon and Rebecca Leadbetter; the barn and homestead behind it were David Tolman's; the barn high on the hill to the right was Captain Thomas Beverage's. Most of the villagers have been identified: e.g., Horace Leadbetter in foreground with bicycle; the two boys holding the horses, left and right, Walter Parsons and Grover Babbidge; in the front row, Elsie Beverage, Mildred Cooper, and Katherine Parsons...and so forth.
(From Sands Witherspoon glass slides at North Haven Historical Society, courtesy of Samuel H. Beverage, who made the identifications.)

to work the East Boston quarry and later the Harbour Quarry. These were working owner-managers in those early years: Webster worked in the quarries proper, Bodwell drove oxen. S. G. Webster and Joseph Kittredge opened the Diamond Rock quarry in 1853. S. G. Webster and William B. Kittredge operated in partnership for a dozen years on Kittredge (later Armbrust) Hill. In 1863 Garrett Coughlin and others worked a quarry on Dyer Island. And so forth.[5]

The Bodwell Granite Company was organized in 1871 and for more than forty years played the dominant role in Vinalhaven quarries. It absorbed most of the quarries of the earlier firms. At times the company employed more than fifteen hundred quarrymen, inevitably taking many from the fisheries. For many years Bodwell Granite handled lucrative government and private contracts across the nation. One of the earliest was stone for the Brooklyn Bridge. Another, in 1879, was a monument to be erected in Troy, New York (to General John E. Wool), that weighed 650 tons and is believed to have been the largest shaft quarried in the United States up to that date. Oxen provided the principal power; a hundred yoke were used at one time. The most famous contraption used by the Bodwell company was the *gallamander*, a derrick on wheels that raised huge pieces of stone from the ground and underslung them between the two hind wheels, as teams of oxen (later horses) pulled the contraption from quarry to cutting shed, then to the granite schooners.

But all was not prosperity and happiness during the Bodwell years. In the early 1890s, during a period of deep economic depression throughout the country, a lockout by the company to break the growing power of the Granite Cutters' International Association (a branch was organized on Vinalhaven in 1877) brought in outside strike breakers and elevated tensions in town to a dangerous level. Although the stoppage lasted only three weeks, it did effectively curb the power

[5] A fuller story of the Vinalhaven quarries is told by Sidney L. Winslow in *Fish Scales and Stone Chips* (see Bibliography for full listing).

Ferry linking North and South Islands across Fox Island Thorofare, early 1900s; view is southeast from North Haven.
(Courtesy of Vinalhaven Historical Society.)

Carvers Harbor from the 1859 map of Waldo County, showing roads and residents around harbor and on Lane Island. Two quarries have been opened—J. Carver's, north of the harbor, and another east of Indian Creek; this was before the peak of the quarrying era.

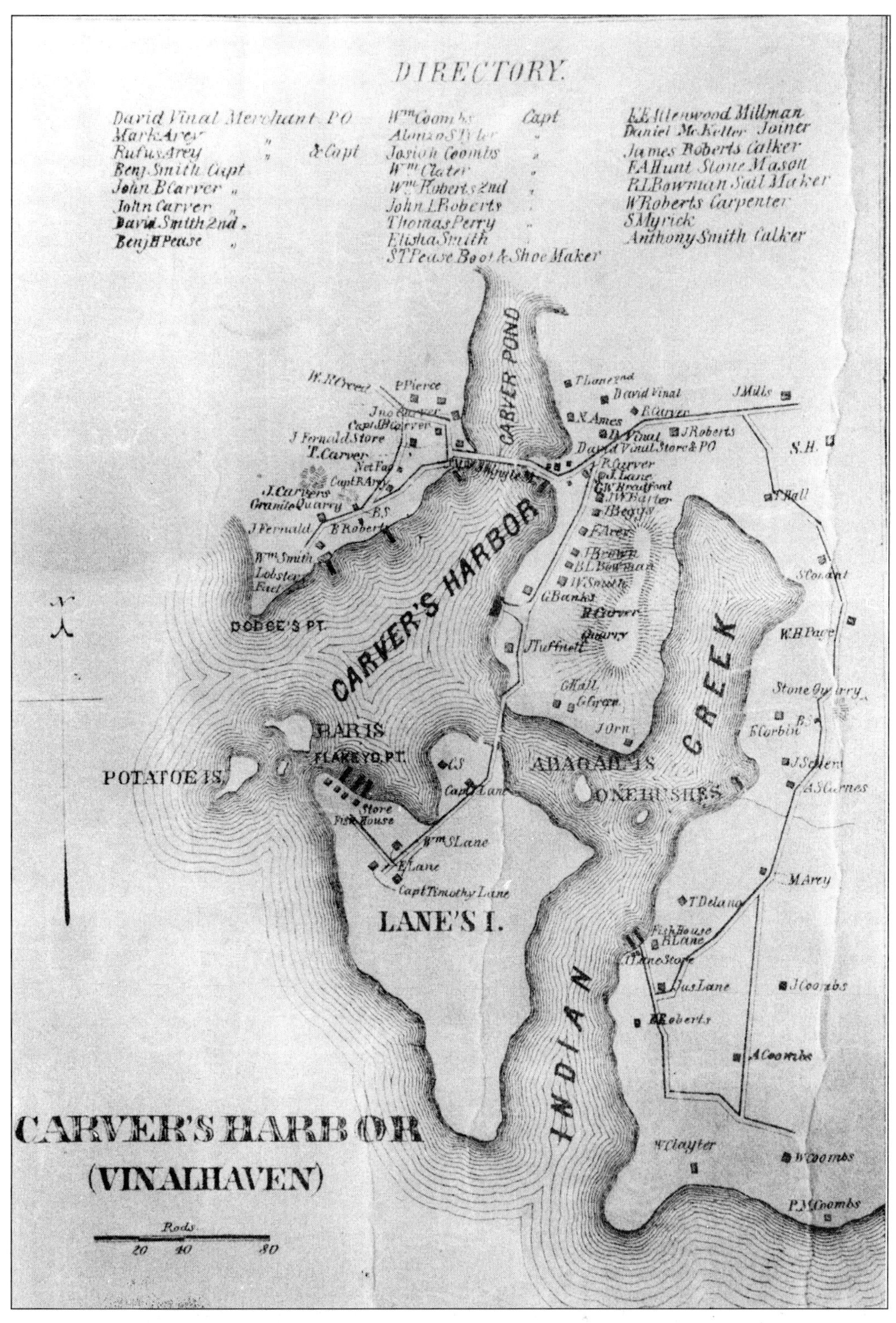

of the unions, and worker-employer relations thereafter remained cool. Vinalhaven continued to be a company town, with its store for groceries, dry goods, and indeed all life's essentials such as coal, wood, and hay; payment, of course, came out of the quarrymen's wages. The granite industry gradually slowed as cement replaced stone. The Bodwell Company itself closed after World War I. Smaller firms continued to cut paving stone into the 1930s when the last hammers on the island were silenced.

The fisheries appeared to lose ground to quarrying in the last decades of the nineteenth century, but it was more appearance than reality. True, an estimated ninety percent of the labor force on Vinalhaven was in the granite industry according to a Congressional report in 1880 (Goode, 51), but many of the quarrymen were transients—from the British Isles and Scandinavia; they moved on when work grew scarce. The indigenous population on the South Island remained primarily in the fisheries. By the late 1870s fish processing had become a major industry on Vinalhaven. The Vinalhaven Fish Company early in the 1900s was said to be the largest fish curing plant in Maine, a formidable rival locally to the Bodwell Granite Company (Winslow, 680).

On North Haven, meanwhile, the earliest rusticators arrived within two decades of the Civil War. Some had perhaps seen the Fox Islands for the first time passing through the Thorofare on their way from Rockland to Bar Harbor on the early steam ferry MOUNT DESERT.[6] By the 1880s Bostonians such as William and Charles Weld and J. Murray Howe had arrived and built their many-tiered cottages on the shore of the island. The early vacationers (male only) gathered periodically at a small bungalow on the Thorofare which they nicknamed "Paralyzo"—because, said one matron, that was the condition of the men on their evenings out; the men countered that they were "paralyzed" only by good food, delicate wines, and stimulating conversation.[7]

The town's tax records show how much the North Island was taken over by the summer vacationers: in 1890 the ratio of non-resident real estate valuations to resident was about one to four;

[6] President Grant had visited North Haven even earlier, in 1873; but this was in the way of an emergency stop-over when the captain of his yacht felt it prudent to avoid a northeast storm, given the quality of his passengers: in addition to the president, Hannibal Hamlin (Lincoln's first vice-president), James G. Blaine of Augusta, and others. The president stayed at the Mullins Inn, already a hostelry for occasional visitors.

[7] A small volume published in 1992 describes the evolution of the summer community on North Haven: Eleanor Motley Richardson, *North Haven Summer* (see Bibliography for full listing).

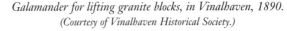

Galamander for lifting granite blocks, in Vinalhaven, 1890.
(Courtesy of Vinalhaven Historical Society.)

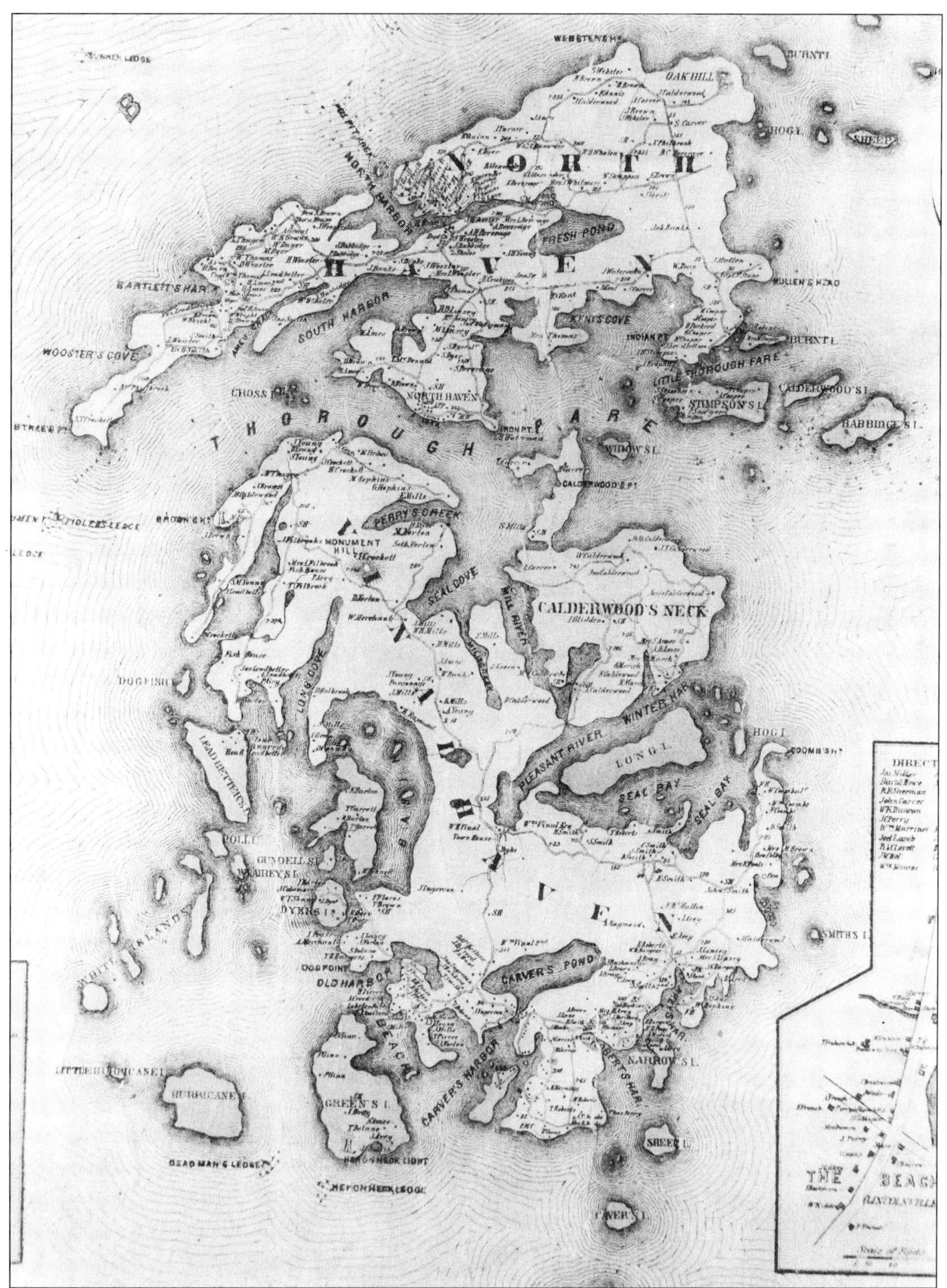

Vinalhaven and North Haven: segment of the 1859 map of Waldo County. (Both islands became part of Knox County when it was created in 1860, but at this date were surveyed in Waldo County.) Householders are named on both islands, but their names can be deciphered only with a magnifying glass. Residents shown on the smaller islands (e.g., Leadbetter, Greens, Stimpson) are discussed in my comments on those islands.

in 1900 it was one to two; and in 1916 it was one-and-a-half to one ($241,765 to $159,115). The land, in short, was being gradually taken over by outsiders and this process continued as the great estates of Cabots, Lamonts, and Gastons were shaped. Did the influx affect the lives of indigenous residents? Inevitably it did—how could it be otherwise? North Islanders became boatmen, builders, groundsmen, and caretakers. The number of farms declined; fishermen became an endangered species. Meanwhile, the differences between North and South Islanders, already more defined because of quarrying on Vinalhaven, became even more so because of gentrification on North Haven. It was a difference based on changing values and occupations—a difference discernible in many neighboring island communities: on Deer Isle in the nineteenth century, for instance, between the prosperous farmlands of the village of Deer Isle proper and the scarred face of the quarrymen's Stonington. It is a difference that waxes and wanes over time. Even before quarrying ended on Vinalhaven, summer colonies had begun to spread to the island. If Vinalhaven and North Haven went through some decades of intolerance toward each other, it is doubtful whether such sentiments are relevant today.

The islands dealt with in this division are in two groups. The first includes those around Vinalhaven, proceeding clockwise, as nearly as possible, from Greens Island on the southwest corner to Lane Island off Carvers Harbor. The second group includes the islands adjacent to North Haven, from Oak on the northeast tip clockwise to Widow Island in the Thorofare.

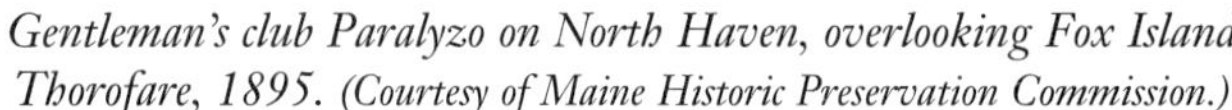

Gentleman's club Paralyzo on North Haven, overlooking Fox Island Thorofare, 1895. (Courtesy of Maine Historic Preservation Commission.)

Group I: Islands Around Vinalhaven

Greens

Greens, not *Green*, is the name of this island, and it was a near thing that it stayed this way: only the boldness of a fourteen-year-old girl, daughter of a recent owner, who wrote the Coast and Geodetic Survey in 1970 that its charts were persistently in error in rendering the island as "Green," restored the original spelling—after the man, that is, not the color. The man was Joseph Green, a stepson of Ebenezer Hall of Matinicus who was massacred by Indians in 1757 (see page 9); Joseph, then fourteen, after surviving some days alone on Matinicus, was taken off by a passing schooner.[8] Green eventually returned to Matinicus but re-moved soon thereafter to the island off the southwest corner of the southern Fox Island that bears his name. Several editions of British Admiralty charts surveyed on the eve of the American Revolution show his homestead on the southeast peninsula of the island (e.g., the 1776 "Atlantic Neptune"). Rufus Putnam, in his 1785 census of the islands (page 473), noted that Joseph Green had lived on Greens Island since 1769. His wife was Dorcas Young of Old York, sister of Susannah who married his surviving stepbrother, Ebenezer Hall, Jr. of Matinicus; Joseph and Dorcas raised fourteen children on the island and are buried there in a small family plot not far from their homestead (see sketch by Joseph Morton).

According to O. P. Lyons, historian of Vinalhaven, Joseph Green invited Eben Pierce to join him on Greens Island as a neighbor and gave or sold him the northern third of the island. It is not known where Pierce came from, but the surname was a familiar one in the St. George and Muscle Ridge area on the western shore, and it is possible he was one of this family. He did not remain long on Greens Island, for by 1785 he had sold his interest to Thomas Ginn and the latter was already settled there; the 1785 census noted above shows Thomas Ginn resident in 1781. Ginn, O. P. Lyons tells us (page 2), was born in Liverpool in 1762 and came to Vinalhaven in the 1780s as a mariner; he sailed a coaster between the Fox Islands and Boston. In 1785 he married Sarah Young of Old York—a sister of Dorcas Young Green, I assume—and the same year built a frame house on Greens Island north of what was later called Delano Cove. The building was still standing early in the twentieth century.

Conveyances during the first half of the nineteenth century are predominantly within the Green and Ginn families and do not indicate the names of additional settlers. Daniel Green, whom I take to be a son of Joseph, figures in deeds early in the century involving the Greens' two-thirds of the island (Knox Lands 1/224 and 1/288). In 1817 Joseph offered part of his holdings to another son, John, on condition the latter provide for his parents in their old age (Knox Lands 1/421 and 1/562). Whether John undertook the responsibility is unclear, for the parcel in question, which appears to have been in the middle of the island, passed to Jesse Calderwood about this time and was deeded by the latter or his heirs to Phineas Ginn in 1854 (Knox Lands 52/398). Greens continued to deed parcels of land on the island after mid-century, but they were then shown as living in Camden: e.g., Freeman and John Green, Jr. to the United States government in 1853—Heron Point Neck, for the light station (Knox Lands 51/4); and the same two Greens to Hannah Bray in 1860—a lot at the south end (Knox Lands 2/319). No Greens are shown as residents on the island in the Waldo County map of 1859. Nor do I find a Green household in census schedules after 1840 (see residence table).

The Ginns were more tenacious. In fact, a deed in 1850 conveying a lot north of Quantity Cove on the west shore, from Phineas Ginn to Isaiah Bray, notes the island as *Ginn Island*—though this was not a name that remained in

[8] Some accounts refer to Ebenezer Hall's stepson as "Daniel" or "David," but according to Charles A. E. Long (*Matinicus Isle*, 20) his name was Joseph.

general use (Knox Lands 74/31). The 1859 county map noted above places three Ginn Families on the island: J. Ginn in Thomas Ginn's original homestead; P. Ginn on the western shore near Quantity Cove; and another P. Ginn at the head of Delano Cove. Other settlers shown on this map are as follows: Nathaniel Ames and Joseph Arey near the southeast tip (Boiler Point on Joseph Morton's sketch); T. Delano westerly of these two on the peninsula; J. (Isaiah?) Bray at the head of Deep Cove; and J. Smith at Heron Neck Light.

There is no census, of course, for Greens Island itself, but I identify as best as I am able in the accompanying table the households resident on the island from 1790 to 1880. The peak years of year-round habitation were in the mid-nineteenth century, but the quarrying boom of the 1880s and 1890s brought nearly as many temporary residents onto the island.

Farming and fishing were the principal occupations of the islanders during the greater part of the nineteenth century. Farming was carried out mostly on the southeast peninsula, where ancient stone walls marking off the fields and meadowlands are still visible in the new spruce forests. It can be taken for granted that the island was cut over several times during the last century, as all islands in the area were. The large number of coves around the island facilitated both the loading of its produce on coastal schooners and the launching of small boats for the fisheries. The short row into Carvers Harbor simplified the island's social and commercial life—so that Greens Island, while enjoying its own distinctive character, was very much a part of the Vinalhaven community.

In the 1880s new enterprises were launched on Greens Island. A whale oil industry was opened in 1885 by General Davis Tillson and his son-in-law William S. White of Hurricane Island (Winslow, *Fish Scales and Stone Chips*, 72). The tryhouse and reservoir were located on the western shore in Sand Cove. The whales were brought in at high tide; an iron ring still visible in a ledge was used for hauling the mammals onto shore.

Opposite page: *Sketch of Greens Island as it was in about 1910; drawn for the first edition of this volume by Lucille Burgess, as dictated by her father, the late Joseph Morton, who was brought up on the island.*

Schooner YANKEE GIRL *bringing Greens Island schoolhouse to Vinalhaven after it was closed, 1916; the building is still in use.*
(Courtesy of Vinalhaven Historical Society.)

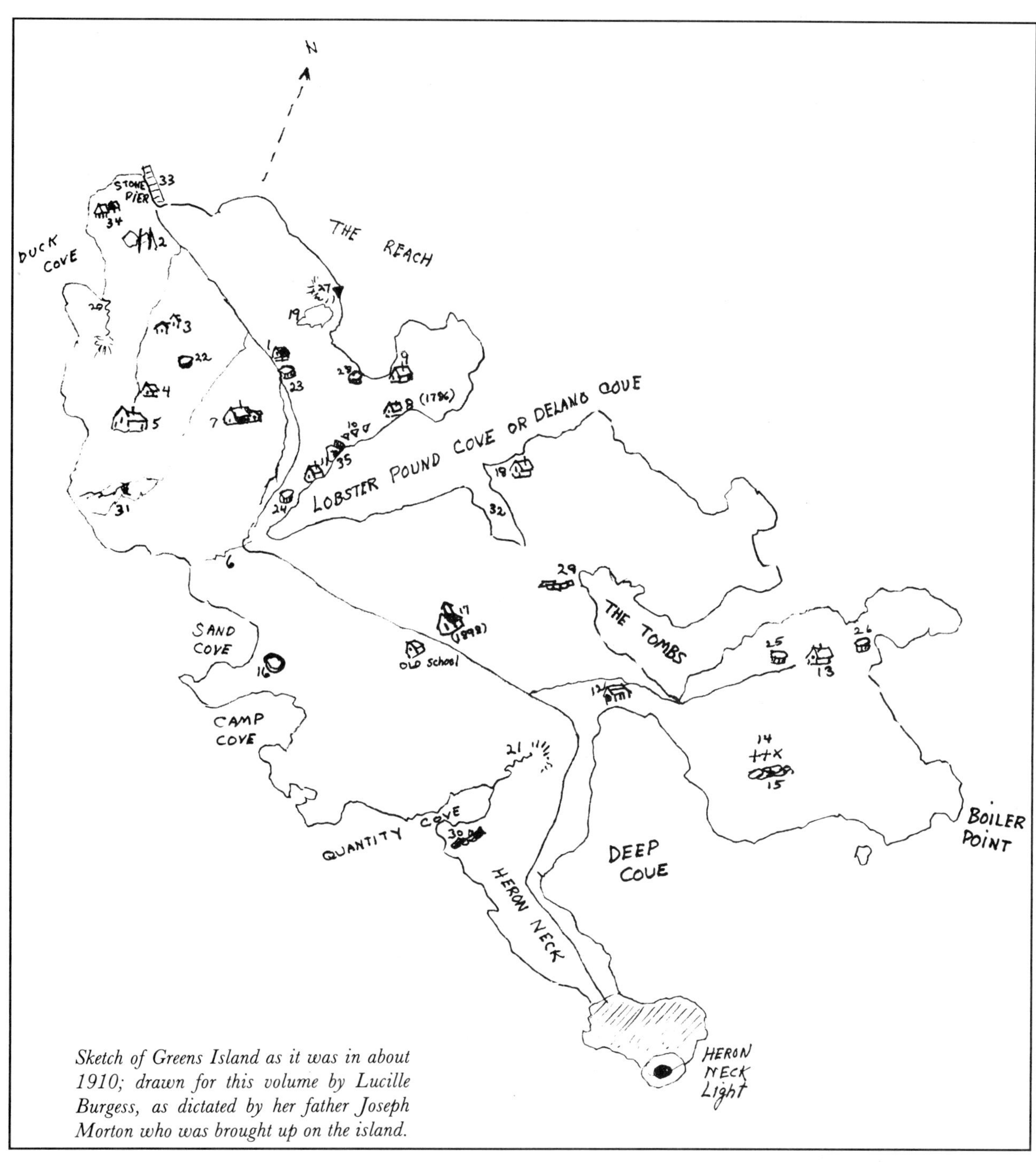

Sketch of Greens Island as it was in about 1910; drawn for this volume by Lucille Burgess, as dictated by her father Joseph Morton who was brought up on the island.

1 Morton House
2 Quarry
3 Big and Little barns
4 Store
5 Boardinghouse
6 Path to back shore
7 Dance Hall
8 Ginn House–1786
9 Yellow barn house
10 Three small houses
11 Delano house
12 Old house ruins
13 Farmhouse
14 Cemetery (Greens)
15 Stone wall
16 Reservoir, for whale tryworks
17 Schoolhouse–built 1898
18 "Bray" house
19 Pond
20 Brook
21 Brook
22 Well
23 Well
24 Well
25 Well
26 Well
27 Indian shell heap
28 Well
29 Cellar
30 Old cellar
31 Flat quarry
32 Dan Green Cove
33 Stone pier (wharf)
34 Blacksmith shops
35 Big boulders

This business continued for several years.[9] Then at the end of the 1880s, the granite boom, which had enveloped the entire Penobscot Bay region, led to the opening of a quarry at the north end of Greens Island. In 1895 forty or fifty quarrymen were employed at this site (Rockland *Courier-Journal*, January 29, 1895). The quarry provided some of the granite for the Mount Holyoke dam in Massachusetts and the Rockland breakwater, but the greater part of the stone was paving block. There were no cutting and polishing sheds. By the standards of stonecutting on Hurricane Island and at Vinalhaven, the quarries on Greens were crude and small, but they quickened the pace of life. Joseph Morton's representation of Greens Island in the early 1900s shows many new buildings, including a company store, a boardinghouse, a blacksmith's shop, and even a dance hall. He estimates that about fifty persons were living on the island, exclusive of the quarrymen who commuted daily from Vinalhaven. Twelve to fifteen pupils were in the new school built in 1897. (In due course this building was removed to Vinalhaven and served for many years as a fish house.) There was never regular ferry service to Greens Island, according to Joseph Morton, but the GOVERNOR BODWELL stopped irregularly to drop off supplies at the granite pier serving the quarries on the northern tip of the island.

The decline of quarrying after 1900 precipitated the evacuation of Greens Island. With the departure of the quarrymen, the store could not continue: the Mortons, who managed the store, left in 1906. The school was closed in 1907. The last "native" family to quit the island, according to Joseph Morton, were the Brays—in about 1910. Bradford Bray, an energetic farmer-fisherman who kept sheep on half a dozen islands in Hurricane Sound, was the dominant personality on Greens Island during the last decades of the community there. The abandoned buildings, as happened on most islands like Greens, were vandalized and quickly fell into disrepair; none of them stood by the 1990s. The road that once extended from Boiler Point to the northern tip of the island can hardly be found today.

Greens was, of course, not wholly deserted. Fishermen continued to summer there and a few even spent the winter; a birth in the Rogers family—the first birth on the island in forty years—was recorded in 1938 (*Vinalhaven Neighbor*, February 2). Meanwhile, many residents of Vinalhaven came regularly to Greens Island for clamming, berrying, picnicking, and other recreation in season. There were weirs around the island, and purse-seining in many of its coves persisted. In 1948 a pulping operation in the interior brought out a crew of lumbermen for some months. Sheep were pastured on Greens into the 1950s, many of them running wild. The most significant commercial enterprise in the twentieth century has been the lobster pound at Delano Cove, now called Lobster Pound Cove; this facility was originally constructed by the Rackliff and Witham Lobster Company of Rockland (out of a load of lumber dumped from a vessel grounded on the Triangles off Metinic Island, acording to a Rockland lobsterman, Woodbury Snow). Later the pound was acquired by the Bickford Company.

There were still occasional year-round residents on Greens Island in the last decades of the twentieth century. This is not the place to explore in any depth their activities, but a few may be noted here. The lobster pound, for instance, normally had attendants throughout the year. The son and family of an owner in the 1970s spent several winters on the island; their horse, Osiris, grazed on Boiler Point, a landmark to mariners. Descendants of early residents (e.g., Brays) maintained cottages on the island for seasonal use. And there were of necessity the keepers of Heron Neck Light before it was automated in 1982.

[9] The try works attracted much interest in Vinalhaven and prompted many expeditions to Greens Island by the curious, as an article in the May 8, 1885 issue of the *VinalhavenWind* explained. One 67-foot finback, brought in from Monhegan, was said to have yielded 1,200 gallons of oil. The whale blubber was placed over fire in the inner of two concentric kettles, bolted together at the lip but leaving an inch and a quarter air-space between to keep the blubber from being damaged; oil was siphoned from the inner kettle. (The article is reproduced in part in Winslow, 73, and in Richardson, *Hurricane Island*, 36).

Heron Neck Light

The lighthouse dates from 1854, when it was built on an appropriation of $5,000, according to records in the National Archives. The station underwent the usual trials and tribulations of similar facilities along the coast—perhaps even more than its allotment. It was acknowledged in an 1890 report that five deaths had occurred in the keeper's dwelling because, it was alleged, of insufficient mortar used in the original construction: the premises were "leaky and unhealthy… unsuitable for occupancy." A benevolent Lighthouse Service agreed to correct the problem by constructing a new building with more mortar.

I do not have a list of all keepers, but here are a few:

Name	Dates of Service	Remarks
James Smith	1850s–1870	See residence table, 1860
John Green	1870–1883	Died in service[10]
Mrs. Sara J. Green	1883	Acting keeper, one month
Nathaniel Hartwell	1883–1890	
Edward K. Tapley	1890–1900	Transferred to Blue Hill Bay light
Levi L. Farnham	1900–1911	Transferred from Blue Hill Bay
Joseph A. Farnham	1911	Acting keeper, three months
Fred M. Robbins	1911–1930	
Andrew Bennett	1930–c. 1950[11]	

[10] John and Sara Green appear in the 1860 census, in the household of Joseph Arey (see table), but do not appear in 1870 and 1880 schedules; however, they were clearly in residence, according to National Archives records.

[11] Robbins is the last keeper listed in the National Archives file I consulted; Andrew Bennett's service is verified by his son Clarence (a resident of Vinalhaven).

Heron Neck Light on Greens Island, early 1900s; Hurricane Island in background. Note keeper's wife on porch in white dress.
(Courtesy of Vinalhaven Historical Society.)

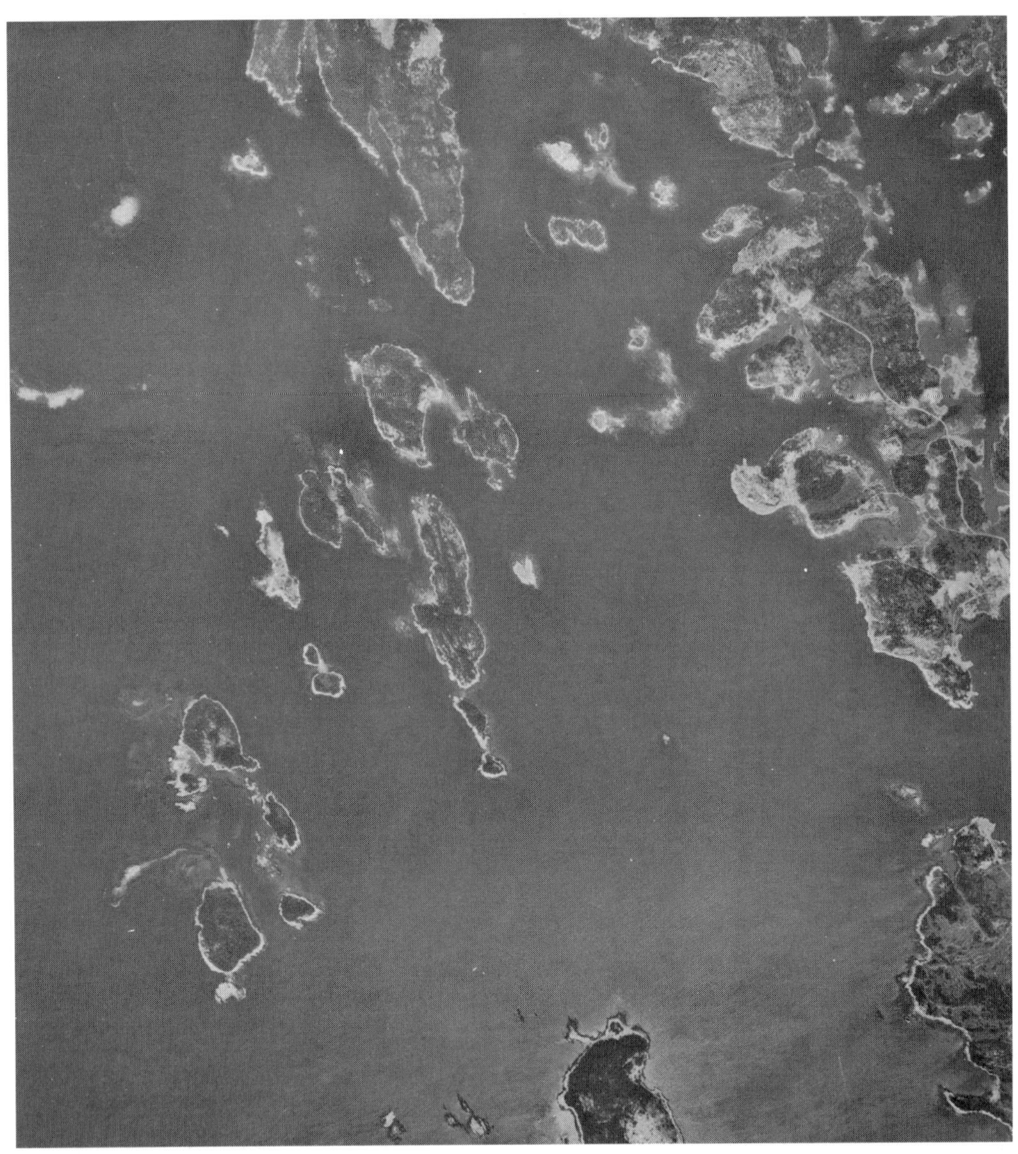

Aerial view of Hurricane Sound west of Vinalhaven, 1955. Leadbetter Island is top center, Greens is lower right, White Islands lower left; the road at right winds from the village of Vinalhaven (off photo) to Granite or Barton Island, west of the Basin. (United States Air Force photo.)

Residents of Greens Island, 1790–1880

Note: The householders listed below, taken from Vinalhaven census schedules, are believed to have resided on Greens Island between 1790 and 1880. Age, if shown, is at first appearance. Spouses, if known, are in parentheses. Householders are fishermen unless otherwise indicated: e.g., Fa, farmer. Dollar amounts after some householders represent the highest combined real estate/personal valuation between 1850 and 1880, as estimated by the census-taker. Males are to left of slash, females to right, in decennial columns.

Householder	**1790**	**1800**	**1810**	**1820**	**1830**	**1840**	**1850**	**1860**	**1870**	**1880**
Green, Joseph, -45	6/5	8/4	3/4	1/1						
Ginn, Thomas, -45	2/3	4/4	5/4	2/2						
Green, Daniel, Fa, -45			1/2	1/2	1/1	3/2				
Delano, Stephen, -45			4/2	5/1						
Green, John, -45, Fa				3/2	8/7	6/8				
Ginn, Sally, 45+				2/4	2/3	1/1				
Ginn, James, 30s (Lucy), sailor $1,500					3/5	-	5/3			
Ginn, Thomas II, 30s					4/6					
Delano, Theophilus, 27 (Patience) $1,100						2/0	3/1	3/2	3/2	2/2
Ginn, Joseph, 41 (Rachel/Deborah), Fa $800						1/4	2/3	1/1		
Delano, Joseph, 49 (Hannah), Fa $1,500							2/3			
Brown, Samuel, 39 (Polly)							5/3			
Ginn, Margaret, 49							0/1			
Bray, Isaiah, 34 (Hannah) $1,400							1/5	2/5	3/3	2/3
Ginn, Jonathan, 26 (Eliza)							3/1			
Ames, Nathaniel, 41 (Charity) $1,000							4/3			
Ginn, Phineas, 43 (Nancy) $2,500							4/4	4/5		
Arey, Joseph, 23 (Susan) $900								2/2	5/2[12]	
Arey, Lewis, 27 (Malinda)								2/4	4/3	
Smith, James, 52 (Ann), lightkeeper $1,200								3/2		
Delano, Stephen II, 50 (Jane), Fa $1,500									3/2	3/2
Arey, Joshua, 30 (Abigail)									2/2	
Bray, John H., 26 (Rosetta)										1/1
Warren, Charles, 35 (Mary)										4/2
Delano, John G., 35 (Annie)										2/1
Arey, Edwin, 23 (Margaret), quarryman										1/1
Total:	**16**	**20**	**25**	**26**	**40**	**28**	**56**	**43**	**34**	**22**
	1790	**1800**	**1810**	**1820**	**1830**	**1840**	**1850**	**1860**	**1870**	**1880**

[12] This household includes John Green, forty, and wife Sara; and Francis Brown, twenty-three.

Hurricane and Little Hurricane

Note: Since the publication of the first edition of this volume, a book-length study of Hurricane Island has appeared, written by a fourth-generation summer resident in the area, Eleanor Motley Richardson: The Town that Disappeared *(Rockland: Island Institute, 1989). In the present revised notice of Hurricane Island for the second edition, I naturally make use of Richardson's new findings, but readers are encouraged to consult her study for fuller coverage of this remarkable island.*

Although Hurricane Island is lettered *Island R* in the first official map of Vinalhaven (Map 1785 Knox County), it is given its present name in a deed as early as 1772: in that year William Heard sold it, along with eight others in the vicinity, to James Heard (Knox Lands 6/142). James Heard was one of the successful petitioners to the Commonwealth of Massachusetts for possession of the Fox Islands in 1785, and I assume his title to have been validated. I do not find his conveyance to the Crockets, who lived on Crocket's (now Leadbetter) Island in the 1780s, but assume that Hurricane, along with most of the islands lying to the west of Hurricane Sound, was conveyed from James Heard to Isaac Crocket sometime during the decade following the American Revolution. In 1807 Ephraim Crocket sold the two Hurricane islands to George Gardiner, a mariner from the Kennebec region; the sale price was $60 (Knox Lands 1/294). Gardiner sold the two islands to Oliver Brown of Vinalhaven in 1831 (Knox Lands 3/57); Brown, who according to tax records defaulted on his 1840 tax ($11.21) but regained title, sold the larger island to George W. Vinal in 1848 (Knox Lands 47/223); and Vinal sold to Joseph Ginn of Greens Island in 1852 (Knox Lands 48/643). Other conveyances are recorded, but none that enlarge our perspective of Hurricane Island or suggest settlement. No structure is shown there on the Waldo County map of 1859.

It may be assumed, then, that prior to the Civil War this island, like others in the area, was used primarily for pasturage, for the fishing privilege, and for seasonal residence by a few fishermen. At least one year-round residence predating the quarrying era, however, survived the massive transformation of this island after the Civil War: a site remains near the northern tip, with a cellar hole and dug well of uncut fieldstone characteristic of construction in the first half of the nineteenth century. I find no record of who this settler was, and can hardly envy his husbandry with so little fertile land to cultivate and no anchorage for his boats. But the ancient cellar hole and well are unmistakably there.

Harold Vinal, in his poem "Hurricane," asserts that his great-great-grandfather, William Vinal, sold the island to the "granite breakers" for $50, and he considered this a "preposterous bargain." He is in error concerning William Vinal's title, for it was a nearer antecedent (George W.) who owned Hurricane. It is certain, in any case, that in 1870 the island was acquired by General Davis Tillson, a pioneer "granite breaker" in the area. Tillson was born on a farm outside Rockland. Although he attended West Point for two years, he resigned before being commissioned because of the amputation of part of a foot following a mishap. His rank of brigadier general dates from the Civil War, during which he rose rapidly after organizing an artillery battery in Maine; he fought in several battles and served in Ohio, Kentucky, and Tennessee. After the war he returned to Rockland and resumed his business activities. He formed a company for his quarry operations together with two other pioneer quarrymen, Patrick McNamara and Garrett Coughlin, and quarries were opened on the east side of Hurricane Island by 1873. As early as 1872, according to Vinalhaven tax records, there were already a dozen polls and taxpayers on the island, in addition to the Hurricane Granite Company.[13] There were also nineteen "scholars," implying that a school was already established. The

[13] For the record, the residents were listed as follows (only Garrett Laughlin is unmistakably from Vinalhaven, though a number appear to be Maine residents):

Garrett Laughlin	M. T. Fitzsimonds	Charles Shields
Michael Coyne	George Northrope	Noah Twiss
Mathew Comefry	Thos. Philips	Richard Williams
Andrew Carr	Charles Parker	Charles Ward

Hurricane company was assessed for ninety-five acres of land with buildings, wharf, derrick ($800), eight oxen ($900), a steam engine ($600), stock and tools ($1,000). Four years later Vinalhaven tax records show 130 individual taxpayers on Hurricane Island, most with their own homes.[14] The Hurricane Granite Company had a total valuation of $36,670: the island itself was valued at $5,000; five boardinghouses at $5,500; a "new blacksmith shop" at $2,500; two steam cars at $3,500; stock-in-trade at the store at $2,000; a post office at $250. There were also numerous cutting sheds and engine houses, four named administrative buildings, eight oxen, and several horses.

In the forty or more years that the Hurricane quarries were worked, stone was sent to most states in the Union, and finished granite was contracted for such diverse structures as the St. Louis Post Office, the Boston Art Museum, the Cathedral of St. John the Divine in New York, the Washington Monument, and the Brooklyn Bridge. The number of workers fluctuated according to the orders on hand, but there were several hundred in the most prosperous periods and many more persons living on the island because of the quarries; estimates of two thousand, seasonally, are perhaps exaggerated, but a year-round population of between two and three hundred was normal. There were 231 in the 1880 census. The island was incorporated as a separate township in 1878—it already had its post office, since 1875—and promptly provided for a town hall, firehouse, and other facilities; a four-cell lockup was built in 1895 (*Courier-Gazette*, January 29, 1895).

Hurricane was conducted as a company township during the era of General Tillson, and this caused some grief to its inhabitants. Called "Lord of the Isles" by most of his immigrant subjects (and *Bombasto furioso* by the Italian stonecutters), Tillson was an autocrat of another age, contemptuous of the democratic tendencies that prevailed along the coast. He owned most of the sixty or more dwellings on the island, the stores, and the boardinghouses (where the "blue-eyed Swedes, the dark Italians with weather-beaten wives and trooping children, and a mere handful of Americans," as Harold Vinal describes the stoneworkers, were normally segregated). All necessities had to be bought at the company store, deductions being made regularly from the weekly paychecks. Deductions were also exacted, it is said, for the island chapel.[15]

Such a figure was certain to have a mixed press. The Rockland *Gazette*, for instance, in a February 1880 piece, gave a glowing picture of life on the island in consequence of General Tillson's efforts. Not only were the company store and market well laid out and provisioned, but there was a "first-class boardinghouse" where visitors were astonished by the "ever preparedness" of host Captain E. Pendleton and his "most estimable lady." There were also a number of other boardinghouses as well as forty small cottages. From the outside a stranger might think them "temporary and slight" but inside "he will find more than ordinary taste manifested in chromos, good steel engravings, and fair oil paintings in good frames on the walls; books, magazines and newspapers on the tables; organs, pianos and other musical instruments scattered about." A cultural paradise, in short! And how was this managed on a rock-bound island peopled by Irish and Italian quarrymen? By the absence, the author eulogizes, of "the great enemy of the working man...the rum fiend."

The island was indeed dry and kept so by General Tillson's zealous superintendents. Any worker found drunk or even in possession of liquor was summarily dismissed and banished from the island. Raids were carried out periodically, especially against the luckless Italians to whom wine was an ethnic habit and who sometimes managed to secrete a bottle or two from fishing smacks that called at the island.

The rival Rockland newspaper, the *Opinion*, pro-labor and militantly anti-Tillson, gave a very different picture of life on the island, needless to say. For the slightest insubordination or lack of respect for the company—indeed, for the sin of possessing or reading the *Opinion*—workers were

[14] Again, as a partial record, here are those assessed at $500 or higher:

Ellen Kendricks (boardinghouse keeper)	Persia Dean
Rodney Sullivan (boardinghouse keeper)	M. H. Drinkwater
George Crabtree (keeper of a "Public Hall")	Alden Crockett
Michael Cogan (Coyne?)	Samuel Spofford

[15] I assume this was a Protestant chapel, built by General Tillson in the early years. Subsequently there was a Catholic church, supported by the Italian and Irish workers.

Quarrymen's dwellings on Hurricane Island, c. 1910.
(Courtesy of Hurricane Island Outward Bound School.)

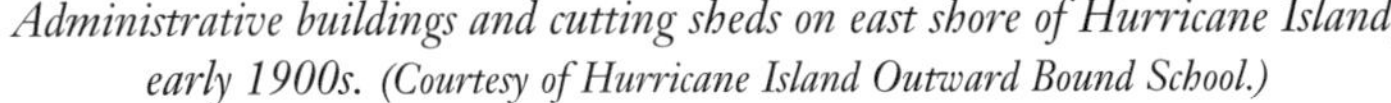

Administrative buildings and cutting sheds on east shore of Hurricane Island, early 1900s. (Courtesy of Hurricane Island Outward Bound School.)

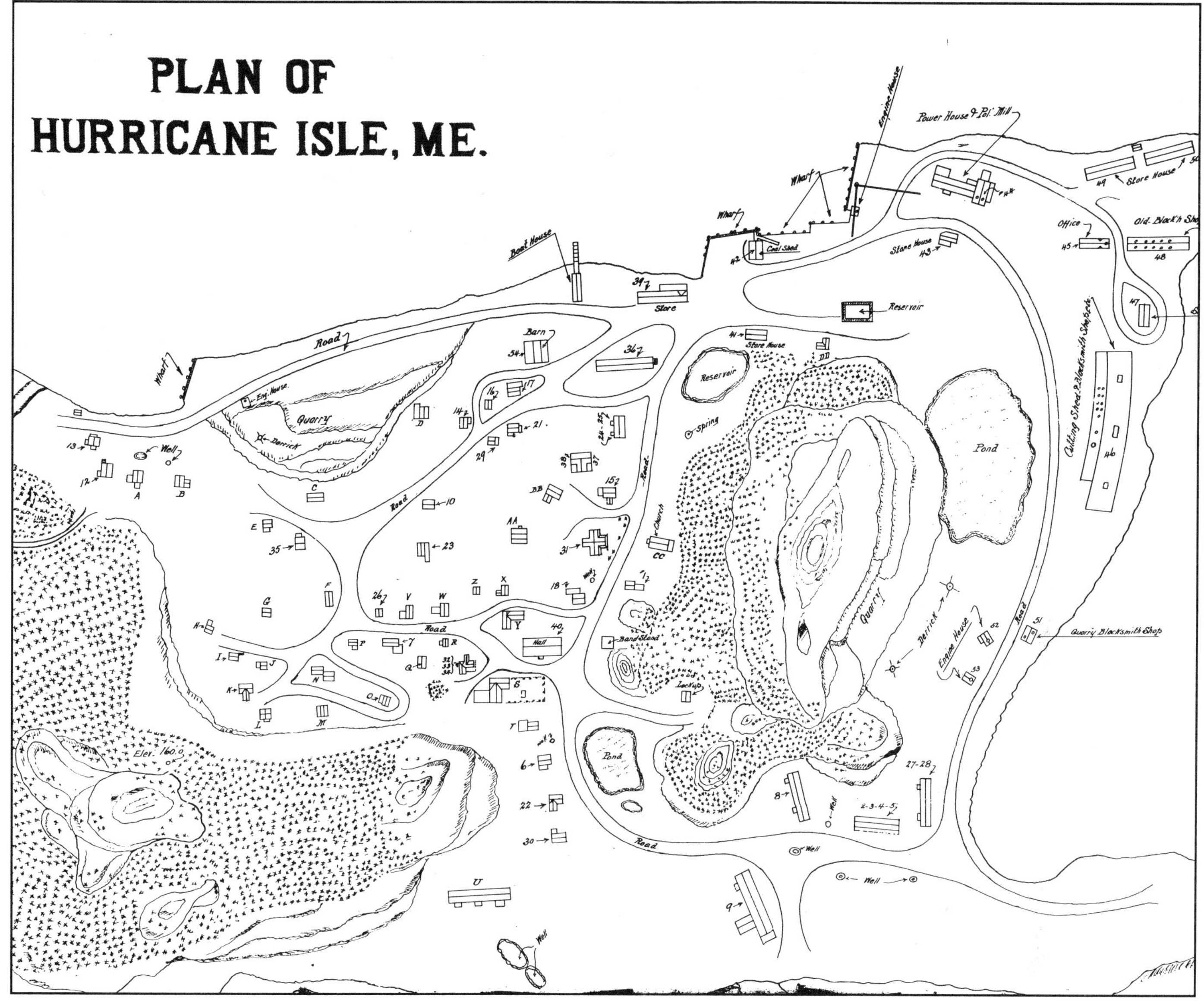

Plan of Hurricane Island in 1910, showing dwellings and other insallations shortly before the end of the quarry era; nearly all buildings have long since been taken down. Outward Bound uses expanded store, top right.
(Plan is at Knox County Registry of Deeds, Rockland.)

A – W.F. Shields
B – J. Testa. Est.
C – Rowling. Est.
D – Frank Ferrigno
E – W.G. Cogan
F – Jos. Gallasini
G – Mrs. Ant. Barsuglia
H – Mrs. Condon
I – Wm. Martin
J – V. Cassini
K – H.I. Packard. Est.
L – R. Rowling. Est.
M – I.W. Sullivan
N – M.E. Landers
O – J. Testa. Est.
P – O. Piatti. Est.
Q – Socialist Hall
R – D. Fabrizo
S – Thos. F. Landers. Est.
T – E.C. Patterson
U – J.W. Sullivan & Others
V – G. Pantoni. Est.
W – T.W. Sullivan
X – T.W. Sullivan
Y – Mrs. Moses Smelds
Z – Mrs. Moses Smelds
ZZ – N. Coletti
BB – Mrs. T.F. Halen
CC – Catholic Church
DD – Mrs. Alex Smith

Buildings owned by Heirs of Davis Tillson are numbered to 1, 18, and 21 to 54.

fired. Pay, the newspaper protested, was not infrequently withheld for capricious reasons: on one occasion work on a government contract was halted entirely by a strike over wages withheld—until the government itself intervened at the workers' request.[16] In the 1875 presidential election the reported returns for Hurricane Island were so one-sided (130 Republican votes *vs* sixteen Democratic) that they defied credulity. As the *Opinion* observed, "everyone knows that the great body of stonecutters—and especially Irish stonecutters—are naturally Democratic.... The intimidation was not brought to bear to keep men from voting, but to make men vote Republican."[17]

General Tillson, though the acknowledged force behind the Hurricane quarries, did not spend much time there. He had many other investments in Maine: a large commercial wharf, for instance, in Rockland, mining interests in Vassalboro, a try-works on Greens Island, as well as a canning factory (the Ocean Packing Company) on Hurricane itself which in 1888 employed fifty female workers from Vinalhaven.[18] He spent winters in Florida, where indeed he occupied himself with investments in oranges and cabbages. Tillson died in 1895, having already built his crypt in Achorn cemetery in Rockland.

What epitaph should we give Davis Tillson? He aroused little affection in his vigorous life. Compassion and tenderness of any sort were absent from his character. But he was a pioneer developer of the region, a late-nineteenth-century replica of Samuel Waldo or Henry Knox. Almost singlehandedly he launched an island community of between 300 and 1,000 residents and transient quarrymen which lasted forty years and produced granite for hundreds of public edifices across the nation.

The Hurricane Granite Company was under some strain at the time of Tillson's death, as a result of the general economic depression of those years and the 1892 "lock-out" (see page 134).[19] Relations between workers and management improved under Tillson's son-in-law and successor, William S. White, but the granite industry as a whole was failing in Maine: cement was replacing granite in foundation work, the ornamental stonework of the 1870s and 1880s was going out of vogue, and railroads were everywhere replacing sailing or steam vessels as the transport of choice, which favored the quarries near Barre, Vermont. The Hurricane company was reorganized and limped along until 1914 when two events within a fortnight signaled the end: the sinking of a scow loaded with Hurricane granite in Rockland Harbor during a September gale (an episode hardly unknown in the trade, but disheartening at this particular juncture) and the premature death from typhoid fever of the energetic young superintendent, John T. Landers, son of Thomas Landers who preceded him. Father and son had managed the quarries from their opening in the 1870s.

The quarry workers quit the island immediately, leaving homes, furniture, and most personal effects behind them. The company retained Ansel Philbrook (skipper of the ill-fated scow in Rockland Harbor) as caretaker, and his large family remained on Hurricane until 1924 when the island was sold. A few of the old quarrymen returned for their possessions, but little of the once bustling community was salvaged. The buildings were torn down one by one except for the best of the sheds and company dwellings, and the Philbrook homestead. The "last inhabitant," according to the *Portland Press-Herald* of September 28, 1926, died in that month—Vin Preston; his effects were removed by the steamer VINALHAVEN on its last call at the once-crowded landing. Normal ferry service had been discontinued a dozen years before.

For some years the buildings left on the island were plundered by vandals, and abandoned machinery—including a giant compressor—rusted near the water-filled quarries. Fishermen again summered there, as they had in the distant past. In the late 1930s the new owners, who were vacationers in the area, conceived the idea of transforming the island into a granite museum (on the model of the seaport museum at Mystic, Connecticut) and of organizing an exclusive club for wealthy yachtsmen and other guests. The island had reverted to Vinalhaven's control in

[16] Labor unions had existed on the island from the mid-1870s, but their ability to operate freely in this climate was crippled.

[17] The *Opinion* and *Gazette* articles are given in some detail in Eleanor Richardson's volume.

[18] The women came daily from Vinalhaven by ferry, since it was considered imprudent for them to live on the largely male island.

[19] Three unions operated on Hurricane Island early in the twentieth century, enrolling 175 workers; there were occasional brief, but successful, strikes (Maine: *Industrial Statistics*, 1905, 1907, 1910).

Outward Bound pulling boat (or towing barge) in Penobscot Bay—a typical sight in the bay from May to June. (Courtesy of Hurricane Island Outward Bound School.)

1937, and this in the end punctured the vision—for the owners were unable, after repeated attempts, to secure the liquor license they needed to make a success of phase two of their plan, on which phase one depended (*Portland Press-Herald*, February 18, 1949 and March 24, 1964).

In 1964, half a century after the quarrymen left, Hurricane Island was leased to Outward Bound and since then has served as the base for a succession of Outward Bound "generations." The students—originally all male, now mixed—live on the steep eastern slope of the island, most of them in tents perched over the quarrymen's cellar holes. They scale the quarry walls, they simulate sea rescues off the granite piers, and they steel themselves in countless exercises on and off the island. Outward Bound Headquarters, located on the same site as the headquarters of the Hurricane Granite Company, crackles with incoming radio calls from watches at sea in the famous 30-foot, ketch-rigged pulling boats, Outward Bound's hallmark. Trainees, in addition to extended expeditions in the pulling boats, spend three-day "solos" on many of the smaller islands dealt with in this study. Eight or nine months each year Hurricane Island is reborn in a worthy blending of the past and present.

Little Hurricane Island has no distinctive history of its own. It normally belonged to the owners of Hurricane itself in the last century—ordinarily for the fishing privilege—but in recent years it has been owned by out-of-state vacationers quite separately from the parent island.

Residence on Hurricane Island, 1880

Note: The following households are shown on Hurricane Island in 1880 federal census schedules. Spouses are in parentheses. Males are to left of slash, females to right Quarrymen and stonecutters are shown as "Q"; other occupations are spelled out.

Bagley, A. J., 41 (Caroline), boardinghouse keeper;10 boarders, all Q	14/3
Gilman, (illeg), 28 (Belle), Q	2/1
Elbridge, Rolf, 47 (Hellen), Q	1/1
Cogan, William, 23 (Isabelle), teamster	1/2
Landors, Thomas S., 39 (Joanna), Q; 5 boarders, all Q	8/4
Robinson, James, 55 (Kate), Q	4/2
Bragg, Austin, 57 (Eliza), machinist	1/2
Wood, Fred, 45 (Mary), engineer; 5 boarders, various occupations	8/4
Hall, Augustus, 29 (Ellen), blacksmith	1/2
Murphy, Michael, 35 (Mary), Q	3/4
Butler, Daniel, 34 (Julia), Q	4/2
Pendleton, Elbridge, 44 (Lizzie), trader; 6 boarders, all Q	10/2
Gilmore, Alvin, 31 (Mame), teacher	1/1
McDonald, John, 40 (Elizabeth), Q	2/4
Clark, Willson, 57 (Clara), Q; 5 boarders, all Q	7/1

Rentilla (?), Foant, 30 (Jane), Q	2/2
McFarland, E., 41 (Addie), watchman	2/1
Roland, Richard, 41 (Lucy), Q	4/3
Hill, William,. 49 (Catherine), Q	1/2
Beer, Richard, 30 (Mary), Q	2/3
Bowdon, Stephen, 29 (Adna), blacksmith	1/2
Cronin, John, 26 (Kate), Q	2/1
Ogston, William, 36 (Annie), Q	4/1
Bollo (?), James, 42 (Mary), Q	7/2
Bowen, John, 34 (Ann), Q	2/2
Donahue, John, 40 (Mary), Q	2/3
Connovallo, Joseph, 37 (Annie), Q	1/3
McG...(illeg), John, 40 (Ellen), Q	4/3
Brogene (?), Jacob, 30 (Annie), Q	1/1
Fillmore, Charles, 59 (Catherine), Q	2/1
Phillips, Thomas, 40 (Ellen), engineer	5/1
Landors, Michael, 33 (Maria), Q	2/3
Snowman, Fred, 22 (Emma), Q	1/2
Coyne, Michael, 40, laborer	2/0
McIntyre, Martin, 38 (Rose), Q	3/1
Pietti, Joseph, 30 (Louise), Q	2/1
Bettizi, Carlo, 30 (Jane), Q	1/2
Remi (?), Joseph, 24 (Margaret), Q	1/2
Brightman, B. F., 49 (Ida), carpenter	2/4
Fulton, Richard, 33 (Fannie), Q	1/1
Pasetts, John, 42, Q; 9 boarders, all Q	10/0

Totals:		
	Quarrymen	68
	Machinists, engineers	3
	Blacksmiths, teamsters	5
	Teachers, clerks, officials	5
	Male	125
	Female	83

White Islands, Spectacle, and Bald

The legend running through these islands on John Vinal's map of 1786 reads: "Ragged Islands and Ledges—of no Value." Subsequent owners would disagree with Vinal's appraisal, and indeed this cluster of islands has known considerable activity over the years. How many of the cluster are properly called White Islands is conjecture. The earliest charts suggest that six or seven might be in the group—all those southwest of Crotch Island in Hurricane Sound—and even the Waldo County map of 1859 leaves the same impression. But deeds make sharper distinctions, usually separating the four most westerly islands as the White Islands proper; the others are sometimes left unnamed.

The earliest conveyance of these islands—

and it is very early indeed— was in 1772 when William Heard sold to James Heard nine islands west of Great Fox Island from Hurricane northerly to what is now Lawrys (Knox Lands 6/142). Although there are more than nine islands in this area, it is likely that the White Islands, Spectacle, and Bald were all included in the conveyance. James Heard sold most or all of these islands to Isaac Crocket (or Crockett), of modern Leadbetter Island, after the Revolution. In 1805 Crocket sold "the White Islands, so called" to several Thomaston buyers, including John Ulmer, an agent for General Knox; he named them *Great White*, *Ram*, *Flat*, and *Harbor*—"four islands making the White Island Harbor"—and I take these to be: the most southwesterly of the four, from whose white boulders facing seaward the group takes its name; the most northerly; the one south of the latter; and the smaller bold island east of the first (Knox Lands 42/233). In 1832 Philip Ulmer sold a third interest in the White Islands to Oliver Fales of Thomaston and called these "the same he and others bought from Isaac Crocket" (Knox Lands 42/123). The same year Fales acquired another undivided third interest in the White Islands from Hannah Torrey, along with two other islands to the northeast called Spectacle and Western (Knox lands 42/121). The latter two had been conveyed to Elijah Torrey by Isaac Crocket in 1805 (Knox Lands 1/350). The name *Spectacle* was erroneously given by charters to the more northerly of the two islands lying northeast of the White Islands, and the error persisted to recent times; in reality, according to those familiar with the area, Spectacle Island is the southerly of the two, and, indeed, on a map it looks like a pair of spectacles with a thin nosebridge. The northerly island, called *Western* in the deed cited above, is known as *Bald* today, though it is not named on coastal charts. Reference is first made to this name in an 1850 conveyance: "Bald or Western Island lying westerly of Truman Garrett's island"—that is, Crotch (Knox Lands 48/359).

A new file of names for the White Islands proper appears in an 1877 mortgage deed: *Big* and *Little White* and *Big* and *Little Garden* (Knox Lands 48/88). The name Big Garden, for the most northerly of the four, has survived, though it is not shown on current charts. This was the island given to the Charles A. Lindberghs by Dwight A. Morrow, father of the bride, at the time of their wedding on North Haven in 1929, and given by the Lindberghs to the Nature Conservancy in 1969.

Leaving aside this fragmentary and baffling title record, what *use* did the various titleholders make of these islands? The Thomaston owners, it is reasonable to assume, bought them for the pulp to be used in the Ulmer lime kilns. Joseph Ginn, a farmer and sheepherder on Greens Island, undoubtedly wanted the islands for pasturage. All owners gained some profit from the fishing privilege that went with ownership, or from shore rentals to fishermen known to have summered on these islands from the early 1800s. At least one fisherman, Joseph Dyer, lived in the White Islands with his family through the winter of 1814, according to his own testimony many years later (Winslow, *Fish Scales and Stone Chips*, 254). But year-round habitation was presumably the exception, to judge from the absence of deep wells and cellar holes, which alone could verify permanent residence on any of these islands. On the other hand, maps and charts surveyed from the 1860s on show half a dozen structures or more in the area, usually on the southwest shore of Big Garden and the north tip of Bald. Such dwellings on Big Garden were doubtless occupied seasonally by fishermen from early in the nineteenth century (Maps 1880 CGS 4 and 1904 Vinalhaven quad). The buildings on Bald or Western Island, however, were associated with quarrying there: tax records in Vinalhaven for 1898 name the New England Dredging Company as operator on Bald Island and show a valuation of some $2,500 for office building, wharf, several engine houses, blacksmith shop, and two boardinghouses; 146 quarrymen, mostly Italians and Irishmen, were in residence.[20] The New England Dredging Company defaulted on its 1903 taxes, and Bald Island reverted to the town of Vinalhaven.

Summer settlers in the White Islands are said to have played a part in the War of 1812, when a British privateer named FLY brought several prize coasters into the harbor one July evening and

[20] The company's total valuation of $2,850 included Crane Island as well—which, however, had little if any activity.

worked all night to transfer cargo to the largest captive vessel. A solitary whaleboat coming in at dusk, however, had sighted the privateer and, after the alarm had been spread, local fishermen attacked the FLY at dawn. The captain was shot, the prize coasters were liberated, and seventy-five of the FLY'S crew taken hostage, but an early-morning breeze carried the privateer itself out of danger before the fishermen could secure her (Lyons, 18–20).

The White Islands proper escaped quarrying during the granite age on Vinalhaven and Hurricane islands, but Bald was stripped by the Bodwell Granite Company. All of the group came into the hands of vacationers in the area during the twentieth century, and in recent years have been used more frequently by day picnickers than by squatting fishermen.

Crotch (Hurricane Sound)

This island was among the nine in Hurricane Sound deeded in 1772 from William to James Heard (see page 146). In 1808 Isaac Crocket, who acquired a number of these same islands from James Heard after the American Revolution, sold Crotch Island—by that name—to Amos Andrews for $50 (Knox Lands 1/249). The origin of the name is obvious, from the island's twin coves that nearly cut it in half, but I do not find the name on maps before the twentieth century. In 1833 the administrator of Amos Andrews's estate sold for $30 to Truman Garrett a seven-acre island named Crabtree as well as a small island northeast of it (Knox Lands 50/303, recorded in 1852). There is, indeed, such a small (miniscule) island, and the identity of Crabtree is not in serious doubt, though to my knowledge this name never appears again for Crotch Island. It is possible that Truman Garrett lived there briefly: deeds in mid-century refer to the island by his name, Truman Garrett's Island, as though he lived there (e.g., Knox Lands 48/359).[21] In 1852 Garrett sold the island to Phineas Ginn for $75 (Knox Lands 50/304)—not an escalation in price that indicates significant improvement. In the early 1870s the island, which was appraised at $200, was owned by Patrick McNamara, a well-known quarry operator in the region; no quarrying, however, was undertaken. The island changed hands several times during this restless era in the granite industry (e.g., Knox 41/339, 46/411, and 48/88).

No one appears to have settled for very long on Crotch Island; there is no cellar hole to suggest year-round residence. A chart surveyed in the 1870s shows a structure on the bar separating the two crotches, probably a fisherman's summer camp (Map 1880 CGS 4). I find no record of who this fisherman was, but we know that shortly after 1900 Samuel Dyer, from Gilkeys Harbor on Islesboro, who lived or squatted on numerous islands in the bay, spent two seasons there with his family (interview with Frank Dyer, Samuel's son). Such summer tenants probably came regularly to Crotch Island up until the time it was acquired by the forebears of the present owners for use as a vacation residence. The island's most glamorous history was undoubtedly during the 1930s when one member of the family, who lived in an elegantly furnished log cabin on the northeast tip, played host to a succession of celebrities and female companions. Of the latter, it is said locally, one would not infrequently arrive on the same ferry that was to bear her predecessor away. The celebrities included John Barrymore, Michael Strange, and Clare Booth, who is said to have written her play *The Women* while a guest on the island.[22] The extraordinary two-story outhouse on the island's eastern shore, named the "Johnson Memorial" after a female guest who wanted a better view, is presumably a creation of that heroic era.

[21] Truman Garrett, seventy-eight, is shown in the 1850 Vinalhaven census with his wife, Abigail, sixty-nine; their precise place of residence is not indicated.

[22] *Maine Sunday Telegram*, August 1, 1971—article by Bill Calderwood, special reporter for the *Telegram*.

Crane

I do not find this island named on maps or charts printed before 1859, but Crane is named in deeds at least from the 1840s. In 1841 David Larry (Lawry is the usual spelling, a family that owned other islands in the vicinity) sold Crane Island to Jabez Brown for $100, and he explicitly stated he was living on it at the time (Knox Lands 52/51). Brown sold to Phineas Ginn of Greens Island in 1850, Ginn to Timothy Lane in 1861, and Lane to Joshua Dyer in 1870 (Knox Lands 74/30; Knox 5/433 and 26/454). Since the purchase price of the island in thirty years rose only from $100 to $150, it seems unlikely that any significant improvements were made; two shallow wells are on Crane Island, but no deep cellar holes that would indicate prolonged year-round residence.

In 1874 Joshua Dyer sold to John Carr and James H. H. Hewett, of Rockland and Thomaston, respectively, for $1,000, and the sharp increase in price suggests quarrying operations were under consideration (Knox Lands 35/508). In fact, apart from a few exploratory motions, there was no quarrying on Crane Island, though its neighbor to the east—unnamed on charts today—was surface stripped. The barred islands to the south, also unnamed on charts, are collectively known as Little Crane.

Title to Crane Island became extremely complex in the last quarter of the nineteenth century as a result of mortgages among off-island granite interests. One owner was the New England Dredging Company, which in 1898 was taxed by the town of Vinalhaven for Crane and Bald islands: a total appraisal of $2,850. The company defaulted on its 1903 taxes, and Crane Island was sold to Thomas J. Lyons of Augusta and by him in 1918 to Bradford Bray of Greens Island for $550 (Knox Lands 177/307). Bray used the island for a decade or more for sheepherding, and possibly for lumbering, before selling to vacationers, who sold to forebears of the present owner in the 1930s.

Lawrys and Cedar

The earliest deed affecting these islands was the 1772 conveyance, noted above (page 153), which conveyed from William to James Heard nine islands lying west of Great Fox Island, running northerly and northwesterly from Hurricane to "Heards Island"; the latter is described as "southerly from the next adjoining Beaver Island" (Knox Lands 6/142). *Beaver* is surely Leadbetter (no other island in the vicinity provides beaver a congenial habitat), and *Heards* is today's Lawrys. The name Heards surely came from claim of ownership, not residence; had a Heard[23] settled on the island, he would have appeared there in Rufus Putnam's 1786 census and the island would have been named in the first post-Revolutionary map of the region about the same time (Map 1786, J. Vinal).

In 1809 Isaac Crocket, then of Prospect, acquired the nine-island archipelago from the Heards and sold two of the islands to Isaac Phillips of Vinalhaven for $30: the islands were then named *Heard* and *Potato* (Knox Lands 1/254). In 1822 Phillips sold the pair to William Lawry, "a small dwelling house, smoke and fish house on each island"; the sale price was $106.61 (Knox Lands 1/408). The two islands assumed the name *Lawrys*—Big and Little—although the spelling varied: Larrys, Lowrys, and usually Laireys. The Lawrys, a prolific family on the western shore of Vinalhaven, owned the two islands into the 1860s and appear to have lived there, at least seasonally. The 1830 federal census shows three Lowry households on an island in Hurricane Sound: John, in his sixties, with a household of six (five males, one female); Thomas, twenties, a household of four (three males, one female); and Wil-

[23] William Heard, though he gave his residence as the Fox Islands in the 1772 deed, had quit the area before 1785. This is the same William Heard who settled on Ash Point in South Thomaston in the Revolutionary era and owned a number of islands in the Muscle Ridges. James Heard was a signer of the 1786 petition of the Fox Islanders, but settled elsewhere on the South Island.

liam, thirties, a household of five (two males, three females). The 1859 map of Waldo County shows no residence on the island,[24] but deeds in 1863 indicated there were "buildings." The Lawrys sold three-quarters of the two islands to Reuben Leadbetter of neighboring Leadbetter Island; the price was $150—which does not suggest the "buildings" were worth much. Leadbetter sold immediately for $190 to James Fuller of Searsmont, an active land speculator in the 1860s (Knox 8/142 and 9/289).[25]

In 1866 the Bodwell Granite Company acquired the two Lawry islands with the intent of opening a quarry on one or both. Apart from a few exploratory motions on the western slope of Big Lawry, however, no operations were undertaken—despite a natural deepwater landing and easy access to the granite which, as one admirer of the site wrote, "is practically quarried for you before you start" (1960 letter to a recent owner from a former quarryman turned lawyer). There continued to be intermittent residents on the larger island, to judge from charts surveyed in the last decades of the century which show a dwelling on the eastern shore near the bar as well as several fish camps (Maps 1880 and 1905, CGS 4 and 310). The cellar hole and dug well of the homestead provide the best evidence of year-round residence on Lawrys Island at some point in the nineteenth century. I have been unable to identify the settlers—presumably fishermen, since the cellar hole is close to the water and the island has few stone walls or other evidence of farming.[26]

Little Lawry Island is called *Cedar* in deeds from the 1880s on, when it was sold for the first time separately from the larger island. J. R. Bodwell sold it for $45 in 1883 to E. P. Walker, another quarry contractor from Vinalhaven (Knox Lands 58/488). Old names die slowly, however, and maps early in the twentieth century continued to show the island as "Laireys" (e.g., Maps 1904–06 Vinalhaven quad). The modern name, according to a recent owner, comes from a ground cedar that proliferates on the island—and whose berries, he liked to think, were used in local gin. If the island ever had year-round residents, they left little trace, for there is no certain evidence of a foundation and none at all of a root cellar; there is, however, an excellent spring on the island, reported to be the only natural source of fresh water in the White Island group.[27]

Cedar Island, meanwhile, has had another name that is almost as well known locally as its official name: *Treasure Island.* Owners gave it this name when they took possession in the 1930s, then created a setting to give the name substance: the family residence was a log cabin built like a ship; the doors were from a Civil War frigate; outdoor lights were the running lights from a ship named the MAGGIE MULVEY, which, it was claimed, sailed from Belfast with women of easy virtue to give pleasure to fishermen at sea; the guest house was the forward quarter hull of the CASTINE, salvaged and turned upside down on the shore; a small barred island is called Skeleton Island. Ben Gun's cabin played a part in the complex—I have forgotten just what; and the island's flag was—what else?—the skull and crossbones. Even today, if you pass close to Treasure Island, certain you are unobserved, and suddenly hear a bell sound close to your masthead, fear not, it is not Long John Silver's warning he is about to board you—it is the owners' way of sending greetings by remote control.

Big Lawry—today, plain Lawry—has also become a summer residence of vacationers in recent years. The island was bought in the 1950s by a New York yachtsman who cruised so much in Maine that he felt he should have a base there. He sank an artesian well near the site of the old homestead, but balked at the cost of a pier and sold the island in 1960, to the dismay of his progeny. The successor owner completed the pier at a cost (he says) of $600—which proved to be a fraction of the cost of the well.

[24] This county map names the island *Poll,* a name that signifies nothing to me. In subsequent maps the name is rendered as *Pole* and even *Cole* (Colby atlas of the State of Maine, 1888) but the island continued to be called *Lawrys* in deeds.

[25] The grantors in the first deed above were, in addition to William Lawry, Mary Young and Henry Sellars, apparently relatives. Sellars, nineteen, is listed in the 1870 census in the household of William Lawry, Jr., on Vinalhaven proper.

[26] According to a recent owner of Little Lawry Island, a family named Ames lived on Big Lawry at the end of the nineteenth century—but this could be a confusion with the Ames family of Leadbetter Island (page 161).

[27] Ivan Calderwood, it should be noted, has one of his characters in *Days of Uncle Dave's Fish-house* (page 232) state that Lawrys lived on the island and that William Lawry indeed was born there. I believe this is unlikely.

Barton, Gundell, and Dyer

Brown's Island, *Island P*, and *Burge's Island* are the names given to Barton, Gundell, and Dyer in the first surveys of the Fox Island Division (Knox County Plan Book, 1785, and Map 1786 Vinal). Brown's was later known as *Granite Island*, and is still known locally by this name, though on charts it has been *Barton Island* since at least the 1850s—after a family that lived there in the nineteenth century. Island P became Gundell; the origin of the name is obscure (see below). Burge's Island (which should have been spelled Burges') was settled in 1783 by John Burges, or Burgess, and later by various Dyers, who gave the island its modern name.

Barton Island has been bridged by a short, narrow causeway to Vinalhaven proper for a hundred years or more, and its residents are not distinguished from those on neighboring Vinalhaven in tax or census records. One can pass from Vinalhaven to Barton Island, indeed, without being aware of it. Yet it is an island, surrounded by the waters of The Basin and Hurricane Sound. The households on the island in 1859, according to the Waldo County map of that date, were two Bartons, two Garretts, and one Bennett. First names are not shown on the county map, but the Garretts could be Thomas and Truman Garrett, and one of the Bartons was undoubtedly Watson Barton: all three names figure in an 1871 deed from Thomas Garrett to John S. Hopkins. This instrument conveyed to Hopkins, for a whopping $2,200, seventy-five acres in the northeast sector of the island (Knox 37/464). Quarrying began soon thereafter. John S. Hopkins was taxed in 1876 for the "Granite Island Quarry"—sixty acres rather than seventy-five—including oxen and a wharf. Hopkins, a Vinalhaven contractor in an era of granite giants (Joseph R. Bodwell, Davis Tillson, Moses Webster, Garrett Coughlin, Patrick McNamara), did not prosper on Granite Island. In less than a decade he was bankrupt. Booth Brothers of New York acquired the premises in 1888, and the Bodwell Granite Company followed two years later. In 1896 tax records show Bodwell with twenty acres, miscellaneous buildings including a boardinghouse, the

Granite Island school children, early 1900s.
(Courtesy of Vinalhaven Historical Society.)

whole assessed at $7,100. It is clear the Granite Island Quarry never became a primary enterprise in Vinalhaven. By 1930 the quarry (called the Conway Place Quarry, but long inactive) occupied only fifteen acres of Barton Island; fifty acres on the Basin were designated as a woodlot. The rest of the island has remained residential, a bedroom community for commuters into Vinalhaven village as well as the ancestral home of local fishermen. Sixteen homesteads are shown on Barton Island early in the 1900s (Map 1904 Vinalhaven quad). There were thirty pupils in the Granite Island school (District 9) in 1915.

Gundell is so persistently spelled *Gundellow* (or some variant thereof) in early deeds and tax records that one must assume the name derives not from any surname (there are, in any case, none like it on Vinalhaven) but from the flat-bottomed vessel once used for transporting livestock: *gundelo*, though what connection there might be between the island and the vessel is unclear. The island was first transferred in 1807, from Thomas Brown to Thomas Brown, Jr., along with sizeable acreage on Vinalhaven proper (or perhaps on "Brown's Island"): "Gondalow and Rasbury" islands with all salt marsh (Knox Lands 1/282; "Rasbury" is presumably one of the small islands lying to the west of "Gondalow"). A single resident is shown on the island in the 1859 county map: a Dyer, with two fish camps; the dwelling was still in the center of the island early in the twentieth century (Map 1904 Vinalhaven quad). John B. Dyer was taxed for the island in 1896: seven acres, with buildings, valued at $650. There was no quarrying reported on the island, and there was never a bridge, though access was easy.

Dyer Island, like Barton linked to Vinalhaven proper by a bridge for well over a century, knew quarrying: as early as 1828, according to O. P. Lyons (71), when a Captain Nelson Spear of Rockland quarried a small cargo there (Winslow, *Fish Scales and Stone Chips*, 21). John Burgess had already left the island and Dyers were presumably in residence at this date. The county map of 1859 shows three Dyer households; one of them was surely Joshua Dyer, who figures in deeds relating to the island from the 1820s to the 1850s (e.g., Knox Lands 1/503 and 50/222). These transactions—mortgages or conveyances of tiny lots—do not reveal much about activity on the island.

Quarrying resumed on Dyer Island in 1863 and continued with few interruptions through the century. The first contractors were Garrett Coughlin, Edward Russell, and James Sprague; when Sprague retired, Bodwell and Webster bought into the enterprise, which became known in due course as the Dyer Island Quarry (Knox 99/608). There was a boardinghouse near the quarries, which were located on the southwest shore with easy access to a deepwater quay. The number of quarrymen surely fluctuated with the orders for cut stone; there were periods when the quarries on Dyer Island were reduced to cutting paving block, or closed down altogether. Meanwhile, small lots on the island continued to change hands, as on Barton and Gundell islands, between local fishermen and commuters into Vinalhaven. In the twentieth century Dyer Island, without any appreciable change in its appearance, became a retreat for vacationing cottagers.

Leadbetter

It will come as a shock to the uninitiated, but the proper pronunciation of this island's name omits the "d" entirely and places a single strong accent on the first syllable with a flat "e": LEHbetter. Why it came out this way I do not know. The island was named after residents in the nineteenth century, descendants of Increase Leadbetter of nearby Crocketts Cove, a signer of the settlers' petition to the Commonwealth of Massachusetts in 1786.

The Leadbetters were not, however, the first settlers on the island. Several editions of the British Admiralty charts surveyed between 1764 and 1775 show a dwelling on the northeast corner of the island. Though the names of neither island nor settler are shown, the latter was presumably Isaac Crocket, who in Rufus Putnam's 1786 census was said to have been on "Crocket's Island" for twenty years. The earliest post-Revolutionary maps (Maps 1785 Knox County and 1786 Vinal) also name the island *Crocket's*. An even earlier name for this island was *Beaver*, mentioned in the 1772 conveyance of islands lying south of it (see Lawrys and Cedar islands above).

The Crockets (or Crocketts) appear to have remained on the island into the early 1800s. In 1806 Isaac Crocket sold 150 acres, including "dwelling house, barn and fish house," to Amos Andrews, and the sale price of $1,000 suggests the island had not been neglected (Knox Lands 1/228). Amos Andrews, a restless fisherman who lived briefly on many islands in the western bay, owned this one only three years: in 1809 he sold the eastern two-thirds to Eliakim Darling for the same price he had paid for it (Knox Lands 1/252). Eliakim sold the next year to Thomas Darling, a "trader"; both were said to be from Boston (Knox Lands 1/275). In 1815 Thomas Darling sold the same premises to Reuben and Luther Leadbetter, yeomen, for $800—and this is the first appearance of Leadbetters in the island's ownership (Knox Lands 1/371). In 1823 Luther sold his half of the island to Reuben, who was already in residence there (Knox Lands 3/43).[28] Reuben eventually acquired the whole island and lived there for more than half a century.

The Leadbetters were a prolific family, extending over both the northern and southern Fox Islands (see the abbreviated genealogical table, below). Only Reuben and his descendants, of the Leadbetter family, settled on Leadbetter Island proper, though his brothers Luther and John lived on the peninsula across Leadbetter Narrows, apparently in close communication. Reuben's household was not large, as the residence table shows, and he doubtless employed farm workers who crossed the Narrows daily to help him. A brother-in-law, Samuel Carver, was reportedly living in the household in 1829 when one of Reuben's children was born;[29] he appears on the island in the 1830 census.

[28] The 1823 deed suggests there were buildings at that time on the *southern* half of the island, though it is believed Leadbetter residence was generally confined to the northeastern quadrant.

[29] This information is from the notes of Samuel Beverage of North Haven, a Leadbetter descendant.

Reuben Leadbetter homestead on Leadbetter Island, from an engraving on the border of an 1859 map of Waldo County; the building, which was elegantly constructed for its day, was built before 1840 and still stands. *(Courtesy of Mrs. Alexander M. White.)*

RES. OF HON. REUBEN LEADBETTER.
ON LEADBETTER'S ISLAND VINALHAVEN.

Reuben Leadbetter, who is shown in census schedules as both farmer and trader, was a prosperous settler, judged by the standards of the times. His real estate valuation in 1860, according to the census-taker, was $2,500; his personal valuation was a resounding $10,000. His 1872 tax valuations, while more modest, were still substantial (150 acres valued at $2,600, a yoke of oxen, two cows, twnety sheep, and $6,380 in his personal estate). He leased quarry rights on the island to Carlton Brothers in the 1840s, and this unquestionably brought him assured income, though serious quarrying was not undertaken until later in the century. The 1859 Waldo County map shows five or six buildings clustered around the handsome two-and-a-half-story dwelling built a few years before; an engraving of the homestead is on the margin of the map as one of the county's showpieces, "residence of the Hon. Reuben Leadbetter." The title "Honorable" is said to derive from Reuben's service in the Maine state legislature.

Reuben died in 1875, and the bulk of his estate passed to his grandson, Charles E. Kimball, son of his only surviving daughter on the island, Mercy, who married Luther Kimball; Luther Kimball was a quarryman who came onto the island in the late 1840s. He died prematurely in 1863, and Mercy married again in 1872—George Kimball, possibly a relative of Luther's—and he, too, died soon thereafter. In the 1870 census Mercy is shown as a widow in the household of Charles Littlefield.[30]

Charles E. Kimball, Mercy's son, was the successor patriarch of Leadbetter Island after Reuben Leadbetter. He managed the island much as Reuben had for thirty years, farming and leasing quarry rights. He and his wife Sabra Jane Leadbetter (a cousin, once removed—see genealogical table) raised five children on the island. One son, Frank, remained on the island for some years after his parents died; he was apparently not of robust health and, after marrying the nurse who cared for him, he removed to Rockland in the 1920s.

Farming was the main occupation on Leadbetter during most of the nineteenth century. There is little record of Reuben Leadbetter's long and productive life, but elder residents of Vinalhaven whom I interviewed in the 1970s recalled Charles Kimball and the scope of his activity. Nearly half the island was cleared by 1900 for his hay fields and pastures. He kept fifty or more sheep and a herd of cattle. His oxen were butchered in the fall, and the meat not needed by the family or Sabra Jane's "boarders" was sold at Hurricane Island. Charles had fish weirs, principally on the eastern shore. His son Frank tended these weirs after Charles's death and was joined on the island for a few years by his sister Bertha and her husband, Walter Greenlaw. Frank and Walter both took part in an historic catch of 20,000 bushels of herring in 1921 (correspondence with Alfred E. Greenlaw, Walter's son). Charles Kimball also kept a fish house and lobster pound at his wharf on the Narrows; he stocked a store with supplies for fishermen in the area. Charles and Sabra Jane's children attended school across the Narrows on Vinalhaven. In some seasons one could cross the ice, but there were hairy moments: Elsie Calderwood of Vinalhaven recalls a winter dance at the Kimballs' in 1905 when ice clogged the Narrows and the boys were able to escort the girls home after the party only by working their way carefully around the ice floes when the tide changed. The Kimballs' life appears in all respects to have been full and self-sufficient, made possible by a combination of successful husbandry, catering to fishermen in the area, and leasing the granite outcroppings for ever-new motions.

Quarrying was the second occupation of the island—and, for a time, probably the most active. There are few sectors of the island where there is no evidence of surface quarrying in the nineteenth century. Three granite landings were in use at one time or another—two on the eastern shore and one on Lobster Cove (also known as the Back Cove)—and the graded approaches to these landings from the quarries may still be discerned today. The schooner YANKEE GIRL was one of several that loaded granite from these piers. The steamer GOVERNOR BODWELL, although not stopping regularly at the island, called on demand in the 1890s. The stone was mainly for paving block and curbing; there is no indication of sophisticated cutting or polishing done on the island.

[30] Charles Littlefield, a blacksmith, is given two households in the 1860 Vinalhaven census: one with Mercy Kimball and another with a quarryman named Charles Shurburn.

How many quarrymen were in residence at any one time is not known; some older residents suggest as many as fifty or sixty, and this is not improbable. There are said to have been three boardinghouses on the island, but I believe not operating at the same time; one (no longer in use) was still standing in 1900 near the stone landing on the eastern shore, which is clearly visible today. At that date, which was near the close of the quarrying era, the stonecutters boarded at the Kimball farm—that is, the dwelling built by Reuben Leadbetter in the 1840s. The most intensive period of quarrying was probably during the 1890s, when Joseph Leopold, a New York businessman with extensive quarrying interests on Vinalhaven, secured the rights on Leadbetter Island, as well as on Greens Island, to provide stone for the Mount Holyoke dam in Massachusetts (*Vinalhaven Neighbor*, December 29, 1937). The guest register of the Central Hotel in Vinalhaven in 1895–96 shows a steady flow of visitors who gave Leadbetter Island as their residence: the Charles Halls, the John Monaghans, Daniel Doherty, James Barry, who was superintendent for a time, and Owen Sheehy, who signs "Boss, Leadbetter Isle, Maine—U.S. Navy." [31]

At least one other family lived on Leadbetter Island in the early decades of the twentieth century: the Ameses, who summered for many years in a camp on Lobster Cove. I believe three generations of Ames fishermen lived in this camp or in one near it: James Harvey Ames, who appears in several photographs of Leadbetter Island in Ivan Calderwood's *Days of Uncle Dave's Fish-house*, his son Bert, and Bert's sons Kenneth and Leonard. The family continued to summer on the island until the late 1920s, principally as weirmen—and there were surely other weirmen and summer lobstermen who camped on Leadbetter but whose names have been lost with time. Farming ended after the Kimball era, but sheep were pastured on the island in the 1920s and 1930s and made free use of the great house. The fields, of course, grew up quickly, and only the northeast end of the island was open by the end of the twentieth century.

Passing yachtsmen in 1936 noted a "For Sale" sign on Leadbetter Island and subsequently bought it from the Kimball estate. Continuity was preserved when it was discovered that one of the new owners, a Kimball, shared a common ancestor with the island Kimballs—a Richard Kimball who came to the American colonies in 1634 (owner's questionnaire). The two families that bought the island in the 1930s have used it as their summer residence through the twentieth century. Like most of their predecessors, they, too, have congregated in the northeast sector facing the Narrows. The Reuben Leadbetter homestead, cleared of sheep and debris, was restored and returned to use.

[31] The register is now at the Vinalhaven Historical Society. (I know nothing of these "residents" of Leadbetter, but list them for the benefit of anyone who might.)

Leadbetters and Kimballs of Leadbetter Island

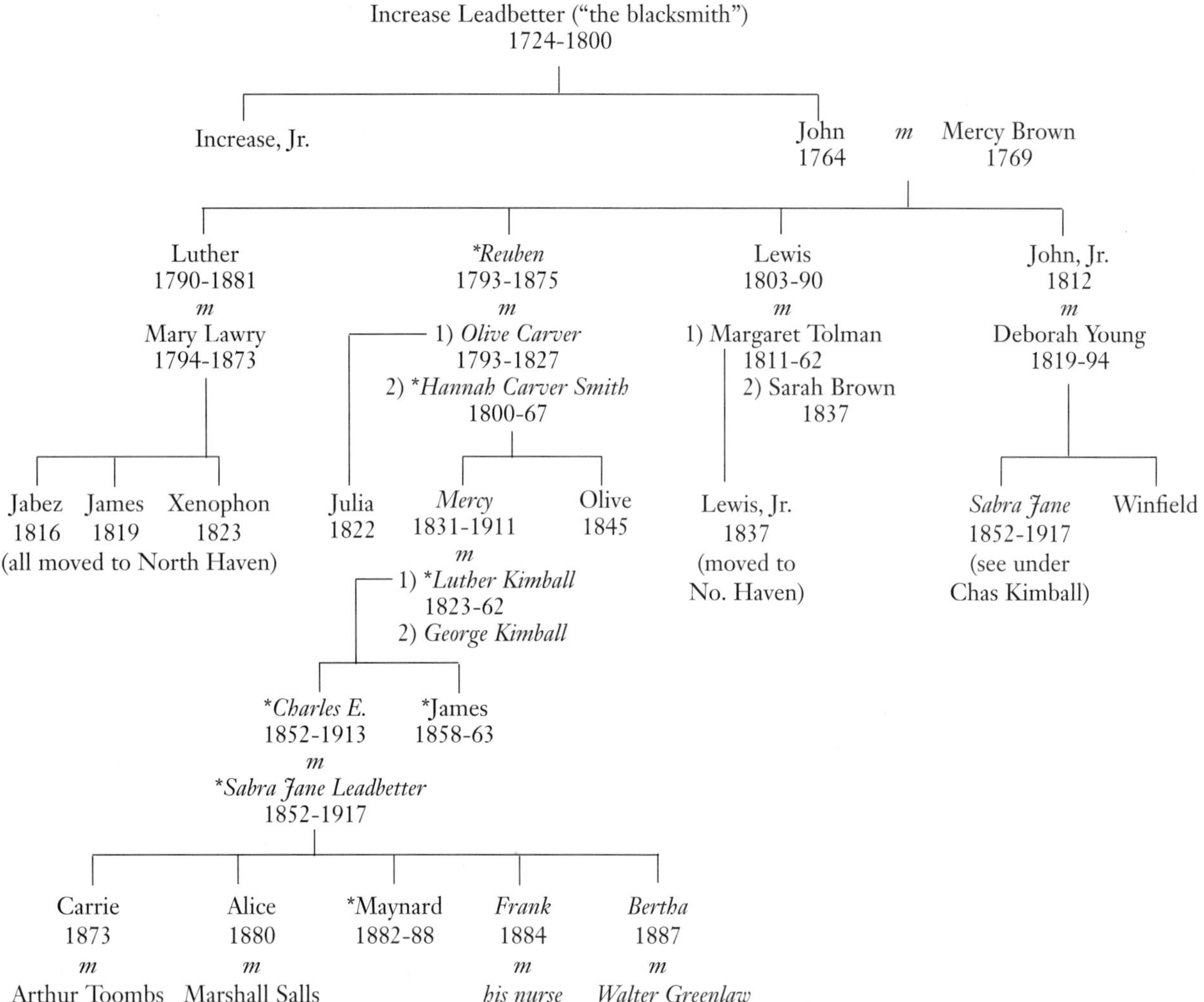

Note: This table is drawn from data in J. E. Ames, Leadbetter Records *(see Bibliography for full listing). Those in italics lived on the island as adults. Those with asterisks are buried on the island. Single dates are birthdates.*

Residence on Leadbetter Island, 1820–1880

Note: The data below are from federal census schedules, but do not include many transient residents—especially quarrymen. Age is at first appearance in census. Spouses are in parentheses. Occupations are shown as follows: Fa, farmer; Q, quarryman; T, trader, merchant. Males are to left of slash in decennial columns, females to right.

Householder	**1820**	**1830**	**1840**	**1850**	**1860**	**1870**	**1880**
Reuben Leadbetter, 26 (Olive/Hannah), Fa/T	1/2	3/2	2/2	3/3[32]	1/2	1/0	
Samuel Carver, 20s		1/2					
Luther Kimball, 36 (Mercy), Q					3/1		
Joel Philbrook, 37 (Mary), Fa					2/6[33]		
Charles Littlefield, 30 (Rebecca)						1/2[34]	
Frank Myric, 28 (Jane), boardinghouse keeper						6/1	
including: Michael Maloney, Q							
Loring Powers, Q							
James Hunfrey, teamster							
Samuel Savage, Q							
Charles E. Kimball, 28 (Sabra), Fa							1/3

[32] Household includes Luther Kimball, twenty-six, and James Fuller, thirty, both quarrymen; also Mercy Leadbetter, Luther Kimball's wife-to-be.
[33] I know nothing of Joel Philbrook's residence on Leadbetter Island, but his position in the census indicates he was there.
[34] This household includes Mercy Kimball, widow of Luther Kimball.

Dogfish

This island is named *Dogfish* on the first maps of Vinalhaven (e.g., Map 1786, J. Vinal) and has never had another name. It was first owned—or claimed—by Increase Leadbetter of Crocketts Cove, and he sold it to Jeremiah Philbrook for £50 in 1789 (Hancock 7/196). I do not know why Dogfish Island fetched such a handsome price in those days. No natural water supply was on the island, and for this reason, if for no other, no one ever lived there, apart from summer clammers and fishermen. According to Elsie Calderwood, who was brought up in Crocketts Cove, there was a fish shack on the cove opposite Leadbetter Island early in the twentieth century, which was used by her brother-in-law, Osborn Calderwood. The island was also used for pasturing sheep, as Sunday picnickers from Rockport in 1913 testify (item in *Down East* magazine, May 1968, p. 20). But beyond this I find no "history" for this engaging island.

There is, however, a legend—and, not surprisingly, it has to do with buried pirate treasure. Two Vinalhaven boys in the 1890s went to look for it, the legend runs, and many years later the widow of one of them, at the age of ninety, wrote a poem about their adventure. The poem, it must be confessed, has little artistic merit and is too long to reproduce in its entirety—yet a few verses might not be amiss here, starting from the point when the two boys, having penetrated deep into the island "forest," discover a faded sign nailed to a tree trunk:

> It said, "My Friend, this is no joke.
> T'is a warning, so beware!
> And do not touch a single thing
> That we have buried here.
> There is a barrel in the hole
> And if you touch it, damn your soul!
> And a spade hangs in the tree
> Take my advice and let it be."
> And sure enough, they found the spade
> Hanging on a tree
> And there it was all old and bent
> For anyone to see.
> I wonder if there really was
> A treasure buried there.
> And is it still there in its hole
> Upon that island fair?
>
> Mary Lowry (courtesy of Elsie Calderwood)

The last owner of Dogfish Island native to the area, I believe, was Captain Ed Mills, who kept the Fish Market in North Haven. Another North Haven personality, Captain Goldie MacDonald, served for many years as caretaker for owners who summered in a cottage (or cottages) dating from the 1920s; Captain Goldie was succeeded in the 1990s by a nephew, James MacDonald.

Bluff Head and Islands in Seal Bay

Bluff Head, easily visible crossing East Penobscot Bay from Merchant Row or Deer Island Thorofare, is well named. It marks the entrance to Seal Bay (the only one of this name along the Maine coast, as distinct from many Seal coves and harbors), an excellent anchorage used from Revolutionary times. A very early deed (1771) conveys the Seal Bay area, including the islands, from Zebulon Howard to Job Philbrook, in return for the northeast corner of the Great Fox Island, or Vinalhaven (Lincoln 9/85). Two tidal mills are shown in the bay on maps drawn in 1785, and another, William Vinal's, is close by (Maps 1785 and 1786, Knox County and J. Vinal).

The names of the islands in the bay, including Bluff Head, have changed over the years, and even today several are obscure. The only one shown on the 1785 maps is *Long Island*, the large island at the north side of the bay. It was still Long Island (valued at $75) when it appeared in William Vinal's estate in 1821, and this continued to be its usual name until changed to *Penobscot Island* in 1965. However, it is shown as *Calderwood's Island* or *Great Hog Island* in an 1828 deed from Solomon Crockett to Joseph Rider (Knox Lands 1/566); other islands named in "Ceil Bay" in this deed are *Rider's Point*, for Bluff Head, and *Little Hog Island*, for Hen, the island being conveyed. *Hog Island* (that is, Hen) shows on subsequent local maps, according to residents of the area. The two small islands southerly of the Hen islands are known locally as *Ram* and *Mink*. The island barred to and south of Bluff Head is called the *Neck* and has been known as *Sheep*. The two barred islands lying in tandem east of Penobscot are known as *Big Smith* and *Little Smith*—presumably after the St. George family that for many years owned a number of islands in Seal Bay. The two islands south of Penobscot—*Burnt* and *Hay* on current charts—have names of obvious origin; I do not know when they were named.

There is a richer history of nomenclature for the Seal Bay islands than of human habitation. None, as far as is known, was genuinely settled, though all were used for timber, hay, grazing, hunting, and fishing. A few of them had transient squatters: early in the twentieth century, for instance, an elderly hermit is said to have had a camp on Ram Island; there was also a camp on Big Smith at some point, for part of a chimney still stands; there is a summer cottage on Penobscot. But no cellar hole to my knowledge exists on any of these islands, and there is a dug well only on the Neck—evidently for sheep or cattle, for which there were also stone corrals. Signs of a few granite motions are on Bluff Head, possibly for foundation stone for the ancient homestead north of Coombs Hill to whose resident Bluff Head and the Neck have usually belonged. Bluff Head and the Neck were charged to Freeman F. Coombs in 1900.[35]

Bluff Head has been for more than a century and a half linked to the episode of the ROYAL TAR, one of the most extraordinary maritime disasters in the area. The episode is so overlaid with legend and lore that an accurate description of the mishap is probably beyond the capabilities of the most conscientious historian. But let us try. The steamer was launched at St. John, New Brunswick, in April 1836, and the accident occurred six months later, on a passage from Yarmouth, Nova Scotia, to Boston. She had aboard, in adddition to Captain Reed, a crew of twenty, seventy-two passengers, and an assorted menagerie of animals that had been on display at Yarmouth: these included

[35] I am indebted to the current owner of Bluff Head, the Neck, and Coombs Point itself for most of the foregoing information about the Seal Bay islands.

camels, circus horses, two lions, a leopard, a tiger, a gnu, various other species, and an elephant. The ROYAL TAR, encountering strong northwesterly winds off Isle au Haut, made for the lee shore of Vinalhaven and dropped anchor off Bluff Head (as nearly as we can tell). Fire broke out: one explanation is that the wooden reinforcements for the deck to support the elephant pressed on the boiler and ignited first; another version is that fire broke out after the stoker let the boiler go dry. According to Captain Reed there was some disorder among the crew, a number of whom made off with a few passengers in the largest lifeboat. Another passenger, a sea captain named Edward Waite, claims to have slipped the anchor and raised some emergency sails in the hope of beaching the vessel, but the sails caught fire and left the stricken ship drifting seaward before the gale. Some animals leapt or were backed overboard and presumably drowned (though tales of strange beasts on nearby islands persisted for some years). The elephant, it is said, resisted all persuasion until, singed by flames, he too plunged overboard; his carcass was later discovered on Brimstone Island. The only hero of the episode was Captain Dyer of North Haven who came out in his revenue cutter VETO and saved forty passengers before the ROYAL TAR was totally consumed on its seaward course; residents of Matinicus reported seeing the glow of the ROYAL TAR long into the night.

There is some uncertainty whether the surviving passengers were first taken to Isle au Haut or North Haven, but forty-three were saved in the end, along with eighteen of the crew; the losses were twenty-nine passengers, including eleven of the dozen children aboard and twelve of the sixteen women, three crew members, and all the animals. The accident was gruesome enough, especially with the high percentage of surviving crewmen compared to passengers, but its measure was hardly taken by Vinalhaven's historian half a century later. "In these days of frequent marine disaster," he wrote, "we get accustomed to such appalling recitals, but fifty years ago an occurrence of this kind was talked about *for many days*"—which must, to judge from the legends that have grown up around this disaster, be the understatement of the century.[36]

[36] In addition to O. P. Lyon's account (*Sketch of Vinalhaven*, 25–26), see "The Burning of the Royal Tar," in *Vinalhaven Pilot*, No. 2, 1837; see also Beveridge, *North Island*, 41–42, and Winslow, *Fish Scales and Stone Chips*, 249–53.

Browns, Stoddart, and Smith

These three islands, lying off the east shore of Vinalhaven or barred to it, may be treated together. All three are bare today, but they were not always so, for maps in the 1880s show Stoddart thinly wooded; and Browns, according to the present owners, would return to spruce if they let it. None of the three was ever inhabited, to my knowledge, except seasonally perhaps by transients or squatters.

The earliest name I find attached to any of them is *Eastmost Island* for Smith, which appears in a 1770 mariner's account of the region; New Harbor is the name he gives to the anchorage behind it, and he judges it "but an indifferent harbor" (Owen, "Narrative of American Voyages," 741). Smith is referred to as *Shroud Island* in an 1823 deed; I do not identify its origin. The name Smith, as shown on maps for the mid-nineteenth century, is after the large family of that name in this vicinity who presumably were owners of the island.

Browns Island was similarly named after the Browns who settled in the Coombs Hill area and laid claim to the island. Thomas Brown sold it to Seba Pease in 1823 for $40, and in 1825 the latter, then living in the Kennebec region, sold to William Roberts of Vinalhaven, yeoman (Knox Lands 1/482 and 1/548). The island eventually returned to the Browns, one of whom farmed the land to which it was barred and kept cattle there; the island indeed was called *Cow Island* locally for some years—to distinguish it from its barred neighbor Stoddart, which was known as *Bull Island* (though I doubt the bar was a significant obstacle to a mingling of the sexes). The Browns sold the island out of the family finally in the 1940s.

The origin of the name Stoddart is less clear to me, for I do not identify a settler of this name in the area. According to Kenneth Webster of Vinalhaven, who once kept sheep on Stoddart, the island normally went with the old Kittredge farm on the facing shore.

Narrows

Airies Island is the name given this one on early maps of Vinalhaven (Maps 1785 and 1786, Knox County and J. Vinal). It was named after the Arey family that settled in this vicinity and laid claim to the island. The first Arey was Isaac, a petitioner of twenty years' residence for the incorporation of Vinalhaven in 1785; he appears in the 1790 census with a household of ten (six males, four females). According to O. P. Lyons (page 45), he came from Cape Cod in 1770 with his wife and child, en route to Mount Desert Island, and settled on the east side of Vinalhaven at what came to be called Arey's Harbor (now Arey Cove). In due course he moved onto the island that makes the harbor, which also took his name. The Ebenezer Arey in the 1790 census is probably his son. There were numerous John Areys in the nineteenth century, and locally they were known by identifying sobriquets—e.g., "John the Baptist," and in our case "straight-legged John of Narrows Island" and sometimes simply "John of the Island." Born in 1801 (according to family records), he married Hannah Arey in 1825 and had ten children, most of whom, it is believed, were born on Narrows Island (interview with Joseph Morton, a descendant). The dwelling was located on the northwest hook of the island facing southwest, and one may judge from ancient stone walls in this vicinity, as well as from the remains of a root cellar, that John was as much farmer as fisherman.

How long the Areys lived there is uncertain, but it is likely that they removed about the middle of the century. The family is shown on the island in the 1830 census: John is in his thirties and there are six in the household (two males, four females). In 1850 John Arey sold a small parcel to John Bray (Waldo 95/99)—quite possibly the father of Emery Bray, who married one of John and Hannah Arey's daughters in 1856. It is not known whether the Brays lived on the island, and indeed no building or resident is shown there on the Waldo County map of 1859.

Charts in the 1880s (e.g., Map 1880 CGS 4) show as many as four structures on the northwest bulge. Two are in the midst of cleared land north of the cove and could be the old Arey farm (overlooked in the 1859 survey); the other buildings are on the narrows itself and are probably fish houses. I am inclined to think that even if the Arey farm was still standing at that time, farming was incidental to fishing. The last year-round resident on the island was a fisherman, William Young, of the Matinicus Youngs, whose home was on the narrows. It is not known when he came onto the island (he was born in 1849), but he left some years before World War I. According to Lyons (page 42), the island was owned in 1889 by Smith Hopkins. In the twentieth century, Narrows Island has been used for sheepherding; an occasional fisherman and his family have summered there.

Brimstone

Remarkable Rock is the elegant designation given this island in one edition of the 1776 "Atlantic Neptune." Brimstone, however, is the name affixed in post-Revolutionary charting (e.g., Map 1785 Knox County), and this name has persisted. It comes from the sulphurous black stone that abounds on the island. This name appears in early deeds—for example, from Anthony to Benjamin Coombs in 1815, for $300 (Hancock 37/53); the State of Massachusetts to John Arey in 1831, for

$30; and from John to Thomas Arey in 1840, for $200. There is no explanation of the fluctuation in the value of the island, and I am at a loss to say why it fetched as much as $300 early in the last century. Thomas Arey and both Coombses are shown as yeomen (farmers) and presumably used the land for pasturage—a usage that rarely required a high fee, if indeed any at all.

There is no indication that Brimstone was ever "settled," except seasonally by fishermen and hunters. Ivan Calderwood in his reminiscences (*Days of Uncle Dave's Fish-house*, 200) notes the intermittent use of the island by lobstermen and duck hunters and includes a photograph of a cabin there around 1900, replacing another "washed overboard during the big Portland breeze" of 1898. One can easily imagine Brimstone used for transient residence as far back as Revolutionary times: the harbor formed by the Little Brimstone cluster to the south is a better anchorage than one usually expects to find off a seaward island, and the usual delicacies of an uninhabited island are in abundance.

This island, in a mid-twentieth-century conveyance, was a Christmas-stocking island: the gift of one fond spouse to another on Christmas morning.

Roberts, Carvers, Otter, Hay, and Sheep

These are called *Stroud's Islands* on one edition of the "Atlantic Neptune"—and this is perhaps as good a reason as any to deal with them as a group. Early mariners found little pleasure in this "parcel of islands, rocks and breakers," as one sea captain unceremoniously labeled them in 1770 (Owen, "Narrative of American Voyages," 740); but they have played a not insignificant role in the economy of the area. Sheep have grazed on one or another of these islands for nearly two centuries; summer camps were erected on Roberts and Otter and show on charts surveyed in the nineteenth century (e.g., Map 1880 CGS 4); all of them have been highly valued for the fishing privilege. None of the group, however, ever had year-round habitation to my knowledge—at least on a continuing basis.

The names of these islands have changed several times over the years, so nomenclature—I suppose—becomes the most relevant feature in the slender history of this cluster. Who Stroud was I do not know, but it is enough like *Shroud*, once the name of Smith Island (see page 165), to suggest that an early settler of some such name was in the region. I do not, however, recognize him. Islands take either the names of their owners or of some striking characteristic. Sheep Island was thus *Jewel's Island* on the earliest local maps, after the Jewells of Calderwood Point (Map 1786 J. Vinal). The Roberts Islands were once *Brown's Islands*, before they changed families. Carvers Island is, of course, named after the large family of that name in Carvers Harbor (that is, the village of Vinalhaven). The Hay Islands yielded hay, I assume, for whoever owned them (though the yield must have been small), and Otter Island must have been overrun with otter; it is also called *Yellow Island* in an early deed.

Tracing title records will not advance significantly our knowledge of these islands, and I therefore omit this exercise—except to make one observation: summer visitors have never been much interested in the group, and with one exception, the Roberts Islands, ownership through most of the twentieth century remained in local hands.

Lane

Today's Lane Island[37] was *Hamelton's* Island in the earliest post-Revolutionary maps of the region (e.g., Map 1786, J. Vinal), presumably after John Hamelton (or Hambleton) who in 1786 was a petitioner for the incorporation of the Fox Islands. He had been in residence on the island, according to Rufus Putnam, since 1770 (see page xx). It is not clear, however, that he had good claim to the island. A 1776 deed transferred from Francis Cogswell of Ipswich to Thaddeus Carver all of the land around what is now Carvers Harbor, including the island, then called *Griffin's*. Thaddeus in 1797 sold the sixty-acre island for £22 10s to Benjamin Lain (Lane); thus began the Lane connection, which lasted into the twentieth century.

Not all descendants of Benjamin Lane lived on the island, but many members of this prolific family did. In the 1859 map of Waldo County four of the five dwellings shown on the island belonged to Lanes: Captain Timothy, William Lane, E. (Edwin) Lane, and another Captain Lane.[38] According to Roy Heisler, a contemporary resident of the island, this would be father (Timothy) and three sons.

The 1860 census shows the following Lanes in Vinalhaven, of whom the first four (at least) appear to be living on Lane Island[39]:

Timothy Lane I, 55 (Rebecca), trader ($10,000/15,000)	4/4
William Lane, 29 (Mercy), fisherman	3/4
Edwin Lane, 28 (Rebecca), clerk	3/2
Francis Lane, 25 (Susan), fisherman	1/2

[37] Although the island is named *Lane* on contemporary charts, it has always been known locally as *Lane's*.

[38] The only other Lane shown as a master mariner in census schedules is Hiram, but it is believed this householder was Francis Lane.

[39] The sequence in the listing is as follows: householder, age, (spouse), occupation, (real/personal estate), males/females in household.

Lane Island from Armbrust Hill, 1880; note the absence of vegetation. The large inn is at the home of Timothy Lane.
(From a stereopticon slide, courtesy of Vinalhaven Historical Society.)

Hiram Lane, 30 (Susan), sea captain[40] (-/$3,500)	6/4
Joseph Lane, 60 (Abigail), farmer ($2,000/500)	3/1
James Lane, 58 (Lydia), caulker ($1,500/500)	6/2
Benjamin Lane II, 33 (Mahala), trader	3/2
Timothy Lane II, 32 (Amanda)	3/3

I believe these Lanes are descended from the original Benjamin (see genealogical table below); Benjamin's brother Isachar left the area before 1800. Timothy I, who was an outfitter, was one of the wealthiest merchants in Vinalhaven; he was said to have owned twenty to twenty-five vessels and in 1865 to have paid the highest tax assessed in the township to that date—$1,328 (Lyons, *Brief Sketch of Vinalhaven*, 45). Other Lanes were partners in a fish curing business on the island (Edwin and H. V. Lane). Some were involved in the lucrative net industry, which dated from the 1840s (including Benjamin II). Still others later in the century ran weirs in Indian Creek off Lane Island (H. V. and F. M.) [41]

In the 1870s the large Lane homestead near the center of the island (once Captain Timothy's) was converted to a hotel named Ocean House. According to the *Maine Register*, it functioned as a hotel from 1874 to 1891. F. M. Lane was shown as its proprietor on the Colby map of 1881. The retreat was predominantly for actors—Otis Skinner among them—and they occasionally performed in Boman's Hall or the Granite Hotel in the village: productions, as varied, it is reported, as Shakespeare and "Ten Nights in a Bar Room" (Winslow, *Fish Scales and Stone Chips*, 221).

As time passed, more settlers came onto the island, but fewer Lanes. The residents in 1902 were as follows, with their occupations (*Vinalhaven Directory*, 1902):

Charles F. Lane, fisherman	F. M. Lane, farmer
W. S. Lane, farm laborer	George Smith, sea captain
Ira E. Smith, sea captain	Lucy Smith, schoolteacher
Walter Tolman, fisherman	Mrs. M. S. Dolham

A 1900 tax bill noted A. J. Barrocas, a nonresident, as owner of two "tenements" on Lane Island assessed at $1,250. The inn was still operating, but under different management. Later renamed the Rockaway Inn, the facility lasted well into the twentieth century.

In the 1960s, when this bedroom community was seriously threatened by development, townspeople raised funds to buy the island for preservation. Under the Nature Conservancy, the southern two-thirds of the island became a preserve, protecting forever the four-thousand-year-old sites of Indian settlement along Indian Creek.

[40] Both Captains Timothy and Hiram Lane, according to Sidney L. Winslow (*Fish Scales and Stone Chips*, 212–13), commanded coastal vessels built in Vinalhaven.

[41] According to a coastal chart surveyed after the Civil War (between 1867 and 1875), there were at least eight dwellings on Lane Island (Map 1882 CGS 309).

Lanes of Lane Island

Note: The following table, drawn with the help of Roy Heisler, includes Lanes who lived on Lane Island as adults.

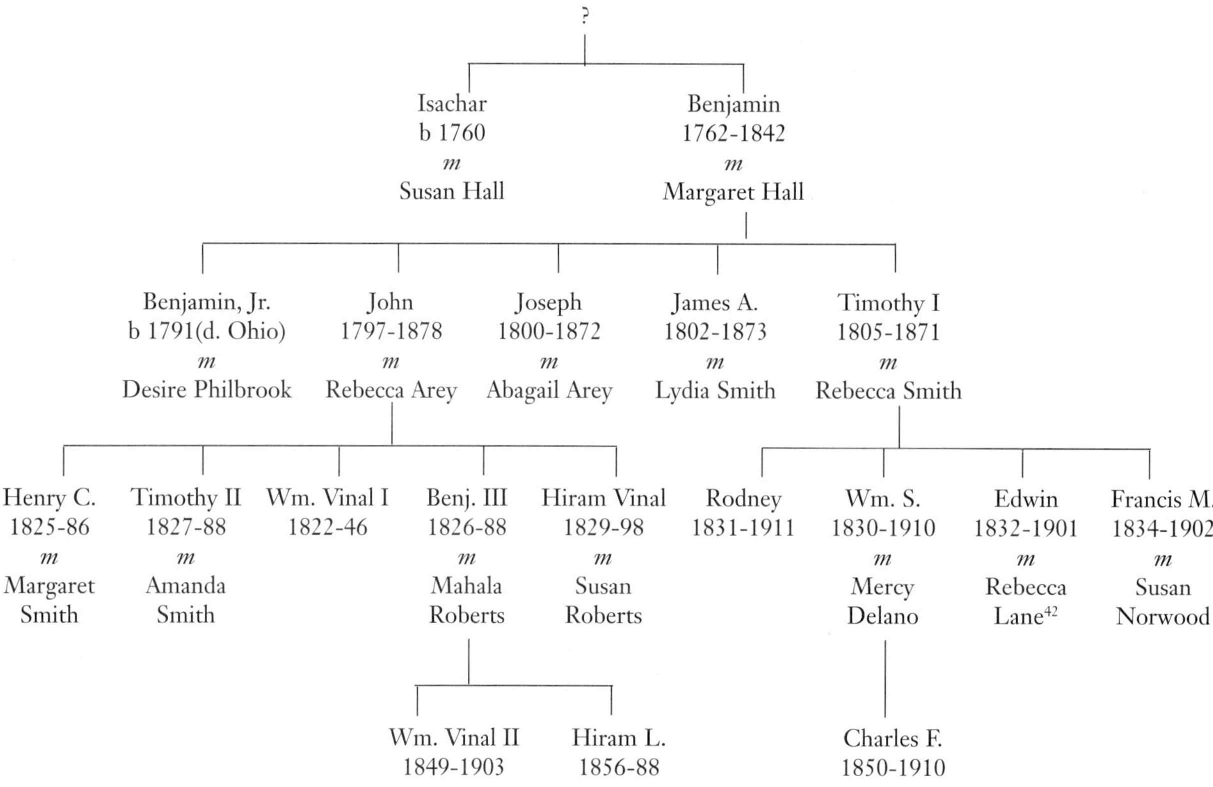

[42] Rebecca Lane was a cousin of Edwin, daughter of Joseph and Abagail.

Group 2: Islands off North Haven

Note: These islands off the eastern shore of North Haven are described from northeast to southeast—that is, flanking Little Fox Island Thorofare.

Oak (off North Haven)

This island is given its current name on surveys completed soon after the American Revolution (Maine Plan Book I: 31). It must have been named after an ancient stand of oak that once existed here, as on many islands in this sector of the bay—for example, Great Spruce Head, once named Stave Island after the oaks there used for barrel staves. Today Oak is bare, apart from a few scrub oak struggling bravely to keep up the name, and has been for at least a century. Calderwoods of Vinalhaven owned Oak in the first half of the nineteenth century and Quinns of Eagle Island in the last half, according to deeds in Ellsworth and Rockland; both families probably used the island for grazing sheep. A building on the northeast shore, apparently a fish shack, is shown on maps of the 1880s (e.g., Map 1882 CGS 309), and this may have been the same camp stocked by Fred P. Frye after he acquired the island in 1910 (Hancock 471/119). According to a descendant,

Frye left provisions and firewood in the camp for stranded fishermen, but after it was several times vandalized he abandoned the service. The camp has long since gone, but the descendants of Fred Frye, down to the fifth generation, still owned Oak in the 1970s and used it in season for day visits. (Outward Bound soloists have also used it—but with small thanks from the owners, one careless soloist having set the island juniper afire.) A variety of birds nest on Oak Island, including Arctic terns and ruddy turnstones.

A true tale of human interest concerns a local celebrity, Marian Howard of Eagle Island: once during the years when she worked in the telephone exchange on North Haven, her father, unable to put her properly ashore because of ice, left her at her insistence on Oak Island, whence she maneuvered her way across the floes to Oak Hill, then on to her post.

Burnt, Dagger, Downfall, and Sheep

Three of these four small islands off Oak Hill Point on North Haven were named on post-Revolutionary maps of the area: *Burnt, Daggers,* and *Sheep* (Map 1786, J. Vinal). Early naming, however, did not guarantee the islands significant history, and there is little to tell of them. Deeds in Rockland show that Burnt and Dagger were conveyed by Thomas Cooper to Benjamin Stanley in 1825; by the latter's widow to Nathan Philbrook in 1836; and the same year by Nathan Philbrook to Norwood Beveridge (Knox Lands 1/550 and 3/215); a descendant of Norwood Beveridge today owns Sheep Island. Local families residing at the eastern end of North Haven, then, appear to have figured prominently in the ownership of these islands, used principally for grazing sheep. There must surely have been seasonal residence by fishermen on the two largest of them, Burnt and Sheep, but the only certain residence is on the smallest, Downfall—known locally as *Mall Rock.* Here, early in this century, an energetic local fisherman named Will Sampson, a victim of hay fever, regularly spent his summers in a small camp, to escape the pollen of North Haven; the camp was eventually removed and now stands at Fresh Pond (correspondence with Samuel Beverage).

A pair of eagles nested on Burnt Island not many years ago, but so many curious visitors came to see them—including often the entire complement of Camden schooners—that at last report they had removed.

Bald (off North Haven)

This bald island, one of a chain dividing the inner eastern bay from the outer, is without harbor and without a spring; it has therefore been without habitation. The Quinns of Eagle Island used it, like most others in the vicinity, for grazing. Other than this, I know of no history that attaches to Bald Island. It was acquired by a vacationing family during the Depression—for back taxes. In 1974 the island was eased to Acadia National Park as an eider nesting ground.

Burnt (Fox Island Thorofare)

The earliest deed I find to Burnt Island was in 1789 from Jonathan Robbins of North Fox Island to John Day: the island is included in a reasonably large tract of farmland in the Indian Point area conveyed to Day in return for his maintenance of Robbins in the latter's old age (Hancock 1/472). I lose sight of John Day's disposition of the island, but in 1812 the western two-thirds was deeded from John Douglass to James Cooper and the remaining third from William Norwood to Cooper in 1816; as in the 1789 deed, the island parcels accompanied parcels on North Haven (Knox Lands 1/329 and 1/577). Lieutenant James Cooper, a Revolutionary War veteran whom we know to have settled during the post-Revolutionary era in the Indian Point vicinity, was the progenitor of most of the Coopers on North Haven. In 1824 James Cooper for $500 sold the eastern third of Burnt Island to Walter Stimpson, together with one of his North Haven lots, four cows, and twenty-eight sheep (Knox Lands 1/513).

Although there is no indication in these conveyances of residence on Burnt Island, it is likely that Coopers were settled there as early as 1809; a Cooper descendant, John Ferdinand Cooper, born in the 1850s, states that all but one of his uncles (there were at least six) were born on Burnt Island, the eldest in 1809 (Cooper typescript, see Bibliography). These were the children of Lemuel Cooper, a son of Lieutenant James Cooper. I have discovered nothing further of this family, except that most were sea captains. A "Mrs. Cooper" is shown on the west end of the island in the first Waldo County map of 1859; according to genealogical data compiled by Samuel Beverage, this would have been Lemuel's widow, Margaret MacDonald Cooper. A year earlier, she had sold the island to one of her sons, Warren K. Cooper (Knox Lands 55/135), and before 1860 had either removed or died. She does not appear in the 1860 federal census for North Haven.

A family that may well have been in residence on Burnt Island in 1860 is that of James Leadbetter, forty-one, a farmer, with wife Abigail, thirty-eight, and three minor children; an English fisherman named Stephen Noble, according to the federal census, was also in this household. It is uncertain where the James Leadbetters lived on the island, if indeed they were there: in 1850 Captain Seth Cooper, eldest son of Lemuel, sold a house and land to James and Xenophon Leadbetter, and it would be reasonable to assume that the James Leadbetters settled in this homestead, wherever it was; alternatively, they could have been living in 1860 on the farm vacated by Lemuel's widow Margaret. John F. Cooper, in his memoirs, recalls the latter homestead in his childhood—"a little house near the shore and the cellar for vegetables which was away from the house and covered or arched over"—but he does not say whether it was then occupied. The site is still visible on the northwest corner of the island on Mullens Cove.

There is greater certainty about the next resident, Lewis Leadbetter, Jr., a cousin of James, who settled on the southwest corner of the island in about 1870 and remained there until 1885. It is unclear from whom Lewis acquired title to the island—both Coopers and Leadbetters appear to have had claims—but he evidently was the sole owner by 1885 and was almost certainly the sole resident, with his family, by that date. According to John Ferdinand Cooper, Elisha Cooper, who had been living on Stimpson Island, moved for a time to Burnt Island where he built a home, but it is not likely he remained there long.

Lewis Leadbetter, Jr. built his farm on the southwest shore of Burnt Island. A photograph of the farmhouse in about 1880 shows it as a story-and-a-half structure, surrounded by cleared fields, wooden fencing, and various outbuildings. Lewis was married to Mary Ann Calderwood (1862) and they had four children before they moved onto Burnt Island. The Leadbetter children crossed the bar to attend the "new" Little Thorofare school (District 4) along with Stimpsons and Coopers from Stimpson Island and others from the Indian Point sector of North Haven. A tragedy in the Little Thorofare—the drowning of two Kent schoolmates within sight of the farm—is given in family records as one reason for the Leadbetters quitting the island in 1885; the perils of island life appear to have shaken Lewis and Mary, and they moved to Auburn, well away from the coast.[43]

Lewis continued to own Burnt Island for several years after the family's removal. He had the island farmed and kept sheep there (according to letters he wrote his son-in-law Samuel C. Beverage), engaging George Leo Gillis for certain services, possibly even as resident caretaker. Leo Gillis, a Prince Edward Islander, subsequently bought the island from him. He lived there more as fisherman than farmer until about 1907 when he dismantled the old homestead and removed it piecemeal to North Haven village, where it still stands. According to a recent owner, he did this after selling the island and buildings to a yachtsman named Philip Wrenn who had cruised in the area; Wrenn returned the following season to find his farmhouse had vanished.

During the twentieth century the island has been used by families that summer on North Haven. They drew their picnic water from the old Leadbetter well-head, equipped (in the 1970s) with a new mechanical pump. The island has long since lost the "burnt" appearance that gave it its name; indeed, the Leadbetters' meadows are now covered with a dense growth of spruce, unendangered for three-quarters of a century by the pulpman's saw. In 1993 the island was given to the town of North Haven by the most recent owners—and within a year the town was advertising urgently for the return of the mechanical pump, missing after a quarter century of service.

[43] I am indebted to Samuel Beverage, a great-grandson of Lewis Leadbetter, for this record of the Lewis Leadbetter family on Burnt Island.

North Haven Harbor and east end of Fox Island Thorofare, June 1971. Local islands are: at right, Stimpson, beyond Goose Rock Light; Calderwood behind (not separable at this angle); Babbidge, upper right; Burnt, across Little Thorofare from Calderwood. Islands in left distance, beyond North Haven, are from right to left: Sheep, Bald (not separated), and the Porcupines.
(Photo by Robert Hylander.)

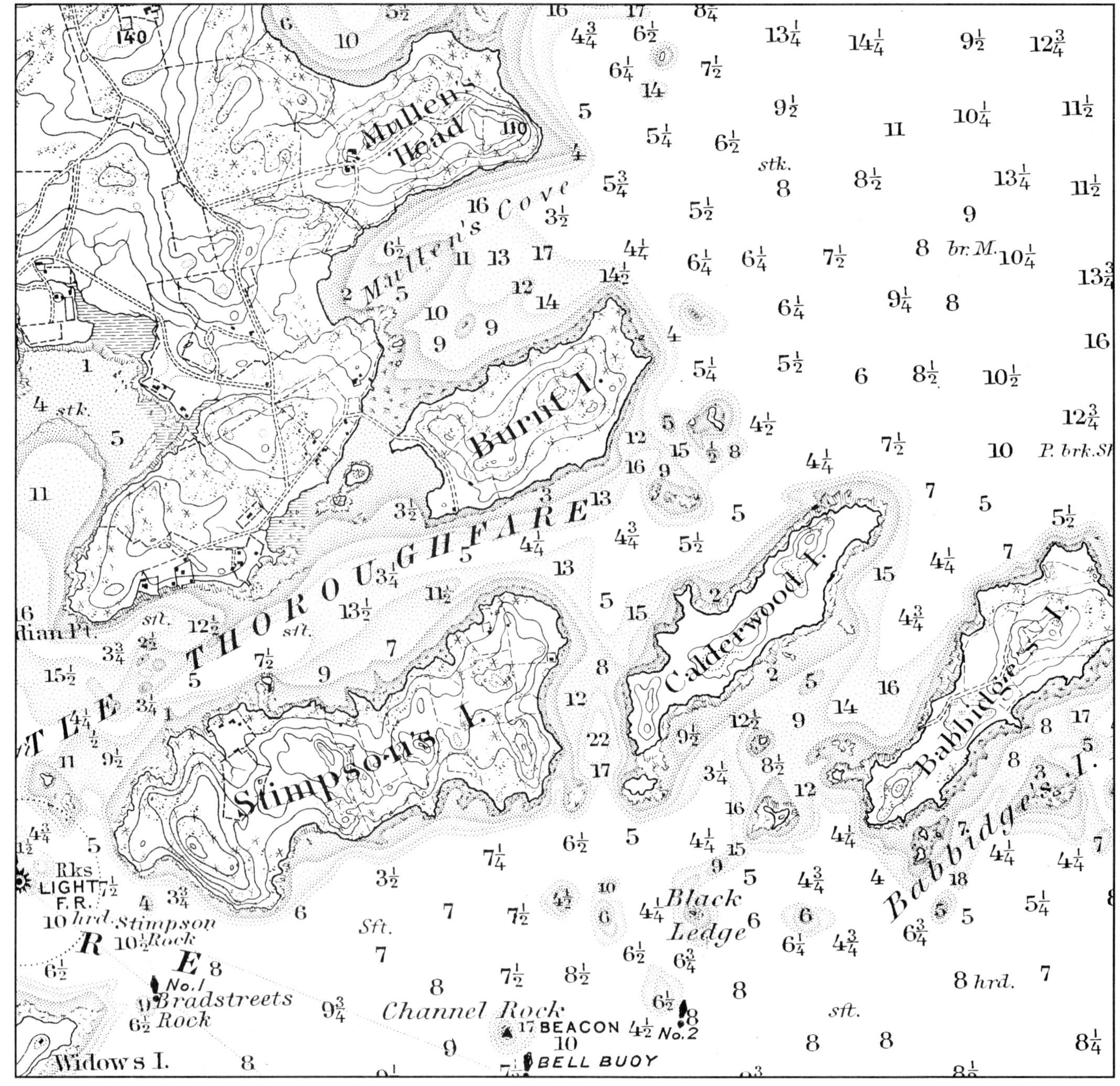

Segment of CGS 309, East Penobscot Bay, 1882, showing islands flanking the Little Fox Island Thoroughfare off North Haven. Five or six farms with cleared fields and stone walls show on Stimpson Island, one farm each on Burnt and Babbidge, and the Naval Hospital on Widow.

Lewis Leadbetter farm on Burnt Island in Little Fox Island Thorofare, 1880s. This farm, built in about 1870, was later moved to the village of North Haven, where it still stands. (*Courtesy of Samuel H. Beverage.*)

Babbidge

The earliest designation I have seen for this island, in surveys made after the American Revolution, is *Island D* (Maps 1785 Knox County and 1786 J. Vinal). There is a nice legend passed down through Babbidge descendants that an eccentric ancestor lived alone on the island and occasionally came into the village of what is now North Haven for supplies, dressed in a blue swallow-tailed coat with brass buttons, and muttering: "There's only one Tory lives on Babbidge's Island." The Babbidge descendant who passed this story on to me writes: "It fascinates me that this family story is so precise in its detail of his dress, and yet nobody in the family has any idea which Babbidge this was or whether he even owned the island."

Babbidges did, in fact, own the island at one time, and at least one Babbidge is said to have settled there briefly, but this was some fifty years after the outbreak of the Revolution.

According to the Deer Isle historian George Hosmer (page 198), a Roger Merithew "many years ago resided upon, and owned, what is now [1896] called Babbidge's Island." The phrase "many years ago" is hardly helpful, but if Roger Merithew, as Hosmer stated, was the father of Benjamin Merithew, an earlier settler on the south end of Isle au Haut, Roger's residence on Babbidge must have been in Revolutionary times, or soon thereafter. Benjamin L. Noyes, Deer Isle genealogist, also notes that a Merithew lived on the island (Noyes, Family histories: Merithew). A Merithew connection with the island is confirmed in a deed executed in 1799 conveying *Ames' Island* from James Cooper to William Merithew for $210 (Hancock 7/410). I do not know the relationship between Roger and William Merithew, but the identity of Ames' Island as the modern Babbidge is not in serious doubt since the connection is clear in the title record. The Ames in question was presumably one of the family of that name (Ames or Eames) settled on both the northern and southern Fox islands in post-Revolutionary times, but we have no assurance that he resided on the island named for him. James Cooper is recorded in the 1799 deed as "of Deer Isle," but it is more likely he was already resident at this date in the

Little Thorofare area—that is, off the southeast corner of the northern Fox Island—for he is shown in a 1794 tax list for North Haven (Beveridge, *North Haven*, 29); he subsequently acquired Watermans (later Stimpson) Island as well. In 1808 William Merithew sold his island, "formerly Ames' Island or Cooper's Island," to Ephraim Stinson (or Stimpson), a yeoman from Prospect; the purchase price was $500 (Hancock 32/31). Ephraim died within a decade of this conveyance, and his heirs sold half the island to Courtney Babbidge for $300; the other half was left to Ephraim's widow Catherine, who married Courtney Babbidge (Knox Lands 45/445). Were Ephraim Stinson and Courtney Babbidge both living on the island before Ephraim's death? Did Courtney marry his neighbor's widow out of compassion (he, too, was a widower)? We may never know. Babbidge, in any case, remained on his island until his death in 1834, long enough—to judge from his estate (a remarkable inventory from probate records follows this entry)—to have constructed an impressive husbandry. He appeared in the 1830 census schedule in his sixties, with a household of seven (four males and three females).[44]

Courtney Babbidge's heirs were his widow Catherine, his son Calvin by his first marriage, Catherine's daughter Rebecca by an earlier marriage, and Rebecca's husband George Shaw. In 1847 these four heirs conveyed 61/64ths of the island—now called *Shaw's Island*—to Melzar Waterman, and the deed explicitly states that the Shaws were living there at the time (Knox Lands 46/46); very probably they had been there since Courtney Babbidge's death. Federal census records in 1840 show George Shaw with a household of eight (three males, five females). Whether the sale to Waterman signaled the Shaws' departure is not clear, but in an 1857 conveyance of Shaw's Island from Melzar Waterman to Ephraim Stimpson, Jr. and Paul Sawyer, it is described as "the same on which George Shaw *formerly* lived"; the sale price was $800 (Knox Lands 55/219).

There is a possibility that Paul Sawyer settled for a time on Babbidge Island, and, if so, this would have been in the late 1840s—that is, soon after the conveyance to Melzar Waterman: North Haven town records for 1849 inspected by Samuel Beverage mention, in connection with school districting, two islands in the Little Thorofare vicinity—Waterman's Isle and a *Sawyer's Isle*. I know of no island in the area that this latter could be other than Babbidge, and infer from the name that the Paul Sawyer family *might* have been living there on the old Shaw farm. (Only one homestead site is on the island, and it is unlikely that two families could have been living there together.)

If this hypothesis is correct, the Paul Sawyers' residence was brief. The 1859 map of Waldo County, which normally shows residence on the inhabited islands, shows nothing for Babbidge (*Babbidge*, incidentally, is the official name appearing on maps from this time on, though other names continue to be used in deeds). The omission could be the surveyor's oversight, or it could mean that the island was in fact uninhabited for a few years. Babbidge appears, in any case, to have been repossessed before 1880, for charts at that time show a well-established farm on the island, with many walls, cleared fields, and a wagon track running from the farm and barns in the center of the island east of the salt marsh to a stone pier on the northern shore near the west end (Maps 1880 and 1882, CGS 4 and 309). The same buildings and improvements also appear in surveys completed early in the 1900s (e.g., Maps 1904–06 Vinalhaven quad). The walls, the well-laid cellar foundations, and the sturdy granite pier still stand as evidence of a prosperous husbandry.

But *who* lived there after George Shaw—or if the hypothesis above is correct, after Paul Sawyer? The decennial census is of little help, since island residents are not distinguished from those on North Haven, and in the 1860 census—where they are at least put at the end of the tally—I find no family I can place on Babbidge Island with any confidence. Nor do the deeds provide any clues. Paul Sawyer sold his share in the island to Ephraim Stimpson II in 1858, a year after they both bought from Melzar Waterman (Knox Lands 55/220); Ephraim Stimpson II we know to have been resi-

[44] There were several Courtney Babbidges on Deer Isle in the late seventeenth and early eighteenth centuries. Deer Isle historian George Hosmer states that this one was a Revolutionary War veteran (page 110)—but that is not likely given known census data. Hosmer describes Courtney Babbidge as "a man of decided political opinions," a characterization that lends some support to the family legend: perhaps his Toryism came late.

dent on Stimpson Island at the time. Paul Sawyer is presumably the "P. Sawyer" shown on Stimpson Island in the 1859 Waldo County map, but he does not appear in the 1860 census, and thereafter I lose sight of him. During the next forty years Babbidge Island changed hands several times among residents of the area—from Ephraim Stimpson II to Seth Calderwood in 1862; from Seth Calderwood to John Smith in 1864; from John Smith to Otis B. Kent in 1874; and from Otis B. Kent to Hollis Leadbetter in 1900—but none of these conveyances mention past or present residence. Nor does John F. Cooper, in his detailed recollections of the Little Thorofare area in the 1870s (see page 181), make any mention of residents on Babbidge Island; surely he would have done so had there been any. Elder residents of North Haven in the 1970s professed to remember hearing of the Shaws on Babbidge or Shaw's Island: ten children hardly knowing any contemporaries until they began school on North Haven. Ten children is a good guess for an island family, and their isolation can be taken for granted, but I doubt whether any details reported in the 1970s about a family that the deeds tell us quit this island more than a hundred years before can be considered very precise. It is possible, of course, that one of George Shaw's sons returned there after the family's initial departure, and that it is his barns and walls we see in the surveys of the 1880s; it is even possible that Babbidge descendants farmed the island, for there are Babbidges in the 1860 and 1870 census schedules for North Haven. But I have another theory: it was neither Shaws nor Babbidges but Stimpsons who farmed the island in the latter decades of the nineteenth century. The Stimpsons were numerous enough to overflow onto Babbidge and it would have been logical to extend their farming there, using the facilities left by Courtney Babbidge, George Shaw, and possibly Paul Sawyer. In support of this thesis is the fact that the island is called *Stimpson's Island* in conveyances noted above from the 1860s to 1900 (a matter of some inconvenience to title searchers, since it meant two Stimpson Islands in the same vicinity). Ephraim Stimpson II surely did not own the island long enough—barely five years—to give it his name, and it is very unlikely that he lived there; I am suggesting that others in his family did, at least seasonally. The island was still called Stimpson's (or Stinson's) when title passed from Hollis Leadbetter to the first non-native owner in 1906: "...known by the name of Stinson, sometimes called Shaw's or Babbidge's" (Knox 141/294).

To recapitulate these diffuse findings: the island has had at least half a dozen names—*Island D, Ames', Cooper's, Babbidge's, Shaw's, Sawyer's,* and *Stimpson's,* with Babbidge the official name since the 1850s. Half a dozen settlers or more have farmed it—Roger Merithew reportedly in Revolutionary times; possibly an Ames at the end of the eighteenth century, and Ephraim Stinson I in the second decade of the nineteenth; Courtney Babbidge from 1819 to 1834; then George Shaw until the 1840s or 1850s; possibly Paul Sawyer for a few years in mid-century; and unknown—probably seasonal—settlers from the 1860s or 1870s to around 1900. At least a dozen families were involved in the island's ownership prior to 1906, including, in addition to the families indicated above, several others well known in the area, such as Watermans, Calderwoods, Smiths, Kents, and Leadbetters.

Since 1906, Babbidge Island has been used principally as a summer retreat. The former owner, Mrs. Amey D. S. Peters, permitted sheep-grazing on the island, and for some years the fields were kept open. She built a small cottage on the west end, but this was removed before World War II when title passed to the present owners; the house is still standing in the village of North Haven. Since the war the island has reverted to its natural cycle of growth, decay, and rebirth, and the present owners plan to keep it this way.

And now to the remarkable inventory of Courtney Babbidge's estate in 1834 (remarkable, among other things, for not having a single misspelling, unless one chooses to quibble over "chattels"). I list the items exactly as shown in the probate record, with a few explanations in parentheses. Readers should remember that these household items were accumulated on this remote island, not in a lifetime of residence, but, it is believed, in a dozen to fifteen years.

Inventory of Courtney Babbidge Estate, 1834

Inventory of the Real Estate and chattles, rights and credits of Courtney Babbidge late of Vinalhaven in the County of Hancock, Yeoman, Deceased, to wit:

Real Estate. Consisting of three fourths of two thirds of a certain Island lying at the Eastern entrance of the Foxisland Thoroughfare the whole of said Island containing sixty seven acres of land, with three fourths of two thirds of a Dwelling house and Barn standing thereon

Valued at the sum of	$300.00
A Pew in the Meeting House in Deer Isle	10.00

Personal Property consisting of the following, to wit,

1 yoke of Oxen value of	$59.00
4 cows at $12 each	48.00
4 cows at $10 each	40.00
1 Yearling bull	6.50
1 Last Spring Calf	4.00
30 sheep and Lambs, $1.50 each	45.00
2 fatting swine at $10 each	20.00
2 Lean swine at $4 each	8.00
2 small pigs at 50¢ each	1.00
6 Geese at 25¢ each	1.50
14 Tons of hay at $7 per ton	98.00
20 bushels of wheat at $1 per bu	20.00
120 bushels of potatoes at 15¢ per	18.00
144 pounds cheese at 5¢ per	7.20
1 Clinch work boat, sails & oars	10.00
1 Cart	14.00
1 Plough	4.00
1 Harrow	1.00
1 Sled	.50
2 manure forks at 50¢ each	1.00
3 rakes at 10¢ each	.30
1 Iron bar	.50
1 Pitch fork	.25
2 hoes at 12-1/2¢ each	.25
2 Scythes at 30¢ each	.60
2 Scythe Sheaths at 17¢ each	.34
1 pair Ox bows [*collar for oxen*]	.25
1 Iron ring and staple	.50
1 large Iron kettle	.40
1 large Iron pot	.50
1 small Iron pot	.25
1 small dish	.25
1 frying pan	.25
1 wrought iron pan	.25
1 Tea kettle	.20
2 Cranes [*arm in fireplace*]	.75
4 Crane hooks	.33
1 meal chest	.50
1 pair Steelyards[*scales*]	.20
2 Iron candlesticks	.10
2 Brass candlesticks	.20
1 pair Handirons [*andirons, obs*]	.34
1 shovel & tongs	.75
1 Tea pot	.06
1 Grindstone	.75
2 Axes at 50¢ each	1.00
1 Cross cut Saw	.75
1 Square	.10
1 chain	.45
1 chain	.25
1 Negro saw [*not identified*]	.50
1 short jointer [*a plane*]	.25
1 fore plane	.10
1 smoothing plane	.06
1 Auger	.10
1 Draw shave [*for spokes*]	.16
3 empty barrels, 25¢ each	.75
2 empty barrels, 6¢ each	.12
1 Churn	.25
1 firkin [*cask for liquids*]	.12
1 Cheese tub	.75
1 bag	.12
3 wooden pails at 17¢ each	.51
1 Tin pail	.08
9 tin pans at 17¢ each	1.12
14 Earthen pans at 5¢ each	.70
1 wash dish	.06
1 Callender	.06
2 tin Bakers at 25¢ each	.50
2tin coffee pots at 5¢ each	.10
1 wooden Mortar	.12
1 Brass kettle	1.50
5 case bottles	.20
2 glass lamps	.40
Snuffers & Tray	.10
1 small shovel &tongs	.42
1 pair dogs [*andirons*]	.10
5 wooden chairs	.25
7 old Kitchen chairs	.20
1 old Table	.12
1 Table	.50
1 Table	1.00
1 case knives & forks	.20
3 knives & forks	.10
1 Chest	.30
1 Bureau	5.00
1 wooden clock & case	2.00
1 Looking Glass	1.00

4 Table spoons	.06
6 Earthenplates	.12
8 Earthen plates	.17
7 Earthen plates	.12
4 cups & saucers	.10
1 Tea pot	.16
1 Sugar bowl	.20
2 Cream pitchers	.12
2 Bowls	.08
1 Mug	.12
1 Pitcher	.17
2 Decanters	.25
6 wine glasses	.12
2 Glass plates	.16
1 Tumbler	.03
1 Tin Server	.10
1 wash bowl	.10
2 bowls	.10
2 Soup platters	.16
1 funnel	.06
6 silver teaspoons	1.50
1 underbed sack [*for storage*]	.49
1 pair Blankets	2.50
2 Sheets	.60
1 Coverlet	1.25
1 Comforter	1.00
1 woolen quilt	.50
2 pillows	.84
4 pillow cases	.16
1 Bolster	.42
~~1 underbed sack~~	~~.10~~
1 bed Cord	.10
1 bed stead	1.00
1 feather bed	4.00
1 bed Cord	.16
2 pair blankets	2.00
1 pair blankets	1.20
1 Coverlet	1.50
1 bed quilt	.50
1 Comforter	.75
1 Comforter	.50
1 bed quilt	.20
1 bed quilt	.12
1 pair blankets	1.20
4 pillows	1.67
1 Butter tub	.25
1 Bible	.75
1 History of S. America[45]	.25
1 of Law's serious calls	.20
1 Hymn book	.25
1 Prayer book	.15
1 Spinning wheel	.75
1 High bed stead	2.00
1 Feather bed	7.00
1 under bed sack	.42
2 pair blankets	2.50
2 sheets	.40
1 Counterpane	1.00
1 Coverlet	2.00
1 bed quilt	.33
2 pillows	.84
2 pillow cases	.08
1 Bolster	.42
1 Bed Cord [*for bedsprings*]	.16
1 half high bedstead	1.50
1 Feather bed	7.00
11 pillow cases	.44
1 bed stead	.50
1 Straight bodied coat	6.00
1 frock Coat	1.25
1 Over Coat	2.50
1 Old Coat	.50
2 pair drawers	.50
1 black silk vest	1.00
1 waistcoat	.12
1 pair pantaloons	.75
1 pair pantaloons	.50
4 shirts	1.00
1 woolen shirt	.25
1 shirtee	.10
1 silk Handkerchief	.25
1 Cambrick Handkcf [*linen*]	.12
1 hat	1.00
1 hat	.40
6 pair stockings	1.00
1 Table cloth	.50
1 Table cloth	.40
1 short towel	.16
1 Long towel	.20
	$516.12

Vinalhaven Novr 20th 1834 Appraisers: John Kent
James Beverage
Benjamin Beverage

[45] This item is surely a book, since it is in Babbidge's small library, but I do not identify its content.

Calderwood

If this island ever had habitation, it must have been at the end of the eighteenth century when a 1797 conveyance uses the phrase "together with all the buildings thereon." The conveyance in this case was from John Barbrick (also spelled Barberick or Barbick) to Samuel Calderwood (Knox Lands1/93). John Barbick we know to have settled on the northern Fox Island a few years earlier—he is on a 1794 tax list, though not a signer of the 1785 petition (Beveridge, 24, 29)—but I know nothing of his residence or the use he made of his seventy-five-acre island. Samuel Calderwood was an early member of this large family of Scottish descent that came to the Fox Islands in 1769 and settled on the southern island, according to Samuel Beverage, a descendant. Samuel Calderwood's island, which had been called *Island B* on the earliest town surveys (e.g., Map 1786 J. Vinal), was given the family name. It has never had any other.

A complete title record thoughtfully provided by a previous Calderwood owner shows a remarkable continuity in the ownership of the island among Samuel Calderwood's descendants, but indicates no residence. We are bound, then, to believe there was none of any permanency, despite the fact that the island's three neighbors—Burnt, Stimpson, and Babbidge—were all inhabited for many years. Sheep were regularly put on Calderwood, and a shallow well was dug in some distant era to slake their thirst; the island was even burned over in recent years to stimulate the growth of grass for grazing. Once the island was presumably covered with forest, despite its shallow soil and ledges, and with most of the sheep now gone, the spruce are gradually regaining dominance.

Stimpson

Waterman's is the name given this island in the earliest surveys of the area (Maps 1785 Fox Island Division and 1786 J. Vinal). This would be after Joseph Waterman, who settled north of the Iron Point area during or just after the Revolutionary War: he is listed as a veteran of the war, with the rank of Captain, in Norwood Beveridge's *North Island* (page 72), but does not appear in Rufus Putnam's list of residents in 1786 (see Appendix 1). He was, however, a signer of the petition for incorporation the year before and so must have been in residence.[46] In 1818 Joseph Waterman willed the island to his three daughters, while leaving his farm on the North Island to his son (Knox Lands 4/190), a disposition of his property that suggests the island was not then inhabited; had it been, Waterman would presumably have left it to a male heir. Another conveyance in 1820, making no reference to the daughters' title, recites the sale for $500 of the western half of Waterman's Island to Samuel Calderwood by James Cooper, who was said to be occupying a farm opposite the island—that is, on the Little Thorofare (Knox Lands 1/438).

In 1825 another Cooper—Thomas—conveyed for $400 the rest of the island, one-half interest each, to his son Thomas, Jr. and to Paul Sawyer, a shipwright; it is explicitly stated that their land extended to "the line of Ephraim Stimpson" (Knox Lands 1/549); this would be Ephraim Stimpson II (at least) since another Ephraim in the area is known to have died before 1819. In 1832 Thomas Cooper, Jr. for $120 sold thirty acres—that is, his share of the island—to Josiah Stimpson, who was probably a brother of Ephraim II (Knox Lands 3/87).

Conveyances on the island during the 1840s and 1850s are bewildering and do not always appear to reflect residence. In 1843, for instance, Paul Sawyer sold ninety-five acres on the east end of the island to Stephen S. Lewis, a Vinalhaven trader; I find no record of Lewis's disposition of his property, apart from ten acres to Horatio

[46] The assertion in Lyons, *Sketch of Vinalhaven*, 51, that the island is named for a *Thomas* Waterman appears to be in error: according to Samuel Beverage, there was a Thomas Waterman on the North Island in Revolutionary times—indeed, two of them, father and son—but neither owned this island.

Brown, who was also a non-resident (Knox Lands 43/511 and 46/15). In 1845 Ebenezer Calderwood and Barnabus Philbrook, non-residents, conveyed seventy acres on the western end of the island to Ephraim Stimpson II, who was already in possession (Knox Lands 46/599). A quitclaim? A mortgage? There is no explanation of the maneuver. A clearer transaction occurred in 1852 between Melzar Waterman, descendant of the original claimant, and the two principal residents, Ephraim Stimpson II and Paul Sawyer: for $1,500 Waterman quitclaimed to the two a 105/106th part of "Waterman's Island"; payment was to be staggered over four years, the deeds to follow (Knox Lands 47/537).

Through all this conveyancing, the permanent residents, as nearly as I can make out, were Ephraim Stimpson II, Josiah Stimpson, Paul Sawyer, and by the 1850s their descendants (see residence table, below; I have not been able to fix the relationships between the three families with any certitude). The Waldo County map of 1859 shows the following six households on what is now called *Stimpson Island*: T. Cooper at the eastern end; A. Cooper midway along the northern shore; S. Stimpson, S. Cooper, and another Stimpson at the west end; and P. Sawyer on the south shore. (The house sites given on these county maps—I know from working with them—are often inaccurate.) If one estimates five persons to a family, a conservative estimate, this means a settlement of approximately thirty on Stimpson Island at the end of the 1850s.

Given the uncertainties of census tallies (since census-takers never distinguished between residents on North Haven and those on the smaller islands), we can do worse than consult the recollections in the 1920s of a former resident on the Little Thorofare: John Ferdinand Cooper (see Bibliography for the listing of his memoir). J. F. Cooper notes the following families on Stimpson Island when he was a boy (1860s and 1870s):

Isaac Stimpson, wife and seven children (two boys, five girls); family moved west in J. F. Cooper's "early manhood."
Note: This family is in the 1850, 1860, and 1870 censuses.

Asa Cooper, five children (four boys, one girl).
Note: In 1850, 1860, and 1870 censuses.

Horace Sawyer, son-in-law of Asa Cooper, boat builder and fisherman.
Note: In 1880 census for North Haven.

Elisha Cooper, wife and five children (three boys, two girls); family moved to Burnt Island and later to Beverly, Massachusetts.
Note: In 1870 and 1880 censuses.

Stephen Sawyer, wife Lydia, four children (two boys, two girls).
Note: In 1870 and 1880 censuses.

Benjamin Merchant, eccentric bachelor living on east end of island; died there.
Note: In 1850 and 1870 censuses.

J. F. Cooper draws a picture of an agreeable childhood in the Little Thorofare sector. There were some thirty pupils in the school that served the islands and Indian Point (District No. 4).[47] Baseball, or round ball, was the activity of choice for boys after school, and anticipation of the games was enough to ensure regular attendance. Those from Stimpson Island (or *Sawyer's*, as it was generally called in that era) came by boat and often in winter across the ice.[48] As the boys grew older, dancing replaced baseball as the principal preoccupation, and opportunities for it were generous. J. F. Cooper recalls one winter evening when, with two Stimpsons from the island, he and a friend attended a dance at the village. A "heavy blow" came up before they started home, and their clothes were frozen by the time they reached the island. They were warming themselves with a hot drink at the Stimpson house—and apparently waxing "a bit too enthusiastic" from its influence—when from upstairs came a preemptory order to put out the lights and go to bed. J. F. Cooper and his friend finished the journey to the Indian Point shore, duly chastened. "Looking back now," J. F. Cooper had the grace to recall from his sixty-year perspective,

[47] According to Seward E. Beacon, *White Schoolhouses on an Island*, this district was created in 1852 and lasted until 1904; there were at times as many as sixty pupils. The teachers are listed in Beacon's booklet, including numerous Watermans, Coopers, and Leadbetters from the area. J. F. Cooper's memoir covers residents of Indian Point as well as those of the islands.

[48] There was a "Waterman's Isle" district when North Haven separated from Vinalhaven in the 1840s, but it is uncertain there was ever a schoolhouse there. In 1847 and 1849, according to town records (cited by Seward Beacon and Samuel Beverage), Waterman Isle pupils were taught in the East and South districts. Three teachers, however, are shown on Waterman's Isle, respectively in 1848, 1849, and 1851: Obediah B. Hewett, John Woster, and Jason R. Grant—all males, be it noted, presumably the better to cope with the rigors of passage.

"I realize that we had given the heads of three families an uncomfortable night."

Maps printed in the 1880s (e.g., Map 1882 CGS 309), which are more accurately surveyed than the 1859 county map, show ten or twelve buildings on the island in clusters that suggest at least half a dozen separate homesites. Two or three sites appear to be at the northwest end facing the Little Thorofare; one is in the middle of the island; one or two are on the northeast promontory; and another is on the cove facing Calderwood Island. About two-thirds of the island is cleared, and there is considerable fencing.

Most of the residents, it is believed, removed during the 1880s, though tax records show that some farming and significant sheepherding continued into the 1890s (see page 183). Maps surveyed after 1900 (e.g., Maps 1904–06, Vinalhaven quad) show no more than one or two buildings on the island; J. F. Cooper said in his 1915 memoir that only two buildings remained at that date. One of these may have been occupied by Frank Cooper, who is said to have lived on Stimpson Island while serving as caretaker for the summer retreat for the "convalescent insane" on Widow Island (see next entry). In 1905–07 the various parcels of Stimpson Island, by then many times subdivided between Coopers, Sawyers, Carvers, Calderwoods, and Stimpsons, were acquired by Martha P. Lawrence, a cottager on North Haven. The Lawrences maintained the two dwellings on the western shore for some years, and Lawrence descendants continued in possession of their "summer island" through the twentieth century (correspondence with Lisa F. Shields, a descendant).

Probable Residents of Stimpson Island, 1830–1880

Note: The following households, according to the author's reading of the federal census, were on Stimpson Island between 1830 and 1880. Age is at first appearance. Spouses are in parentheses. Occupations are shown thus: ***Fa****, farmer;* ***Fi****, fisherman;* ***L****, laborer;* ***C****, carpenter. Dollar figures after some householders represent highest real estate valuation (over $1,000) in 1860, 1870, or 1880. Males are to left of slash, females to right. Dashes mean not found in census schedule for that year.*

Head of Household	**1830**	**1840**	**1850**	**1860**	**1870**	**1880**
Stimpson, Josiah, 27 (Lucy), **L**	4/2	-	5/2			
Stimpson, Ephr'm, 33 (Susan), **Fa**, $2,000	3/3	4/3	3/2	2/1		
Sawyer, Paul, 40 (Diadama), $4,000	6/3	6/5	3/2	3/2		
Cooper, Eben, 29 (Susan), **Fi**			2/2	3/3		
Cooper, Asa, 32 (Irene), **Fi**			3/6	4/5	6/2	
Stimpson, Isaac P., 26 (Lucy), **Fi**, $2,256			1/2	4/4	3/7	
Cooper, Thomas, 50 (Mercy), **Fa**			7/2	7/3[49]	5/1	
Merchant, Benjamin, 33, **Fa/L**			2/1[50]	-	1/0	
Cooper, Elisha C., 30 (Eliza), **Fi**					5/2	5/2
Sawyer, Stephen, 43 (Lydia), **Fi/Fa**, $1,500					3/3	4/1
	1830	**1840**	**1850**	**1860**	**1870**	**1880**

[49] Two adult sons and three elderly gentlemen boarders in the household.

[50] Mary Cooper, sixty-three, and Robert Cooper, twenty-nine, also in this bachelor's household.

Little Fox Island Thorofare: Island Valuations, 1890s

Note: North Haven town records show the following valuations on islands of Little Fox Island Thorofare. The date of the valuation is shown after taxpayer. Key to the headings is as follows: ***Acre****, number of acres owned;* ***Valu****, value of acreage ($);* ***Hors, Oxen, Cow, Shep****, number of horses, oxen, cows, or sheep;* ***Boat****, value of vessel. None of the taxpayers are believed to have been in year-round residence on the islands at the time, but their livestock shown below were there.*

Taxpayer	Acre	Valu	Hors	Oxen	Cow	Shep	Boat
Stimpson Island:							
Ephraim S. Cooper (1892)	13	450	1				
Azariah S. Cooper (1892)[51]	75	300			1		400
Francis P. Cooper(1892)	60				2	32	
Ulysses Prescott (1898)	60		1		2	64	
Cyrus Carver (1896)	75					52	
Lewis Crockett (1896)	60	713	1		1	35	
Burnt Island:							
Howard D. Dean (1892)	60	875					50
Leo Gillis (1896)	42	713		2	1	19	
Robert Steward (1898)	50[52]						
C. S. Stapler (1898)	25						
Babbidge Island:							
Otis B. Kent (1896)	60	360					
Calderwood Island:							
Charles Kittredge (1892)	40	350					
John Mullen, estate (1898)	40	130					

[51] Azariah Cooper appears in later schedules with gradually diminishing acreage; in 1898 his ten-acre lot includes a dwelling.
[52] Robert Steward owned two-thirds of Burnt Island in 1898, C. S. Stapler one-third.

Widow

Called *Sheep Island* on John Vinal's map of 1786, Widow was uninhabited until the last decades of the nineteenth century. The island was part of the Winslow farm on North Haven and is named for Josiah Winslow's widow, Penelope Kent Winslow. Josiah, according to Samuel Beverage, died in 1820, leaving Penelope a widow for nearly fifty years. Widow Island was divided among the Winslow heirs, and a profusion of quitclaim deeds are recorded in the Knox County Registry as the title was cleared for conveyance to the United States government at the end of the 1850s; Seth Calderwood, who had bought half the island from the heirs, was also involved in these transactions (Knox Lands 49/406, 51/108, 55/232-235, 56/42).

The United States government initially wanted the island for a light station at the eastern entrance to Fox Island Thorofare, but after a decision to locate the light at Goose Rock[53] instead, the United States Lighthouse Board transferred Widow Island to the Navy in 1884. The Navy

[53] Goose Rock hardly qualifies as an island, yet it was "inhabited" for some years, and its early keepers should be noted here. Many of them, it will come as no surprise, served very brief terms on this lonely aerie. According to the National Archives, the following served from 1896 to 1912 (K signifies keeper; AK, assistant):

Angier W. Tapley, K	1896–99; transferred
Charles A. Doliver, K	1899 (one week)
Arthur R. Miller, K	1899–1912 (intermittent)
Henry Wilson, AK	1904 (three months)
Charles E. Barber, AK	1904 (one month)
Augustin Linnekin, AK	1905 (appointed, never served)
Alonzo Morong, AK	1905–06
Marmal Newman, AK	1906–07
Clarence D. Wallace, AK	1907 (two months)
Clarence W. Guptill, AK	1907 (six months)
Nelson L. Kelley, AK	1908–09
George P. Merritt, AK	1909–11

The station was automated in 1963.

thought it needed a quarantine station—for sailors who might contract yellow fever in the Caribbean and especially at Panama—as a replacement for an aging facility at Portsmouth, New Hampshire. Dr. A. C. Heffenger was transferred from Portsmouth to Widow Island, and in 1885 he supervised the construction of temporary buildings by a Rockland company. A 127-ton steamer was placed at his disposal. But, no patients came. The transition to steel hulls from wooden vessels—whose putrid bilges and rotting planks, it was believed, spawned the "yellow fever poison"—and new knowledge about the disease obviated the need for the quarantine station. Such are the ways of bureaucracy, however, that in 1888 the temporary facilities were replaced by an elaborate two-and-a-half-story structure capable of housing fifty patients, or more in an emergency. No emergency, needless to say, arose, although the station was kept in readiness for half a dozen years. A caretaker watched over the buildings—and presumably nourished the trees set out on the previously bare island. Mr. G. B. Ames, a retired lighthouse keeper from Portsmouth, was the first caretaker, followed by Frank Calderwood and his sister Rebecca from Vinalhaven. From 1894, when the surgeon general first advised there was no longer a need for the Widow Island hospital, it was nearly a decade before the transfer of the island and its buildings to the State of Maine was finally authorized.[54]

The state was apparently not enthusiastic at first about accepting the facility on Widow Island. However, at the urging of a trustee of the Maine State Mental Hospitals, a Mr. Chase, the island buildings were transformed in 1905 into a summer retreat for the "convalescent insane" and functioned in this capacity for a decade. According to Mr. Chase's daughter, his scheme was subjected to some abuse by his colleagues, one of whom demanded whether he himself would risk spending the summer with the patients; his reply was that he was obliged to support his family, but he would be willing to send his children. Which he did—to their great enjoyment, as his daughter described those summers from a perspective of fifty years (Virginia Chase, "Sanctuary"; see Bibliography for full listing). In addition to the original buildings, a new frame house was erected and a swimming pool and wharf constructed; the inmates also had a schooner at their disposal, in which they used to explore the vicinity.

[54] The foregoing details about the quarantine station are drawn from a well-documented account in the *Rockland Courier-Gazette*, October 8, 1970.

United States Naval Hospital on Widow Island, about 1900; the hospital was built in 1888 as a quarantine station but was never used for this purpose; it was demolished in the 1930s. (Courtesy of Mr. and Mrs. Garnet Thornton.)

Occasionally they stopped at North Haven for postcards and ice cream—the suspicious local inhabitants hurriedly gathering-in their children when this occurred. Male patients came to Widow Island during one month, female the next, and there was, of course, a trained staff to care for them; some thirty or forty were on the island at a time. Frank Cooper of Stimpson Island was caretaker of Widow Island during this period, and he ferried the patients and staff to and from North Haven as they arrived and departed.

After the end of Mr. Chase's experiment in 1915, the buildings were used briefly as a school for the children of lighthouse keepers. They were torn down in the 1930s as a WPA project. Subsequently the island was used as a bird sanctuary, and eventually became the property of a cottager on Vinalhaven. But the decade of the summer retreat for the "convalescent insane" is what is most remembered about the island by elder residents of the area—some of whom link the "widow" and the Chases in calling it "Widow Chase's Island."

The Islesboro Group

Islesboro (Islesborough, 1789–1890)

Les Isles Perdues, as Champlain called these islands on his 1607 chart of the region, were not as "lost" as he implied, lying as they did in the much-traveled channel to Pentagoët—both the trading center (Castine) and the river (Penobscot). Mariners through the seventeenth and eighteenth centuries surely stopped along the shores and in the magnificent harbors of *Long Island* (as the main island, presently labeled Islesboro Island on charts, was long known). An expedition in 1692 stopped on Seven Hundred Acre Island and found a few French and Indians, who immediately fled (Farrow, *History of Islesborough*, 1); nothing is known of these French visitors, but it is doubtful that they were settled permanently on either Acre Island (as Seven Hundred Acre Island is known locally) or Long Island. Seasonal Indian settlement, of course, one takes for granted. Long Island, incidentally, is named on charts as early as the late seventeenth century (e.g., Map 1691 New England).

Early Settlement

By the 1760s permanent settlers began to arrive. An observant (but scornful) mariner in 1770 noted "but a few families settled...and most of their business seems to be cutting cordwood for the Boston vessels and planting a few potatoes" (Owen, "Narrative of American Voyages," 737). By 1776 some two dozen "potato-planters" were on the large island and several of the smaller ones. The British controlled Long Island during the Revolutionary War—to the benefit of the settlers, as it turned out: though not intentionally disloyal to the American cause, they yielded to the exigencies of the times and, in direct contravention of orders by the Continental Congress, sold their produce to the British and their allies in Castine.[1] In 1780 the British granted permission to a team from Harvard University to observe a solar eclipse from Long Island on the condition that no communication be held with the settlers.

Lying less than three miles from the Western Penobscot shore, the island was claimed under the Muscongus or Waldo Patent and early titles came from holders of this famous grant. In 1771, for example, Isaac Winslow, a claimant by virtue of his marriage to a daughter of General Waldo, leased 620 acres of *Winslow's* or *Long Island* to William Pendleton for twenty-five years, at the end of which time Pendleton or his heirs were to receive title to fifty acres, on condition of suitable development of the land in the interim (Farrow, 93–94). Few early settlers, in fact, went through this process; they simply squatted on whatever lands they found vacant to await the outcome of the impending struggle for independence. In 1788, after the war, twenty-five settlers on Long Island petitioned for the incorporation of a township to be called *Winchester*, and the possession of its lands. By that date sixty families resided on Long Island and the other islands to be included in the proposed township. Eight of these other islands were explicitly named—Seven Hundred Acre, Ensign, Little Long Island (Job), Lime, Lazdels (Lasell), Mouse, Saddle, and Western Mark—but the intent was to include all islands barred or adjacent to the main island. The petitioners, seeking to escape a settlement with the Waldo heirs for the lands they occupied, argued that the *center* of the main island was more than three miles from

[1] Farrow, 71, 123. John Pendleton Farrow's *History of Islesborough, Maine* (1893) and its sequel by a team of local historians, *History of Islesboro* (1984), cover all important facets of the island's history.

the mainland, which at certain points was true enough. The Massachusetts legislature was silent on the three-mile claim, but in 1789 passed, over Isaac Winslow's protests, the act of incorporation—for "Islesborough," not Winchester (I am not aware how or why the name was changed). Only four of the original nine islands mentioned in the petition were included: Long Island, Seven Hundred Acre, Job, and Lime.

The question of title was eventually settled after General Knox came into full possession of the Waldo Patent in the 1790s: in 1799, he and the Islesborough settlers agreed to submit the three-mile issue to a new team of surveyors and to abide by their findings. The center of the island was indeed found to be within three miles of the nearest point on the mainland, and General Knox quieted the original settlers, in accordance with the laws of the Commonwealth, and in due course sold off the rest of the lots.[2]

This is the time to name the twenty-five petitioners of 1787, who are the forebears of most indigenous residents on the island today. I include the approximate dates of their arrival; where they settled (on Seven Hundred Acre Island or, if on the main island, north, central, or south);[3] and male offspring who remained on the island (asterisks indicate petitioners among the offspring).

The petitioner's dispersal indicates that settlement was spread over the entire thirteen-mile length of the main island: six in the north sector, nine in the center, four in the south. Farrow names another twenty families settled on Long Island by 1790, most of them in the north sector. The first federal census in 1790 shows a total of 382 persons.

Sectors of Islesborough

The three sectors of Long Island acquired their distinctive characteristics over time. The same families tended to remain in each sector, though there was, naturally, migration and intermarriage. Each sector had its own school, or schools: the north sector had four schools late in the nineteenth century (known as Ryders, Sprague, Bluff, and Parker); the center, two (Creek and Pendleton, the largest school on the island); and Dark Harbor, one.[4] Each sector also had its church.

[2] Farrow covers most details of the Waldo Patent controversy and the incorporation of the township (Chapters I–III). Additional documents may be found in the Baxter manuscripts ("Documentary History," XXI: 360) and *Bangor Historical Magazine*, II: 216/446.

[3] The north sector is clearly divided from the central at the narrow waist of the island; the south sector is less clearly distinguished, but the line comes between Dark Harbor and Jones Cove off Gilkey Harbor.

[4] The High School, when it was established in 1905 in response to new state laws, was in the central sector. It was still in existence at the end of the twentieth century (a dozen to fifteen students, as a rule).

Name	Date	Settled	Sons (*Petitioners);	Other
Shubael Williams[5]	1764	North	*Samuel, *Amos, Joseph, Benjamin	
Samuel Pendleton	1764	Central		
William Pendleton	1769	South	John, *Job, Harry, *Jonathan, Oliver	
Thomas Eames	1770	Central	*Jabez; Elder Thomas removed	
John Gilkey	1772	Central	*Thomas	
William Philbrick	1774	700		
Joseph Philbrick	1774	700		
William Griffeth	1774	700		Removed
George Minor	1774	700		Removed
Joseph Boardman	1774	South		
Thomas Pendleton	1775	Central	Thomas, Samuel, *Gideon, *Joshua, Nathaniel, Stephen	
Jeremiah Hatch	1780	Central		
Charles Thomas	1783	700	Son of David Thomas, 1783	
Peter Coombs	1784	North		
Noah Dodge	1784	Central	Son of Simon Dodge, 1784	
William Grinnell	1791	North		
Godfrey Trim	1792	North		

[5] It was claimed at one time that Benjamin Thomas was the first settler, in 1769 (*Bangor Historical Magazine*, I: 167/173); Islesborough historian John P. Farrow has disputed this claim and gives preference to Shubael Williams.

The original Baptist Church, built between 1794 and 1804, was called the Meeting House and was maintained at town expense; it was in the northern part of the central sector and still stands (much altered) as the Islesboro Historical Society. In 1843 the Free Will Baptists built their church in the north sector, where most of them lived. In 1845 members of the original Baptist Church, who were most numerous in the southern half of the island, built the South Islesborough Baptist Church, later named the Second Baptist Church. The location of the latter irritated other members of the original congregation, who therefore in 1853 built yet another church in the north sector; this came to be called the Middle Church. With the arrival of the rusticators two additional churches were built in the Dark Harbor sector: Christ Church, an Episcopal chapel in 1902, to accommodate the cottagers, and St. Mary's of the Isles, an edifice to satisfy their mainly Catholic servants.[6] Each sector also had its own communal center, named locally Pripet (the north), Guinea (the center), and Dark Harbor (the south).

The delivery of mail to Islesborough over the years provides a fair way of profiling the island's growth and relationship to neighboring mainland communities. The earliest regular mail route, according to Islesborough historians, was via Lincolnville once a week by packet. Since John Gilkey, who lived on Grindle Point at the entrance to Gilkey Harbor, was the first postmaster with the post office at his home (1834), the packet evidently came straight across the western bay as modern ferries do. At that time it would appear that the largest segment of settlers lived in the central sector. Some years later the mainland terminal shifted to Northport, and mail delivery, said to have been by rowboat, was apparently to one of the coves on the island's northwest shore. A new post office was established in the north sector, and the original office was closed. Of the three postmasters Farrow lists in his 1893 volume, the first (Nelson Gilkey) lived in the middle sector, the other two (Otis Coombs and William P. Sprague) in the north. The heaviest concentration of population had by mid-century shifted to the north end of the island. The North Islesborough Post Office was formally opened in 1880 at Ryders Cove. The first post office for the rest of the island, located in the Guinea sector, was opened in 1889; the next year the spelling of the township was changed to *Islesboro*. The North Islesboro Post Office remained in service another fifty years, but the principal facility remained at the Pendleton store in mid-island. There were, in fact, four post offices on Islesboro during most of the first two-thirds of the twentieth century: the North Islesboro Post Office (1880–1940); a post office called Pripet in the north sector (?–1966); the central post office in the village of Islesboro (1889 to the present); and a seasonal post office at Dark Harbor (1895–1966).

The routing of mail from the mainland, meanwhile, changed many times. Belfast became the mainland point of transfer in 1892, after the Islesboro residents petitioned for and were granted direct daily service. A mailboat (initially the steamboat ELECTRA, followed by others—most of them owned by Pendletons) left Ryders Cove each morning except Sunday and left Belfast on the return trip each afternoon, stopping at Hewes Point. Mail was normally called for at the different post offices during this era, but there was also informal delivery by carriers who were paid (if at all) by those receiving mail. In 1916 the Hewes Point delivery terminated, and in 1918 the Ryders Cove wharf was carried away in a winter storm. Mail thereafter was delivered from Belfast to Lime Kiln Wharf at the northeast end of the island and driven by team from there to the several post offices. This, in the era before motor vehicles, was an all-day undertaking. The decision in 1933 to allow motor vehicles on the island (of which more below) changed many patterns of life on Islesboro, including the delivery of mail. The new car ferries from Lincolnville to Grindle Point henceforth brought mail directly to mid-island—as the packets had a century before. All other routes were suspended, including, in due course, seasonal delivery to the Dark Harbor Post Office from the steamers that carried summer passengers from Rockland to vacation points in the bay.

[6] The Isleborough churches are discussed in some detail in the updated *History of Islesboro*, 47–63.

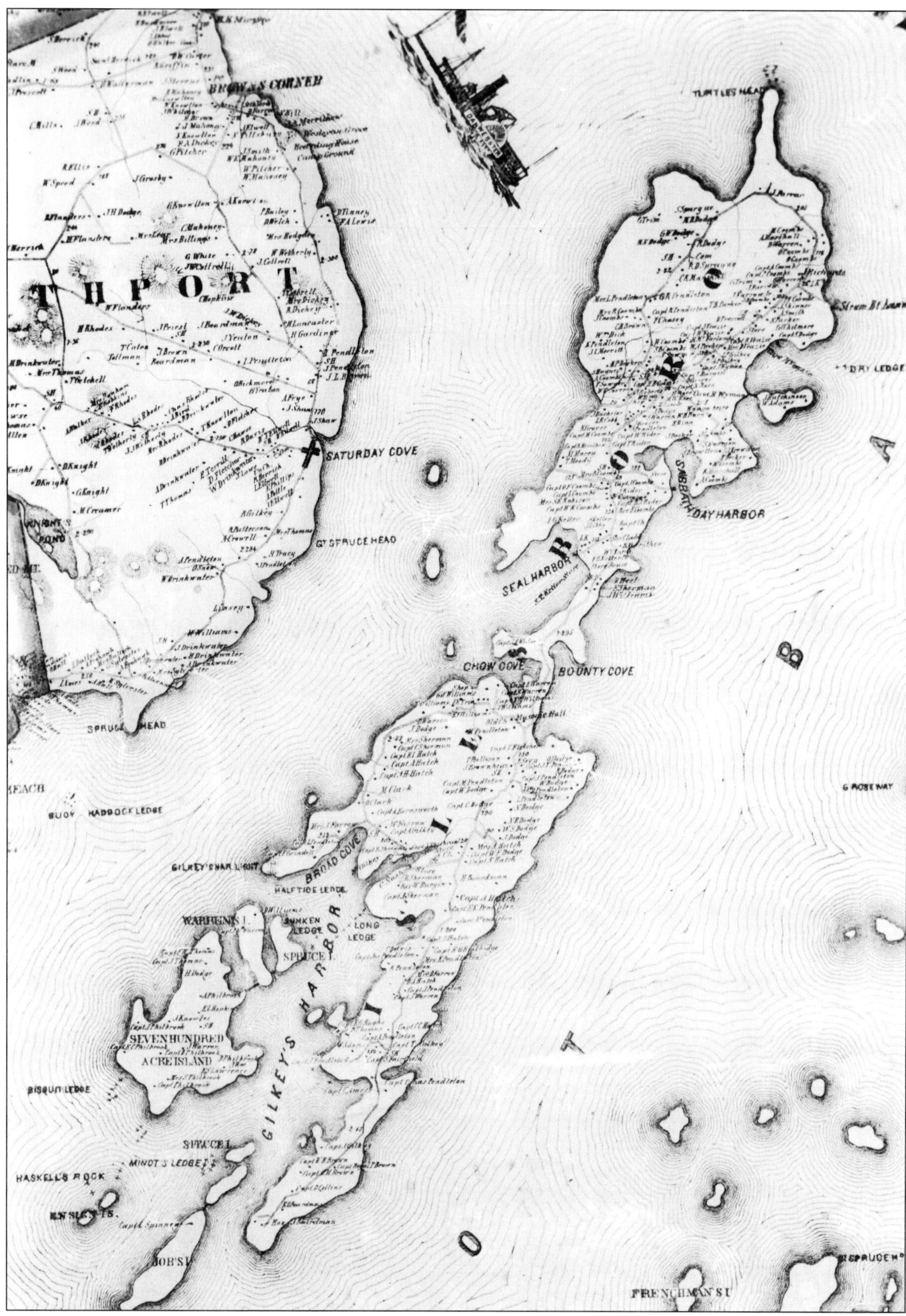
BROWNS CORNER
TURTLES HEAD
DRY LEDGE
SATURDAY COVE
GT SPRUCE HEAD
SABBATH DAY HARBOR
SEAL HARBOR
CHOW COVE
BOUNTY COVE
SPRUCE HEAD
BUOY HADDOCK LEDGE
GILKEY'S HAR LIGHT
BROAD COVE
HALFTIDE LEDGE
WARRENS I.
SUNKEN LEDGE
LONG LEDGE
SPRUCE I.
SEVENHUNDRED ACRE ISLAND
BISQUIT LEDGE
GILKEY'S HARBOR
SPRUCE I.
MINOT'S LEDGE
HASKELL'S ROCK
ENSIGN'S IS.
JOB'S I.
FRENCHMAN'S I.

Occupations of Settlers

What then did the residents of Islesboro do—apart from "planting potatoes" and "cutting cordwood" for the Boston market? They were predominantly farmers and fishermen in early days. The elongated shape of the island encouraged settlers to be both: all lots in the original town plan in the 1790s included both shorefront and interior land (Farrow, 93). The historian Williamson, writing in the 1820s, reported a saying that "Islesborough has neither a rich man nor a poor man in it" (Williamson, II: 542). This may well have been true in that era, but long before the arrival of the rusticators, significant differentials in income had become apparent as residents sorted themselves into prosperous merchants or sea captains on one side, and subsistence fishermen and farmers on the other. Farrow lists sixty-nine Islesborough sea captains in the 1840s; in the 1880 census eighty-five are shown. Farming may have preempted fishing by 1880, according to census tallies, but mariners outnumbered both farmers and fishermen by a wide margin. Shipbuilding was also an occupation on Islesborough in early days: according to Farrow (pages 109-12), a 175-ton brig, two sloops, and twenty schooners over one hundred tons were built on the island between 1792 and 1837. But this was not an enterprise that rivaled the great shipyards of Waldoboro and Damariscotta.

The coming of the cottagers inevitably opened up new opportunities for work and at the same time elevated income differentials among the islanders. I devote the balance of this notice to the era of the cottagers on Islesboro.

Cottagers and Indigenous Residents

Summer vacationers began to arrive on Islesborough soon after the Civil War, not from Boston, Philadelphia, and other Eastern cities which provided the largest number of visitors to Maine over time, but from Bangor. These early vacationers stopped at Sabbathday Cove in the northeast sector of the island. Some built modest cottages, but most stayed at a guesthouse built in the 1860s and soon expanded as The Islesborough. Steamboat service grew to meet the ever-expanding traffic to and from wharves on the east shore of the island: Lime Kiln, Ryders Cove, Hewes Point, and, after it was developed, Dark Harbor. West side service began more slowly, from Smith's Landing to Belfast and, eventually, from Grindle Point. (The ferry from Lincolnville to Grindle Point has been the only regular ferry service to Islesboro since 1936; it was owned by the town until 1959 and since then by the state.)

In the 1880s the heart of the summer community moved down island from Sabbathday Cove to Dark Harbor, where there was established over the next few decades a bastion of opulence, social preeminence, and high fashion unparalleled at the time anywhere in Maine. (Bar Harbor, which had previously been dominant in these respects, was in decline by the end of the century.) Great estates were fashioned out of the fields and hillsides once farmed by William Pendleton and his descendants. The Islesboro Land and Improvement Company, organized in the late 1880s, bought up all available land at the south end of the island to sell to prospective cottagers. The Islesboro Inn was built overlooking Dark Harbor proper, near the steamboat landing. Vacationers of breeding who lacked the means to build the palatial "cottages" of the Dark Harbor sector, or could not find the land for it, or simply wished to avoid the bother of housekeeping, stayed at the inn. With its eighty guest rooms, ballrooms, stage for theatricals and concerts, and huge covered verandah for rainy days, the inn was meant to cement the summer community together.[7]

Development on such a scale inevitably had an enormous impact on the island economy. Land values soared. The fishing industry lagged as many were lured to the more profitable construction trades while the elegant cottages were being built. Later they stayed as gardeners and caretakers. Not household servants, however: cooks, nannies, and domestics were invariably brought by the cottagers from their winter homes.[8] The subsistence

Opposite page: *Islesborough in 1859, a segment of the Waldo County map. Use a magnifying glass to decipher names of residents. (Courtesy of Vinalhaven Historical Society.)*

[7] The Islesboro Inn burned in 1915, but it had played so large a part in the life of the community that it was promptly rebuilt; ex-President Theodore Roosevelt, visiting a daughter at Dark Harbor, spoke to 2,000 people at the dedication in 1917 (*History of Islesboro*, 218).

[8] The comparatively large number of domestic servants shown in the 1880 federal census (twenty-six) were working at the numerous inns and boardinghouses already in operation by this date.

Yacht Club at Western Jetty in Gilkey Harbor, Isleboro, c. 1910; the gentleman in the "lady boat" is Captain George Farrow Pendleton. (Courtesy of Isleboro Historial Society.)

Jeffrey C. Brackett cottage, Islesboro, built 1890s. (Courtesy of Islesboro Historical Society.)

Steamer BOOTHBAY *arriving at Dark Harbor, before 1900. (Courtesy of Maine Historic Preservation Commission.)*

agriculture of the island flourished for a time but was not always sophisticated enough for the cottagers' palates; much food was accordingly imported. This gave a boost to storekeepers on the island and they, too, multiplied. The 1984 Islesboro history identifies some three dozen different stores and markets in operation on the island in the twentieth century (pages 107–13). Livery stables sprang up to meet the needs of carless cottagers. Boatmen were needed at the yacht club, groundsmen at the golf club.

But the interaction of cottagers and native population, when all is said and done, was not large in those early days. Had local women served in the cottagers' households as housekeepers and domestic servants, as they did in less pretentious summer communities in Maine, there might have been a different story to tell. Boatmen, groundsmen, and carpenters (the latter often working under off-island contractors) are not part of households and do not necessarily interact with their employers. The Dark Harbor summer community, then, was superimposed upon what had been an integrated and moderately prosperous island polity. The two communities had little to do with one another beyond the normal civil intercourse between those sharing the same premises. Year-round residents, of course, continued to set town policies and fix tax rates, given their exclusive vote at town meetings. Cottagers, however, were not without influence. This was especially apparent in the bitter struggle over the issue of vehicles on the island, a debate that raged for more than two decades.

In 1913 (the same year Mount Desert voters agreed to allow automobiles there), the Islesboro cottagers and their supporters were able to press through the state legislature a bill forbidding motor vehicles of any description from operating on the island. This was not the beginning of the debate, but it ratcheted the intensity upward. Periodically at town meetings, efforts to repeal the prohibition were defeated, yet a growing number of local residents wanted repeal. The islanders had had telephone service from the 1890s, acquired electricity in the 1920s, and felt increasingly bitter at being denied twentieth-century transportation because of the sensitivities of seasonal visitors. The cottagers, meanwhile, were adamant in their stand, threatening to "secede" from the island if the prohibition were lifted. In 1933 the town did at last vote for repeal, and the state promptly complied (only one cottager, it is said, "seceded"—by selling her property and moving away).

With time, native residents and cottagers have become accustomed to each other. Many of the latter now spend much of the year on the island, and some maintain their legal residence there. Though the differences in incomes and lifestyles are as great as ever, natives and non-natives meet in the local stores and at the post office, serve together on town committees to shape municipal policy, cooperate in the Historical Society and library. They are, in short, no longer strangers. The bonds that link them together grow stronger than the barriers that kept them apart.

Mark, Saddle, and Mouse

Mark Island is named on British Admiralty charts surveyed before the Revolutionary War; on some editions it is shown as Western Mark to distinguish it from Resolution Mark farther up the bay (Map 1776 "Atlantic Neptune"). All three islands are named in the settlers' petition for the incorporation of Islesborough in 1788 (*Bangor Historical Magazine*, II: 216/446) and so far as I know never had other names. These islands were *not* included in the incorporation of Islesborough for reasons that are unclear, and subsequently they were attached to mainland communities for tax purposes. It made little difference, since none of the three was ever settled. Mark was large enough to sustain a family, and there are reports that it was once inhabited—but whenever I try to track down these reports, the island in question proves to be Resolution Mark, not this one. Fishermen used it periodically for summer residence: Willis Rossiter of Islesboro reports that his father and uncle fished in a dory from Mark Island for one or two seasons early in the twentieth century, living in a small fish shack at the north end. It can be taken for granted that other fishermen or clammers used Saddle Island as well, but Mouse Island was too small and inhospitable for residence. Saddle Island was owned in 1921 by Grace Cilley Tibbetts, owner of part of Lasell Island, and assessed at $500—a not inconsiderable valuation for that era (see Appendix 4B).

In 1844 Mark Island was conveyed by Massachusetts and Maine to James Smith (Waldo 51/219). It passed in due course to John Adams and from him to his heirs early in the twentieth century; I know nothing of these owners or of the use they made of the island. In 1916 it was acquired by a family that vacationed in the area (Waldo 322/99). A descendant, a former Secretary of the Navy (Garrison Norton), presented the island to the Nature Conservancy in 1969 in memory of his son.

Lasell

The spelling of *Lasell* has varied so much over the years that one wonders whether the name derives consistently from the same family. Some of the spellings, as they appear on charts and deeds dating from the 1780s, are as follows: *Laselle's*, *Lassel's*, *Lazdel's*, *Lassell's*, *Laisdell's*, and *Lazell's*. The island has also been called both *Smith's* and *Maker's Island*.

The earliest inhabitant, according to John Pendleton Farrow (*History of Islesborough*, 13, 229), was Ellison Laselle, who apparently settled on the island before 1786 when it is called *Lassell* in a map of that date (Map 1786 Penobscot Islands). Several of his children were born there before the family moved to Turtle Head at the north end of Long Island (Islesborough) in about 1799. Other settlers were on the island in the 1820s, according to Williamson (I: 71), but it is not known who they were.

In 1830, according to the federal census, two families were living on *Lasdell Island*: John Smith, in his forties, with his wife in her twenties, and four minor children—a son and three daughters; and William Ureh, in his twenties, with his wife of about the same age, and two minor daughters. I know nothing about the second family, whose name may be misspelled in the census, but the Smiths evidently remained on the island until 1852. In late December of that year, according to an item in the *Republican Journal* of Belfast (January 14, 1853), John Smith and his wife met with tragedy while returning to the island from Camden. The couple had gone ashore to trade and to make "some little preparations for the new Year just at hand." They had left their children on the island and left Camden to rejoin them "not long before dark...as there was quite a strong headwind with some sea, it is probable they found themselves unable to make the passage [four miles]." They were driven up the bay and capsized while attempting to come ashore at Belfast; both were drowned. Assuming this to be the same John Smith as in the 1830 census, he would have been in his sixties at the time of the accident. His children would have been old enough, one presumes, to care for themselves: bereft, surely, but not abandoned and destitute, as later historians make out (e.g., Eaton, *History of Thomaston*, I: 20).

Ownership of the island after the Smiths is complex (and probably not a suitable topic for amateur title searchers like the present writer). The surviving Smiths apparently quit the island after the accident, and no successor immediately settled there: the 1859 map of Waldo County shows no residents on the island. In 1863 John Carver, a land broker from Lincolnville, began to acquire portions of it from the heirs of John Smith and from other claimants (Knox Lands 56/508–510). The exact proportion acquired by John Carver is uncertain, since ownership had been divided into multiple shares, but it appears to have been well over one half of the total 148 acres. Sometime before 1874 the family of James R. Maker moved onto the island: an auction held that year by the State of Maine, involving islands that had never been properly deeded by the state, took note of his widow's residence there with her children and appears to have acknowledged the legitimacy of her deed to five-sevenths of the island, for which she paid $1,500 (Maine Archives, "1874 Island Sales"). I find no other record of her deed and assume it was either acquired from John Carver or was in competition with his title; Mrs. Maker could, of course, have been an heir of John Smith, though I have no record of this, either. The remaining two-sevenths of the island at the time of the 1874 auction was conveyed by the state to George S. Ames. At the end of the 1870s Carver and Ames combined forces and sold one-seventh of the island to Frances L. Lazell of Rockland and another seventh to George L. Maker, eldest son of James R. (Knox Lands 57/67 and 57/73). This appears to have disposed of the Carver-Ames interest, for neither figures in subsequent conveyances.

The James R. Maker legacy evidently did not go in its entirety to his widow and children, despite her claim at the 1874 auction. In 1881 a fraction of the island—"one undivided seventh of five undivided sevenths," to be precise—was sold to Frances L. Lazell by the guardian of two young Lassells who had inherited the fraction from their mother Rose S. Lassell, described as an heir of James Maker (Knox Lands 57/66). At this point the relationships between the original Laselles, Smiths, Makers, and now back to Lassells begin to overset the mind, and I leave it to genealogists to sort out. As to Frances L. Lazell, who continued to acquire shares in the island, there is nothing in the deeds to suggest that she was related to Laselle or Lassell descendants and no reason beyond the similarity of names to believe that she was. She appears to have been a land speculator, unmarried, and in addition to Lasell Island claimed title to half a dozen others in the area through a very ambiguous release in 1879 from the State of Maine (Waldo 189/9); none of these titles proved substantial when tested against titles passed down over the years through private conveyances. She did, however, have good title to shares in Lasell Island and because of the similarity in the names, it was referred to for some years as *Lazell's*.

Since the shares were undivided, George L. Maker, who continued with his brother Henry and sister Etta to occupy the island after their mother's death, applied for partition in 1882. Together with Henry and Etta, he claimed 24/49 interest in the island and acknowledged that Frances L. Lazell held 25/49. The partition was made in 1892 by a court-appointed commission—not on the basis of acreage, but of value: the Makers were assigned the southern two-thirds of the island, Frances L. Lazell the northern third (Waldo 259/314, recorded in 1900). When, some years later, the boundary of this division was in dispute between the current owners, their lawyers had occasion to inquire into the circumstances of the 1892 partition and discovered some interesting details: the smaller size of the northern parcel was explained by the fact that the land here was of greater value and that there was a very satisfactory cove from which schooners had taken considerable gravel, to the profit of Frances L. Lazell. It was also pointed out, by the widow of Henry Maker, that Frances Lazell's lawyer, General J. P. Cilley, may have antagonized the members of the commission and so secured a smaller parcel for his client than might otherwise have been the case. General Cilley himself seems to have had some interest in Lasell, for he had four or five small cottages at the northern end; moreover, when Frances Lazell sold her portion of the island in 1902, she sold to Grace Cilley Tibbetts, whom I assume to be a relative of the General. (I am indebted to a recent owner for the documentation relating to the 1892 partition.) Grace Tibbetts is shown in state tax records of 1921 as the owner of 148 acres on the island, valued at $1,480—a high valuation for the era (see Appendix 4B).

The children of James R. Maker lived on the island from the 1870s until about 1900. I am not certain whether their home was the same used by the Smiths, and perhaps by their father, but it is the same that was in use in the last decades of the twentieth century—with notable improvements—by a recent owner. The Makers farmed the central portion of the island, principally for themselves, and kept sheep, cattle, oxen, pigs, and hens. It appears to have been a subsistence farm, rather than the semicommercial operation run by the Fryes on neighboring Lime Island. George Maker was married, and at least one of his children (later Mrs. John W. Haigh of Salem, New Hampshire) was born on the island in 1880. Henry Maker left in 1889, and the rest of the family removed in 1898 or 1901; the testimony of descendants differs on the date. The Makers' residence thus spans some three decades or more, long enough to justify the name *Maker's Island*, which appears as alternate to Lasell's in most subsequent deeds.

The Makers sold their portion of the island in 1900 to Chauncey Keep, who had a caretaker there for ten or a dozen years before World War I: Samuel Dyer, a lobsterman from Islesboro. During his eventful life, Samuel lived on many islands in Penobscot Bay—Minot, High in the Muscle Ridges, Crotch in Hurricane Sound, Wooden Ball off Matinicus, and, not surprisingly, Dyer Island off Vinalhaven (interview with Frank Dyer, his son). The southern portion of Lasell passed next, in 1934, to Ira Reed of Bangor, who cut much of it for pulp during the 1930s; he loaded the wood onto barges in the large cove on the eastern shore, where he built a wharf. He sold the island to summer vacationers in 1939, and this family used the island as a summer residence during the rest of the century. Frances L. Lazell's sector, meanwhile, was held by Grace Cilley Tibbetts until 1945 when it was sold to the parents of the present owner.

An island legend, which may be more than that, though I cannot vouch for it, is that some thirty British sailors were buried on its eastern shore, not far from the boundary line dividing the two sectors. Some say they were victims in the fighting at Castine during the War of 1812, though why they should be transported so far for burial is unexplained; some say they perished of scurvy; and still others claim they died of yellow fever on a ship anchored offshore. It is said that field stones marked the graves at one time, but I believe no sign of either stones or graves has been detected for some years.

Lime

For an island of its size, Lime has an unusual and varied history. It is named on several editions of the 1776 "Atlantic Neptune," and its lime kilns are shown; the lime, it is believed, was used principally in the manufacture of mortar at Castine. In one edition of the "Atlantic Neptune" a dwelling is indicated where there is nothing but a sand spit today, north of the island, with the designation *Burbuder I.* This was probably the Little Bermuda Island referred to in later deeds: "Little Bermuda containing one third of an acre" was conveyed along with several other islands in the area to Charles and William Crooker of Bath by the States of Maine and Massachusetts in 1839 (Knox Lands 41/308; the conveyance did not include Lime Island proper). The act of incorporation of the town of Islesborough in 1788, meanwhile, mentions specifically the *Lime Islands*, "with the inhabitants thereon" (*Bangor Historical Magazine*, I: 172/178). The miniscule Burbuder Island has presumably been eroded by the seas, for its name no longer appears on contemporary charts.[9] I have no clue as to what prompted the British Admiralty's choice of the name.

Another early reference to Lime Island of historical interest is during the War of 1812: an American privateer hid behind the island to await two British vessels loading at Castine and destined for Boston; when they appeared in the eastern channel, the privateer gave chase and forced the British vessels ashore on Deer Isle, where they were taken as prizes (Noyes, Family Histories: Small).

The earliest deed I have discovered for Lime is dated 1813 and conveyed 9/16ths of the island from the owners of the Waldo Patent to Erastus Foote of Camden for $60 (Knox Lands 4/385). The entire island was released to Erastus Foote in 1838 by Massachusetts and Maine after their separation; the price was now $150 (Knox Lands 4/281). Fifteen years later Foote sold a half interest in the island to Albert J. Averell and his wife of San Francisco for $2,000, "and in consideration of love and affection" (Knox Lands 51/391). It was love and affection well paid for, inasmuch as Erastus Foote, then "of Wiscasset," appears neither to have lived on the island nor to have improved it significantly. The above deed includes a one-and-a-half-acre exception on the southeast point, representing a lease dating from 1832, with ten years still to run, to Brown and White; I have no information on Brown and White, but imagine them to be fishermen leasing a small plot for a summer camp. No major building was on the island during this period, for had there been it would surely have shown on the Waldo County Map of 1859.

Sometime after mid-century, according to Willis Rossiter of Islesboro, his grandfather David Williams used to come regularly each summer from Bath and camp on the island under his wherry.[10]

In 1885 Albert Averell, then living in Chicago, and Erastus Foote's heirs sold their respective half interests in the island for $100 each to James Frye of Pulpit Harbor (Waldo 204/480 and 482). The transaction may have been facilitated by the fact that Footes and Fryes, according to a Frye descendant, Mrs. Margaret Babcock of Camden, were related by marriage. Fryes were associated with Lime Island for the next quarter of a century, principally as summer farmers. James built a farmhouse and outbuildings, valued by Islesborough assessors in 1893 at $250; he had apparently abandoned his operations by 1896, when the island was sold "with the buildings thereon" for non-payment of taxes. Belle M. Gilkey was the buyer, and the price she paid was $8.13—surely a bargain (Knox 253/386). The island returned to the Frye family, however: it was reconveyed to Edmund C. Frye in 1900 (Knox 255/80) and farmed until 1913, when it was sold again.

This thirteen-year period was probably the most prosperous on Lime Island. According to Mrs. Babcock, three generations of the Frye family customarily lived on the island from early spring to

[9] "Little Bermuda" did, however, appear in a State of Maine tax record in 1921: owned by Grace Cilley Tibbetts and valued at $25 (see Appendix 4B).

[10] John Pendleton Farrow, the Islesborough historian, wrote a fictionalized version of David Williams's voyages—*The Romantic Story of David Robinson, among the islands off and on the coast of Maine* (Belfast: Belfast Age Publishing Company, 1898).

late fall under conditions of self-sufficiency and prosperity that were very nearly idyllic. The island's produce—garden crops and poultry, as well as lobsters and clams—was loaded onto boats at a sturdy wharf and sold, mainly at Dark Harbor.[11]

In 1913 Edmund Frye sold the island—I am not clear why—to Guy Norman; the price had now escalated to $6,000. Norman's widow sold to a weir-fishing syndicate in 1919, and weirmen dominated the island for the next quarter century.

[11] An abstract painting of the Frye farm is included in Peter Blume's *Maine and its Role in American Art, 1740–1963*, New York: The Viking Press, 1970.

The Frye homestead stood until the late 1930s, I believe, but had burned before Duane Doolittle (later editor of *Down East* magazine) bought Lime in 1942. The last weirman to live on the island was Howard Kimball of Rockport, who built a cabin over the old Frye cellar hole in 1942 or 1943; this dwelling suffered the same fate as its predecessor. I believe no one has "lived" on Lime Island since that time, apart from transient clammers, an occasional solo from Outward Bound, and, not many years ago, Mr. Doolittle himself, when a plane scheduled to pick him up after a brief visit, failed to keep the appointment because of engine trouble.

Job

Together with its barred neighbor Middle Island, Job is shown in the pre-Revolutionary "Atlantic Neptune" as *Long Island*—or, in some editions, as *Little Long Island*, to distinguish it from Long Island proper (Islesborough). By the time Islesborough was incorporated in 1789 the island was known as *Job's* and so appears on the town's first surveys by Samuel Warren (Map 1795 Islesborough). Locally it was called *Billy Job's*, and that name has persisted into this century. "Billy" was William Pendleton, one of the early settlers of Islesborough who had a lot on the southern end of the larger Long Island, and Job was his son, to whom William is said to have deeded Little Long Island in 1765. Job Pendleton himself, in a petition to the General Court of Massachusetts in 1789, claimed to have "settled" the island twenty years earlier, together with James Mathews and Shubael Williams; whether "settled" meant actually lived on, or merely taken possession of, is unclear, but Job said he bought out James Mathews's and Shubael Williams's interests in 1769 and 1772, respectively. What Job was seeking in the 1789 petition was: "how I may still be in quiet possession of my land" (Farrow, 96–97).

I think it unlikely that the General Court responded to Job Pendleton's petition, for had it done so there would doubtless be some record of the fact and a title case in 1843 would not have been necessary. In this case Charles Pendleton, grandson of Job, successfully defended his title against litigants who claimed the island from a release granted by the States of Maine and Massachusetts in 1829, following their separation. Charles Pendleton, it is true, could show no document proving the original grant of the island to his forebears, but he testified to having *seen* such an instrument among his grandfather's papers and to always having believed the title was in order; after all, he argued, Pendletons had been living unmolested on Job Island for some seventy-five years. The judge agreed with this argument, against the petitioners' claim that the Pendletons never had received a proper grant and merely passed title back and forth among themselves. But let the judge speak for himself: "It is not essential that it should appear, beyond a doubt, that a grant had been made. The presumption may be deemed one rather of law than of fact.... The object is to quiet ancient possessions, and to promote repose, after such a lapse of time, as that it may well be deemed difficult if not impossible, to prove the existence of a regular grant.... The presumption is bottomed upon the same principle as the statute of limitations, and is analogous to it."[12]

[12] Waldo County, Court Records, July Term, 1843, pp. 339–343. I am indebted to the present owners for bringing this case to my attention.

With regard to Charles Pendleton's claim of his forebears' settlement on the island before the Revolution, some editions of the "Atlantic Neptune" show that the upper—that is, northeastern third of the island—is cultivated and fenced, but none that I have seen show a building. Farrow (page 139), however, places Job in residence on his island by 1769 and states that he lived there until his death in 1794 at the age of forty-seven; his will, as probated, records that he left the upper half of the island to his second son, William, father of Charles; and for all we know William settled there in his father's home. Williamson (I: 71) notes that the island was inhabited in the 1820s. William Pendleton died in 1837, and we know Charles to have been residing on the island in 1843, the year of the case cited above; that same year he bought a parcel of the island from his brother Jefferson, a master mariner of Camden, and the deed recites that another brother, William F. Pendleton, was part owner as well (Waldo 46/322). There is, then, quite apart from Charles Pendleton's claim in court, good evidence of the family ownership of Billy Job's Island from the Revolutionary era to the 1840s and presumptive evidence of their continuous residence.

This was close to the end, however, of Pendleton residence. In 1845 Charles, then living in Camden, sold Billy Job's Island and Spruce (now Minot) to George Fisher of Cambridge, Massachusetts, for $2,250, a figure that suggests residence and improvements on one or both islands. In 1848 George Fisher conveyed the same islands to two Camden yeomen, Nathan W. Eaton and William G. Barrett (Waldo 52/578 and 65/88). A description of certain Penobscot islands in 1847 mentions Job as a "desirable residence" for someone wishing to retire from the world (Dakin, *Monterey*, Appendix). The island was surely inhabited in the 1850s, for the 1859 map of Waldo County, surveyed a few years earlier, shows Captain J. Spinney living near the northeast tip, possibly in the homestead vacated by Charles Pendleton. I have no information about Captain Spinney.

Another Charles Pendleton, Charles A., a second or third cousin of the above Charles, appears in the chain of title in 1863 when he acquired the island—apparently all of it—from Isaac Gregory (Waldo 121/287); I do not know the origin of Gregory's title, but doubt that either he or Charles A. Pendleton lived on Job.[13] The next owner, however, did: William L. Wagner bought it from Charles in 1874 (Waldo 171/217), and according to a subsequent resident, the late Harold Barton, the Wagners lived there for some years, farming and tending a small herd of cattle; on a chart printed in 1880 two buildings are shown near the northeast end, presumably the farmhouse and barn, and a wagon track runs two-thirds of the way down the island (Map 1880 CGS 4). William L. Wagner and Wilburt Robbins, a co-owner to whom Wagner sold an undivided half interest, conveyed Job Island to Jeffrey R. Brackett in 1882 (Waldo 201/150); the valuation of "Wagner's Island" was $5,000 in 1883, according to town tax records. Brackett was a professor who summered on Islesborough and was active in real estate development there. Billy Job's Island remained in his family's possession for more than eighty years.

I am not certain whether the Wagners remained on the island after the sale—valuations for the island are markedly lower in 1893 than a decade earlier ($2,500 for "Jobes Island" as a whole, with only two cows and twenty sheep)—but two other tenant families are known to have lived there during the Bracketts' ownership: the Charles Dyers, about the turn of the century (again at the northeast end, where all residents of the island lived), and from about 1910 to 1918, the Edward E. Bartons. Edward's son Harold, shortly before his death in 1975, provided me with some details of the family's tenancy on Job's Island in the second decade of the twentieth century, and I pass them on as interesting evidence of the continuity of traditional life there in the midst of the opulent summer colonies then in full sway on Islesboro and Seven Hundred Acre Island. Edward Barton was both farmer and fisherman: he tended weirs, he clammed, he put out lobster traps, and he had a flock of sheep whose wool he sold; he also kept a small vegetable garden for the family's use. The island supported more wildlife

[13] Charles A. Pendleton appeared in 1875 tax records for Islesborough with a total valuation, including the island, of $855—moderately high for the era. He had eighty sheep, presumably herded on Job Island.

then than now, for there were—in addition to the ubiquitous deer, rabbits, and water fowl—several pairs of eagles, occasional moose, and a large colony of blue herons on the southwest side. The Bartons were tenant farmers, rather than caretakers for the Bracketts, but they apparently had close relations with the professor's family; Harold, at the age of seventeen, was captain of the Bracketts' yacht. After the senior Bartons removed to Camden, Harold Barton and his wife remained another year on the island—in 1919—and they, I believe, were the last year-round residents.

The farm has long since disappeared, leaving only the cellar hole, some moldering beams that were once the barn, and the ancient well.[14] The open fields have grown in, and the forest lands, which were cut over for pulp at least once during the twentieth century, are returning to their natural state—a state the present owners, who live on Islesboro, wish to preserve.

[14] The location of the original Pendleton site is uncertain: if it was at the later site on the northeast shore facing Pendleton Point on Islesborough, the foundations were absorbed into the existing cellar, which was clearly constructed in the nineteenth century; if, on the other hand, the first Pendletons settled on the northernmost tip, where Captain Spinney's residence is shown in 1859, a shallow depression discernible in this sector could have been their cellar hole.

Minot

This pleasing and sheltered island, well inside Saunder's (now Gilkey) Harbor, must have had many early visitors, but I am unable to discover who settled there, if indeed anyone, until the latter third of the nineteenth century. There was apparently little surface water supply on the island, and this may explain the absence of a cellar hole (although one may be under the present cottage). Moreover, the absence of a name for this island before the late 1850s also suggests no early settlement, for islands were usually given the name of their settlers if no earlier name was established. Job Pendleton, in a petition to the Massachusetts General Court in 1789 for clarification of his title to Little Long Island (Job), seems to have taken it for granted that his island embraced what are now known as Job, Middle, and Minot islands (Farrow, 96). It was not until 1859, in the first map of Waldo County, that this island was given a name of its own—*Spruce*; the ledges to the west are labeled *Minot's* on this map, which suggests it was the ledges that eventually (after 1900) gave their name to the island, not vice versa. Minot may be a misspelling of Minor: a George Minor was an early settler on the facing shore of Seven Hundred Acre Island.

Minot Island was indeed considered part of Job Island until the 1860s, and since there were no settlers, no one disputed the assumption. In 1866 Charles A. Pendleton, a great-nephew of Job who had somehow managed to isolate Minot (that is, Spruce) from Billy Job and Middle, sold it to two other Pendletons—Peleg and Charles C.—for $200; it was identified in this conveyance as an island "at the southern entrance to Gilkey's Harbor and connected to the Job Islands so called" (Waldo 196/213). The latter grantee, Charles C. Pendleton, was the first known resident of the island. He appears in the 1880 federal census along with other residents of smaller islands in the area: a farmer, aged forty-seven, with wife Elizabeth, forty-nine—no children in his household. In conveying his share in Spruce Island to Jeffrey C. Brackett in 1881, "with all the buildings thereon," Charles C. Pendleton explicitly notes that the island had been "occupied by me for many years past" (Waldo 195/186); the same year, the heirs of Peleg Pendleton conveyed the other half interest in "Spruce Island" to the same J. C. Brackett.

Professor Brackett, who had an elegant "cottage" on the south end of Islesboro, made little use of Spruce or Minot Island and in 1902 conveyed it to Cleveland H. Dodge, another cottager on Islesboro. The conveyance stipulated that "no manufacturing or mechanical business whatsoever" be conducted there, including hotels, entertainment facilities, and so forth (Waldo 266/91). I judge this must be one of the earliest conservation easements on the coast of Maine. Mr.

Dodge and Professor Brackett were both involved in the Minot's Island Company that was set up the same year—1902—to manage the property, but the company apparently lasted less than a decade, for in 1912 title reverted to Professor Brackett, who sold all rights that year to Frederick R. Kellogg, yet another cottager. Both parties were evidently enough concerned about the confused identity of the island to have writen into the conveyance an explicit statement that "Little Spruce or Minot's Island" was *not* part of the "Job Islands," which Jeffrey Brackett also owned (Waldo 309/232).

The principal resident on Minot Island during the Brackett-Dodge era was Elijah Dyer. He appears in the 1900 census, a fisherman, aged seventy-four, with wife Rebecca,[15] sixty-five, and a son, thirty-one; he was doubtless on Minot Island at this date, having removed from Warren Island (see page 210). The next household in the census, probably also on the island, is that of Charles Dyer, thirty-two, wife Minnie, and family of four. Elijah was still on Minot Island when the Kelloggs took possession in 1912. A photo of him about this time at the Islesboro Historical Society—unfortunately, too scarred to be reproduced—shows him a tall, craggy man in his eighties.

The Kelloggs summered regularly on the island in their sizable cottage until after World War II when Minot Island was conveyed to new owners; the cottage still stands.

A final note of historical interest is the visit of President Nixon to Minot Island, as the guest of these owners, in August 1971. He flew in by helicopter from Bangor, landing in his hosts' front yard, a swarm of Secret Service officers having preceded him. The visit occasions a few remarks on prior presidential visits to the Penobscot Bay region. President Grant was probably the first, coming in 1873 on an informal excursion from Rockland to Mount Desert Island—an excursion that aborted because of fog, driving the revenue steamship McCULLOCH, which bore the presidential party, into North Haven; President Grant spent the night ashore, at the home of a Mr. Mullins, and proceeded directly to Bangor the next day.[16] Theodore Roosevelt visited Islesboro, probably on several occasions, but not, I believe, when he was president; he addressed a meeting at Dark Harbor in 1917 while visiting a daughter there (see page 191). Grover Cleveland may have visited his sister on Seven Hundred Acre Island, but not while he was President, since Rose Cleveland acquired her estate there after his terms in office. Franklin Roosevelt must have cruised numerous times through Penobscot Bay on his way to and from Campobello, both before and during his presidency. His last passage through the region, carrying him down Eggemoggin Reach and past Islesboro, was on a cruiser in 1941 after he signed the Atlantic Charter. And finally John F. Kennedy, an enthusiastic sailor, must also have cruised among the islands of Penobscot Bay before he became president; as president, he visited Johns Island off Pemaquid in August 1962 at the invitation of the Gene Tunneys (see Volume IV of this series, page 53). But Richard Nixon's visit to Minot Island in 1971 is the only presidential visit I know of to any of the islands dealt with in the present study.

[15] Rebecca Dyer, according to a Kellogg descendant, was addicted to smoking clay pipes, and is said to have died from clay poisoning (though the latter detail is presumably unreliable).

[16] Williamson, Joseph D., "Presidential Visits to Maine," *Historical Magazine*, No. 22, (1873), 340–45.

Ensign Islands

According to John P. Farrow (page 241), these islands were named after Jonathan Pendleton, who was appointed ensign for duty in the Islesborough area. The thesis is improbable on two counts: first, the islands are already named on British charts surveyed before the Revolutionary War when Jonathan Pendleton, who was born about 1750 or later, was presumably too young to have been named ensign—least of all by the British Admiralty; secondly, there is no record of Jonathan's possession of the two islands until the 1790s, long after the name *Ensign* was attached to them. It is quite possible, on the other hand, that they were named for some earlier ensign, and it is true that Jonathan Pendleton bought them from his father William in 1794 for £14 at the same time that he acquired the southern half of Seven Hundred Acre Island (Hancock 2/448). In 1814 William Pendleton, who was one of the early settlers on Islesborough, conveyed most of his extensive holdings there to Jonathan, in return for maintenance in his old age (Pendleton, *Brian Pendleton and his Decendants*, 110).

There is no evidence that Jonathan Pendleton, or indeed any early settlers, lived on the Ensign Islands. They were too small to sustain farming and at the most could have been used for limited pasturage. This does not, of course, mean that fishermen did not occasionally squat there; indeed, it would be surprising if they did not.

Title to the Ensign Islands was occasionally confused after the separation of Maine from Massachusetts in 1820, as a result of the land agents twice conveying them to different parties: in 1839 to Charles and William D. Crooker of Bath (Knox Lands 41/308); and in 1879 to Frances L. Lazell (Waldo 189/9). Since we are not contending with residence on the Ensign Islands, at least so far as I have discovered, there is no need to trace out here the consequences of the land agents' absentmindedness.

The Ensign Islands were acquired in 1910 by Charles Dana Gibson, whose summer home was on the east shore of Acre Island. He built a lodge on the easterly of the two islands for family outings, and this building was still standing at the end of the twentieth century, the summer residence of a grandson.

Seven Hundred Acre (Acre Island)

A voyager in 1770 calls this *Little Long Island*, to distinguish it from Long Island proper (Islesborough), and wrote disparagingly of the few "potato-planters" on the two islands (see page 187). According to British Admiralty charts, two families were on Seven Hundred Acre Island before the American Revolution—one at the northern tip, the other at the southern (Map 1776 "Atlantic Neptune"). We cannot be certain who these set-tlers were, but they are presumably among the six shown in a 1785 survey as having settled on the island "before the war": William Griffiths, George Minor, Joseph and William Philbrook, Joseph Hardy, and Nathaniel Pendleton (Maine Archives: Plan Book VIII: 44). A seventh settler, listed in the survey as having been on the island one year, was David Thomas, Jr.

Details of these early settlers are sketchy, but a few may be extracted from Farrow's *History of Islesborough* and from deeds. William Griffin (presumably Griffiths) took up a lot of 114 acres on the island in 1774, according to Farrow (page 7), and appears to have settled there immediately; nothing further is known of him, and he evidently quit the area sometime after 1785. George Miner (Minor) in 1790 conveyed a lot of similar size to Simon Dodge, and reference is made to the adjoining lot of William Griffeth (Farrow, 97). Both of these lots appear to have been in the southeast sector of Seven Hundred Acre Island—or Acre Island, as it is known locally. It is not certain whether Simon Dodge lived on the island—Farrow makes no mention of it—but a nephew, or possibly grand-nephew, Hiram Dodge, did: he acquired a lot at the northern end of the island from the owners of the Waldo Patent before 1817 (noted in Hancock 39/225), and according to Farrow (page 195) lived and died there. William and Joseph Philbrook were probably brothers, sons of an eminent early settler in Bath named Jonathan Philbrook; they appear to have come onto the island together in 1774, the year Joseph acquired a one-hundred-acre lot from Elihu Cheesbrook (Farrow, 7). It is unlikely that the latter ever lived on Acre Island. William Philbrook was drowned in 1789, but his son William, Jr. spent most of his life on the island, as did *his* sons Jabez and Ambrose. Joseph's descendants are unknown. The original Philbrook lot was on the western shore, stretching around what is still known as Philbrook Cove. I do not identify Joseph Hardy; he apparently left the island soon after 1785.

Nathaniel Pendleton—if I identify him correctly in Farrow (page 250)—would have been under twenty at the outbreak of the American Revolution and so a young, unmarried settler. It is not clear whether he lived on Acre Island proper or on Warren Island, which is called *Nat's Island* on early surveys (e.g., Map 1795 Islesborough) and, being barred to the larger island, may have been considered a part of it. Nathaniel Pendleton is noted in this vicinity in a 1783 deed. Nathaniel, according to Farrow, drowned while crossing the bay—the date is not given—but a brother, Gideon, lived for some years on the northern part of the island before removing around 1814. Another Nathaniel Pendleton (no immediate relation of the Nathaniel above) lived briefly on Acre Island in the 1820s, after quitting Mark (Resolution) Island where his father lived and before moving to the mainland (Farrow, 256). Other Pendletons, meanwhile, were associated with Acre Island in ownership but did not settle there: William Pendleton, one of the earliest settlers on the south end of Islesborough (1767), apparently claimed most of the outlying islands, including at least the southern half of Acre, which he "sold" to his son Jonathan for £14 in 1794 (Hancock 2/448). I am not certain where the boundary between the northern and southern halves of Acre Island might fall, assuming this Pendleton conveyance to have had any validity, but it surely overlapped several of the lots already described.

The 1783 deed noted above conveyed from Samuel Turner of Islesborough to a new settler, David Thomas, Jr. of Marshfield, Massachusetts, a one-hundred-acre lot on the northern tip of Acre Island; the price was $500 (Hancock 2/404). Turner had taken up this lot in 1772, according to Farrow, but there is no evidence that he had settled there or "improved" it despite the high price he exacted—a price that must have seemed altogether exorbitant to David Thomas when he was obliged, thirty-four years later, to buy his lot again from the owners of the Waldo Patent (Hancock 39/225). According to a contemporary cottage owner in this sector of the island, a grave there marks the resting place of David's wife Marcy, who died in 1788. David's second wife Abigail, who lived to 1867 and bore ten of his twelve children, was a daughter of his neighbor Nathaniel Pendleton (Farrow, 284). Another early settler was Robert Trim; his residence in the northern part of the island is referred to in a conveyance between members of the Philbrook family in 1826 (Hancock 18/356).

There appear, then, to have been at least seven or eight families living on Seven Hundred Acre Island by the 1820s—and I have undoubtedly overlooked others. Williamson (I: 71), writing about this time, describes the island as "of very good land" and indicates the principal occupation of the settlers there was farming. A traveler in 1847 writes that fourteen families were on the island, totaling one hundred persons, and "a good school house near the center" (Dakin, *Monterey*, "Appendix"). The 1850 federal census (as I read it) shows fifteen households on the island, the 1860 census sixteen (see page 206). The first map of Waldo County in 1859, meanwhile, shows fifteen families on Acre Island and the approximate location of their homesteads. I use this list of residents and a more accurate map of the island surveyed some years later to plot as nearly as I can the mid-nineteenth-century settlers; where I have supplementary information as to previous or later residence, I have indicated it in the legend accompanying the map drawn for

Seven Hundred Acre Island, c. 1859.

the original edition of this volume by A. Vogt.[17]

The names given in the legend should not be understood to represent *all* the inhabitants of Seven Hundred Acre Island in the last half of the nineteenth century; indeed, there may be as many families again that lived there for a time. Lewis Fairfield, for example, mentions the Charles Pendletons; Ed Eames who ran a packet to Camden; Billy Coombs; and several other households. However, the sites shown on the sketch are the only ones that can be identified with any confidence.

There is little concrete information about the lifestyles and habits of these settlers on Acre

[17] This supplementary information comes principally from an interview in 1916 given to John Jay Chapman by Charles E. Philbrook, then in his sixties—a great-grandson of William, Sr. (I am indebted to William A. Chanler for the transcript, which also appears in Chanler's 1984 reminiscence of Acre Island, *And Did Those Feet in Ancient Time*; see Bibliography for full listing). Further information of residence changes comes from the recollections of another former inhabitant of the island, Lewis Fairfield; and from overlays of property ownership early in the 1900s prepared by Jesse Rolerson of the Islesborough Historical Society. The detailing of house sites and roads, which is identical on various maps produced after 1880, appears to be copied from a government chart surveyed between 1863 and 1875 (Map 1880 CGS 4).

Acre Island Map Legend

Note: The italicized names below are as they appear on the 1859 map. Subsequent information, including given name, where identified, comes from the sources described in Footnote 17.

1. *Capt. F. W. Thomas.* Later Isaac Thomas.
2. *Capt. J. Thomas* (Jacob). This was near site of original home of Deacon David Thomas, a post-Revolutionary settler.
3. *H. Dodge* (Hiram). Later the Charles Hunt home (burned).
4. *A. Philbrook* (Ambrose). Later the Scott Cookson house. Ambrose's daughter married Jackson Philbrook, who built across the road (that house had been taken down by 1915).
5. *E. L. Hopkins* (Ebenezer). House down by 1900.
   Note: From Charles E. Philbrook's evidence, the sequence from north to south of the above three homesteads should be: Hopkins, Dodge, Philbrook. A property diagram around 1900 prepared by Jesse Rolerson also indicates this sequence.
6. *J. Knowles* (Joseph). The location of this homestead is uncertain.
7. *Capt. J. Philbrook* (Jabez). Built by Jabez's brother William, and later lived in by Jabez's son, Charles E. Philbrook; early in the 1900s owned by Emmetts (cottagers).
8. *Capt. E. C. Philbrook* (Elbridge). Built in 1840 by Elbridge Philbrook, son of Job Philbrook; cottage of John Jay Chapman after 1900, still standing.
9. *Capt. Philbrook.* Uncertain which Philbrook this was; later summer home of George M. Nowell (cottager).
10. *Mrs. S. Philbrook.* Presumably Sylvina, widow of Job and mother of Elbridge; later the Drinkwater house.
11. *Capt. D. Philbrook.* Probably David.
12. *J. Warren* (Jeremiah). Later home of Miss Rose Cleveland. Jeremiah, Jr. lived in house to south (unnumbered), later Miss Cleveland's cottage.
13. School. One plan of the island, based on the recollections of Lewis Fairfield, shows the school farther north along the ridge road—but I believe this is the correct location.
14. *E. S. Lawrence.* I identify neither this settler nor his homestead, apparently long since gone.
15. *J. Roe* (John Rowe). This homestead, formerly lived in by Captain Trim, was down before 1900; it is near site of Miss Cleveland's Beach House, later the Chanlers' summer cottage.
16. *D. Philbrook* (David). Later Edgar Knowles' home.
   Note: A sketch in William A. Chanler, And Did Those Feet..., *places the Knowles homestead closer to Cradle Cove.*

Island. We do, however, have good evidence of their occupations. The principal occupation on the island continued to be farming through the nineteenth century. Charles Philbrook, for example, recalling his childhood on Seven Hundred Acre Island in the 1860s, noted farming rather than fishing as the main source of revenue. Each farm had its yoke of oxen or team of horses, a few cows, sheep, hens, and ducks. A tax schedule for the island in 1884 shows individual holdings—though the valuation schedule seems short on cattle for that era (page 208). There must also have been fairly continuous lumbering as one sector of the island or another became reforested.

Meanwhile, the high number of master mariners shown on the 1859 map and in census schedules indicates that coastal and perhaps more distant shipping played a part in the economy of the island.[18] Each of these captains was presumably master of a vessel at some point. Several of them are named in Farrow's list (page 112) of Islesborough captains in mid-century, and the profits they earned must have greatly augmented the islanders' income. No shipbuilding took place on Acre Island prior to the boatyard of this century, as far as I know, but coasters were frequently rafted in Cradle Cove during the winter months; the name of this cove, indeed, according to Willis Rossiter, comes from the "cradling" (or careening) of vessels for caulking and other repair work.

There appears never to have been a store on the island in the nineteenth century—at least not one established long enough to be remembered—but in the 1890s an inter-island steamer called twice a week at Jabez' Head in Philbrook Cove to pick up produce and leave supplies; a town road, now wholly grown over, was maintained to the landing. As for a church, I have never heard of one on Acre Island, but it would surprise me greatly if services were not held more or less regularly at the school. If not there, then they were surely held in private homes—e.g., the Thomases', for the original David Thomas was a deacon of the Baptist Church, and I believe his youngest son Jacob followed in his father's footsteps.

[18] See also the occupations on Islesborough proper in 1880: table on page 278.

Despite the apparent prosperity of Seven Hundred Acre Island in mid-century, the population began to fall off after the Civil War and declined sharply in the late 1890s. Charles Philbrook noted that forty-five children were in the school in the 1860s, out of sixty registered on the island. In 1893, according to a teacher of that era (a Miss Pendleton, cited in William A. Chanler's booklet), there were twenty-three pupils in the District 1 school. The next year the school report noted that "new seats, desks and floor have been put in the school house on Acre island and the building put in thorough repair." In the spring of 1902 the school was temporarily suspended when enrollment fell to three. It was closed for good in 1905.

The inhabitants quit this island for many of the same reasons that caused a general exodus from Penobscot Bay islands at the turn of the century: farming, once favored because of the easy access to markets by sea, was no longer profitable with the improvement of rail communication on the mainland; the end of the sailing era put into retirement a category of mariners who had had the luxury of living on distant islands like this one between voyages; as secondary school education became more general, island families moved to larger communities when their teenage children came to high school age. An additional factor in the depopulation of Seven Hundred Acre Island was the insatiable thirst of the cottagers for land. As early as 1890 Acre Island was surveyed by the Islesborough Land and Improvement company with a view to locating new cottage sites.[19] The Thomases sold land at the north end of the island—and themselves moved—before 1900. Soon after 1900, Miss Rose E. Cleveland, sister of Grover Cleveland, and Miss Evelyn O. Ames of Boston began buying lots that when finally put together constituted a domain of some four hundred acres. George M. Nowell of Boston had extensive acreage at both the north and south ends of the island. Charles Dana Gibson, meanwhile, bought eleven acres on the northeast point where he constructed a "cottage" that over the years took on baronial proportions.

[19] See the Aspinwall and Lincoln Survey at the Islesboro Historical Society.

It is not the object of this study to explore the residence of cottagers on Acre Island, but the activities of Miss Cleveland and Charles Dana Gibson form such a prominent part of the island's history that to ignore them altogether would be capricious. Miss Cleveland's object in acquiring such a large portion of this land was to create a model farm, which she proceeded to do. She had both tenant and paid farmers, and this for a time had the effect of bringing back the population—or at least curbing the exodus. She built a seawall along the southwest cove, behind which the hay in her salt marsh grew to a height of seven or eight feet; she cultivated many acres of meadowland along the ridge with teams of magnificent horses and oxen; and she raised livestock. Her home was near the highest point of the island in the old Warren homestead, as shown on the Vogt map. She also had a large wharf and an elegant beach house on the main channel opposite Minot Island.

Sketch of Rose E. Cleveland's cottage on Seven Hundred Acre Island, drawn from a photograph in the Boston Sunday Globe *of September 25, 1904; the cottage was remodeled from the Warren farm. (Courtesy of Earle G. Shettleworth, Jr., in whose volume* Summer Cottages of Islesboro *Islesboro, ME: 1989, this sketch appears.)*

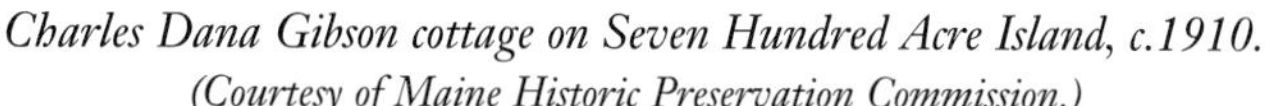

Charles Dana Gibson cottage on Seven Hundred Acre Island, c.1910. (Courtesy of Maine Historic Preservation Commission.)

The distance between the wharf and her house being nearly a mile, Miss Cleveland kept a carriage and coachman on the island for her convenience and that of her guests.

Farming did not preoccupy her entirely, for she entertained generously and is said to have been a spirited and engaging conversationalist. According to William A. Chanler, a summer resident on Acre Island for many years,[20] the monologuist Ruth Draper gained inspiration for her subsequent career from listening to Rose Cleveland, whom she often visited as a teenager while vacationing at Dark Harbor.

The Cleveland-Ames farm was given up in the 1920s and the land sold to other cottagers. The Chanlers, who owned much of it and used the beach house as their summer home, carried on something of Miss Cleveland's husbandry in raising sheep for several years and later mink and rabbits. But Miss Cleveland's farm buildings are long since down, and the site—I regret to say—is now the island dump.

I have less to say explicitly of Charles Dana Gibson, but the mere mention of his name—and that of his wife Irene Langhorne, model for the famous "Gibson girl"—evokes an era to which much sentiment attaches. Among the many creations on the Gibsons' point was a medieval stone chapel, a landmark to all who pass to and from Gilkey Harbor; it was used for social gatherings more often, it is said, than for baptisms. Franklin Roosevelt, an admirer of Charles Dana Gibson, sent an amphibious plane to remove him from the island when he was stricken there during World War II. Gibson descendants still summer on the point and now own most of the island.

There is a last enterprise on Seven Hundred Acre Island that should be recorded: the Norton boatyard in Cradle Cove. Sidney Norton, a native of Camden who was captain of Miss Cleveland's Friendship sloop, founded the yard in the 1920s after the farm was given up; the equipment was transferred to Acre Island from a defunct boatyard on Islesboro, and the land on Cradle Cove was acquired from the Knowleses, the last of the old families to live there. Albert Norton, Sidney's son, ran the yard from 1933 until the early 1970s when it was sold to Gibson descendants. For some years the boatyard induced a number of employees to live on the island, but by the 1990s—while the boatyard, which serves all of Islesboro, carried on—only a few year-round residents still lived on Acre Island itself.

[20] William Chanler grew up on the island during the transition from the year-round indigenous community to predominantly seasonal residence. His booklet noted above (*And Did Those Feet...*) illuminates the transition.

Seven Hundred Acre Island Residence, 1800–1880

Note: This table shows the residents of Seven Hundred Acre Island from 1800 to 1880, according to the author's reading of federal census schedules. Age of resident is as shown at initial appearance in schedules. Wives, if shown, are in parentheses. Occupations are indicated as follows: Fa, farmer; Fi, fisherman; S, sailor, mariner; M, master mariner, or sea captain; C, carpenter; L, laborer. Males in a household are to left of slash, females to right. Sums following householders in 1850–1870 represent the highest valuations of those years (real estate and personal valuations combined).

Head of Household	1800	1810	1820	1830	1840	1850	1860	1870	1880
Griffen [Griffiths], Wm., 45+	3/3								
Dodge, Simon, -26	2/1	4/3	4/3						
Philbrook, Joseph, -45	4/4	3/6	-	2/2	1/1				
Philbrook, Wm., Jr., 45+, Fa	7/3	7/2	8/5						
Thomas, David, 45+	6/1	5/5	5/6	5/4	2/2				
Hardy, Joseph, 45+	1/3								
Philbrook, Job, -45 (Sylvina), $1,100	2/5	5/6		5/6	5/6	2/3[21]	1/2	0/1	
Philbrook, Jonathan, -45	2/4								
Philbrook, Elisha, -45, Fa		1/5	3/5						

Head of Household	1800	1810	1820	1830	1840	1850	1860	1870	1880
Trim, Robert, -45 (Lucy), Fa, $1,000		2/5	4/3	4/2	5/1	1/2			
Philbrook, David, 30 (Margaret), Fa, $800			2/5	3/3	5/4	2/3			
Thomas, Daniel, 30s				2/3					
Warren, Jeremiah, 22 (Abagail), Fa, $1,250				2/2	4/2	4/2	3/1		
Dodge, Hiram, 34 (Elizabeth), S/Fa, $1,450				3/3	5/5	3/5	2/3	0/1	
Drinkwater, James, 23 (Henrietta), Fa				1/3	-	-	-	-	2/1
Philbrook, Jabez, 28 (Julia/Eliza), S, $1,500				1/5	4/3	4/2	4/3	4/2	1/3
Smith, John, 30 (Sally), Fa				3/4	-	2/6			
Warren, George, 50s [22]				6/4	2/2				
Philbrook, David II, 20s					1/3				
Philbrook, Ambrose, 36 (Lydia), S/Fa, $900					3/2	3/3	2/3		2/2
Warren, Thomas, 30s					2/1				
Thomas, Isaac, 30s					2/0				
Thomas, Jacob, Jr., 26 (Julia), Fa, $800					3/1	-	4/3		
Drinkwater, William, 30s					5/3				
Philbrook, Job Jr., 37 (Alice), S					3/4	7/2			
Hutchins, Albert, 20s					1/2?				
Philbrook, Ruel, 60 (Submit), L						1/1			
Smith, John, Jr. (Julia), S, 300						2/3			
Knowles, Robert, 25 (Grace), Fa, $900						2/3			
Philbrook, Elbridge, 31 (Angela/Elizabeth), S/Fa, $1,300						4/2	5/4	1/1	2/8
Knowles, Joseph, 27 (Lenora), S, $400						3/2	3/5	-	3/5
Philbrook, Daniel, 35 (Lydia), Fa/M, $2,400						4/5	4/3	2/2	1/2
Philbrook, James Jackson, 28 (Lydia), M $600							2/3	3/3	
Cookson, Walter S., 21 (Almira), S/M, $600							2/1	3/2	2/3
Warren, Jeremiah. Jr., 29 (Marinda/Charlotte), M, $1,100							1/2	4/4	
Warren, George W., 35 (Martha), Fa, $1,050							5/1		
Thomas, William, 30 (Ann), S, $100							1/1		
Norton, Vincent, 40 (Clarinda), Fi, $400							5/4		
Hopkins, Eben L., 37 (Elizabeth), Fi, $300								3/3	
Hunt, Caroline (widow of John W. Hunt)								2/3	
McFarland, Zedoc, 32 (Susan)								2/1	
Warren, Martin V., 31 (Cindarella), S/M, $1,400								1/3	2/4
Philbrook, Ambrose, Jr, 31, S								1/1	
Philbrook, Elbridge, Jr., 25 (Georgianna), S								5/2	
Thomas, Castanus, 33 (widow)								2/2	
Coombs, Wm. R, 70 (Emily), Fa, $1,100								2/4[23]	1/2
Hassell, George F., 38 (Medora), Fi									2/1
Philbrook, Charles, 28 (Lucy), Fi									1/3
Totals:									
Number of households	6	8	7	12	17	15	16	15	11
Number of residents	38	61	64	78	95	88	89	64	52

[21] Sylvina is head of household in 1850 and thereafter.
[22] George Warren and several of his sons (e.g., Jeremiah, above) lived some years on Warren Island.
[23] Including Climona Marshall and family.

Seven Hundred Acre Island: Valuations, 1884

Note: The taxpayers on Seven Hundred Acre Island in 1884 were valued as shown below. ***NR*** *designates a non-resident taxpayer. There was one additional resident on the tax list, with no valuation: Simeon Dyer. The key to the columns is as follows:*

1 Acre	Acreage owned	**6 Ox**	Number of oxen
2 Valu	Value of acreage ($)	**7 Hors**	Number of horses (all ages)
3 Hom	Value of homestead	**8 Cow**	Number of cattle (all ages)
4 Barn	Value of barns, outbuildings	**9 Shep**	Number of sheep
5 Tre	Value of total real estate	**10 Total**	Total valuation

Householder	**1 Acre**	**2 Valu**	**3 Hom**	**4 Barn**	**5 Tre**	**7 Ox**	**8 Hors**	**9 Cow**	**10 Shep**	**Total**
Drinkwater, James	60	480	275	10	765		6		12	885
Hassel, Joseph	20	160	200	15	375		2			410
Pendleton, Jenni	40	320	200	50	570		5		12	2,597
Philbrook, Jabez	15	120	75	10	205		3	4	8	273
Philbrook, Elbridge G.	35	280	250	75	605	2	4	2	6	717
Philbrook, Daniel	70	560	250	40	850	2	4	5	8	1,102
Thomas, Cartman M.	30	240	150	20	410	2	3		10	525
Warren, Martin V. (heirs)	40	320	350	35	705					705
Warren, Jeremiah	20	160	250	10	420		1		2	449
Knowlton, L. A. **NR**	14	154	100							504
Thomas, Fred (heirs) **NR**	15	120	10		130					130
Philbrook, J. J. **NR**	15	120								120
Young, Sarah **NR**	8	96								96

Warren

There was residence on this island before the Revolution, according to some editions of British Admiralty charts: a single homestead near the center of the island. The settler may have been Nathaniel Pendleton, who is said to have been living before the Revolutionary War in the northeast sector of Seven Hundred Acre Island; this sector may well have embraced Warren Island, since the latter is barred to Acre Island. The island is named *Nat's Island* in a 1795 survey, which strengthens the supposition of Nathaniel Pendleton's residence (Map 1795 Islesborough). The island appears to have had an even earlier name, *Marshall's* or *William Pendleton's Island*—one of six inhabited islands, according to Williamson (II: 542), that were included in the petition for incorporation of Islesborough in 1789. Marshalls were settled in the area at this time, and one of them may well have been living on the island along with Nathaniel Pendleton; William Pendleton, meanwhile, Nathaniel's father, was one of the largest landowners on Islesborough, and it would not be in the least surprising for him to lay claim to this convenient island in Saunder's (now Gilkey) Harbor. The name Marshall's or William Pendleton's, however, is not found again, and indeed the *official* act of incorporation of Islesborough names only four islands, excluding this one.

By 1803 the island had another resident and another name, and here we are on firmer ground: George Warren at the time of his marriage to Lydia Hatch, according to town records, is said to be "of *Warren's Island*" (Farrow, 294). Although he did not acquire title from the Pendletons until 1822 (Hancock 43/347), he and his descendants appear to have lived on the island for about sixty years. A traveler in the 1840s reports the Warren family living in a sturdy farmhouse at the highest point of the island, with abundant cleared acreage surrounding the farm (Dakin, *Monterey*, Appendix). This farm does not appear on the Waldo County map of 1859, but the map shows Captain J. W. Warren—presumably Jeremiah, son of George—living on the northwest shore opposite Acre Island. Another residence shown on the same map is that of J. Williams on the northeast tip; I am assuming that this was the home of *David* Williams.

In 1861 George Warren, by then a very old man, sold the island for $600 to Mansfield Clark of Islesborough, "reserving one acre now owned by David Williams" (Waldo 116/325). Williams, who came from Bath, was married to a widow from Acre Island, Mrs. Samuel Haskell: according to her grandson Willis Rossiter, this family lived midway along the northeast shore of Warren Island. David was reportedly still on the island in 1878, when another conveyance set aside "one acre now owned and occupied by David Williams" (Waldo 179/181). The family apparently removed soon after this date; David died in Lincolnville in 1891 (Farrow, 301).

From later deeds we learn of two additional residents in the 1880s and 1890s: a conveyance in 1891 from Henry Harwood notes that the parcel in question on the east side of the island was "formerly occupied by Joseph McKinney and now by me" (Waldo 232/85). Willis Rossiter, a lifelong inhabitant of Islesboro, gives further evidence of residence on Warren Island. Elijah Dyer, he reports, lived there for a time with his family before removing to Minot Island. McKinneys and Dyers appear side by side in the 1880 federal census for Islesborough, and I believe they were then living on Warren Island: Joseph McKinney, fisherman, aged forty, with wife Phebe and five minor children; Elijah Dyer, fisherman, aged sixty, with wife Rebecca, a son Samuel A., nineteen, and three minor sons; also Elijah's in-laws, Andrew

Mon Rêve and guests on Warren Island; this was the cottage William H. Folwell built to entertain customers of his woolen mills in Philadelphia. It was built early in the 1900s and burned in 1918.
(Courtesy of Maine Department of Parks and Recreation.)

and Mary McKinney, respectively aged seventy-five and seventy. Elijah is shown in the 1880 agricultural census with twenty acres under cultivation, fifty-five in pasture, and twenty sheep (see Appendix 3). Islesborough tax records for 1884 show Elijah Dyer on *Dyer's Island* with a considerable estate: a seventy-five-acre farm valued at $600; livestock, including sheep and horses, valued at $127; a boat valued at $50—total, $777. Another resident, Henry Harwood, is also shown on "Dyer's Island," with a total valuation of $45. Although I find nothing to show that Elijah Dyer held title to the island and although the name "Dyer's Island" does not appear in other records, I believe this was in reality Warren Island and that Elijah Dyer was its principal resident in 1884. The island, however, was not long occupied year-round after this date, though it continued to be used by transient clammers. The Elijah Dyers removed to Minot Island in the 1890s.

In 1899 the then-owners of the island, Joshua and Benjamin C. Adams of Camden, sold it outright to a cottager from Philadelphia, William H. Folwell. Folwell, who already had a summer home on Seal Island, built an elaborate cottage on Warren—which he named *Mon Rêve*—to lodge the customers of his Philadelphia woolen mills. Folwell himself did not live to see the completion of this cottage, but it played its part in Folwell family and other celebrations for a dozen or more years. Gradually, however, the un-supervised building was vandalized until in 1919 it mysteriously burned. The island went to the town of Islesboro for delinquent taxes and in 1960 was given to the State of Maine as a state park; indeed, it is the *only* island in the state park catalog. The name *Mon Rêve* never took hold (mercifully)—perhaps because it violated local ears.[24]

[24] An account of the Folwell era is in *Island Journal*, VI: 17, "Island Park Place," by Mike Brown.

Spruce

This island is called *Spruce* on maps of the late eighteenth century (e.g., Map 1795 Islesborough), and the name has evidently never changed. It was conveyed by John and Thomas Pendleton to John Gilkey early in the nineteenth century (mentioned in an 1822 deed, Hancock 43/347), but neither Gilkey nor later owners lived there. It was used for pasture land, especially by residents on Warren, and perhaps for periodic cutting of the spruce that gave the island its name. A visitor in the 1880s called them fir trees and wrote ecstatically of their "most gorgeous development, rivalling the noted groves of arbor vitae that have been established at enormous expense on Lake Windermere in the English Lake District" (Cook, *An Eastern Tour*, 258). Perhaps this stand of fir and the island's prominent position in Gilkey Harbor, facing a host of elegant "cottages" built at the end of the century, had something to do with its remaining uninhabited: the Dark Harbor Improvement Association, in which all property owners had a significant interest, was able to keep Spruce Island from being developed.

Pendletons again figure in ownership of Spruce Island in the twentieth century, Lorenzo Pendleton acquiring title by 1909 and willing it to his heirs in 1921 (Waldo 340/158). It subsequently passed to summer residents on Islesboro. Spruce Island was inadvertently burned over in 1937, possibly by careless picnickers, and its famous groves were still struggling back to maturity in the 1990s.

Flat, Seal, and Ram

These three islands changed hands numerous times during the nineteenth century and often changed their names in the process. An 1877 deed of the islands to Lewis A. Knowlton from Samuel T. Kellar, who claimed title through a conveyance from Mrs. Frank Russ "about twenty-five years ago," named them *Flat*, *Spruce*, and *Rain*—surely a mistranscription of *Ram* (Waldo 176/248); this island has also been named *Hog* (e.g., in a 1937 edition of CGS 310). Spruce became *Seal* and appeared on all *official* maps after the 1880s under this name; in the Islesboro summer colony, however, it was known as *Folwell's Island*, after William H. Folwell, who bought it from Warren Reed, a rusticator acquaintance in Northport, and built an elegant summer cottage there in the 1890s. He named the island fancifully *Isola Bella* (after an island in the Italian lake district), but to my knowledge the name never had currency outside the family.

William H. Folwell died in 1901 and left his island archipelago to his wife and children: the three islands noted here and Warren (see page 208). Only Ram Island remained in the family; it is still used seasonally by descendants. Seal Island (*Isola Bella*) was sold in the 1940s to Horace Hildreth of Bangor, who restored the cruelly vandalized cottage, and in due course sold to other cottagers at Islesboro. The Hildreth family acquired Flat Island as well and gave it to the State of Maine as a bird sanctuary (*Island Journal*, VI: 19).

Hutchins

The names *Hutchins* and *Hutchinson* were evidently interchangeable, for maps and deeds show both. According to Farrow (page 226), the island is named after John Hutchins, Jr., who lived there in the middle of the nineteenth century. His home is shown at the east end of the island, as that of J. Hutchinson, on the Waldo County map of 1859. A recent survey of the island notes (without source) that John Hutchins, Jr. lived there with his wife and four daughters ("Hutchins Island," prepared for the Island Institute). Another resident shown on the 1859 map, on the south shore, is W. Adams, whom I take to be William C. Adams, son-in-law of John Hutchins, Jr. (Farrow, 166).

In 1874 Annis Hutchins or Hutchinson, said to be the widow of John, conveyed a lot on the island to William C. Adams (Waldo 164/418). Then in 1879 Annis Hutchinson and Rhoda A. Page, whom I do not identify, conveyed a fourteen-acre lot to Lewis Knowlton (Waldo 190/320); in this deed the lot is described as on what was "formerly Fields Coombs Island," implying that the Coombs family, which also settled in this sector of Islesborough, owned the island before the Hutchinses. Lewis Knowlton, who dabbled in island properties, also acquired a mortgage on a seven-acre parcel from Sybil J. Weed in 1874 and foreclosed in 1889—at which time, if I read the conveyances correctly, Knowlton was in full possession. Knowlton is shown as the owner in 1883 tax records, the island proper valued at $243, a dwelling at $75. The survey noted above states that residence on the island ended in 1884, apart from a squatter early in the twentieth century named Iver Johnson.

Coastal charts surveyed in the 1860s and 1870s show four buildings together in the center of Hutchins and indicate walls enclosing cleared fields (e.g., Map 1882 CGS 311). There were also at least three dug wells, as well as an apple orchard. It is apparent, then, that the residents were predominantly farmers, not fishermen.

The 1986 Island Institute profile of Hutchins Island, the purpose of which was to generate a stewardship plan for limited public access, identified no fewer than eighty-five species in its flora inventory—from the common lowbush blueberry to the pipsissewa.

Mid-Penobscot Bay Islands

A common feature of this scattered group of islands in the middle of Penobscot Bay is that none has ever been part of any community. They are still called "unorganized lands" of the State of Maine. Deer Isle, it is true, once sought to reclaim the closest of the islands—for tax purposes—on the basis of an ancient ship channel that was said to have been the dividing line between its lands and the great beyond; nothing came of its suit. The mid-Penobscot Bay islands themselves were unified for a brief time only, during and after the Civil War when the settlers banded together, first, to resist recruitment, and later, to claim compensation for their volunteers. The organization, which included Eagle, Butter, Bradbury, Bear, and Great Spruce Head islands, was called the Eagle Island Military Plantation; nothing is heard of it after 1873 when State of Maine officials awarded the residents $433.33 for their wartime efforts (Enk, *Story of Eagle Island*, 211–13).

Even without formal ties, however, the inhabitants of these islands—a dozen of them were settled for varying periods of time—had close relationships. They assisted each other at harvest time; they traded their produce; the children often attended school together, on Eagle Island or later at high school on Deer Isle or North Haven; and not infrequently they intermarried. The islands are distinctive, however, and their histories diverge more often than they merge. I include a list of State of Maine taxes on the mid-Penobscot Bay islands in 1887 and 1896, from records in Augusta, as well as valuations for 1912 (Appendix 4A).

The islands in this division are noticed clockwise in a large, loose circle, beginning with Western off Cape Rosier and ending with Beach.

Residents of the Mid-Penobscot Bay Islands, 1800–80

Note: The following lived on mid-Penobscot Bay islands between 1800 and 1880 (in a few cases until 1900), according to the federal census. Spouses, if known, are in parentheses. Age, if shown, is at first appearance. Occupations are indicated as follows: Fa, farmer; Fi, fisherman; S, sailor or mariner; K, lightkeeper. Males in a household are to left of slash, females to right. Dollar amounts after some householders represent their highest real estate and personal valuations calculated by the census-taker between 1870 and 1880. Annual totals are shown for the larger islands.

Beach Island:	**1800**	**1810**	**1820**	**1830**	**1840**	**1850**	**1860**	**1870**	**1880**
Pendleton, Mark		3/1							
Miller, Asa			1/2						
Haycock, Ralph			1/1						
Appleton, Francis			2/1						
Grover, George				5/3					
Linzey [Lindsay], James				2/2					
Gray, Jesse, 35					4/4				
Dodge, Joseph, 30 (Rebecca), Fa						2/1			
Ranlett, Daniel, 27 (Jane), Fa $600						3/3			

	1800	1810	1820	1830	1840	1850	1860	1870	1880
Stockbridge, Robert, 46 (Laura), ropemaker							5/5		
Lloyd, Elizabeth, 22							0/2		
Staples, James, 59 (Rosanna), Fa $775								3/6	1/3
Staples, John, 41 (Almira), Fa									4/6
Total (Beach Island):		**4**	**8**	**12**	**8**	**9**	**12**	**9**	**14**

Bear Island:	1800	1810	1820	1830	1840	1850	1860	1870	1880
Monroe, James				4/3					
Eaton, Peter Hardy, 40s					6/5				
Eaton, Jonathan H., 28 (Martha), Fi						5/2	5/2	2/2	1/1
Eaton, John, 23, Fi							2/1		
Eaton, Peter H., Jr., 37 (Louisa), Fa/Fi $950							4/1	4/1	3/1
Harvey, Joseph, 30 (Mary A.)								2/2	
Total (Bear Island):				**7**	**11**	**7**	**15**	**13**	**6**

Bradbury:	1800	1810	1820	1830	1840	1850	1860	1870	1880
Vickery, John (Elizabeth)						?[1]			
Staples, James, 49 (Rosanna), Fa $780[2]							9/3		
Staples, James, Jr., 24 (Esther), Fi								4/2	

Butter Island:	1790	1800	1810	1820	1830	1840	1850	1860	1870	1880	1900
Annis, Ralph	11										
Small, Job (tenant)		?[3]									
Witherspoon, John, 44 (Abigail), Fa			6/4	4/4	3/2	3/2					
Witherspoon, Unadilla, 24 (Eliz.), Fa $4,400				1/1	2/4	5/3	5/1	3/3	4/2[4]		
Dyer, Walden, 38 (Louise), Fi										4/2	
Blaisdell, James W., 46 (Jennie), Fa										6/4[5]	
Shephard, Eldridge, 39 (Elvira), caretaker											2/6
Total (Butter Island):	**11**	**-**	**10**	**10**	**11**	**13**	**6**	**6**	**6**	**16**	**8**

Eagle Island:	1810	1820	1830	1840	1850	1860	1870	1880	1900
Banks, William	7/2								
Quinn, Samuel, 31, Fa $800		5/2	5/5	7/7	4/6				
Spear, John, K			2/1	2/2					
Quinn, Samuel, Jr., 29 (Louise), Fa $2,160					3/1	7/2	8/2	4/4[6]	
Quinn, Joseph W., Fa					2/4	4/6			
Quinn, James, 37 (Sylvia), Fa/Fi					3/5	2/4	1/1		
Carver, Israel, 39 (Sarah) $800					2/4	4/3	1/1		
Smith, William, K					5/3				
Quinn, John L., 34 (Mary), Fa/Fi						2/2	1/2	1/1	
Carver, Moses, 31, Fi						2/2			
Dyer, George, 33						2/2			
Clay, Russell, 40, K						2/2			

[1] The Vickerys are not shown on Bradbury Island in the 1850 census, but are known to have lived a few years on the island in the late 1840s.
[2] James Staples moved to Beach Island in the 1860s.
[3] I do not find this household in census schedules, but believe it to have been on the island in 1801.
[4] Household includes three farm workers: George A. Briggs, eighteen; Levi Gould, fifty-seven; and Wilbert Carver, thirteen.
[5] Household includes U. D. Witherspoon, eighty-nine.
[6] Louise, widowed, is head of household in 1880.

	1810	1820	1830	1840	1850	1860	1870	1880	1900
Quinn, William, 35 (Orena), Fa $1,835							2/2	1/3[7]	
Carver, Seneca, 24 (Clara), Fi							1/3		
Witherspoon, Rodney, 39, K							1/2		
Sweetland [Swartland], Anbar, 58, K								2/2	
Brown, George, 25 (Abbie), Fi								1/2	2/5
Quinn, Edgar, 21 (Alze), Fa/Fi								1/1	
Stewart, Robert H., 34 (Lizzie), Fi								3/1	
Raynes, Charles, 23 (Ada), S								3/1	
Ball, Howard, 36 (Lucy), K									4/4
Quinn, John H., 42 (Hattie), Fa									2/2
Howard, Charles (Elva)									3/3
Quinn, Edgar, 38									2/1
Smiley, Mary, 46									0/2
Totals (Eagle Island):	**9**	**7**	**13**	**18**	**42**	**49**	**26**	**31**	**30**

Eaton Island:	**1810**	**1820**	**1830**	**1840**	**1850**	**1860**	**1870**	**1880**	**1900**
Gardiner, Cephas, 60, Fi						1/0			

Great Spruce Head:	**1810**	**1820**	**1830**	**1840**	**1850**	**1860**	**1870**	**1880**	**1900**
Walton, Paul, 40s (Abigail), Fa	6/3	5/3	4/3	4/4	2/2				
Dow, John	3/4								
Staples, William	3/3								
Wright, William, -45, Fa		1/1							
Thomas, William, 45+, Fi		1/1							
Munroe, James, 20s (Sally), Fa		1/1	4/3	-	2/2				
Eaton, Peter Hardy, 30s			3/3						
Haskell, Thomas P., 20s (Phebe)				2/2					
Walton, Ambrose, 40 (Adelaide), Fa $1025					2/2	4/2	4/2	2/3	
Parsons, Josiah, 32 (Margaret), Fi $1160					4/3	7/5	7/5		
Herriman, Josiah, 52 (Margaret), Fi							1/3		
Eaton, John B., 30 (Hannah), Fa/Fi									7/1
Total (Great Spruce Head):	**22**	**14**	**20**	**12**	**19**	**18**	**22**	**5**	**8**

Hog Island:	**1790**	**1800**	**1810**	**1820**	**1830**	**1840**	**1850**	**1860**	**1870**	**1880**	**1900**
Morrison, James M., 38, Fi								2/6			
Turner, Austin, 27 (Eliza), Fi									3/1		
Turner, Warren, 29 Sarah), Fa									1/1		
Carver, Fred A., 30 (Etta), Fa/Fi										2/3	-[8]

Little Sprucehead:	**1790**	**1800**	**1810**	**1820**	**1830**	**1840**	**1850**	**1860**	**1870**	**1880**	**1900**
Richardson, John			7	2/3	3/3	3/3					

Pickering:	**1790**	**1800**	**1810**	**1820**	**1830**	**1840**	**1850**	**1860**	**1870**	**1880**	**1900**
Pickering, Samuel, 45+	3/3	1/1									
Pickering, Daniel, -45	1/2	1/3	?								
Pickering, Samuel, Jr., -26		1/3	2/6								

[7] Orena, widowed, is head of household in 1880.
[8] I do not know the size of Fred Carver's household in 1900, but it would have included a number of hired hands.

	1790	1800	1810	1820	1830	1840	1850	1860	1870	1880	1900
Simpson, Samuel, 40s					6/3						
Gray, Josiah, 40s						5/4					
Black, Samuel, 30s						2/3					
Green, Charles T., Fa $2,000							4/2	7/4?			
Staples, James, 39 (Rosanna), Fa							6/1				
Edburg, G. W., 40 (Eliza), Fa $3,136									1/2		
Dow, Amos, 27 (Lydia), Fa										5/2	
Total (Pickering Island):	**9**	**10**	**8**	**-**	**9**	**14**	**13**	**11**	**3**	**7**	

WESTERN:	**1800**	**1810**	**1820**	**1830**	**1840**	**1850**	**1860**	**1870**	**1880**	**1900**
Sawyer, William, 66; David, 47; Fred, 18, Fi									3/0	

PUMPKIN:	**1800**	**1810**	**1820**	**1830**	**1840**	**1850**	**1860**	**1870**	**1880**	**1900**
Tibbetts, John L., 62, K							1/2			
Babson, Charles. L., K								-[9]		

RESOLUTION (MARK):	**1800**	**1810**	**1820**	**1830**	**1840**	**1850**	**1860**	**1870**	**1880**	**1900**
Pendleton, Joshua, 30s		5	7/1	3/2						

[9] Charles L. Babson was keeper of Pumpkin Island Light from 1870 to 1902, but may have had his normal residence on Little Deer Isle; I do not find him in census schedules for the mid-Penobscot Bay islands.

Western

This island has been called *Western* from Revolutionary times, obviously because of its position as the most westerly of the three islands off Cape Rosier: Hog, Pond, and Western. Western's early history, associated with the other two, and it is no surprise to find that ownership of one often entailed ownership of all three. In 1833, if not earlier, Western and Pond appear to have been temporarily separated from Hog in ownership when they were conveyed from Hezekiah Rowell to Joshua Carpenter, both land brokers (Hancock 57/374).

I know of no sustained habitation on Western Island before the last quarter of the nineteenth century, and I doubt that there was any. Its size (twenty-seven acres) and topography did not recommend Western for individual farming; the most use any farmer could expect to have had was pasturage. Sheep from farms on Cape Rosier presumably grazed on the island throughout the nineteenth century, and we know Western to have been used for this purpose by Fred Carver after he moved onto Hog Island in 1880. He owned Western, Pond, and half of Beach Island at one time, as well as Hog, and his farming activities extended over all four.

Fishermen, not farmers, were the only year-round residents known to have lived on Western. The 1880 census lists for *West Pond Island*: William Sawyer, sixty-six; David Sawyer, forty-seven, a brother; and Frederick, eighteen, a nephew and seaman. A chart printed in 1882 shows their dwelling at the narrowest point of the island facing Cape Rosier (Map 1882 CGS 309); the same building appears on surveys twenty years later (e.g., Map 1907 Penobscot Bay quad). According to a recent owner, there is no evidence of this homesite today, which suggests it had no cellar. There is, however, a brick-walled well on the island that may have been dug in this era.

I have no further information concerning the Sawyers, or how long they remained on Western, but it is more than likely that they engaged in weir fishing. A map of 1873 in the possession of David Littleton-Taylor of Lincolnville shows a salmon weir off Western Island; and several herring weirs are known to have been set between Western and Pond islands around the turn of the century. Fred Littlefield of Brooksville, who used to help tend these weirs for his uncle, Lou Herrick, speaks of catches that sometimes amounted to $5,000 in one night and an annual catch of $50,000 after expenses.

Another activity on Western Island around the turn of the century brought additional persons periodically to the area. It was more recreational than commercial, I assume, and hardly sportsman-like by today's standards, but it was a popular entertainment at the time: this was the shooting of sandpipers, which abounded on both Western and Pond islands. According to Clara Orcutt Jesse Bakeman Drexel of Isles-boro organized hunting parties during the sandpiper season to both Western and Pond islands, which he "rented" for the purpose from Orcutt's stepfather Fred Carver.

Title to Western Island passed eventually to Fred Carver's heirs. After World War II it was sold by Clara Orcutt to the Robinsons of Cape Rosier, and eventually, in 1972, it was sold to a theologian who summered on Little Deer Isle.

Pond (off Cape Rosier)

This island, which has been called Pond from the post-Revolutionary era and has never to my knowledge had another name, has been closely associated in ownership and history with its neighbors, Hog and Western. Of the three, Pond appears to have been the most regularly used by Indians, to judge from the extensive middens on the southerly shore.

The pond at the southeast end, which gives the island its name and occupies nearly half of its total area, was once a freshwater pond, it is said. Inevitably legends have sprung up about treasure hidden there: French treasure from the pre-Revolutionary era, a British paymaster's chest from the War of 1812, and, of course, Jacob Astor's fortune. At some point in the past the ocean broke through, so that it is now a saltwater pond, filling and emptying with the tide. Moreover, it is gradually silting in and may someday be no more than a marsh, and later still meadowland.

The island is a mecca for birdwatchers during seasonal migrations, for both waterfowl and land species abound here. Pond normally has its family of osprey in residence, and eagles have infrequently been sighted. There is also a species of vole on the island, whose part in the ecological balance is unclear to me.

Human habitation has been considerably less important than avian in the last two centuries. There is indeed no record of year-round residence, and summer residence has been irregular. Weirmen camped on the island, presumably in tents or fish shacks, during the peak of the weir-fishing era at the end of the nineteenth century. Scallopers, too, have undoubtedly made the island a temporary home over many seasons. And there were Jesse Bakeman Drexel's sandpiper hunters from Islesboro, who probably joined weirmen and scallopers for overnight visits (see Western Island, above).

The most regular summer resident on Pond Island was Miss Augusta (Annie) Johnson, matron of a home for the handicapped in Boston, who boarded for several years early in the 1900s with the Carvers of Hog Island and then bought Pond Island from Fred Carver; he had acquired it for $250 from Andrew Sinclair of Brooksville in 1888 (Hancock 225/409). Miss Johnson was described by one acquaintance as "large, imposing and eccentric" (Fred B. Littlefield interview). She had a cottage built at the highest point on her island, and she summered there for half a dozen years in the 1920s; she left in 1931. There is some uncertainty as to whether her cottage burned or was taken down, but no trace of it exists today. Only a dug well remains as witness of Annie Johnson's tenure.

In recent years Pond Island has been left to its own cycle of change, and the only "residents" have been occasional kayakers or soloists from Outward Bound. In 1980 ownership was transferred to the National Audubon Society via the Philadelphia Conservationists, Inc.

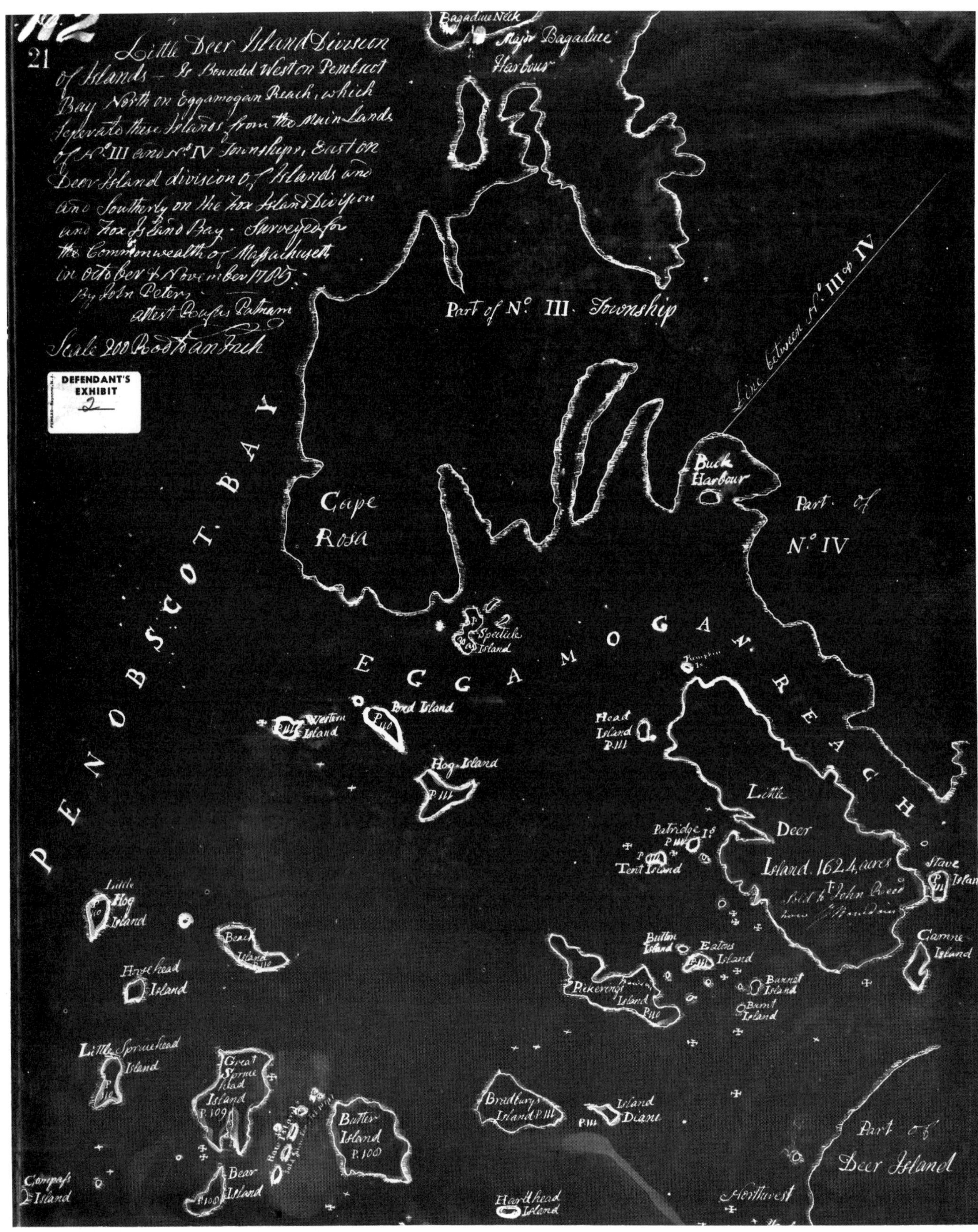
21
Little Deer Island Division
of Islands – Is Bounded West on Penobscot
Bay North on Eggamogan Reach, which
Seperate these Islands from the Main Lands
of No. III and No. IV Townships, East on
Deer Island division of Islands and
and Southerly on the Fox Island Division
and Fox Island Bay. Surveyed for
the Commonwealth of Massachusetts
in October & November 1785:
By John Peters
attest Rufus Putnam
Scale 200 Rods to an Inch
DEFENDANT'S
EXHIBIT
2
Bagaduce Neck
Major Bagaduce
Harbour
Part of No. III Township
Line between No. III & IV
PENOBSCOT BAY
Cape
Rosa
Buck
Harbour
Part of
No. IV
Spectacle
Island
EGGAMOGAN REACH
Bird Island
Western
Island
Head
Island
P. 111
Hog Island
P. 111
Little
Deer
Island 1624 acres
Patridge Is.
Tent Island
Stave
Island
Little
Hog
Island
Horsehead
Island
Button
Island
Eaton
Island
Pickering
Island
P. 110
Barred
Island
Camme
Island
Little Sprucehead
Island
Great
Spruce
Head
Island
P. 109
Butter
Island
P. 100
Bear
Island
P. 100
Bradburys
Island P. 111
Island
Diane
P. 111
Part of
Deer Island
Compass
Island
Hardhead
Island
Northwest

Hog (off Cape Rosier)

It is not likely that this island sustained habitation before or during the Revolutionary era, although Indians surely used it for many seasons to judge from extensive middens in the area. Indeed, Indians were still coming to the island in the twentieth century, searching for sweetgrass for their basketmaking. Hog Island has never had another name, as far as I am aware, and since it is explicitly mentioned in the Hancock County survey of 1785 (Hancock Plan Book II: 2), there is the implicit suggestion that it was at least farmed, if not settled, by someone who kept hogs—for, why else would the island be given the name? It is not clear who this early farmer might have been, if the supposition is correct. The first reference I have seen to ownership is in Farrow (History of Islesborough, 250), who states that Samuel Pendleton, a settler on Islesborough in 1772, "bought all the islands which lie west of a south course from Cape Rosier, including seven small islands." This purchase would surely have included Hog, and it may have been a Pendleton who put hogs on the island. Samuel Pendleton's title, in any case, must be considered tenuous, for few land titles acquired before or during the Revolution had subsequent validity unless explicitly confirmed by the Commonwealth of Massachusetts. We find no such confirmation, and indeed in 1787 Massachusetts agents convey these same islands to Cotton Tufts, a land trader from Weymouth (Hancock 1/166). Tufts sold Hog to Richard Hunnewell of Castine, along with Pond and Western; and Hunnewell, in 1799, conveyed all three islands to Richard Blake of Castine, in return for a $1,000 bond and a promise to deliver one ton of hay annually to Hunnewell's wharf in Castine during the six years of payment (Hancock 6/377). Whether the hay was to come from Hog or Pond—Western would be unlikely—we do not know.

Opposite page: *Little Deer Isle Division, surveyed by John Peters and Rufus Putnam in 1785; page references are to Plan Book I for the State of Maine. Note that most of the larger islands retain their post-Revolutionary War names. (The survey, which was used in a civil suit involving Buck Harbor Island, is at the Registry of Deeds in Ellsworth.)*

Farming appears to have continued during the first half of the nineteenth century, but not residence.[10] The island changed hands fifteen times during this period, according to a title search in the possession of the present owners, and several of these conveyances indicate the harvesting of hay—for example, an 1836 deed from George Kimball to Isaiah Barber, "reserving however to said Kimball the right of taking off the grass on said Island, the growth of 1836" (Hancock 62/437).

The owners of Hog Island, for the possible enlightenment of future researchers, were as follows: Jacob Orcutt and William Patten (1800–06); Josiah Waterman (1806–07); Robert Moore (1807–08); John Faxon (1808–17); Timothy Condon (1817–21); Samuel Bartlett (1821–22); Timothy Barnes (1823); Joseph Bryant (1823–24); Noah Mead (1824–34), with Samuel L. Valentine holding a partial interest in the island from 1824 to 1828; George Kimball (1834–36); Isaiah Barber, or Barbour (1836–39); Reuben Carver and Timothy Lane (1839–42 for the former, 1839–63 for the latter); and finally Elisha Smith (1842–63). None of these owners is believed to have actually lived on Hog Island, for if they had, their names would surely have appeared in the federal census schedules for "unorganized lands" (see page 215, above). Indeed, the owners from the 1830s to the 1860s appear to be from well-established families on Isle au Haut and Vinalhaven.

In 1860 the federal census does for the first time show residents on Hog: James M. Morrison, a fisherman, thirty-eight, with wife and five children, and his father, seventy-one. The agricultural census for the same year shows James Morrison, although a fisherman, with sixty acres of land under cultivation, one cow, six sheep, but no oxen. In 1863 he bought the island from Timothy Lane and Elisha Smith, and the deed makes explicit reference to the Morrisons still living there (Hancock 118/413). They did not

[10] There is a possibility that the "Hog Island" occupied by James Gray in 1820, according to the federal census, was *this* Hog Island, rather than the one at the other end of Eggemoggin Reach—but I believe not; Grays were numerous in both Brooksville and Brooklin.

Haying on Hog Island, early 1900s: Fred Carver, his wife Amelia (on top of hayrick), and mother-in-law Sarah Brown; unidentified hired man. (Courtesy of Clara Orcutt.)

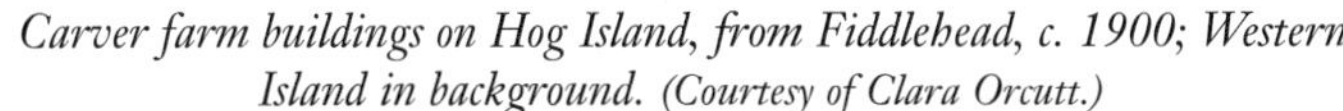

Carver farm buildings on Hog Island, from Fiddlehead, c. 1900; Western Island in background. (Courtesy of Clara Orcutt.)

remain long, however, for in 1865 Morrison sold the island to Benjamin Rea, who sold to Rowland Carlton of Brooklin in 1872, together with the house standing on the island (Hancock 142/550). The 1870 census shows another family—actually two households—living on the island, presumably as tenants: Warren W. Turner, twenty-nine, a farmer, and his wife Sarah, thirty-two; and Austin Turner, twenty-seven, a fisherman, with his wife Eliza and two children. Warren Turner is shown with seventy-five acres under cultivation (very unlikely—this was the total acreage of the island), two cows, two oxen, and ten sheep. They also ran a small pogy press on the west end of Hog Island. They lived there until the next residents, the Fred Carvers, moved from Cape Rosier in 1880. Carvers owned Hog Island for nearly eighty years.

The Carver era is rich in lore and recent enough to evoke vivid memories in elder citizens of the region whom I interviewed in the 1970s; my principal informant was Fred Carver's step-daughter, Clara Orcutt, then living in Stonington. Frederick Augustus Carver, born in 1850, was one of sixteen children and so was "boarded out" with relatives on Eagle Island. He lived until he was nineteen with Orena Quinn, then moved to South Brooksville where he was carpenter, boatbuilder, and eventually farmer. He first owned a farm on Cape Rosier, then moved to Hog Island after buying it for $400 from the Carltons (Hancock 168/494). The federal census for 1880 lists Fred A. Carver on Hog Island with his wife Etta, thirty-one, and one child, Ada May; living with them were Dan Howard, Jr., forty-one, and Elthea Howard, fifteen, Etta's brother and niece.

Fred Carver started off in a small way on Hog Island. The 1880 agricultural census shows him with two acres of tilled land, ten in meadows, and fifty-eight "unimproved." At this time he had a small herd of cattle, for which he took in

Fred Carver farm on Hog Island, c. 1900; the house was built in 1891 and still stands. Cape Rosier is in background. (Courtesy of Clara Orcutt.)

twenty-eight tons of hay, but kept only three sheep. Some fifteen to twenty years later, according to Clara Orcutt, he had one hundred sheep, most of them on nearby islands that he owned or leased. He owned both Pond and Western islands at one time and had a one-half interest in Beach. He used two yoke of oxen in rotation, and it is said that his voice could be heard on Cape Rosier when he bellowed at them; he had numerous barns and outbuildings to hold his produce; and he had various other animals, including a sizeable herd of cattle. There is a tale that when a bull he was leasing to the Quinns of Eagle Island balked at boarding a scow, he heaved it bodily in with his massive shoulders. He was a powerful, vigorous, warm-blooded, and full-bearded farmer.

He was also a fisherman. He hauled one hundred lobster traps from a catboat and sold his catch to a smack from Portland which passed every fortnight. He did not keep weirs himself, but leased rights (at five percent) to other fishermen who summered on the island in rented cabins or in tents: e.g., William Babson, Chester Bridges, Arthur Newman, Joseph Ladd, Elmer Orcutt, and Abraham Bryant. The Carvers also took in summer boarders, either in their own new farmhouse (which was completed in 1891) or in several cottages built for the purpose on the east shore of the island. On summer Sundays as many as twenty visitors customarily dined at their table. Among their regular guests were his second wife Amelia's parents, Henry and Sarah Brown from Pennsylvania; and Reverend Charles Snedeker, pastor of Grace Church in New York City, and his wife, author Caroline Dale.

Fred Carver's second wife Amelia was behind much of this activity on Hog Island. Fred had suffered many tragedies during his first marriage: two children had died in infancy; his wife Etta died in 1885; and his only remaining child, Ada May, succumbed after a long illness in 1889. Amelia, indeed, had first joined the household as nurse to Ada May; she brought her own child Clara with her.[11] She married Fred Carver in 1888.[12] Amelia was Fred Carver's partner in his many ventures on and off the island. And in due course she cared for him—as she had for his child Ada—when he suffered cancer of the spine in his last years and was obliged to turn over the farming to tenants or hired hands. John Davis was the first; he lived on Hog Island with his wife Cora and a large family for eleven years. The Davises were followed by Amelia's younger sister Melinda and her husband Albert Farr, who remained on

[11] Amelia Brown was first married to Thomas Vivian, and Clara was their child; Clara took the name Carver after her mother's second marriage.

[12] Lydia Dunham, Fred Carver's widowed sister-in-law, was housekeeper on the island the first year after Etta died. Fred's brother, George Carver Dunham, was a deserter in the Civil War—the reason he took his mother's maiden name.

the island two years with four children. Meanwhile, Fred Carver had died in 1919. Amelia and a widowed sister, Louisa Randall, managed the island farm into the 1930s, with the help of Davises and Farrs and of Clara and her younger half-sister Augusta (born to Fred and Amelia in 1894). Clara and Augusta attended school on Cape Rosier and on Eagle Island (often no more than a single ten-week term a year), but spent most of their childhood on Hog Island, helping on the farm.[13]

Amelia Carver remarried in the 1930s—her third husband was Arthur Mussels—and moved to north Deer Isle, returning to Hog Island each summer. The enterprises on the island were now beginning to run down, and the island itself was vacated much of the year. Arthur Mussels died of a heart attack in a boat off the island in 1938, and Amelia herself succumbed two years later, leaving the island to Clara and Augusta; Clara bought Augusta's interest and owned the island until the 1950s, when it was acquired by Eugene Meyer III (to whom I am indebted for a full record of the conveyances).

The facilities on Hog Island deteriorated during the quarter century between Amelia's departure and the full reorganization of the island as a summer residence. Since so many people had grown accustomed to using the island in Fred Carver's day, they continued to come, but without proper supervision the buildings were quickly ravaged. As Clara Orcutt wrote me: "Vandals destroyed the buildings faster than I could have them repaired." It was the senseless depredation on the uninhabited island that eventually persuaded Fred Carver's heirs to surrender all save Fiddle Head, the knob barred to the island's eastern tip, which is preserved forever as a memorial to Fred and Amelia.

Hog Island, fully restored with the help of Lewis Black and his son Edward of Cape Rosier (caretakers for the Meyers), has flourished as a family residence in the last half of the twentieth century. A 1930 cup defender, SHAMROCK V, restored to all its ancient glory by a Meyer descendant, is sometimes moored off the island.

[13] Clara and Augusta both married in due course and left the island. Clara, however, continued to be actively involved: she and her husband Myrle Orcutt kept weirs off the island in the 1920s; they also raised strawberries, herded sheep, and used Amelia's smokehouse to cure bacon and hams. Clara's children were also dedicated to Hog Island: Jeanne Fifield, for instance, Clara's oldest daughter, spent the first summer of her married life on Hog Island, in 1941.

Pendletons of Mid-Penobscot Bay Islands, Early 1800s

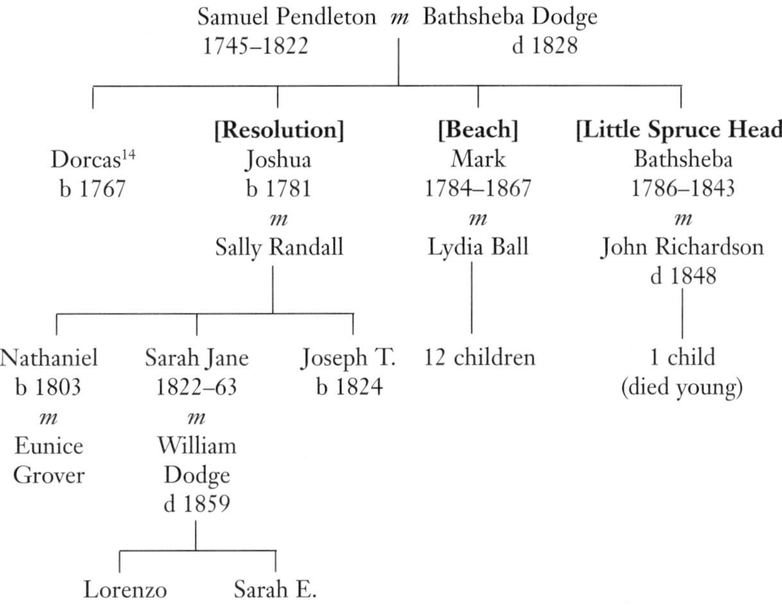

[14] Janet Rhodes suggests (page 28) that this Dorcas might have married the Bela Nichols who spent a few years on Little Spruce Head; if so, she would be the fourth child of Samuel and Bathsheba Pendleton to live on an island in the mid-Penobscot Bay.

Pumpkin

There being no significant settlement at the north end of Little Deer Isle until some decades after the Revolution, little use was made of this island until the 1850s when a lighthouse was erected on it. The owner at that time appears to have been a John C. Tibbets—but there was uncertainty as to title: an inspector reported to the Lighthouse Board in 1855 that "plans and estimates have been prepared and submitted for the lighthouse on Pumpkin Island, the construction of which has been delayed in consequence of not being able to find an owner who can give a good title" (United States Lighthouse records: Pumpkin Island file). Tibbets' title was finally accepted and the island purchased for $50 (Hancock 97/519). The State of Maine, meanwhile, had given the United States government a quitclaim to the island, which at the time did not even have a fixed name—at least in the mind of United States Attorney General Caleb Cushing; he wrote of the island in 1854, "It is a barren rock, in a bay where such islands are so numerous as to exhaust the inventive faculties of the navigators in furnishing them with names." But there was a name: Rufus Putnam had given it a name, *Pumpkin Island*, in his 1785 plan (see page 474); and Tibbets, in conveying the island to the United States, was said to be "of Pumpkin Island." Whether he was living there at the time is uncertain—other instruments identify him as "of Brooklin"—but it is certain he was the first keeper after the lighthouse was completed. He is shown as keeper in the 1860 census, aged sixty-two, living with his wife and one child.

The next keeper served for thirty-two years, one of the longest tenures in the Lighthouse Service: Charles L. Babson, appointed in 1870. A figure of great vitality, despite the loss of a leg in the Civil War, he built a number of cottages at Indian Cove (now Eggemoggin) and ran an inn for summer guests. One visitor to the area in the 1880s—an out-of-state gentleman with a tendency to disparage all he discovered of local origin—referred to the community as a "sprinkling of cottages...for the accommodation of summer visitors of moderate means" (Drake, *Nooks and Corners of the New England Coast*, 287). Most of the cottages Captain Babson built are still standing, and few would describe the means of their owners as "moderate." Captain Babson had excellent relations with islanders in the region and was counted a close friend of many of them, especially Fred Carver of Hog Island.

The next keeper, serving from 1902 to 1911, was Charles S. Holt; he is shown with his wife on Pumpkin Island in the 1910 census. The last keeper I find in National Archives records is C. M. Newman, appointed in 1912. Weir privileges off the island were given in 1918 to Arthur E. Newman, undoubtedly a kinsman of the keeper. The light was extinguished in 1934 and the island and facilities sold for $552 to George Harman of Bar Harbor. It has served as a summer residence through the last decades of the twentieth century.

Pumpkin Island, though a stone's throw from Little Deer Isle, has remained one of the unorganized lands of the State of Maine since the Revolution.

Birch

This is called *Head Island* on the first post-Revolutionary survey of the islands in Hancock County (see page 218), meaning, I suppose, near the "head" of Little Deer Isle. In 1823 Head Island was conveyed to John R. Redman (Maine Archives: Island titles). I have not traced the title record of this island since it was never settled; it belongs to the group considered unorganized lands of the State of Maine and in recent years has been the residence of out-of-state vacationers.[15]

Captain Walter Scott, long a resident of the area, has said that the name comes from the birch on the island that was removed many years ago for a spindle mill in North Penobscot; spruce came in after the birch (Walter Scott papers). I have no confirmation of this explanation, still less of the following romantic tale concerning Birch Island. In the early seventeenth century when Samuel de Champlain, Jean Rosier, and others were exploring the region, a French seaman fell in love with a local Indian maiden, whom he used to meet at night on shore. His wooing being discovered, the unhappy seaman was thrown into the brig and before he was released his Indian lover, feeling she had been abandoned, threw herself into the bay and drowned. When the seaman was at last set free, on the first moonlit night he could slip away from his ship he discovered the body of his maiden floating in the Reach; with nothing further to live for, he rowed deliberately out to sea and was heard of no more. The sounds of his oars in the locks are the phantom sounds one still hears on clear, windless nights from the landing on Birch Island.[16]

[15] I share with readers the substance of a letter from a Birch Island owner, written in 1985 after the publication of the first edition of this volume. It makes a point that devotees of Maine islands might ponder, especially those piecing together their history. After regretting my decision to pass lightly over ownership of those islands not inhabited year-round, he writes: "The history of summer residence also has its fascination, and is not without importance for the history of the Maine coast and its economics.... I perfectly understand that you could not have followed this line of investigation out systematically, but I hope someone does someday before this information, too, is forgotten." He goes on to point out the following artifacts of summer residence on his island in the twentieth century: the shed where a Boston spinster of 1899 (the first out-of-state owner) kept her cow; the overgrown tennis court of a 1920s millionaire (possibly H. W. Park, listed in state tax records as owner); the black-out curtains put up at a boys' camp during World War II. My correspondent is right, of course: summer residence need not be an inferior part of an island's history. It has not indeed been the focus of our research, but it could well be that of others'.

[16] From a piece by Rosemary Poole in *Farmstead Magazine*, Winter 1975—called to my attention by Dorothy Carman.

Scott Islands

These two islands are named *Tent* and *Partridge* (the westerly and easterly islands, respectively) on Rufus Putnams's survey of Hancock County islands in 1785 (see page 218). An 1804 conveyance of three small islands west of Little Deer Isle probably includes the pair, and if so, this would explain the modern name, for the islands were deeded by Nathaniel Scott, an early settler on Deer Isle; the sale price for all three was $40 (Hancock 15/24). Another deed, in 1824, shows the islands conveyed formally by the State of Maine to Hezekiah Rowell—a step that normally extinguished prior claims (Hancock 46/393). I have not followed title search further inasmuch as the Scott Islands were never settled: since they were unorganized lands of the State of Maine, any settler would have appeared prominently in the decennial census. Edwin Blaster of Deer Isle was listed by the state as the owner in 1921, the island then valued at $300.

The Scott Islands are more celebrated in fiction than in history, for these are the islands where Robert McCloskey's Sal and Jane, of *One Morning in Maine*, *A Time of Wonder*, and other stories, lost their teeth, found Indian shell heaps under uprooted firs, and ate clam chowder for lunch—all before they grew up and became mid-Penobscot Bay matrons in their own right.

Pickering

Samuel Pickering, descendant of early settlers in Portsmouth, New Hampshire, and the sixth or seventh of this name, came first to Isle au Haut in the 1770s, then to Deer Isle, and eventually to this island which has ever since borne his name (Dr. Benjamin Lake Noyes, *Courier-Gazette*, Rockland, September 13, 1932). He took possession in 1775, according to Rufus Putnam's survey a decade later (see page 474). In 1786, when the Commonwealth of Massachusetts sold the island to John Reed, Samuel Pickering was given a settler's deed of one hundred acres in accordance with Massachusetts law. The first federal census in 1790 shows Samuel and his son Daniel living on the island with their families, a total of nine. A Deer Isle tax record of 1792 shows Samuel Pickering and his son, with four acres planted to hay and grain (four and five tons, respectively), two oxen, three cows, and one pig. This was modest husbandry, but it was a start. In 1793 Pickering Island, along with Conary and Merchant islands, was exempted from the Deer Isle school tax, meaning that these islands were presumed to be conducting their own school. The next census, in 1800, shows Samuel and Daniel with households respectively of two and four, and Samuel, Jr. with four, presumably still on Pickering Island. Samuel Pickering, Sr. probably quit the island after 1806, when he sold a seventy-five-acre parcel on the eastern end, including buildings, to Ignatius Haskell. The fee was $500. I have no information concerning Samuel's death. According to Dr. Noyes, he was married three times, each time to a Mary—the last, Mary Dunham of Deer Isle (Noyes, Family Histories: Pickering). I lose sight of Samuel Pickering, Jr., but Daniel apparently remained on the island after his father departed: an entry in the Hancock Registry of Deeds in 1816 notes his having lived there a total of thirty-eight years. The deed in question was a quitclaim from Daniel to Ignatius Haskell, in consequence of a lawsuit brought by Haskell that was decided in his favor. Daniel probably left Pickering at this time, if not before; he was the last Pickering to have been associated with the island so far as I am aware.

Before considering other residents, it is helpful to turn back for a moment to the vast holdings of the Bowdoin family, which included Pickering Island. John Reed's purchase in 1786 included—in addition to Pickering—Long Island in Blue Hill, Little Deer Isle, Great Spruce Head Island, and Bradbury Island, less "settlers' deeds" as required by law; the price was £1,814, which must be considered one of the best real-estate

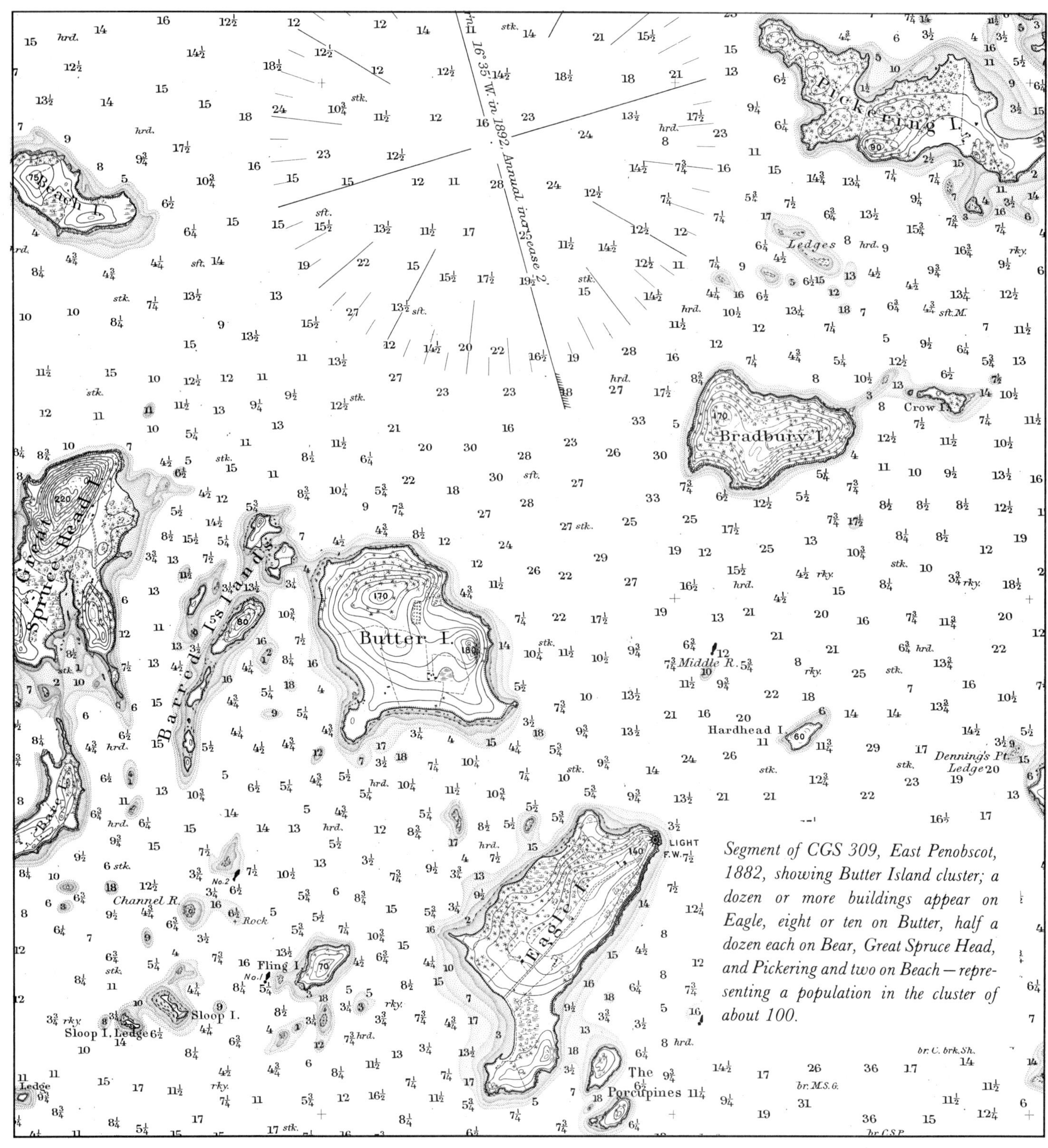

Segment of CGS 309, East Penobscot, 1882, showing Butter Island cluster; a dozen or more buildings appear on Eagle, eight or ten on Butter, half a dozen each on Bear, Great Spruce Head, and Pickering and two on Beach—representing a population in the cluster of about 100.

bargains of the time. In 1787 Reed sold the same islands, with the same reservations and for the same price, to James Bowdoin, who was then governor of Massachusetts. On Governor Bowdoin's death in 1789 his estate was divided between his wife and two children, James, Jr. and Lady Elizabeth Temple; his widow gave her share to the two children four years later. In 1797 the two heirs divided the island empire as follows: Long Island (with 1,130 acres reserved at the north end) and Bradbury to James, Jr., and Little Deer Isle, Great Spruce Head, and Pickering to Lady Elizabeth. I do not find a conveyance of Pickering Island, but this might be because there was in reality little left to convey of the 220-acre island after the Pickerings had been quieted.

Turning now to residence on the island after the Pickering era, I offer a table (page 230) that shows in parallel columns residence and ownership. What strikes one is how infrequently the two are in correlation; in contrast to most other islands in the mid-Penobscot Bay region where one finds resident owners, there is a certain impermanence to habitation on Pickering.

The conveyances shown in the 1820s involve only one resident: Abraham Moor (or Moore), who is described in 1831 and 1834 deeds—not listed in the table because they involve other property— as "of Pickering Island" (Hancock 57/428 and 58/460). Financial difficulties, to judge from numerous mortgage deeds on which his name appears, evidently drove Moore from Pickering before 1840, and he spent the remainder of his life on Holbrook Island, owned by Benjamin Hook of Castine (see page 399). Concerning Samuel Simpson in the 1830 census, I have no clue as to his identity; he does not appear in census schedules for other islands in the region. Of Josiah Gray we know that a Mrs. Eaton of Deer Isle worked for him, whether or not on Pickering Island is uncertain. According to Mrs. Eaton's son, Samuel Newell Eaton, Josiah Gray sold to a Mr. Cook of Boston, and it was this gentleman or his son who put Charles Tilden Green on the island as caretaker (Dr. Noyes's interview with the seventy-four-year-old Samuel Eaton in 1907). I have not verified Josiah Gray's ownership, but the conveyance to Samuel Cook in 1844 is confirmed. Gray was said to have been living on the island at the time, but did not remain. Samuel Black in the 1840 census, meanwhile, came and went; the surname suggests he was from Little Deer Isle. James Staples in the 1850 census removed during the next decade to Bradbury Island and later to Beach; he was the progenitor of the large family associated with those two islands for more than a quarter century (see pages 232 and 267).

Charles Tilden Green, who appears in both the 1850 and 1860 census with a large family, and who owned the island briefly at the end of the 1860s, was undoubtedly the settler who lived longest on Pickering Island (with the possible exception of Daniel Pickering). He was a fairly prosperous farmer according to agricultural census data: in 1850 he is reported to have had 125 acres of improved land, seven milking cows, two oxen, and sixty sheep; in 1860, he had fewer cows but a hundred sheep. While these are not extraordinary achievements compared to those of, say, the Witherspoons of Butter Island, they reflect an energy that is not demonstrated by any other farmer we know to have inhabited Pickering Island during the nineteenth century.[17] I am not certain why the Greens quit the island, especially after paying $500 for it in 1868 (to a Bangor agent who had managed to gain title several years earlier by paying up two delinquent tax bills of $12.87 and $21.81), but it may have had to do with a fire on Pickering: Clara Orcutt of neighboring Hog Island recalls hearing in her childhood of a fire in the Green household in which several children were lost.

The Greens' residence on Pickering coincided, in its last years, with a fish-oil business there. The principal person involved was apparently John Marland, who is noted in several deeds as resident on the island in the 1860s as the "agent" for Martha L. Punchard; she appears in a series of conveyances in 1863–64 and was apparently the owner for some years. Not much is known of this pogy factory, which was probably comparable to many such fledgling enterprises that sprang up throughout the region in the 1860s and 1870s before the vast schools of menhaden

[17] An item of interest in Captain Henry Lufkin's diary—whether reflecting sound husbandry or simply excess energy, I could not say—notes a visit by Charles Green to Deer Isle in 1854 to pick up three barrels of ashes to keep the rats off his potatoes (Lufkin, July 26, 1854).

quit the Penobscot Bay region. The enterprise gave its name to the northeast cove, still known locally as Pogyhouse Cove.

The buildings on the island during the Greens' tenure—and I believe always—were concentrated at the east end, at the narrow point between the above-mentioned cove and Sunset Cove, facing south. A topographical map dated 1873, in the possession of the present owner, shows a large farmhouse on the easterly side of this isthmus that I assume to be the Greens' homestead; several barns are near it, and a small building is on the southerly shore east of the bar. The same buildings, plus two or three others, show on maps early in the 1880s, along with numerous stone walls or other fencing; most of the eastern third of the island is cleared (see the segment of Map 1882 CGS 309, page 226).

Two other families were resident on Pickering before it passed altogether from local hands. One was a Swedish family named Edburg, shown in the 1870 census; I know nothing at all of this family except that he was a moderately prosperous farmer (to judge from the census-taker's estimates). The other—the twelfth or thirteenth separate household on Pickering Island—was the family of Amos Dow, who acquired the island in 1879, as shown in the table. The agricultural census of 1880 shows him with six acres of tilled land, sixty-five acres in meadow yielding twenty-five tons of hay; he had thirty-eight sheep. This was a good deal more than subsistence farming. Amos was still a young man when in 1885 he sold both Pickering and Eaton islands to Dr. Stacy B.

John Scott farmhouse on Pickering Island, 1892; one of his nineteen children is on the porch. (Courtesy of Deer Isle Historical Society.)

Dr. Collins's cottage on Pickering Island, which gave rise to mysterious legends of ill-doing; photo taken shortly before demolition of the cottage after World War II. (Courtesy of Gerald Brace).

Collins of New York for $2,000 and moved elsewhere. This marked the end of farming on the island.

Dr. Collins's residence on Pickering, which lasted more than two decades (summers only, of course), is clouded by awesome rumors of his strange behavior and doubts as to his sanity. Enough time has elapsed since those days to place many of the legends about him in a sensible perspective, but a few years ago one had only to talk to elder residents who lived in the area when Dr. Collins was on Pickering Island to appreciate the tenacity of those legends. Most of them concerned the curious cottage he built soon after his arrival, with its square turret projecting from one corner and the windows even up to the second floor heavily barred. The bars, it was said, were to keep inside his deranged wife, or mother-in-law, or mental patients on whom he was experimenting; one version suggested his "victims" were barmaids he collected each season in Boston, with whom to while away the summer hours.

Where did the rumors start? Captain Walter Scott, son of an early caretaker of the Collins estate, explained that they were fabricated by a dissolute clammer from Castine who was once chased off the island (Scott papers). This is indeed plausible. Dr. Collins was known to have had a strong sense of privacy and apparently kept a band of ferocious dogs to protect it. Few ventured on the island unless the dogs were on leash. Whatever the merits of the rumors about Dr. Collins, it is undeniable that they gave to Pickering an exotic, even haunted reputation. So measured an observer of island life as the late Gerald Brace recalled episodes from childhood picnics on Pickering, after Dr. Collins's departure, that to his impressionable mind suggested the supernatural: the distinct image of a bearded farmer sharpening knives in a barn (probably Fred Carver of Hog Island over on one of his occasional visits, Gerald Brace later judiciously proposed); or the front of Dr. Collins' shuttered and abandoned cottage unaccountably bursting into flames, which the picnickers beat out (this was too real to explain away).

Dr. Collins's caretaker during the early years of his tenure was Captain John Scott, whose diaries for the years 1888–1890 (now at the Deer Isle Historical Society Library) give a vivid picture of island life at that time. The diaries cover the winter of 1888, one of the most formidable ever recorded along the coast of Maine, when the inner bay was frozen solid, allowing wagons to cross from Islesboro to Belfast. On Pickering Island, the ice stood eighteen inches thick in Pogyhouse Cove in mid-April, and blizzards continued into May. The Scotts had no fewer than nineteen children, most of them resident on the island during the years Captain Scott was caretaker, from 1886 to 1891. He was followed by other year-round caretakers until Dr. Collins mortgaged the island to Elmer P. Spofford in 1907 and moved onto Deer Isle.

Residence on the island has been periodic in the twentieth century. In the 1920s, when the island was owned by the E. O. Ladds, at least two couples lived there seasonally: Rufus Black, caretaker for the Ladds, lived in the old farmhouse; Harry and Lois Smith of Little Deer Isle lived in the Collins cottage. The Blacks and the Smiths had up to five weirs around the island and ran a clam and fish business (Dorothy Carman interview with Cecil Eaton of Little Deer Isle). According to state tax records, the island was valued in this era at $5,000—the second highest valuation, after Butter, among the unorganized Penobscot Bay islands.

In 1946 Grace Ladd sold Pickering Island to James H. Wakelin and since that date the restless sequence of tenants has ceased. Pickering is now a family island with simple accommodations and appropriate scenic and conservation easements, which permit timber harvesting when needed. The old farmhouse and barns are long down, and Dr. Collins's cottage, for many years an object of ghoulish curiosity around the bay (more than one uninvited visitor fell through the second floor planking), was demolished in 1954.

Residence and Ownership of Pickering Island

Note: Householders are in left column; size of household, from decennial census, in brackets (see residence table, pages 215–216, for fuller data). Ownership data, in right column, show only critical conveyances.
The symbol > means "conveyed to."

Residence	Date	Ownership
		1786 Mass. > John Reed, except 100 xres for S. Pickering
		1787 Reed > Jas. Bowdoin & heirs
Samuel Pickering [6][2]	C. 1790 C. 1800	
Daniel Pickering [3][4]	C. 1790 C. 1800	
Samuel Pickering, Jr. [4][8]	C. 1800 C.1810	
	1806	S. Pickering > Ignat. Haskell: 75 acres east end
	1816	D. Pickering > Ignat. Haskell (court ruling)
	1825	Haskell > Thos. Adams
	1829	Adams > Josiah Hook > Benj. Hook & Abraham Moore
Samuel Simpson [10]	C. 1830	
	1836	Hook > Ed. Renouf (foreclos.)
Josiah Gray [9]	C. 1840	
Samuel Black [5]	C. 1840	
	1844	Renouf > Samuel Cook
Charles T. Green [6]	C. 1850	
James Staples [7]	C. 1850	
Charles T. Green [11]	C. 1860	
	1863-64	Cook > Blaisdell & Emerson > Martha Punchard > E. Avery, Wm. & Geo. M. Hobbs
	1866	Tax collectors > I. R. Clark
	1868	Clark > Charles T. Green
G. W. Edburg [3]	C. 1870	Green > Avery & Hobbs
	1879	Avery & Hobbs > A. F. Dow
Amos F. Dow [7]	C. 1880	
	1885	Dow > Stacy B. Collins
	1907	Collins > Elmer P. Spofford
	1920?	Spofford > E. O. Ladd
	1946	Grace Ladd > Jas. H. Wakelin

Eaton

The origin of this island's name is surely no mystery, Eatons abounding in the area as they do, but after which particular Eaton this island was named it would be impossible to say; it has been called *Eaton's Island* since Revolutionary times (see page 218).

Surveyed initially as twelve acres but doubtless larger,[18] Eaton has normally been bought and sold along with Pickering and used by residents of the latter as adjunct to their operations. For example, Charles T. Green, who farmed for twenty-five years or more on Pickering, owned Eaton Island; and when the fish-oil enterprise was in progress in Pickering's Pogyhouse Cove in the 1860s, John Marland, who was behind this enterprise, bought Eaton for his weirs. Later Amos Dow, the last resident farmer of Pickering, also owned Eaton and sold both islands to Dr. Stacy Collins when he removed to Deer Isle (Hancock 197/506).

The census schedules in the last century show a solitary resident on Eaton, a sixty-year-old fisherman named Cephas Gardner who is listed there in 1860. A conveyance from the heirs of Hezekiah Rowell to Cephas Gardner, "now in

[18] The present owner measures the island at sixteen acres, intertidal, plus four acres for Little Eaton, barred to it.

occupation," is recorded in 1861; Gardner paid $50 for his island—or islands, for there are in reality two (Hancock 114/323). I have no further information about this resident. Nor do I have information about an activity reported in the Colby atlas of 1881: a silver mine shown at the east end of Eaton island, called the Clam Ledge Mine. My supposition is that a mine may have been staked out for this area—as happened on a number of islands in the Penobscot region during this era of mining euphoria—but that it was never worked. The owner in the 1990s (a geologist) assures me that no silver was ever mined on Eaton Island.

Crow (off Bradbury)

Island Diane is the name given this spot in Rufus Putnam's survey of 1785 (Hancock Plan Book II: 2; see page 218), and in 1824 it was conveyed to Hezekiah Rowell as Diana (Maine Archives: Island Titles). I do not know after which local maiden the island was named, but certainly after none who ever lived on it. Only crows inhabited it—thousands of them in the nineteenth century, according to a former resident of Pickering Island, because of the excellent feeding grounds on the clam-filled mud bar. When eventually the mud washed away, leaving only gravel, the crows departed (Scott papers). But they left their name. The island, having passed through various ownerships and tax defaults, is now owned by the State of Maine.[19]

[19] Some excitement was aroused in 1982 when curious markings on a rock on the shore of Crow Island were translated by an amateur cryptologist: "Haakon brought his cog here." It was thought (by the credulous) to be evidence of a Viking landfall—why on this tiny outcropping was never explained (*Ellsworth American*, August 12, 1982). The "finding" has been dismissed by archaeologists.

Bradbury

The 1776 "Atlantic Neptune" calls this *Bear Island*, and it would indeed have been and could still be a formidable redoubt for bears. It is named *Bradbury* in the earliest deeds of the 1780s, when it was acquired from the State of Massachusetts by John Reed (or Read), a land speculator. From Reed, title passed to James Bowdoin of Boston in 1787, and the island was part of the vast Bowdoin properties in the region that went to his heirs following his death. Who Bradbury might have been is unknown, although the surname was a familiar one, especially among British forces in the Pemaquid region before the Revolution. Two further deeds—in 1817, when Hezekiah Colby conveyed to Hezekiah Torrey, and in 1825, when the latter conveyed to Pearl Spofford (Knox Lands 1/559)—do little to advance our knowledge of any early settlement.

The first settler on Bradbury appears to have been John Vickery, an Englishman who emigrated to the United States alone—probably in the 1830s—and then summoned his wife and two children to join him. They perished during the voyage, and John married Elizabeth Bridges of Castine. The banns were published only in 1847, according to Deer Isle records, but the couple had four children by this date; another was apparently born on Bradbury Island in September 1848. There is uncertainty over the date of John Vickery's death, but it was apparently on Bradbury, and during the winter months; reports of his widow's suffering on the island before her rescue persist among residents on the facing shore of Deer Isle. The best guess as to the date is 1849 or 1850, for the census of the latter year does not show the Vickerys on Bradbury and places the oldest daughter Lydia, aged nine, in the household of John P. Johnson on Deer Isle; it is known that Mrs. Vickery bound out all her five children before she married Joseph Morey of Deer Isle and raised another family of seven.

John P. Johnson was the owner of Bradbury Island in 1855. I have not been able to discover when he acquired it, but if from Pearl Spofford, then we may assume John Vickery to have been a tenant farmer; if from John Vickery's estate, this may have been a return for his care of Lydia Vickery.[20]

The next settler on the island was James Staples, who is shown in the 1850 census on Pickering and apparently moved into the Vickery farm a few years later. He is said to be "of Bradbury Island" when he and Henry Brookman of Bucksport bought it in 1855 from John P. Johnson; the price they paid—$600—suggests the buildings were in good repair when the Stapleses arrived (Hancock 104/289). The 1860 census shows James Staples, a farmer, with his wife Roxanna, two adult sons, John and Samuel, who were fishermen, and eight minor children—a total of twelve; he is shown to have had a hundred acres of "improved land" (which is quite improbable), three cows, twenty sheep, but no oxen. The same year, James con-veyed his half interest in the island to his son John (Hancock 111/526). During the next decade James and Roxanna moved to Beach Island, where they are shown with most of their family, including John, in the 1870 census. James Staples, Jr., with his wife Esther, two minor children, and two younger brothers, Justus, twenty-two, and George, twenty-one, are still listed on Bradbury in 1870; all three brothers are shown as fishermen. This is the extent of information in census reports (see page 214). Samuel Staples, we know from a petition he signed in 1873, fought in the Civil War, enlisting from Bradbury Island in 1863 (Enk, *Family Island*, 213). The Staples farm, of which the cellar hole is still visible, was located near the high ground at the western end, with most of the plateau cleared to the east. A wagon track wound down to the only possible landing place, on the northeast tip; if there was a wharf, no evidence of it remains. It is unlikely that the Staples children had any formal education, since there was no school in the area before the establishment of one on Eagle Island sometime during the 1870s—by which time the family had presumably removed. No buildings appear on county and coastal maps early in the 1880s; they would surely have been shown had they been occupied.

After the departure of the Staples family, the open fields on Bradbury were used for some years by neighboring islanders for pasturage and hay, and later for berrying. Fishermen occasionally used the island for shelter. A dramatic rescue is reported during a severe northeaster in November 1887 when two scallopers, vainly seeking protection on the exposed northeast beach where they were driven ashore, were safely brought off the island by Captain John Scott and two of his sons, who had spotted their fire from Pickering Island; the return journey to Pickering in an open dory against fierce headwinds was broken at Crow Island, where a fire was built in the lee to thaw out the half-frozen scallopers (Scott papers).

In 1900 title passed from the Staples family when John Staples sold to Massachusetts investors; they held the island without introducing significant changes until it was sold in 1936 to Frederick B. Littlefield of Brooksville. Logging operations were conducted on Bradbury twice in the twentieth century, and during Prohibition it was reportedly used to store contraband (but so, reportedly, were most other islands in the bay). During the 1940s, according to Mr. Littlefield, more than a hundred sheep were pastured there; the paddock used for shearing was located at the site of the old farm, and its remains were still evident in the 1970s. But the island has not been "inhabited" since the 1870s, except by an occasional Outward Bound soloist or a stranded fisherman. Its fortress-like cliffs and poor anchorages undoubtedly discouraged residence, by farmer and fisherman alike, so that Bradbury Island, perhaps more than any other in the bay has reverted easily to its natural wild state. Part of the island has already been made over to the Nature Conservancy, and the remainder is scheduled to be transferred by the present owner.

A final, ornithological note: one summer evening in the 1970s when my wife and I were anchored off the northeast cove, waves of crows came from every point of the compass steadily for ten or fifteen minutes, congregating at a point high on the western head not far from the Staples farm site. A rough estimate would be a thousand crows. The racket was deafening for a half hour, then subsided as the meeting broke up or the crows cawed themselves to sleep. There was no sign of congregation at dawn, and we did not stay another day to see if this was a regular evening occurrence.

[20] The above account of the Vickerys is pieced together from Noyes, Family Histories: Vickery; Noyes, Robbins interviews; and the recollections of the late Dorothy Carman from her forebears.

Hardhead

This island has borne its name since shortly after the Revolution. In 1787 the Massachusetts Land Commission conveyed it by this name to John Lee, along with Eagle and Butter islands and eight or ten smaller islands in the vicinity (see next entry). In 1795 Lee sold to Jonathan Eaton of Deer Isle with the stipulation that while Eaton could make improvements, he was "not to cut trees off they being considered for a mark for the guidance of Sailors" (item at Deer Isle Historical Society). Anyone seeing this nearly soilless granite outcropping today will marvel that a tree ever grew there. The reference to Hardhead as a marker for navigators is interesting, for some forty years later the island was apparently considered as a possible site for the lighthouse that in 1839 was constructed on Eagle Island. Captain Walter Scott argues that Hezekiah Rowell bought the island in the 1820s with the idea of fetching a good price for it from the United States government (Scott papers)—an argument that would be difficult to prove specifically inasmuch as Rowell bought dozens of islands in the bay during this era, all for purposes of speculation. In 1859 his heirs sold Hardhead to Henry Brookman, another land speculator, for $20.

Hardhead, losing the light station, remained in its natural state. The Quinns of Eagle Island used it for pasturage—when they could persuade a cantankerous ram they wished to isolate to go ashore.

Eagle

Note: The late John C. Enk, a retired schoolteacher from New Jersey who summered near Belfast, completed a full-length monograph on Eagle Island before his death (c. 1975). His study was based on extensive interviews with Captain Erland L. Quinn, a native of Eagle Island and probably the most knowledgeable authority at the time on the mid-Penobscot Bay islands. I accordingly refer readers interested in the minutiae of island life to John Enk's volume Family Island in Penobscot Bay *(see Bibliography for full listing) and confine myself here to essential historical detail and to speculation as to why the Eagle Island community outlived so many like it.*

This island appears never to have had another name. Although it is unnamed on the 1776 "Atlantic Neptune," it is called *Eagle Island* on the initial survey of Hancock County in 1785 (Hancock Plan Book I: 31) and so appears in the earliest known conveyances.

According to Rufus Putnam's census of 1785 (see page 473), the earliest settler on Eagle Island was Allin Calf (or Allen Calef—the spelling varies) who came there in 1778. A conveyance of the island in 1787, from the Commonwealth of Massachusetts to John Lee of Castine, notes that Allin Calf was still there and was to be quieted with one hundred acres (Lincoln 21/82). A list of early residents in Castine, meanwhile, includes Allin Calef in 1770, but notes him as "absent," which means he could have been on Eagle Island, then considered under Castine's jurisdiction (*Bangor Historical Magazine*, VIII: 57/1843). Allin Calef is not listed as a resident of Hancock County islands in the 1790 census, so it may be assumed he had removed by that date.[21] Ten or a dozen years is a respectable island residence in the late eighteenth century, but we know nothing of Calef's husbandry, nor of immediate successors. I find no other settler on Eagle Island before 1810. From 1810 to the present, however, the island has never been without inhabitants (except in some years for a few months in winter), and this must be very nearly a record for residence on an island of comparable size in the Penobscot Bay region.

[21] An Allin Calef is shown in Ducktrap on the western shore of the bay (now Lincolnville) in 1793 (*Bangor Historical Magazine*, VI: 244/1466).

The residence table on pages 214–15 shows the households from 1810 to 1900. Since the great majority of them are Quinns, an abbreviated genealogical tree is given below.

The Generations of Quinns

Of William Banks in the 1810 census I know nothing; the surname was well known in Penobscot Bay in this era. Samuel Quinn (spelled with two "n"s in most records, though with one on his gravestone) evidently settled on Eagle Island soon after his marriage in 1815, and it is likely that all but one of his thirteen children were born there; he and his wife Lucy Carver apparently came from Vinalhaven, or North Haven, with which Eagle Islanders appear to have had close ties through the nineteenth century. It is not clear why Samuel did not buy the island until 1844, a quarter century after he had settled there, but the price he paid ($1,500) suggests that the improvements at that date were of some significance; he bought from John C. Gray, who had acquired title to the island in the 1820s from the estate of his father, William Gray, a wealthy Boston merchant who had secured title from the Lees (Enk, Chapter II). In 1837, meanwhile, John C. Gray had sold a six-acre tract of land at the northeast tip of the island to the United States government, which in 1839 built and commissioned a lighthouse there (of which more below).

Five of Samuel Quinn's sons settled on Eagle Island, at least for a time. James and his wife Sylvia, daughter of a Nova Scotian fisherman out of Gloucester, lived their lives out on the island, as did Samuel, Jr. and his wife Louisa from North Haven; Samuel, Jr., according to John Enk, inherited the "mantle of leadership" from his father. John L. Quinn, married to Mary Carver, appears in three census schedules, but removed in 1884. Joseph W. is shown in the 1850 and 1860 census and inherited one of the four farms left by his father, but removed soon after Samuel, Sr.'s death. Finally, William N. also inherited land and settled on a farm with his wife Orena, who remained on the island after he drowned in 1873 and later married another islander, Allen Briggs; they removed to Camden before 1890.

This was the second generation of Quinns (fuller accounts of their activities are given in John Enk's study). Israel Carver, shown in the 1850, 1860, and 1870 schedules, was a younger brother of Lucy Carver Quinn and the father of Moses Carver; the Carvers, according to the census, were fishermen rather than farmers, but I am uncertain where on the island they settled. Walden Dyer in the 1860 census was presumably one of the North Haven Dyers who married into the Quinn family, but I do not identify his relationship precisely; he was on the island during the Civil War and appears as signer of a subsequent petition for reimbursement of funds raised to procure substitutes during the war—a common practice (Enk, 212). The Walden Dyers removed to Butter Island before 1870.

I pass now to the third and fourth generations of Quinns to fill out the profile of island residence. Of James's four children, three daughters married islanders—or brought their husbands to Eagle Island after marriage. Abbie married George Brown, a fisherman from North Haven who settled on the West Cove in the 1880s and spent the rest of his life there. Their five children (not shown on the family tree) lived off island after maturity but were closely associated with it for many years. Ada's husband was Captain Charles Horace Raynes (known as Horace), an Englishman who fished at the Grand Banks with the brother of Sylvia Kelly Quinn before marrying her daughter and settling on the southwest tip of the island sometime before 1880; he was a boatbuilder. The family remained on the island to about 1900 (they are omitted from the census of that year). Alice, after her marriage to Ellington Carver of North Haven, lived there for a number of years before returning with her husband to Eagle Island in 1917; he was a fisherman, and she was for a dozen years postmistress and storekeeper before they returned to North Haven in 1936. James Quinn's only son, Edgar, is shown in the 1900 census as a fisherman, apparently a widower with two sons and his widowed mother. Edgar's grandson James (Jimmy) O. Quinn played a significant role in the comparatively recent history of Eagle Island. Having left the island as a young man, he returned to fish in the late 1930s and 1940s; then, from 1948 until his death in

1976, he ran the mailboat from Sunset on Deer Isle to Eagle and the nearby islands. (See *New York Times*, August 26, 1973, page7: 7.) His son I. Robert Quinn succeeded him as ferryman.

The children of Samuel, Jr. and Louisa—there were thirteen born, though no more than half a dozen reached full maturity—constitute the balance of the third generation of Eagle Islanders of Quinn descent. Augustus, who married Charity Arey, drowned with his uncle William N. Quinn, when returning to Eagle Island from Deer Isle with supplies in 1873; his widow married Augustus's brother John. Elva married Charles Edwin Howard in the early 1890s, and after a year at Brooksville they settled in the old William Quinn farm in the center of the island for the remainder of their lives. Charles Edwin Howard (known as "Uncle Ed") was a dynamic figure on Eagle for many years—farmer, fisherman, herdsman, caretaker at "Dirigo" (Butter Island), mail carrier from Sunset for thirty years, and generally adept at all trades. Two of his children also played a large part in the island's life. Clarence E. Howard, living in an era when the ambitions of an energetic man could not easily be confined to a single island, was active in many localities and many fields, but mainly in fishing: together with his cousins Erland and Bonney Quinn (noted below) he engaged in a number of seining, dragging, and processing operations, described in some detail by John Enk. His sister Marian Howard was for many years a legend in Penobscot Bay: returning in 1953 for a "short vacation" from her position in Camden, she spent the next quarter century on Eagle Island, alone with her cats during the winter months, until her death in December 1979 at the age of eighty-five. (The only complaint against her, it is said, during her fifteen years of service as a North Haven telephone operator, was that she persistently and unabashedly extolled the superior virtues of Eagle Island over all others.)

Frank Quinn—and I am back again with the children of Samuel, Jr. and Louisa—lived only briefly on Eagle after reaching maturity; he was

Charles Edwin Howard of Eagle Island, known familiarly as "Uncle Ed," for several decades one of the forceful personalities that held this community together; photo is a tintype made in Belfast c. 1900. (Courtesy of Robert L. Quinn, Eagle Island Association.)

John Hemmingway Quinn, son of Samuel, Jr. and father of Erland and Bonney; a tintype from the 1880s. (Courtesy of Robert L. Quinn.)

Capt. Erland Quinn of Eagle Island (1901-1991); he spent many years of his life on private yachts and windjammers. (Courtesy of Robert L. Quinn.)

lobster buyer for the island fishermen during the 1880s but removed before 1900. Finally, John H. Quinn was to the latter decades of the nineteenth century what his father and grandfather had been to an earlier era: mainstay of the island community, both in its economic and in its social life. His first wife, Augustus's widow Charity, bore him one son, Louis E. Quinn, who married his second cousin Vivian Raynes and lived on Eagle Island as a carpenter until 1915, when the family removed to Camden. John Quinn's second wife, Harriet (Hattie) Littlefield,[22] bore him two sons, Erland L. and Carl Bonney, both of whom—along with Clarence Howard—were central figures in the last decades of active community life on the island. (Robert L. Quinn, son of Erland's first wife Beulah Allen—both his first and second wife, Edith Ball, were daughters of keepers of Eagle Island Light—is noted below).

The foregoing analysis, focusing primarily on the Quinns, inevitably omits the few non-Quinns in the residence table, along with others

[22] Hattie Littlefield Quinn's brother John came to the John H. Quinn farm in 1904 at the age of twenty and remained there until his death in 1972—surely one of the longest unbroken residences on Eagle Island.

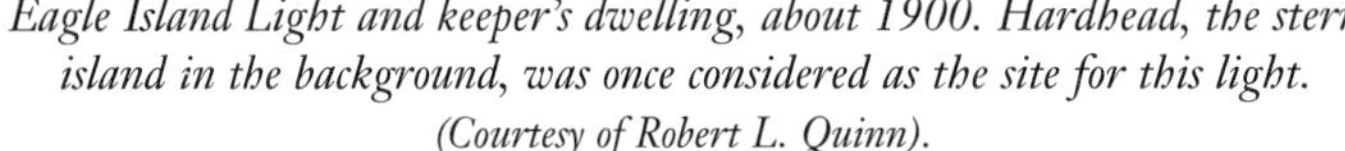

Eagle Island Light and keeper's dwelling, about 1900. Hardhead, the stern island in the background, was once considered as the site for this light. (Courtesy of Robert L. Quinn).

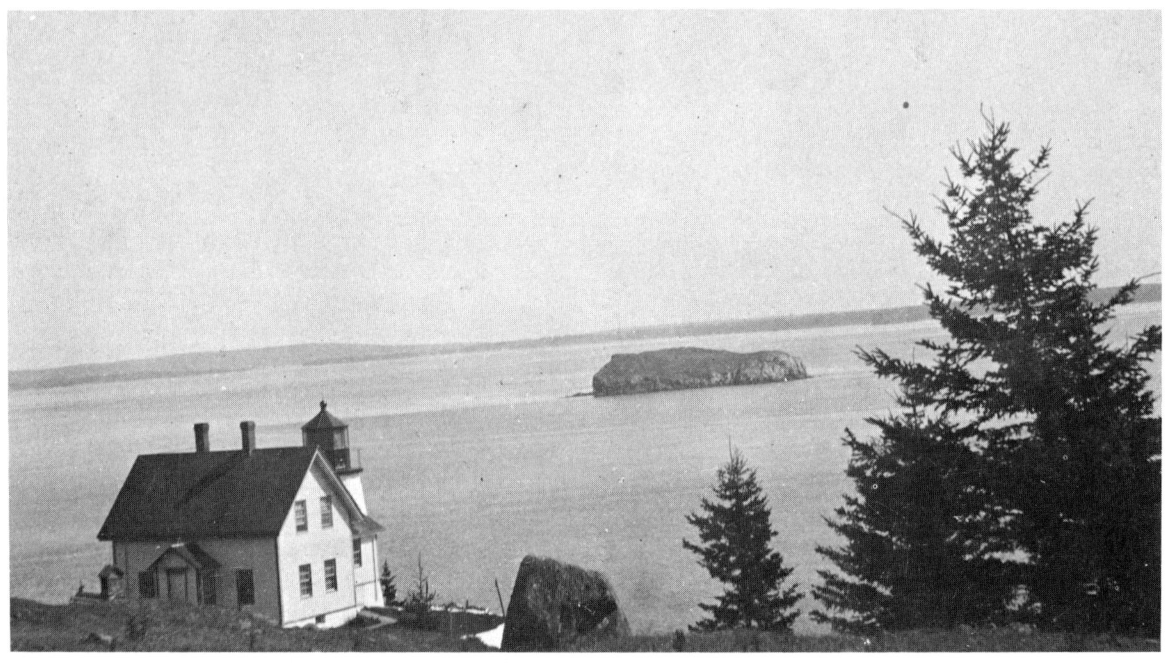

who lived briefly on Eagle Island between the visits of the census-taker (especially during the last two decades of the century). There was, in short, more happening on Eagle Island than revealed in the recitation above. But John Enk had it right: this was a "family island" through the nineteenth century and beyond (as we shall see). The continuity of Quinn leadership was remarkable.

The Eagle Island Light

Before considering in more detail the occupations of the Eagle Islanders, I turn briefly to the light station. A list of the keepers, from the light's establishment in 1839 to 1945 when it was taken over by the Coast Guard, appears below. The keepers inevitably played an important part in the island community. The daughters of some keepers married islanders; island girls often cared for the keeper's children in times of stress; the early impetus for a school on the island, it may be imagined, came from these government employees whose children needed to be educated.

In 1959 Eagle Island Light was automated and the last crew departed. It was a sad denouement to this long and fruitful association of the station and the island community that the keepers' handsome landmark was crudely demolished by Coast Guardsmen in 1964, although there were islanders ready to preserve it; the episode left a lingering residue of ill will toward this service among islanders and their neighbors.

Eagle Island Lightkeepers, 1838–1945

Name of Keeper	Dates of Service	Notes
John Spear	1833–41; 1843–48	In 1830 & 1840 censuses; died in service (widow served a year as acting keeper)
Nathan Philbrook	1841–43	
Daniel Moore	1849–50	
William Smith	1850–53	In 1850 census
R. C. Clay	1853–58; 1859–61	In 1860 census
Rodney Witherspoon	1861–71	In 1870 census; see also under Butter Island
A. P. Sweetland	1871–83	In 1880 census; died in service
John Ball	1883–98	
Howard T. Ball	1898–1913	In 1900 census; died in service (widow Lucy served two months as acting keeper)
Edward S. Ferran	1913–18	
Charles W. Allen	1919–31	
Frank E. Bracey	1931–45	

Note: Coast Guard personnel manned the station from 1945 to the light's automation in 1959.

Occupation of Eagle Islanders

The Quinns were primarily farmers. The agricultural census for the years 1850 through 1880 shows four separate farms on the island, each with a yoke of oxen, a few milking cows, a flock of sheep, and varying amounts of land under cultivation (see the 1880 agricultural census in Appendix 3, page 476). It was subsistence farming—not agriculture for profit as on neighboring Butter Island—but subsistence was normally the object of island farming in the nineteenth century. Moreover, the Quinns outlasted the Witherspoons on Butter Island by two generations.

Although farming continued on Eagle Island well into the twentieth century, third-generation Quinns turned increasingly to other occupations. One was boatbuilding. From 1875 on, according to John Enk (Chapter XIII), no fewer than five boatshops operated on Eagle Island at one time or another, normally in barns along the ridge. The best-known product of this industry was the double-ender or peapod, long a prized possession in Penobscot Bay; but larger vessels were also built, including a 36-foot schooner. The children of James and Samuel Quinn, Jr. were the most active boatbuilders, but later arrivals on the island,

Quinn House from Hill House on Eagle Island, 1910; the cluster of people at the flagpole beyond the tennis court includes Hattie Quinn, her sons Erland and Bonney, and her brother John Littlefield. Porcupine Islands are to left. *(Courtesy of Erland Quinn.)*

Horace Raynes and Allen Briggs, also contributed to the industry.

And then, as always, there was fishing. The Israel Carvers are listed as fishermen in the census from 1850 on; George Brown was a fisherman in the 1900 census; as noted above, Clarence Howard, together with Erland and Bonney Quinn, fished extensively away from the island in this century. All Eagle Islanders, indeed, were to some degree fishermen, and the census-taker must have been hard put in certain years to determine whether his subject was more fisherman or farmer. Eagle Island fishermen followed prevailing trends in the industry. In the 1860s and 1870s, when menhaden were abundant in Penobscot Bay, a pogy factory operated on the northwest cove. The building was later used as a boatshop and later still for storing fishing gear; its long dock, built for seiners, is still used as the island's principal landing. After the menhaden quit the coast in commercial quantities in 1879, Eagle Islanders turned to mackerel, and when mackerel, too, left the area, to weir-fishing; six weirs were constructed around Eagle in the early decades of the twentieth century. Later, herring were caught in purse seines. Meanwhile, there was the steady, if diminishing, take of lobster; scallop dragging in the winter out of Wood Landing Cove on the southeast shore; and harvesting whatever else the sea would yield. But fishing replaced farming only gradually, and Eagle Island never became a full-fledged fishing community like Great Gott Island, Frenchboro, Matinicus, or Isle au Haut.

Another occupation not usually found on islands of this size but critical to the history of Eagle was "hospitality," as John Enk calls it—specifically, Quinn House. This unusual hostelry opened soon after 1900 to absorb the overflow from the resort Dirigo on Butter Island (see page 246 ff) and soon developed its own style and clientele. Quinn House was the original homestead of Samuel Quinn, Sr., at the north end of the island, greatly expanded to accommodate some thirty or forty summer guests. Not all could find beds in Quinn House proper, but all took meals in Samuel, Jr.'s converted boatshop and found recreation in the dance hall above it; Hill House was built to accommodate the overflow. A boardwalk connected the two buildings so that rusticators could keep their feet dry. John H. Quinn was proprietor of Quinn House until his death in 1917, and after a hiatus of a year Hattie Quinn, with the assistance of her sons, carried on until 1931.

Until 1915, when Dirigo closed, guests came on the steamer that touched at Butter Island, where they were picked up by the Quinns' launch or, earlier, their sloop; after 1915, guests were met at Rockland or North Haven. A few summer guests, soon after Quinn House opened, built their own cottages and came regularly each season, forming the nucleus of a summer colony. But the colony was quite constant without cottages, since many of the same guests returned to Quinn House year after year. This circumstance, Erland Quinn felt, contributed to the closing of Quinn House: "The same group over the years resented new faces...[and] gradually put us out of business" (Enk, 141). But this, of course, was not the only reason for the closing of Quinn House in 1931. Indeed, with the changing patterns of transportation and changing styles of summer vacations by the 1930s, the wonder is that Quinn House lasted as long as it did.

Why the Eagle Island Community Endured

This leads to a question that it is appropriate to ponder in concluding this entry—the reverse of that raised about many islands in the present survey—the question being not what took the islanders away, but what kept the community on Eagle Island alive so long? I believe, first of all, that farming creates a more stable base than fishing for marginally small communities like this one: farmers build solid and permanent homes away from the shores and winter gales, while fishermen normally live by the sea in dwellings that are more fragile and therefore more vulnerable. Accordingly, when the usual pressures to remove arise—the awkward separation from high-school-age children on the mainland, the economic advantage of marketing a harvest from land or sea in a large community, the inevitable restlessness of the young in the modern era—the temptation to leave is invariably greater for the fisherman than for the farmer. The fisherman has merely to take his boats and his gear, and leave; the farmer must be concerned with his machinery, his livestock, his great investment in the land, not to mention the troublesome question of where to find another place half as suitable in which to reestablish himself.

Another factor in the survival of the Eagle Island community was its location at some distance from any important center where islanders might prefer to live. The residents of Long and Bartlett islands in Blue Hill Bay, for

Eagle Island, c. 1910, looking north from the Raynes dock on the southwest end of the island; the dwellings across the cove, from left to right (as identified by Robert L Quinn), belong to Owen Quinn (this house burned c.1938), Laura and Earle Brown, and George and Abby Brown.
(Courtesy of Deer Isle Historical Society.)

example—and these communities were comparable to Eagle Island in many ways—lived but a short distance from villages on the mainland and moved back and forth at will; many had quit their island homes before they themselves were fully aware of it. Not so for Eagle Islanders, to whom the decision to remove to Deer Isle or North Haven or Camden was a matter of some moment. Eagle Islanders, therefore, developed a keener sense of the separate identity of their community—an identity that was strengthened by the island always having been counted among the "unincorporated lands" by the State of Maine, never attached to any incorporated township in the area.

A third factor in the prolonged vitality of the community was surely the fortuitous sequence in the generations of Quinns: there was never too long a gap between the time the elders of one generation passed their prime and the heirs matured to take their places. Perhaps it was a near thing after the Civil War when the population fell sharply, but by 1880 it was back to a viable level; the success of Quinn daughters in persuading off-island husbands to settle on Eagle Island was undoubtedly a factor in this demographic turnabout. Meanwhile, the unpredictable but always-to-be-expected tragedies—the twin drownings in 1873, for example, or the high mortality in the family of Samuel Quinn, Jr.—were staggered over long enough time periods to prevent an exodus arising from grief or despair, causes of the evacuation of more than one Penobscot Bay island. Add to these considerations the good fortune of there

Pupils at old school on Eagle Island, 1909. Top row, left to right: *Marian Howard, Minnie Ball, Minnie Howard, Lottie Brown;* middle row: *Edith and Marcia Ball;* front row: *Clarence Howard, Erland Quinn, Arthur Ball, Bonney Quinn, Elmer Johnson, Maurice Ball, Herman Howard.* *(Courtesy of Robert L. Quinn.)*

The late Marian Howard in 1979, holding one of her famous cats, with a cousin from Islesboro, Ralph Gray. She was at this date the island's only year-round resident. (Courtesy of Marian Howard.)

appearing in each generation at least one, and often two or three, who could and did assume the responsibilities of leadership.

Finally, I note the diversity of occupations that contributed to the vitality of the Eagle Island community. If there was drought, one fished; and if lobsters were in short supply, Eagle Islanders could and did build boats. Meanwhile, from 1900 on there was hospitality—and I am not inclined to underestimate Quinn House as a force in keeping this island community intact: for more than thirty years after most island communities of this size disintegrated under one pressure or another, this one was assured a steady revenue from summer vacationers. There was not an islander who did not profit in some way from these guests. And the fact that they remained *guests* on an island predominantly of natives was also important in preserving the essentially indigenous character of the community; apart from a few lots sold early in the century on which cottages were built, there was no large-scale influx of cottagers until after Quinn House had closed its doors.

The Eagle Island community did dissolve at last, and as in many other cases three or four decades earlier, it was education that triggered the exodus. Erland Quinn decided in December 1941 to remove his family to Camden, thus lowering the school population from eight to four; the school closed for good the following June. The post office and solitary store, which was in the Erland Quinn home, ceased operations when the Quinns departed, and there was little to keep the remaining families with children on the island. A few individuals stayed on, to be sure—Hattie Quinn most years to her death in 1952, her brother John Littlefield until his death in 1972, and Marian Howard until 1979—but since 1941 a "community" has existed on Eagle Island only in the summer. This community of about fifty persons is made up predominantly of cottagers; their caretaker and general factotum is Erland's son Robert L. Quinn, who with his wife Helene (they are several times related as the genealogical tree shows) live on the island year round in Quinn House. Few descendants of the early settlers, then, are associated with Eagle Island today, yet I know of no other island, apart from those still actively inhabited by native islanders (such as Frenchboro and Matinicus), where the character and pace of the old life is more poignantly preserved than here.

The Quinns of Eagle Island

Note: This table includes only Quinn descendants who lived on Eagle as adults. Those with asterisks are buried on the island.

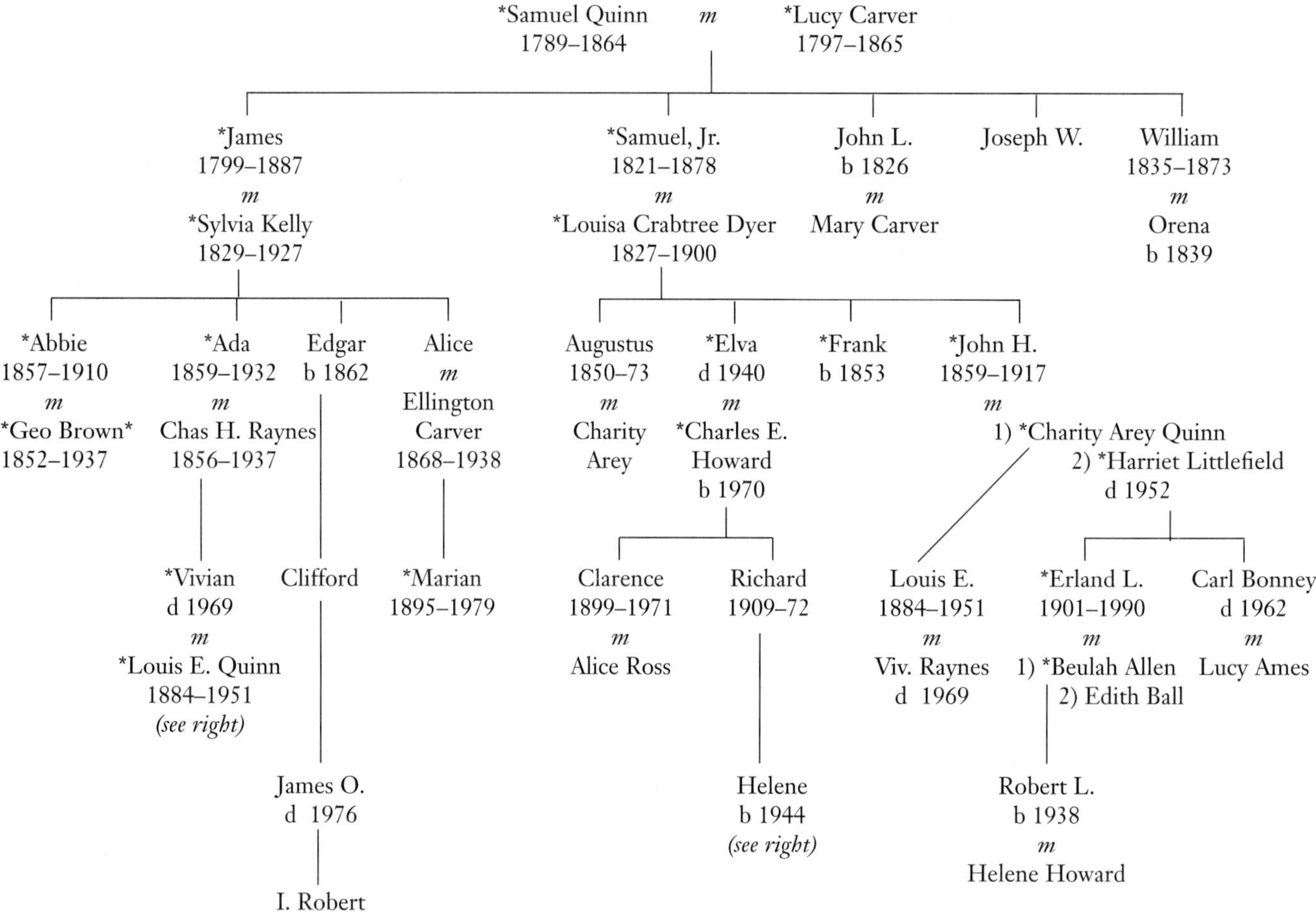

The Porcupines (off Eagle Island)

The origin of the name is clear enough and since it was in use early in the last century, it suggests these twin islands were cut over sparingly in post-Revolutionary times. The Quinns of Eagle Island owned The Porcupines during most of the nineteenth century and pastured sheep there. In the twentieth century the islands have been owned by cottagers from Sunset on Deer Isle, who have used them for day outings. Sheep were still pastured on them as late as World War II, and in recent years Outward Bound soloists have proven themselves on The Porcupines. Hurricanes Carol and Edna in the 1950s removed the bristling hump from Outer Porcupine, and the hedgehog-like aspect of the pair was less pronounced for a time than that of their famous namesakes in Frenchman Bay. Nature, however, is doing its work, and the islands will soon again grow up to their name.

Fling

This island had its present name as early as 1787, when it was conveyed to John Lee along with Butter, Eagle, and other neighboring islands (Enk, *Family Island*, 14), but I have no knowledge of the origin of the name *Fling*. (I reject as unworthy of mid-Penobscot imagination the legend that it derives from a bear having been somehow "flung" from this island to Bear Island, two miles away.) Fling never had a settler, since there is no water, but for a hundred years, the 1840s to the 1940s, it was used as pasturage by various Quinns of Eagle Island. Title, needless to say, became complicated as shares in the island multiplied from generation to generation; one of the two present owners acquired his undivided half at a tax sale.

Captain Walter Scott, son of a former caretaker on Pickering Island, tells a grim tale of two young Deer Isle clammers who were spending a winter on Fling Island in 1903; they were lost in a February storm returning to Deer Isle to a Saturday night dance. They were last seen by the wife of the keeper of Eagle Island Light, battling their way toward Northwest Harbor (Scott papers).

Butter

There are two theories, according to local pundits, concerning the origin of the name of this island. One is that its goldenrod in late summer, seen from a distance, suggested butter; the second is that early settlers trafficked in dairy products with the British at Castine during the Revolutionary War. The first theory is faulted by the great probability, as a recent owner observes, that very little goldenrod overspread the island when the name took hold in the mid–1780s. The second thesis is at least plausible, though we know too little about the politics of the early settlers to confirm it.

Early Settlers

The first European resident on Butter Island, according to a petition dated 1789, was John Grindlow (probably Grindle), who was said to have settled briefly there twenty years earlier (Massachusetts Archives, Eastern Lands, Box 14). He was followed by Benjamin and Ralph Annis (or Annes), who are noted on the island in Rufus Putnam's census of 1785 (see page 474); Ralph Annis was the author of the 1789 petition mentioned above. Title to Butter had apparently already been assigned by the Commonwealth of Massachusetts to John Lee of Penobscot who in 1787 had acquired Butter, Eagle, and a host of smaller islands for the absurdly low price of £89 4s (Enk, *Family Island*, 13–14). The sole condition was that Lee quiet the settlers with one-hundred-acre lots. Benjamin Annis quitclaimed his interest in Butter to John Lee in 1788 (Hancock 1/183), which may mean that he left the island at this time. Ralph Annis remained on Butter Island at least until 1790 when he appears in the first federal census, with a family of eleven, on one of "the smaller islands in Hancock County." The same year a Mrs. Rebecca Annes "of *Annes Island*" married a Sedgwick man, according to Sedgwick town records. Who was Rebecca Annes (or Annis)? She could have been the widow of either Benjamin or Ralph. Dr. Benjamin Lake Noyes, Deer Isle genealogist suggests that the title "Mrs." did not necessarily mean she had previously been married, though she probably had children (Noyes, Family Histories: Annis); that is, she could have been one of the young women in Ralph Annis's household. As to Ralph (or Rolfe) and Benjamin, Dr. Noyes notes merely that they were father and son, born respectively in 1734 and in 1758 in Haverhill, and settled on Butter Island together before 1784. We also note both as signers of a 1785 call to the first pastor of the Church of Christ on Deer Isle (Hosmer, *Sketch of Deer Isle*, 265).

I assume the Annis family removed from Butter Island in the last decade of the eighteenth century. The 1800 federal census gives no indication of the island residents in Hancock County, but in 1801 Job Small appears to have been living on the island. A lease agreement that year between John Lee of Castine, still the owner, and Job Small "of Butter Island" provides, in addition to evidence of the latter's living there, interesting testimony to the development and cultivation of Butter Island at this very early date.[23] The livestock on the island included four oxen (two was the norm for most of the small inhabited islands early in the nineteenth century), seven cows, one heifer, a three-year-old bull, a steer, and twenty-three sheep, which increased to fifty during the period of the lease, in addition to two other bulls to be removed "as soon as convenient." The agreement called for John Lee to pay the wages of a hired man for Job Small and to provide cedar posts for fencing and the required seed for crops of corn, grain, potatoes, and flax, of which Mr. Lee was to receive one half; he was also to receive, in return for the lease, "one half of the Butter and Cheese, half of the Increase of the meat Cattle and Sheep and half the wool, half the Geese and Feathers and half the pork that shall be fatted on said farm." His share was to be delivered to the farm "landing." Job Small was also to deliver to Lee all the cut cordwood on the island, an estimated fifty cords, and Lee was to receive a third of any additional wood cut during the period of the lease.

The Witherspoons

The duration of Job Small's stay on Butter Island is not known; it was probably not long, for if Witherspoon family records are accurate, this remarkable family was settled there by 1802; they remained for more than eighty years (Witherspoon, "John Witherspoon," 29). I find title record to the island perplexing during the early decades of the nineteenth century—no novelty, to be sure, to anyone working in this field. According to the title search in the possession of current owners, John Lee and his heirs held title to the island until 1816, when it was sold to William Gray in a court-ordered auction of Silas Lee's estate; the sale price was $946. An heir of William Gray sold to the Witherspoons only in 1844 (Hancock 76/34). What I find perplexing is that by then the Witherspoons had been the sole residents of the island for forty years, and from what one knows of this family, it is not likely its members would have allowed a cloud to remain over their title for so long. I can resolve the perplexity only by suggesting that there were conflicting claims to Butter Island and that the 1844 sale was in reality a quitclaim—an expensive one, perhaps, at nearly $1,000, but not beyond the Witherspoons' resources; they wished to extinguish all liens on their island.

John Witherspoon, progenitor of the Butter Island line, was a nephew of the Reverend John Witherspoon, President of Princeton University and a signer of the Declaration of Independence. He came to Maine in the 1790s, having already married Abigail Mills of Amherst, New Hampshire, and managed the estates of General Henry Knox: first at Knox's home, Montpelier, in Thomaston and later on Brigadier (now Sears) Island. In 1800 he is shown in the federal census in the township of Prospect, which then embraced Brigadier Island; his wife and two children are shown with him. In 1802, according to family records cited above, he acquired Butter Island from General Knox, who held title to vast properties in the Penobscot region through his possession of the Waldo Patent, and lived there for thirty or more years. He and Abigail apparently removed to the mainland in their old age, but they were brought back for burial: their graves in the center of the island, their stones being the only ones in the burying ground today,[24] are maintained by the present owners.

Two of John and Abigail's five children remained on the island after maturity: Unadilla (or Unadella) and James. A third son, Rodney, was a sea captain living in Bucksport, but he died before he was forty. James remained until the 1850s when he removed to North Haven, where his descendants still live. Unadilla, then, was the true successor of John as the patriarch of Butter Island. He was born in New Hampshire before the family moved to the region, and was with his

[23] The lease is in the possession of one of Job Small's descendants, Mr. Harrison Small of Castine.

[24] According to material at the Deer Isle Historical Society, there were once as many as ten gravestones in the Witherspoon burying ground (Noyes, "Butter Island").

father at Montpelier and on Brigadier Island before coming onto Butter. According to family records, he farmed for a time on his own at Bucksport, or it may have been at Bucks Harbor in Brooksville, for his wife, Betsy Kench, came from this area.[25] By 1840, Unadilla had taken over supervision of the Witherspoon farm on Butter Island, and it was he who secured the quitclaim from the Grays in 1844.

Unadilla was by all accounts a prosperous farmer and a towering personality in the area. The agricultural censuses of 1850 through 1870 show him to have had over two hundred acres under cultivation, twenty-five cows, six oxen, more than two hundred sheep, and pigs; his real estate valuation was $3,000 in 1870, and his personal valuation was $1,400—both high figures for farmers in that era. The farm, with its outbuildings and dammed pond, was on the south side of the island, facing Eagle. Charts surveyed in the 1870s show nine or ten buildings, five in the central cluster and the rest in the direction of the southwest nub where the landing was then located (Maps 1880 CGS 4 and 1892 CGS 309). Fencing is shown at various points on the island, and an orchard—still discernible today—was planted in a ten- to fifteen-acre plot between the two high knolls; approximately two-thirds of the island was cleared.

The 1860 census shows two of Unadilla and Betsy's seven children working on the farm: Rodney II and Charles. Charles apparently left the island soon thereafter, and I lose sight of him. Another son, Thomas, settled in Charlestown, Massachusetts, according to family records, and sent his daughters to Radcliffe and Smith colleges. Rodney also spent most of his adult years off the island, yet of all Unadilla and Betsy's children he maintained the closest ties to it; he bought an undivided half interest from his father in 1877 (Hancock 159/518) and apparently inherited the rest at his father's death. Rodney was keeper of Eagle Island Light from 1861 to 1871, and so was well known to Eagle Islanders (Enk, 236). According to Mrs. L. C. Quinn of Eagle Island, whose 1896 deposition is appended to the title record in the possession of the present owners, Rodney Witherspoon reurned to Butter Island in the mid-1870s and remained there for several years, "farming and raising stock," before removing again and leasing the island on shares. During this period, in 1879, he ran unsuccessfully for the State Legislature from Deer Isle (Hosmer, 261). He removed to Camden—apparently before 1880, since he is not shown on Butter Island in the census of that year—and his father, now widowed and in his eighties, later joined him there.

Unadilla died in 1886, and his obituary in a Camden newspaper, excerpts from which follow, gives an idea of his character: "a man of more than ordinary intelligence...a great reader of history...he attributed his long life of ninety years to his strict habit of 'temperance in all things'...he was not a member of any Church, [but] a great reader of the Bible and firm believer in its doctrines...originally a Whig, he became a warm supporter of the principles and policy of the Republican party" (Witherspoon, 30).

Rodney returned once again to Butter Island, according to Mrs. L. C. Quinn. This was in 1887, after his father's death, and apparently following a suit he launched against one of his tenants on the island, John Door. I know nothing about this suit or about John Door, but I doubt that Rodney—now in his late fifties—was in a mood to resume serious farming. He apparently returned soon again to the mainland, where he kept a grocery store and restaurant at Lincolnville. The island was sold in 1895 to the Harriman brothers of Boston. Albert Eels, Rodney's son-in-law, husband of his only daughter Lizzie, was instrumental in gathering the various family interests in the island for proper conveyance to the Harrimans; the value of the quitclaims, according to the title record, though I doubt this was the final sum paid by the Harrimans, was $2,800. I am under the impression that the Eels family never lived year round on the island—Albert was a quarryman from Brooksville. According to Erland Quinn, Albert Eels for several years took ice from the farm pond to sell on the mainland.

Before proceeding to the Harriman era, we should check out other persons mentioned in the census record through 1880 (see page 214). The farm workers in the 1870 census, after Unadilla's

[25] Betsy Kench was the eldest daughter of Thomas Kench, an early settler on Swans Island, and sister of Mrs. Ross, who was at one time married to the notorious Jeptha Benson of Marshall Island.

children had quit the island, were hired hands, living in his household; the surnames are well known in the area, but I do not identify any of the individuals. Walden Dyer, in the same census, came from Eagle Island. James Blaisdell, in the 1880 census, was presumably the first tenant farmer Rodney Witherspoon engaged to run the farm after his father's retirement, and to judge from the fact that Unadilla was a "boarder" in this household, I assume the relationship to have been cordial. It is also testimony to Unadilla's half-century of agricultural husbandry that the Butter Island farm in 1880 was the most prosperous in the mid-Penobscot Bay region, according to the census-taker's valuations: ten acres of tilled land, fifty in pasture, seventy tons of hay, and 190 sheep (see Appendix 3).[26]

The Harrimans and The Dirigo Colony

The next episode on Butter Island, which lasted from about 1896 to World War I, was unlike any other in the region covered in this study. George and Emory Harriman were architects, unmarried at the time of their handsome purchase, and they conceived of Butter Island as a summer vacation-

[26] The higher figures for "cultivated" land in mid-century (cited above) refer to acreage in use, not necessarily tilled.

Plan of projected tent-city at Dirigo (Butter Island), 1896. A few sites were deeded. Points on compass show nearby centers of attraction: Dark Harbor, Castine, Camden, and so forth.

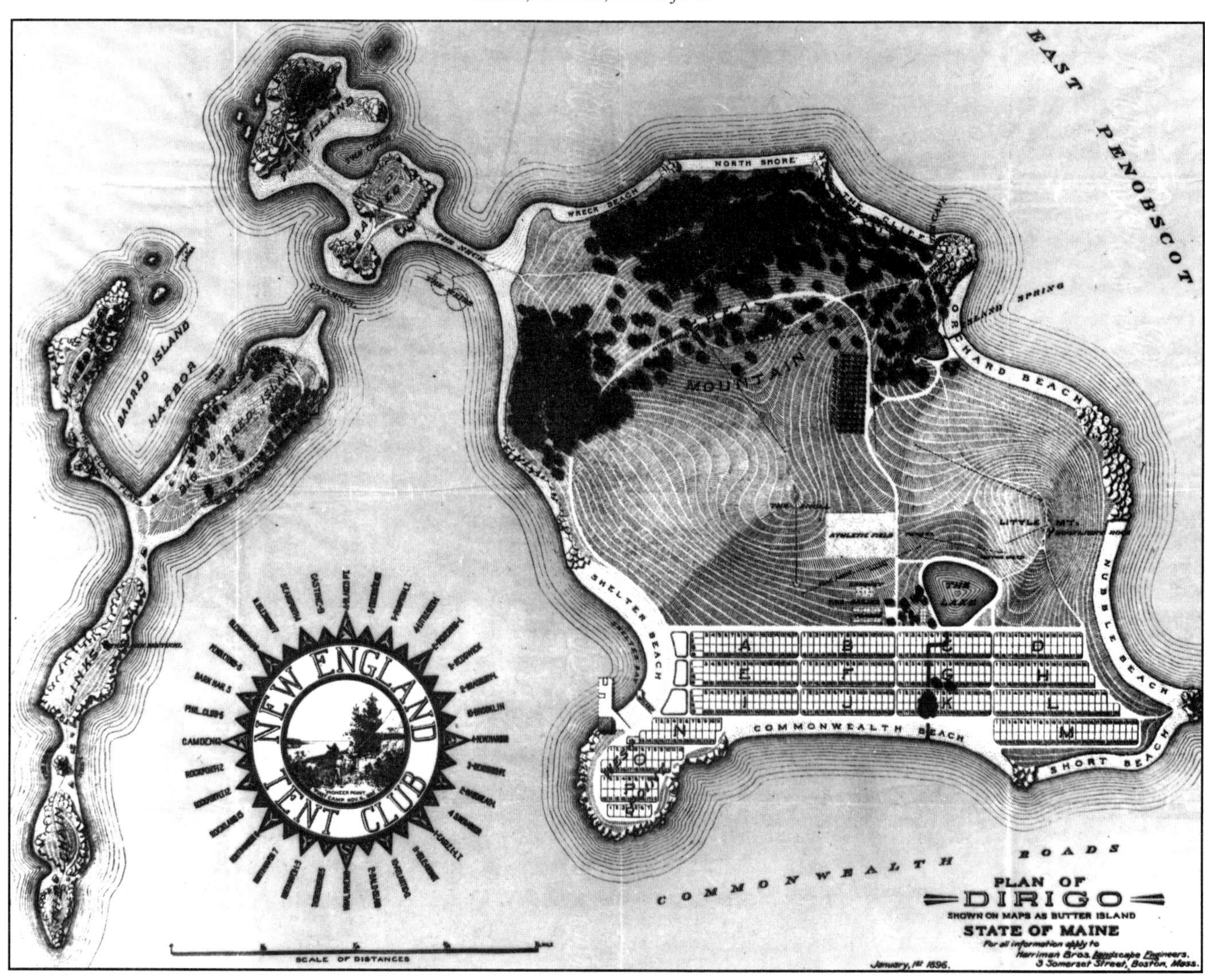

land for genteel Bostonians and other pedigreed guests. Their early brochures and publicity for what they called the New England Tent Club emphasized clean, wholesome outdoor living in an "Arabic-like town of tents and cottages."

Appeal was made especially to "the young merchant, club man, college student, graduate professional man, of good social standing and reference" who, upon acceptance, would be offered "an opportunity of becoming an individual landowner in this exclusive club." The first deeds for such tent sites in 1896 underscored, in addition to a ban on dogs and any commercial activity, a prohibition of "intoxicating liquors." The island was renamed *Dirigo*, after Maine's state motto "I lead," and although the name was never officially acknowledged beyond the printing of ferry schedules, its letters were emblazoned in whitewashed stone on the east slope of Little Mountain, facing Eagle Island.[27]

As matters developed, the Arabic tent-town, for which 497 sites were set aside in the ambitious prospectus of 1896, never materialized. Instead, most of the guests stayed in the Pavilion, or Casino, a capacious building near Unadilla's pond, reconstructed from one of the Witherspoon barns, or possibly built afresh from lumber taken from the outlying farm buildings no longer in use. The atrium of the Casino rose two stories and was the general gathering place for the guests; it was comfortably furnished, with a large fireplace at

[27] Copies of the brochures and other memorabilia are in the possession of the present owners, as well as at the Deer Isle Historical Society and elsewhere.

Covered walk connecting Casino and Club Room at Dirigo (Butter Island), c. 1900. The Club Room was remodeled from the old Witherspoon farm house; the Casino was constructed from a standing barn. *(Courtesy of Thomas D. Cabot)*

Well-sweep at Dirigo. (Courtesy of Robert L. Quinn.)

one end and a raised stage at the other, for recitals, concerts, and other entertainment. The bedrooms opened off this assembly hall—some ten or a dozen of them at ground level and as many again off a balcony on the second floor. The island post office, run by Mr. Harriman, Sr., was in a corner of the Casino. The guests ate in another building (I believe the original farmhouse), which was reached via a covered verandah; it was attached to a cookhouse, behind which the Harrimans themselves had their living quarters. Water was drawn in part from the Witherspoon well, with its colorful well-sweep, in part from a spring on the northeast side of the island above Orchard Cove and hauled by oxcart over the saddle; later a pump was rigged to bring fresh water to the height of land, whence it flowed by gravity to its destination.

Dirigo could accommodate up to eighty or a hundred guests by 1900, and the Harrimans increased their capacity as the enterprise flourished. In the years 1905 through 1910, as many as a hundred and fifty guests were at Dirigo seasonally, some living in cottages of their own on leased or deeded land. (A 1911 blueprint of Dirigo, showing these conveyances, is in Hancock Plan Book III: 52.) The Harrimans built a landing on the southeast tip of the island to ensure ferry service, and in the early years of the colony Captain Crockett's JULIETTE and CATHERINE stopped two or three times a week during the summer runs between Rockland and Blue Hill; after Oscar Crockett sold to the Eastern Steamship Company in 1905, there were daily stops at Dirigo in season on the Sedgwick run—actually two stops, going and coming. The round trip by steamer from Boston, which cost $5.50, left Boston at 5:00 P.M. and arrived at Dirigo, with a change at Rockland, at 7:00 P.M.; the return trip, on about the same time schedule, was shorter.

For staff, the Harrimans used many combinations of local help. A year-round caretaker was hired and lived on the island. Eldridge Shephard (or Shepherd) in the 1900 census, a Nova Scotian who had settled on Little Deer Isle, was one of the Harriman caretakers. Lewis Shepherd, Eldridge's brother, was also a caretaker on Butter Island and lived there with his family from 1908 to 1912; according to his daughter, Abbie Shepherd Weed of Little Deer Isle, six Shepherd children were on the island during most of these years. Lewis's sons Albert and Kimball assisted

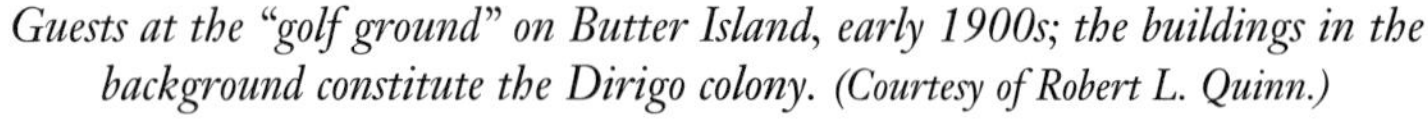
Guests at the "golf ground" on Butter Island, early 1900s; the buildings in the background constitute the Dirigo colony. (Courtesy of Robert L. Quinn.)

their father when they became of age. Abbie (to whom I am indebted for many details about the Dirigo colony in its last years) worked as a chambermaid in the Casino for several seasons. A couple managed the cookhouse, assisted by various teenaged girls from the area who served as kitchen help and waitresses. Some of the guests brought personal servants, who also helped in the running of the establishment. Ed Howard and the Quinns of Eagle Island sheared and cared for the large flock of sheep the Harrimans kept. Erland Quinn, growing up on Eagle Island in the heyday of the Dirigo colony, described the opening of the resort each season as one of the more stirring moments in life—surpassed only by its closing in late September, when the fairytale island was left deserted for young lads to explore.

While the Harrimans' concept of the colony inevitably changed with the passage of time, the general spirit of robust outdoor living prevailed. There were endless trails about the island and, when the tide was right, across to the Barred Islands where collectors could search for stones and seashells. There were excursions by sloop and motor launch to nearby islands; the Harrimans retained William Hendrick of Deer Isle for this purpose. There was tennis and swimming, and if the advertised yacht basin, under the aegis of "Captain Bullard of the Harvard crew," never fully materialized, every August a two-day regatta brought dozens of sailboats and yachtsmen to Dirigo from around the bay. Meanwhile, true to the original admonitions of the Harriman brothers, there were no dogs, no children (or at least very few), and no intoxicating liquors. Some guests came for a night or two, the majority for a week or a fortnight, and a few of the most dedicated for the entire four-month season from June through September. The Harrimans did all they could to give reality to John Greenleaf Whittier's couplet, which they displayed prominently in their brochures:

They seek for happier shores in vain
Who leave the summer isles of Maine.

By World War I, Dirigo had begun its decline. The opening of the coastal highways for the new "horseless carriages" and the paring of steamer schedules sharply reduced the Harrimans' clientele. The collapse was quick and irrevocable; by 1916 ferry service was suspended and the Dirigo colony for all practical purposes no longer existed. The Harrimans themselves returned for a few more seasons, but after Emory's death even these visits ended. Howland Harper remained on the island as caretaker until about 1920, but with

Page from a promotional brochure for Dirigo, 1895.
(Courtesy of Thomas D. Cabot.)

shores of myriad islands, the warmth of a summer breeze mingling with the ceaseless song of receding waves over the sandy and pebbly beaches, one stands enraptured and amazed.

From the heights, to which our inspirations have carried us in this commune with Nature, our eyes commence the descent again, stopping upon a living, acting scene at West Point Wharf, bringing us back to the actual pleasures of our existence and a summer vacation. The whistling of the steamboat, the flapping of sails and halyards, the grating keel of a row-boat on the beach, and a near-by old abandoned schooner, its journeys long since over, are enlivened by the salutations and his departure depredations on Butter Island, according to the scavengers' code of the era, became severe. Whole buildings were carried away, some to Deer Isle, others never traced. The larger buildings, such as the Casino, were dismantled in more orderly fashion: part of the lumber went to build a barn that stood until a few years ago opposite the cemetery on Eagle Island; part to construct a home for James Hardie, Lewis Shepherd's son-in-law and the new caretaker on Bear Island. By the end of the 1920s no buildings were left standing. The fields were kept open for a time by the Harriman sheep, but these, too, were eventually sold. The last lumbering on the Great Mountain was carried out in the 1930s, before the island was sold to the late Thomas D. Cabot, also a Bostonian as well as a life-long yachtsman and conservationist. He put sheep back on the island in the late 1940s in an effort to keep the few remaining fields open, but without success. By the 1970s, the farm pond was a tangled alder swamp, its man-made dike barely discernible; the meadows were choked with young spruce, and many sectors of the island were virtually impenetrable—testimony to the speed with which nature, left alone, reverts to its own.

Eagle Island Light in the 1970s, after demolition of the keeper's dwelling. Butter Island in near background, all signs of Dirigo obliterated by overgrowth; behind Butter, at left, is Barred Island in front of Great Spruce Head; Beach Island is behind right end of Butter. (Photo by Robert Hylander.)

One uninvited "settler" was able to find his way about the island. In the 1980s, he built a camp with stone walls in the midst of a spruce thicket, carefully concealing all approaches by crawling under low-hanging branches; he planted a garden, laid in a supply of books, and apparently intended to stay indefinitely. When in due course he was confronted by Mr. Cabot, he proposed himself as caretaker—a proposition that came to nothing when Mr. Cabot counter-proposed references and proof of license to carry the firearms in evidence at the camp. This twentieth-century Robinson Crusoe eventually removed, taking his library and his arsenal with him.[28]

[28] Butter Island is part of the Maine Island Trail, whose 1996 guidebook describes it as the largest wild island—"by a large measure"—in the MITA system.

Witherspoons of Butter Island

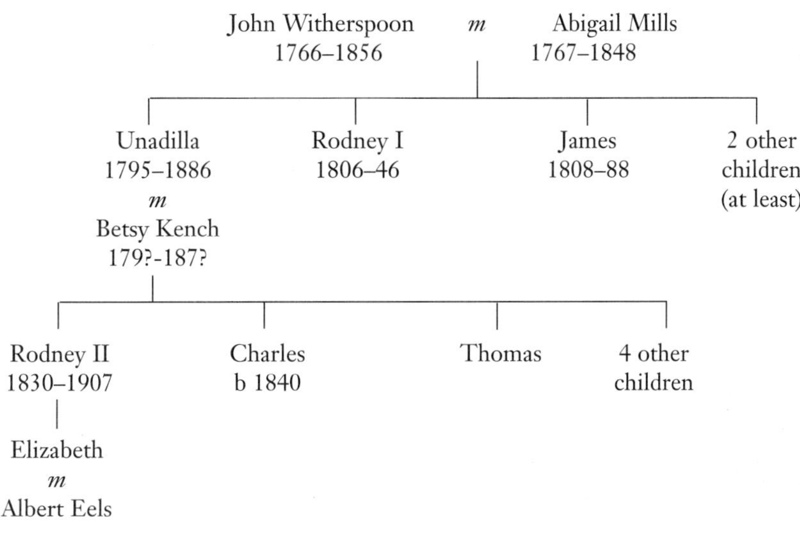

Barred Islands (off Butter)

The Barred Islands lie between Butter Island and Great Spruce Head Island, and early deeds indicate some confusion as to how many there were in the group. The State of Massachusetts apparently intended to convey them all to John Lee in 1787—they are called the *Bow Islands* in this conveyance (Enk, *Family Island*, 14)—but by the 1820s, with the separation of Maine from Massachusetts, there is uncertainty as to ownership and number. In 1828 the State of Maine sold four of the islands, "containing one acre each, more or less," to Hezekiah Rowell, and later in the year Rowell sold these same four to Paul Walton of Great Spruce Head (Hancock 51/319 and 51/314); it is uncertain which the four were, but they manifestly excluded the largest of the group, which no one could mistake for a one-acre island. In 1829, meanwhile, a conveyance among the heirs of William Gray, who had acquired John Lee's title to various islands, including the Bow, or Barred, group, mentions "one called Barred Island containing about six acres" (Hancock 54/166); this is about the size of the larger island and inasmuch as no others are mentioned, one assumes that the Grays had acquiesced in their loss of title to the group as a whole. What happened to title to the remaining three, for there are eight altogether—at least eight distinguishable at high tide—I do not know.

I lose sight of the title record until the 1890s, by which time all eight of the Barred Islands were owned by the owners of Butter Island. They are shown in the Dirigo plan prepared by the Harriman brothers in 1896 as a recreational extension of the summer colony. The Harrimans appear to have been the first to attach separate names to the Barred Islands, and several of these designations, though unofficial, have remained in use, while subsequent owners have made additions. The most northerly of the group, for instance, was called *Peak Island* on the Harriman map and its neighbor toward Butter simply *Barred*; the present owners call these two *Escargot* and *Bartender*, respectively. To the south—this cluster is now owned separately—the larger island continues to be called *Big Barred Island*, as on the Harriman plan, and the connected islands stretching southerly, the *Chain Links*. To the west, what was called *Harbor Island* is now called *Shelter*, or *Little Barred*, and the tiny one connected to it is called the *Osprey Nest* for obvious reasons.

There is more nomenclature than history, however, to these islands. They were never inhabited, except by transient fishermen, more recently by Outward Bound soloists, and, of course, by the family that has summered on Big Barred Island for some decades. The cabin there was built by Louis Quinn of Eagle Island from logs cut off the north end of Big Barred Island itself and floated along the shore to a point near the cabin site; the bricks, according to Erland Quinn, came from the old quarantine hospital on Widow Island in Fox Island Thorofare (see page 184), which was taken down in the 1930s. Big Barred Island, meanwhile, has yielded some profit to Eagle, for a number of its ancient oaks—probably seeded from the stand of oaks on Great Spruce Head in the days when it was known as Stave Island—were used to make "ship knees" in the Quinn boatshops on Eagle Island.

These are the islands that peer through the light summer fog in Eliot Porter's photograph on the back jacket of this volume.

Great Spruce Head

The earliest name I have seen for this island is *Stave*, a name given several coastal islands from which barrel staves were cut for the lively cooperage trade of Revolutionary times. It is shown thus on the 1776 "Atlantic Neptune" and again on Rufus Putnam's plan of Hancock County in 1785 (Hancock Plan Book II: 2). Soon thereafter the island was given its present name, which it has retained ever since: *Great Spruce Head*, or infrequently just *Spruce Head*.

The first apparent resident was a "Mr. Blastow," who is shown living there in Putnam's 1785 plan noted above. In a 1786 document he is named "Mr. Blagdon or Blaston" and is given a settler's deed by John Reed of Roxbury, who had acquired title from the Commonwealth of Massachusetts (*Bangor Historical Magazine*, I: 217/223). No Blagdon or Blaston appears on the "smaller islands" of Hancock County in the 1790 census, nor do I discover such a person in the 1800 census. But in 1804 when Lady Elizabeth Temple, who had inherited numerous Penobscot Bay islands from her father James Bowdoin, deeded Great Spruce Head to Paul Walton, she explicitly reserved one hundred acres to "Mr. Blastow, a settler" (Hancock 14/115). Whether or not the elusive Mr. Blastow/Blagdon/Blaston ever in fact settled on the island is unknown.

Waltons, Parsonses, and Eatons of Great Spruce Head

Paul Walton, in any event, did settle, and was evidently there at the time of the deed from Elizabeth Temple.[29] Federal census data show Paul Walton, an Englishman, living on Vinalhaven in 1790 and again in 1800. According to Deer Isle's

[29] A Porter in-law in the 1960s (who calls himself Dr. Harold Sprague) prepared an elegant spoof of the Waltons, set forth in a pamphlet entitled "John Walton, 1700–1805." There was indeed a John Walton, whose life nearly touched on three centuries; he is buried in the island cemetery and is probably Paul's grandfather. John, the story runs, was the son of a New Hampshire woman of prominent background who gave birth to him six months after her marriage to one George Walton. Scandalized matrons forced the semi-illegitimate son into exile, and the father chose Great Spruce Head as his refuge, sufficiently remote to shield the child from society's scorn. There John lived out his life, in due course siring his own progeny. So the story runs. It takes some imagination, to be sure, to place John Walton in the Penobscot Bay region well before the French and Indian War—but Dr. Sprague was undeterred in his search for John Walton's roots.

historian Dr. Benjamin Lake Noyes, he married Abigail Higgins in 1794 (Noyes, Family Histories: Walton). Paul Walton is shown on Great Spruce Head in the census schedules of 1810 through 1850 (see page 215). His offspring—or all of them I can identify—are in the genealogical table on page 257.

The little we know of the Waltons, in the absence of personal records, comes from Dr. Noyes's late-nineteenth-century notes based on interviews with a descendant (Paul M. Walton). Charles, apparently the eldest child, was a mariner who during his voyages left his wife and children on the island; according to Hosmer (*Sketch of Deer Isle*, 165), she was the daughter of Naylor Small of Deer Isle. William, who died comparatively young, was a bachelor living with his parents; he is buried in the family plot. Of Nancy I know

Aerial photo of Great Spruce Head and Bear islands (upper, lower left), Barred and Butter islands at high water, April 1955. Note shoals around the islands, many of them visible at low tide; note also modest overgrowth on Butter compared to 1970s, previous photo. (Photo by United States Air Force.)

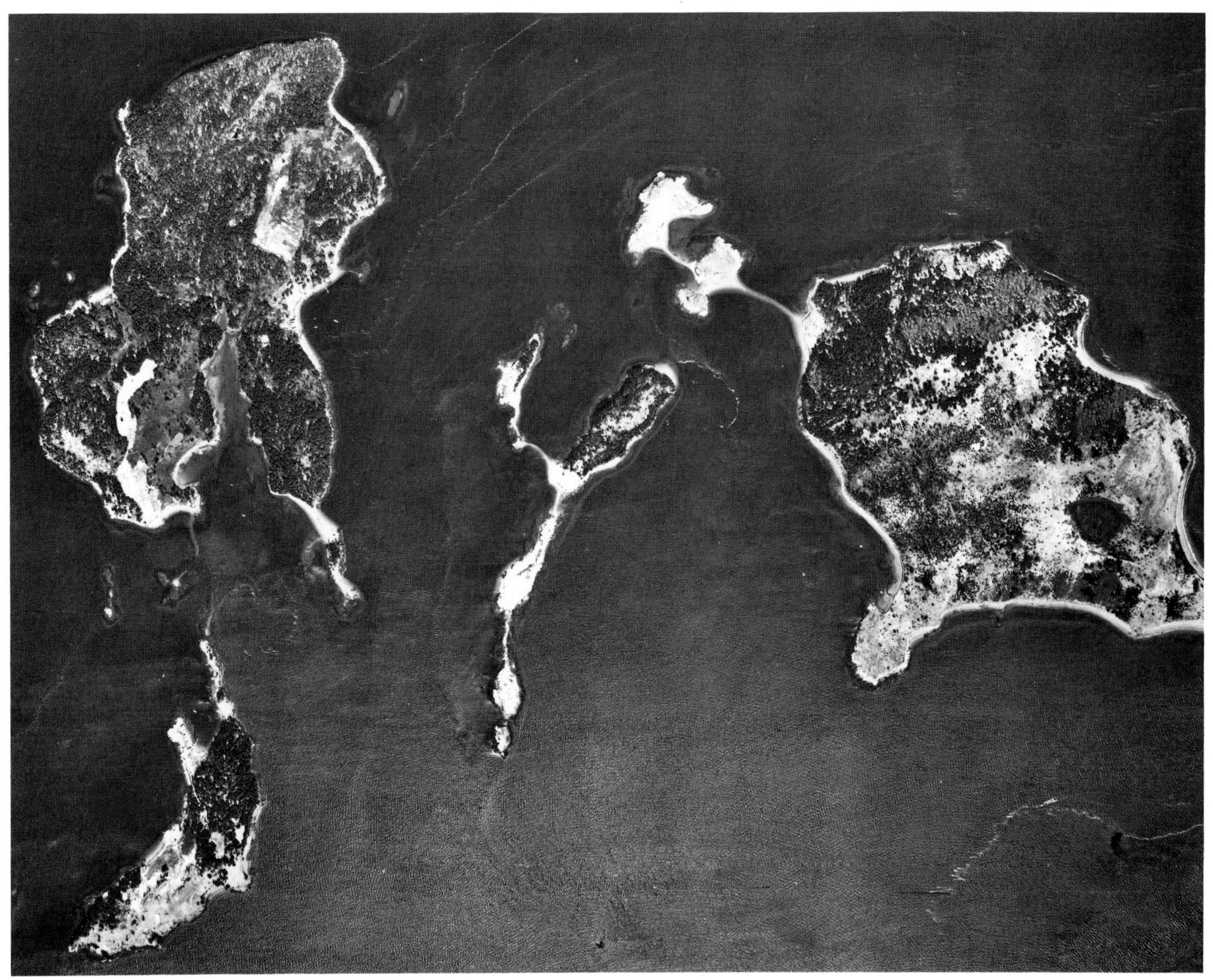

nothing beyond the dates on her tombstone. Ambrose remained on the island as long as our census lasts and presumably until his death in 1884. His children are shown as they are listed in the census schedules: in 1870, James H., twenty-five, and Ambrose, Jr., eighteen, both fishermen, and Helen, housekeeper; in 1880 only Paul M., of Ambrose's children, remained on the island, with his wife and daughter.[30] Paul and Abigail's daughter Sally was married to James Munroe, a farmer who lived intermittently on Great Spruce Head from before 1820 to the 1850s; he was on neighboring Bear Island in the 1840 census. They had a family but I have not made a record of all their children. Phebe, the youngest child of Paul and Abigail, married Thomas Haskell, who settled on the island at least until his wife's early death of tuberculosis in 1843; they had two children, Thomas, Jr. and Almira, who married John Staples of Beach Island (see page 266).

Other families shared Great Spruce Head with the Waltons, as census records show. I know nothing of the John Dows in the 1810 census, except that Susannah Dow, according to Dr. Noyes, married William Staples (also in the 1810 census) in 1797 (Family histories: Staples). Dow and Staples are familiar names in the mid-Penobscot Bay region. Wright and Thomas, by contrast, are not, and I know nothing of the two Williamses and their spouses in the 1820 census. Peter Hardy Eaton in the 1830 schedule was formerly of Little Deer Isle and subsequently of Bear and McGlathery islands; his extended family—prime movers in the RLDS movement (Reorganized Church of Jesus Christ of Latter Day Saints)—are discussed in some detail under those two islands). John B. Eaton in the 1880 census is a son of Peter Hardy Eaton. Josiah Herriman (or Harriman) in the 1870 census is said to have been an Englishman who came to the area before 1868; he eventually settled on Deer Isle, according to Dr. Noyes.

The Parsons family was the most numerous on Great Spruce Head Island after mid-century. Josiah and Margaret both came from Isle au Haut (she was a Hamilton from Duck Harbor), and several of their children were born there before they moved to Great Spruce Head. According to an affidavit prepared in 1812 by Charles W. Parsons, son of Josiah and Margaret, Paul Walton *asked* Josiah Parsons to come to the island, evidently to help him on the farm. The family lived initially on what was known as the Stimson lot; later, after acquiring the lot inherited from his father by Charles, Josiah Parsons built his own homestead there. Subsequently, according to the affidavit, Josiah bought the Stimson lot and another (Sally Munroe's inheritance) known as the Cooper lot. This gave him control of about two-thirds of the island, which he used principally for sheep husbandry; he had a flock of fifty or sixty. The fertile southwest tip of the island, a forty-acre lot, was acquired in 1865 by two sons of Peter Hardy Eaton living on Bear Island, Peter, Jr. and Jonathan; they used it for extra pasturage for their flocks. This lot was eventually sold to Charles W. Parsons and his brother-in-law James S. Eaton, who continued to use the lot, as well as one to the north called the Sargent lot, for their sheep which eventually, according to Charles W. Parsons, numbered between one hundred and fifty and two hundred.[31]

The identity of the lots in the last half of the nineteenth century is sometimes bewildering, as they changed names from owner to owner. The location of the house sites is less perplexing. Coast and Geodetic Survey No. 309, first printed in 1882 and surveyed between 1867 and 1875, shows three distinct clusters of buildings on Great Spruce Head: one west of the cove and about midway across the peninsula below the waist; another at the north end, midway across the island at its widest point and at the eastern base of the mountain; and a third at the neck of the southeast peninsula, close to the large east-facing cove. The sites were linked by farm roads.[32] It is believed that the first site was the Walton home-

[30] James H. Walton enlisted in 1864 at the age of nineteen; he was signatory of a petition in 1873 seeking reimbursement to the mid-Penobscot Bay islands (the "Eagle Island Military Plantation") for recruiting expenses during the Civil War (Enk, *Family Island,* 212–13).

[31] Charles W. Parsons's 1912 affidavit, as well as one by his sister Flora Parsons Eaton (widow of James S. Eaton), were prepared in connection with the Porters' title search of Great Spruce Head; the two affidavits were kindly made available to me by Stephen Porter, the island's contemporary historian.

[32] See page 226 for a reproduction of a segment of CGS 309; the segment shows rough boundary lines as well as house sites and farm roads.

stead, described by Paul M. Walton, who was born there, as a large log cabin with three fireplaces. Josiah Parsons probably lived at the second site. The third could have been the James Munroe homestead, for it is known he lived separately from his in-laws.

Josiah Parsons removed to Stockton Springs in about 1875. His son Charles W. and James S. Eaton remained on the island for a few more years, looking after the combined Parsons-Eaton flock; when they left the island, they hired John B. Eaton (brother of Jonathan) to care for the sheep. He lived on Great Spruce Head about two years before Charles Parsons and James Eaton sold the flock. They leased pasturage for a few more years to John Quinn of Eagle Island before selling their interest in the island. Ambrose Walton, meanwhile, died in 1884.

My impression is that the prosperity enjoyed by Paul Walton in the first half of the century[33] was not extended to Ambrose Walton in the second. Compared with the success of neighboring islanders like the Witherspoons of Butter Island, the Eatons of Bear, the Quinns of Eagle, or indeed the Parsons of Great Spruce Head, Ambrose's achievements seem modest. It is true that his valuations in the 1870 census were quite high ($1,025)—probably based on the real estate he inherited from his father—but the agricultural schedules of 1860 and 1880 show him without cattle or sheep and with small acreage under cultivation, even though the census identifies him as a farmer.

With the departure of the Waltons and John B. Eaton, there were, I believe, no further year-round residents on Great Spruce Head Island until after 1912 (an anomaly when one considers that this was an era of heightened activity on neighboring Butter Island). Most of the buildings shown in the charting of the 1880s still appear on maps in the early 1900s (e.g., Maps 1904–06 Vinalhaven quad), but all were down by 1913 when the island was bought by James F. Porter of Chicago from the Buel sisters of Litchfield, Connecticut. The Buels had made no significant improvements.

[33] The agricultural census of 1850 shows Paul Walton with sixty acres of improved land, a yoke of oxen, five cows, and sixty-two sheep. This was more substantial husbandry than any other islander in the vicinity—except Unadilla Witherspoon of Butter Island—could claim.

I pass over the long and eventful tenancy of the Porters, with two exceptions: the sequence of local caretakers, who played an important part in the year-round operations of the island community, should be noted here; and a word should be said of two remarkable artists who were in some degree nurtured by their years on Great Spruce Head—Eliot and Fairfield Porter.

Caretakers of Great Spruce Head

The first caretaker on Great Spruce Head was Monte Green, who lived there with his wife and three children from 1913 to 1917 before enlisting in the Coast Guard during World War I. He ran the Porters' cabin launch, the HIPPOCAMPUS; he taught the young Porters sailing and navigation; and during winters he cut wood and ice for the following season. He built a small schoolhouse where his children were educated, along with one or two Hardies from Bear Island.

The Greens were followed by Lewis Shepherd, a Nova Scotian who had settled on Little Deer Isle and recently served for several years as caretaker for the Harrimans on Butter Island. One of his daughters, Abbie, had spent several winters with the Greens; another was married to James Hardie, caretaker on Bear Island; and his son Kimball spent a dozen years as Lewis's assistant on Butter and Great Spruce Head islands. Lewis Shepherd retired after a few years and was succeeded by Rupert Howard of Eagle Island, who lived on Great Spruce Head with his wife and two daughters for twenty-five years. After Howard's retirement in 1944, the Porters could not for several years find caretakers able to withstand the solitude of long winters. Erland Quinn, captain of the HIPPOCAMPUS II, helped out during this era. Another resident caretaker was Arthur J. Duncan of Camden (1948–51). Wolcott Hardie, son of James Hardie, long caretaker of neighboring Bear Island, served the Porters in the 1950s and was followed in 1955 by Walter Shepherd, grandson of Lewis, who remained for thirteen years. The caretaker in the 1970s was Reynold Hardie, who is a son of Wolcott and great-grandson of Lewis Shepherd. Caretaking on Great Spruce Head, then, was a distinctly family affair.

Eliot and Fairfield Porter

Now to Eliot and Fairfield Porter. They were respectively eleven and five when their father James, a well-to-do architect, bought Great Spruce Head Island and promptly built a cottage there. They came to Great Spruce Head nearly every summer of their lives, not simply for a rusticator's two-week holiday but as a lifetime rite of passage. It was on the island that Eliot first photographed birds, shells, and lichen-covered rocks, little imagining it would become a career (he was a chemical engineer and physician before he became a professional photographer). It was on the island that Fairfield in turn, completed his first sketches—hardly expecting they would lead him to a lifelong career as a painter (he was a student of Russia and of socialism before he was a confirmed student of art). Fairfield once wrote of the island, protesting a suggestion that he went there in the summers to get away from the hubbub of the Hamptons on Long Island where he spent his winters: "It is my home more than any other place, and I belong there."[34] Eliot once wrote: "Our joy in the island was unbounded and uninhibited."[35]

Eliot and Fairfield Porter shared Great Spruce Head in their background, and they shared also a lifelong preoccupation with the fauna and flora of their surroundings, as anyone who regards their work will acknowledge. There was another affinity between the brother-artists, the consequence of their genes perhaps more than the island itself: both were absolutely independent in their respective fields. Eliot was sometimes criticized for being too conventional, conservative—for instance, when he shifted from black and white to color in the 1940s (Ansel Adams protested the use of color in modern photography as too "literal"), or in his close identity with the Sierra Club in the 1960s ("environmental propaganda," the critics wrote). Eliot replied that the *use* made of his photographs was "incidental to my original motive for making them, which is first of all for personal aesthetic satisfaction." But this, too, was a red flag to certain critics who wanted art not to be the artist's "reproduction of a scene" but an expression of "formal invention."[36] Fairfield Porter was judged "conservative" by some critics because he did not embrace abstract art, as most contemporaries did. "His art," one critic wrote, "stands out against the identity of most modern art like a rock in a stream."[37] Fairfield was oblivious to such criticism. "Painting does not illustrate or prove anything," he wrote with some passion the year he died (1975). "It is a way of expressing the connections between the infinity of diverse elements that constitute the world of matters of fact, from which technology separates us in order to control it and control us. The more effective technological control is, the more destructive it is. Technology is essentially totalitarianism and artists who collaborate with technology are technology's Quislings."[38] This is surely the creed of an independent modern.

Tale of the Eagle Island Bell

I close this account with an episode no competent historian should overlook: the raising of the Eagle Island bell and its installation on Great Spruce Head Island. In the Coast Guard's too-eager dismantling of the Eagle Island lighthouse in the winter of 1964, an event much deplored by everyone in the area, the ancient fogbell was allowed to pitch over the cliff, and it settled on the bottom. Walter Shepherd, spotting the bell as he passed over it during a spring low tide, managed to suspend it beneath his boat with a chain and moved it cautiously to the Great Spruce Head shore; the three-mile voyage took him two hours. In due course, and with the help of two tractors and other equipment, the bell was hauled up from the beach and raised onto new gallows—where for many years to come it will hail passing vessels and summon residents in case of emergency. (See the account of the episode in *Down East* magazine, October 1964, by John Porter, brother of Eliot and Fairfield.)

[34] "Fairfield Porter: Realist Painter in an Age of Abstraction," Boston: Museum of Fine Arts, 1983, p. 11.

[35] James M. Carpenter, "Eliot Porter, Fairfield Porter," Colby College Art Museum Exhibit (catalog), 1969.

[36] Essay by Ann Tucker, Curator of Photography, in "Eliot Porter: Intimate Landscapes" (catalog), Houston: Museum of Fine Arts, 1983.

[37] Peter Schjeldahl, cited in item above.

[38] Statement in a catalog for a retrospective exhibit of Fairfield Porter's work, 1975; cited in John Ludman, "Fairfield Porter: A Catalogue Raisonné of his Prints," Westbury: Highland House Publishers, Inc. (n.d.)

Waltons of Great Spruce Head Island

Note: This abbreviated table is drawn from census data prepared by Dr. Benjamin Lake Noyes. It is not necessarily complete and may contain errors.

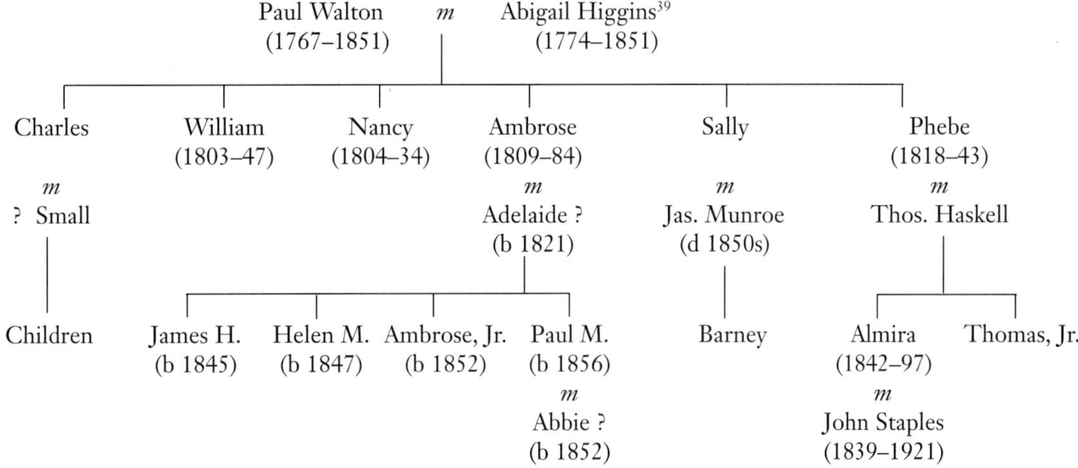

[39] The father of Abigail was presumably Barnabus Higgins, who is buried in the island cemetery (1743–1819). He is believed to have come from Penobscot (*Bangor Historical Magazine*, III: 147/625).

Bear (mid-Penobscot)

The name of this island was shown as *Bear* or *Bare*, interchangeably, from its earliest appearance on charts and in deed records until early in this century. It is, therefore, impossible to guess the origin of the name. I have discovered no evidence of habitation before 1830; Williamson (I: 73), in his relatively complete listing of mid-Penobscot Bay islands at this time, does not even mention Bear Island, and I am unaware of any claims of ownership prior to the separation of Maine from Massachusetts in 1820. In 1828 Paul Walton of Great Spruce Head acquired the island from the State of Maine for the handsome price of $42.50, and this appears to have set in motion the first sustained residence on Bear Island. James Munroe, who is listed on Great Spruce Head in the 1820 federal census, married Paul Walton's daughter Sally and is listed on Bear Island in 1830, in his thirties, with wife, three minor sons, and two minor daughters. The family returned, in due course, to Great Spruce Head, where James Munroe is said to have been buried.

In 1840, the family of Peter Hardy Eaton, totaling eleven, is recorded in the census as resident on Bear Island, and the Eatons play the dominant role on the island for the next half century. The family came from Little Deer Isle. The oldest of Peter Eaton's dozen children were born there; probably not more than two of this generation were born on Bear. We assume the initial residence of the Eatons to have been relatively brief, perhaps four or five years, before the family removed to McGlathery Island south of Deer Island Thorofare. I do not know the reason for this move—unless it was to find mates for the maturing Eaton children. No fewer than five of them married the children of George and Sarah Harvey of nearby Russ Island and either returned to Bear or settled on islands in the Thorofare vicinity (see page 296).

By 1850, according to census records, Peter Eaton's oldest son Jonathan is shown back on Bear Island with his Harvey bride, one son born the same year, and a household of seven; the next two sons died in infancy and are buried on the island—Benjamin F. in 1856, John W. in 1858. By

1860 Jonathan had been joined by his brothers Peter Hardy, Jr. and John, each with *his* Harvey bride and children (see residence table on page 214). The three brothers are listed as fishermen, but the agricultural census for that year shows, under Jonathan's name, that forty acres of land, all that were available, were under cultivation, and that the island's livestock included three cows and twenty sheep, but no oxen.

The 1870 census shows the families of Jonathan and Peter H. Eaton, Jr. still on Bear Island, but their younger brother John had removed.[40] His place is taken by Joseph Harvey, who had married Charlotte Eaton (the fifth Harvey-Eaton union) and, after her early death on McGlathery, married again before moving to Bear.[41]

It is curious that the Eatons, though associated with Bear Island since before 1840, did not gain full title to it until 1865. In that year it was deeded to them by Jeremiah McIntire, a land trader from Camden, who had apparently held it since 1836 when it was conveyed to him by Paul Walton (Hancock 62/455 and 123/572).

The Eatons, measured by the standards of the era, were a prosperous family. They constructed a dozen or more buildings during their long tenure, many of them with well-laid cellars. They had numerous boats, including the pinky that commuted regularly between Bear and the islands in Deer Island Thorofare where the rest of the family lived. The wharf they built on the northwest shore of Bear Island was still in use in the 1920s. And they owned many of the surrounding islands, including by the 1860s a forty-acre lot on the southwest end of Great Spruce Head Island. The Eaton children attended the school on Eagle Island after it was established in the 1870s.

The exodus began in the 1880s and was evidently completed before 1900 when the federal census shows no residents on Bear Island. Peter Eaton and his wife removed in 1885 to Stockton Springs, where Peter died in 1904. Jonathan Eaton died in 1886 and was buried on the island; his grave reads "Elder Jonathan Eaton," and there is an appropriate verse reflecting his strong religious beliefs. His wife Martha is buried beside him; she died in 1897, but I think it unlikely that she was still living on the island at the time. A Parsons family from Great Spruce Head is known to have been living on the island in the 1890s, for three Parsons girls of Bear Island are remembered as pupils at the Eagle Island school at that time (Clara Orcutt interview; this could, of course, have been a summer term—there is no certainty Bear Island was occupied year round in the 1890s). In 1904 Charles W. Parsons and Flora Emmeline Eaton (née Parsons and the widow of James S. Eaton), both living in Stockton Springs, sold the island to Caroline W. Andrews of Chicago (Hancock 414/246). She and her heirs have maintained possession of Bear since that time, using it as a summer residence.

Year-round residence was suspended with the departure of the Eatons and Parsonses, but not for long. The *Maine Register* shows two persons resident on Bear Island in 1910, possibly caretakers for Caroline Andrews who was still alive at this date; in 1913 James Hardie of Deer Isle took up permanent residence on the island as caretaker for Mrs. Andrews's heirs. He and his family lived there for nearly thirty years, until shortly before his death. He built his home at the northeast end, of materials salvaged from the old Casino on Butter Island. He fished the local waters, farmed the island, and kept sheep on neighboring islands, one of which, Scrag, he owned. He even kept a converted Ford truck on Bear and built roads for it to travel.[42] His children went to school on Great Spruce Head Island during the brief period when a school was there, and later on Eagle Island. James Hardie carried on and extended a tradition in the area that still persists, for his father-in-law, Lewis Shepherd, as well as his son Wolcott and eventually his grandson Reynold, served as caretakers for either Bear or Great Spruce Head.

[40] John B. Eaton did not go far evidently, for he is shown in the 1880 census on Great Spruce Head where he was employed by his brother Jonathan and Charles Parsons to tend their flock. He appears in the agricultural census of 1880 with one hundred sheep ("in shares"), forty acres in meadow, and harvesting eight tons of hay.

[41] Dr. Noyes shows Joseph's second wife as Angeline Hutchinson (Family histories: Harvey); the 1870 census names her Mary A.—unless this is the thirty-year-old Joseph's third wife.

[42] See NEAFOH, interview with Wolcott E. Hardie, August 1976.

I pass over the long, full summers in the twentieth century when the descendants of Caroline Andrews vacationed on Bear Island, except to note a feature of historical interest: one descendant, the philosopher-inventor R. Buckminster Fuller, has left the mark of his genius on its shores—a model of his famous geodesic dome, still visible to passing voyagers.

Scrag

Scrag, which as a noun means "scrawny person" or the "lean end of a leg of mutton," seems a misnomer for this island—but those who named it probably knew what they had in mind. It was not so listed on charts until the end of the nineteenth century, and its few acres could not have supported a settler's family. The Eatons of Bear Island owned it for fifty years or more and used it for pasturage. James Hardie, caretaker on Bear Island for the descendants of Caroline Andrews after the Eatons left, bought Scrag from them in the 1920s and used it as a working vacation home both before and after his retirement. He built a house there, which still stands, dug a well, grazed his sheep, and fished. He and his son Wolcott, who succeeded him as caretaker on Bear, lobstered, maintained weirs off the island, and in season scalloped. Scrag passed to Wolcott Hardie after his father's death, and he sold to the present owner in 1960.

Compass

This island is not named on maps before the mid-nineteenth century and when it first appears it is called *Turnip* (Map 1859 Waldo County). If there be truth in legends, the name comes from the quantity of this vegetable that washed up on the island's shores following an ancient spill at Pulpit Harbor: a schooner named JACKIE, the legend runs, passed to starboard of Pulpit Rock instead of to larboard, running in before a squall, and the vessel was a total loss. Not, however, the turnips. Apart from those that came ashore on Turnip Island, others washed up along the shores of North Haven and onto Eagle Island and were judged so great a delicacy that residents planted and replanted the seeds into the twentieth century. Any septuagenarian who has lived on Eagle Island or on North Haven will testify to the delicacy of the turnips.

As far as the name *Compass* is concerned, it would be easy to imagine that, like the numerous Mark islands in the region, this one was named for its early navigational usefulness, were it not for the fact that it does not appear on early charts. A resident of North Haven at Webster Head has discovered on an old map that the stone walls in his immediate area appear to be aligned with Compass Island (Charles Bauer, as reported by Samuel H. Beverage). I do not find that this is generally the case along the northern shore of North Haven (e.g., Map 1880 CGS 4), but if it were so, this would suggest another possible explanation of the island's name.

Compass was conveyed by the State of Maine to Rodney Witherspoon of Butter Island in 1877, on condition that the title was clear—which implied that it might have been conveyed before and the record lost, as was the case with several other islands in the area (Hancock 161/59). The sale price was $13.50. In 1898 Rodney Witherspoon sold it to Freeman C. Leadbetter of North Haven, and in 1905 the latter sold to the owner of Bear Island. Descendants held title through most of the twentieth century (Hancock 327/286 and 420/506). Compass Island was never inhabited.

Little Spruce Head

Little Spruce Head is the earliest name I have seen for this island, even when Great Spruce Head was called Stave (Hancock Plan Book II: 1), and it so appears on deeds. It was one of the islands conveyed from the Commonwealth of Massachusetts to Dr. Cotton Tufts of Weymouth in 1787 and conveyed by him to Richard Hunnewell (or Honeywell) of Penobscot in 1790 (*Bangor Historical Magazine*, I: 213/219). Hunnewell sold Little Spruce Head to Mark Pendleton in 1807, along with Beach, the Horsehead Islands, and "sundry" others (Knox Lands 4/350). In 1813 came the conveyance that initiated habitation: Mark and Lydia Pendleton, then living on Beach, sold Little Spruce Head Island to Mark's brother-in-law John Richardson (Hancock 62/35). John Richardson, though described in the deed as a "yeoman," had been a French naval officer under Napoleon, according to John Pendleton Farrow (page 270), and married Bathsheba Pendleton in 1804. I do not know how he came to Islesborough or why he chose Little Spruce Head as his home. But he did, and he is listed there in federal census schedules of 1820, 1830, and 1840.

According to Farrow, John and Bathsheba had only one child, who died prematurely; in view of the fact that the household totaled seven in the 1820 census, it is likely the Richardson family was larger. In 1830, when both John and Bathsheba were in their forties, a male in his twenties was in the household, as well as one teenager and one minor female.[43] Another settler in 1830 was Benjamin Simmons, in his thirties, no family. In 1840 the Richardsons, again alone on the island, had a household of six. Bathsheba died in 1843, Farrow tells us, and John in 1848. The latter date squares with a tax sale in 1849—State of Maine to Erastus Redman for $6.93, including back taxes and interest (Hancock 88/274)—and this fee is a melancholy comment on the Richardsons' thirty-year tenure. I know nothing further of John Richardson, but it must have been his origins that gave the island the name *Frenchmans*, as it appears on the Waldo County Map of 1859, though his surname, anyone will agree, could hardly be less French. His farm, or homestead, was on the southwest end of the island where a cellar hole and well are still visible today.

[43] The 1830 census calls the island *Spoon*, but the name did not last.

The Richardsons' was the only established residence on Little Spruce Head that I have been able to discover. Doubtless so commodious an island—and so close to other settled islands in the area, such as Great Spruce Head and Bear—had other settlers, but they must have been transient, for no record of them appears in census tallies or in histories of the region.

The name William W. Sargent of Castine appears on a number of deeds at the end of the nineteenth century, as a former owner. He conveyed the island to Eliza W. Gray of Sedgwick sometime before the 1880s, and she to Jonathan Eaton in 1881 (Hancock 178/60). Jonathan was still living on Bear Island at this time, but he removed soon thereafter and sold Little Spruce Head to his son James and his son's brother-in-law, Charles W. Parsons, formerly a neighbor on Great Spruce Head. In 1889 James Eaton and Charles Parsons, having already been settled for some years in Stockton Springs, sold Little Spruce Head for $450 to Freeman C. Leadbetter of North Haven (Hancock 237/428). The Eatons and Parsonses had used the island for pasturage, and Freeman Leadbetter did the same.[44] In 1905 Freeman Leadbetter sold Little Spruce Head for $450 to Richard B. Fuller of Boston and North Haven (Hancock 420/506). Possession of the forty-acre island by rusticators did not immediately elevate taxes on Little Spruce Head: the Fullers paid a mere 90 cents tax in 1912, if I read state tax figures correctly, on a valuation of $250 (see Appendix 4A). Richard Fuller's wife was the daughter of Caroline W. Andrews who had purchased Bear Island in 1904, so the two islands naturally were linked in the family holdings; descendants of Caroline Andrews still owned the two islands at the end of the twentieth century.

[44] State tax records show Little Spruce Head in the years 1887–92 charged not to Freeman Leadbetter, but to J. G. Lambert; I have no explanation of the discrepancy. The tax varied from 68 cents to $1.65.

Horse Head and Colt Head

These islands were named in the first decades of the nineteenth century, if not earlier, presumably by some resident in the area with a generous imagination. Williamson mentions Colt Head in his 1832 volume (I: 73), and Horse Head is mentioned in an 1839 deed, in which the States of Maine and Massachusetts conveyed the island, along with numerous others, to Charles and William D. Crocker of Bath (Knox Lands 41/308). Neither island was ever inhabited or, I believe, extensively used even for grazing—as most neighboring islands were. Horse Head was presumably cut over periodically for pulp. Colt Head never had significant growth, and what there was of it was killed by nesting cormorants in the twentieth century. (See item in *Maine Coast Fisherman*, June 1947, p. 7).

The present owners have prepared so meticulous a title record that it would be negligent of me not to render it here in abbreviated form, though it leads to no insight respecting residence on or even use of the island.

Horse Head Island Title Record

Note: The symbol > means "conveyed to." The date of the conveyance is the first date in the left column.

Dates	Owners	Comment
1787–90	Mass > Cotton Tufts, Weymouth trader	Also Hog, Pond, Western, Little Spruce Head, Beach, and "2 small unnamed islands"; £ 67 16s.
1790–1807	Tufts > Richard Hunnewell, Penobscot trader	Same islands, same fee; RH sold several of latter, 1799.
1807–81	Hunnewell > Mark Pendleton I, Islesborough	Also Little Spruce Head, Beach, & Barred, $1,100.
1839	Mass & ME > Chas & W. D. Crocker, Bath investors	This conveyance, part of an effort by the two states to clear up island titles, was in conflict with the 1807 deed—and did not prevail.
1881–86	Mark Pendleton II > Jon. H. Eaton, Bear Island	This Mark Pendleton was an heir of Mark I; the fee was $20.
1886–1903	Jas S. Eaton, Stockton Spr, heir of JHE, owned island.	
1903–15	Flora Emma Eaton, Stockton Spr, widow of JSE, is owner.	
1915–52	FEE > Isaac E. Gray, Castine (probably weirman)	
1952–67	Rodney F. Gray, Castine, heir of IEG, owned island.	John E. Gray and Frankie Heath, also heirs, gave quitclaims to RFG.
1967	Two Grays and Heath > Godwin W. Wiseman, island realtor	GWW held title only three months.
1967–76	GWW > Judith Lippencott Goodwin (later Mrs. N. Pott)	
1976–	JLGP > current owners	

In 1980 the owners built a cabin on Horse Head Island, and this was in all likelihood the first dwelling ever erected there.

Resolution

The earliest name given this island, according to a 1799 deed from Samuel to Joshua Pendleton (Hancock 6/523), was *Resulation*, presumably a misspelling. Samuel, an early settler on Long Island (Islesborough), claimed possession for twenty-seven years when he deeded the island to his eighteen-year-old son. The name *Mark*, contrary to local impression, came later, probably because the island served as a convenient channel marker for vessels making up the bay on the shortest course to Castine or the Penobscot River. There is, however, a second possibility: another son of Samuel settled on neighboring Beach Island. He was named Mark, and it is imaginable that Resolution acquired the name of Beach Island's owner by mistake. The next deed to Resolution, in 1857, in fact describes it thus: "called by some *Marks Island* more commonly known by the name of Resolution" (Hancock 127/474). In later years cartographers overcame the problem of distinguishing between *this* Mark Island and other Mark Islands in the bay by designating ours *Resolution Mark*.

The 1857 conveyance, from Joshua Pendleton to his daughter Sarah Jane Dodge, came some twenty years after Joshua had quit the island. He lived there a quarter of a century or more and appears in the federal censuses of 1810, 1820, and 1830, with households of five, seven, and five, respectively. According to John Pendleton Farrow (page 254), Joshua was first a mariner, then a volunteer in the War of 1812; after being ordained in the Baptist Church in 1824, he served as an itinerant preacher among the islands for thirty-six years. He married Sally Randall of Lincolnville and had six children, of whom Sarah Jane was the youngest (see Pendleton genealogy, page 223).

The Pendletons were apparently the only year-round settlers on Resolution Island in the nineteenth century; at least there is no record of other residence and no evidence of continued farming. All traces of Pendleton tenure have long since disappeared except for two wells, one of which is still in partial use. Sarah Jane Dodge conveyed the island to John Staples of Beach Island in 1877, and he back to her in 1888 (Hancock 162/296 and 227/138); I do not know the object of these two conveyances, but suspect that John wanted the uninhabited island for pasturage, then no longer needed it after he removed to Castine (see Beach Island, below).

The State of Maine, meanwhile, was confusing title to the island by conveying it haphazardly, along with half a dozen in the vicinity, to different parties: in 1839, for example, to Charles and William D. Crocker (Massachusetts joined Maine in this conveyance) and in 1879 to Frances L. Lazell (Knox Lands 41/308 and Waldo 189/9). I lose sight of the Crockers' claim, but Frances Lazell's title was challenged by Sarah Jane Dodge in 1889, and judgment was in Sarah's favor (Hancock 242/455).[45] Sarah Jane conveyed to her son Lorenzo Dodge the same year, and he mortgaged the island in 1894 to a group of Belfast owners, who foreclosed that year; the latter sold to Charles P. Hazeltine in 1896 and he to Preston Player (or Pleyer) of New York in 1912 (Hancock 276/464, 301/487, and 493/95). There was one further passage at law by Dodge descendants: in 1920 Sarah E. Dodge, Sarah Jane's daughter, attempted to regain title from Preston Player, by extinguishing the 1894 mortgage, but judgment was against her (Hancock 553/350).

Preston Player, an eccentric bachelor of means who summered on Islesboro, built an elaborate experimental farm on Resolution Island. He constructed a farmhouse with an artesian well—probably on the foundations of the old Pendleton farm—and several barns and outbuildings on the southeast shore, east of the cove. He built an elegant guesthouse, with well-laid foundations and cellar, on the northeast tip, and he had a small bungalow for himself nearby on the northwest shore. Much of the granite used in the foundations of these buildings appears to have been quarried from outcroppings on the island. The farm included, at its peak, pedigreed sheep, geese, turkeys, guinea hens, and various other stock. Mr. Player left the running of the farm to a succession

[45] A title abstract in the possession of the present owners traces the course of this judgment.

of resident caretakers, for he himself visited the island irregularly. Manfred Gray was one of the early caretakers. During World War I the Durkees of Islesboro spent a year on Resolution, and they were followed in 1918 by Ralph Collamore, who wintered there with his wife Margaret and two daughters, aged eight and five. Collamore had kept a boat in the water to fetch supplies and ferry carpenters working on the bungalow, but as the bay closed in with ice, he had to haul it out. While rigging a cradle alone, he fell on the ice blocks and broke his leg. His wife found him in due course and helped him home, but without a telephone she could only attract help from Islesboro (two miles away over open water—or ice pack) by lighting and feeding a huge bonfire on the western shore. Help did arrive, but the episode effectively ended winter caretaking on Resolution Island (*History of Islesboro*, 40).

Preston Player himself apparently lost interest in his farm about this time and in 1920 sold off his livestock. Untended, the property soon became subject to vandalism—perhaps the more readily because the owner was considered odd. The farmhouse went window by window, door by door, and vandals would have dismantled the artesian well itself had it not been cemented into the cellar. The guesthouse was saved by being cut in half and moved in the mid-1920s to Islesboro, where it was relocated and still stands, on the shore south of the old Islesboro Inn. The barn, while it stood, was put to a dif-ferent use. During Prohibition it was used as a temporary cache for contraband brought in from offshore vessels and held until the time was ripe to put it properly ashore. Leroy McCorrison of Islesboro, a part-time caretaker during this era, tells of coming out one winter day in performance of his duties, and, noting tracks in the snow, followed them to the barn where he was greeted politely but resolutely—with a gun in his ribs to underscore the resolution—and told to "set" with his captors until morning, for they were removing the contraband that filled the barn that very night. This they proceeded to do as several boats came into the lee of the island after dusk. But all stories have their complement: Leroy McCorrison tells of another occasion when he came out to inspect and found the barn again full of liquor, this time unguarded; and so he made off with as much as he could carry and passed the word up and down the coast. (No respectable historian, needless to say, should vouch for the authenticity of Prohibition stories—any more than of those that affirm Cap-tain Kidd's treasure or Jacob Astor's fortune buried on a dozen islands in the bay.)

Preston Player died in 1932 and left his Hancock County real estate to the Episcopal Diocese of Western Massachusetts for the Susan Preston Player Fund (Hancock 640/439). I do not identify Susan Preston Player. If Resolution Island was included in the will, title eventually returned to Maine, for a Camden family owned and vacationed on the island for twenty years after World War II; they built a cottage on the site of the famous barn. In the 1970s Resolution was sold to three Boston families, who use the island each summer in rotation.

Beach

*Note: Since the publication of the first edition of this volume in 1982, Janet Rhodes, a longtime summer resident of Beach Island, has written a 134-page history of the island (*Beach Island, *1992—see Bibliography for full listing). While more than half the volume is devoted to the summer residents in the twentieth century—Hoagues, Stewarts, Byrnes, and so forth—Janet Rhodes has given careful attention to residents of the nineteenth century as well. I have accordingly revised my earlier presentation of material on Beach Island to include some of her findings.*

Apart from an occasional misspelling, such as *Beech* in Williamson's History (I: 73) and *Buck* in a 1788 deed (presumably a mistranscription), this island has consistently been named, not for the tree, but for its sandy shores. Samuel Pendleton, a second-generation settler on Islesborough, is said to have bought Beach Island before the Revolution, along with six other small islands "west of a south course from Cape Rosier" (Farrow, *History of Islesborough*, 250); from whom he bought the archipelago is not indicated. His title appears to have had little value after the Revolution, for most of these same islands were conveyed in 1787 by the Commonwealth of Massachusetts to Cot-ton Tufts, a land investor (Hancock Plan Book II: 1). In 1788—and here comes the "Buck" Island deed—John Calf "of Buck Island...scituated between Cape Roseway and great spruce head" conveyed his sixty-four-acre possession to Richard Honeywell of Penobscot (Lincoln 22/26).[46] Who was John Calf "of Buck Island," and was he in fact a resident of our island? The surname Calf, or Calef, was well known at Castine: Dr. John Calef was a prominent Loyalist there during the Revolutionary War, but he left the region before the end of the war to settle in St. Andrews, east of Calais.[47] John Calf "of Buck Island" may have been a relative of Dr. John; there was also an Allen Calf resident at this time on neighboring Eagle Island (see Rufus Putnam's 1785 census, page473). But it seems unlikely, without further corroboration, that the phrase "of Buck Island" meant more than possession by John Calf. On the other hand, it is likely that John Calf and/or his successor owner Richard Honeywell made improvements on Beach Island: the price Honeywell received in 1807—$1,100 (Knox Lands 4/350)—was altogether too high for an unimproved island in that era, even when "sundry other islands" (Horsehead, Little Spruce Head, etc.) were thrown in. There is some presumption, then, that there was activity on Beach Island at the end of the eighteenth century of which there is no record—and probably never will be.

Pendletons of Islesborough, we know, played a critical role on mid-Penobscot Bay islands during the first half of the nineteenth century (see the genealogical table of Pendletons, page xx). Mark Pendleton, who bought Beach Island in 1807, was a son of Samuel, the original claimant, though there appears to be no connection between the original claim and Mark's purchase some forty years later. Mark was in residence by 1810 with a household of four. Since there is a nearly complete record of ownership and residence on Beach Island, it is useful to present it in tabular form, and then to make whatever comments are appropriate.

[46] Cotton Tufts sold, or quitclaimed, his interest in the island to Honeywell in 1790 (Rhodes, 26).

[47] Dr. Calef undertook an expedition to England in 1778 to petition for a grant of lands in the Bagaduce to Castine Loyalists, in the hope that any dividing line between the American colonies and Acadia would be far enough to the west to leave the Bagaduce in English hands; his mission failed, and he left Castine with a number of other Loyalists soon after his return from England.

Ownership and Residence on Beach Island, 1770–1919

*Note: The symbol > means "conveyed to." Some deed references are given in the text; others are easily located in the Hancock Registry of Deeds. Dates followed by "**C**" indicate federal census records, with householders and size of household in right column (census data are summarized more fully for Beach Island in the table on pages 213–14).*

Ownership	Date	Residence
Samuel Pendleton claims island	1770s	
Mass > Cotton Tufts	1787	
John Calf > Richard Honeywell	1788	
Tufts > Richard Honeywell	1790	
Honeywell > Mark Pendleton	1807	
	1810 **C**	Mark Pendleton, 4
	1820 **C**	Asa Miller, 4
		Ralph Haycock, 2
		Francis Appleton, 3
Mark Pendleton > Jesse Coombs	1821	
Coombs > James Crawford	1821	
	1830 **C**	George Grover, 7
		James Linzey, 4
Jas Crawford > James B. Crawford	1838	
	1840 **C**	Jesse Gray, 8
Wm Witherle & C. J. Abbott >	1844	

Ownership	Date	Residence
Joseph, Charles & Wealthy Dodge		
	1850 **C**	Joseph Dodge, 3 Daniel Ranlet, 6
Charles > Joseph Dodge: 1/3	185?	
Wealthy > Lucy Dodge: 1/3	1858	
Jos Dodge > Rob Stockbridge: mort	1860	
	1860 **C**	Robert Stockbridge, 10
Stockbridge > John & Sam Staples	1865	
Sam > John Staples	1869	
John > Almira & Rosanna Staples	1870	
	1870 **C**	James Staples, 10
	1880 **C**	James Staples, 4 John Staples, 10
Staples > Fred Carver & J. Quinn	1891	
Fred > Amelia Carver	1904	
A. Carver > Chas H. Snedeker & Henry K. Bush-Brown: mort	1905	
Snedeker & Bush-Brown > Eggemoggin Fish Co.	1917	
Eggemoggin Fish Co. > Caroline P. Williams: mort (foreclosed, 1923)	1919	

The comparatively rapid turnover of homesteaders on Beach Island is not typical of residence on the larger islands in the region: Witherspoons, for instance, came onto Butter Island before 1820 and were there into the 1880s. Waltons lived on Great Spruce Head Island from 1810 into the 1880s. Quinns remained on Eagle Island well into the twentieth century. On Beach Island, by contrast, no homesteader until the 1870s remained through more than one census-taker's visit. Moreover, of the ten householders resident on the island from 1810 to 1860, ac-cording to federal census schedules, only three were owners: Mark Pendleton, Joseph Dodge, and Robert Stockbridge.

What creates stable settlement on islands? Size is surely a consideration. Beach Island is smaller than most of its neighbors (half the size of Great Spruce Head and barely a third the size of Eagle and Butter islands). This meant limited productivity on Beach, rarely enough to support more than a single family. If that family removed for any reason, the island would be abandoned. Not so on other islands where there were always several farms, or, as on Butter, a single extended enterprise; on those islands, when Quinns and Witherspoons occasionally removed, other Quinns or Witherspoons replaced them. But size is only one consideration in the stability of island communities. Settlers themselves normally determined the parameters of settlement. If we knew what persuaded Mark Pendleton to quit Beach Island, after a mere dozen years there, with half the dozen children he eventually had already born and healthy, we might start to unravel the riddle of the island's restlessness.

With Mark and Lydia Pendleton's removal before 1820, Beach Island came under tenancy for the next quarter century, and tenant farmers, it is known, do not put down as deep roots as owning famers. The Pendleton name disappeared from the records of Beach Island, but—for those who place some stock in bloodlines—it is worth noting that the family linkages persisted: George Grover in the 1830 census, for instance, was probably the brother-in-law of Nathaniel Pendleton of Resolution Island, son of Preacher Joshua (Janet Rhodes, 36). Joseph Dodge in the 1850 census was a direct descendant of Pendletons through his mother Wealthy (indeed, Dodge-Pendleton connections are so numerous in the area as to be taken for granted). There were, meanwhile, ties among residents of Beach Island that had nothing to do with Pendletons: George Grover in the 1830 schedule married the sister of Robert Stockbridge of the 1860 schedule; and Samuel Staples, who bought Beach Island in 1865, married Robert Stockbridge's daughter. The appearance of family discontinuity in census tables, then, may be misleading, for linkages were numerous.

As for the husbandry of Beach Island, we know that most residents before 1860 were registered as farmers.[48] In 1850 Daniel Ranlet is shown with thirty acres of improved land worth $600, a pair of oxen, seven cows, and sixty sheep; Joseph Dodge does not appear in the agricultural census. In 1860 Robert Stockbridge is shown with one hundred thirty-six acres of improved land (obviously a typographical error, since Beach Island is not half that size), a pair of oxen, four cows, and two sheep; the farm, valued at $500, produced twenty tons of hay, forty bushels of barley, one hundred and fifty bushels of potatoes, and four hundred pounds of butter. This was creditable farming, especially for a householder who gave his occupation as rope-maker. In both 1850 and 1860 the Beach Island farm was as productive as any of the Quinn farms on Eagle Island, according to the agricultural census.

In 1865 Robert Stockbridge sold Beach Island to John and Samuel Staples, and a quarter century of Staples occupancy began. John and Samuel were the oldest sons of James and Rosanna Staples, who had lived in the 1850s on Pickering Island and at the time of the purchase of Beach Island were living on Bradbury with a sizable household. James and Rosanna moved to Beach with the younger children, leaving the older sons on Bradbury; John, the eldest, who in 1862 married Almira Haskell, granddaughter of Paul Walton of Great Spruce Head, joined his father to help run the farm on Beach. Its productivity in the 1880 agricultural census was comparable to the island farm in the preceding two decades (though the measurements were different): four acres of tilled land, thirty of meadows, and one hundred and thirty of "unimproved land."[49] The farm yielded sixteen tons of hay, and there were forty sheep. Two buildings are shown southwest of the cove on charts surveyed in the 1870s, with fencing; about two-thirds of the island was cleared (Maps 1880 CGS 4 and 1882 CGS 309).

[48] Only Asa Miller and Ralph Haycock in the 1820 schedule are shown as fishermen —or as "manufacturers," which was the designation for fishermen in that census.

[49] This would include Resolution Island as well, which John Staples owned at this time.

Accidents and ill health may well have been the catalysts that led to the Stapleses' eventual removal to Deer Isle about 1890. Two of James Staples's sons, at ages twelve and fourten, were drowned off Bradbury Island in separate accidents in the 1860s. Another child, Rose, according to the 1880 census, was palsied from birth. John's wife Almira Haskell, though she bore ten children (including triplets), suffered through life from tuberculosis. Her sister Melissa Haskell, for whom she cared, was deformed. David Haskell, who married James Staples's youngest daughter Elmira, drowned off the island in 1881 within a year of his marriage. Meanwhile, John and Almira Staples lost six of their twelve children on Beach Island in the 1870s and 1880s. Calamities of this magnitude sap the will to persist.

Beach Island was without year-round inhabitants for some years after the departure of the Staples family and never again had continuous residence outside the summer season. There is, however, a certain amount of history to record before the present owners took possession. In 1891 the Stapleses (Rosanna and Almira by then held title to Beach Island) sold to John H. Quinn of Eagle Island and Fred A. Carver of Hog for $700 (Hancock 259/43). According to Erland Quinn, John's son, the two farmers kept about one hundred sheep on the island and for some years took off hay each summer; the buildings had collapsed by the turn of the century. In 1905 Amelia Carver, Fred Carver's second wife, to whom he had given his share of the island, deeded it to one of her summer boarders, the Reverend Charles H. Snedeker of St. George Episcopal Church in Hampstead, Long Island, and his friend Henry K. Bush-Brown, a Philadelphia sculptor (Hancock 414/439); the two took turns tenting on the island in the summer until World War I. In 1917 the Snedekers and Bush-Browns mortgaged their half share in the island to the Eggemoggin Fish Company (Hancock 533/249).[50] The Quinns, meanwhile, had sold their interest to Pendleton descendants, who held title for forty-five years but manifested no interest in using the island.

[50] According to State of Maine tax records, the island, valued at $1,000, was charged to the Snedekers as late as 1921.

The Eggemoggin Fish Company was primarily interested in weir rights and maintained weirs in season off the northwest end of the island, toward the Barred Islands. A log cabin—indeed, a rather elaborate one—was built at this end of the island for the weirmen, and traces of it are still visible; Rupert Howard was one of the weir-tenders after World War I, as well as caretaker on Great Spruce Head. The pit where the weirmen tarred their nets is still clearly visible north of the cove. The fish company also had other enterprises on the island. Clara Orcutt, Amelia Carver's daughter, recalls hog-raising on Beach Island during this period and speaks of the fine barn and hog shelters built by what she calls the "White Fish Company."[51] There are also the unmistakable remains of a scallop factory on the northwest shore of the cove which presumably operated during this era: no traces of the "factory" itself remain, but the scallop shells are deep in this sector. What was once a stone pier extended into the middle of the harbor, and its fragments are still visible at low tide.

The Eggemoggin Fish Company's diverse operations on Beach Island evidently failed, for in 1922 the island was mortgaged to Caroline P. Williams of Massachusetts, and foreclosure followed the next year (Hancock 555/529). There was some sense of continuity between past and future in the foreclosure: Amelia Carver was official witness to the taking possession by Caroline Williams's lawyer George Hoague, and George was forebear of the two present owners. The latter have shared the still undivided island as summer residents for three-quarters of a century—a residence chronicled in Janet Rhodes's volume.

[51] Warren White of Newton, Massachusetts was a director of the company, which had its headquarters in Rockland; the two other directors were Joseph T. Moore of Thomaston and T. Lewis Thomas of Philadelphia.

The Staples Family of Beach and Bradbury Islands[52]

Note: All but the original John and Abigail Staples lived a part of their lives on either Bradbury or Beach islands.

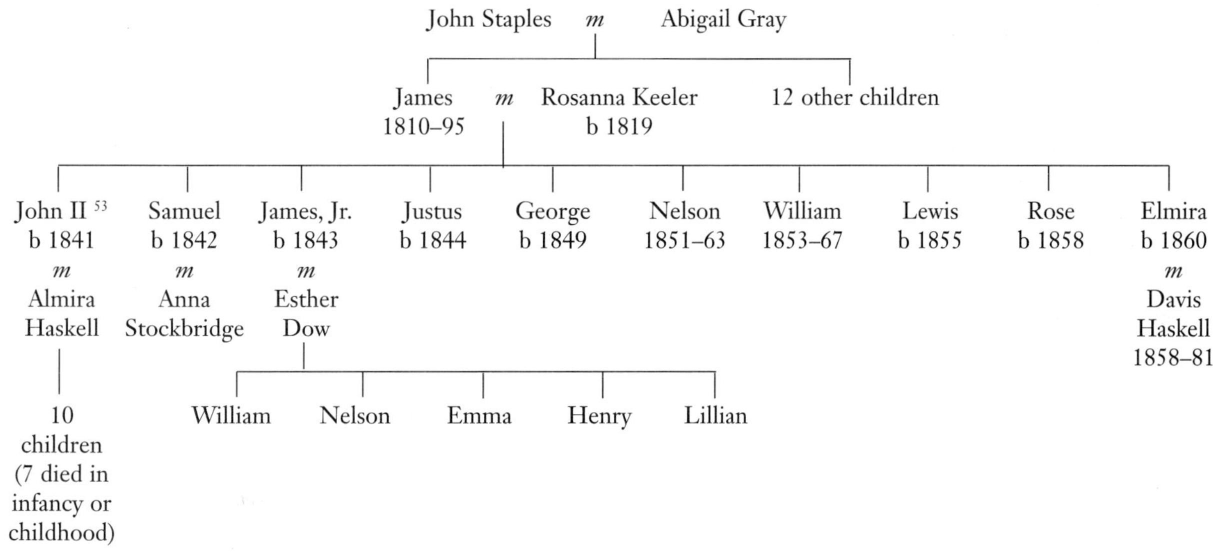

[52] Compiled from data in Janet Rhodes, *Beach Island.*

[53] There were many John Staples—at least one in every generation; I call this one John II to distinguish him from his grandfather.

Barred Islands (off Beach)

These twin islands northwesterly of Beach Island—barred to each other, not to the parent island—were passed in early years from one owner of Beach Island to the next. During the nineteenth century, title appears to have gone astray or taxes were in arrears, for in 1874 the State of Maine sold them for $22 to Tobias L. Roberts of Eden (Mount Desert); they were said to be good "for pasturage only" (Maine Archives, "1874 Island Sales," and Hancock 156/318). They remained in the Roberts family until 1917 when Tobias, Jr. and his wife sold them to the Eggemoggin Fish Company (Hancock 508/189). At this time they were used for weir rights, and since the passing of the weir-fishing era they have been used by summer residents of Beach for short outings.

Deer Isle

Deer Isle and Little Deer Isle

Deer Isle was late in gaining its own distinctive name, compared to the other great islands in the region: Mount Desert Island, Isle au Haut, and Matinicus early in the seventeenth century; the Fox Islands, *Brûle Côte* or Burnt Coat Island, and Long Island (Islesborough) by the end of that century. As late as the mid-eighteenth century, maps showed Deer Isle as part of the Fox Islands or, as often as not, gave it no name at all (Maps 1721, 1754, and 1755). The earliest map I find on which *Great Deer Island* and *Deer Isle* are named is a 1764 survey ordered by Governor Francis Bernard of the Bay Colony (Map 1764 Penobscot). By this date the earliest permanent settlers on Deer Isle had arrived. There were some fifty households on the island (including those of adult sons of original settlers) by the outbreak of the American Revolution.

After the Revolutionary War a census of Deer Isle settlers was taken by Rufus Putnam, surveyor for Massachusetts, showing eighty-six householders in residence (see Appendix 1, pages 472–73, for a facsimile of Putnam's 1785 census). Some pre-war settlers had left the island, including a few Loyalists (Tories) who removed to Loyalist enclaves in New Brunswick; those who remained were the founders of the township of Deer Isle. In 1788 the Massachusetts legislature passed a resolution granting a hundred acres to each settler who had arrived before January 1, 1784. In 1789 the township of Deer Isle was incorporated, embracing Deer Isle proper, Little Deer Isle, Sheep (now Sheephead) Island, and Isle au Haut.[1]

Deer Isle Town Records, 1789–1819

A résumé of selected actions taken by town meetings during the first thirty years of the township (until the separation of Maine from Massachusetts in 1820) suggests the preoccupations of a fledgling community in that era.[2]

1789 The sum of £100 was voted for the minister, Reverend Peter Powers; it was also agreed to build him a one-story house thirty-six by twenty feet.
The sum of £60 was voted for roads, daily labor to be paid as follows: four shillings for a man, three for oxen.

1790 Same allowance for the minister; £80 for defraying town charges. Voted not to send a representative to the General Court.

1791 *Voted:* to divide the township into five school districts: one (schoolhouse already standing) on the west shore, in the present community of Sunset; a second near the mill at Northwest Harbor (the village of Deer Isle proper); a third on the west shore of Southeast Harbor; a fourth at north Deer Isle on the west shore; the fifth on the Reach Road. £36 voted for schools; residents on Stinson Neck to be exempted from school taxes.

1792 *Voted:* that notices for town meetings be posted at the meetinghouse, at Haskell's gristmill (Northwest Harbor), and Tyler's

[1] The islands between Isle au Haut and Deer Isle were considered part of Deer Isle, and in time residents received benefits such as schooling and care of the indigent, but paid no taxes. After the Civil War, the town was no longer willing to provide these services without collecting taxes, and the islanders were unwilling to pay taxes unless they were formally included in the township. Accordingly, in 1868 the state legislature, at the request of the township, redrew the territorial limits of Deer Isle to include the Thorofare islands (Hosmer, *Historical Sketch of Deer Isle*, 37). For the separation of Isle au Haut itself and the islands south of Merchant Row, see page 342.

[2] The early town records are preserved in the Deer Isle town office and summarized (more fully than here) in Hosmer, 211–62.

gristmill (Southeast Harbor). *Voted:* to lay out a "new" burial ground.

1793 Two new school districts were added: Babbidge's Neck (future Oceanville) and Little Deer Isle.

1794 *Voted:* to give men who enlisted voluntarily for military service a sum to bring their wages to $8 a month—if they were called to duty, or three shillings a day if called to form a "detachment."
Note: There was, of course, no compulsory military duty in peacetime in that era, and even in wartime finding and rewarding substitutes was common practice to fill town quotas. The vote here was to entice young men to enlist either in full-time active duty or in reserve "detachments."

1797 Non-residents were forbidden to gather clams from any flats within the township, on pain of a 50-cent penalty per bushel (one half for the town, the other for the owner of the flats).
Note: Currency was gradually shifting from the pound to the dollar during this era, the exchange being at parity; the exchange of cents and shillings was more bewildering.

1799 *Voted:* not to send a representative to the General Court that year, but the vote was later reconsidered: one might be sent if he brought "no additional expense to the town and procured two bondsmen for the purpose"; two bondsmen came forward and George Tyler was elected representative.
Note: The town normally voted not to send a representative to Boston, presumably because of the cost; in pre-Revolutionary times the General Court of Massachusetts levied fines on Maine townships that failed to send a representative (see Vol. IV of Islands of the Mid-Maine Coast, page 41), but this practice appears not to have been followed by the Commonwealth.

1800 *Voted:* that important votes in town meetings should be by written ballot and that the vote, when declared, should not be disputed. The funds voted this year were: $333 for the "support of preaching"; $250 for the schools; $333 for repairing highways; and $100 for town charges.
Note: Annual budget figures fluctuated wildly, but by this date were generally three times higher than at the town's incorporation. ("Town charges" included care of the indigent, which after 1804 was treated as a separate item in the budget—as in other townships.)

1801 The town called on George Tyler's bondsmen (see 1799 entry) to refund the money he had drawn from the treasury in Boston and which was now charged to the town as "representative's pay."
Note: A decade earlier the town had had an awkward time with George Tyler and his brother Joseph (one of the bondsmen), who had improperly represented the settlers in arranging land grants from the Commonwealth; the 1801 action may have been a sequel to the earlier episode.

1803 The sum of $150 was voted "for a town stock of powder, lead, flints, kettles, etc." (The purpose of "kettles" is obscure.) Also voted to give Reverend Joseph Brown a "call" at a salary of $400 and to furnish him a residence until a parsonage was built.
Note: Fourteen years after the parsonage was approved (1789), construction had apparently not begun.

1804 *Voted:* that each district was to raise its own school money.
Note: There continued, nonetheless, to be school appropriations (e.g., $200 in 1805); possibly the action was for 1804 only.

1807 A bounty was voted for the destruction of crows.

1808 A group of religious dissidents led by James Eaton, after asking to be excused from paying the minister's salary (the issue was "passed over"), petitioned the General Court to be incorporated as the First Baptist Society of Deer Isle; a majority at the town meeting voted to remonstrate with the General Court against the petition.
Note: The original church, founded by most of the males on the island in 1785 and funded by the township, was Congregationalist; the minister, who served from 1785 to his death in 1900, was Reverend Peter Powers. His successor, Reverend Joseph Brown, appointed in 1803, alienated some of the parishioners (especially in the southern part of the township) and this led to the formation of the First Baptist Church noted here.

1809 The town voted disapproval of the federal embargo laws then in force and petitioned the General Court for relief. James Eaton and fifteen others were this year released from the minister's tax (that is, the minister's salary voted annually by the town: normally $300–350).

1810 *Voted:* to collect the minister's tax from Baptists, but to return it to the members of that church for their own religious use.

1811 *Voted:* against setting off the District of Maine as a separate state.

1812 *Voted:* to petition the United States government for one or more companies to be stationed on Deer Isle for its defense; also petitioned the Commonwealth for the loan of sixty muskets and four four-pound guns. A resolution was passed strongly criticizing the administration (President Madison) for the declaration of war against England. The record notes that "party feelings ran high and led to acts of indiscretion and violence of language."
Note: The embargo of 1807 and the war itself were unpopular in Maine, which had enjoyed a modest boom in coastal commerce and was suddenly cut off from a major source of income. An episode during the war illustrates the mood of some Deer Islanders (described in Hosmer, 225): an English brig sailing to the West Indies from Castine (which was under British control during the war) grounded in a cove off Deer Isle while attempting unsuccessfully to elude an American privateer. The brig's mate was a Deer Islander, and it may have been he who inflamed residents against the privateer, or it may have been the general irritation of the Deer Islanders against the war and the government's pursuit of it. In any case, unambiguous efforts were made—but failed—to free the brig. It was an action verging on treason, and had the privateer been a United States naval vessel it assuredly would have been treason.

1815 *Voted:* that "no swine should be allowed to go at large upon the commons or highways with or without yokes and rings." Sixteen men were chosen for a committee to assist tithingmen in enforcing due observance of the Sabbath and for the suppression of intemperance.

1816 The vote this year for Maine's separation from Massachusetts was: 160 opposed, none in favor.
Note: The vote is misleading inasmuch as sentiment for separation was very strong after the War of 1812, when Massachusetts had provided little assistance in the defense of Deer Isle from possible British attack. However, a federal law requiring vessels in coastal shipping to put in at the neighboring state but one was prejudicial to an independent Maine (it would have meant an obligatory stop in Massachusetts—Boston—even though Maine's commerce was principally with the Southern states and the West Indies). The lifting of this legislation in 1819 removed the objection to separation.

1817 *Voted:* that "the overseers expose for sale at public auction the poor of the town to the lowest bidder"; this practice (common in many Maine towns) was amended later in the year to allow the overseers the right to find suitable homes for the poor and to apply the town monies at their discretion.

1818 *Voted:* $300 for repair of highways and bridges, $400 for schools, $400 for town charges and the poor.
Note: Budget items had leveled off close to these figures at the moment of statehood, with additional levies for special purposes (e.g., new pounds, public buildings). The minister's annual salary, when reported, was in the $400 range.

1819 Delegates were chosen for the convention to write a State Constitution and the Constitution was approved by the town: twenty-two to one (a meager turnout).
Note: The final vote for separation, after the lifting of the objectionable coastal legislation noted above, is not shown in town records.

Sectors of Deer Isle

It would be presumptuous in this brief survey to attempt a rigorous delineation and description of each of the settlements in the far-flung corners of the township, but some identification of them is necessary for an understanding of the neighboring inhabited islands; and most of the smaller islands surrounding Deer Isle were inhabited within fifty years of the American Revolution.

North Deer Isle, the part of the island settled first (1760s), was predominantly a farming sector at the outset. Lots were laid out in parallel strips from the northwest shore, and some fields cultivated in that era were still under cultivation at the end of the twentieth century; several eighteenth-century homesteads (or parts of them) still stand. The village of Deer Isle, with its saw and grist mills, harness and blacksmith shops, as well

DEER ISLE
NORTH DEER ISLE P.O.
DEER ISLE P.O.
SOUTH DEER ISLE P.O.
WEST DEER ISLE P.O.
OCEANVILLE P.O.
GREENS LANDING P.O.
S. E. HARBOR
S. W. Harbor
N. W. Harbor
Cape Carter
Campbell's I.
Greenlaws Cove
Greenlaw's Neck
Longs Cove
Webbs Cove
Sheep I.
Bold I.
Camp I.
Devils I.
Spruce I.
Thurlow's or Crotch I.
Fifields Pt.
Andrews I.
Marble Quarry
Steamboat Wharf
Bar I.
Conat

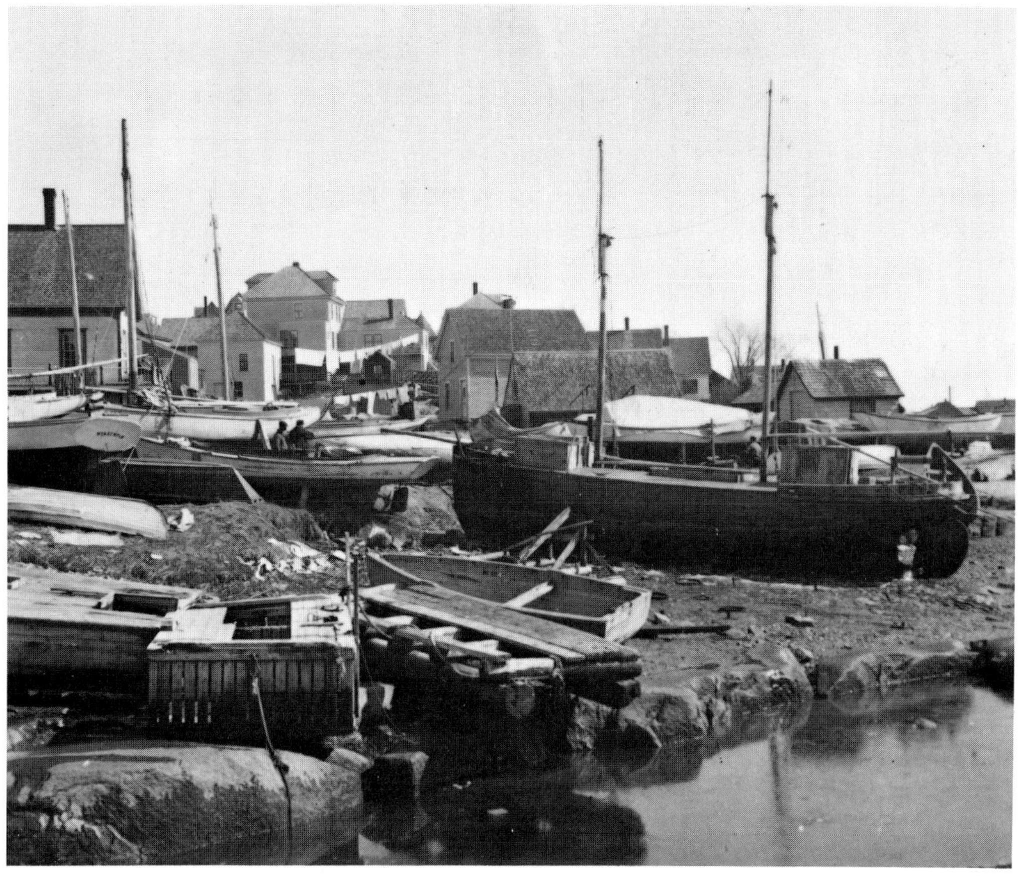

Fishing boats beached in Green Head Cove at Stonington, 1920s.
(Courtesy of Deer Isle Historical Society.)

as the first meetinghouse and church, came into existence to meet the needs of the north Deer Isle settlers and those living south of Northwest Harbor toward Dunham Point. Many of the early settlers on the mid-Penobscot Bay islands came from the western shore of Deer Isle.

Northwest Harbor, however, the interior of which empties at low tide, was not a satisfactory anchorage for coastal vessels or a fishing fleet. Accordingly, maritime activity was concentrated in the deepwater coves on the opposite side of the island, notably Southeast Harbor. Oceanville, on Babbidge's or Whitmore Neck, which makes Southeast Harbor, became a thriving center by the mid-nineteenth century. The large number of fishermen and mariners on Deer Isle in 1850 (see page 278) lived principally in this sector of the island. The 1860 map of Hancock County shows thirty-two dwellings at Oceanville, complete with stores, school, Baptist Church, wharves, and canning factory. The estimated eighty-five vessels that fished from Deer Isle during the peak of the fishing industry between the 1840s and 1860s were berthed in this sector (Goode, *Fisheries of the United States*, 40).

If the communities of Deer Isle and Oceanville were the principal centers of population in the middle of the nineteenth century, there were a number of smaller communities clearly identified: the Reach, Mountainville, Stinson's Neck, and Sunrise (now called Sunshine), on the eastern shore; Sunset on the western; and, of course,

Opposite page: *Most residents on Deer Isle and surrounding islands are shown on this segment of the 1881 county map, but names can be deciphered only with a magnifying glass. The road pattern is much as it is today.*

Haymakers posing on Deer Isle, 1890s. (Deer Isle Historical Society.)

Irvings or House Island in Stonington Harbor—probably the smallest inhabited island in this survey: the house was lived in by Irving Robbins c. 1910. (Courtesy of Deer Isle Historical Society.)

Little Deer Isle, which grew slowly but steadily through the century. Each district had not only its school, but often one or two stores, and sometimes a church.[3]

[3] According to Hosmer (pages 263–78), there were five churches on Deer Isle at the end of the nineteenth century: the original Congregational Church in Deer Isle village, the Baptist Church at Oceanville, a Methodist Church (1842) at what he calls South Deer Isle, a second Congregational Church at North Deer Isle (1858), and a Free-Will Baptist Church at West Deer Isle. There was also activity in the Reorganized Church of Jesus Christ of Latter Day Saints and among certain Adventists, but these parishes were not organized until later.

The one sector of Deer Isle that was not significantly settled in the first three-quarters of the nineteenth century was the rocky southern shore, separated from dozens of small islands by the Deer Island Thorofare. Though Crotch Island (as we shall see) had had a thriving community in the early 1800s, the only settlement on the Thorofare itself was Green's Landing (the future Stonington), where a few fishermen lived to be closer to the seaward fisheries. By the end of the

Home of Dr. Benjamin Lake Noyes in Stonington on Deer Isle, c. 1910; the doctor-historian lived here until his death in the 1930s. (Courtesy of Maine Historical Preservation Commission.)

Stonington waterfront, 1890s. (Courtesy of Maine Historical Preservation Commission,)

1870s, quarrying, already established for some years on Vinalhaven and in the Muscle Ridge Islands, had spread to Green's Landing. Job Goss and his son John L. were the pioneers of an industry that outlasted most similar enterprises in Maine and survived well into the twentieth century (the pink granite on John F. Kennedy's tombstone in Arlington Cemetery was quarried on Deer Isle). The peak of this era was in the last two decades of the nineteenth century, when Green's Landing became a bustling settlement of stonecutters, blacksmiths, teamsters, and other indispensable players in the industry; rough dwellings sprang up among the granite boulders for married quarrymen, boardinghouses accommodated single workers, and two rival music halls (Green's "Eureka" and Eaton's "Olympic") vied for customers. Green's Landing became a regular stop for steam ferries carrying passengers from Rockland to distant corners of Penobscot and Frenchman bays. By 1895 the noisy community on the southern shore of Deer Isle had so outgrown its casual association with Deer Isle proper that by mutual consent it was incorporated separately as Stonington. Stonington embraced, in addition to Green's Landing (which adopted its name), the communities of Oceanville, South Deer Isle, and all of the islands between the Thorofare and Merchant Row.[4]

These small islands, as well as Isle au Haut and *its* satellite islands, were influenced in the nineteenth century more by activities in southern Deer Isle than by those in the northern sector of the parent island. The influence was initially from Southeast Harbor and Oceanville; later it was from Stonington, as quarrying moved through the Thorofare islands. But the dichotomy was always there, as old as the earliest settlement in New England: the frontier versus settled centers; the swagger of exploration versus the smugness of

[4] An 1896 tax record of these three dozen or more islands, with names of owners and their holdings, is on pages 282–84.

Fishing boats hauled up for winter on Clam Flats east of Stonington on Deer Island Thorofare. (Courtesy of Deer Isle Historial Society.)

John L. Goss (on right), son of Job Goss and principal quarry owner on Crotch Island, with Elmer P. Spofford, his wife's cousin, 1880s. (Courtesy of Deer Isle Historical Society.)

consolidation; the leaky homesteads among the boulders versus the white clapboard farms of northern Deer Isle.

Occupations of Deer Islanders

A comparison of occupations on Deer Isle over a sixty-year period, 1850–1910 (table on page 278), reflects observations already made about the evolution of the island economy as well as one dimension often overlooked.[5] The 1850 data (the first year census takers tabulated specific occupations) show fishermen and mariners outnumbering other wage-earners by a margin of three to one. This year was close to the peak of the maritime industries, both fishing and coastal trade. The categories had not at this time been sufficiently refined to give the profile made possible in later decennial schedules. We cannot, for instance, distinguish between a simple sailor or fisherman and a sea captain, or between a farmer owning his own farm and a farm laborer. Wide differentials in income and influence are thus obscured in these data.

By 1880 the categories used give a sharper profile of the economy. The number of wage-earners had fallen since 1850 despite the fact that the number of residents was slightly higher (3,268 compared to 3,037). Unemployment is responsible in part for the drop in the number of wage-earners, but the principal reason for it appears to have been an aging population: many of the young left to find jobs in the cities (or to seek berths on vessels out of Portland or Gloucester); the aged remained. The number of farmers was up, the number of fishermen and sailors down—not surprising, since the peak of maritime activity had passed. The author of a Congressional report on the fisheries in 1880, the same report that praised Deer Isle's fishing industry in mid-century, wrote that "Deer Isle today owns the poorest class of vessels of any town on the entire coast" (Goode, 40). The 1880 census shows no quarrymen, not because none were there but because no *local* residents had yet learned the trade: the original stonecutters were brought in by the contractors, often from abroad, and, living in boardinghouses, were considered as transients by census takers.

The data for 1910 provide a more detailed and accurate profile of the island's economy. (It is necessary here to consider Deer Isle and Stonington together, since they both contributed to the island profile.) The large number of quarrymen in Stonington reflects the continuing vitality of the granite industry there; the small number of quarrymen in Deer Isle (seven) merely means that a few *resided* there—no quarries were opened within the perimeters of Deer Isle proper. The statistical difference in the number of farmers and fishermen/mariners in 1910 as compared to 1880 does not appear to be significant: fewer farmers, as island agriculture failed to provide the stable livelihood it had in the nineteenth century; more fishermen, as the lobster fisheries in particular expanded. The most arresting figure in the 1910 data (reflecting the "new dimension" noted above) is the high number who considered themselves "yachtsmen"—that is, serving as masters or crews on pleasure or racing yachts either in Deer Isle

[5] The data in the table for other large islands (Islesboro, etc.) are for purposes of comparison and are discussed in the essays on those islands. The 1850 and 1880 data are from the federal census; 1910 figures are from Chatto & Turner, *1910 Register*.

waters or further afield. The heroic days of the AMERICA's Cup defenders manned by Deer Isle crews (DEFENDER and COLUMBIA) had ended by 1900,[6] but the occupation of "yachtsman" persisted; doubtless it was a matter of pride for a Deer Islander, when asked in 1910, to give his occupation as "yachtsman"; federal census takers were less fastidious and called these "yachtsmen" mariners—unless they were, in fact, masters of their yachts (twenty-one were).

[6] For an account of the role of Deer Islanders in the defense of the AMERICA's Cup, see Clayton H. Gross, *Island Chronicles*, 34–38.

Occupations on Deer Isle and Other Major Islands in Penobscot Bay

Note: This table shows the occupations of wage-earners in selected townships, according to census schedules in certain years. The total number of wage-earners is in parentheses after the year in question. The key to the occupations is as follows (dashes mean no count was given for that year):

Fa Farmer, farm laborer
Fi Fisherman
S Sailor, mariner
M Master mariner, sea captain
Y Yachtsman (1910 only)
Ca Carpenter, shipwright
Q Quarryman (all jobs)
Blk Blacksmith
Tmr Teamster, liveryman
Skl Skilled worker[8]
La Unskilled laborer
Trd Trader, businessman
Prof Professional class[7]
Off Town official; clerk
Tch Teacher
Dom Domestic servant

	Fa	Fi	S	M	Y	Ca	Q	Blk	Tmr	Skl	La	Trd	Prof	Off	Tch	Dom
DEER ISLE:																
1850 (756)	148	-	520[9]	-	-	36	-	4	-	23[10]	-	21	3	-	1	-
1880 (572)	162[11]	34[12]	257	34	-	9	-	3	1	22	13[13]	13	6	7	7	4
1910 (770)	104	105	59	66	169[14]	48	7	5	9	26	24	48	5	36	27	32
STONINGTON:																
1910 (665)	34	123	23	20	27[15]	21	173	21	8	46[16]	31	64	4	27	16	20
ISLESBORO:																
1880 (373)	80	29	110	85	-	10	-	1	-	8	3	9	1	4	7	26
VINALHAVEN:																
1880 (912)	63	162	39[17]	-	-	47	366	38	30	29	46	26	10	21	16	19
NORTH HAVEN:																
1880 (227)	67	105	-	7[18]	-	4	-	2	-	9	7	7	2	7	10	-
SWANS ISLAND:																
1850 (117)	46	12	51	-	-	6	-	2	-	-	-	-	-	-	-	-
1880 (224)	37	152[19]	-	2	-	7	1	2	-	7	4	4	-	-	2	8
ISLE AU HAUT:																
1880 (71)	6	42	7	3	-	1	1	-	-	2	-	4	-	-	-	-
MATINICUS:																
1880 (75)	9	48	-	-	-	2	1	-	-	5	3	2	-	2	2	
FRENCHBORO:																
1880 (48)	1	45	-	-	-	-	-	-	-	-	-	-	-	1	-	1
	Fa	**Fi**	**S**	**M**	**Y**	**Ca**	**Q**	**Blk**	**Tmr**	**Skl**	**La**	**Trd**	**Prof**	**Off**	**Tch**	**Dom**

[7] E.g., doctors, lawyers, clergymen.
[8] E.g., masons, coopers, sailmakers, milliners, shoemakers, machinists, engineers, etc.
[9] Sailors on Deer Isle in 1850 included fishermen as well as all mariners.
[10] Sixteen skilled workers on Deer Isle in 1850 were coopers.
[11] Seventy-three farmers on Deer Isle in 1880 were farm laborers—meaning they did not own their own farms.
[12] Eight fishermen in 1880 were specifially designated as clamdiggers and seven as lobstermen.
[13] Most of these unskilled workers on Deer Isle in 1880 worked in a silver mine at Dunham Point on the western shore.
[14] Twenty-one yachtsmen on Deer Isle were yacht captains—that is, master mariners.
[15] Seven yachtsmen were yacht captains.
[16] Thirty-eight skilled workers at Stonington were engineers.
[17] Master mariners are not distinguished from sailors or mariners in this Vinalhaven schedule.
[18] Sailors are not shown on North Haven in 1880—only mariners, who may be master mariners.
[19] Sailors on Swans Island in 1880 are not distinguished from fishermen.

This, then, is a brief sketch of Deer Isle, most populous and, indeed, the largest territorially in the Penobscot Bay area.[20] To treat Deer Isle in any significant detail in the twentiety century would exceed the objectives of this volume. A landmark development in the twentieth century was the completion in the 1930s of the long-awaited Deer Isle–Sedgwick suspension bridge, replacing the ferry service across Eggemoggin Reach—for more than a century the islanders' principal access to the mainland. The bridge, of course, made Deer Isle more of an extension of the main than ever before: island housewives could henceforth shop as easily in Blue Hill or Ellsworth as on the island proper; Deer Isle teenagers could go to mainland high schools, and vice versa. Meanwhile, the influx of summer cottagers escalated sharply, which meant that non-residents soon owned most of the island real estate, as they already did on other summer islands in Penobscot Bay such as North Haven and Islesboro. Still, many of the indigenous communities of Deer Isle and Little Deer retained their distinctive outlook and orientation. The famous bridge may have brought the two islands into more intimate contact with the mainland but did not destroy their identity: Deer Islanders, it could be said, maintained more control over their affairs than did their counterparts in Islesboro and North Haven.

The islands in this division are treated in two groups: first, those from Merchant Row northward, sweeping from west to east, east to west, and back again—that is, from Scraggy Island to Shabby, back to Western Mark, and back again to include the islands south and north of Deer Island Thorofare; second, islands close to shore, clockwise around Deer and Little Deer Isle from Stonington, beginning with Sheephead Island and ending with the Freese Islands in Southeast Harbor.

[20] The ten largest coastal islands in Maine, in order of their size, are as follows:

1. Mount Desert
2. Deer Isle
3. Vinalhaven
4. Georgetown
5. Islesboro
6. Swans
7. North Haven
8. Isle au Haut
9. Westport
10. Arrowsic

Residence on Islands of Deer Island Thorofare, Nineteenth Century

Note: Hundreds of Deer Islanders lived on the Thorofare islands in the nineteenth century, most of them leaving no trace of their residence—or even of their identity. Despite gaps in our data, it is helpful to attempt a profile of residence using material in the notices that follow. Title record is less help than usual in tracing settlement since there were few resident-owners. Our best evidence of settlement is, as usual, the federal census, which, if we can interpret schedules correctly, provides us with hard data on Thorofare islanders (householder's age is at first appearance, 1850 on; spouses are in parentheses; occupation of householder is assumed to be fisherman unless otherwise noted—e.g., K, lightkeeper; size of household is in decennial column, males/females).[21] Other data in this table are taken from interviews Dr. Benjamin Lake Noyes had with Thorofare islanders early in the twentieth century; these data, flagged with the letter **(N)**, *are of varying reliability, depending on the credibility of Dr. Noyes's informants. Three other sources are used: indication of residence in the 1860 Walling* **(W)** *and 1881 Colby* **(C)** *county maps and in the 1896 Stonington tax record* **(T)**. *These data are entered in the closest decennial column. An "x" indicates decade of presumed residence if no census data available. There is a separate residence table for Crotch Island (page320).*

Island/Householder	**1800–1850**	**1850**	**1860**	**1870**	**1880**	**1900**
Bare						
Harvey, John, Jr.	Residence reported early 19th C **(N)**					
Harvey, George	Residence reported, 1830s (see Russ I. below)					
Bold						
Harvey, ? (Mr.)	Resided briefly before 1825 (according to deed)					
Camp						
Merchant, Nathaniel	1820s **(N)**					
Merchant, Robert	1830s, 1840s **(N)**; 1840 census, 6 in household					
Robbins, Hezekiah, 58 (Lucretia)			5/2[22]			

[21] Data for 1900 are sparse, since much of the Deer Isle and Stonington schedule for that year was illegible in copies available to me.

[22] Hezekiah Robbins moved onto Camp Island in 1850, or soon thereafter, and removed to Kiah's Island in about 1860.

Island/Householder	1800–1850	1850	1860	1870	1880	1900
COOMBS						
Coombs, Abizer	Reported 1829 **(N)**					
Coombs, Francis, 45 (Experience)		5/6	1/6			
Thurlow, Ben					x **(N)**	
DEVIL						
Coombs, John	Reported there, 1835 **(N)**					
Thurston, Nat'l and George Grover	Reported, 1840s **(N)**					
GREEN						
Gross, Charles	Reported 1830s **(N)**					
Harvey, Bill and Ben	Reported 1840s-60s **(N)**					
Robbins, Joseph (Catherine Eaton)	Reported 1840s **(N)**					
Robbins, David, 32 (Deborah)			4/2	12		
Robbins, Elijah, 48 (Elizabeth)					3/3	
Robbins, Amos, 20 (Martha)					1/1	
MARK						
Small, Thomas, 53 (Eliza), K			4/1			
Morris, James, 45,K				4/1		
Gott, Charles A., K (1881–87)						
Gilley, Howard M., K (1887–96)						
Tapley, Will C. (1896–1905)						
Stanley, Charles E., K (1905–12)						
MCGLATHERY						
Eaton, Peter Hardy, 55 (Catherine)	Arrived early 1840s **(N)**	5/3	3/3			
Eaton, Samuel, 22 (Margaret)		1/1	2/3			
Eaton, Daniel, 24 (Philena)		2/1				
Eaton, George Washington, 28, Hannah)			1/3			
Black, Samuel, 52 (Hannah)			3/3 [23]			
Harvey, Joseph, 24 (Charlotte)			1/1			
Harvey, William, 19 (Sophronia)			2/1	5/1		
Harvey, Benjamin, 27 (Susan),				2/3		
Robbins, James, 23 (Louise)				1/2		
Conary, Levi G., 32 (Abigail)					1/2	
MOOSE						
Allen, George W., 32 (Climentia) [24]			x **(W)**	1/2	x **(C)**	
Allen, Samuel, 63 (Susan)				5/1		
Allen, Henry A. [25]					x **(C)**	
Allen, W. C.					x **(C)**	
Robbins, Hiram (Clementine) [26]						x **(T)**
Clegg, James						x **(T)**
Island/Householder	**1800–1850**	**1850**	**1860**	**1870**	**1880**	**1900**

[23] It is not known where in the Thorofare Samuel Black lived in 1860, but his position in the census makes it likely he was on McGlathery.
[24] George Allen's home was bought by Ezra and Nellie Kenney in the 1880s and, after his death, by James Clegg.
[25] Henry Allen's homestead was rented in the 1880s by Eben Small and his daughter Minnie Gross.
[26] The Hiram Robbins family arrived from Wreck Island in 1884 (see below); Clementine owned most of the island in 1896—see page 323.

Island/Householder	1800–1850	1850	1860	1870	1880	1900
Round						
Holbrook, Elisha	Reported in 1830; census tally, 4/5					
Robbins, Hezekiah, 49 (Lucretia), S	Bought island 1835, settled soon thereafter	6/4				
Russ						
Harvey, ?	Reported in 1825 deed					
Harvey, George, 50s (Sally/Polly)	Bought island 1838 and settled immediately; 8 in household in 1840 census	4/3	0/4 [27]	1/1		
Dunbar, Elijah, 29 (Lucretia)			1/1			
Robbins, Elijah, 33 (Margaret)			4/1			
Saddleback						
Cooper, James, 30s	Bought island, 1837, settled there **(N)**; 1840 census: 30s, 3/3					
Frye, James	Reported living with Coopers **(N)**					
Morey, Elias	Reported residence, mid-century **(N)**					
Sand						
Small, E(ben)			x **(W)**			
St. Helena						
Barter, O(rrin), 45 (Experience)					x **(C)**	2/3
Morey, O.					x **(C)**	
Gross, Thomas and wife Adelaid						x**(N)**
Spruce						
Harvey, Bill				x **(N)**		
Robbins, James, 33 (Louisa)					3/3	
Wreck						
Barter, Robert, 43 (Mary), Fa/S	Arrived 1830s; 1840 census, 3/5	4/4	3/3			
Barter, Henry, 25 (Julia)			4/1			
Barter, Levi, 23 (Abigail)			3/2	5/2	2/2	
Merchant, Shubael, 26 (Hannah), Fi			2/2			
Barter, Stephen, 29 (Eliza)				2/2	2/1	
Robbins, Hiram, 22 (Clementine)				1/2	3/2	
Barter, Oscar, 22 (Nancy)					1/2	
Island/Householder	**1800–1850**	**1850**	**1860**	**1870**	**1880**	**1900**

[27] Polly Harvey, widowed, is head of household in 1860.

Deer Island Thorofare Islands: Valuations and Ownership, 1896

Note: The following valuations on islands in Deer Island Thorofare were made in 1896, the first year of Stonington's jurisdiction. The owners appear under each island (NR means non-resident). The acreage, if shown, is the first figure in the middle column, followed by any further detail (e.g., house, quarry equipment). Except for Crotch and Moose islands, no islands at this date are believed to have had year-round residents. The total dollar valuation is in the right-hand column.

Island Owners	Acres; House	Value ($)
BARE		
Thayer Tyler (NR)	30; house	140
BOLD		
Robert Knowlton heirs	30	60
CAMP		
Winfield S. Thurlow	68	136
COOMBS		
Thomas S. Fifield	20	40
CROTCH		
Lucy A. Small (NR)	5	2,000
George W. Robbins (NR)	house	10
Arthur McMillin (NR)	39; house	1,010
Elvira Collier (NR)	2-1/2	25
Delia H. Petrie (NR)	3; house (1/2)	35
Casey & Sherwood (NR)	20	800
Fred A. Wesgott	3[28]; house (1/2)	55
Eliza S. Thurlow	5	25
Laura J. Small	3	400[29]
Amos Robbins	3/4; house	135
Edson L. Morse (resident)	1/2; house	30
Parris G. Merrill	19; quarry equipment	900
Hiram L. Morey	5; house	80
Minnie E. Gross (resident)	1; house	88
Simeon Goss	43; quarry equipment	159
Violet Goss	3	400
Job G. Goss (resident)	2; house	105
John L. Goss	much quarry equipment	1,932
Israel Eaton (resident)	1/2; house	158
Eaton brothers	1; house, stock-trade	310
George W. Colby	1/2	5
Gilman L. Bray	5; quarry equipment	855
Stephen E. Allen	32; house and quarry	1,230
Goss & Small	shop and stable	65
DEVIL		
George M. Nelson (NR)	45; boardinghouse	545
EASTERN MARK		
Not listed		

[28] "... formerly occupied by the late Jos. Dufore as a quarry."
[29] Revalued at $36.

Island Owners	Acres; House	Value ($)
Enchanted		
Not listed		
Georges Head		
Jeanne B. Stinson	30	60
Gooseberry		
Not listed		
Green		
Scott Geyer (NR)	4; quarry equipment	600
J. A. McCarty (NR)	3	100
— Barnard (NR)	5	30
Elizabeth W. Green	20	82
Amanda R. Green	1; quarry equipment	175
Goss & Small	quarry equipment	90
Grog		
Peter Powers heirs	5	10
Johns		
Wilmot B. Thurlow	2	—
Kimballs [Farrel]		
Eben S. Fifield	7	14
Mark		
Not listed (United States government)		
McGlathery		
Levi K. Stinson	75; house	175
Millet		
Whitfield Gross	20	20
Moose		
Nellie Kanney (NR)	1/2; house	145
Clementine Robbins (resident)	32; 2 houses	428
James Clegg (resident)	house; quarry	910
John L. Goss	3 derricks, equipment	640
No Mans Land		
Not listed		
Otter (northwest of Devil)		
Eben S. Fifield	8	16
Peggys (now Scraggy)		
Unknown		50
Phoebe		
Not listed		
Potato (west of St. Helena)		
Unknown	2	16
Potato (southeast of Russ)		
Thomas H. Eaton	3	25
Russ		
Thomas H. Eaton	45; quarry equipment	420
Dougal McKinnon	shop, quarry equipment	312
Rock		
Not listed		

Island Owners	Acres; House	Value ($)
Round		
Robert Barter heirs	20	40
Robbins (Webb Cove)		
William L. Stinson	4	6
Saddleback		
Winfield S. Thurlow	67	134
Sand		
Rebecca D. Eaton	5	10
Scott		
Phebe E. Thurlow	8	50
Joseph H. Robbins	3/4; quarry equipment	140
Herman Eaton	blacksmith shop	55
Sheep		
George W. Taft (NR)	34	68
Shingle		
Not listed		
Spruce		
Frank S. Warren	30	60
St. Helena		
A. A. Leason (NR)	1/2	37
Charles S. Grant (NR)	18; house, equipment	87
John L. Goss	derrick	15
Wreck		
Robert Barter heirs	25	50
Unknown	15; house	105

Group 1: Islands South of Deer Isle (Deer Island Thorofare)

Scraggy and Sparrow

Flanking the western end of Merchant Row, a passage used more frequently in the eighteenth century than today, these sentinels might have been called the Western Mark Islands. The outermost of the two, once called *Peggy's Island*, was in fact briefly considered as a site of the lighthouse that was built on Mark Island in the 1850s (see page 322). The two islands appear on charts with their present names only in the last half of the nineteenth century. *Scraggy* (or *Scrag*) *Island* was owned by David Thurlow of Crotch Island and was among the numerous islands he deeded to his daughter-in-law, Charlotte Thurlow, in 1856, in return for maintenance of himself and his wife in their old age (Hancock 109/441). Scraggy and probably Sparrow as well were used for grazing sheep. Scraggy presumably was cut over at least once, the slash left behind suggesting its modern name; the island is not "scraggy" today. With Merchant Row serving as a boundary between Deer Isle and Isle au Haut, the two islands are in different townships.

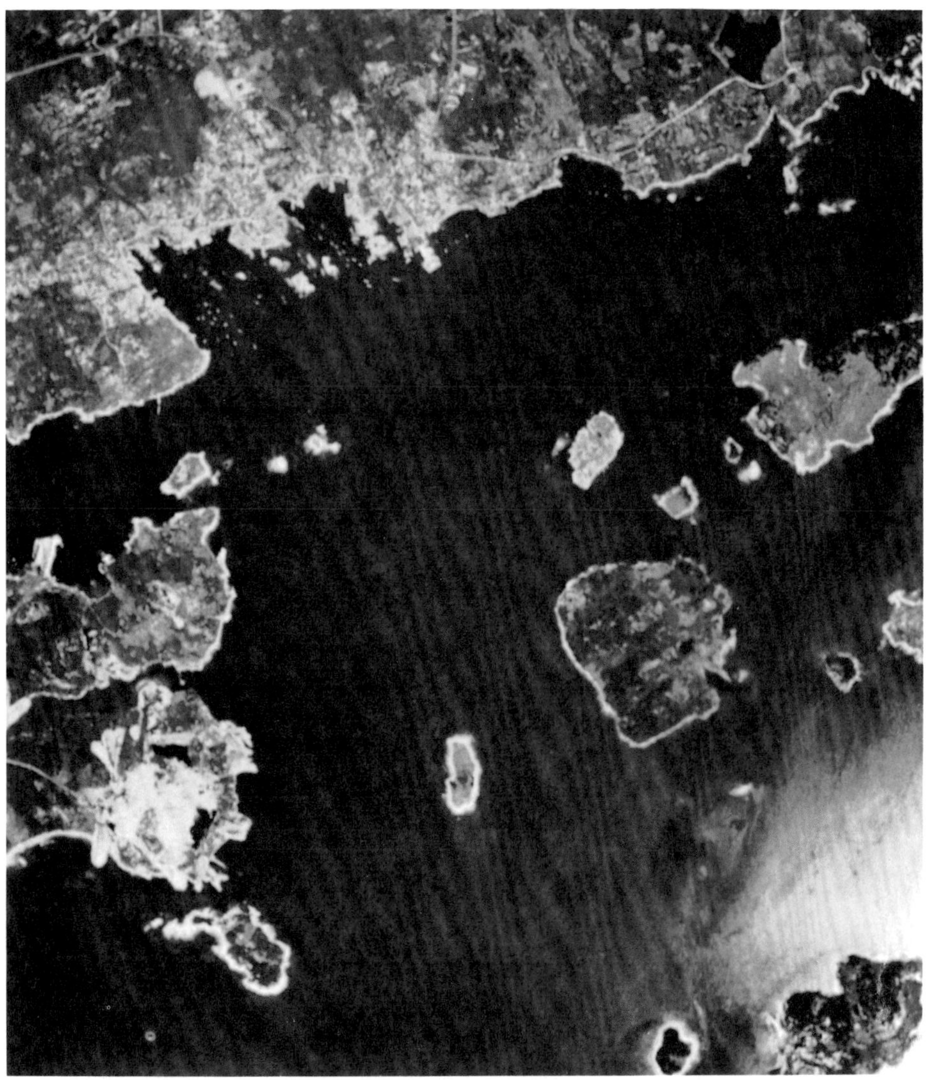

Aerial view of Stonington and part of Deer Island Thorofare, June 1944: Crotch Island at left, Green Island, right center, Russ Island. upper right. Apart from vegetational changes, there are no significant transformations in the half century since this photo was taken.
(Photo by United States Air Force, courtesy of Alan C. Bemis.)

Farrel

This is known as *Island N* or *Kimball's Island* in the earliest conveyance I have seen—a will from George Allen to his sons in 1828 (Knox Lands 5/134). George was probably the son of the Reverend Samuel Allen, who lived near to and owned Moose Island in Deer Island Thorofare; this George, according to Hosmer (page 154), died at sea. The next conveyance was in 1833 from Daniel Allen, another son of the Reverend Samuel Allen who married his brother's widow, to Silvious Simpson. The island is called Kimball's, and its location makes it unmistakably Farrel; the sale price was $25 (Knox Lands 5/74). Silvious Simpson sold to Eben T. Simpson for $100 in 1869 (Hancock 133/508). In 1876 the State of Maine, evidently judging that the island had never been properly conveyed, deeded it to J. M. Mason (Maine Archives Book 19/221). Mason presumably

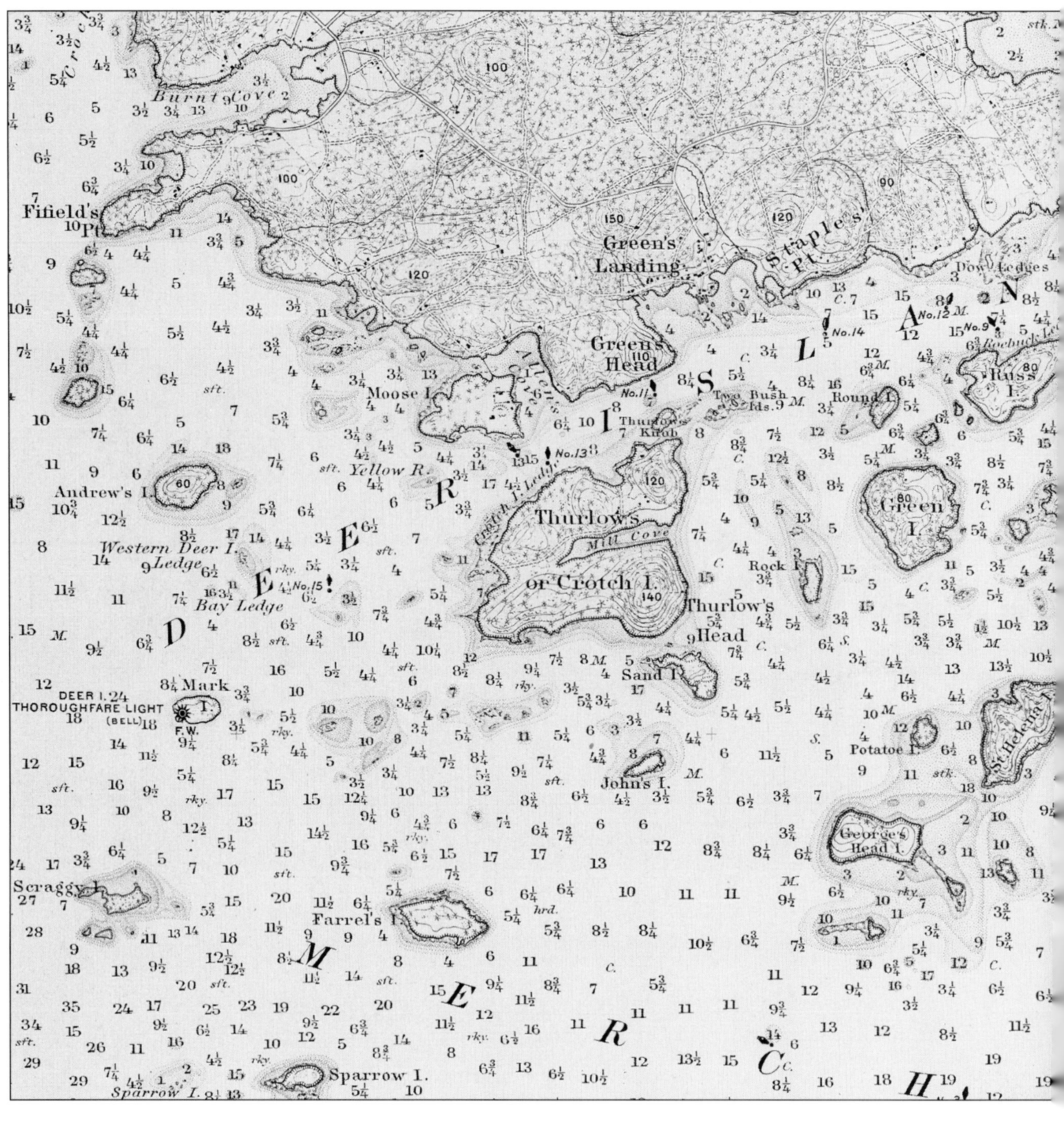

Segment of CGS 309, East Penobscot, 1882, showing islands in Deer Island Thorofare. Habitation is shown on Crotch, Russ, Devil, Wreck, and McGlathery.

sold to Ebenezer Fifield, for in 1878 the latter conveyed it to Dudley Fifield, along with several other islands in the area, in return for support of himself, his wife, and daughters (Knox Lands 5/431). The island has remained in the Fifield family to the present day. This is the title record, as nearly as I

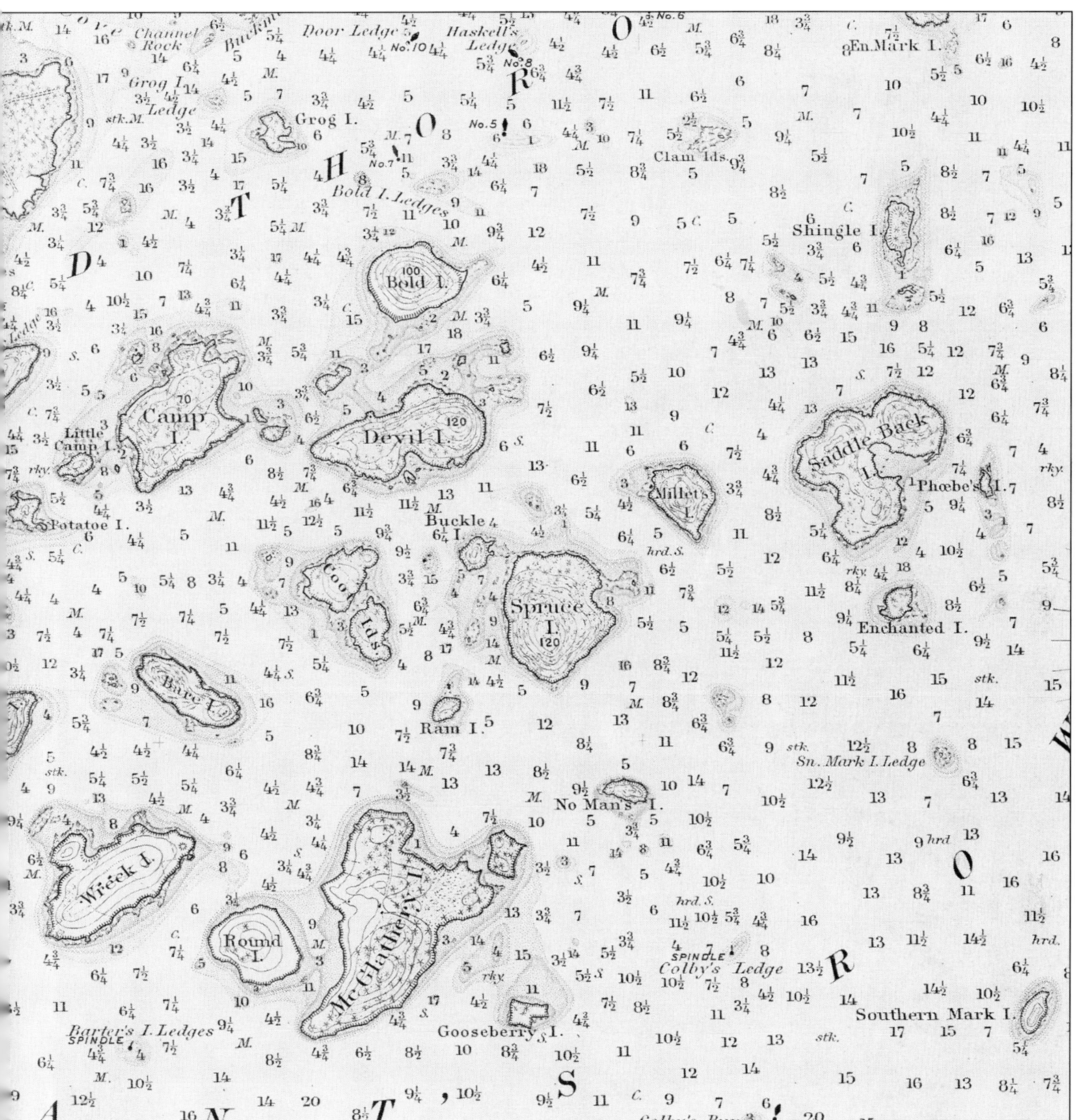

have been able to reconstruct it, but nothing here gives us a clue as to the origin of either name—Kimball or Farrel—unless the latter is somehow a corruption of Fifield. The island is shown as *Farrel*, or *Farrels*, on maps dating from the 1880s (e.g., Map 1880 Hancock County, Colby).

It is certain that Farrel never had year-round residents, although it was cut over several times, to judge from its changing appearance on coastal charts, and was undoubtedly used periodically for grazing as well as by fishermen in season.

George Head

This is *Island R* in Rufus Putnam's survey of the Thorofare islands in 1785 and is marked "sold" (Hancock Plan Book II: 23). To whom it was sold I do not know, and it is unlikely that the buyer made good his title; in 1824 the land agents of the State of Maine sold Island A (Bare) and Island R to David Thurlow of Crotch Island for $40.75 (Hancock 46/397). David may have sold Island R before 1856, for it does not appear in the long list of islands in the area conveyed to his daughter-in-law Charlotte in return for care of himself and his wife Mercy during their lifetime. The island reverted to the town in the 1860s for non-payment of taxes; and in 1868 it was sold under its present name to Henry Eaton of Clinton; three years later, Eaton conveyed it to Stephen Colby and Jack Stimpson of Deer Isle for $100 (Hancock 155/80). In 1885, Colby sold his half-interest in the island to Stimpson, who conveyed to his wife Joan in 1894, and she to vacationers on Deer Isle in 1900 (Hancock 201/470, 281/131, 350/259). George Head Island remained in the hands of non-residents through the twentieth century.

The title record, then, shows no year-round residence at any time on George Head Island, and maps over the years confirm this. Moreover, the relatively low prices fetched by it in conveyances during the last decades of the nineteenth century—never exceeding $125—do not suggest significant improvements. Why an island of this size remained uninhabited, when most others nearby of similar and even smaller size were settled, is a mystery to me—as, indeed, is the origin of its name. Rutherford (page 73) suggests it is after a family named George on Deer Isle, but it is more likely to be after someone's given name, since the surname George is not a common one in the area.

St. Helena

In Rufus Putnam's "Isle of Holt Division" of 1785 this is shown as *Island P* and marked "sold" (Hancock Plan Book II: 23). I have found no indication who the initial owner was and doubt that early settlers were on the island. According to those familiar with the area, neither a building nor cellar hole was on St. Helena before the quarrying era in the 1880s (Noyes, Dennis Robbins interview). This may seem curious, since most islands of comparable size in the Thorofare were settled at one time or another in the post-Revolutionary War era; presumably there was no certain water here or the soil was too shallow for farming.

Undoubtedly, transient fishermen were on the island from time to time. Two are shown on the south shore in the Colby atlas of Hancock County in 1881 (surveyed a few years earlier): O. Barter and O. Morey. O. Barter would be Orrin, the son of Levi Barter of Wreck Island. The only other O. Barter I identify is Orrin's brother Oscar, who appears in the 1880 census as still resident on Wreck. O. Morey would be one of the large Morey family associated with the Thorofare islands, notably Russ and Crotch, in the last half of the century. Neither of these two squatters appears on St. Helena in the 1880 federal census, which suggests they did not tarry long. Another transient at the end of the century, according to Dr. Noyes, was Thomas Gross, who was married to Adelaide Dow, a descendant of Paul Walton of Great Spruce Head (Noyes, Family histories: Walton).

Hezekiah Rowell, who acquired many Thorofare islands after the separation of Maine from Massachusetts in 1820, owned Island P for a few years before selling to Thomas Buckmaster, Jr. of Deer Isle, who sold a half-interest in 1835 to Samuel Whitmore and Daniel Doroty (sic) and Sidna (sic) Smith; the sale price in the latter conveyance—$18—suggests few improvements to that date and confirm our impression that Island P was uninhabited (Hancock 62/103). Half a century later (1883) Seth and Charles Webb, having bought the same half-interest from the estate of Samuel Whitmore, sold to A. A. Lesan of Winterport (Hancock 188/366). The other half-interest passed about the same time to Tyler Thayer of Winterport, a near relation of A. Lesan. Sometime during this half of the century, Island P acquired its present name. Rutherford (page 83) suggests that it was named after the island where Napoleon was imprisoned off Africa, and this is plausible, but I mistrust his explanation that the connection was the use of prisoners in the quarries of *our* St. Helena: no quarry was opened here until the 1880s, sixty years or more after Napoleon had died on *his* St. Helena, and prison labor was surely never used on the islands in Deer Island Thorofare.

The Lesans and Thayers of Winterport, who jointly controlled St. Helena for twenty years or more, opened the quarries. The initial motions in the 1880s were modest, but by the 1890s when Hollis and Joshua Thayer, sons of Dr. Tyler Thayer, took over operations and built a boarding-house for the workers, the enterprise prospered. Two large piers were constructed on the west side for loading. In 1909 an account of a fire on the island made reference to power and engine houses "and other buildings" (*Ellsworth American*, January 6, 1909). About this time the Benisch family of Brooklyn, New York, bought into the quarrying operations on St. Helena and eventually took full control. In the 1920s H. F. Robbins of Deer Isle was the superintendent and John Wood of Blue Hill the boss-cutter. According to John Wood's daughter Esther, a schoolteacher in Stonington in the late 1920s, about fifty men were still employed on St. Helena; quarrying continued on St. Helena longer than on any other Thorofare island except Crotch. Since there were no buildings on the island at this time, the stoneworkers lived in Stonington and were ferried to work daily, from April to November; the quarries were closed in the winter. The ornamental stone cut on St. Helena went principally into the exterior of the Catholic Church Our Lady of Perpetual Help in Brooklyn—an edifice larger than St. Patrick's Cathedral in New York (letter from Henry J. Benisch to a recent owner, Dec. 14, 1981).

In about 1929 the Benisch operation ceased. Frank Maguire of the Deer Isle Granite Company acquired the island with the intention of reopening the quarries, but by this date island quarrying had become unprofitable and the project was abandoned. Superintendent Robbins, the last year-round resident of St. Helena, remained as caretaker until the equipment had been sold; he removed to Stonington with his family before World War II. The Robbins home, which he built, was on the west side of the island near the quarries and was still standing—or the shell of it was—in the 1990s.

Our information on St. Helena, then, is meager. While the island had a number of transient residents—many more than I have identified—it had few settlers, and probably none who stayed as long as the H. F. Robbins family in the twentieth century. Harold Robbins, son of H. F. Robbins, served as caretaker for the successors of Benisches and Frank Maguire, who use the island as a summer residence.

Wreck

The earliest name I have seen attached to this island, on Rufus Putnam's survey of 1785, is *Bear*. It is indicated as "sold," and the owner was undoubtedly Joseph Colby, Jr., whom George Hosmer (page 36) identifies as Wreck's first resident. A descendant of Joseph Colby, Margaret Hundley, says that he was one of the two children who rowed with their mother Sarah Colby to deliver the news of Cornwallis's surrender to the British garrison at Castine. Mrs. Hundley describes Colby as a sea captain of great size and physical strength; he was associated for some years with his brother-in-law Captain David Thurlow in shipbuilding on Crotch Island. Why Captain Colby should have chosen Bear Island as his home—remote, with poor anchorage and few neighbors—is unclear, but in the absence of any contrary evidence we may take Hosmer's word for it that he did, at least for a time. In 1805 he signed an affidavit testifying to Anthony Merchant's residence on Merchant Island prior to 1784, which suggests he had been familiar with the area for some years.

Whether residents were on Bear Island between the departure of Joseph Colby early in the eighteenth century and the arrival of the Barters in the 1830s is uncertain. There is a possibility that Harveys lived on the island for a time, but I will not go into that here since I discuss it in some detail under Bare Island. After the separation of Maine from Massachusetts, Bear Island was resold by Maine land agents in 1827 to Hezekiah Rowell, a Deer Isle investor (Hancock 50/252). Rowell sold to Henry Wilson, another investor in the area, and Wilson sold to Anthony Merchant, Jr. in 1831 (Hancock 53/466 and 67/305). It was from Anthony, Jr. that Robert Barter eventually acquired title to the island, to which he moved during the 1830s and where he remained until his death in 1867; he was a nephew of Anthony Merchant, Jr. and a son of Henry Barter of Isle au Haut and later Burnt Island.

I pause to note one deed in 1838, not so much for its prime relevance to the history of Wreck Island, but as an indication of the difficulties these early settlers had in keeping titles straight. The deed is a quitclaim from Eliza Cottrell of Northport to Anthony Merchant and notes the earlier conveyance to Anthony Merchant from Henry Wilson. Then the deed continues: "...and the said Merchant deeded the Island aforesaid to the s[d] Eliza Cottrell and which deed has not been recorded and is now lost or misplaced to the best of her judgment" (Knox Lands 5/329). I have no knowledge who Eliza Cottrell may have been and doubt she ever lived on the island she claimed to own. But Anthony Merchant "quieted" her with $100 in order to be able to convey the island properly to his nephew Robert Barter.

Since the Barter family of Wreck Island is complex, the rudimentary family tree that follows this entry will be helpful, even though it has some gaps and uncertainties as to dates. The known householders on the island from 1840 through 1880 are shown on page 281.

Robert Barter and his wife Mary or Polly—both names appear in records—had at least five children who played a role in the island's history. Deer Isle records show a school on Wreck Island as early as 1842, evidently for Robert and Mary's three older children (Clayton Gross, *Island Ad-Vantages*, May 14, 1976). Their eldest daughter, Martha, according to Barter descendants, gave birth at an early age to an illegitimate child whose father was David Robbins, eldest son of Hezekiah, who was living on Round Island when the Barters moved onto Wreck. Dr. Noyes writes in his account of the episode: "Martha would have been David's first wife had not a 'family jar' on the part of Martha's father, Robert, and her brother Levi prevented the carrying out of the marriage before Hiram was born" (Family histories: Robbins).[30] Orrin Barter described David Robbins to Dr. Noyes as "a good looking fellow and dressed up flashing"; after he got Aunt Martha "in a fix," Levi

[30] If Levi Barter intervened in the episode, as Dr. Noyes states, then, at the age of twelve, he took a very precocious interest in his sister's amours.

Horse and sleigh rick carrying hay across ice to island sheep; Deer Island Thorofare, c. 1915. (Courtesy of Deer Isle Historical Society.)

got "up a tree ... and a hell of an uproar happened" (Noyes, Family histories: Barter). Martha is shown on the island in the 1850 census, but she eventually moved to Camden; David moved from island to island in the vicinity. Hiram, meanwhile, was brought up in the Robert Barter household, though keeping his father's surname; he married Clementine Small of Isle au Haut in 1866 and settled on Wreck, removing to Moose Island off Stonington in about 1881.

Another of Robert Barter's daughters, Eleanor, married Shubael Merchant, her first cousin (Anthony Merchant, Sr. was their common grandparent), and she bore two children on Wreck Island before the family moved away. I do not know where they moved, but Shubael is said to have died eventually in Rockport where his son was living (Noyes, Family histories: Merchant). Henry, Robert's oldest son, married and had seven children on Wreck Island before removing after 1870. Levi was born shortly before the family came to Wreck from Burnt Island (Deer Isle records and the family Bible are in conflict over the year of his birth), and he lived there for over half a century. His wife, Abigail, the daughter of Peter and Catherine Eaton, was born on McGlathery Island, within sight of the Barters' farm. They were married before either was twenty and had six children, of whom three sons survived; one child died of "fits" in infancy and another in the diphtheria epidemic of 1873 (Noyes, Family Histories: Eaton). Orrin, Levi's oldest son, left the island before 1880, but Oscar remained and is listed as a fisherman in the 1880 census, married but as of that date without children (the second female in his household is a boarder). Robert Barter's youngest son Stephen also settled on the island: he lived in Henry Barter's home after the latter's departure and appears in the 1880 census.

The men on the island in 1880 are listed in the census as fishermen, though it is clear from the appearance of Wreck Island on maps of that time, as well as from the testimony of descendants, that much farming was carried on as well. Most of the central ridge, where the Barter homesteads were located, was kept clear by good-sized herds of cattle and sheep. Levi's farm was a short distance north of his father's; Hiram built at the west end of the island. According to the 1850 agricultural census, the island farm, utilizing fifty acres with livestock valued at $300, yielded two hundred pounds of wool and three hundred pounds of butter; the total valuation was $1,000. This was better than average for an island farm in that era.

There are a few non-Barters in census schedules for Wreck Island. Rosetta Holbrook in the 1860 census, for instance, was one of a large family that moved from island to island in the Thorofare, like the Robbins family; I do not know her parentage—and it may not have been widely publicized. (We will encounter her again in the notice of Russ Island, below.) The fifty-three-year old George Higgins in Hiram Robbins's household in the 1880 census was apparently a drifter without fixed residence. Annice Cole, boarding with Oscar Barter in 1880, was probably the schoolteacher; the school district included McGlathery Island as well as Wreck and classes alternated from one island to the other.

I have been referring to the island as *Wreck Island*, which is the official name appearing on most maps and charts in the latter decades of the nineteenth century, but locally it was known as *Barter's Island* for forty or fifty years. I do not know what particular mishap on its shores led to the change from the original Bear to Wreck, but there were undoubtedly plenty to choose from. (The special local pronunciation of the name, incidentally, accounts for it often appearing in Deer Isle records as "Wrack" or "Rack.") The designation Barter's Island is reflected today only in the name of the reef lying due south—Barter Island Ledge.

The Barters quit Wreck Island during the 1880s, the last of them about 1888. Levi and Abigail removed to Clam City in Stonington, where their son Orrin and his wife Experience Ames watched over the couple in their last years. Wreck was sold piecemeal by the heirs of Robert Barter to Winfield S. Thurlow, distant kin of the original settler, Joseph Colby, Jr. The island was never settled again for year-round use, and the buildings quickly fell into disrepair. Maps at the beginning of the twentieth century show no sign of habitation, permanent or temporary; an 1896 tax record, however, shows one dwelling still standing—or tottering (see page 284). Today not more than two of the four Barter homesites can be easily identified; the stones from the family burial ground, where Robert and Mary and a number of their descendants are buried, have long since been removed. Sheep grazing until recent years, as well as a procession of summer visitors, have kept portions of the island open, but the alder and spruce are steadily gaining.

Wreck Island was acquired in the 1960s by the Nature Conservancy, which seeks to keep it in its natural state, "forever wild."

Barters of Burnt and Wreck Islands

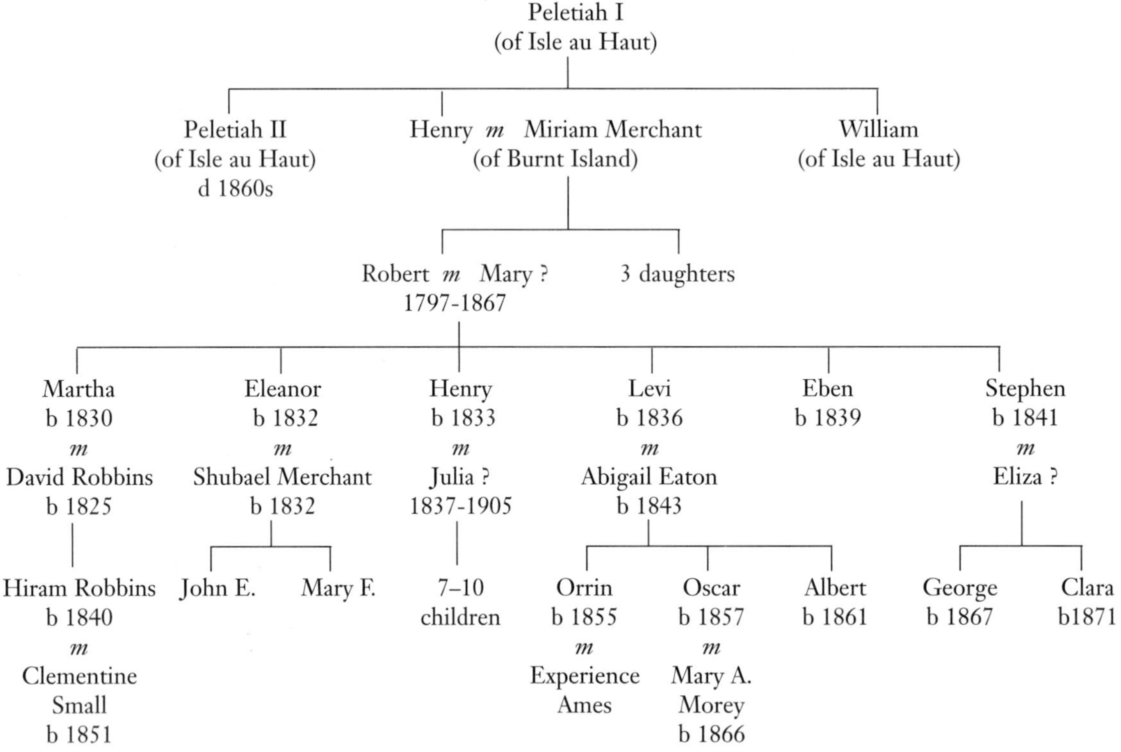

Bare

This is called *Island A* on Rufus Putnam's survey of the "Isle of Holt Division" in 1785 and is indicated as "sold." To whom it was sold is not shown. The sale must have been tentative, for in 1824 Island A, falling to Maine's portion in the separation from Massachusetts, was conveyed to David Thurlow of Crotch Island (Hancock 46/397). I have not found Captain David's disposition of the island. Sometime during the second quarter of the nineteenth century, the island received its present name, the only one it has ever had.

Early settlement on Bare Island presents a problem to historians for two reasons: the easy confusion between "Bare" and "Bear" (the latter was the commonly known name of nearby Wreck Island until the later decades of the nineteenth century), and conflicting evidence respecting the first settler on Bare Island, John Harvey, Jr. There is nothing I can do regarding the first dilemma, except speculate that where "Bear" is written, "Bare" was often meant—and vice versa. Regarding the second, I can merely present the conflicting evidence; I cannot resolve the contradiction. George Hosmer (pages 181, 201) states that John Harvey, a veteran of the Revolutionary War, lived for some years on Bare Island. He had settled first in Northport, where he married in 1789; and after living on Bare Island, he returned to Northport. Unable to procure a pension, he fell into penury and, being chargeable to Deer Isle, was returned there, where he died in 1837. Meanwhile, in an interview in 1911, John Harvey's grandson William, who was sixty-six at the time, said that his grandfather and grandmother lived on "Bear Island close to McGlathery" and died there (Noyes, Family histories: Harvey). I am assuming that "Bear Island" is Bare—both Bare and Wreck are equally close to McGlathery—and that the only discrepancy in the two accounts is where John Harvey died. According to Hosmer, he had two sons: John, Jr., who lived most of his life on Isle au Haut, and George, William's father, who settled in the 1840s on Russ Island; William states that he was born there in 1845.

If there is lingering uncertainty about Harvey residence on Bare Island (as distinct from Bear/Wreck), there is no question about *some* settlers on this island in the first half of the nineteenth century. Two cellar holes are still in evidence, one on the northeast side, in from the shore, the other in open meadowland on the southwestern shore. There is also a dug well in the center of the island. The residents appear to have been primarily farmers rather than fishermen, for fishermen usually spent only summers on isolated islands like this and did not build cellars. Though the island is small for farming and rocky, there is enough deep soil to support at least one small farm; there is no suggestion, of course, that two farms were in operation at the same time. The best reason for imagining residence in the first half of the century rather than the last is not necessarily lack of reference to it by our usual informants (Bester Robbins, for example), but the fact that maps and charts surveyed after 1850, on which one normally relies for hard evidence of habitation, show nothing for Bare Island. Doubtless, transient residents were there after 1850—indeed, it would be extraordinary if there had been none—but permanent settlers are unlikely.

The island was acquired by a quarryman sometime early in the twentieth century, but no motions were begun. His daughter, who paid taxes on the island for some twenty years but never saw it, sold it to summer cottagers in 1957; they used it as a summer residence, maintaining a flock of sheep to keep the meadows open, then sold to still other summer vacationers in the 1980s. It is an island I pass with particular pleasure because it is where I am most likely to catch a glimpse of a beloved yawl we owned for some years, before selling it to the owner of Bare Island.

Round

This island may describe a less perfect sphere than several others in Penobscot Bay, but its appearance, inside the curving southwest arm of McGlathery Island, has always suggested roundness. And *Round Island* has accordingly been its name since Revolutionary times. It appears thus, for example, on Rufus Putnam's survey of 1785. It is marked "sold" on this survey, but there is no indication to whom. Nor is there clear indication that anyone lived on it before the separation of Maine from Massachusetts in 1820, after which it was resold, along with Bear (Wreck) Island, to Hezekiah Rowell (1827) and by him to Henry Wilson (about 1829) and by Wilson to Anthony Merchant (1831).

The earliest *probable* settler on our island was Elisha Holbrook, who is shown on a *Round Island* in the 1830 census: in his fifties, with a wife in her forties, three sons, and four daughters. These details are appropriate for the family of the Elisha Holbrook who settled on Isle au Haut in about 1800, according to Hosmer (page 193). But was *his* Round Island the one we are discussing? The best evidence that it was is an assertion by Bester Robbins to Dr. Benjamin Noyes that he always understood that when his father Hezekiah bought the island from Anthony Merchant in 1835 and built his homestead there, a cellar hole was already in place. In short, someone had preceded Hezekiah Robbins. Why not Elisha Holbrook?

Elisha Holbrook eventually settled on Deer Isle.[31]

Hez Robbins, according to Bester, was born on North Fox Island (North Haven) around 1800 and spent most of his life among the smaller islands in Deer Island Thorofare. His wife was Lucretia Morey and they had ten or more children. The eldest was David, born in about 1828, a peripatetic islander like his father. Bester—or Bestis, as he was named—was the fourth child and second son; it is not known how many of Hezekiah's and Lucretia's children were born on Round Island. Hezekiah sold the island to William Barter the same year he bought it (Hancock 59/313, 62/118), but the family remained there for some years. Hezekiah's household of ten is shown in the 1850 census—Hezekiah, forty-nine; Lucretia, forty-three; David, twenty-five; Hannah, twenty-four; Rachel, eleven; Bester, eleven; Amos, eight; Lewis, six; Susan, three; and Samuel, one—but whether the family was still on Round or had removed to Camp Island is unclear; Hezekiah's last child, Joseph, is known to have been born on Camp. Hezekiah remained some years on Camp before removing to Kiah's (short for Hezekiah) Island at the head of Webb Cove on the south side of Deer Isle; he died there in the 1880s (Noyes, Bester Robbins interview).

I do not precisely identify the William Barter who bought Round Island in 1835, but he was undoubtedly one of the large Barter clan on Isle au Haut and so related to Robert Barter of Wreck Island. Robert acquired Round Island in due course, and it passed to his heirs after his death and was eventually sold by them, along with Wreck itself, to Winfield S. Thurlow; this was near the end of the nineteenth century.

In the interim another resident was on Round Island, according to Dr. Noyes. This was Samuel S. Eaton, who was brought up on McGlathery on a farm facing Round Island and before 1850 married Margaret Harvey of Russ Island. Samuel, aged twenty-two, and Margaret, nineteen, appear in the 1850 census in their own household, but it cannot be said for certain that this was on Round Island. They had several children, and it is altogether probable, as Dr. Noyes argues, that the family lived for a decade or more on Round Island before returning to McGlathery, where Samuel Eaton is known to have been living in the family homestead early in the 1870s (Noyes, Family histories: Eaton). Samuel never owned Round Island, so far as is known, but the matter of rent was in all likelihood not a serious question, since the Barters and Eatons were on good terms.

Apart from the residence of Samuel Eaton, Hezekiah Robbins, and possibly Elisha Holbrook, I know of no other on Round Island, at least on a year-round basis. The island was doubtless used for pasturage after the Eatons' departure, for it appears almost entirely bare on maps of the 1880s (e.g., Map 1882 CGS 309). It must have been cut over at least once in the nineteenth century, but I think not in the twentieth, to judge from the maturity of the spruce stand that covers the island today. Fishermen have used it periodically, and a fish shack, normally located on the northeast shore, shows on most geological surveys of the island in the twentieth century; one was still standing in the mid-1970s.

Round Island was acquired by the Nature Conservancy in the 1960s and thenceforth follows its own course of forest renewal.

[31] According to George Hosmer, Elisha Holbrook's wife, a daughter of Abiathar Smith of Isle au Haut, died about the time of their presumed residence on Round Island, and the family broke up. Elisha, according to Dr. Noyes, had been "published" to Eunice Dunham in 1842, but they were not married (Noyes, Family histories: Morey). He appeared in the 1850 federal census: seventy-four, married to Phebe Morey, thirty-eight, with six childtren in his household, most of them Phebe's illegitimate offspring; he was still living in 1860, listed with Phebe in the home of his son Abram.

McGlathery

The origin of the name *McGlathery* for this island is puzzling. It would appear to be after William McGlathery, an early trader in Penobscot Bay island properties (including *Little Island Hoalte*, or Kimball Island, in 1773), but there is no record that McGlathery or any of his descendants ever owned this island. He is listed in various deeds as a resident of Bristol, Camden, Islesborough, and Frankfurt, but never of Deer Isle or any island near it. Still, William McGlathery—there is no other with that surname known to me in the Penobscot Bay region in Revolutionary times—must have had some early and long-forgotten association with the island, for it bears his name in the first post-Revolutionary War survey.[32]

In 1802 the island was sold by Massachusetts to David Coffin, a land speculator from Newbury; the price, with Crotch Island thrown in, was $220.55 (Hancock 11/258). In 1815 Coffin sold the island "formerly called McGlathy's" to Ignatius Haskell of Deer Isle for $500 (Hancock 35/122). Why "formerly" is unclear, since the name persisted: in 1835, when Ignatius Haskell sold to William Frye, it is referred to as "a certain Island called McGleather" (Hancock 62/219). The island, then, has had the same name since Revolutionary times, if we make allowance for the casual spelling used by early traders. There is less perplexity over the origin of *Blaster's Rock*, off the northeast tip of McGlathery: this is surely named after one of the Deer Isle Blastows, though as a result of what particular exploit or incident we do not know.

It is highly probable that so felicitous an island had residents from Revolutionary times. Nearby Merchant was settled in the 1770s, Kimball and Isle au Haut to the south about the same time; and much of the Southeast Harbor sector of Deer Isle, not to mention many of the islands in the Thorofare, were settled by 1800. But who McGlathery's settlers were, if there were any in the first decades of the nineteenth century, is not known. There is no evidence that the Haskells, Norwoods, Adamses, and other Deer Isle owners who appear on deeds through the 1830s ever lived on this island.

The first settlers we can identify with assurance are Peter Hardy Eaton and his large family who removed from Bear Island, near Great Spruce Head, to McGlathery during the 1840s. By 1847 there were enough Eaton children, along with the Barter children of Wreck Island, for the town of Deer Isle to create a special school district. This school appears to have run more or less continuously for the next thirty years, alternating from one island to the other.

This is the place, I believe, to sort out the family of Peter Hardy Eaton and his wife Catherine Billings, for without an understanding of this family it is impossible to trace residence on either McGlathery or Bear island, or to a lesser degree Great Spruce Head, Round, and Wreck islands as well. I include a rough genealogy of this extended family, no fewer than five of whom, it will be noted, married the children of George and Sarah Harvey of Russ Island (which must be a record for inter-island liaison). Peter Hardy Eaton was a son of Eliakim and Mary Bunker Eaton (whose forced union is discussed under Stave Island, below, pages 328–29). For probable residents on McGlathery from 1850 to 1880, see the table on page 280.

The oldest children of Peter and Catherine Eaton are known to have been born on Little Deer Isle, the original home of the Eaton clan before the family moved westward onto the mid-Penobscot Bay islands. The family is shown on Great Spruce Head Island in the 1830 census and on Bear Island in 1840. At least three more children were born in this area before the family moved to McGlathery; all of the Eaton children, it is believed, lived for a time on McGlathery, and most were there at the time of marriage. Jonathan, the eldest, presumably spent the least time on the island—long enough, in any case, to woo and marry Martha Harvey—for he is listed in the federal census as back on Bear Island in 1850, the year his first child was born. Peter Hardy, Jr. was married to Louisa Harvey before Jonathan's

[32] William McGlathery (1748–1834), a native of Ireland, was one of the fifteen wealthiest men in Hancock County in 1815, judging from a tax record of that year (*Bangor Historical Magazine*, IV: 15/739).

Peter Hardy Eaton Family of McGlathery and Bear Islands

Note: The data for this genealogical table are adapted from census schedules and from Dr Benjamin Lake Noyes's family files at the Deer Isle Historical Society. Single dates are birth dates.

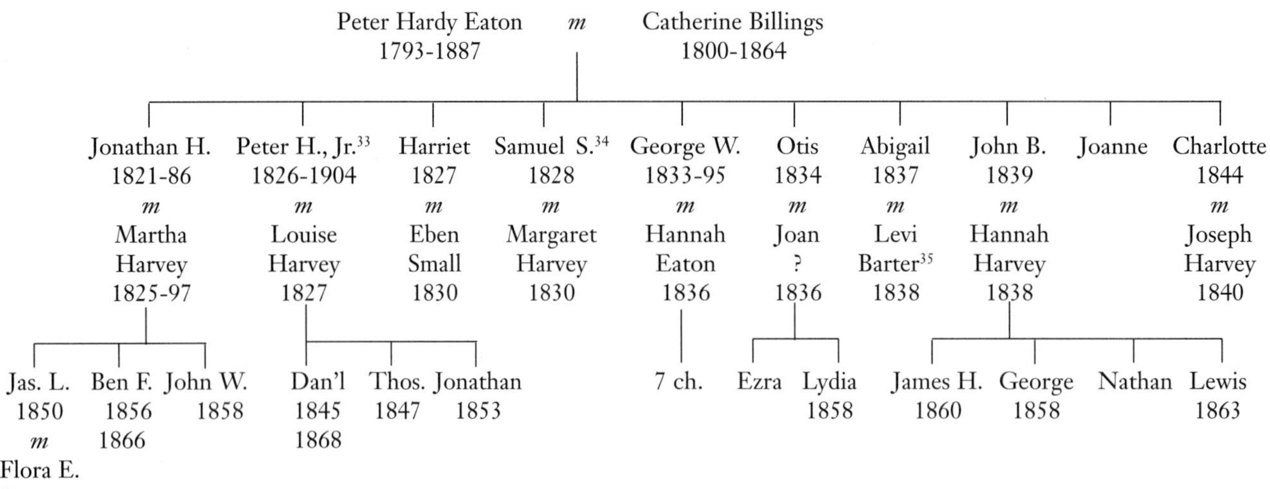

[33] This Peter H., Jr. was apparently named for a brother who died in infancy.

[34] Samuel and Margaret Eaton had several children before her early death: one died in the diphtheria epidemic on McGlathery Island in 1873; another married Frank Hassel of Islesborough.

[35] For the five children of Abagail and Levi Barter, see Barter genealogy, page 292.

marriage, and the birth of their first child in 1845 suggests that the family's removal to McGlathery was in the early rather than the late 1840s—for Eaton lads were unlikely to find Harvey wives over so great a distance as that between Bear Island and Russ. Peter, Jr. and Louisa had joined the Jonathan Eatons on Bear Island by 1860, according to the federal census, and may have been there as much as a decade before; none of their children returned to McGlathery. The next Eaton son, Samuel, remained in the vicinity of McGlathery and after marrying *his* Harvey, Margaret, settled for a time on Round Island, according to Dr. Noyes. Subsequently he settled on McGlathery, on his father's farm on the west side facing Round Island; this homestead was still standing as late as the 1920s. Of Samuel and Margaret's children, one died in the diphtheria epidemic of 1873 and is buried on the island; the others removed. It was Samuel who eventually acquired title to the island and mortgaged it in 1874 to Levi K. Stinson.

George Washington Eaton, Peter and Catherine's fourth son, was a wanderer, according to Dr. Noyes's account. He had seven children: three were born on McGlathery and died of diphtheria on Campobello Island where George had gone in the 1860s, possibly to avoid recruitment during the Civil War; a son was born on Campobello and another child on Bear Island. Together with his brother Sam, George built the schooner LAVINIA, which he used on expeditions downeast.

It was on one of these expeditions in the 1860s, according to elders of the Reorganized Church of Jesus Christ of Latter Day Saints (RLDS) in Stonington, that George and Samuel Eaton were converted by an itinerant missionary named Landers. They brought Elder Landers back with them to McGlathery, where, according to local church lore, the first conversions in the Deer Isle area to the RLDS were accomplished. George subsequently, it is said, went to Palestine as a crew member on the schooner NETTIE CHAPIN, which took a contingent of RLDS faithful to the Holy Land. George moved to Green's Landing in the mid-1870s and lived there until his death in about 1895, an elder in his church and a respected figure in the community.[36] According to Dr. Noyes, he died when his schooner foundered off Wreck Island in a December storm; one of his sons was lost with him.

Otis Eaton (overlooked in Dr. Noyes's summary of the Peter Hardy Eaton family) was another son who remained on McGlathery Island for several years after his marriage; he lived in his father's household and removed before 1890. John B. Eaton, Peter and Catherine's youngest son, is shown on Bear Island, with his older brothers Jonathan and Peter, Jr., in the 1860 census, but he apparently removed before 1870. He, too, married a Harvey, Hannah, who bore six sons between 1858 and 1874. The John B. Eatons are listed as living on Great Spruce Head in 1880 (see page 215). Abigail Eaton married Levi Barter of Wreck Island and is noted in the account of that island.

[36] I am indebted to Mr. and Mrs. William Wilson of Stonington for some of the details of George W. Eaton's colorful life.

Charlotte, finally, the youngest of the family, married Joseph Harvey, but died of consumption at an early age; she and her only child, who died in infancy, were buried in the family plot on the island.

I believe this account of the Peter Hardy Eaton family to be reasonably accurate, though it tells little of their character and way of life. The dominant influence in their lives and the force that held the family together was unquestionably their adherence to the Reorganized Church of Latter Day Saints. This association established close ties between members of the family remaining on McGlathery and Round islands and those who returned to Bear, and these ties were doubtless strengthened by extensive intermarriage with the Harveys. The LAVINA, it is said, made frequent visits between the two rather separated communities of Eatons. Measured by the standards of the time, the Eatons were reasonably prosperous in their prime—especially the sons

McGlathery and Round islands at high tide, 1944. Most of the land shown as open pasture on McGlathery in 1944 was grown over by the 1970s; the well-known yachting anchorages, with the shoals to avoid, show clearly. (United States Air Force photo, courtesy of Alan C. Bemis.)

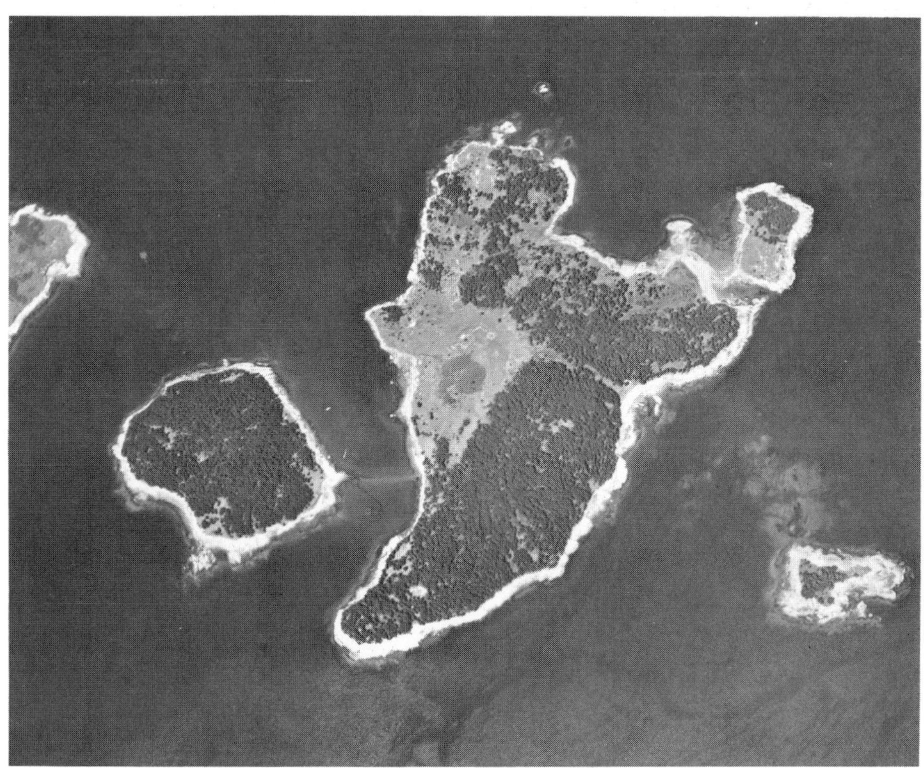

who settled on Bear Island. The McGlathery Eatons were later reduced in circumstances, and there were tragedies in the family. Catherine Eaton is said to have committed suicide on the island in 1864—I do not know for what reason. Then, the diphtheria epidemic of 1873 must have taken a heavy toll of Eaton grandchildren. I have no record of how many died in this epidemic, but on the evidence of Sam Judkins, who taught school on McGlathery Island that winter, fifteen of his eighteen pupils died during the year; this total, assuming it is accurate, would, of course, have included Barters on Wreck Island and the children of several other families in the vicinity.

Others said to have been living on McGlathery in the 1860s or 1870s were two sons of George Harvey of Russ island: Ben, who removed to Green's Landing before 1873, and William, or Bill. Both Ben and Bill Harvey were married, and Bill lost at least one child in the epidemic. Ben Harvey's house, which I believe was near the point closest to Wreck Island, was used for the school after he vacated it. Bill's was in the vicinity of the northeast cove. Another adult resident on the island in 1870 was James Robbins: there are many of this name in Deer Isle census schedules, but this may have been the one shown at the age of three in Peter Hardy Eaton's household in 1850, come back to settle with his bride twenty years later. There was perhaps another Eaton living on McGlathery in mid-century: Daniel Billings Eaton, a nephew of Peter Hardy Eaton, Sr. He, too, married a Harvey and had four children. Dr. Noyes believes this family had removed to Bear

Aerial view of a segment of Deer Island Thorofare, May 1944. The tip of McGlathery Island is at bottom of photo, Spruce Island above it; Saddleback is right center, Camp left center
(United States Air Force photo, courtesy of Alan C. Bemis.)

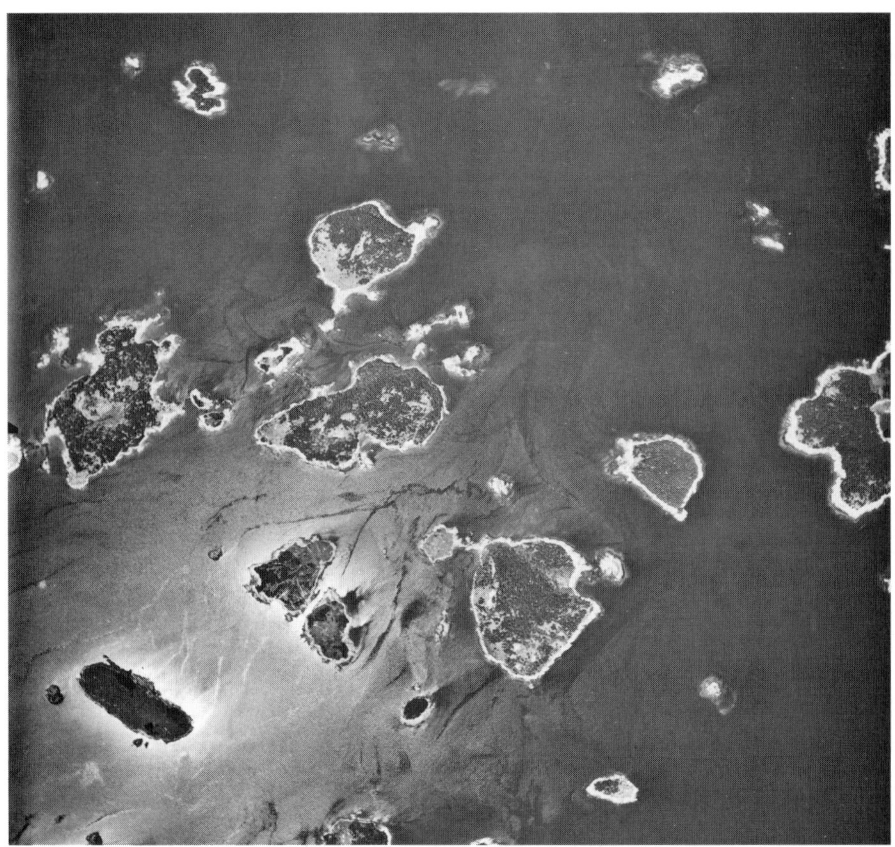

Norman Gray, grandson of Levi Stinson, near the old Eaton homestead on McGlathery Island, 1912; Round Island is in the rear left, Wreck in the distance. Eaton gravestones are under tree at right.
(Courtesy of Cora Stinson Gray.)

Stinson family and friends in front of Peter Hardy Eaton farmhouse on McGlathery Island, c. 1910. From left to right *(as identified by John Havice, a descendant): Sadie Simpson,* on ground *(family friend); Lydia Ann Thurlow (widow of Levi Stinson)* —in dark dress, sitting; *Elizabeth, daughter of Cora Gray,* holding baby; *Cora E. Gray (wife of Capt. Harry W. Gray)*— seated in white; *Helen Gray,* in front of Cora; *Mel Stinson (son of Levi and Lydia)*— bald man, right rear; *three children,* right front—*Albert (son of Sadie), Carrie (daughter of Cora), and Edith Gray. The projections on the roof appear to be lightening rods— evidently the rage in this era.*
(Courtesy of Cora Stinson Gray.)

Island soon after 1850, but a descendant recalls the Daniel Eatons still living on McGlathery some years later. I do not find this family in census schedules.

The diphtheria epidemic may have been the cause of the Eatons' quitting McGlathery Island in the 1870s. George, we have seen, moved to Green's Landing (Stonington) in the mid-1870s, and Samuel removed to Campbell's Neck about the same time. Peter Hardy Eaton, Sr. must have removed before 1870, for I do not find him in the census; he died in Samuel's home in 1887 and was brought back for burial beside Catherine. Ownership of the island had in the meantime become confused by Peter, Sr.'s inability—or refusal—to pay taxes in 1867: the tax collector of Deer Isle that year assigned Peter, Sr.'s holdings on the island, 130 acres, to a Peter Eaton (possibly, but not certainly, Peter, Jr.); title to the entire island eventually returned to Samuel in 1871, and he in 1884 mortgaged to Levi K. Stinson, a sea captain, apparently about the time Samuel and his father were preparing to quit the island (Hancock 150/217). The mortgage was foreclosed in 1877, and Levi Stinson and his heirs maintained possession of the island until the 1950s.

Eaton and Harvey departures from McGlathery Island in the 1870s did not mean the end of year-round settlement. The 1880 census for McGlathery shows Levi S. Conary there. The Colby atlas of 1881 shows the Conarys, the only family on the island, living in the home of Peter Hardy Eaton, Sr. The remaining three or four buildings shown standing on the geodetic survey of about the same era (Map 1883 CGS 309) had apparently been abandoned. The Levi Conarys, it is believed, were the last year-round residents.

McGlathery has, of course, not been out of use because of lack of year-round occupancy since the 1880s. The Stinsons used it as a base for summer operations for many years and apparently used the abandoned Eaton homestead (see photos); they also kept hens and sheep. Local lobstermen and yachtsmen have also shared the island for many decades, for its two anchorages provide protection from storms, and its shores are an endless source of fascination to the curious. Two episodes in the twentieth century deserve historical notice. In 1929 the Lindberghs— Charles A. and his bride Anne Morrow—reportedly spent part of their honeymoon here, eluding a relentless band of airborne photographers and reporters by camouflaging their launch with spruce boughs and thereby managing a day or two of seclusion; the cove where they stayed, on the northeast shore, is still known locally as Lindy's Cove. (I have been unable to confirm this story with any Lindberghs, but the legend lives on.) That same year, the three-masted schooner WAWENOCK foundered on a ledge off McGlathery and, after being abandoned by her crew, drifted onto the southeast shore, where she was quickly stripped by unauthorized "wreckers." According to Vernal Hutchinson, who witnessed the dismantling of the WAWENOCK, the entire business was completed in a week, leaving nothing but the massive keel and a few timbers too solidly fastened to remove.[37] The keel is still visible at low water.

The Friends of Nature, a conservationist group, acquired McGlathery Island in 1955 from the heirs of Levi Stinson and managed to arrest some of the wanton destruction of the island's artifacts, but not soon enough to prevent the desecration of the burial ground; most of the headstones were carried away. By way of recapitulation, the persons known to have been buried there are: Catherine Billings Eaton, in 1864; her daughter Charlotte Eaton Harvey and *her* infant daughter about the same time; a number of young victims of the 1873 diphtheria epidemic, including children of Samuel Eaton and William Harvey; various other Eatons and Harveys who died in infancy; and finally, Peter Hardy Eaton, Sr., in 1887. His stone was still standing the last time I visited the island.

[37] Note from Vernal Hutchinson to Dorothy Carman, April 1975, in Deer Isle Historical Society files.

Coombs Islands

These are *Islands K* and *L* on Rufus Putnam's survey of the "Isle of Holt Division" in 1785, and they still went by their letter designations when they were sold to Hezekiah Rowell by the State of Maine in 1825. In 1829 Rowell sold the pair for $32 to Abizer Coombs, who was already in residence according to the deed (Hancock 53/263). Apparently something went awry in this transaction, for in 1835 we find Henry Wilson, another island broker in the area who claimed title from Rowell, selling the two *Otter Islands*—"otherwise the islands on which Abizer Coombs now lives"—to Avery Fifield of Deer Isle (Hancock 62/100). I believe Abizer (or Abiezer) Coombs to have been the son of an early settler on Islesborough, and if John Pendleton Farrow's genealogical data are accurate, he would have had six young children at the time he is reported on the Otter Islands (Farrow, *History of Islesborough*, 180). What prompted him to move to two such small islands at such a distance from his home is unknown, but he apparently did not stay many years; according to Noyes ("Devil Island," page 5), he returned to Islesborough, leaving only his name behind.

The eastern Otter Island was known locally in the last century as *Bijah Coombs' Island*, after Abizer, while the larger island continued to be called Otter. Maps, however, normally showed both as Coombs—or sometimes *Coot Islands* (probably a cartographer's confusion with the even smaller pair of Coots lying between Devil and Camp islands). Fifields continued to own one or both during the last half of the century: Otter was included among the islands deeded from Ebenezer to Dudley Fifield in 1878 in return for support in his old age (see Farrel Island, above).

Bester Robbins speaks of a "conspicuous cellar" on Bijah Coombs's island in the late nineteenth century (Noyes, Robbins interview), but I am uncertain whether other settlers lived there after Abizer's family in the 1830s. The 1850 census, in the section of its schedule where many known Thorofare residents are listed, shows the household of Francis Coombs, forty-five, with his wife Experience and nine children. Francis's relationship to Abizer is unknown, but according to Dr. Noyes he was a brother of William Coombs, who settled for a time on Burnt Island off Isle au Haut (Noyes, Family histories: Coombs).[38] Francis *could* have settled on Bijah Coombs' Island after Abizer, but there is no certain evidence that he did.[39] The Walling Map of 1860 shows no habitation on either island. A single structure shown on the southeast shore of the larger island in the 1880s appears to be a fish shack (Map 1882 CGS 309) which, according to Bester Robbins, belonged to Ben Thurlow. The federal census of 1880, which listed the inhabited islands in the Thorofare separately, shows no residents on Coot, Coombs, or Otter islands. Seasonal residence by local fishermen into the twentieth century can be taken for granted—but I have no details on such residence.

[38] Readers should recognize the strong probability that, despite the coincidence of the surname, Abizer Coombs was unrelated to other Coombs settlers in the Thorofare: Abizer appears to have come from Islesborough, the others from Deer Isle and Isle au Haut.

[39] Francis, Experience, and five children—all girls—are shown in the 1860 census, but the listing here does not group the islanders as explicitly as the 1850 schedule. Francis's first wife was Abigail Barter of Isle au Haut, his second Experience Arey of Vinalhaven.

Spruce

This high-domed island has been close to prosperous island communities, but never sustained prolonged settlement itself so far as I have discovered. There is report of a settler named Bill Harvey who lived on the southeast shore for three years at an unspecified time, and there is indeed a small and ancient cellar hole on the easterly cove; his house is said to have burned (Noyes, Robbins interview). There are too many William Harveys in the Deer Isle census to speculate, without more detail, which this one might have been. Another residence around 1880 is more certain: James Robbins, a thirty-eight-year-old fisherman, is shown there in the 1880 census, with his wife

Louisa and four minor children (two boys and two girls). His home is shown near the northwest corner of the island on the Colby map of Hancock County in 1881. It is not shown, however, on the 1882 Coast and Geodetic Survey of the area (Map 1882 CGS 309). I have found no trace of his dwelling.

Quarrying activities appear to have been carried on for a brief period at the end of the century. The motions were confined to surface granite, which was lowered down the steep northwest slope, itself granite, by block and tackle (the eyebolts and flywheels are still embedded in the rock). The stone was apparently loaded front-end onto barges nosed in to the sloping granite shore; the twin jetties, which were held in place by steel cables and still stand, served as breakwaters for seas making in from the southwest or northeast. There were no cutting or polishing sheds and no evidence that quarrymen lived on the island. The entire operation, to judge from the amount of granite removed, seems to have been brief—perhaps no more than a half a dozen years—and it may have ended abruptly, for the northwest slope is strewn with blocks of granite that never made it to the barges.

Spruce is called *Black Island* in 1785 (Hancock Plan Book II: 23) and still had this name when it was assigned by Massachusetts commissioners to Hezekiah Rowell in 1825 (Maine, Forestry Commission, *Report*, 1914). Sometime between the latter date and 1860, when the Hancock County map shows it as Spruce, the name was changed.

The conveyances I have seen concerning the island in the nineteenth century shed no light on residence, but I would not discourage others from seeking further. The first Stonington tax schedule in 1896 showed the forty-acre island owned by Frank S. Warren, valued at $60. Ownership of Spruce Island passed out of local hands early in the twentieth century when Ella M. Warren, then living in Boston but with roots on Deer Isle, sold to C. A. Higbee of Philadelphia (Hancock 401/112); his family owned the island for more than half a century before selling to another island owner in the area, also from out of state (Hancock 864/159). From the latter, title passed to vacationers, who have used Spruce for occasional summer residence.

Millet

This is *Island F* in the Isle au Haut Division of 1785 and is marked "sold"; the buyer is not indicated. The owner's title may not have been too secure, for in 1827 the State of Maine sold the island, without reference to any previous title, to Hezekiah Rowell (Hancock 50/252). In 1854 Sarah Rowell, Hezekiah's widow, sold the island for $25 to Moody Buckminster of Webb Cove and Asa S. Pinkum (owner's title record). I lose sight of conveyances in the last half of the nineteenth century; in 1901 Winfield S. Thurlow bought Millet for $225 from Whitefield Gross (Hancock 367/336). Thurlow obviously thought more of the twenty-acre island than town assessors, who in 1896 had valued it at $20. From Winfield Thurlow, title passed normally to the present owner, who is a descendant.

The history of this island in the nineteenth century is obscure. The first name other than Island F to appear on any map is *Milet's* on the Walling Map of Hancock County in 1860. This might provide a clue at least to ownership, if not to residence, were it possible to identify such a family; I have been unable to. Meanwhile, the Colby Atlas of Hancock County, which appeared two decades later, gives no name to this island, although all others in the Thorofare are named and residence shown where there was any.

It is a reasonable assumption, I believe, that no one settled on the island on a year-round basis, for had this been so there would have been some report of it in existing records as well as a defined cellar hole and some evidence of cleared land. It is equally reasonable to assume that the island was used seasonally by fishermen, and there is some evidence both of a dwelling and of an ancient spring on the west side. The present owner (herself a student of island history) recalls having heard that these fishermen were exceptionally tall; if her recollection is correct, they were probably Buckminsters, for according to George Hosmer (page 122) the males in this family, long residents of the southeast corner of Deer Isle, were "remarkable for their stature."

Saddleback

This island, alone among those in the Thorofare, is given its modern name on the 1776 "Atlantic Neptune." On the earliest post-Revolutionary surveys it is named *Saddleback or Ash*, and these twin names, whose origins are obvious enough, survive in deeds into the twentieth century.

Unfortunately, our certainty concerning the island's name does not extend to habitation on it. George Hosmer (page 180) states that a settler named Edward Howard lived there early in the nineteenth century. He came to Deer Isle, according to Hosmer, as early as the mid-1760s, married a Deer Isle girl after the death of his first wife (an Eaton), and in about 1820 removed to Brooksville, where he died. It would be capricious, I think, to deny out of hand the reality of this residence—yet in the absence of evidence to support Hosmer's claim, one remains skeptical.

The next reported residence, in the late 1830s, is buttressed by several sources, and despite discrepancies, appears credible. According to Bester Robbins, James Cooper "of North Haven" lived some years on Saddleback with his wife Eunice Bridges, and both died there. James Frye, also of North Haven, lived with them—that is, in his half of what Bester describes as a "double house." The two men, Bester adds, were "splendid chums" of his father, Hezekiah Robbins, who was living on one of the nearby Thorofare islands. Frye removed to Rockland after the Coopers died (Noyes, Robbins interview). Bester's brother Joseph, in a later interview with Dr. Noyes (1927), added several details to this account: Eunice Bridges was in reality Eunice Dunham[40] and was not married to James Cooper; she had with her a "foolish" (that is, retarded) teenage girl—presumably an illegitimate daughter by a previous liaison—who died on the island before her mother. Daughter, mother, and James Cooper, according to Joseph Robbins, were buried near a stone wall leading to the north cove. Two others lived on the island for a time, Joseph Robbins tells us, though Bester curiously omitted this information in his interview with Dr. Noyes—or if he did not, Noyes neglected to record it. Elias Morey, the down-at-the-heel son of Elijah Morey and reportedly a drunkard, moved into the well-stocked Cooper homestead with his daughter Phebe when his own home in Mountainville burned (Noyes, Family histories: Dunham).[41]

If proof of the Cooper residence on Saddleback rested only on the testimony of Bester and Joseph Robbins, who could hardly have remembered James Cooper (Bester was born in 1839 and Joseph in about 1850), we might be justified in placing this occupancy in the doubtful column. There are, however, several bits of confirming evidence. First, a James Cooper *did* own Saddleback Island, which he purchased from Anthony Merchant in 1837 (Hancock 65/73); moreover, the price he paid for it—$200—suggests the island already had "improvements" and held greater attractions for him than incidental pasturage. He still owned the island in 1843, according to a quitclaim deed from another James Cooper living at Vinalhaven (Hancock 77/153). Second, Deer Isle records show that banns were published for James Cooper and Eunice Dunham in 1845 (Noyes, Family histories: Dunham). They were never married, to be sure, but the publication of the banns establishes a strong link between James and Eunice.[42] Third, the 1840 federal census for Deer

[40] Either surname could be correct, for Eunice Dunham lived with a number of Deer Islanders at one time or another and may once have been married to a Bridges.

[41] A relationship between Moreys and Eunice Dunham may have given the former some claim on the latter's household: Elias Morey's elder daughter Polly was the third wife of Eunice's father Elijah Dunham, though many years younger than he, and even a few years younger than Eunice herself; Elijah died in 1884. For more on Phebe Morey, see the next entry.

[42] It is somewhat disconcerting that banns were published between Eunice and two other Deer Islanders at about the same time: Elisha Holbrook in 1842 and Daniel Pickering in 1846, neither of whom she married.

Isle lists a James Cooper in his thirties, head of a household of six: a female also in her thirties—Eunice would have been in her forties, but such errors were common—two minor males, and two minor females. This listing does not account for James Frye and the Moreys, who may, of course, have been on the island at a different time, but does at least establish the existence of a James Cooper household in the town of Deer Isle in 1840. So, why not on Saddleback? Whether this James was a descendant of the large family of Coopers who had settled in post-Revolutionary times on North Haven and owned extensive property there (see page 172), I cannot say for certain—nor why, if he was, he should have chosen to settle on a remote island like Saddleback. All that can be reasonably claimed is that *a* James Cooper, said to be from North Haven, undoubtedly settled on Saddleback Island for a time in the 1830s and 1840s.[43]

Saddleback had no known settlers after the middle of the nineteenth century, though there were surely transient visitors: lumbermen who came periodically to strip the timber, fishermen who squatted in summer months, farmers who grazed sheep or raised an occasional crop in the saddle. I know nothing of these visitors, but there is record of transient Indian settlements on Saddleback at the end of the century. How many seasons these Indians from Pleasant Point (near Eastport) came to the island is unknown, but a clipping from an 1899 newspaper (called to my attention by Dorothy Carman of the Deer Isle Historical Society) suggests that they may have returned for some years. In the 1890s they made rustic furniture from the native ash and sold it in Stonington, together with gulls' breasts and other curios that might "turn over a dollar or two from some of the summer visitors." The newspaper piece gives a very favorable account of this "highly civilized and cultivated" Pleasant Point tribe and of their colorful settlement on Saddleback. It even names the braves who managed the canoes: Chief Joseph L. Dana and his son Lolar, Daniel Sockovy, Sabattis and Swissin Lolar, William Toma, and Tom Loring—not all of them convincing Indian names to the untutored ear, but described as "all genial and jolly fellows and most of them speak the English language very fluently." Assuming that these Pleasant Point Indians came regularly to Saddleback, season after season, this would have discouraged prolonged settlement by Deer Islanders.

As far as ownership of the island is concerned, the deeds I have seen are not instructive in suggesting other residence. It was owned at one time or another in the last half of the nineteenth century by Webbs, Whitmores, and Thurlows of Deer Isle. The assessment of $134 for the sixty-seven-acre island in 1896 (the assessment was to Winfield S. Thurlow) does not suggest significant usage. Early in the twentieth century timber rights to the island were held for a time by Dr. Benjamin Lake Noyes of Stonington, who had similar rights from Thomas W. Lawson on several other islands in the area. In 1925, Thomas Lawson having apparently defaulted on taxes, the Town of Stonington sold Saddleback to A. Cressey Morrison of New York (Hancock 607/328), and title passed out of local hands. A summer cottage, which still stands, was built in the 1930s.

[43] See page 378 for an account of this, or another, James Cooper "of North Haven" on York Island off Isle au Haut.

Enchanted and Phoebe

These two handsome islands have no history of human habitation, beyond transient fishermen and vacationers in season.

Enchanted was *Island E* in Rufus Putnam's 1785 survey of the area, but had its present name on maps of the 1880s. Rutherford states that its name comes from an echo that follows one around the island and persists even after one has stopped moving—undoubtedly from subterranean caverns full of Spanish gold.

Deer Isle

Phoebe Island is probably named after Phebe Morey, who is believed to have lived for a short time with her father on nearby Saddleback Island in the 1830s. A younger sister of Polly Morey of Russ Island, Phebe appears to have had as many husbands, lovers, and illegitimate children as her notorious sibling (see page 310).

Southern Mark

A mariner passing through Merchant Row in 1770 noted this "small, tufted island" and mentioned a shoal bearing north by west of it (Southern Mark Ledge), which was "covered only on high spring tides ... and is one with a flat woody island (Enchanted)." He goes on to say—superfluously, one would suppose: "...this ledge should be attended to, especially in the nighttime or thick weather" (Owen, "Narrative of American Voyges," 742). Our island, then, was an early navigational reference point, and it is not surprising that it was named on the first post-Revolutionary surveys; it was, indeed, the only *Mark Island* named between Deer Isle and Isle au Haut, where there are now three (Hancock Plan Book II: 23). The island is indicated as "sold" and the buyer was probably one of the Barters of Isle au Haut. In 1843 Robert Barter, describing himself as a "yeoman," sold one-half of a "serting island known by the name of Mark Island" to Francis Coombs of "Deearisle" for $5 (Knox Lands 5/449). Barters and Coombses may have put sheep on it periodically, but it is more likely that they and their successors used it for the fishing privilege. In the 1860s a structure of some sort appears to have been on the island, either for a fisherman or a shepherd: an 1868 tax default by Levi Barter on "a dwelling House situate on Mark Island" led to the sale of the island by Deer Isle assessors to Henry Eaton for $8.63—a price that does not say much for the quality of the dwelling (Hancock 137/399). I have not discovered how Henry Eaton disposed of his prize. Yachtsmen continue to use Southern Mark as a point of reference in altering course between Merchant Row and Jericho Bay—and curse the fickle winds that play around it.

Shingle

This is *Island D* on Rufus Putnam's 1785 survey. The name *Shingle Island* appears in deeds in the mid-nineteenth century (e.g., Hancock 103/367, Samuel Whitmore conveying it to Josiah Webb for $25), and on charts in the last half of the century. No evidence exists of even short-term habitation. Perhaps lack of water warned off early settlers—apparently, no water was available on the island before a well dug in 1940 when the existing summer cottage was built. Shingle is small and with only average soil; the anchorage is poor, and the island is vulnerable to easterly gales. Passamaquoddy Indians, who came regularly to neighboring Saddleback during summer months through the latter years of the nineteenth century, may also have discouraged local settlers. Still, perhaps there was habitation of which we have no record. Shingle, most easterly of the islands in Deer Island Thorofare, evokes more mystery than history.

Shabby

Unless a later eighteenth-century surveyor erred in his calculations and confused this island with the *Sheep Island* at the entrance to Southeast Harbor, Shabby had that name at an early date (Map 1795 Deer Isle). And sheep were surely pastured there, for how long I do not know. The present name appears on all charting since the mid-nineteenth century—and most voyagers in recent years agree that the name is appropriate. The island, denuded of its growth by nesting seabirds, does indeed have a shabby appearance, but the birds provide compensation: more than one summer sailor, coming out from the Thorofare islands on no particular course and finding thick fog in Jericho Bay, has found the channel markers of Long Ledge after navigating past the western shore of Shabby Island by the sound (and sometimes the stench) of gulls and shags (cormorants).

Eastern Mark

Dumpling was for many years the name of this island, and it has persisted in some topographical maps into recent years. It became *Eastern Mark* to distinguish it from Mark island, at the opposite end of Deer Island Thorofare, only after the lighthouse was built on the latter in the 1860s. Hezekiah Rowell acquired the island, along with many others in the area, after the separation of Maine from Massachusetts in the 1820s, and his widow sold it to Josiah Webb for $5 in 1859 (Hancock 108/368). The State of Maine apparently felt that title was not clearly established, and in 1874 reconveyed the island—still as Dumpling—to Josiah Webb (Maine Archives: "1874 Island Sales"). The island at the time was described as having "considerable soil and few trees." Trees, to judge from mapping over the years, matured, were cut off, and grew again. I have not discovered that the "considerable soil" sustained any settlers, but if the soil did not, shipwrecks undoubtedly attracted transient scavengers and wreckers: the shoals off Eastern Mark were the nemesis of many vessels making into Southeast Harbor in foul weather.[44]

[44] See, for instance, the account of an 1885 wreck in "Warren's Diary," *Island Ad-Vantages*, January 10, 1975: an incoming schooner foundered and broke up utterly in two days' time.

Bold

This is *Island M* in Rufus Putnam's 1785 survey. Later it was called *Bold*—occasionally misspelled *Bald*—and this is the name that appears on maps after 1850.

The only resident that I have heard of was a Mr. Harvey, who is noted in an 1825 deed as having "lately" lived there before moving to Russ Island; the deed is a conveyance from Hezekiah Rowell to Avery Fifield of Deer Isle (Hancock 62/106). This is as far as we can trace habitation on Bold Island. While good springs are on the island—springs where early mariners are reported to have filled their water casks—there are no dug wells, no cellar holes, and no stone walls to suggest sustained settlement. One can surely imagine fishermen summering there, and perhaps occasionally wintering as well, but these must be considered transients. George Harvey bought Bold Island from Avery Fifield in 1838 at the same time he bought Russ Island, where he lived (Hancock 67/367). I have not traced ownership systematically from George Harvey, but in all likelihood he used the island for pasturage until he lost title in a mortgage foreclosure.

In 1877 Robert Knowlton appeared to convey the seventy-acre island to Joseph H.

Judkins, both of Deer Isle (Hancock 155/390), but a few years later Knowlton's heirs still had possession, according to 1896 tax records, assessed at $60. The island is shown as heavily wooded on charts of the 1880s, then partially cleared on the western and southwestern slopes on the topographical maps of the 1940s, indicating that some pulping was carried out early in the twentieth century.

Bold Island has been owned through much of the twentieth century by summering musicians, whose cottage is on the southwest corner of the island.

Devil

This is *Island I* on the 1785 survey (Hancock Plan Book II: 23), and the island retained this designation, at least in the deeds, until 1866. Locally it was called *Devil Island* before this—the origins of the name coming *inter alia* from reports of diabolic behavior on islands in the vicinity (e.g., Camp Island, see page 308). "Some of the better classes," Dr. Noyes piously observes, "in honor of the belief that a Satanic atmosphere pervaded this region, gave to Island I the name of Devil Island" (Noyes, "Devil Island," 4).[45]

According to deeds reviewed by Dr. Noyes, the earliest known settler on Island I was John Coombs, who is said to have been living there at the time he purchased it from Hezekiah Rowell for $85 in 1835; Rowell had bought it, along with many others in the area, from the Commonwealth of Massachusetts in 1825. How long Coombs had been living on the island is uncertain, but he quit it in the spring of 1837, according to another deed conveying title to Avery Fifield in June of that year (Hancock 29/232). Nathaniel Gamage Thurston is believed to have been the next resident of Island I, together with George Grover, both of them newcomers to the region. They presumably lived in John Coombs's homestead near the highest point of the island—a rough cabin, it may be imagined, for none of the three settlers so far mentioned were married at the time they lived there (Noyes, Family histories: Merchant).

Avery Fifield's son and heir Thomas sold the island for $180 in 1866 to William Small of Stonington—the deed identifying it for the first time as Devil Island (Hancock 43/418). William Small owned it for twenty-five years, taking hay from the cleared fields and possibly collecting a modest rent from occasional squatters. A building shows at the western tip on a map of the early 1880s (Map 1882 CGS 309). As the granite boom gathered momentum in the Deer Isle area, Small leased quarrying rights to a Canadian company under the name of Nelson and Shields. When he sold the island to this company in 1891 for $1,200—a handsome price for those days—a granite wharf had already been built on the southeast end and a quarry was in full operation (Hancock 253/3322; see also Noyes, "Devil Island," 5). Neelon and Shields, however, who had already given up a quarry at Stonington, fared poorly on Devil Island. The wharf, battered by storms, was in frequent need of repair; "recklessness and lazity," as Dr. Noyes puts it, contributed to the company's failures. In 1895 the quarry workers themselves attached the island for back pay, and it was put up for auction. By a legal maneuver too complex for this layman to follow, it wound up in the possession of a judge involved in the case, and several years later he sold it for a handsome profit to William W. Frazier of Philadelphia (Hancock 341/476). In 1896, meanwhile, the island and facilities (which included a boardinghouse) were appraised at $803, chargeable to George Neelon, a son of the original contractor.[46]

I have no record of the residents on Devil Island from the 1830s to the end of the century—and there may, indeed, have been no regular

[45] The suggestion by Rutherford (*Dictionary of Maine Place Names*, 71) that the name derives from the prison island in French Guinea—where men sentenced to hard labor were obliged to work in quarries—is fanciful: the quarries on our Devil Island were not opened until some years after the island was given its name, and prison labor, so far as is known, was never used on the Thorofare islands.

[46] The assessment breakdown for the equipment is as follows:

Boardinghouse	$300	Dwelling house	$75
Office	50	Blacksmith shop	15
Stable	75	Blacksmith shop	30

settlement. A few of the transients may be buried in the small cemetery on the southern slope of the island's highest hill, where Dr. Noyes counted seven to nine graves in 1929. All the headstones are gone today. Not all these graves belonged to resident or transients: two were reportedly those of the young sons of Robert Merchant of Camp Island (see below); one was that of Mary Ann Holbrook, a feeble-minded girl of fourteen who died at the Deer Isle Poor Farm (Noyes, Family histories: Dunham). The Devil Island cemetery was apparently considered an appropriate resting-place for the maimed and unwanted from anywhere.

Four generations of Frazier "devils," as they call themselves,have summered on Devil Island since 1900—their family cottages stretched along the south cove, a clubhouse perched near the old stone wharf, and trails to Cape Sunset, Devil Bay, and other favorite retreats quartering the island. If true devilry ever plagued the island, its sting has long since been extinguished.[47]

[47] An account of the Fraziers' summer pastimes on Devil Island may be found in *Down East* magazine, June 1967, pp. 58–67.

Camp

This island is named *Camp* on the Rufus Putnam survey of 1785, the name presumably deriving from the fact that some early unknown squatter "camped" there. The earliest inhabitant, according to Hosmer (page 183), was Nathaniel Merchant, eldest son of the original Anthony of Merchant Island (see Merchant family tree under Merchant Island, page 371). Nathaniel, after marrying John Pressey's widow (daughter of the ill-fated Mr. Sheldon who drowned off Fog Island early in the century), is said to have lived "many years" on Camp Island before his death around 1830. According to Dr. Noyes, Nathaniel lived at some point, out of wedlock, with Nancy Harvey (either a sister or a niece of George Harvey of Russ Island) who had been three times married to Isle au Haut fishermen (Noyes, Family histories: Harvey).

Nathaniel's second son, Robert Merchant, remained on Camp Island after his father's death, married Sarah Smith of Swans Island, and in a dozen years, according to one account by Dr. Noyes ("Devil Island," pages 3–4), built up as unsavory a reputation as anyone ever had in the Thorofare islands. Dr. Noyes is not inclined to be charitable about some of the early residents of these islands, especially those who inhabited the ones nearest to Clam City on Deer Isle. "A large group of nomads sought a lowly form of livelihood on most of these islands," he wrote—and went on to identify these families by name: certain Harveys, Dunbars, Holbrooks, Blacks, and Robbinses. "They promiscuously mixed up with each other's wives and families that to be specifically mentioned would be out of place here. Not half of these cohabitants were married and a few were the limits of squalor. It was not uncommon for one man to take the other man's spouse and appropriate the same to himself." But Robert Merchant, according to Dr. Noyes's account, took the prize for devilry, and it was his behavior more than anyone else's that caused Island I—not Camp Island, ironically—to be named Devil Island. He is credited with causing the death of two of his sons, both buried on Devil Island—one from a severe beating, and the other from drowning after being ordered to fetch the cattle off Little Camp Island at a time when it was known he would be trapped by the tide rising over the bar. Robert's wife, distraught by his severity, eventually hailed a passing schooner whose captain, after hearing her tale, carried her home to Swans Island.

Another account of Robert Merchant's occupancy of Camp Island, which also comes to us through Dr. Noyes, is benign by comparison: Bester Robbins reports that Robert, whom he calls the first settler on the island, built a substantial home there before tragedy struck—the death of his two children in an epidemic, presumably diphtheria. They were buried on Devil Island, which was then uninhabited, to limit the danger, as it was believed, of contagion (Noyes, Robbins interview).

Deeds do not help us greatly in resolving

discrepancies in the above accounts or in unraveling the character of Robert Merchant, but they do fix certain important dates in the island's history. In 1836 Robert acquired title from Hezekiah Rowell for $100 (Hancock 66/23). The conveyance is silent concerning his residence at this date, but Deer Isle records show a school on "Robert Merchant's island" in 1842 (Clayton Gross, *Island Ad-Vantages*, May 14, 1976). This school was presumably for the Merchant children—four are shown in the 1840 census—and, after 1850, for the numerous children of Hezekiah Robbins who moved from Round Island to Camp about this time: Hezekiah's son Joseph has stated that he was born on Camp Island in 1851—Noyes believes several years earlier (Noyes, Family histories: Robbins). In 1845, according to Hosmer, the island was conveyed by Robert Merchant to Captain David Thurlow of Crotch Island, and a decade later David Thurlow willed Camp, along with a number of other islands, to his daughter-in-law Charlotte (Hancock 109/441). In 1859 Charlotte Thurlow sold Camp Island, "now occupied by me," to John G. Knowlton (Hancock 123/30). Charlotte herself was surely not in residence, but she may have retained Hezekiah Robbins as caretaker. Hezekiah, according to his children, lived eighteen or twenty years in Robert Merchant's homestead on the southeast shore at Camp Island before removing in his old age to the head of Webb Cove on Deer Isle. He appears in the 1860 census, aged fifty-eight, head of a household of seven, including several adult males. The Robbinses were surely fishermen (or clammers) for the island, though generous in size and reasonably fertile, shows little evidence of extensive farming. Another Robbins died on Camp Island in the 1870s: Mary Reed Robbins, third (or fourth) wife of Elijah, a much-married island fisherman who was the illegitimate son of Phebe Morey. Neither the cause of Mary Robbins's death nor the reason for her being on Camp Island are indicated by Dr. Noyes's sources (Noyes, Family histories: Robbins). Robert Merchant, finally, whose wife did in due course leave him (for whatever reason), wandered from island to island during the last years of his life—Wreck, Moose, Crotch—and died at last on Swans.

In 1896 Camp Island came back again to Thurlows, Winfield S. Thurlow acquiring it from George Knowlton, a descendant of John G. (Hancock 305/495). Tax records in 1896 show Winfield S. Thurlow as owner of the sixty-eight-acre island, assessed at $136. Timber rights on Camp Island were granted in several deeds in the 1920s—one of them, incidentally, to our Dr. Noyes; by this date, title to the island had passed out of the hands of Deer Islanders to summer vacationers. The last local resident of the island is believed to have been John G. Merchant, with his wife Betsy Harvey and two daughters, noted in a 1910 census (Chatto and Turner).

Russ

Indian Island is the name given this one on Rufus Putnam's 1785 survey. It is still called Indian Island in a conveyance in 1825, from Hezekiah Rowell to Avery Fifield, but "generally known as *Russ* and now occupied by Mr. Harvey" (Hancock 62/106). Why it was ever called Russ is unclear, since no Russ is known to have lived there and to my knowledge the Russ family, which was prominent in Deer Isle affairs in the latter half of the century, was not active in island purchases before 1825. Harveys, on the other hand, lived on this island for thirty or forty years, and the local designation *Harvey's Island* would have been more appropriate as the official name.

The identity of "Mr. Harvey" referred to in the 1825 deed noted above is also unclear. It is not likely that it was John Harvey, Sr., the veteran of the Revolutionary War, for depending on the evidence one accepts, John Harvey, Sr. at this date was either on Bare Island or back in Northport, having left the area (see Bare Island above, page 292). Nor is it likely that it was John's son George, for according to George's son William, the George Harveys moved onto Russ Island only around 1840. John Harvey, Jr., meanwhile, is believed to have been living with his family at Duck Harbor on Isle au Haut at this time. The strongest probability, then, is that the "Mr.

Harvey" noted in the deed was some relative of John, Sr. and his sons, about whom we have no information.

The 1840 census shows George Harvey in his fifties, with eight in his household—whether yet on Russ Island is not indicated. In 1850, when the family was surely on Russ Island, seven were in the Harvey household: George, Sally (or Sarah), Mary (or Martha), Jeremiah, Joseph, Ben, and William.

George Harvey, a fisherman primarily, and his first wife Sarah Stone of North Haven raised a large family on Russ Island. The youngest of their dozen or more children were born there, the older ones on Bare Island. A veteran of the War of 1812, according to Hosmer (page 201), George settled on Bare Island for a number of years before moving his household—farm and all, according to his son William—to Russ Island (Noyes, Family histories: Harvey). Five of his children—four daughters and a son—married children of Peter Hardy Eaton who headed an extended and moderately prosperous family on McGlathery and Bear islands (that is, Bear Island by Great Spruce Head, see page 257). These Harveys were converted to the Reorganized Church of Jesus Christ of Latter Day Saints, and a number of their children were buried on McGlathery. William Harvey, born in 1845, settled on Swans Island. Another son was Ben Harvey, whose widow Susan provided Dr. Noyes with much of the information on the family. One daughter, probably Nancy, died on Russ Island at the age of twenty-five and was buried on the south shore.

If George Harvey's children did reasonably well in life, the same cannot be said of George himself. He appears to have been frequently in debt, to judge from mortgage deeds that show his island put up as security for loans (e.g., Hancock 73/397 and 77/258), and he was in debt when he died; his estate was sold at auction to cover claims against him. His stepson Stephen Morey acquired title to all of the island except a seven-acre piece set aside for George Harvey's widow—that is, his second wife, Polly Morey (Hancock 121/538).

After the death of his first wife, who was also buried on the island, George married Polly Morey, one of the most colorful and controversial personalities in the region. She was born in 1802, the daughter of Elias Morey, a hapless drunkard, it is said, who squandered a considerable property inherited from his father Elijah. Elias's daughters Polly and Phebe were apparently left to their own devices at an early age and contracted multiple alliances among Deer Isle fishermen—Robbinses, Dunhams, and Holbrooks in particular—which have confounded local genealogists ever since. Dr. Noyes describes Polly with some awe—and, for him, even restraint: "Her career was one of widespread, romantic, sensational, notorious and, finally, of pathetic interest—similar to that of her younger sister Phebe. She was a strong, wiry character and frequented the clam flats and associated with boating during her early days the same as the men of her time" (Noyes, Family histories: Harvey). She was married for a while to Elijah Dunham, Jr. when he was very old, but bore him no children. Her six or seven illegitimate children—"the father of all or each being a matter of conjecture," Dr. Noyes tells us—went under the names of Dunham or Morey, and most of them prospered. Stephen Morey, the eldest, was brought up in the family of Avery Fifield, Sr., who adopted him at the age of five after discovering him with his mother on the clam flats off Devil Island. After Polly married George Harvey in the 1850s and settled on Russ Island, Stephen "helped George Harvey to a living"—a circumstance that may have facilitated his control over the island after George's death. We know George Harvey died before 1860 because he is not in the census for that year and the Walling Map of Hanock County printed in 1860 shows only "Mrs. Harvey" resident on Russ Island.

Some controversy surrounds Polly Morey's regime on Russ Island after her husband's death. According to Harvey descendants, Polly drove George's children off the island and proceeded to lead a debauched and riotous life there. It is true that no Harveys appear in Polly Harvey's household in the 1860 census[48] and that they are replaced by Polly's own kin: her daughter Lucretia Dunham, for instance, with her husband Elijah

[48] Ben Harvey, George Harvey's next to youngest son, appears in the 1860 census schedule with his first wife Susan in a household listed immediately after his stepmother; he may have been still living on Russ Island, in his own home, before he moved to McGlathery.

Dunbar and their children; Polly's youngest illegitimate child Charles Morey, then fifteen; and her sister Phebe's illegitimate son Elijah Robbins, then thirty-three. There is evidence of violence on the island: Rosetta Holbrook Robbins, second wife of Elijah, suffered an "upset" by her husband when five months pregnant and died—she was under twenty at the time (Noyes, Family histories: Robbins). Rosetta was buried in the family plot on Russ Island, as was her sister Sukey Holbrook Harvey, first wife of Ben. Polly herself came to a violent end under circumstances that have never been explained: she was found dead one morning on the northwest point—some say from a fall after an island brawl, others from foul play, and it was even suggested her own son Charles "had a hand in this act" (Noyes, Family histories: Morey, citing Susan Hutchinson Harvey, widow of Ben). The date of her death was sometime after 1870, when she is shown in the federal census with a single member of her household: Silas Harwood, aged seventy. Polly Morey was also buried on Russ Island.

Polly's death heightened the feud between Stephen Morey and the Harvey heirs. According to one report, William Harvey, Ben's youngest son, brought suit against Stephen Morey and recovered the family homestead; he even lived there a few years before selling it to his nephew Thomas Eaton. Another version is that in the end Stephen Morey prevailed and tore down the house to prevent it from falling into Harvey hands (Noyes, Family histories: Harvey, citing the evidence of various Harvey descendants). The continuing controversy, needless to say, explains in part the severity of the Harveys' judgment of Polly Morey and her entourage, though most appraisals of Stephen Morey are favorable. Permanent residence on the island appears to have ended soon after Polly's death; had there still been residents in 1880, they would have appeared in census schedules of that year, which for the first time listed the inhabitants of the Deer Island Thorofare island by island.

Quarrying began on Russ Island in the 1880s when four sons of Paul Thurlow bought the west end from Stephen Morey and organized the Harvey Island Granite Company (Hancock 182/486). The quarry is shown as the Thurlow Bros. Stone Quarry on the 1881 Colby map of Hancock County; locally it was known as "Eaton's Quarry," after Thomas Eaton and his son, who ran it. The principal contract, it is said, was for the towers supporting the Brooklyn Bridge cables. The cutting was mainly on the north and northwest shore, where several buildings are shown in maps of the 1880s (e.g., Map 1882 CGS 309). Operations were said to have been handicapped by the graves of George and Sarah Harvey, which their descendants would not allow to be disturbed. In 1896 the two owners of the island shown in Stonington tax records are Thomas H. Eaton and Dougal McKinnon, assessed $420 and $312 respectively for their share of the island and for quarry equipment.[49] The quarries are shown as still in operation on a map early in the 1900s (Maps 1904–06 Deer Isle quad). I do not know when quarrying ended on Russ Island, but presumably before World War I, when the industry waned on smaller islands like this.

Since quarrying days, it is doubtful that anyone beyond an occasional squatter or clammer has lived on Russ Island for any appreciable time. Meanwhile, it has been for many years a favorite and handy picnic spot for Deer Islanders willing to ignore the ghosts of the 1860s. In 1970 the Island Institute of Rockland acquired the island, which is now part of the Maine Island Trail.

[49] McKinnon's equipment included two derricks ($100), an engine and boiler ($200), and a shop ($12).

Harveys and Moreys of Russ Island

Note: The data for this table come from interviews Dr. Benjamin Lake Noyes had with various Thorofare islanders early in the twentieth century; their evidence is sometimes contradictory and is not easily verified. The accuracy of the table can, therefore, not be taken for granted. Those with italicized names lived for a time on Russ Island; those with asterisks are believed to have been buried on the island.

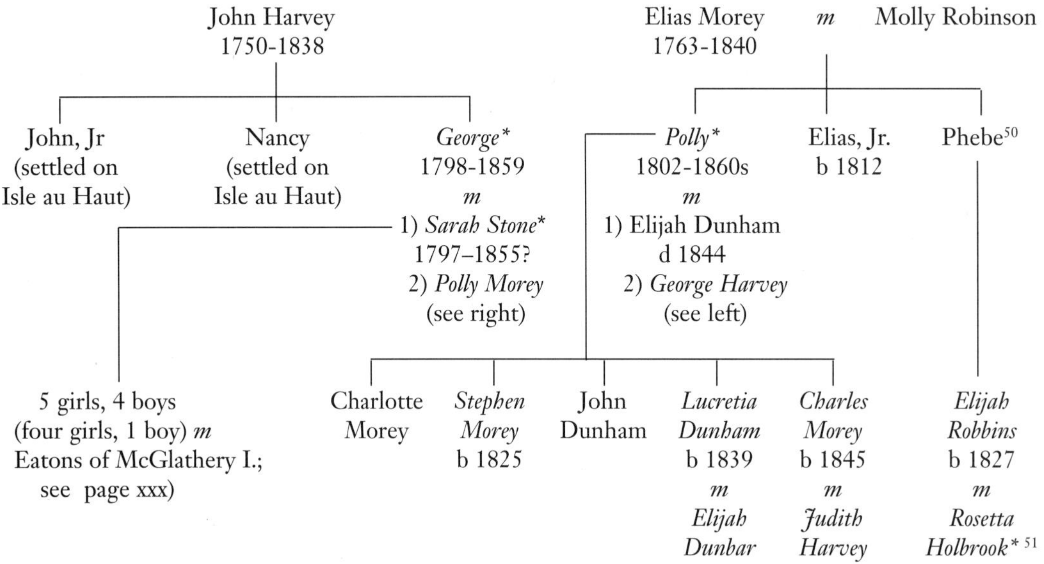

[50] Phebe Morey was married to Elisha Holbrook, but bore him no children.

[51] Elijah Robbins had other wives, but only Rosetta Holbrook while he lived on Russ Island.

Scott (or Round)

This small island opposite Stonington was ignored in the first survey of Hancock County islands, for almost alone among islands of its size it is assigned no name or letter. Perhaps to make up for the oversight it has two names today: *Scott* and *Round*, and they appear with equal frequency on current maps. The name Scott presumably comes from owners of that surname early in the last century. If so, their title was doubtful, for in 1874 the State of Maine sold the island at auction for $3.50 to Charlotte Thurlow (Maine Archives: "1874 Island Sales"); the price was, of course, derisory, even for real estate values in the nineteenth century. I have not traced conveyances of the island forward from Charlotte Thurlow, daughter-in-law of David Thurlow of Crotch Island, but by the end of the century quarrymen had come onto the island, and the value rose. Tax returns of 1896 show the heirs of Charlotte Thurlow as owners, Joseph H. Robbins with quarry equipment valued at $140, and Herman Eaton with a blacksmith shop valued at $55.

Quarrying would have eliminated any sign of earlier habitation, but it is unlikely that there was any: neither nineteenth-century maps nor local report give a hint of it. After the quarrying era, the island was used for many years as sheep pasture. Indeed, unauthorized grazing obliged a recent owner to place notices in the *Island Ad-Vantages* asking the intruder to remove his flock.

Green

This island has had many names. It is *Island Poor* on Rufus Putnam's 1785 survey (Hancock Plan Book II: 32) and still went by this name in 1825 when it was conveyed by the land agents of the State of Maine to Hezekiah Rowell. Hosmer (page 180) calls it *Worthy's Island* and states that it was occupied for some years by Charles Gross; when the latter failed to pay rent to Hezekiah Rowell, he was forced off in 1839. Sullivan Green of Green's Landing (the future Stonington) then bought the island from Rowell. Sullivan probably never lived there, but he gave it his name. He married a daughter of Captain David Thurlow of Crotch Island and eventually played an important role in Deer Isle affairs, but went through bankruptcy proceedings in 1843 (Hancock 75/11). According to Bester Robbins, William (Bill) Harvey settled on the island after Charles Gross removed; he lived on the south side of "Charlie Cove," where there is indeed a cellar hole (Noyes, Robbins interview). I do not identify this Bill Harvey if his residence, as Bester Robbins suggests, was as early as the 1840s; if, however, the residence was in the 1860s, this could be George Harvey's youngest son William, born in 1843, whom Bester Robbins mentioned as a transient resident on a number of Thorofare islands. Bester also mentioned the residence of Ben Harvey on the north end of Green Island—again, without date; I am assuming this to be another son of George Harvey, and I place the residence after 1860, when I locate the two brothers on McGlathery Island (see page 280).

If these Harvey settlers, or squatters, on Green Island are uncertain,[52] there is better evidence of Robbins residence. Joseph Robbins, according to Dr. Noyes, married Catherine Eaton in 1846 and had a son born on Green Island: James Turner Robbins (Noyes, Family histories: Robbins). This may be the James Robbins shown in the 1850 federal census, aged three in the Peter Hardy Eaton household on McGlathery Island; I am not sure *why* he was there, since his mother was not of this immediate family, but some mishap in the Joseph Robbins family could have caused his adoption by the Peter Hardy Eatons. A second Robbins known to have lived on Green Island (no near relation to the first) was David, oldest son of Hezekiah. His son James is known to have been born on the island in 1871, in the farm on Charlie Cove (Dennis Robbins interview; Dennis is the son of this James Robbins). David Robbins, married to Deborah Lindsay of Isle au Haut, is shown in the 1870 census with ten children; in the 1860 census he was living with his father—probably on Camp Island—and according to his grandson Dennis, he spent the Civil War years in Webb Cove on the south shore of Deer Isle. I do not know how long the David Robbins family remained on Green Island, but they had removed before 1880. The third Robbins to settle on Green was Elijah, who according to the 1880 census was a fisherman aged forty-eight, living with his wife Elizabeth, thirty-five; a son Amos by a previous marriage was also on the island with his wife Martha (daughter of David Robbins, above) and a household of six. The census lists the island as *Charles Island*, presumably after Charles Gross of Charlie Cove; the identity of the island is certain, in any case, for Elijah Robbins' homestead is shown on the north end of Green Island on the Hancock County map surveyed about this time (Map 1881 Hancock County, Colby). Elijah, illegitimate son of Phebe Morey by Mark Robbins (whom I do not identify), eked out a marginal existence on many Thorofare islands during his long life. He married or cohabited with half a dozen different local women and fathered ten or a dozen children. Amos, according to Dr. Noyes, was killed in a quarrying accident on Crotch Island, where he was living in the 1890s with a family of five or six (Noyes, Family histories: Robbins).

The Colby map of 1881 shows a quarry on the south end of the island called the Russ Stone Quarry; Bester Robbins refers to it as the Latty Bros. Quarry and says that Courtney Snell was a major figure in the company (Noyes, Robbins interview). Stonington tax records in 1896 note

[52] If Bill and Ben Harvey came later onto the island rather than earlier, as I suspect, there were surely *some* settlers in the early 1840s, for a school is shown there in Deer Isle records in 1842 (Clayton Gross, *Island Ad-Vantages*, May 14, 1976).

several non-resident operators with significant valuation: Scott Geyer with four acres and miscellaneous equipment ($600); J. A. McCarty with three acres ($100); and Goss and Small with equipment valued at $90. In addition, there were descendants of Sullivan Green who owned part of the island: Elizabeth W. Green, twenty acres ($82), and Amanda R. Green, one acre with quarry equipment ($175). The quarry was still operating in 1909, according to an item in the *Ellsworth American* (January 20, 1909) that notes the chartering of a schooner to remove stone from the island.

This is the extent of the information I have been able to gather about this island, although it is obvious from its location and its size that there must have been more settlers and more activity than I have shown.

Crotch (off Stonington)

The longest-surviving of the granite islands of Penobscot Bay, this island was named *Smith's* in British Admiralty charts surveyed before the Revolution, presumably after some long-forgotten squatter of that era. Smith is not a name that figures in early Deer Isle history. In 1785 it appeared as *Crotch Island* on Rufus Putnam's survey (Hancock Plan Book II: 26), and this remained its official name from that time forward; though in deeds and locally it was more often than not called *Thurlow's Island* during the sixty or seventy years that this family owned the greater part of it. What Indian settlement there had been on Crotch Island before European habitation is, as usual, speculative, but there are middens to signify the Indians' presence. One recent find suggests an activity that could be associated with either Indian or early white settlers in the area: the skeleton of a whale in the mudflats well up the "crotch." The supposition is that the whale was caught off the island, or possibly beached by the tide, then hauled up to this more secure area for dressing (Clayton Gross, *Island Ad-Vantages*, June 5, 1970).

Early Settlers

The first deed I have seen for Crotch Island is dated 1796 and conveys "rights, title and interest" to a sawmill and landing already on the island, from Edward Small to Thomas Colby; the price was a yoke of oxen (Hancock 4/440). Small and Colby were brothers-in-law, both of them living at the time in the vicinity of Southeast Harbor on Deer Isle.

I include below an abbreviated genealogical tree, drawn from data provided by Margaret Hundley, a descendant, to illustrate the relationship between the Smalls, Colbys, and Thurlows who appear in early deeds concerning Crotch Island. No title was secure until transmitted directly or indirectly from the Commonwealth of Massachusetts, so it is not surprising to find Thomas Colby and his brother Joseph, Jr. buying the island—or two-thirds of it—again in 1801 from David Coffin, a land agent or speculator who had acquired title from the Commonwealth; Coffin sold the remaining third to Paul Thurlow and an interest in the mills to Paul's brother David, a cousin and brother-in-law of Joseph Colby, Jr. David Thurlow was the principal figure in the early settlement of Crotch Island.[53]

David Thurlow, born in Newburyport on the eve of the American Revolution, came to live with an aunt on Deer Isle at the age of ten, following the accidental death of his father. In due course he married Mercy Trundy of Sunset and moved onto Crotch Island, in all likelihood sometime before 1800; Thomas Colby was either already there or came onto the island soon thereafter. The mill interests noted in the deeds were what initially brought the Colbys and Thurlows to Crotch Island. Whether they built the mill noted in the 1796 quitclaim deed—that is, before acquiring title—is unknown, but the sawmill was their first operation. It was located at the upper end of the crotch and was operated by tidal power; timber was readily available from the nearby islands. Thomas Colby left Crotch Island early in the

[53] The early deeds concerning Crotch Island were transcribed by Dr. Noyes and may be found in the Deer Isle Historical Society; they are also well summarized by Clayton Gross ("Crotch Island," pp. 29–30).

Tintype of Captain David Thurlow of Crotch Island, 1774–1857: mill owner, shipbuilder, and merchant. (Courtesy of Margaret Hundley.)

nineteenth century, but David Thurlow remained and eventually acquired title to the entire island, as well as to many smaller ones in the area. In addition to the mill, David also ran a boatyard that he constructed lower down in the crotch—or *basin*, as it was then called, before narrowed by quarrying. The first of seventeen vessels constructed on Crotch Island was launched in 1805, a schooner named MERCY, after David's wife. David owned several of these vessels personally and used them in coastal trade as far as the West Indies; he also owned mackerel vessels which he sent to Bay of Chaleur in the Gulf of St. Lawrence. The Thurlow home, in which David and Mercy reared twelve children, was located north of the basin. According to the 1850 agricultural census, David Thurlow had fifty "improved" acres (three hundred "unimproved") and his farm homestead was valued at $1,000.

Other families were on the island as well; in 1828 Deer Isle records show a special school district established on Crotch Island. Captain David —the title came from his rank in the militia in the War of 1812, not from seafaring—served a term in the State Legislature in 1829. In 1839 the mill was destroyed in a storm and was not rebuilt; the last vessel left the ways soon thereafter. Captain David died in 1857 at the age of eighty-three.[54]

He had lived a full and dynamic life on his island and, more than anyone else, was responsible for attracting settlers to the once neglected southern end of Deer Isle at Green's Landing. Before he died he made over most of his holdings to his son Paul, and Paul's wife Charlotte, in return for care of himself and Mercy during the remainder of their lives. The 1860 map of Hancock County, which was surveyed shortly after Captain David's death, shows three Thurlow households on the island—those of Mercy (who died in 1860), Paul, and David, Jr.—and two other homesteads under F. Shea and L. Babbidge. Levi Babbidge married David and Mercy's oldest daughter, Ann; Francis Shea may have married another daughter named Mercy (see residence table at end of this notice). All of the homesites are shown along the north side of the crotch. An 1882 chart (CGS 309) shows five homesteads in the same area with connecting roads north of the millpond, as well as a large structure on the northeast shore on the Thorofare, and two smaller buildings on the eastern shore south of the millpond. The David Thurlow homestead passed from Paul to his sister Elvira Collier and remained in the Collier family until 1905.[55] Probably none of these sites could be identified today, for this entire area was to be transformed beyond recognition.

[54] The foregoing details concerning David Thurlow's career come from notes assembled by a descendant, Margaret Hundley; from Clayton Gross's article on Crotch Island (see Bibliography); from Noyes, Family histories: Thurlow; and from Hosmer, *Sketch of Deer Isle*, 153–54.

[55] The deed of transfer of the Thurlow homestead suggests that Elvira's marital relations were not altogether satisfactory: the homestead was conveyed "to her sole and separate use, free from the control and interference of her husband." This deed is in the possession of Margaret Hundley.

Benvenue Quarries on Crotch Island, c.1910; note locomotive in center. Moose Island is at right, across Deer Island Thorofare.(Courtesy of Nathaniel Barrows of Island Advantages.*)*

The Quarrying Era

The quarrying era began on Crotch Island about 1870, after most of the Thurlows had moved to Green's Landing, taking their houses with them in several cases as well as the caskets in the family burying ground. Job Grant Saunders Goss was the prime mover in the Crotch Island operations. According to interviews Dr. Noyes had with Job Goss in 1903, which are summarized in the Noyes Collection at the Maine Historical Society (Box 14/21), as well as statements by Clayton Gross ("Crotch Island," 22ff.), Goss came to the area from Massachusetts in about 1860, already a stonecutter, and after living for a few years on Vinalhaven and Isle au Haut, began quarrying operations first at Greens Head—that is, the high headland on Deer Isle opposite Crotch island—and then on Crotch itself. He invited his son-in-law, George Small of New Hampshire, to join him in the business and in due course his son Job Goss, Jr. joined them as well. I pass over the family squabbles the Gosses are said to have had over shares, but the profits of the quarrying itself far exceeded the skeptically received estimates Job Goss, Sr. made at the start of his venture. In due course two Goss companies emerged—Goss and Small, and the John L. Goss Company (organized by another son of Job, Sr.)[36]—with ample contracts for both. Meanwhile, a third company, organized by Charles A. Russ, an early partner of Job Goss in the Greens Head operation, acquired land south of the crotch (or *millpond*, as it was now called) and quarried there from the mid-1870s on.

The contracts handled by the Crotch Island companies prior to 1900 included many small orders for paving and construction block as well as several larger ones—for example, the Mount Holyoke dam in Massachusetts, bridges in Providence and New York, the post office in Lowell, and so forth. These orders, to be sure, were less impressive than some received by the stone companies operating on Dix and Hurricane islands in the 1870s and 1880s, but the work was steady and there was rarely an interval between contracts.

[36] According to the recollections of an adopted son of John L. Goss, Jr., the Job Goss enterprises encountered difficulties at the end of the century and were resurrected by John L. Goss (Lawrence N. Button, "Rocky Road of a Famous Granite Quarry," paper at Deer Isle Historical Society).

The 1880 census shows forty persons living on the island in five households (see residence table, page 320). This listing does not, of course, represent all the quarrymen working on the island. Some lived at a boardinghouse at the mouth of the crotch (by the old mill dam); many more lived in Stonington and were ferried to Crotch Island daily. These men were considered transients and were not included in census schedules. The number of quarrymen working on the island in most years numbered in the hundreds.

An 1896 tax list for the new township of Stonington lists the property owners on Crotch Island (see page 282). Most of them appear not to have been residents, but the range of activity on the island is apparent. Dr. Benjamin Lake Noyes has left notes on some of these owners as well as a rough sketch of the island, drawn in 1908, showing where they lived. I summarize from Dr. Noyes's notes and sketches:

> The *Stephen Allen* house, formerly belonging to Levi Babbidge (a Thurlow heir) was on the north side of the millpond; part of it was rented to an early quarryman from Vinalhaven, Lorenzo Young, who spent some years on Crotch Island; he built several homes there: e.g., the Howland Gray house and the McGuire bungalow, both north of the crotch.
>
> *Hiram (Haight) Morey*, a lifelong islander, lived in the two latter homesteads in the 1890s.
>
> *Simeon Goss* ran a store and wharf on the north side of the millpond, at the mouth.
>
> *John L. Goss* (Dr. Noyes calls him John Ed Goss) bought one of Lorenzo Young's homesteads—but normally lived in Stonington; he rented the house first to Robert Cleveland, then sold to Bill Smith of Greens Head; Smith eventually sold to the Benvenue Company. Cleveland, meanwhile, removed for a few years to Rockland, then returned to Crotch Island to live in the house of Sullivan Green (another Thurlow in-law).
>
> *Amos Robbins* in the 1880s built on land owned by Sullivan Green, north of the crotch. He was killed in a quarrying accident early in the 1900s; his wife stayed on the island a few more years before selling to Benvenue.
>
> *Fred Wesgott* built near Amos Robbins's homestead, then sold to Walter Sweetland, who later sold to Robert McGuffie.

Subsequent notations on Dr. Noyes's 1908 sketch showed additional details: the boardinghouse was taken down the next year (1909) to make room for a power house and dock extension on the south side of the millpond; a house was built by Eugene Cousins on the north shore of the millpond; quarries are shown belonging to Ryan and Parker (southeast sector of island), Casey and

Sherwood (northeast sector), John L. Goss (new and old quarries south of the millpond), and the Benvenue Company (north sector on the Thorofare); various new roads were opened south of the millpond.

Finally, to complete what we know of residence on Crotch Island during the quarrying era, here are the households on the island in 1910, according to the Chatto & Turner *Register* (the 1910 census schedule for Stonington is illegible):[57]

Baldisare, Giulo	1/0
Bartlett, Augustus (Virginia), trader	2/2
Crega, Antonio and John	2/0
Emerson, Frank (Nellie)	4/2
Goss, Simeon (Blanche), trader	1/1
Grava, Joseph (Victoria)	1/2
	11/7

This represented a sharp drop in the year-round population from the peak years of the granite age. The Crotch Island school remained open through 1908, according to Stonington town records, but it could hardly have lasted much longer with the small number of pupils indicated in the listing above.

A distinctive turning point in the granite industry on Crotch Island, according to Clayton Gross, had occurred about the turn of the century. The local companies could no longer finance the more complicated equipment and improved transportation necessary to meet the continuing urban demand for granite. Accordingly, out-of-state companies with far greater capital at their disposal appeared on the scene: for example, Casey and Sherwood of New London, Connecticut, which operated along the north shore of the island and in due course sold out to the Benvenue Company of New York, which already operated quarries on Vinalhaven, Hurricane Island, and elsewhere. In 1901 the Ryan and Parker Construction Company bought out the properties of the Goss and Small Company and introduced a modern compressed-air plant to run the pneumatic drills; artesian wells provided local water for steam operations, thus avoiding dependance on the water supply from Deer Isle, already a sizable industry in itself, organized by resourceful Deer Islanders. Stonecutters, meanwhile, were increasingly imported from Europe: from Ireland, Scandinavia, and principally, at the bottom of the social ladder, from Italy.

Like the rest of the state, the island was theoretically dry, but this did not prevent the free flow of illegal spirits, especially in Stonington, which naturally grew with the granite boom at the end of the nineteenth century and gained a somewhat hoary reputation as the quarryman's playground in his off-duty hours. According to Clayton Gross, a 1908 newspaper account reported that liquor was openly hauled through the streets of Stonington and sold even on Sundays until halted "out of deference to the complaints of the local clergy." And drink was not the only accompaniment to quarrying: there was gambling, prostitution, rape, and larceny—not to mention several grisly and unsolved murders at the quarries.

But the elaborate operations of Ryan and Parker and of the Benvenue Company were the last gasps of the great granite boom on Crotch Island. The Benvenue handled only two contracts—the Boston Museum of Fine Arts and a portion of one of the Manhattan bridges—before suspending operations in 1910. Ryan and Parker continued in operation until 1914. Both companies in due course sold their equipment to the John L. Goss Corporation, which had continued in existence on a less pretentious scale—less pretentious, that is, in financial terms, but not necessarily in creativity, for it was at the moment of the decline of the industry that the John L. Goss Corporation completed the famous "Rockefeller Bowl" for the family compound in Tarrytown, New York. The bowl, a piece in a mammouth fountain, weighed 225 tons and was 22 feet square and five or six feet thick when first cut in a single piece; gradually it was shaped and polished until it weighed a mere 50 tons when shipped to Tarrytown (*Down East Magazine*, May 1968; also Gross, "Crotch Island," 46).

There was no sudden end to the Crotch Island quarries, as on Dix and Hurricane islands. The John L. Goss Corporation and the newly organized Deer Isle Granite Corporation continued intermittent operations during the 1920s

[57] Spouses are shown in the *Register* in parentheses; occupation of householder was quarryman unless otherwise shown; males are to left of slash, females to right.

Thurlows of Crotch Island

Note: There are many Thurlow descendants other than those named below, but none directly associated with Crotch Island.

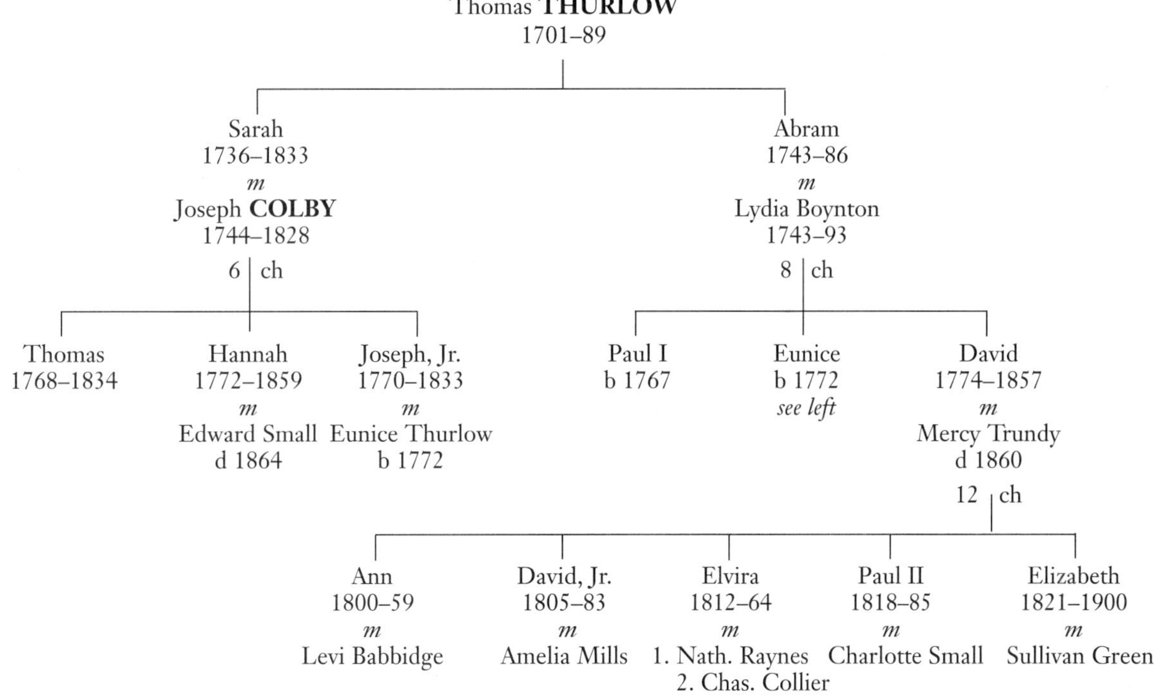

Solid granite bowl cut on Crotch Island for Rockefeller fountain at Pocantico Hills, Tarrytown, New York, 1913 . Stonington is in background.
(Courtesy of Deer Isle Historical Society,)

and 1930s, both on Crotch Island and at the Settlement quarries at Oceanville; they filled various contracts and employed a handful of stonecutters even after World War II—until both finally suspended operations, as had their earlier competitors. In 1953 the John L. Goss Corporation sold its equipment and rights on Crotch Island to the Deer Isle Granite Corporation, which with the help of federal laws was able to continue operations until the 1960s. One of its last orders was for fifteen hundred pieces of "Sherwood pink" for the grave of John F. Kennedy in Arlington Cemetery.

With the gradual decline and final termination of the quarrying industry, Crotch Island was left devastated, with large sections of the island uninhabitable. The basin where David Thurlow had built his schooners and brigs had been cut to a third of its original size by discarded slag, the tops

Residence on Crotch Island, 1850–80

Note: Residents on Crotch Island are not as a rule distinguished from those on Deer Isle proper in census schedules, making their identification difficult. The following appear in schedules in a position that suggests residence for the years indicated. Age is shown at first appearance. Spouses are in parentheses. Males are to left of slash in decennial columns, females to right. Householders are fishermen unless otherwise shown.

Householder	**1850**	**1860**	**1870**	**1880**
Thurlow, Jeremiah, 46 (Dorothy)	5/2	3/1[58]		
Babbidge, Levi, 56 (Sarah)	1/2			
Thurlow, Paul, 32 (Charlotte)	3/2	6/2	4/1	
Wilson, William, 20 (Clarissa)	1/2			
Thurlow, David, Jr., 43 (Amelia)	1/0	2/2		
Green, Sullivan, 38 (Elizabeth), trader	4/6[59]			
Trundy, Joseph, 56 (Hannah)	3/4			
North, Joseph (Mary), cooper	2/4			
Thurlow, Moody, 25 (Hannah)	6/4	5/3	4/2	
Shea, Francis H., 36 (Mercy)		3/3		
Lydiard, Charles, 43 (Jessie)		2/3		
Small, Ebenezer, Jr., 40 (Harriet)		4/5		
Holbrook, Abram, 69		2/2[6]	1/3	
Holbrook, Elisha, 75 (Phebe)		2/4	0/2[61]	
Thurlow, Stephen B. 27 (Ella)			1/2	
Emerson, Charles, 31 (Lydia), quarryman			1/1	
Keller, Washington, 62 (Dorothy)			1/1	
Thurlow, John, 32			3/2	
Goss, Job, 63 (Amelia); 2 quarrymen boarding				4/5
McGee, John, 29 (Lizzie)				4/3
Gray, Charles, 26 (Olive); 4 quarrymen boarding				8/1
Taylor, Israel, 52 (Susan)				2/3
Robbins, David, 38 (Deborah)				7/3
Number of full-time residents	47	54	29	40

[58] Dorothy is head of household in 1860.
[59] By 1850 Sullivan Green may have already removed to Green's Landing, where he was to become a prosperous merchant (valued at $4,500 in 1870, for instance).
[60] Household includes Elisha Holbrook's daughter Lucy with two children—also in 1870.
[61] Phebe is head of this household in 1870.

of the haughty granite hills were lopped off, and the island was abandoned by its inhabitants. Only one of the homes standing at the end of the nineteenth century was still standing at the end of the twentieth. A haunting beauty nonetheless pervades the island. An abandoned quarry on an island keeps a dignity usually lost by its counterpart ashore, where realtors are too quick to hide scars and start afresh. A group of New Age environmentalists acquired title to Crotch Island in the 1970s and for a few years spoke bravely of reclaiming and "humanizing" the island—with words that would have been strange to David Thurlow, like "psycho-architecture," "bio-feedback," and "psychosynthesis." They published a single issue of their *Crotch Island Journal*, then disappeared as soundlessly as they had come.

Rock, Sand, and John

These are, respectively, *Islands V, Z,* and *Y* in the first post-Revolutionary survey of the Thorofare islands, and it was not until the nineteenth century that their names appeared on deeds. Sand Island is known to have been conveyed by the State of Maine to David Thurlow in 1824 (Maine State Archives), but whether under this name is unclear. David apparently claimed title to all three islands, for they are included under their present names in a list of properties he conveyed to his daughter-in-law Charlotte in 1856. I have not followed title to Rock Island, but John Island appears to have been conveyed twice in the 1870s—and not by Charlotte Thurlow but by the State of Maine: first, at an island auction in 1874 to Thomas W. Holden of Bangor (Maine Archives, "1874 Island Sales"); then, in 1876, for $28, to three men from Camden, Portland, and Limerick, Ireland (Hancock 5/591), a dispersion that suggests no obvious object to their joint purchase unless they were quarrymen on Crotch Island seeking a bivouac. The island is in both cases called *Kimball's*—the same name that was given to Farrel Island for many years (see page 285)—but its identity is not in serious doubt; I have no explanation of the double sale. It is called *John's* again in maps of the 1880s (e.g., Map 1881 Hancock County, Colby). Ownership often came full circle amongst the Thorofare islands, and this was the case with John Island: in 1896 the owner of the two-acre island was Wilmot B. Thurlow, descendant of David, and the island, according to Stonington assessors, had no value.

Sand Island is the only one of the three to have been inhabited, and this merely for a few years in the late 1850s and 1860s. A homestead under the name E. Small is shown on Rock Island, which is not named, on the 1860 topographical map of Hancock County, but this is surely an error: it should appear on Sand Island. Eben Small is known to have lived there with a sizable family before moving onto Crotch Island; a son, Warren Arthur Small, was born there in 1866 (Noyes, Family histories: Merchant). Warren later married a daughter of Anthony Merchant, Sr. Whether other families settled on Sand Island before or after the Smalls is unknown, but none are shown in the 1880 census. The cellar hole of the homestead is visible in the center of Sand Island, in a clearing long grown over with young spruce.

In 1870 Charlotte Thurlow sold Sand Island to Charles Eaton for $45—so any "improvements" the Smalls made must have been minimal (Hancock 138/246). Rebecca D. Eaton is shown as owner of the five-acre island in 1896, valued at $10. The island passed eventually to the John L. Goss Corporation of Crotch Island, which conveyed to the present owners in 1964.

Mark (off Stonington)

This island was not named on the pre-Revolutionary "Atlantic Neptune," apparently because the unmarked channel now known as Deer Island Thorofare was not much used then by mariners and the bold island at its western end served no navigational purpose. Rufus Putnam on his 1785 survey named it *Island V* (a letter he assigned to several small islands). It was not until the 1850s that the United States government felt it expedient to erect a light at the western end of Deer Island Thorofare and pondered Mark Island (it was by then named Mark) and "Peggy's," now Scraggy. Mark Island was chosen and purchased from David Thurlow in 1856 for $175 (Hancock 104/210); the lighthouse was completed on a $5,000 appropriation in 1858. A machine-struck bell was installed at the west end of the island in 1885 (United States Lighthouse records: Mark Island file).

We have a partial list of keepers, drawn from census schedules and the National Archives. Thomas Small, who appears in the 1860 census (aged fifty-three, with wife Eliza and a household of five), was probably the first keeper. He may have been succeeded by James Morris, who is shown in the 1880 census, aged forty-five, with a household of five. According to National Archives records, the next four keepers were as follows (with dates of service): Charles A. Gott (1881–87); Howard M. Gilley (1887–96); Will C. Tapley (1896–1905); and Charles E. B. Stanley (1905–12).[62] The keeper after the reorganization of the Lighthouse Service in 1912 was John E. Purrington, who in 1916 traded stations with Allen Carter Holt of Nash Island off Cape Split; the Holts remained to about 1920.

The recollections of the two Holt children, Carl and Louise—teenagers at the time—will give some idea of the life of a lightkeeper's family in this era. The light was kerosene-powered and was lit each evening at dusk. The bell was operated by weights and activated manually when the fog came in. The family had no neighbors short of Stonington and so created its own society and pastimes. Carl and Louise scavenged on the shores after storms, discovering endless surprises, including entire deckloads of lumber and laths. In foul weather and in the evenings the family played cards or read aloud. Mrs. Holt, a former schoolteacher, had herself educated the two children when her husband was keeper of Nash Island Light (off Cape Split), so they were ready for Stonington High School when the family moved to Mark. They boarded ashore during the winter months but sailed to and fro in fall and spring, or were taken ashore in the keeper's motorized dory. One winter's day when the ice was fast across the Thorofare, their father fetched them with a sled, but sent them back hastily by foot later in the day when the wind shifted; they disappeared into the rain and mist as the ice broke up, and it was some weeks before Allen Holt could negotiate the passage himself to learn that his children had made Deer Isle safely.

There were few visitors at Mark Island. The Light Service inspector came periodically, and there was a frantic last-minute brushup as his sail came into view; he invariably stayed for a meal. The Maine Seacoast Mission sloop HOPE—this was the era before the steam vessel SUNBEAM—also called and left Christmas candy in season and installments of reading material, usually Westerns, since this seemed to be the preferred fare of keepers. There were accidents and rescues, of course. A vessel once went ashore near Andrews Island, and Keeper Holt went to the rescue, hailing a passing tug for help; but the tug captain and his engineer were drunk and a fistfight ensued before the rescue was effected. On another occasion, two passenger boats collided in the fog off Mark Island, and Allen Holt brought the passengers ashore for safety while the damage was assessed; for this he won a commendation from his superiors in Washington.

Mark Island Light was automated in the 1960s, and the island was vacated. The keeper's house had burned in an explosion some years before, and the last of the wooden structures were

[62] Captain Stanley appears in the 1910 census with wife Hattie and one son.

razed in 1975. But the light signals and horn are still there, of course, guiding mariners into the narrow Thorofare channel. On a foggy afternoon in August, before the era of Loran, you were likely to find as many as half a dozen yachtsmen hovering about the western end of Mark island, summoning courage to go in—or perhaps waiting for a nonchalant lobsterman to show the way.

Andrews, Second, and Fort

These three small islands, it will come as no surprise, have never had inhabitants. Even sheep-grazing has probably been intermittent, given the relatively small number of settlers on the facing shore of Deer Isle and the availability of more accessible and verdant offshore islands elsewhere. The name *Andrews* is presumably after some early owner, or perhaps after an owner's given name, since Andrews is not a common surname on Deer Isle. *Second Island* must be so called because it is the second of the three, counting either way. The origin of the name *Fort*, Vernal Hutchinson tells us, is from duck hunting many years ago, when the sounds of the shotguns made it seem a battle was in progress there (Vernal Hutchinson's recollections to Dorothy Carman). Fort Island was called *Sheep* in the 1870s when it, together with other islands, was deeded under this name by Ebenezer to Dudley Fifield in return for Dudley's care of Ebenezer, his wife, and daughters (Knox Lands 5/431).

Moose

Moose is surely an island, but is not often thought of as such since it has been connected by road to Deer Isle for a century and a half.

The name dates to at least the 1780s, when it is shown as *Moose Island* on the first post-Revolutionary survey (Hancock Plan Book II: 26). The first known owner was the Reverend Samuel Allen, a Baptist minister who came to Deer Isle in about 1810; he lived at Allen's Cove west of Green's Landing (Hosmer, 154). He bought the island in 1819 for $25 (Noyes, Family histories: Allen). Hosmer indicates that most of Samuel Allen's sons quit the area, but a number of descendants were associated with the island at least into the 1880s: a "G. Allen" (possibly a grandson, George W.) is shown in residence on the island in 1860 (Map 1860 Hancock County, Walling). George W., a fisherman aged thirty-two with wife Climentia and a daughter, is shown in the 1870 census for Deer Isle in a position that suggests residence on Moose Island. There is also a Samuel Allen in the same census, aged sixty-three with wife Susan and a household of six (five males, one female); this would be a son of the Baptist minister, who had surely died by 1870. George W. Allen is still shown on the island on the 1881 Colby map of Hancock County. Other householders on the island in 1881 were Henry A. Allen and W. C. Allen; all lived at the east end near the causeway. The Allen Brothers quarry was located near the center of the island.

In 1884 Hiram and Clementine Robbins moved from Wreck Island, where they had lived for fifteen or twenty years, to Moose; they had a family of five. They bought a homestead from Steve Ed Allen. Several company workers boarded with them: Jim Clegg, Jim Gamble, and Jim Rainey. Other residents on the island, according to Fred Shales Robbins (a son of Hiram and Clementine), included: Eben Small and his daughter Minnie Gross, renting the Henry Allen house; Ed McCormick, who boarded in the George Allen house (and died there about the time the Robbins family arrived); Ezra and Nellie Kenney, who bought the George Allen house after title was cleared. (Ezra, a stone cutter from Frankfort, drowned in the Thorofare soon thereafter.[63]) Jim Clegg bought the homestead from Nellie Kenney, then sold it to Clementine Robbins, who was

[63] Fred Shales Robbins's recollections are summarized by Dr. Benjamin Lake Noyes in a paper entitled "Moose Island History" (1933) at the Deer Isle Historical Society.

Moose Island and causeway from Deer Isle; Crotch Island is in background across Deer Island Thorofare.
(Courtesy of Maine Historical Preservation Commission.)

emerging as the matriarch of Moose Island. Stonington tax records for 1896 show Clementine owning thirty-two acres of the island, as well as two dwellings valued at $428. The George Allen house, which she was about to acquire, was valued at $145. James Clegg's valuation, meanwhile, for the quarry equipment he had from his lease of the Allen Brothers works, was $910. The John L. Goss valuation for another quarry leased in the southeast sector of the island was $640. There was a total valuation for the island, then, of $2,123—the highest in the Thorofare except, of course, for Crotch.

Clementine Robbins died on the island in 1905. She was initially buried there, but when quarrying operations expanded a few years later, all those interred on Moose Island were removed to the Weed Cemetery on Deer Isle. Hiram Robbins sold the family holdings after his wife's death to the Benvenue Granite Company, which worked the quarries until the 1920s. In the last decades of the twentieth century Moose Island was given over to a boatyard, Billings Diesel and Marine, with lobster pounds started by Ralph Barter flanking its causeway.

Grog

This small island south of Webb Cove on Deer Island Thorofare is called *George Island* in the Colby atlas of Hancock County (1881) but is named *Grog Island* in a conveyance of 1876 as well as in other charting of the period (e.g., Map 1882 CGS 309). Grog, of course, may be merely a corruption of George, but local legend (not surprisingly) has other options: the island was a smugglers' lair, a handy place to cache contraband before delivering it ashore; the name reflects the quantities of rum consumed on holiday picnics on the island. Grog was never inhabited, there being no natural water there. Even the water in the artesian well recently drilled by the present owner is brackish and rises and falls with the tide. In 1896 the island was owned by the heirs of Peter Powers (a Deer Islander); the value of the five-acre island was assessed at $10. Grog has been owned by summer vacationers since early in the twentieth century. The current owner, after a prolonged battle with the town of Stonington for a building permit early in the 1970s, has erected a complex of structures for a family vacation home.

Sheep (off Southeast Harbor)

This island undoubtedly had a livelier history in the eighteenth and nineteenth century than in the twentieth: situated as it was at the entrance to the busy trading centers in Southeast Harbor, it could hardly fail to attract attention. It is, in fact, one of the first islands in the vicinity to be conveyed, if we properly identify it in a 1777 deed from Seth Webb to Joseph Whitmore: "...one half of a Small Island known by the name of Sheep Island, together with half of a 600-acre lot on Deer Isle" (Hancock 1/316). There were, to be sure, many Sheep islands at that date—more then than now—but a reason for believing that the deed refers to this one is that both Seth Webb and Joseph Whitmore were settled in the vicinity. The island appears as Sheep Island on the first post-Revolutionary surveys (Hancock Plan Book II: 4) and is shown as "sold to A. P. Thurston," that is, deeded properly by the Commonwealth of Massachusetts, not merely *conveyed* by one claimant to another. The notation of sale was probably added at a later date, for the deed conveying the island from Massachusetts to Amos and Solomon Thurston, for $73.72, is dated 1815 (Hancock 35/315).

Here my history of this strategic island comes virtually to an end. There was no known habitation on it in the last century, and I have no record of transient squatters. It was undoubtedly used, as its name suggests, for grazing sheep and periodically for pulping. The Buckminsters, who were settled on the facing shore, owned the island in the latter years of the nineteenth century, and since they were fishermen they presumably held it for the privilege. Louise Buckminster sold to Winfield S. Thurlow in 1896 for $200, a figure that is not high enough to convince us there had been significant improvement (Hancock 302/26). The same year the island is shown in Stonington tax records under the ownership of George W. Taft, a non-resident, assessed at $68. Sheep Island has been owned by cottagers on Deer Isle during most of the twentieth century and in the 1990s was the first privately owned island to be included on the Maine Island Trail.

Group 2: Islands West of Deer Isle

Sheephead (Sunset)

This was named *Sheep Island* on Rufus Putnam's survey of Deer Isle in 1785, and Timothy Saunders was said to have been in possession for fourteen years (see page 472). Whether this meant he was in residence is uncertain, but it is likely, since he was first listed on Deer Isle itself, and then his name deleted. Sheep Island is explicitly mentioned in the incorporation of Deer Isle in 1789—and it is the only smaller island to be so singled out. The reason for this is unclear: if it was because it was inhabited, so were several islands in Deer Island Thorofare and Merchant Row that are not named; if it was because it was barred to a major island, so were Moose, Carney, and Stave, none of which are mentioned. Hosmer's map of early Deer Isle settlers shows that access to the island was across the dam of Emerson's Mill Pond, thence over the half-tide bar. In any case, Sheep

Island gained a momentary distinction by being linked with the three larger islands that constituted the original township: Great Deer Isle, Little Deer Isle, and Isle au Haut.

James Jordan was the first certain settler on Sheep Island, and he may already have been there at the time of incorporation. According to George Hosmer (pages 104–06), he served for some years under the British government on Sable Island off Nova Scotia, aiding the crews of vessels wrecked on the legendary shoals there and providing for them until rescued. He lived elsewhere in Maine before coming to Deer Isle, spent an undetermined number of years on Sheep, or *Jordan's*, Island, then removed to Deer Isle proper before his death in 1818 at the age of eighty-five. He sold the island to his son Ebenezer in 1805, and this may have been at the time of his removal. Ebenezer farmed the island, and after his death in 1836 it was passed on to Ebenezer, Jr., who also farmed it and lived there until his death in 1852. He is shown in the Deer Isle census of 1850: a farmer, aged forty, with his wife Maria and eight children. The farm where the Jordans settled was on the northeast side of the island, where teams could cross to Deer Isle at low tide; Jordan children also crossed the bar to go to school in Sunset (Lufkin Diaries). Most traffic to this island, however, came from Sylvester Cove by boat. The widow of Ebenezer, Jr., Maria Eaton Jordan, stayed on the island after her husband's early death. She appears in the 1860 census, fifty-three, with a son Eben, seventeen, two minor daughters, and Pearl Pressey, fifty-four. According to a descendant (Dorothy Carman), Maria Jordan remained on the island until her death in 1879. The 1881 Colby atlas of Hancock County shows the Jordan homestead, but it was presumably empty at this date.

I do not know how farming was conducted on Jordan Island during the quarter century that separated the deaths of Ebenezer, Jr. and his wife; but to judge from detailed topographical maps printed in the 1880s, the fields had been kept cleared and the walls maintained. The island continued to be used for grazing, and hay was removed regularly into the twentieth century. The abandoned farm was torn down by a Jordan descendant in the 1890s and used to construct a barn in Presseyville.

Jordan heirs owned Sheephead into the twentieth century, though there was also a Lufkin interest in the 1890s through a mortgage loan (Hancock 282/401). Lufkins and Jordans were connected through marriage. In 1919 Jordan, or Sheephead, Island was sold to Henry E. Sheffield, a cottager at Sylvester Cove, and continued to be owned by Sheffield heirs through the century. The cottages that Henry Sheffield built on the northern tip of the island still stand.

The present name of the island appears on maps in the 1880s (e.g., Map 1882 CGS 103) and was probably selected to distinguish it from several other Sheep islands around Deer Isle.

Heart

This is *Dow's Island* on the first post-Revolutionary surveys of the area, after Nathan Dow, who settled on the facing shore of Deer Isle as early as 1767 (Hancock Plan Book II: 26). I am not certain when Dow lost title or when the name was changed. It was apparently called *Hart Island* in the 1840s, when Captain Henry Lufkin wrote in his diary of towing away two masts (Lufkin diaries, March 8, 1847). It was Hart's Island when the State of Maine conveyed it for $7.50 to Rodney Witherspoon of Eagle Island in 1874 (Maine Archives: "1874 Island Sales"). On the Colby map of Hancock County in 1881 it is shown as *Heart* and has kept this name to the present. Meanwhile, if Dows lost control over the island in the nineteenth century, they evidently regained it in the twentieth, for the present owner received his deed from various Dows in the 1950s (owner's questionnaire).

The island has a legend which once again involves buried treasure, this time Captain Kidd's: this treasure, the legend runs, was buried between two basswood trees, which the Captain himself planted to mark the site. The treasure was never found again, but the basswoods flourished—and one still stands today to confirm at least half the tale.

(Some years ago, the late owner of Butter Island, having put out too short an anchor on a rising tide, returned from an inspection of his premises to find that his yawl had disappeared into the fog; he found it a few hours later—with the help of a passing lobsterman and the Coast Guard—riding nicely off Heart Island.)

Carney

Michael Carney, according to Deer Isle historian George Hosmer (page 39), was an Irishman who settled on the northwest shore of Deer Isle in about 1762 and subsequently removed from there to the island that bears his name. We have little to underpin this claim except the name of the island (called *Carne* in most early maps and deeds), for Michael disappeared without a trace soon after he arrived. He, in any case, has the honor, according to Hosmer, of being Deer Isle's earliest known settler.

Nathaniel Scott, a post-Revolutionary settler on the northern end of Deer Isle (near the old steamboat landing), is the first person I find assuredly associated with the island. *Carne Island* is shown as sold to him on a survey prepared in 1785 (Hancock Plan Book II: 4). Payment appears to have been put off to 1791, after Nathaniel's death, when the Commonwealth of Massachusetts conveyed "Carnne Island" to his heirs; the fee paid—$46.50—is high enough for that era to suggest that the island had some value and perhaps improvements by Michael Carney (Hancock 36/539; the deed was not recorded until 1811). The Scott heirs, to be on the safe side, also paid six shillings in 1791 to a neighbor, William Eaton, apparently to extinguish his claim to a third of the island (Hancock 1/64).

I have not traced title of Carney from Nathaniel Scott's heirs to the present owners since there is no evidence that the island was ever settled. It has been cut over, presumably half a dozen times or more since the days of Michael Carney. It has been camped on summers by weir-men and clammers, and undoubtedly it was used for grazing. But there is no cellar hole, no well, and there are no stone walls to my knowledge to indicate more permanent habitation. Even local residents with long acquaintance of the area whom I interviewed in the 1970s—e.g., Abby Weed and Orrin Eaton—had little to tell of Carney Island.

Sheep (off Little Deer Isle)

This island off the west shore of Little Deer Isle has been known as Sheep since post-Revolutionary times (Hancock Plan Book II: 4). It has never been inhabited, and its principal use, as its name suggests, has been for sheepgrazing—unless reports of its precious metals have more validity than I suppose. This island, it is rumored, has a vein of flint on it, although a recent search for it proved fruitless. Eugene Eaton of Barstow's Cove has long held that a stone found on Sheep, with which he buffs jewelry pieces, is jasper. If so, it must have spilled over from Captain Kidd's treasure on Heart Island. Sheep Island now has a scenic easement.

Author's Note: The Scott Islands, Birch Island, and Pumpkin—which might easily have been included in this section covering islands on the west side of Deer Isle—are in fact noticed in Division V, Mid-Penobscot Bay Islands (pages 223–25).

Group 3: Islands East of Deer Isle

Stave

This island bears a name once common in the region. Numerous Stave Islands appear on maps dating from the Revolutionary era—Great Spruce Head, for example, was one of them. The name obviously reflected a stand of oak suitable for cooperage; in the present case, the oak trunks were doubtless rafted to the coopers at Castine. The earliest naming I have found of the island is on a map of Deer Isle dated 1795, and to my knowledge it has never had another name. It is the only Stave Island left today in the Penobscot Bay region. As far as the oaks are concerned, one ancient tree was still standing when the present owners acquired the island in 1936, and this has seeded itself so that today there is a substantial grove of young oaks on the western side.

There may be more to say about the oaks of Stave Island than about its early inhabitants. Indians used the island evidently over a long era, to judge from the depth of the kitchen middens on the eastern shore; numerous artifacts have been recovered from these middens. The earliest recorded owner of the island is Eliakim Eaton, oldest son of William, who was one of the original settlers in the area as early as 1762. Eliakim Eaton was quieted in the initial conveyance of Little Deer Isle in 1786 from the new Commonwealth of Massachusetts to John Reed, who immediately sold to Governor James Bowdoin (Hancock 13/466); as a settler on Little Deer Isle before 1784, Eliakim was entitled to a hundred-acre lot, which, being at the southeast corner of Little Deer Isle, was presumed to include Stave Island. Hosmer (page 168) notes that Eliakim's lot included the island, but he does not suggest that Eliakim settled there.

Eliakim's wife was Mary Bunker of the Cranberry Isles, and the circumstances of their marriage are worth recording. A pre-Revolutionary voyager in our region, Captain William Owen, had as his pilot Aaron Bunker, Mary's brother, who naturally asked permission to visit his kin when Captain Owen's ship anchored off the Cranberry Isles one October evening in 1770. Captain Owen explains the sequel in his narrative of the voyage: "Alas! the dire mishap! he popped in very unexpectedly, I suppose, and found his maiden sister bundled a-bed with the son of a

Stave Island against Little Deer Isle, viewed from Sargentville across Eggemoggin Reach east of present Deer Isle bridge, c. 1910. The causeway linking Deer Isle and Little Deer Isle is not yet built, though wagons could cross the bar at low tide. Vessel under tow moving up reach, as Rockland ferry approaches Sargentville landing. (Courtesy of Deer Isle Historical Society.)

wealthy settler on Deer Island. The enraged pilot swore he would cut the gallant's throat, if he did not repair the honour of the family by marrying his sister: the trembling swain declared his willingness to do so as soon as he had an opportunity, but observed there was no parson in the district..." (Owen, "Narrative of American Voyages," 731). The "trembling swain," needless to say, was Eliakim (or Eliachim)[64] Eaton, and the resourceful Aaron persuaded Captain Owen himself to perform the ceremony next day—after which, "a good substantial, and plentiful entertainment was provided...and a real and genuine Yankee frolic ensued." Some weeks later Captain Owen went ashore with his pilot at the northern tip of Deer Isle, "for here" (to continue Captain Owen's relation) "lived the parents of Eliachim Eaton, who I helped to a rib at Cranberry island—their greetings were not the most cordial, neither did the family seem to be much obliged to the priest, but as they did not dislike my money I bought a few necessaries, laughed at their self-consequence, and we returned on board again."

Eliakim and Mary Bunker raised a family of seven or more children on Little Deer Isle, but I am doubtful they settled on Stave Island. It would seem unlikely, given his hundred-acre lot from the Bowdoins, all of it excellent farmland, and the awkward access to Stave Island over clam flats at low tide. On the other hand, *some* family was living there around 1790. A French traveler in Eggemoggin Reach at this time—the exact date is unclear—reports a family on the island engaged in fishing rather than cultivating the land, but with sheep, several cows, and good pasturage; the voyager, caught by night, would have built a fire ashore except that the settler proposed three shillings for every tree cut.[65] In the absence of more precise evidence, it would be idle to speculate on the identity of this settler, beyond his being some member of Eliakim's family or a tenant.

The island is believed to have remained in the Eaton family through most of the nineteenth century, though continuous habitation is unlikely. The Walling map of Hancock County in 1860, for example, shows no residence on Stave Island, and it would have, had there been settlers at the time. The Colby atlas of 1881 shows B. Eaton there in a farm on the eastern slope. This was Benjamin H. Eaton, son of Solomon and grandson of Eliakim, and it is known that he lived there until near the end of the century. The cellar hole of his farm is still evident; the wells he used, of which one, dug in a bubbling spring, is still in use today, ring his farm; and sections of his stone walls can still be found. I do not find a conveyance of the island from Ben Eaton, but conveyances in the twentieth century make explicit reference to the fact that he "occupied and inhabited the island for a number of years" (e.g., Hancock 387/409).

The island passed out of local hands for the first time in 1905 when sold by W. J. Grindle to Alanson H. Reed of Boston (Hancock 425/276). Reed, an organ manufacturer, built a large summer cottage near the highest point of Stave, but after his death his son allowed the island to go for taxes, and it was held for some years by banks and realtors in Ellsworth before being offered for sale in 1935, together with the eleven-room cottage, for $2,000. The new owners restored the premises for family residence; it was also used during several seasons as a boys' camp. The cottage, a relic of early-twentieth-century "cottage" architecture, fell victim to a freak accident in March 1958—a spark from a small garden fire ignited the roof, and the building was destroyed. The owners moved to a boathouse on the western shore. Canoeists, working their way up or down Eggemoggin Reach, not infrequently against contrary tides (for the tides meet off Stave Island under the Deer Isle Bridge), have occasionally taken refuge here—much as generations of Tarratine Indians did before the first Europeans came.

[64] However spelled, the accent is on the first "i."

[65] *"Journal de Notre Voyage dans la Contrée de l'Est,"* by Mme. de Leval de la Roche, *Proceedings*, American Antiquarian Society, Vol. 51 (April 16, 1941), page 207.

Campbell

This island was named for John Campbell, an early Scottish settler from Argyllshire, who lived on the eastern side of Deer Isle in the vicinity of Campbell's Neck (Hosmer, 50). It is called *Campbell's* on Rufus Putnam's survey of Hancock County in 1785 (Hancock Plan Book II: 4); John Campbell appears in Putnam's census of the same date, a settler on Deer Isle since 1763 (page 472). In 1791 John Campbell and a neighbor, Ignatius Haskell, petitioned the Massachusetts Commission on Eastern Lands for legal possession of the island which they claimed to have "improved" for twenty years (Massachusetts Archives, Box No. 14). I do not discover the outcome of the petition, but in 1811 John Campbell wrote the same committee again, seeking to reduce the value placed on the island, which he said had been in his possession since he first settled on Deer Isle and which he had been cultivating "more or less yearly"; the $15-an-acre price was for "first quality" land and everyone knew, he wrote, that the island was "second quality" (a quarter of the western end was boggy, the eastern end "falls into low flat and clay," and unknown persons had been stripping the woods).[66] In due course the fee was settled: before his death in 1820, John Campbell paid $69 for a proper conveyance, and title passed to his heirs in 1824 (Maine, Forestry Commission *Report*, 1914, p. 110).

The question of settlement on Campbell Island poses a problem, since there is dispute among local residents as to the existence of wells and a convincing cellar hole. Census records are no help, for the census-takers did not distinguish between residents on offshore islands like this and Deer Isle proper. Although at least one of John Campbell's heirs occupied his lands on Campbell Neck, it appears that none concerned themselves with the island; even its ownership remains obscure. Late in the nineteenth century two Grays apparently built dwellings on the island and lived there briefly: Oliver Gray, according to information compiled by Dr. Benjamin Lake Noyes, settled on the north side of the island. It is not known how long he remained, but he eventually "sold" to Roswell Davis and moved to neighboring Mountainville, taking his dwelling with him. His son Benjamin built a camp on the west side of the island but appears not to have remained very long. The residence of both Oliver and Benjamin must be considerd questionable and brief, but probably occurred. An 1882 chart shows a relatively large structure in from the southeast shore, with cleared land around it—possibly a barn used for herding cattle and sheep (CGS 309). Sheep have been pastured on Campbell for many years: the widow of Samuel S. Eaton of McGlathery Island, for example, told Dr. Noyes in 1911 that she used the northern end of the island, which she owned, for sheepgrazing, and she believed Roswell Davis, who owned the southern end, did the same (Noyes, Family histories: Eaton).

Eatons and Davises of Deer Isle, then, were clearly involved in the ownership of Campbell Island in the late-nineteenth century. In 1897 Oliver B. Gray sold to Rodney M. Gray, and he, living in Castine, conveyed in 1901 for $240 to Ellen M. Davis (Hancock 355/46 and 359/338). In 1929 Roswell P. Davis and Fred R. Sullivan sold to Robert F. Herrick, and from this last Deer Isle owner the island passed in due course to a Boston buyer. There is no mention in any of these instruments of residence on the island. In the 1980s Campbell Island was donated to the Island Institute, which is conducting a long-term study of the two sites on the island used by the Maine Island Trail.

If Campbell Island seems to have been curiously neglected by eighteenth-, nineteenth-, and twentieth-century settlers, it may have hosted seventeenth-century visitors. In 1899 an archaeological expedition from the Smithsonian Institute, headed by the ethnologist Frank Hamilton Cushing, unearthed three skeletons on Campbell Island, one of them unmistakably a European and in armor. To dispel rumors that this was an early Norseman who had accompanied Leif Erikson, Joseph Williamson of the Maine Historical Society

[66] John Campbell was, in fact, a relatively prosperous farmer, according to a 1792 Deer Isle tax return—though his assessments surely come from his property on Campbell Neck, not on Campbell Island: he mowed twenty acres for fifteen tons of hay; tilled an additional four acres for forty bushels of grain; had ten acres in pasturage; and kept a yoke of oxen, nine cows, and three pigs.

wrote Dr. Cushing about the find, and the latter's conclusions were as follows: the European was possibly a French refugee from the St. Sauveur settlement in Somes Sound on Mount Desert Island that was sacked by the British in 1613. His companion, lying prone next to him, without armor and with beads, was probably an Indian woman; no violence appears to have been involved in their death, Dr. Cushing wrote, since the blunderbuss buried with them was blunted—a sign that whoever buried the pair wished them well. The third figure, buried in a sitting position in a ring of stones, was probably an Indian chieftain and was apparently buried at a later date (Maine Historical Society, Collection 110, 20/9).

Conary

This island has had several names over the years, the names often overlapping in time. It is shown as *Greenlaw's Island* on the 1776 "Atlantic Neptune," because a Greenlaw of Greenlaw Neck claimed it; however, no Greenlaw, so far as is known, ever lived there. After the American Revolution it was named *Black Island* (Map 1785 Hancock County), and this name was still used locally by older residents late in the twentieth century.[67] The name *Conary* or *Conaway*—the spelling varies—was in use by the 1820s: William D. Williamson in his history published at that time (I: 75), for instance, uses this name; he stated "the island has a bold shore, a good soil and several families."

Thomas Conary was an Irishman who came to the Penobscot Bay region on the eve of the American Revolution.[68] He settled first at Brooksville, where he married Margaret Lymeburner, a native of Ayrshire in Scotland. The couple had half a dozen children before Margaret died in the early 1780s. Thomas Conary moved to Deer Isle—he appears in Rufus Putnam's 1785 census (page 473)—and there married Olive Staples who bore him nine more children. A number of the latter were undoubtedly born on Conary Island.

In 1789 Jonathan Greenlaw, then living in St. Andrews, New Brunswick (whence as a Tory he had fled after the Revolutionary War), for £30 sold half of Black Island to Thomas Conary. In 1796 Thomas Conary bought the other half from William Foster, who had acquired it a dozen years earlier from another Greenlaw (Hancock 4/135). Thomas Conary is in the 1790 census schedule for Deer Isle (not specifically shown on Black Island, but probably already there): in his forties, with a wife (Olive Staples) between twenty-five and thirty-five, and ten children (six boys and four girls). In 1802 he is known to have bought land on Deer Isle—from his son Thomas, Jr., in fact—and he probably moved to Deer Isle proper soon thereafter. Thomas, Sr. died in 1829.

At this point it is necessary to interrupt the sequence of our presentation to consider a possible glitch in the title record of Black Island. In 1786, according to a source not easily set aside (an item in the Maine Historical Society's "Farnham Papers"), the Commonwealth of Massachusetts concluded a treaty with the Penobscot Indians which, in return for the Indians' surrender of claims on the Penobscot River, awarded them "two islands in the Bay called White Island and Black Island, near Naskeag Point...."[69] The gift of Black Island, in particular, seems appropriate since the island had long been used by Indians, to judge from the wide if only averagely deep middens on the south shore. But what happened to this grant?

[67] A retired lobsterman in the area (Leslie Thompson) suggested the name came from a Rufus Black who once lived there and whose daughter married a Conary. If this detail is accurate, it is coincidence, for the island was named Black Island, presumably to contrast with its neighbor White Island, long before any Rufus Black could have appeared there. *Black* and *White* were common contrasting names for neighboring islands in early days—designating the prominence of vegetation or exposed rock surface.

[68] An item in the *Bangor Historical Magazine* (VIII: 14/1,800) places Thomas Conary on Black Island as early as 1763. There is no basis that I know of for this claim. The details of the movements of Thomas Conary and of his family are from the meticulous research of a descendant, William R. Conary of Reading, Massachusetts. I include here only the details necessary to our story.

[69] The treaty further awarded the Indians three hundred and fifty blankets, two hundred pounds of powder, plus shot and flints, and promised that the lands along the Penobscot River outside the surrendered claims would be considered "hunting grounds," not to be settled by the Commonwealth or by individuals (Maine Historical Society, *Collections and Proceedings*, II: 80; *Documentary History*, XXI: 237).

There is no evidence that Penobscot Indians either occupied the islands or surrendered title of either to Greenlaws, Conarys, or to anyone else. Indeed, the Commonwealth's gesture of amity with the Penobscots simply disappears from view.

Who, then, was left on Black or Conary Island after the departure of Thomas Conary? Thomas had two sons old enough by 1800 to farm the island; he had another two by 1810—not to mention numerous sons-in-law (see genealogical table). Residence on the island, however, is not explicitly shown in census schedules until 1830, although there is a presumption that the island continued to be occupied and farmed. We do know that Conarys continued to own the island: Thomas, Sr. conveyed the island to his son Isaac Knapp Conary in 1821, and if the purchase price—$1,000—was fair market value, it indicated the island had not deteriorated (Hancock 53/99).

The householders on Conary Island from 1830 to 1850, according to federal census schedules, are as follows (males in household left of slash, females to right):

Householder	1830	1840[70]	1850
David Conroy, 20s	3/1		
Joshua Conroy, 20s	4/1		
Israel Conway, 40s			5/3
Joshua Saddler, 40			7/5

David and Joshua "Conroy" were the youngest sons of Thomas Conary, with small families in 1830; Israel "Conway" in 1840 was an older brother (the census-takers were nothing if not imaginative in their spelling). Swans Island historian Dr. H. W. Small corroborates the residence of Israel Conary: he lived "for some years" on Black Island before removing to Swans Island and thence to Blue Hill (*History of Swan's Island,* 154). Dr. Small also notes the brief residence on the island of Thomas Colomy, who was "greatly deceived" in the prospects there and so returned to his native Swans (page 122); this residence was probably in the 1840s. Joshua Saddler in the 1850 census was a Swans Islander, probably a tenant farmer; he had a real estate valuation of $500, according to the census-taker, but was never an owner.

[70] A second "Conways Island" appears in the 1840 census schedule for Hancock County which I am unable to identify (it could, of course, have been simply the same "Conways Island" with an additional homesteader). Its resident was Isaac Cousins, in his thirties, with a household of ten (five males and five females).

Ownership had become cloudy by this time. Isaac Knapp Conary, who had acquired title in 1824 (noted above), conveyed the island to Daniel Merrill of Sedgwick in 1827—possibly a mortgage (Hancock 53/99); he moved to Blue Hill as a brickmaker about this time. Twenty years later George M. Campbell of Blue Hill (but in all likelihood originally of Campbell's Neck, next to Black Island) had acquired title to the entire island and sold twenty acres at the east end to William Conary for $600, "together with all buildings standing thereon" (Hancock 80/187). This was the site of the principal farm on the island (to judge from cellar holes in evidence today). William Conary, a grandson of Thomas, Sr., is not known to have lived on the island—indeed, no one is shown in residence on the Walling Map of Hancock County of 1860; nor do any buildings appear to be standing. William remained an owner for thirty years or more: in 1874 at an island auction at which disposition was made of coastal islands not properly deeded by either Maine or Massachusetts, the claim of William Conary of Blue Hill and Hardy Lane of Deer Isle to Conary Island was allowed on the grounds that though they were absentee owners, the island was "mostly under cultivation" (Maine Archives "1874 Island Sales"). Under cultivation by whom? I identify no year-round residents on Conary Island in census schedules after 1850, yet charting in the 1880s shows buildings on the island—a cluster at the east end and another in the southwest sector (Maps 1880 CGS 4 and 1885 CGS 307).

The memories of local residents I was able to contact in the 1970s did not reach back into the years when Conary Island was last inhabited; the buildings themselves, of course, have long since been removed, burned, or returned to dust. There are no burial grounds to help us.[71] Alder have long since claimed the once-ploughed fields, still marked off by stone walls, especially at the eastern

[71] The only rumored burial on Conary Island was of an Indian who appears in a legend of different versions (none of them particularly edifying). In one version a rum-loving Indian named Swunksus is put to death in a stupor by an early Conary, and thereafter his drunken snores reverberated around the island as he stalked his murderer (Charles M. Skinner, *Myths and Legends of our Land,* Philadelphia: J. B. Lippincott Co., 1895, I: 188). In the other version the drunkard and firebrand is a Conary, who kills the poor Indian to gain undisputed claim to the island.

end. Even sheepgrazing, which persisted into the 1970s (after the last Conary owner, Judge Wiley Conary, sold to two families who summer there), was not able to halt the alder tide. Only the stone foundations and cellar holes—there appear to have been at least four sites occupied at one time or another—remain as evidence of a habitation that must have stretched intermittently over more than a century, most of the inhabitants descended from an early Irish immigrant.

Conarys of Conary Island

Note: This is an abbreviated genealogical table of descendants of Thomas Conary of Conary Island. The children of Margaret Lymeburner were born in Brooksville; Olive Staples's children were born on Deer Isle or Black Island. I am indebted to a descendant, William R. Conary, for the details here.

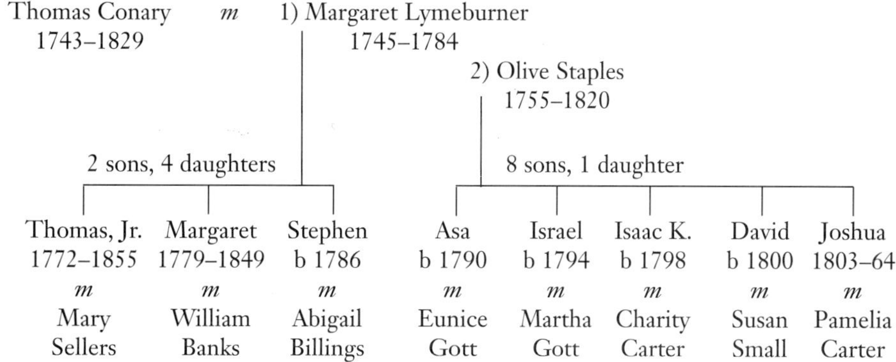

White

The first known claimant of White Island was Thomas Stinson, a settler on Stinson Neck of Deer Isle before the American Revolution.[72] A deed in 1785, in which Stinson conveyed the island—it was White Island even then—to Benjamin York for £18, noted that the grantor had been in possession of the island for ten years (Lincoln 18/41). It is interesting that Thomas Stinson undertook to defend title against any persons residing on Deer Isle, "but no further"; did his reluctance have anything to do with the grant of White and Black (or Conary) islands made by the Commonwealth of Massachusetts to the Penobscot Indians (see pages 331–32 for a discussion of this grant)? We may never know. The Indians did not take up their islands; the curious grant of the Massachusetts legislature remains a mystery.

The Yorks, however, are no mystery. At least the existence of the family is not in doubt. Benjamin York—he went by the title of captain—was the sixth or seventh to bear the name. He came to Blue Hill from Falmouth, in Casco Bay, in the mid-1760s and moved to the Naskeag area a few years later. Sometime between 1785 and 1790 he apparently settled on White Island: he was not there in the fall of 1785 when Rufus Putnam surveyed island residents in the region (Appendix 1), but he is shown with his family in the Deer Isle census of 1790—that is, presumably resident on White Island.[73]

[72] Vernal Hutchinson, in his Revolutionary War volume (*When Revolution Came: the Story of Old Deer Isle During the War for American Independence*, Chapter V), places the privateer John Robinson on White Island—or "Robinson's Island," as he calls it. Mr. Hutchinson, I fear, is in error: John Robinson did indeed live on "Robinson's Island," but this island, now named Tinker Island, is in Blue Hill Bay.

[73] Benjamin York's claim to the island may have been earlier than 1785: Dr. Noyes finds evidence of a 1779 complaint by York against a Castine man for trespassing on White Island; the charge was later dropped (Noyes, Family histories: York).

The Yorks were a prolific family, and it is not easy at this distance from their residence to determine which of them farmed the island and for how long. Benjamin York, Jr., who married Abigail Reed of Naskeag, was living on the island in 1800 and was apparently still there when his mother, Captain Benjamin's second wife, died in 1807; Benjamin, Jr. removed about this time to Naskeag (Noyes, Family histories: York). Captain Benjamin conveyed the island "with dwelling house and barn and other buildings" to Solomon York in 1817 (Knox Lands 4/420), the year before he died at the age of eighty-six. It is doubtful he was living on the island at his death (he had other properties in Sedgwick), but he is said to be buried on White, together with two of his three wives; local residents have always believed that three mounds near the York homesite at the northwest end of the island are their graves. Susannah, the last of the wives, appears to have died in poverty, despite Captain Benjamin's considerable wealth during his lifetime; Deer Isle records of 1828, according to Dr. Noyes, show that the town paid for the expense of her grave-digger.[75]

Although York residence on White Island—or *York Island*, for the names were used interchangeably on charts and in deeds—probably ended in the first quarter of the nineteenth century, the family remained associated with the island in ownership for another twenty or thirty years. Solomon York was the heir principally involved in the years following Benjamin's death, and the one who received formal title from the Commonwealth of Massachusetts in 1824 when these matters were regularized following the separation of Maine from Massachusetts (Maine Archives: Massachusetts conveyances). But the names of George, James, John, and other descendants of Captain Benjamin appear in various deeds affecting the island until mid-century. In 1844 James York conveyed nineteen acres to John Conary, and six years later George York, through his guardian Samuel Freethy, conveyed seventy acres at the western end of the island to William Conary, who already owned the east end of Black or Conary island (Hancock 76/324 and 90/318). This began the Conarys' possession of White Island, which lasted for more than a century. Buildings are not mentioned in the two deeds above, and none are shown on the Walling Map of Hancock County in 1860. By the 1880s buildings are again mentioned in mortgage deeds between various Conarys (e.g., Hancock 184/65 and 188/432); a dwelling is shown at the northwest end of the island on several charts printed in the 1880s and again in the early 1900s (e.g., Maps 1880 CGS 4, 1885 CGS 307, and 1904–06 Castine quad). The last Conary owner—in the 1960s—was Lester, a fisherman at Sunshine who inherited the island from his father Herman; Herman, who was married to his cousin Abigail Conary, daughter of Lemuel, had weirs in the early twentieth century off the southwest shore of the island.

Tracing title to White Island is relatively easy compared to tracing residence, and it is indeed ironic (as it is in the case of neighboring Conary Island) that we know more of settlers in the eighteenth and early nineteenth centuries than we do about residents in more recent years. The absence of reference to any buildings in the 1850s, as noted, suggests that White was then vacated for about a quarter century before new settlers moved onto the island around 1880. I have been unable to distinguish such residents in census schedules from residents of Deer Isle itself. Early in the 1900s, a Bridges family from Brooklin is known to have lived on the island: Leslie Thompson of Sunshine recalls two Bridges girls at the Sunshine grade school. Their father kept Herman Conary's weirs, but how long the family lived on the island is unknown.

When White was sold in the 1960s—to summer vacationers who have built two cottages there, one near the original site on the northwest end, the other on the southwest shore facing Sunshine—the island was still devastated from a pulping operation a decade earlier by Eugene Lymburner and the subsequent burning of the slash by Lester Conary. The scarring was not, of course, permanent. By the 1990s the island was returning to healthy secondary (or tertiary or quaternary) growth.

[74] Census data tend to support Dr. Noyes's account of the Yorks on White Island: in 1910 both Benjamin, Sr. (four males and three females) and Jr. (three males and two females) are in Deer Isle census schedules; in 1920, only Susannah is shown alone.

Bear (off Stinson Neck)

George Hosmer, Deer Isle's historian, tells us (page 136) that James Gibson, a veteran of the Revolutionary War, came to Deer Isle before 1800 and probably settled and died on this island. We do know that it was called Gibson Island for some years, and we know that James Gibson, Jr. owned land at Greenlaw Neck facing this island (Hancock 24/216), but the suggestion of residence on Bear should be treated cautiously. No cellar hole or well exists as evidence of it. They should be there if Gibson lived year-round and with a family, as Hosmer tells us; and I know of no other verification of Hosmer's hypothesis.

Human habitation aside, Bear Island has been used for grazing and surely for pulp, though the latter not in all probability in the twentieth century. It remained in the possession of Deer Islanders until the 1960s, when it was sold to nearby vacationers. The Camden windjammers frequently anchor off its northerly shore on summer cruises. (Several of our children, indeed, have tested their endurance in informal "solos" on the small outcropping northwest of Bear, called Black Island, which is in line of sight from my study on the Naskeag shore.)

Sheep and Crow (off Sunshine)

Sheep Island, which helps to make the harbor at Sunshine, was once named *York Island*, after the York family that settled nearby White Island. Crow Island, farther offshore, has appeared under this name on charts for more than a century. Neither has been settled, but both have been used by Deer Islanders for sheepgrazing and fish staging. Conarys living in the area appear to have owned both islands during the latter half of the nineteenth century: in 1874 John Conary's claim of ownership by will from his father Thomas was recognized by the State of Maine and his title verified (Maine Archives, "1874 Island Sales"); Sheep Island was deeded along with White Island in several conveyances among Conarys in the 1880s. In recent years both islands have been acquired by summer vacationers.

Lazygut Islands

"Glutton," says the Oxford English Dictionary, is the meaning of *lazygut* . "Excrement" is the meaning to Philip Rutherford (*Dictionary of Maine Place Names*, 77). I lean to a more seamanlike definition: the tide pulling gently though a defile. The islands, in short, would seem to be named from the passage, not vice versa.

The islands were already shown on the "Atlantic Neptune" of 1776. Some maps show the Lazyguts to be only the seaward island and its two thrumcaps, but I believe the name applies to the inner island as well. The half-tide passage between the outer Lazygut and its first thrumcap is known locally as the "Narrow Escape," alleged route of the salvation of a Deer Isle mariner under pursuit by—depending on which version of the legend is current—pirates, a British war sloop, or the Feds.

It is likely that Hezekiah Rowell was deeded the Lazyguts after the separation of Maine from Massachusetts: a claimant named George Saddler asserted ownership in 1874 from Rowell's heirs, but the claim was denied by the State of Maine and the islands were auctioned to Josiah Webb (Maine Archives, "1874 Island Sales"). I have not traced subsequent ownership of the islands in detail, but the inner Lazygut has been owned by the Heansslers of Sunshine for many years and the outer by the town manager of Stonington until 1954, and since then by summer vacationers who have built a cottage on the gut. The islands were never settled, but the inner island has been used for grazing sheep and the outer has been pulped—probably several times over.

Freese Islands

There are two Freese islands, but only the larger of the two is suitable for habitation—and, indeed, it has been inhabited intermittently since Revolutionary times. The island's location, well protected within the arm of Stinson Neck and close to Southeast Harbor, a major trading center on Deer Isle in the late eighteenth century and through much of the nineteenth, made it inevitable that the island should be settled. The sequence of settlers, however, the length of their residence, and the chronology of building on the island are not easy to sort out.

The earliest name for the two islands was *Hazlett's*, appearing on several editions of the 1776 "Atlantic Neptune." This may be a rendering of Haskell, the surname of half a dozen settlers on Deer Isle before the American Revolution. There is, in fact, reference to possible Haskell possession, although several years after the printing of the "Atlantic Neptune": in 1778 Isaac and Abraham Frees (then of Orono) for £200 sold land near Long Cove on Deer Isle to Ignatius and Solomon Haskell (Hancock 1/367, cited in *Bangor Historical Magazine*, II: 144/374). To be sure, no island is mentioned, but it may have been included in the Freeses' lot. A number of Freeses had lived on Deer Isle, and several continued to live there: George Frees, for instance, was said to have removed to Orono in 1764 (*Bangor Historical Magazine*, VIII: 14/1,800); the 1800 census for Deer Isle, meanwhile, shows another George and Abraham Frees still there (under twenty-six and forty-five, respectively). George Hosmer (page 111) doubts that any Freeses settled on the island that took the family name, but George Frees's son-in-law, Thomas Warren, did live there: his son Richard (who was to serve several terms in the state legislature) was born on the island in 1786. Thomas is shown on the island—which indeed bears his name, *Warren Island*—in a 1798 survey of Deer Isle by John Peters.[75] Thomas Warren drowned about this time (he fell, it is said, from a log canoe), and his widow Ruth married William Ring; the birth of their child was recorded at Deer Isle in 1802. William Ring farmed both his own lot on Greenlaw Neck and the Warren lands on the island. The Ring family left Deer Isle and Warren Island in due course and moved to Ellsworth. The island, meanwhile, continued to be called Warren: it so appears on a Deer Isle survey in the 1820s (Hancock County Roll Map of Deer Isle, 1827, at the Registry of Deeds in Ellsworth).[76]

Freese or Warren Island was probably uninhabited for several decades after the Rings removed—at least, I find no record of residence. According to later owners,[77] Zaccheus Stinson owned the island in mid-century; it was he who built and lived in the large farmhouse in the center of the island. Zaccheus sold to Billings P. Hardy, who lived on the island for twenty or more years. He appears in the 1860 federal census, aged forty-nine, with wife Comfort and six children; he is also shown on the Walling map of Hancock County the same year (the island is misnamed *Frasier's Id* on this map). In 1862 tax records he is shown on "Freezes Island," with a dwelling (valued at $100), one ox, four cows, and nine sheep—modest but sufficient husbandry; his total real estate and personal valuations were, respectively, $276 and $334. According to a descendant of later owners, the MacDonalds, the Hardys had eleven children, taught by a schoolteacher who lived on the island seasonally (memoirs of Louise MacDonald Eaton, at the Deer Isle Historical Society). Census records do not show Billings Hardy with so large a family: in 1870, for instance, his household had shrunk to four. Another household on the island in this schedule is that of Dudley Hardy, twenty-two—probably a son—with wife Adriadne and one daughter; there were indeed two dwellings on the island, to judge from cellar holes.

In 1876 Comfort P. Hardy—Billings had probably died, for we hear no more of him—sold

[75] The Peters map of 1798 is redrawn as a frontispiece in George Hosmer, *Historical Sketch of Deer Isle*.

[76] A significant amount of Frees—or preferably *Freese*—genealogy has been provided by a descendant, Constance Hanscom, who took the trouble in 1983 correspondence to correct many of my misconceptions.

[77] The informant is Mrs. Isaiah Pickering, whose husband acquired the island in 1901; her information comes from her father, who is not named (manuscript at Deer Isle Historical Society).

the two Freese Islands for $650 to Louisa Jane MacDonald, first wife of Angus MacDonald. Angus MacDonald is shown on the island on an 1881 plan of Deer Isle (microfilm plan at the Deer Isle Historical Society). A coastal survey of the same era shows the island with cleared fields and fencing (Map 1882 CGS 309). Louisa died on the island in 1888, and Angus moved to Sunshine a few years later. He sold the islands to Isaiah Pickering in 1899. Pickering took down the farmhouse, and Jonathan E. Eaton, to whom Pickering sold the island in 1901, demolished the barn (Mrs. Isaiah Pickering, notes).[78]

Residence after the Hardys and the MacDonalds is obscure. Jonathan E. Eaton willed the island to his wife, then to their children, who sold in due course to Ralph Barter. One of the Eaton heirs was doubtless Hattie A. Smith, who in 1916 leased weir rights for five years to Charles E. Smith and Freeman Sprague; both fishermen, the lease stated, "now used and occupied" the island (Hancock 533/392). Other fishermen surely "used and occupied" Freese Island as well during the first half of the twentieth century. Marshall Rice of Sunshine remembered when there were enough males on the island in season to field a creditable baseball team; Rice also recalled that there was a boys' camp on the island in the 1920s where Harvard football players conditioned themselves (correspondence with owner).

The island, long without permanent structures, was bought by a Massachusetts family in 1968 from the Barters, the last Deer Isle owners; since that time it has been used as a summer retreat. The three-acre Little Freese, separated in ownership from the larger island during the twentieth century, has had different non-resident owners and remains in its natural state.

[78] There may have been another resident on Freese Island in the 1870s, according to Louise MacDonald Eaton: Fulton Dow, a sea captain sailing out of Oceanville. He married an Oceanville girl and in 1820 moved her to Freese Island where, it is said, she bore nine of her eleven children; the captain rowed across the bay at each lying-in and walked three miles for a midwife or doctor. (I believe there is more romance than reality in Fulton Dow's tenure, which I cannot verify in standard histories—e.g., Hosmer—or deeds; it is, however, recorded in an item preserved by the Deer Isle Historical Society.)

Isle Au Haut

Isle au Haut

Note: This island—jewel of Penobscot Bay, to many—was noticed only briefly in the first edition in the hope that a full monograph on the island's history would appear. It has not, to date, and it would seem capricious to pass over Isle au Haut again, especially since much of its record is available to historians in materials assembled at the Revere Memorial Library on the island. There is not the space here for a detailed account of Isle au Haut, but at least a portion of its rich past can be captured.[1]

Early Settlement

There are different claims of earliest settlement on Isle au Haut.[2] Dr. Benjamin L. Noyes states that Samuel Pickering of Portsmouth settled on Isle au Haut Thorofare briefly in the early 1770s before moving on to Deer Isle and eventually onto the island off Little Deer Isle that bears his name (article in *Courier-Gazette*, September 13, 1932). Noyes offers no convincing proof of the residence, but refers to his many volumes of Deer Isle history and genealogy for the evidence; I have not discovered it, but Dr. Noyes was no casual historian, and tucked away in these volumes there are doubtless data that support his thesis. A more traditional claim of earliest settlement is that Peletiah Barter came from the Muscongus Bay region in 1788, followed by his sons Henry and William in 1792 (*Bangor Historical Magazine*, III: 1/480 and Hosmer, *Sketch of Deer Isle*, 187–88).[3] The best evidence of early settlement is probably that of the island's first surveyor, Rufus Putnam, who lists five occupants of Isle au Haut in his census of 1785 (see Appendix):

> James Barton (settled 1783)
> Nathaniel Sheldon (1783)
> John Barton (1785)
> Reuben Nobel (1785)
> John Holman ("on an old possession")

The only one easily identified from this list is Reuben Nobel, who in 1791, giving his address as Mount Desert, conveyed a one hundred-acre lot on Isle au Haut to Solomon Kimball of Little Isle au Haut, or Kimball Island (Hancock 1/104; of Solomon Kimball, more in due course). We hear no more of Reuben Nobel. As for the Bartons, it is tempting to think that they were in reality *Barters*, the surnames simply mistranscribed, but the given names are wrong for Barters; there were, meanwhile, Bartons in Castine, including both a James and a John (*Bangor Historical Magazine*, I: 58/64)

[1] There is only one full-length book about Isle au Haut: Charles Pratt's *Here on the Island*—an account by a descendant of cottagers, including many contemporary photographs by the author (see Bibliography). Among other pieces on Isle au Haut are: G. S. Wasson, *Sailing Days on the Penobscot*, Chapter V; George Hosmer, *Historical Sketch of the Town of Deer Isle*, pages 178ff; "Isle au Haut Church, 1957" (centennial brochure at the Revere Memorial Library on Isle au Haut); "Isle au Haut Papers," *Bangor Historical Magazine*, III: 1/479; Roger F. Duncan, "Isle au Haut," *Down East* magazine, June 1968, pages 36–39; numerous items at the library on Isle au Haut (including the memoirs of W. G. Turner and William S. Bowditch); and a scrapbook assembled by J. Williamson at the Maine Historical Society.

[2] The proper way to pronounce *Isle au Haut* has been much argued, and the only conclusion one can reasonably reach is that there is no accepted pronunciation. Perhaps the clearest expression of the differences is in a jingle I learned many years ago—from whom, I do not recall (possibly from Samuel Eliot Morrison, with whom at the age of thirteen I was sailing from Mount Desert to Matinicus when I first saw Isle au Haut):

> The yachtsman says, when the fog hangs low,
> "There's a bridal wreath over Isle [eel] au Haut."
> The fisherman says, when he launches his boat,
> "It's gosh-durned foggy off Isle [I'll] au Haut."

[3] Hosmer considers William and Henry *brothers* of Peletiah, not *sons*. There has always been some confusion about these early generations of Barters in the region. There was another Peletiah Barter in Muscongus Bay, but he remained there and was buried on McGee Island in 1825 at the age of eighty-five (*Islands of the Mid-Maine Coast*, III: 76). It is conceivable, of course, that this Peletiah was the father of the Barter who came to Isle au Haut.

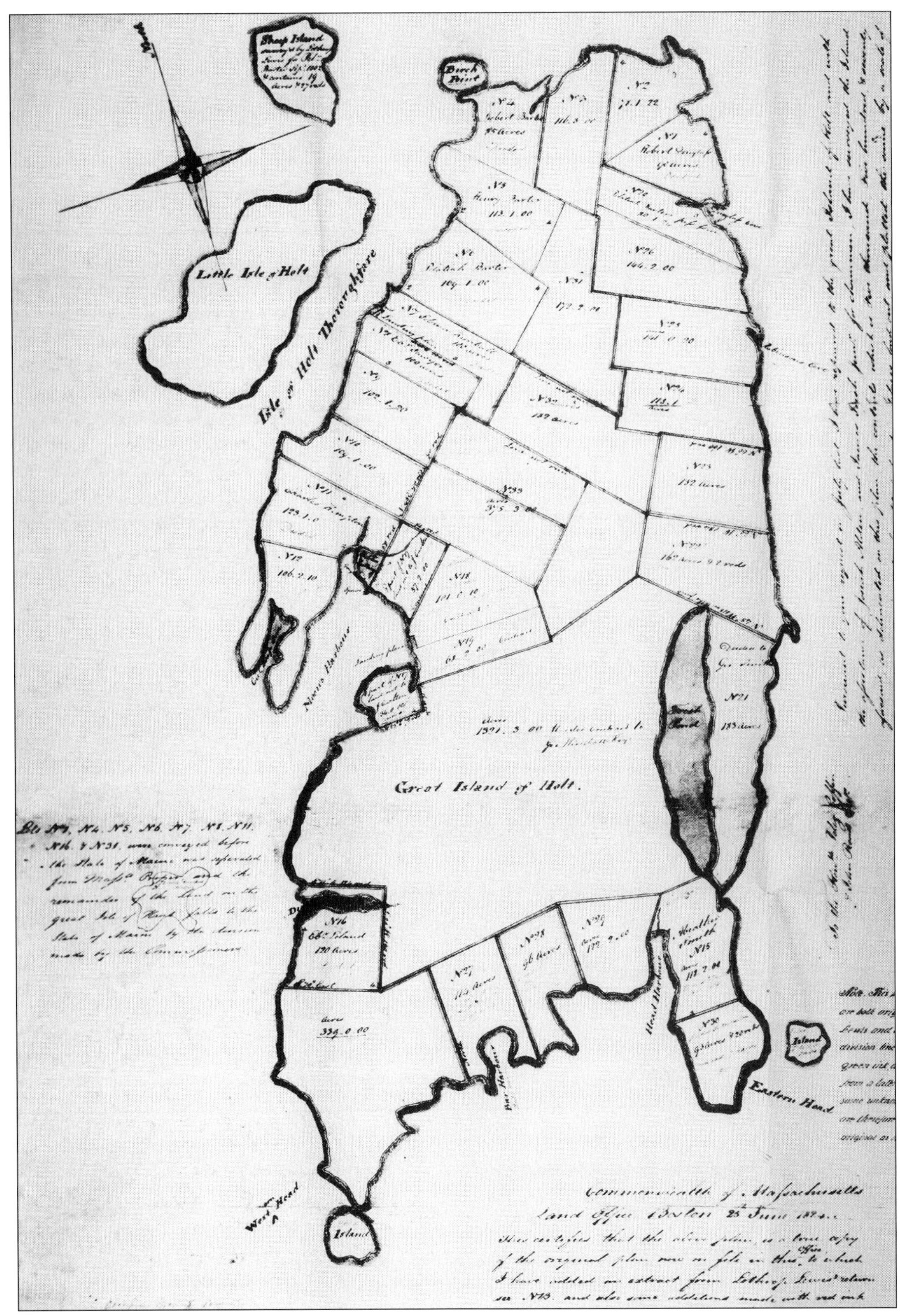
Sheep Island
Beech Point
Little Isle of Holt
Isle of Holt Thoroughfare
Great Island of Holt.
Eastern Head
West Head
Island
Commonwealth of Massachusetts
Land Office Boston

Plan of Isle au Haut Division, 1803

The statement by the surveyor, Lothrop Lewis, is on the right margin, facing right. It reads:

To the Honble Peleg Coffin & John Rand, Esqr

Pursuant to your request in July last, I have repaired to thee great Island of Holt and with the assistance of Josiah Alden and James Irish, Jr. for chainmen, I have surveyed the Island aforesaid, as delineated on this plan the contents which is Five thousand, Five hundred & seventy-two acres, including all the lots & landing places laid out and plotted the same by a scale of eighty-one rods to one Inch.

January 1803 Lothrop Lewis, Surveyor

N.B. I have designated on the plan the different qualities of the settlers' lots by the figures 1, 2, 3, & 4, Figure 1 denoting the first quality, etc. The lands & rocks remaining to the Commonwealth besides the Settlers lots I am of opinion (if sold) ought to be sold in a body together. I have reserved convenient landing places on every part of the Island where they could be of any use which are also distinguished on the plan by a yellow shade. January, 1803

Lothrop Lewis

The text on the left margin notes conveyances of certain lots before the separation of Maine from Massachusetts (see below). The entries at the lower right were made at the time of subsequent official transcriptions of the plan (1824 and 1892). Words such as "Deeded" on some lots were also written in at later dates.

The lots were conveyed as follows, according to records at the Registry of Deeds in Ellsworth (Hancock County):

BEFORE 1820:

Lot 1 — *Robert Douglas, 1819*
Lot 4 — *Robert Barter, 1814*
Lot 5 — *Henry Barter, 1803*
Lot 6 — *Peletiah Barter, 1804*
Lot 7 — *Ebenezer Sawyer, 1806*
Lot 11 — *Charles Kempton, 1808*
Lot 16 — *Ebenezer Leland, 1816*
Lot 31 — *Abiather (Abiatha) Smith; later George Smith*

BETWEEN 1820 AND 1840:

Great Lot (in center, 1321 acres) George Kimball
Southwest Head (between Lots 16 & 27) Noah Mead, David Thurlow
Lot 2 — *John Rich*
Lot 20 — *Thos. Tyler*
Lots 25 & 26 — *George Smith*
Lots 23 & 24 — *Daniel Gilbert*
Lot 22 — *Asa Turner*
Lot 29 — *Isaac Dunbar*
Lot 28 — *Nathaniel Merchant*
Lot 27 — *Benjamin Merithew*

---

and they were perhaps these transients. I know nothing of the other 1785 settlers, none of whom remained on the island.

In 1802 two dozen "inhabitants" of the Great Isle of Holt, led by Peletiah Barter, petitioned the Commonwealth of Massachusetts for a grant of the island. The island, they said, had been "burdened with taxes," was poor, without mills, "with no communication except by water." The signers were as follows, those actually in residence shown with an asterisk.[4]

* Peletiah Barter
* Henry Barter
William Barter
* Robert Barter
Rodgers Barter
Ebenezer Ball[5]
* Jona. Carlton
Jona. Carlton, Jr.
* Robert Douglas
John Dow
Asa Worster
James Cooper
* Solomon Kimball
Geo. Kimball
* Chas. Kempton
Geo. Robinson
Nathan Robinson
William Ring
Peter Goulding
* Ebenezer Leland
Stephen Sawyer
* Ebenezer Sawyer

[4] The petition is found in many places: Massachusetts Archives; *Bangor Historical Magazine*, III: 3/481; and at the Revere Memorial Library. One resident settler is noted who for some reason was not a signer: Alex Nutter.

[5] This signer had the dubious distinction, a dozen years later, of being the first person tried, convicted, and hung by the county court in Castine; his crime was counterfeiting (*Bangor Daily News*, April 25, 1938—item at the Deer Isle Historical Society).

The Commonwealth ordered a survey of the island that was released the following year, showing thirty-five lots of one hundred to a hundred and fifty acres and one thirteen hundred-acre lot running through the middle of the island between the fresh pond and Duck Harbor (see page 340). This survey remained the basic instrument for property transfers on the island, and subdivisions, of course, multiplied geometrically over the years.

Isle au Haut and Deer Isle: Contrast in Style

If it was the intention of the 1802 petitioners to separate from Deer Isle, as well as to gain legal rights to their lands, this was not achieved at the time. Isle au Haut remained a back district of Deer Isle for another three-quarters of a century, paying its share of taxes (when they could be collected) and gaining what benefits it could from the association. The benefits were surely modest. We know little of schooling during those years (and may never learn much more, since most nineteenth-century records of Deer Isle were destroyed in a fire in 1972). The roads, it goes without saying, were execrable. There were apparently no roads as such, except for a mile or so parallel to the Thorofare; there were ox-cart tracks over the saddle and around the island's northern end. According to George Wesson, a teenage girl on Isle au Haut as late as the mid-1880s had never seen a horse (Wesson, *Sailing Days in the Penobscot*, 128). The landings along the Thorofare and in coves around the periphery of the island were built by the settlers themselves and rebuilt each season as winter storms destroyed them. Isle au Haut remained a frontier community with few of the amenities of the parent island.

Small wonder, then, there was little natural affection between residents of Isle au Haut and Deer Islanders. Despite the many ties between them—one need only glance at genealogical records for proof—the two communities were not congenial. Even Baptists on the two islands quarreled, an historian of the Church tells us: in 1836 the tiny Isle au Haut parish broke with the Great Deer Isle parish and cast its lot with more distant but more kindred brethren on Little Deer Isle (Millet, *History of the Baptists in Maine*, 303). To genteel Deer Islanders, especially those living settled and orderly lives in the northern and interior sectors of Deer Isle, the residents of Isle au Haut were red-necked fishermen, many of them spending as much as half a year on the Banks—and (it was believed) spending half of their profits on rum when they came home. To those on Isle au Haut, Deer Isle was a metropolis of elegant frame homesteads where they invariably felt unwelcome.

Isle au Haut natives may indeed have been short on gentility in much of the nineteenth century and lacking in white-framed homesteads, but they enjoyed a robust economy based on the fisheries. Fishermen they assuredly were, first and foremost. By 1825, according to a Congressional report, Isle au Haut sent as many as forty vessels to the fisheries off Labrador, the Magdalen Islands, and Newfoundland, as well as the Gulf of Maine. Off season, the islanders were engaged in the herring fisheries and annually smoked ten to fifteen thousand boxes for coastal markets (Goode, "Fishery Industries of the United States," 42). After mid-century, as the cod fisheries declined, lobster fishing took up the slack; the first canning factory on the Thorofare was built in about 1860. The number of settlers on Isle au Haut, meanwhile, grew incrementally to provide the work force for these operations: from eight-households in 1800, totaling thirty-nine individuals, to fifty-three in 1830, totaling three hundred and nine (see table, page 355).[6] An 1862 tax schedule (pages 356–57) indicates, if not opulence, a sufficient prosperity for the times: homesteads valued at $200–300 on a remote island reflect substance; livestock are abundant, especially for a fishing community; the fifteen "stores" on the island, whether fully stocked or not, were at least places to conduct business and suggest a developed sense of commerce.

The building of a church in 1857 is also testimony to the vitality of the islanders. There was no regular minister on Isle au Haut in the first half of the nineteenth century, though there were occasional ventures in religious instruction—e.g., a four-week "mission" to the island in 1816 (according to materials at the Revere Library).

[6] George Wasson suggests (page 148) a significant drop in the population of Isle au Haut before mid-century: more than half the settlers removed, he argues, many in the 1840s to join the Gold Rush to California. Census schedules do not support this argument: though there was indeed a sharp drop between 1830 and 1840, thereafter the totals remained fairly constant.

Then, in 1851 the Reverend Joshua Eaton was engaged by the parish, though he was not in permanent residence. Four years later a church was raised overlooking the Thorofare, its white steeple the first glimpse one has of the "village" coming from Deer Isle; the cost was $1,645. It was the *building* of the chapel, some decades before such facilities appeared on comparable islands (e.g., Matinicus, Monhegan, Head Harbor Island off Jonesport), that marks the energy of Isle au Haut residents in mid-century. They did not, in truth, prove to be particularly religious, and services over the years were held erratically. There was only one settled clergyman on the island—a Dr. Snell, who served for four years as pastor and physician (correspondence with Virginia MacDonald; I do not have his dates). After the establishment of the Point Lookout summer colony, the parish could sometimes secure the services of a retired clergyman or a student-theologian from among its residents. A survey of the islanders conducted in 1897 by the parish itself acknowledged that of forty-one households then on the island, only half were church-goers. The handsome chapel, elegantly maintained by parishioners from Point Lookout, still stands.[7]

The Golden Years

In 1874 Isle au Haut at last separated from Deer Isle. The new township embraced all the islands south of Merchant Row, including four that were regularly inhabited (Kimball, Merchant, York, and Burnt) and one irregularly (Fog).[8]

George Wasson draws a sympathetic picture of Isle au Haut at its zenith, in the decades after the separation. Perhaps he exaggerates the number of residents supported by the fisheries—he suggests eight hundred, though census schedules

[7] In the twentieth century, periodic visits by the Maine Sea Coast Mission's SUNBEAM substituted for regular church services. The author and his wife were passengers on the SUNBEAM during one of these pastoral visits in January 1973: conversation between the Mission's staff and islanders who came aboard centered mainly on the prospects, with the good offices of the SUNBEAM, for a meeting between the Isle au Haut and Matinicus volleyball teams.

[8] Isle au Haut remained in Hancock County another thirty-eight years, then petitioned to be shifted to Knox County—pundits argued that the residents of Isle au Haut could not tolerate existing in the same *county* with Deer Islanders, let alone township. The true reason was less visceral: by 1913 Isle au Haut's communications, thanks to steam ferries, were chiefly with Rockland, not Ellsworth, and the new association was thus more logical (e.g., the prompt registering of deeds and wills).

Part of mackerel fleet in Isle au Haut Thorofare, seen from Kimball Island, 1896. (Courtesy of the Revere Memorial Library, Isle au Haut.)

indicate no more than two hundred and fifty permanent residents on the island at a given time—but he does not err in his grasp of the quality of life in the Thorofare. All sorts of vessels gathered there to drop their loads, to seek shelter from autumn storms, to escape fog mulls[9]: "bankers" from off Newfoundland, "baymen" from the Baie de Chaleur, Labradormen, mackerel schooners from Gloucester, coasters from Machias. And all manner of seamen appeared in the Thorofare: a cobbler in his pinky, a grocer in his smack, a postman in his sloop hauling a peapod, an itinerant preacher or Latter Day in his gig. And if a "fiddler of coast renown" dropped by, the word would pass quickly to all points on the island, and the next evening an impromptu country (contra) dance would materialize in the hall above the old lobster factory, reputed to have the best floor in Maine. During intermissions the men disappeared downstairs to Turner's store where cooling draughts laced with spirits circulated. It would be idle to suppose that ardent spirits never interfered with the smooth flow of conviviality on Isle au Haut—this was the same era when General Tillson banned the "demon rum" altogether from Hurricane Island on the other side of Vinalhaven (see page 147)—but there is no precise record of any troubles. Meanwhile, the contagion of these impromptu evenings must have been palpable.

The "village" at the Thorofare was always the heart of the Isle au Haut community, with its anchorage, fish houses and landings, its complement of stores (one always, from the 1870s, sometimes two),[10] the canning factory, and—when needed—the church. There were other centers of habitation around the six-mile-long island, with shifting populations as times changed. Duck Harbor, for instance, south of the Thorofare, early home of Ebenezer Leland, had half a dozen homesteads in the late nineteenth century, mostly belonging to Hamiltons. Head Harbor, at the southeast extremity of the island, inside Eastern Head, counted up to a dozen households in its peak years. The hazards of wind and tides at this exposed site were very real—a tidal bore in certain long, drawn-out storms could empty the entire basin in seconds—but the rewards of being close to proven fishing grounds, those who lived there

[9] But not, as a rule, to refit: Castine was the refitting center for the fishing fleets in this sector of Penobscot Bay. The ice extracted in the late nineteenth century from the fresh pond (later Long Pond) on the east side of Isle au Haut by the Knickerbocker Company (ice so clear it was said locally one could read a newspaper through twenty-four inches of it) was for destinations far to the westward, not for the Thorofare.

[10] Little has been discovered of stores on Isle au Haut before its separation from Deer Isle in 1874. By that date, or soon thereafter, William G. Turner opened a store below the lobster factory, and a facility has existed at that location to the present era under a succession of storekeepers (mostly Barters and Turners in the early years). Another store near the landing was opened by Sammy Rich—probably in the 1890s; he was succeeded by Clyde Turner. This store is no longer in existence.

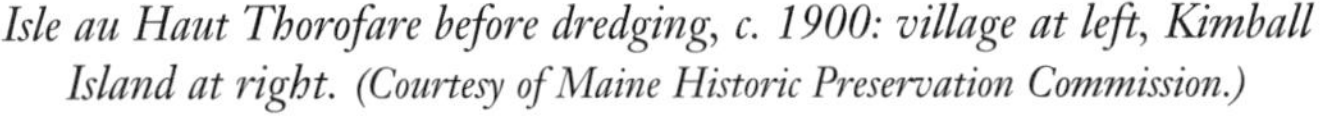
Isle au Haut Thorofare before dredging, c. 1900: village at left, Kimball Island at right. (Courtesy of Maine Historic Preservation Commission.)

believed, outweighed the hazards. This was home to Smiths and Grants; Gooden Grant lived to ninety-eight, the oldest fisherman on the island.[11] On the northeast shore of the island Douglas and Rich's coves, half a mile apart, became the nucleus of a third sub-community, settled principally by families with those surnames.[12]

With the incorporation of Isle au Haut, more precise records of municipal activity were kept than when the island was part of Deer Isle. There is, for instance, a surer grasp on Isle au Haut schools after 1874. By the late 1870s there were six districts in the township, one for each of the centers noted above and one each for York and Merchant islands. In those times there were normally two terms a year, summer and winter, each lasting eight to ten weeks. Terms, however, were not always held as scheduled. In 1878, for instance, District 4 (Duck Harbor) reported that "having but a small sum of money...[it] would like to postpone its school until another season." School funds were raised for the township as a whole, then apportioned to the several districts, as elected school officials thought best. The annual school budget varied: in 1879 it was $412; it dropped to between $250 and $350 in the 1870s, as enrollment fell, then climbed again early in the 1900s, although enrollment continued to decline. Registration in the six districts in 1879 was as follows: District 1 (Village), fifty; District 2 (Rich's Cove), sixteen; District 3 (Head Harbor), six; District 4 (Duck Harbor), ten; Merchant Island, eight; York Island, three. Attendance, it should be noted, was not mandatory in that era and rarely exceeded eighty percent of registration, in the summer even less with many teenage males already at sea. Some of the teachers of that era (late 1870s and 1880s) can be identified, mostly local girls and matrons who frequently changed districts; few had Normal School training:[13] Mrs. R. E. Collins, Florence Davis, Etta G. Turner, Clara Rich, Lizzie Conley, Lottie Robinson, Ms. C. A. Rich, Celestia Hamilton, Clara Barter, and George Chadbourne (not a local resident). Pay was derisory, especially for female teachers in small districts: Clara Barter, $2 a week in District 3 in 1880, a total of $12 for the six-week term.[14]

Enrollments continued to fall in Isle au Haut schools in the first decades of the twentieth century. In 1900 there were two districts left: the village, which averaged registrations of twenty to twenty-five (fifteen to seventeen attending), and the east side school, with registrations of fourteen to fifteen (ten to twelve attending). By the early 1920s so many islanders were leaving during the winter that the school committee decided to drop the winter session altogether; the remaining three terms were held at the Thorofare, which necessitated long walks for east side scholars before school transportation was properly organized.[15]

Why the Exodus?

What caused the gradual exodus from Isle au Haut, reflected in school enrollment figures in the twentieth century? There are reasons common to all islands where indigenous settlers removed; and there are reasons unique to Isle au Haut. Among the former is the coming of the gasoline engine: the fishing grounds suddenly came closer to settled communities on the mainland (or in this case, Deer Isle); there was no longer an advantage in living on an outer island in order to have instant access to the best fisheries. Another reason was the advent of compulsory high school education, which came even to remote communities like Isle au Haut early in the 1900s: as teenagers (especially daughters) went to Deer Isle to high school, mothers felt obliged to go with them; husbands inevitably followed.

The reasons for the exodus unique to Isle au Haut are more speculative. One, for instance, was the lack of a sufficiently large, protected anchorage. True, fishermen and seafaring visitors made do for a century or more with the existing anchor-

[11] Lynn Franklin, "Gooden Grant of Isle au Haut," *Oceans*, May 1974, 20–25.

[12] The distribution of households between the four communities in 1881 (according to the Colby atlas of Hancock County) and in 1910 (according to Chatto & Turner's *Register*) was as follows:

	Village	Duck Harbor	Head Harbor	Riches Cove
1881	24	4	2	5
1910	24	2	12	4

[13] The Normal Schools in the region in that era, specializing in teacher training, were in Castine and Bucksport; few island teachers managed to attend them.

[14] The pay for an unskilled quarryman in this era, by contrast, was about $5 a day.

[15] Contrary to expectations, the Isle au Haut school was never obliged to close down for long. Enrollments in the last decades of the twentieth century sometimes dropped to a single pupil, but normally fluctuated between three and a dozen.

age in the Thorofare. Why, then, the delayed dissatisfaction after 1900? In 1907 a light was installed at Robinson Point at the southern entrance to the Thorofare;[16] the north channel, meanwhile, was periodically dredged to six feet at mean low tide to accommodate shallow-draft vessels. But the shortcomings of the Thorofare anchorage could not be overcome by lights, signals, or dredging. The problem lay in the absence of a breakwater to block the relentless southwesterlies. In early days, when the pace of life was slower, a fleet of seiners might come into the Thorofare and wait happily as long as it took for the fog to lift or for a favorable wind. With the passing of the age of sail, the tempo of maritime life quickened; seamen were no longer content to bob endlessly about on southwesterly seas waiting to load or unload. If Isle au Haut had had a breakwater to protect its anchorage—as Matinicus had in 1911—the island's commercial viability might have been extended many years. No petition that I know of was ever sent to federal or state authorities.

Finally, did the emergence of the summer colony at Point Lookout (described below) affect the fortunes of the indigenous community? If the question is meant to inquire whether rusticators drove native settlers away, the answer is surely negative. Although they promptly acquired vast segments of the island (see the 1882 tax table, for instance, page 360), the cottagers themselves—unlike those on Mount Desert, North Haven, and Islesboro islands—never moved significantly beyond their small sector on the northeast corner of the island. It cannot be denied, however, that the coming of summer people and their creation of a vigorous, albeit seasonal, community next to the village had an impact on the lives of all indigenous residents. Since this community is now older by some years than the original community that preceded it, it deserves more particular attention.

The Point Lookout Community

In 1878 (or 1879—the exact year appears to have been lost in time) Ernest Bowditch, returning to Rockland by steamer from Bar Harbor, stopped at Green's Landing (now Stonington) and found a fisherman to take him to the large and imposing island which, going east, he had seen seven miles seaward. His reception on the island, he tells us, was cool until he mentioned he was a descendant of Nathaniel Bowditch, author of the *Practical Navigator*, bible to all mariners in the nineteenth century. Squire Ezra Turner then happily put him up, and a fruitful relationship was launched.[17] Within a year or two the Point Lookout clubhouse was built (by Clarence Turner) with a half a dozen cottages around it. The club was originally for bachelors: "no dogs, no women, no children"; the restrictions were lifted, needless to say, as the bachelors married. The club flourished. There were fifty members by 1910, with a dozen or more cottages linked by boardwalks (hallmark of summer colonies in that era). A ferry stopped daily in season on the Rockland–Bar Harbor run, but only for a few years. It was not the intent of the exclusive club members of Point Lookout[18] to encourage uninvited visitors. The club president's yacht, DAY DREAM, provided the only regular ferry service to the island, and its crew became adept at denying passage to any without proper credentials.

There were some who sought a more ambitious resort on Isle au Haut. One breathless developer wrote in 1880: "A Sabbath-like stillness prevails over the island, broken only by the bleating of sheep and lowing of kine." Mount Desert Island, this person wrote, would always be the premier resort, "but Isle au Haut will rank next, attracting such tourists as seek a quiet and beautiful summer home and desire to avoid fashion and great expense" (Alsop Leffingwell, *Republican Journal* of Belfast, Maine, October 28, 1880; in J. Williamson's Scrapbook at the Maine Historical Society).

[16] A light had been recommended by the Lighthouse Board numerous times before being authorized in 1906 with a $14,000 appropriation. The light and signal were operational in December 1907 (United States Lighthouse records, Isle au Haut file). The light was automated in due course, as all lighthouses were on the coast of Maine, and in the 1990s the keeper's house became a bed and breakfast, the only one (at the time) on the island.

[17] Memoir by William S. Bowditch at the Revere Memorial Library.

[18] Among the early cottagers who shaped the colony, in addition to Ernest Bowditch its prime mover, were: Charles C. Beaman, Elihu Chauncey, F. F. Thompson, H. P. Shortridge, and John G. Shortall.

One resort hotel was, indeed, opened on the island, the Hotel des Isle, built on the east side in 1885 by Edwin DesIsle and H. C. Sproul of Bar Harbor. The hotel was served by a steam ferry from Deer Isle which stopped at a landing opposite York Island. The hotel operated for two seasons before it burned down in 1888 (item at the Revere Library).

Isle au Haut, happily for the Point Lookout community, was not destined to become a major resort. A few villagers took in boarders, mostly Point Lookout members, but the large influx of cottagers that altered the pace of life on many coastal islands never occurred on Isle au Haut, thanks principally to the vigilance of the cottagers themselves.

How, then, did natives and rusticators get along? Anyone asking this question on Isle au Haut would probably receive as many answers as the number of people asked. I pass along two. The late Charles Pratt, a descendant of cottagers, an author and devotee of the island, argued that while islanders who worked as servants at Point Lookout perhaps became "domesticated," the islanders in general never assumed "servitude" and so kept on equal terms with their wealthy neighbors. A lobsterman, on the other hand, who lives on the island today (and who shall remain nameless), said, when it was suggested to him that the summer colony on Mount Desert brought certain benefits to local inhabitants: "They're lucky. Here, the summer folk come in June with a shirt and a ten-dollar bill, and they don't change either 'fore they go." The remark sounds as though he had in mind the later *trekkers*, not the Point Lookout *cottagers*, but the hostility toward all outsiders is evident. In reality, the concrete benefits brought by the early cottagers were apparent: the improved roads (designed initially to enable cottagers to reach different parts of the island with their horses and carriages, but of course open to all); the Revere Memorial Library and town office in 1911[19]; the restored church, as noted. Not to mention the decades of livelihood to carpenters like Clarence Turner, ironmongers like A. J. H. Turner, and mariners like C. R. Chapin, captain of the DAY DREAM. But the relations between two communities as different as the cottagers of Point

[19] The stone structure, between the village and Point Lookout, was built in memory of a cottager, Mrs. Paul Revere, who died on the island—widow of a descendant of the Revolutionary War patriot.

View north from the church on Isle au Haut, 1880s: Point Lookout beyond church with early cottages; Pell Island in center distance; McGlathery (wooded) beyond, left of schooner in Merchant Row. (Courtesy of Revere Memorial Library, Isle au Haut.)

Lookout and the natives of the village and Head Harbor cannot be measured by benefits and visceral resentments. Best leave this one alone.

Acadia National Park

In 1942 Richard L. Bowditch, grandson of Ernest, offered some thirteen thousand acres of Isle au Haut to the federal government for Acadia National Park; he spoke on behalf of the stockholders of the Isle au Haut Land Company. Harold L. Ickes, President Roosevelt's secretary of the interior, accepted the gift in January 1944. The village and the lands owned by the islanders, as well as Point Lookout itself, were not directly affected by the gift, but the character of the island in the next fifty years obviously underwent a significant transformation. By the 1990s the mailboat provided daily service to the island in the

Point Lookout landing, Isle au Haut, with guests descending to the colony's steam ferry, DAY DREAM.
(Courtesy of Maine Historic Preservation Commission.)

Summer cottages at Point Lookout, Isle au Haut, about 1900.
(Courtesy of Maine Historic Preservation Commission.)

North end of Isle au Haut, 1944, showing (southwest to northeast) the "village" on Thorofare, Point Lookout, Birch Point , and Burnt Island; York Island is off east shore. Note the narrow, winding channel (once used by the Rockland-Bar Harbor ferry) between Isle au Haut and Burnt Island.
(United States Air Force photo, courtesy of Alan C. Bemis.)

summer months, stopping at the Thorofare and Duck Harbor. Most visitors—hikers, nature lovers, the curious—go to the latter and roam the trails in the spectacular southern end of the island; trail bikers are more ubiquitous (there are, of course, no cars on the island except the few owned by natives). There is only one campground on Isle au Haut, at Duck Harbor; it has limited accommodations, and reservations are necessary months in advance. Visitors are therefore kept somewhat apart from residents, cottagers, and natives alike, yet their coming, it is fair to say, has brought lasting changes to Isle au Haut—greater, indeed, than the introduction of electricity, telephone service, or UPS delivery.

This is not the place to explore relations between islanders and park authorities, except to note that the areas where tensions have run highest concern roads (which from World War II have circled the island), fire prevention,[20] and the fixed perimeter of park lands.

[20] A major fire on the north slope of the island in 1949—fought by the Park Service, the Stonington Fire Department, Southwest Harbor Coast Guardsmen, and the crew of the SUNBEAM—brought some of these problems into focus. An earlier fire, in 1894, denuded Isle au Haut up to its twin peaks.

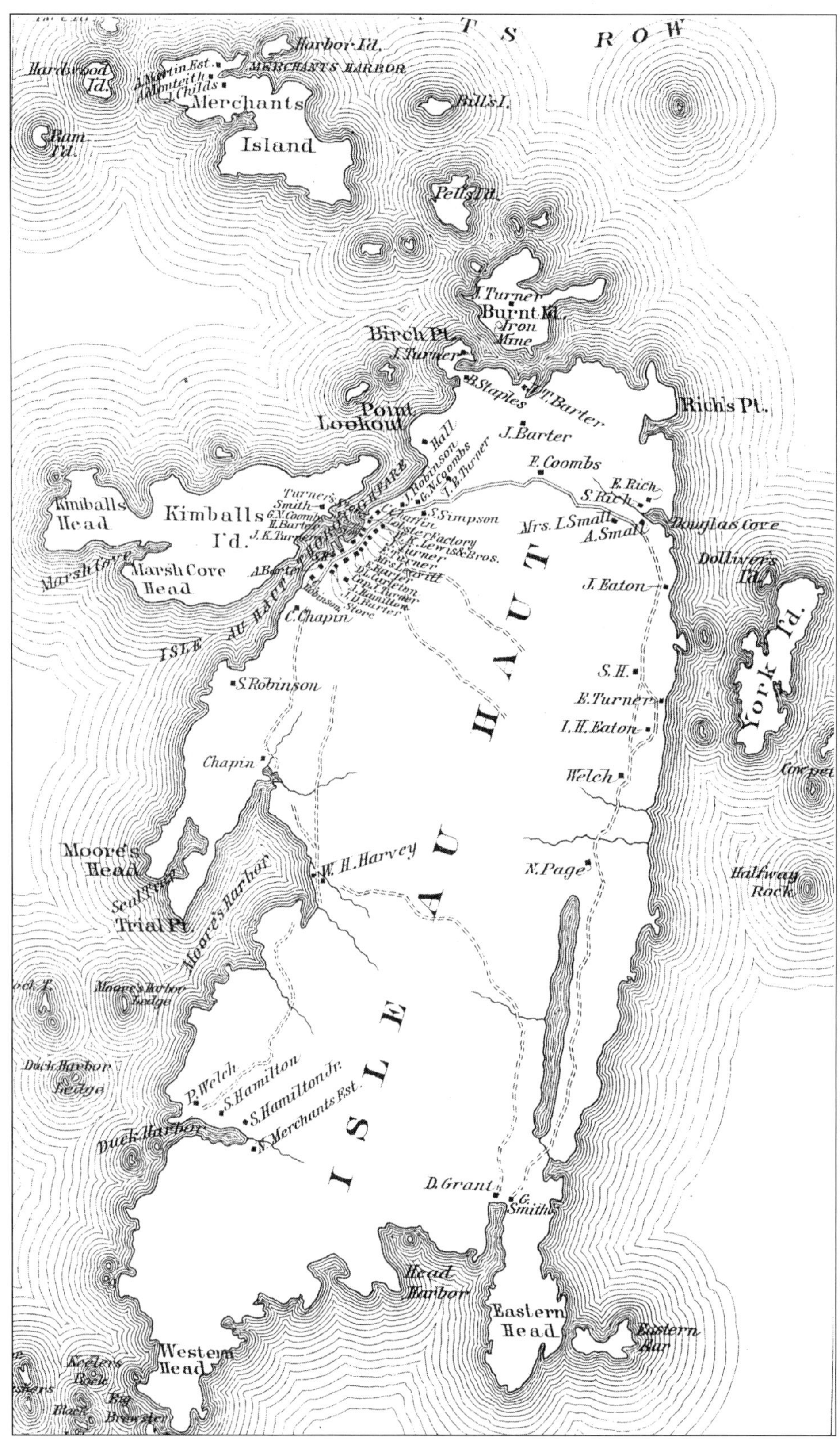

Isle au Haut and surrounding islands with residents in 1881, from the Colby Atlas of the State of Maine.

Isle au Haut Residence, 1800–1880

Note: This table attempts to identify, from decennial census schedules, householders on Isle au Haut proper from 1800 to 1880 (residence on the surrounding islands belonging to Isle au Haut plantation—Merchant, Kimball, York, Burnt, and Fog—is discussed under notice of these islands). Age of householders is given at first appearance in the table. Wives, where shown, are in parentheses. Occupations, if known, are indicated as follows: Fa, farmer; Fi, fisherman; S, seaman; C, carpenter; T, trader or merchant; M, master mariner or sea captain. The dollar figure after some householders is the census-taker's highest real estate estimate for householders between 1850 and 1870. In the decennial column, males are left of the slash, females to the right.

Householder	**1800**	**1810**	**1820**	**1830**	**1840**	**1850**	**1860**	**1870**	**1880**
Barter, Henry, -26, Fi/Fa	2/2	2/3	2/5	-	3/5				
Barter, Peletiah, -26, Fi		1/3	2/6	3/2	2/1				
Carlton, Jonathan, -45	4/2								
Cooper, Thomas, -45	2/2								
Kempton, Charles, 30s, Fa	3/1	3/4	3/4	2/3					
Sawyer, Ebenezer, 30s	4/4	4/4	3/2	1/1					
Robinson, Nathan, -26	2/1								
Groce (Gross), Jacob, -45	4/2	5/2							
Barter, William, 20s, Fi/Fa		2/3	5/5	6/7	6/5				
Knowlton, Eliza, 45+		3/1							
Turner, Calvin, 45+		2/3							
Turner, Samuel, -26		1/1	3/3	7/5					
Douglas, Robert. -45, Fi/Fa		5/3	7/2	4/1	2/1	1/1			
Turner, Asa, -26 (Abigail), Fa		3/1	5/3	7/3	6/5	4/3			
Barter, Robert, -45, Fi			2/2						
Carlton, John			1/3						
Collins, David, 45+			3/2						
Carlton, Jacob, -45			2/3	8/4	7/4				
Holmes (Homes), Chauncy, 50s			2/2	2/2					
Collins, Asa, -26, Fi			1/4	2/5	2/3				
Collins, David II, 20s, Fi $150			3/2	4/3					
Gilbert, Daniel, -45 (Lois), Fa $600			2/2	2/2	1/1	2/6	4/7	4/2	
Harvey, John, 45+			2/3						
Knowlton, Robert, -45, Fi			3/2	-	5/4				
Knowlton, Joseph, -26, Fi			1/1	4/6	2/4				
Knowlton, Benjamin, -45, Fa			2/1						
Lindsey, Huldah, 45+			2/5						
Leland, Ebenezer, -45, Fi			2/2	2/2					
Merithew, Benjamin, -45 (Sarah), Fi			2/5	6/6	-	5/3			
Merithew, Aaron, -45, Fi			3/5	3/7					
Merchant, Nathaniel, -45, Fi $400			2/1	2/4	-	-	1/1	1/1	
Rich, John, -45 (Elinor), Fi			7/1	8/2	2/2	3/2			
Robinson, Samuel, 45+			2/3						
Householder	**1800**	**1810**	**1820**	**1830**	**1840**	**1850**	**1860**	**1870**	**1880**

Householder	1800	1810	1820	1830	1840	1850	1860	1870	1880
Sawyer, Nathaniel, 30s, Fi			2/2	4/4					
Robbins, Nathaniel, 30s			5/4	2/3					
Grover, William, 45+			1/5	3/5					
Yeaton, William, -45			1/8	5/7					
Coval, Josiah, 45+			1/2	1/2					
Crockett, Isaac, -26			2/3	3/7					
Smith, George, -45 (Sarah), Fa			4/5	4/5	3/3	2/1	1/1		
Tyler, Thomas, 45+			2/1	1/1	2/2				
Coombs, Francis, 29 (Experience), S $400				2/1	-	-	1/6	2/5	
Collins, John, 20s				2/3					
Robinson, James, 50s				7/2					
Hamilton, Daniel, 20s				2/2					
Sawyer, Ebenezer, Jr., 20s				3/1					
Douglas, Robert, Jr., 20s				6/1	7/1				
Barber, William, Jr., 20s				3/2	3/1				
Kendell, Francis, 30s				1/0					
Wilson, Henry, 30s				3/4					
Babbidge, James, 20s				2/1					
Coombs, Henry B., 20s				1/2					
Crockett, John, 40s				2/2					
Wentworth, Joshua, 50s				2/3					
Kempton, John, 31 (Hannah), S $1,200				2/2	5/4	4/4	2/2		
Crockett, Thomas, 30s				2/1					
Matthews, James, 20s				1/2	1/2				
Norton, Esther, 30s				0/2					
Hamilton, Solomon, 35 (Mary), S/Fa				2/6	4/7	5/4	3/2	2/0	
Norton, Joseph, 40s				4/6					
Curtis, George, 20s				2/1					
Merithew, Aaron Jr., 20s				1/3	3/5				
Collins, James, 30s				3/1					
Carter, Asa, 30s				1/5					
Fife, Nathan, 30s				2/1					
Plummer, Rufus, 30s				1/0					
Rich, Jonathan, 29 (Mary), pauper					1/2	1/3	2/1	0/2[21]	
Matthews, Benjamin II, 30 (Nancy) $200					1/2	4/3			
Merithew, Joseph, 20s					1/3				
Barter, Noah, 28 (Ellen), S $200						2/2	3/2	-	2/0
Laine, Dennis, 33 (Margaret), S						2/3			
Laine, Daniel, 34 (Ellen), S						2/2			
Householder	**1800**	**1810**	**1820**	**1830**	**1840**	**1850**	**1860**	**1870**	**1880**

[21] Mary Rich, widowed, is head of household.

Householder	1800	1810	1820	1830	1840	1850	1860	1870	1880
Barter, John, 38 (Eliza), S $1,500						4/3	5/3	2/1	
Eaton, Theophilus?, 38 (Betsy), S $600						4/3			
Halliday, William, 38 (Lucinda), S						1/2			
Collins, David III, 34 (Eliza), S						2/2			
Turner, John, 40 (Lucretia), M/T $2,000						7/4	5/4	4/2	6/3
Dunbar, Isaac, 30 (Irene), S						6/3			
Barter, Stephen, 36 (Abigail), S $300						2/2	4/3	3/1	3/0
Barter, Thomas, 38 (Mary), S						1/6			
Turner, Ezra, 37 (Betsy), M/kept boarders $1,000						1/0	1/2	1/3	1/2
Carlton, Eben, 24 (Mary), M/Fi $450						1/2	1/4		
Carlton, Daniel, 34 (Sarah), M/T $2,000						2/1	3/3	2/2	
Turner, John H., 33 (Hannah), cooper $300						2/1			
Turner, James II, 37 (Matilda), M $1,000						3/4	5/4	2/2	
Haskell, Edward, 73 (Martha), S $200						5/5			
Rich, Perez, 29 (Eliza), S $600						3/2	2/1		
Collins, William, 30 (Amelia), Fi $700						4/3	8/2		
Collins, Davis, 30 (Betsy), S						2/1			
Brown, Henry, 49 (Olive), S $100						1/1			
Barter, Amos, 28 (Betsy), S $150						3/3	4/4	7/3	6/2
Robinson, Spencer, 34 (Lydia), Fa/Fi $600						4/4	-	4/2	3/1
Pattee, Asa, 26 (Diantha), S						3/1	-	-	7/1
Wentworth, Michael, 26 (Harriet)						1/3			
Harvey, John II, 50 (Hannah), S						5/3			
Grant, Elisha, 54 (Nancy), M/T $500						4/1	2/1	1/2	
Smith, George II, 40 (Judith), Fa $800						2/4	3/4	3/2	3/1
Eaton, Isaac, 20 (Barbara/Lizzie) $900						2/2	3/5	3/3	
Appleton, William, 40 (Mary) S/Fi $4,200						2/1	2/2	1/0	
Woodbury, James, 38 (Ephounda), S $200						4/4			
Thompson, Sally, 37							2/4		
Coombs, Francis II, 26 (Mary), Fi							1/2		
Seles, William, 53 (Eleanor), C							1/3		
Collins, David IV, 66 (Experience), Fi $200							1/1		
Merchant, John T., 29 (Charlotte), Fi							3/3		
Coombs, Henry II, 22 (Lucy), Fi							1/3		
Williams, Richard, 33 (Lydia), Fi							1/3		
Livington, George, 29 (Sarah), blacksmith							3/2		
Turner, John K., 43 (Olive), T $300							2/3	-	1/2
Merithew, George, 26 (Hannah), Fi							1/1		
Eaton, Amos, 29 (Sarah), C							2/2		
Simpson, John A. (Mary), S							5/1		
Simpson, Sylvester, 50 (Hannah), Fi $300							4/6	2/1	2/1
Annis, Ellison, (Eliza), Fi $100							5/1	7/1	

Householder **1800** **1810** **1820** **1830** **1840** **1850** **1860** **1870** **1880**

Householder	1800	1810	1820	1830	1840	1850	1860	1870	1880
Conley, William, 34 (Ellen), Fa							2/4		
Corron (Cossan), William, 45 (Mary), Fa							1/3		
Harvey, William, 26 (Mary), Fi $250							3/1		
Getchell, David, 52 (Hannah), Fi							2/1		
Hamilton, Alfred, 24 (Elizabeth), Fi							1/1		
Rich, Stillman, 32 (Hannah/Elizabeth), Fi $250							3/5	-	4/3
Turner, Ezra II, 27 (Margaret), S $440								1/3	3/5
Walsh, James P., 35 (Susan/Abbie), Fi								4/3	5/2
Colby, Seth, 27 (Susan), Fa $800								1/4	-
Grant, David, 41 (Sophia), Fi $400								2/2	3/3
Morse, Adam, 68 (Irene), Fi								1/1	
Morse, James, 42 (Rebecca), Fi								1/1	
Hamilton, Solomon, Jr., 40 (Sarah), Fi								2/4	3/7
Richards, Thomas, 37 (Elizabeth), Fi								4/4	
Kelley, George, 46 (Elizabeth), Fi								1/2	
Chapin, Edward, 52 (Catherine), Fi/Fa								4/1	1/1
Robinson, William, 27 (Laura), Fi								3/1	3/2
Merchant, John, 31 (Barbara), Fi $560								4/2	
Gross, John, 27, teamster								2/1	
Chapin, Clark, 24 (Olive), Fi								1/3	4/4
Brown, Stephen, 75								1/0	
Billows, Benjamin, 48 (Elizabeth), Fi $800								2/2	
Barter, James D., 35 (Sarah), Fi/T $800								2/3	2/2
Hamilton, Abel, 29 (Sarah), Fi $600								4/1	5/3
Kempton, Hannah, 73 $560								0/1	
Done (Dunn), John H., 34 (Abigail), C $400								2/2	
Rich, Alfred, 25 (Mary), Fi								1/2	
Carlton, Davis, 48 (Lydia), lobster factory $800								?/?	
Lewis, George, 60, overseer of lobster factory: 25 workers								13/13	
Robbinson, James, 52 (Hannah), lobster factory								2/2	
Coombs, George, 30 (Eliza), Fi								3/1	3/2
Turner, Isiah, 45 (Mercy), Fi								2/2	2/2
Chapin, Silviuz, 25 (Etta)									1/1
Harvey, William H., 36 (Hannah), Fi									3/1
Hutchinson, A., 20 (Lydia), Fi									1/2
Sawyer, Joshua, 60									1/2
Coombs, Theodore, 25 (Carrie), stonecutter									2/2
Freethy, James, 77, Fi									1/0
Thomas, Henry, 43 (Alfreda), Fi									4/1

Householder **1800** **1810** **1820** **1830** **1840** **1850** **1860** **1870** **1880**

Householder	1800	1810	1820	1830	1840	1850	1860	1870	1880
Cook, John L., 27 (Eliza), shoe factory[22]									1/1
Cook, David, 32 (Ella), Fi									1/2
Emerton, Asa, 63, farm superintendent									1/0
Dow, Percival, 29 (Sarah), gardener									3/2
Page, Noah, 46 (Mary), garderer									2/3
Eaton, Lizzie, 32									1/3
Gross, George, 26, and William, 21									2/0
Small, Albert, 25, Fi									2/3
Rich, Edwin, 29 (Albaretta), Fi									2/1
Eaton, Joseph, 32 (Sarah), Fi									1/1
Barter, Joshua, 29 (Sarah), Fi									1/1
Staples, Benjamin, 41 (Rebecca)									3/3
Turner, William W., 35 (Margaret), S									1/2
Coombs, Francis, III, 42 (Julia), M									1/2
Simpson, James, 61 (Hannah), Fi									2/2
Barter, William L., 24 (Annie), Fi									2/1
Chapin, George, 29 (Mary), Fi									2/1
Barter, John E., 32 (Maggie)									2/1

Householder	1800	1810	1820	1830	1840	1850	1860	1870	1880
Totals:[23]									
No. of households	8	11	35	53[24]	24	42	46	50	47
No. of persons	39	63	210	309	133	236	223	239	201

[22] John Cook and the next five names do not appear in the 1882 tax list for Isle au Haut and may be misplaced in the federal census.

[23] These are totals for Isle au Haut proper, exclusive of the surrounding islands (which are counted in federal census schedules).

[24] The higher number of households and residents shown in 1830 may be due to a more definitive census for Isle au Haut, whose residents were often confused in the tally with those of Deer Isle.

Isle au Haut and Islands South of Deer Isle, Valuations, 1862

Note: The following property owners on Isle au Haut and the islands south of Deer Isle are listed in Deer Isle tax records for 1862. There are ninety-eight persons in the total tax list, only the 36 here (not counting non-residents) with taxable property; twenty-two lived on Isle au Haut (according to my count), fourteen on the smaller islands, as shown in the key below. The key to the data is as follows:

Col. 1 Acre	Acres owned (assessed value in dollars)
Col. 2 Hom	Value of homestead[25]
Col. 3 Ox	Number of oxen owned
Col. 4 Cow	Number of full grown cows/calves
Col. 5 She	Number of sheep
Col. 6 Boat	Vessel tonnage (value thereof)
Col. 7 Stor[26]	Number of stores owned (value thereof)
Col. 8 Re	Total real estate valuation
Col. 9 Pers	Personal valuation (e.g., cash on hand)

Island Key:

BRT	Burnt
CRH	Crotch
KIM	Kimball
MER	Merchant
McG	McGlathery
RUS	Russ
WRK	Wreck
YRK	York

Householder	**1 Acre**	**2 Hom**	**3 Ox**	**4 Cow**	**5 She**	**6 Boat**	**7 Stor**	**8 Re**	**9 Pers**
Annis, Ellison	92 (157)			2/0	6			407	36
Barter, John	100 (133)		2	1/1	20	29(150)		353	241
Barter, James D.	1/4 (15)	250						255	
Barter, Robert **WRK**	50 (295)		2	4/2	37	15(125)		505	299
Babbidge, Levi **CRH**	30 (105)		2					355	28
Coombs, Francis	45 (83)			1/2	2			185	36
Carlton, Daniel L.	48 (210)[27]	200		1/0	10	66(500)	1(100)	875	562
Conley, Patrick **YRK**	115 (106)		2	2/0	40			230	124
Collins, William	100 (102)			2/1	25	23(225)	1(?)	347	294
Conley, William	123 (200)		2	2/2				240	86
Eaton, Eli	304 (209)		2					200	46
Eaton, Samuel L.**McG**				2/1	12	33(140)		50	215
Eaton, George W. **McG**								30	
Eaton Isaac B.	250 (180)		2	1/0				300	60
Harvey, John (est.)	130 (71)							166	
Harvey, Polly **RUS**	12 (32)								
Harvey, Benj., Jr. **McG**	1 (20)					20			
Harvey, Joseph, Jr.						20(70)		30	70
Harvey, William **McG**	40 (40)[28]	30							
Kempton, John	118 (66)	300		1/0				396	14
Kimball, Lucretia **KIM**	400(600)	300	2	2/2	70		3(75)	1,025	181
Householder	**1 Acre**	**2 Hom**	**3 Ox**	**4 Cow**	**5 She**	**6 Boat**	**7 Stor**	**8 Re**	**9 Pers**

[25] Homesteads were assessed in a haphazard way, normally if over $100; many more owned homes than shown.

[26] A "store" evidently meant a fish shack or warehouse—a place to carry on business. There were fifteen "stores" on Isle au Haut in 1862, three on Kimball, and one on Crotch.

[27] Includes Peletiah Barter's island (Pells Island), ten acres, $25.

[28] Includes "Washeys Island" (unidentified).

Householder	1 Acre	2 Hom	3 Ox	4 Cow	5 She	6 Boat	7 Stor	8 Re	9 Pers
Merchant, Nathaniel	550 (175)							25	80
Merchant, Anthony[29] **MER**	150 (400)	200	2	3/0	36			650	179
Merchant, Anth'y, Jr. **MER**		50							
Morse, Adam	140 (100)					20(25)		139	25
Smith, George	242 (350)	150		3/5	42		4(100)	600	174
Turner, James II	60 (128)	275		1/2	42	106(576)	4(80)	483	598
Turner, John K.	195 (150)	350		2/2	10	10(133)	2(100)	650	193
Turner, James I **BRT**	61 (50)	300		1/0				370	14
Turner, Asa (est.)	160 (139)		2	2/0			1(30)	269	
Turner, Ezra	43 (60)	350						455	
Turner, Josiah B.	17 (40)		2	1/1		9(11)		205	81
Turner, John	109 (100)	450[30]		2	3/2		2(60)	660	236
Thurlow, David **CRH**	30 (125)						260		
Welsh, James P.	150 (129)			1/0				239	14
Thurlow, Paul **CRH**	175 (290)			1/0			1(250)	460	14

Non-Residents	Acres ($)	Other property
Herrick, Joseph (Northport)	500 (250)	
Bodwell & Webster (Vinalhaven)	100 (80)	
Eaton, Peter H.	65 (155)[31]	
Adams, Samuel (Camden)	65 (75)	
Doyle, Freeman, or unknown	180 (100)[32]	
Carlton, Daniel (Frankfurt)	40 (300)	Also a lot, store, buildings, and bunkhouse on Isle au Haut formerly owned by D. L. Carlton

[29] Shubael, John L., and John L. Merchant, Jr. are also listed (on Merchant Island), but without valuation.
[30] John Turner owned three dwellings.
[31] Peter Hardy Eaton and Samuel Adams each owned half of McGlathery Island.
[32] Part of the Jerusalem lot on Isle au Haut, near the pond.

Isle au Haut (and Islands South of Deer Isle) Valuations, 1882

Note: The 1882 tax valuations for Isle au Haut and its surrounding islands are taken from plantation records on the island. The key is as follows:

Column 1 Re	Acres of real estate (assessed value in dollars)	**Island Key:**	
Column 2 Hom	Value of homestead	**BRT**	Burnt
Column 3 Brn	Value of barns and outbuildings	**FOG**	Fog
Column 4 Ox	Value of oxen	**KIM**	Kimball
Column 5 Cow	Number of cows, all ages (total value of cattle)	**MER**	Merchant
Column 6 She	Number of sheep (value of flock)	**YRK**	York
Column 7 Stor	Value of store and stock in trade		
Column 8 Boat	Value of vessels, or shares thereof		
Column 9 Tax	Assessed tax on all property, possessions		

Householder	1 Re	2 Hom	3 Brn	4 Ox	5 Cow	6 Sheep	7 Stor	8 Boat	9 Tax
Barter, William G.	1/2 (60)	132							4.17
Barter, James D.	131 (327)	325			3 (55)		367		24.69
Barter, Noah	38 (119)	225	25		1 (15)				?
Barter, John E.	3/4 (25)	275	30						10.79
Barter, Joshua L.	1/4 (125)	75			1 (15)	8 (14)			5.76
Barter, John	78 (188)	200	45	90	3 (35)	50 (87)			14.61
Barter, Albert	11 (38)	25	10						4.67
Conley, Hellen **YRK**	75 (510)[33]	500	65	75	2 (30)	80 (140)			30.35
Chapin, Edward	231 (618)	80	25	60	3 (35)	50 (87)			28.99
Coombs, George, Jr.	20 (225)	225	60		3 (30)	2 (3)	260		22.76
Chapin, Charles R.	75 (130)	150	40		1 (15)	1 (2)			10.74
Coombs, Francis	40 (160)	125	50		4 (50)				8.85
Childs, James **MER**	25 (100)[34]	150	40		3 (45)	15 (26)			11.30
Coombs, Henry	1 (20)	50			1 (15)			4/95	
Chapin, Libbens	26 (52)	80							6.03
Dailey, Michael	150 (600)[35]	175	50	75	2 (15)	25 (44)		150	28.49
Eaton, Joseph	1/2 (15)	100	25		1 (15)	18 (31)			4.29
Gross, George					1 (15)	10 (17)			3.94
Grant, David	182 (56)	100	75[36]		4 (50)	20 (35)			18.06
Hamilton, Solomon, Jr.	1/4 (5)	10			1 (15)				3.87
Hamilton, Abel	2 (20)	175			2 (25)				8.06
Holland, Matt.[36] **MER**					1 (20)				3.46
Harvey, William H.	34 (170)	75			2 (40)				9.55
Monteith, Alex **MER**	25 (100)[37]								
Householder	**1 Re**	**2 Hom**	**3 Brn**	**4 Ox**	**5 Cow**	**6 Sheep**	**7 Stor**	**8 Boat**	**9 Tax**

[33] Including York and Spoon islands.
[34] James Childs owned land on Merchant Island.
[35] Michael Dailey (or Daly) owned land on Merchant Island but did not live there.
[36] David Grant owned an icehouse.
[37] Matthias Holland lived on Merchant Island.
[38] West end of Merchant Island, where Alex Monteith lived.

Householder	1 Re	2 Hom	3 Brn	4 Ox	5 Cow	6 Sheep	7 Stor	8 Boat	9 Tax
Rich, Stillman	120 (288)	225	75	60	4 (70)	80 (140)			22.73
Rich, Edwin			250						5.75
Robinson, Spencer	200 (464)	220	100		4(70)	80 (140)			25.86
Robinson, William S.	3 (15)	200	45		1 (15)				9.32
Robinson, James	1 (25)	200	25		1 (15)				9.09
Small, Albert	60 (141)	100	15			10 (17)			9.29
Small, Fred, est.		50				6 (10)			1.39
Simpson, Sylvester	1 (25)	175	25						5.17
Staples, Benjamin	15 (75)	200	25		2 (25)	10 (17)			10.84
Smith, Simon A.	43 (?)[39]	40				40 (70)			7.50
Smith, Benjamin **KIM**	380 (850)[40]	300	125		6 (80)				34.85
Smith, George	50 (312)	280	50	75	10 (105)	45 (80)			22.40
Smith, Eliza K.						30 (52)			2.40
Turner, James II **BRT**	110 (770)[41]	325	75	70	2 (35)	80 (140)		125	88.42
Turner, Isiah B.	40 (250)	200	130[42]		1 (15)				13.58
Turner, John	196 (293)	425[43]							?
Turner, William G.							400		12.20
Turner, James I	60 (155)	250	25						12.66
Turner, Ezra	29 (71)	275	25	30					12.22
Turner, Ezra II	12 (49)[44]	225			2 (35)			200	13.85
Turner, William W.					1 (15)			200	4.94
Turner, A. J. H.			12	1 (15)					3.73
Turner, Clarence D.	43 (86)[45]					58 (92)			7.10
Thomas, Henry	? (35)		150		2 (20)	14 (24)			8.24
Welsh, James O.	120 (265)	165	72		4 (70)	250 (437)			26.23

The following residents were charged only for their poll tax—$3.00:

Amos Barter	Davis T. Conley	George L. Moore	Rufus Robinson
William L. Barter	Anthony Childs	Alfred Pettee	Charles Robinson
DeForest Bennett **FOG**	William W. Colby	George L. Pettee	Joshua P. Sawyer
Joseph Conley	William Gross	Alphonso Robinson	John C. Turner
Asa Turner			James Thomas

Non-Residents									
Bowditch, Ernest et al	2,000 (4,000)[46]								92.00
Collins, Willard	91 (279)	175	50						11.60
Carlton, Daniel P.	2 (50)	150							4.60
Householder	**1 Re**	**2 Hom**	**3 Brn**	**4 Ox**	**5 Cow**	**6 Sheep**	**7 Stor**	**8 Boat**	**9 Tax**

[39] Simon Smith owned the western part of Kimball Island, but did not live there.
[40] Benjamin Smith ownd and lived on the eastern end of Kimball Island, and owned Flake Island.
[41] James Turner II owned and had a home on Burnt Island, forty acres, valued at $490.
[42] Isiah Turner owned "halls" valued at $100.
[43] John Turner owned two dwellings.
[44] Ezra Tirner owned Pell's Island, twenty-five acres, valued at $50.
[45] Clarence Turner owned land on Kimball Island.
[46] Ernest Bowditch owned a large tract on the south end of Isle au Haut.

Householder	1 Re	2 Hom	3 Brn	4 Ox	5 Cow	6 Sheep	7 Stor	8 Boat	9 Tax
Goss, Job G., Jr.	85 (190)								4.34
Harvey, Emma	? (100)[47]								2.30
Knickerbocker Ice Co.	20 (250)								5.75
Lewis, George F.	45 (90)	200	35				300		14.37
Leffingwell, C. S.	124 (330)	150	35						11.34
Mortland, David A.	85 (190)								4.29
Sproul, Henry C.	40 (150)[48]	25	25						4.60
Smith, Fred. F.	43(86)					30 (52)			3.18
Turner, John K.	98(242)	75	20						7.75
Turner, James A., est.	1/2(25)	200							5.17
Ulmer, W. A.	100(200)								4.60
Woodman, Sproul Co.[49]	755(1,655)	225	215	80	16 (230)	350(612)			71.70
Warren, George	273 (546)								12.55

Totals:

Assessments :		Budgeted:	
Residents	$22,667.50	Poor, contingency	$500.00
Non-Residents	11,338.50	Schools	222.00
	$34,006.00	State tax	148.16
		County tax	53.15
			$923.31

[47] Emma Harvey owned Western Ear.
[48] Henry Sproul owned Fog Island, but DeForest Bennett lived there.
[49] Woodman, Sproul & Co. holdings included Eastern Ear and most of the east side of Isle au Haut; the company also ran a slaughterhouse.

Kimball

This island appears as *Little Isle of Holt* on some early charts, before the spelling of the larger island returned closer to Champlain's original designation (*Isle Haulte*). By the early nineteenth century, the island was called *Kimball* (and has kept this name to the present day) after Solomon Kimball whose descendants—both Kimballs and Smiths—lived on the island from the late eighteenth century to the 1930s.

The earliest conveyance I have found was in 1773 when William McGlathery of Bristol gave a quitclaim deed to "Little Island Hoalte" to Charles Anis of Windham, both communities in the Province of Maine; the price was £6 15s (*Bangor Historical Magazine*, III: 1/479). McGlathery reserved the right to remove wood from the island for a period of seven months. Neither McGlathery, who became an energetic entrepreneur on the western shore of Penobscot Bay, nor Anis lived on the island. There was, however, a resident there at this time—Seth Webb. According to Hosmer (*Sketch of Deer Isle*, 117), Webb was primarily a hunter, who in the 1760s had come with his father Samuel Webb to the south shore of Deer Isle where he acquired land. He traveled widely through the area in pursuit of game and probably lived only intermittently on Kimball Island, although he is believed to have been there during the Revolutionary War. One of the editions of the British Admiralty charts, surveyed between 1764 and 1776, shows one and possibly two settlers on the island facing the Thorofare; no settlers are shown on Isle au Haut itself at this time. Seth Webb married Hannah Winship of Windham, according to Hosmer, and had seven or eight children, but it is unlikely that they were reared on Kimball Island. One of Seth Webb's daughters gave testimony to her father's excellent relations with the Tarratine Indians, with whom he often hunted, and said that Orono, one of the most notable sachems of that era, frequently visited the Webb family homestead; whether this was on Kimball Island or at Webb Cove on Deer Isle is uncertain. Seth is reported to have been captured by Indians in one of the earlier Indian wars and ransomed in 1752 (Massachusetts Archives, V: 544).

Webb, according to Hosmer, died of an accidental gunshot wound on the shore of his island in 1785—ironically, the same year he was listed in Rufus Putnam's census as a resident of eighteen years' standing, which would assuredly have entitled him to a settler's deed (see Appendix 1). He was fifty-three years old. His widow apparently sought to secure his title to the island, as well as to land he claimed on Isle au Haut proper, but according to the Webb family version she was frustrated in her efforts by the agent in charge of the Seth Webb estate. This was Solomon Kimball of Haverhill, who allegedly bought the island from the Commonwealth of Massachusetts, agreeing to quiet the two settlers residing there (their names are not known) with a hundred acres each; Kimball also, it is reported, sold Seth Webb's Isle au Haut interests to a Haverhill buyer at public auction—then bought them back the same day (*Bangor Historical Magazine*, III: 1/479). This was the complaint of Seth Webb's heirs some 180 years ago. George Hosmer, more circumspect in family disputes of this sort, reports the Webb complaint without mentioning Solomon Kimball, and in the section dealing with the latter simply notes that "after the death of Mr. Webb, Mr. Solomon Kimball purchased the island...and resided upon it" (Hosmer, 186). Kimball may have taken up residence immediately, but apparently he did not gain clear title until 1804 when a recorded deed shows conveyance of Little Isle of Holt from the Commonwealth of Massachusetts to Solomon Kimball, yeoman, for $60—a bargain price (Knox Lands 2/30). A Deer Isle tax valuation in 1792, meanwhile, gives us an idea of his husbandry: he mowed twelve acres for eight tons of hay; he tilled another acre for fifteen bushels of grain; he had fifteen acres in pasturage; and he had a yoke of oxen, ten cows, and a pig. His total tax was £2, where neighboring islanders (e.g., Anthony Merchant, Samuel Pickering) paid £1 or less.

There are few details of the Kimballs' long tenure on their island. Solomon, we know, had title to one of the original lots on Isle au Haut surveyed in 1803—No. 7, on the Thorofare—but preferred residence on Kimball Island. I do not have the date of his death, but he is doubtless one of the numerous Kimballs buried in the family plot on the island. His son George W. Kimball inherited the island and lived there until his death in 1839. Lucretia, George's widow, is shown as head of the household in the 1840 census. George was an enterprising farmer and "trader," meaning a man with commercial interests. He owned vessels and was in possession of a considerable property—for example, large holdings on Isle au Haut, including the so-called Great Lot of thirteen hundred acres in the southern half of the island. He represented the town of Deer Isle in the state legislature in 1826, being elected without opposition. He also cleared much of the island to pasture his reported four hundred sheep.[50]

George's eldest son, Benjamin, died in 1842, and several of his children had removed before 1850 (one of them, incidentally, to marry a later Seth Webb—which suggests the ancient feud between the families was not insoluble); William and Solomon left for California soon after 1850 to join another brother, George W., Jr., already there. This left ownership of the island first to Lucretia and, after her death in 1870, to her daughter, Eliza Kimball Smith. Various quitclaim deeds in the 1870s from the California Kimballs confirm Eliza's sole possession (Knox 5/632 and 5/492). Eliza's husband, Captain Ben S. Smith, a Deer Islander by birth but with roots on Isle au Haut (he was a descendant of Abiather Smith, an early settler), had been lost at sea in mid-century. In 1878 Eliza deeded the island to her son Ben A. Smith on condition of his support of her on Kimball Island through her lifetime (Knox Lands 5/605). The 1880 census shows her living with Ben, a farmer and then unmarried, and a daughter

[50] The size of the flock evidently fluctuated: according to the agricultural census of 1850, Lucretia Kimball pastured only one hundred twenty-five sheep, which yielded three hundred pounds of wool; the farm also yielded two hundred pounds of butter. The valuation of the farm was, nonetheless, the highest of any island farm in Penobscot Bay in this era—$2,000. According to 1862 tax records (see page 356), Lucretia owned no fewer than three stores on Isle au Haut.

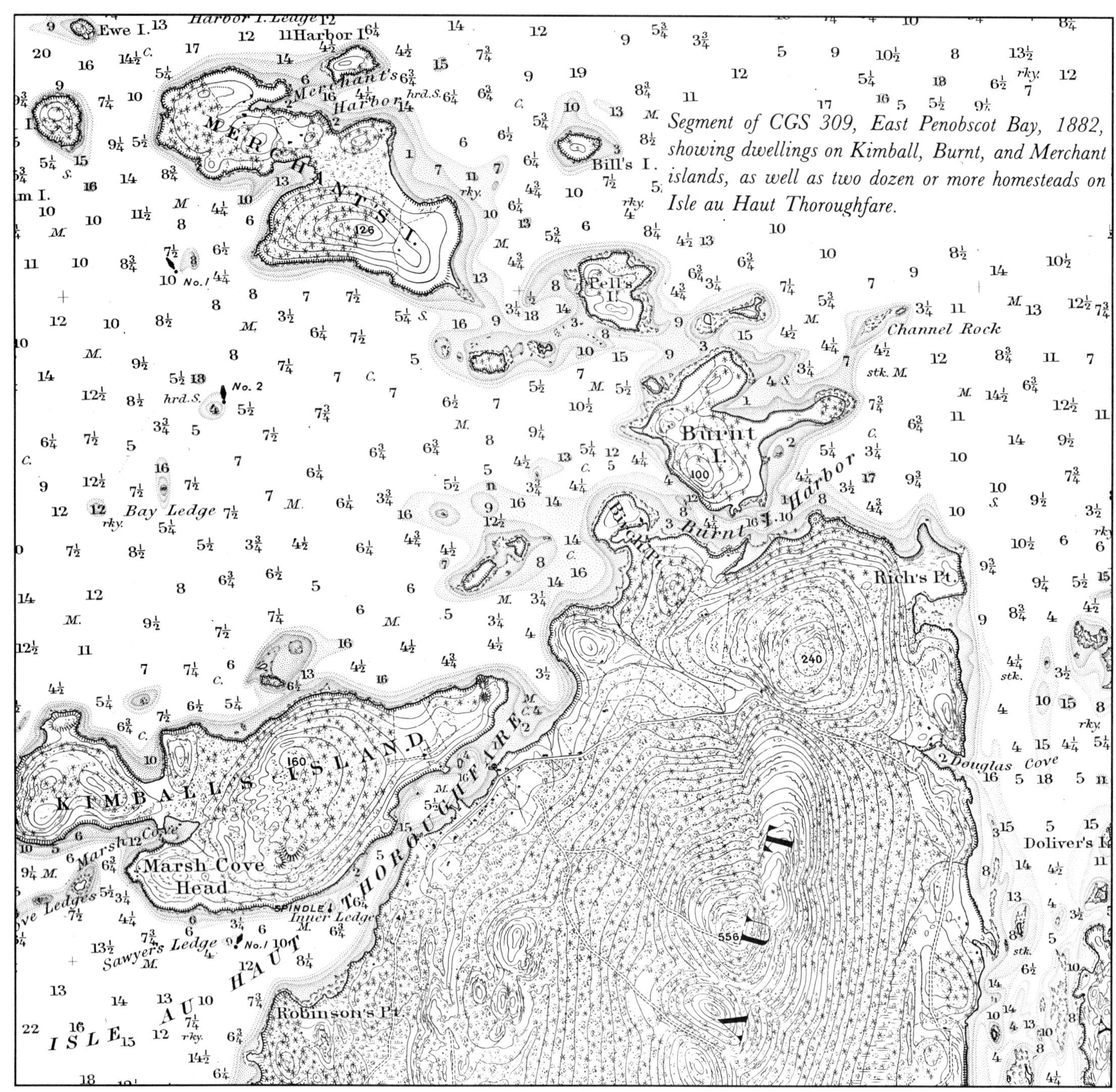

Segment of CGS 309, East Penobscot Bay, 1882, showing dwellings on Kimball, Burnt, and Merchant islands, as well as two dozen or more homesteads on Isle au Haut Thoroughfare.

Fanny, thirty-five, a schoolteacher; another son, Simon, married and with two children, was in a separate household. Eliza died in 1889.

Ben A. Smith was squire of Kimball Island from the 1880s to the 1920s. He was less farmer or fisherman than entrepreneur. In the 1880s, when Isle au Haut, like other coastal areas, was experiencing a tourist boom, Ben Smith remodeled the old farm (its original construction date is unknown), named it Seaside Farm, and advertised for guests. He had room for twelve, though some accounts say he would crowd in many more when there was a need; his rates ranged from $10 to $14 a week. The Seaside Farm ran at least to 1910 and so was perhaps the longest surviving summer inn in the area.

In 1895 Ben A. Smith married Elizabeth Barton, who had come to the island a few years earlier as housekeeper; she was the widow of a doctor and had one son, Frank. Frank married Elizabeth Hamilton of Duck Harbor, known as Lizzie Belle, and they, too, settled on the island and raised a family of seven children. The 1910 census shows eight persons living on Kimball Island in two households: Benjamin Smith, listed as proprietor of the "summer boarding house," and his wife Elizabeth; Frank Barton with *his* wife Elizabeth and their first four children. The island community dissolved after the death of Ben A. Smith and his wife in the 1920s. Lizzie Belle removed eventually to Rockland with the children, and she was still living there in the 1970s; Frank remained on the island. He had inherited the farm from his mother (or stepfather) and whatever land that had not been sold off during Ben's lifetime. Frank lobstered and maintained a weir at one time or another, but he did not prosper. He died in 1954—the last year-round resident of Kimball island in an unbroken sequence of more than 175 years.

This recitation of the principal inhabitants of Kimball Island inevitably omits many transients, squatters, hired hands, and others, a few of whose names have been passed down, most not. Sam Bridges, for instance, Ben Smith's hired man during the Seaside Farm era, was for many years a familiar figure on Kimball Island. A chart of the 1880s shows not only the four or five buildings on the Thorofare that made up the Smith farm complex, but another cluster of four small buildings on the south side of Marsh Cove; these may have been temporary dwellings of lumbermen

Benjamin A. Smith homestead on Kimball Island, overlooking Isle au Haut Thorofare, 1891; this farm was a summer inn from the 1890s to World War I. A residence appears to have existed on or near this location from the late 1700s. (Courtesy of Alice Cain Crowell.)

during one of the periodic logging operations on the island, first for the lime kilns at Rockland, later for pulp. Lobstermen have also summered on the island with permission of the owners.

Title passed, after the Smiths and Bartons, to numerous owners. Guests at Ben Smith's Seaside Farm acquired the western end of the island—Kimball's Head—as early as the 1890s; their descendants owned this sector, including the shore around Marsh Cove, through most of the twentieth century. Descendants of Nathaniel Bowditch, founder of Point Lookout, owned the eastern end of the island. Other cottagers from Point Lookout owned segments in the center. By the 1990s ownership centered in two of these families.

The owners most in residence in the later decades of the twentieth century were Jack and Alice Crowell, who owned the old Kimball homesite on the Thorofare facing the "village" on Isle au Haut. Jack was a cold region environmentalist, a veteran of both World War I and II, and commander of expeditions to both the Arctic and Antarctic. Alice Cain, whom he married in 1927, was born and reared on Burnt Island off the northeast end of Isle au Haut—undoubtedly a compelling reason for the Crowells settling in the area. The Crowells built their home on the foundations of the old Kimball-Smith farm and moved there permanently in 1968 when Jack finally retired; apart from a few months each winter in Rockland, they spent the rest of their lives here. Alice died in the early 1980s. Jack died in his sleep on the island in 1986, more than 206 years after Seth Webb, first settler on the island, shot himself accidentally—probably less than a hundred yards away.

Residence on Kimball Island, 1790–1910

Note: The following lived on Kimball Island at dates shown, according to federal census schedules. Age of householder is at first appearance. Spouses, if known, are in parentheses. In the decennial column males are to left of the slash, females to right. All adult males are farmers, unless otherwise noted. Dollar figures after some householders represent real estate valuations in 1850, according to the census-taker.

Householder	**1790**	**1800**	**1810**	**1820**	**1830**	**1840**	**1850**	**1860**	**1870**	**1880**	**1900**	**1910**
Solomon Kimball, 45+	3/4	5/4	1/1									
George Kimball, -45 (Lucretia)			2/5	5/7	6/7	0/4[51]	1/1[52]					
Isiah Barber, 20s					2/2							
Ralph Haycock, 20s					1/2							
Willard Clark, 41 $2,000							4/1					
Benjamin S. Smith, 35 (Eliza), mariner $2,500							4/2	-	0/1[53]	1/2		
William Kimball, 35 (Fidelia), sea captain $1,800							3/1	2/3[54]				
Simon A. Smith, 30 (Laura)										3/1		
Benjamin A. Smith, 53 (Elizabeth), boardinghouse keeper										2/2	1/1	
Alonzo[55] Barton, 30 (Elizabeth B.)												3/3

[51] Lucretia Kimball is head of household; her sons evidently lived on Isle au Haut and came out daily to work the farm.
[52] All seventeen persons on the island in 1850 are in Lucretia Kimball's household.
[53] Eliza Smith was the sole resident of the island in 1870, but she doubtless had a houseful of retainers and hired hands.
[54] William Conley of Nova Scotia is shown as head of this household in 1860, but I believe he was a tenant farmer.
[55] The census-taker names him Alonzo, but his name was Frank. There was an Alonzo *Smith* on the island in this period, not related to Ben A. Smith.

Kimballs and Descendants of Kimball Island

Note: This genealogy of Solomon Kimball's descendents on Kimball Island has been worked out from census data and other materials.

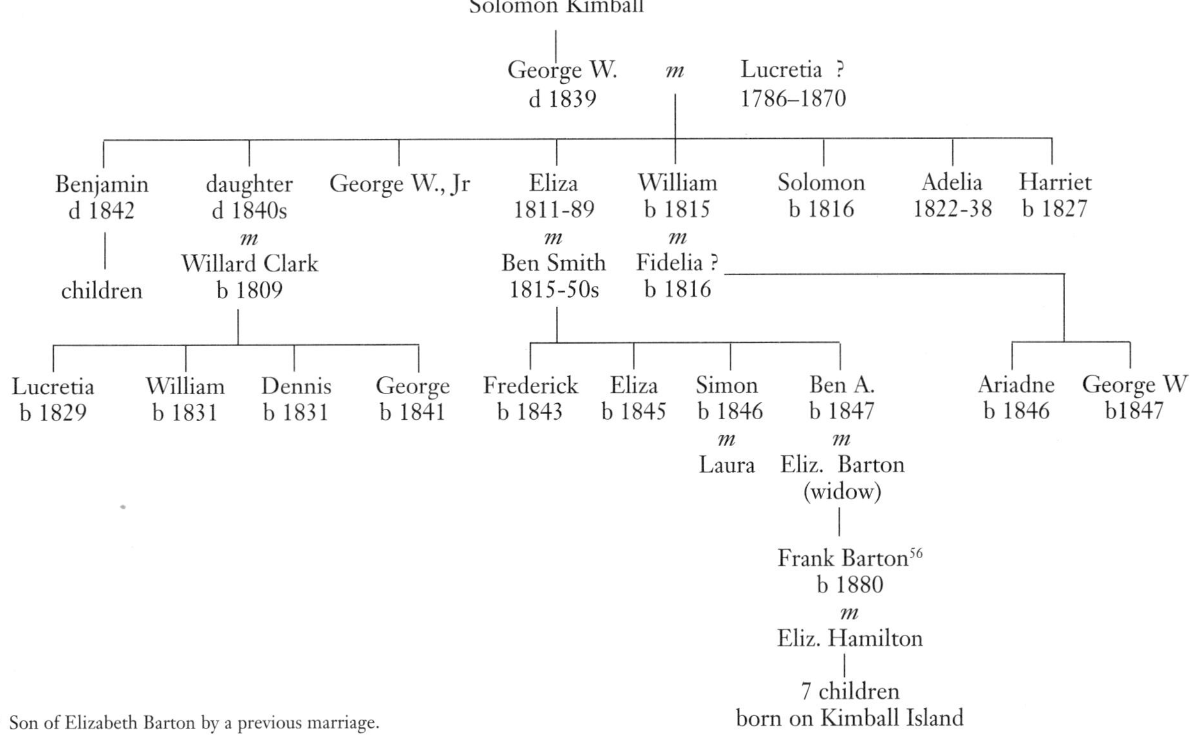

[56] Son of Elizabeth Barton by a previous marriage.

Merchant

The 1776 "Atlantic Neptune" appears to show one residence on Merchant Island, at the southeast end, though the island itself is not named. The house designation is fuzzy, but it is properly shown, for we know that Anthony Merchant settled there in about 1770 (see Appendix 1). He was the first settler on any island among those lying between Deer Isle and Isle au Haut. Rufus Putnam's survey of 1785 names the island *Marchants or White*, and the word "sold" (whether of that date or later is unclear) appears under it (Hancock Plan Book II: 23). In 1804, according to Dr. Noyes, Anthony Merchant petitioned the Commonwealth of Massachusetts for title to two hundred acres on the island, one hundred for himself and another in the name of his erstwhile fellow resident, Daniel Austin, whose interests he bought out; the petition argues that he and Austin had lived on the island since the early 1770s and "there built two houses and made such other improvements" prior to 1784, as the law required for grants of one hundred acres. An affidavit in support of the petition, signed by Joseph Colby and Thomas Stinson, testified to the residence of the two settlers before 1784 (Noyes, Family histories: Merchant). The petition affecting Merchant Island was granted, but Merchant's further request that he be allowed to purchase Sheep (Pell's) and Burnt islands "at a reasonable price," also on the basis of pre-1784 "improvements," was satisfied only with respect to the latter. Pell's Island, as far as I am aware, remained in the possession of Peletiah Barter of Isle au Haut. Anthony Merchant's successful petition in 1804 did not excuse him from the necessity of acquiring legal title to his island once again when Maine and Massachusetts were separated in 1820. In 1826, then, the State of Maine formally conveyed one hundred acres at the east end of "Mark Island, otherwise Merchant's Island" to Anthony Merchant, for a modest fee ($15); in 1831 the state conveyed the remainder to Anthony (Knox Lands 2/105 and 2/106).

Since Merchants and their descendants played the major role on the island in the nineteenth century, an abbreviated genealogical chart follows this notice, including those who had something to do with Merchant Island itself or neighboring islands. I also include a table drawn from federal census schedules showing the householders on Merchant Island from 1800 to 1900, with the size of these households; this table inevitably omits residents who lived on the island between the census-taker's visits (including the period 1880–1900).

Anthony Merchant, Sr., according to George Hosmer (page 182), was a master mariner from York, Maine, who accomplished the "improvements" on his island between voyages to the West Indies. Some of these improvements are reflected in a 1792 Deer Isle tax valuation: he mowed six acres for ten tons of hay, tilled two acres for twenty bushels of grain, and had five more acres in pasturage; he had a yoke of oxen and three cows. This was sound husbandry for that era, especially on an island. Anthony Merchant lived to about 1833. (He died of typhoid fever on Christmas Day, according to descendants, and was buried on the island.[57])

Anthony, Sr. had eight children. Nathaniel, the oldest, lived on Camp Island, which he left to his second son Robert (see page 308); his eldest son, Nathaniel, Jr., settled on the south end of Isle au Haut; and Abigail, a daughter, married John Gott, Jr. of Swans Island—none of Nathaniel's family, then, were associated with Merchant Island. A daughter of Anthony, Sr., Miriam, married Henry Barter of Isle au Haut, and they lived for many years, and died, on Burnt Island (page 373); their son Robert lived on Wreck Island (page 291). Another daughter of Anthony, Sr., Eleanor, married John Smith of Vinalhaven, and his name appears in several early deeds relating to Merchant Island: in 1810 John Merchant, another son of Anthony, Sr., who had removed from the island, sold his interest in both Merchant and Burnt islands to John Smith for $1,000, and in 1814 John Smith sold most of this back to Anthony Merchant, Jr. (Knox Lands 2/21 and 2/19).

Anthony Merchant, Jr., youngest child of Anthony, Sr., appears by this time to have replaced his father as the dominant personality on the island and remained so for the next fifty years. He was a farmer primarily, one judges from the stone walls that crisscross the island, and he kept sheep. Captain Henry Lufkin (writing in a style one could not invent if one tried) tells of picking up lambs off Merchant in 1853 for the Bangor slaughterhouse: "Lite SSW wind went to Isle Holt to Gilberts worfe & tuck in 51 lambs and back to Marchats Isle while they ware after the sheep cought 2 frying of fish ready for the pan." And two days later: 'Flying fog left Groses Cove [Merchant Harbor] & went to Barter's [Wreck] & got 20 sheep & left for Bangor lite S. wind came tue at Butteriland fog" (Lufkin Diaries, August 15 and 17,1853). Hosmer tells us (page 184) that Anthony Merchant, Jr. was for some years tax collector for the Isle au Haut district and a much respected figure in the area (if the two are indeed compatible).

Anthony Merchant, Jr. had two children by his first wife, Eunice Smith, one of the twenty-four children of David Smith of Swans Island, and at least five more by his second wife, the widow Maria Robertson Gross. His oldest son, David, lived for some years on the island after his marriage; he is shown with a household of nine in the 1850 census, before he removed to Deer Isle where he died in 1857. Anthony's eldest daughter married Willard Matthews, then a resident of the island. Shortly after their marriage they moved to Belfast, where Willard became a master mariner; this would have been in the early 1840s. Maria, the first child of Anthony's second marriage, married James Childs, who came to the island in the 1840s and remained there the rest of his life. At least four of their children lived on the island past maturity. Their daughter Catherine married Alexander Monteith, a widower who had been on the island for ten years or more, and they raised four girls on Merchant before Alexander's death there near the end of the century. The two oldest Monteith girls, Ann and Abbie, remained on the island until they

[57] There were two burial grounds on Merchant Island: the principal one (where Anthony, Sr. was buried) was on the south shore facing Isle au Haut; another was on Monteith Point (see sketch below).

married—but I believe not long thereafter. Emma, another daughter, married Simon Knowlton and settled for a time on Merchant. Mina Monteith, who married Edward Dyer, bore three children on the island before the family moved to Isle au Haut—this was the sixth generation of Merchants or their descendants on Merchant Island.

Of James and Maria Childs's other children: Anthony remained on the island with his wife Lucy Dunbar and their two boys Frank and Charles until near the end of the century; James was still living on Merchant when he died in the early 1880s; and Rebecca, who married Mathias Holland, a Nova Scotian, raised six children on the island before removing to Isle au Haut around 1900. Their daughter Mary married Albert Hutchinson of Stonington in 1896, and they, too, lived on Merchant for several years after their marriage. James Childs remarried after Maria's death in 1892: his second wife (not shown on the genealogical chart) was Jane Haggerty, a former schoolteacher on the island. She is shown in the 1900 census, aged seventy-one, living with Elizabeth Childs, twenty-eight, who was presumably a younger daughter of James Childs; James Childs had died before this date.[58]

Turning again to the second family of Anthony Merchant, Jr.: Shubael, who married his cousin Eleanor Barter of Wreck Island, moved onto the latter island before 1860 and is noticed there (page 291). Anthony Merchant III in 1857 married Rebecca Beal, daughter of John Beal of Jonesport, a fisherman who lived on Merchant for some years; Anthony was living in this household with his wife and child in 1860 (he is shown as Anthony, Jr. in the census). He became a sea captain, and neither he nor his large family settled permanently on the island. John, another son, also had little to do with Merchant after reaching maturity, except in the disposition of some lots after his father's death. Martha, the youngest of Anthony and Maria's progeny, married John Gross of Boston, and she bore several of her children on Merchant Island before removing sometime after her father's death.

The Walling map of Hancock County in 1860, which was surveyed a few years earlier, shows the Anthony Merchant, Jr. homestead where it should be—at the west end of the island near the head of Merchant Harbor—and the James Childs family (misspelled *Giles*) at the southeast end—that is, near the original site of the senior Anthony Merchant's farm. J. Beal is shown at the head of the cove directly south of Harbor Island. Two other families had come and gone by this time—the Grosses and the Matthewses. Jacob Gross, according to Hosmer (page 184), lived on the western end of Merchant Island and gave his name to what is now known as Merchant Harbor (as the Lufkin diaries noted above attest). It is not known when he settled on the island, or for how long; I do not find him in the federal census. His widow could have been the Maria Gross who was the second wife of Anthony Merchant, Jr. Jacob's daughter Mary, Hosmer tells us, was the wife of William Matthews, who came to Merchant Island from Boothbay in the 1830s; a deed recorded in the Hancock County registry in 1835 shows the conveyance of a lot to William from Henry Wilson, a resident of Isle au Haut who held many island properties in the area at this time. Willard Matthews, who, as noted earlier, married the eldest daughter of Anthony Merchant, Jr. before removing to Belfast, was probably William's son; it is certain that another son was Stinson Matthews, who settled on Deer Isle and in whose home his parents spent their last years. In 1852 Stinson, having been deeded his father's twenty-five-acre lot on Merchant, sold it to Anthony Merchant, Jr. (Knox Lands 2/211). And in 1865 another Matthews—Annis, whom I do not identify—sold a twenty-five-acre lot known as the "Gross Place" to Alexander Monteith (Knox Lands 2/213). The Matthewses were involved in island properties for thirty years, though their actual residence appears to have been only about half of this period.

One further detail of the era of Anthony Merchant, Jr. is worth noting—if only as a reminder of the swelling population of Merchant Island with the multiple intra-island marriages and births: in 1833, according to Deer Isle records, a special school district was created for Merchant Island, embracing for a few years Wreck and Round islands as well. This district apparently

[58] I am indebted to Mrs. Dennis Robbins of Stonington, a grandchild of Mathias and Rebecca Holland, for much information concerning the Merchant descendants in the latter decades of the nineteenth century.

lasted until Merchant was incorporated into Isle au Haut in 1874.

When Anthony Merchant, Jr. died in 1865, he left his portion of the island—which appears to have been about three-quarters of it[59]—to his surviving children: Maria Childs received the twenty-five acres on Merchant Harbor that was sold to Anthony by Stinson Matthews in 1852; Martha Gross received the house at the east end of the island and several small lots; Shubael and David's heirs also received lots in the south and west, together with Hardwood Island, on condition that they provide for their mother Maria through her lifetime (Knox Lands 2/208). This fragmentation of Merchant Island, I believe, destroyed the sense of its unity that the two Anthonys had managed to preserve over nearly a century despite the comings and goings of Grosses, Matthewses, Beals, and others.

Off-island heirs sold their inheritance as opportunity arose. Those in financial straits mortgaged their lots or had them attached to settle debts: Shubael Merchant, for example, was attached for one-seventh of his holdings on the island a year after his father's death, to satisfy a debt to James Turner (Hancock 127/318); Alexander Monteith, scarcely married to his eighteen-year-old bride, Catherine Childs, apparently used part of her inheritance to satisfy debts to other Monteith claimants (Knox Lands 2/239, 2/243, and 2/355). Meanwhile, a certain instability is reflected in the type of settlers after Anthony Merchant, Jr.: his son David's widow Catherine, according to Noyes, returned to the island to live with a disreputable bootlegger named Ben Leach, who was frequently in trouble with the law (Noyes, Family histories: Merchant).

By the 1880s growing portions of the island were coming into the hands of off-island speculators and investors—e.g., Warren E. Marsh of Belfast, Michael Dailey (or Daley) of Hancock, Edwin G. DesIsle (pronounced locally "Dazelle"), and H. C. Sproul of Mount Desert. Tax records for Isle au Haut reveal their grip on the island. Michael Dailey, for instance, appears in tax records of 1882 with one of the highest valuations in the plantation of Isle au Haut (see page 358); compare his assessments with those of residents of Merchant Island such as James Childs, Alex Monteith, and Mathias Holland. DesIsle and Sproul, who speculated extensively in island properties in the last two decades of the century, farmed extensively on Merchant Island: they had cattle and horses, according to Monteith descendants, as well as gardens and hothouses from which they sent vegetables and flowers to markets in Bar Harbor. Levi Conary, who lived on McGlathery Island during this era, was one of the mariners who carried this produce.[60]

Maps of the 1880s show more buildings on the island than the census would suggest: five or six clustered at the head of Merchant Harbor, two south of the harbor at about the middle of the island, and two more near the southeast tip (Maps 1880 CGS 4 and 1882 CGS 309). While several of these might be barns or outbuildings, it is also possible that with the fragmentation of the original lots, a number of Merchant descendants or their assigns kept small cottages on the island for incidental use, while maintaining their normal residence elsewhere. Certainly Isle au Haut school records for this period suggest more inhabitants on Merchant Island than are reflected in the 1880 census, which shows only one or two children of school age.[61] In 1879, for example, eight pupils were enrolled in the Merchant Island school; the teacher was Addie L. Turner. Other teachers at the island school in the 1880s and 1890s, according to Monteith informants, were: Grace Atwood, Josie Phinney, Lizzie Childs, George Welch, and Liza Toothaker Morey. The school carried on until 1901, before closing for lack of pupils.

The best indication of residence on Merchant Island at the end of the nineteenth century—and indeed earlier—is a sketch showing the island in about 1900, accompanied by a key prepared by Dr. Benjamin Lake Noyes after conversations with two Monteith descendants in 1933. The sketch and the "key" provide a good deal of perspective on the island, and I shall not attempt to improve on them.

[59] The Deer Isle tax record of 1862 (see page 357), a few years before Anthony, Jr. died, shows him with 150 acres valued at $400 (a high valuation for that era).

[60] The Monteith descendants are Ann M. Richardson and Abbie M. Sertz (see genealogical table), who were interviewed by Dr. Noyes in 1933; see also the sketch and key, below.

[61] One family on the island in the 1880s with school-age children in the household was the Atwood family, who lived at what was called the "Old Farmhouse."

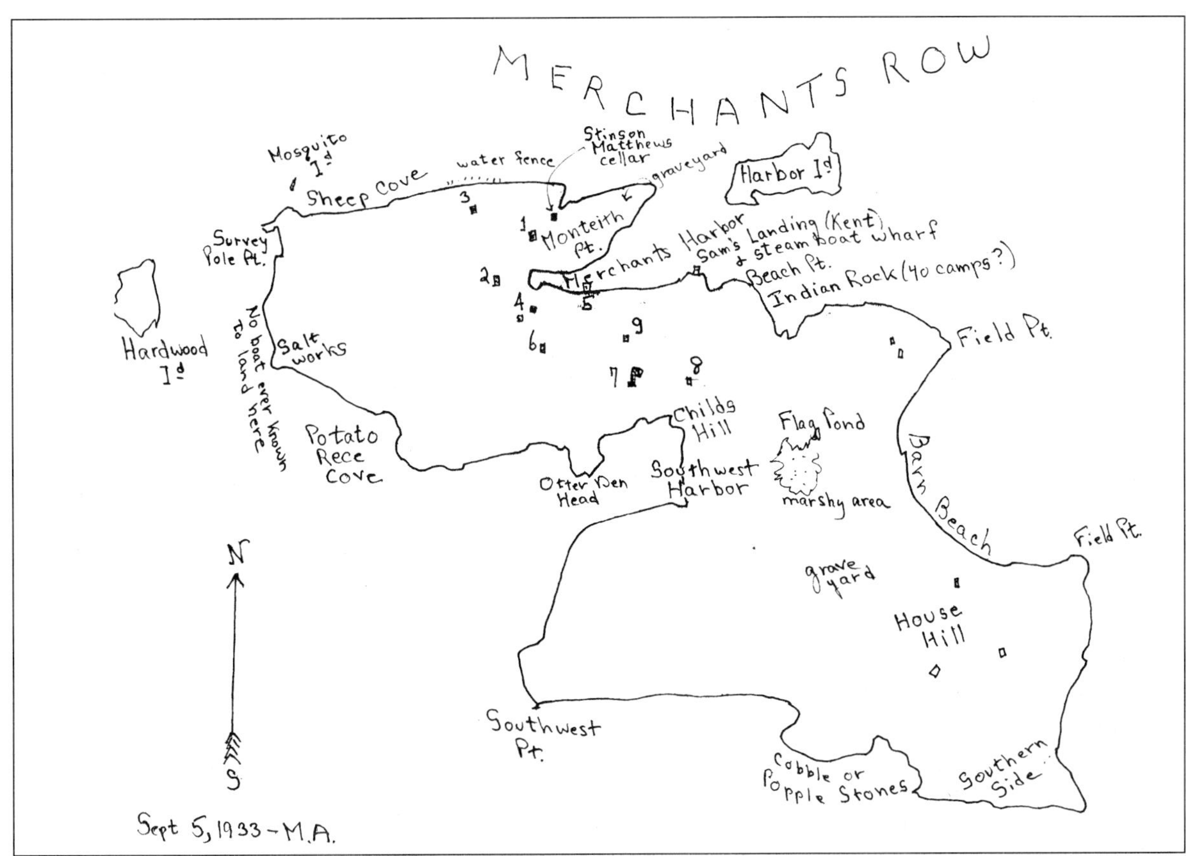

Sketch of Merchant Island, as of 1900 (drawn in 1933 by Dr. Benjamin Lake Noyes—or his secretary Mildred Allen; the sketch has been altered by the author only to enlarge place-names and house numbers).

Key to Houses on Merchant Island, c. 1900

(Notes by Dr. Benjamin Lake Noyes based on interviews with Annie Monteith Richardson and Abbie Monteith Sertz, 1933)

1. Alex. Monteith bought old Mathews house & moved it to his cellar then built his barn on Mathews cellar.
2. Anthony Childs built and squared own lumber. No one else ever lived in it. Cellar can be seen and large orchard.
3. Simon Knowlton had house here built abt 4 years ago. Mrs. Damon tore it down & fixed up Father's[62] house, James Childs.
4. James Childs abt 79 or more years ago [1854], and then Lizzie, the widow [63] lived there. Barn up in field, only roof left now on ground. House dropping down, painted red.
5. First school house & was grandfather Child's boathouse before moved on shore & [?] for school. Al Hutchinson lived there afterwards.
6. Mathew [Mathias] Holland built abt 46 years ago [1887] then A. Hutchinson tore it down and built one now [1933] owned by Grindle Robbins on Green Head, Stonington. Mrs. Damon owned the land and wanted the building down.
7. Anthony Merchant & wife Maria Robinson (great-aunt to Sadie Simpson).[64] Maria got it afire & burnt down & they rebuilt. Mrs. Damon owned it when it burned again & and she built new house seen there today on same cellar and called the Farm House and in good condition. Chas A. Russ bot from HR Sproul to Mike Dailey. Sproul had store.
8. Peleg Thomas from up River [Rockland]. John S. Merchant probably first & brother Anthony in other tenement. Sproul turned it into hot house & sent flowers & farm produce to Bar Harbor where he was in business.
9. Last school house & can be seen there now. John Gross who m. Martha Merchant lived in one of the houses not numbered. Osborne Sterns lived in one, wife Emma.
10. Old Anthony Merchant & James Childs had homes on House Hill before building at other side of Island. Annie Richardson & Abbie Monteith said the houses on House Hill, as their mother called it, were gone before their day. That was the part of the island first settled.
11. On Walling Map of 1860 on Merchants Island will be seen J. Beal (John) whose dau. Betsy m. John,[65] son of Anthony Merchant on the Island & Rebecca, Betsy's sister m. Anthony Merchant, Jr.

[62] That is, *grand*father of informants, James Childs.

[63] Unidentified.

[64] Not identified in our genealogical table.

[65] Betsy Beal may have been John Merchant's second wife; according to other records, he married Barbara Robbins (as shown in the family table).

The island's inhabitants appear to have removed rapidly around 1900. The senior Childses, James and Maria, had both died by this time, and their family, as we have seen, was dispersed. The Staples family, shown in the 1880 census below with numerous stepchildren, also removed before 1900—I do not know where. A 1907 atlas shows a single homestead standing near the center of the island south of the harbor. This is inaccurate, for in addition to the two school-houses at this date, at least three other homesteads were still up—the James Childs farm and the former homes of his son and son-in-law, Anthony Childs and Alex Monteith. The two latter home-steads were in poor condition and were razed about 1916, but the James Childs home remained serviceable for several more years, according to descendants. The building south of the harbor was used as a caretaker's cottage and was occupied in 1910 by Asa Hopkins, his wife, and two grown children; these were the only year-round inhabi-tants of Merchant Island at that date (Chatto and Turner).

I pass over the twentieth century. Miss Theresa Damon, a cottager on Isle au Haut, acquired the island soon after 1900 from the descendants of Anthony Merchant, and her descen-dants vacation there still. A number of boats, including lobster boats, may still be seen in the harbor on a summer day, but it is a small fleet compared to that of the heyday of Merchant Island, when two dozen or more settlers stretched across the island from the "Gross Place" to the southeast tip where Anthony Merchant, Sr. first put down his roots.

Residence on Merchant Island, 1800–1910

Note: The following households on Merchant Island appear in federal census schedules between 1790 and 1910. (Many others, of course, lived on this island between visits of the census-taker.) Age is at first appearance. Spouses, if known, are in parentheses. Occupations are shown as follows: Fi, fisherman; Fa, farmer; S, sailor.

Householder	1790	1800	1810	1820	1830	1840	1850	1860	1870	1880	1900	1910
Anthony Merchant, 45+	4/7	3/4	3/1	-[66]								
Anthony Merchant II, 38 (Mariah), Fa					2/3	5/6	3/3	2/2				
William Matthews, 77 (Mary), Fa						1/2	1/1					
James Childs, 25 (Maria), Fa/Fi							1/1	3/3	3/3	5/2[67]		
David Merchant, 31 (Catherine)							6/3					
John Beal, 43 (Ann), Fi								4/3				
Anthony Merchant III, 20 (Rebecca), Fi								1/1				
Peleg Thomas, 55 (Lucy), S									3/3			
Alexander Monteith, 39 (Catherine), S									1/2	1/4	1/4[68]	
Alonzo Hutchinson, 21 (Cynthia/Lydia), Fi									2/1	1/2		
John E. Staples, 56, Fa										3/4		
Elizabeth Childs, 38											0/2	
Mathias Holland, 50 (Rebecca), Fi/Fa											1/4	2/1
James Holland, 20, Fi											1/0	
Charles Parker, 42 (Lillie), Fi											2/2	
Frank Gross, 25 (Sarah), Fi												1/1
Asa Hopkins, (Fannie), Fa												1/2
Earl Hopkins, 22 (Lizzie), Fi												1/1
	1790	1800	1810	1820	1830	1840	1850	1860	1870	1880	1900	1910

66 No Anthony Merchant is listed in the 1820 schedule for Deer Isle (which is alphabetical); residents, however, were surely on Merchant Island.
67 The household includes son-in-law Mathias Holland, twenty-eight, a fisherman.
68 Catherine, seventy-nine, is head of household; son-in-law James Dyer, twenty-seven (wife Mina), a fisherman, is in household.

Merchants and Descendants of Merchant Island

Note: Those in italics lived on the island as adults.

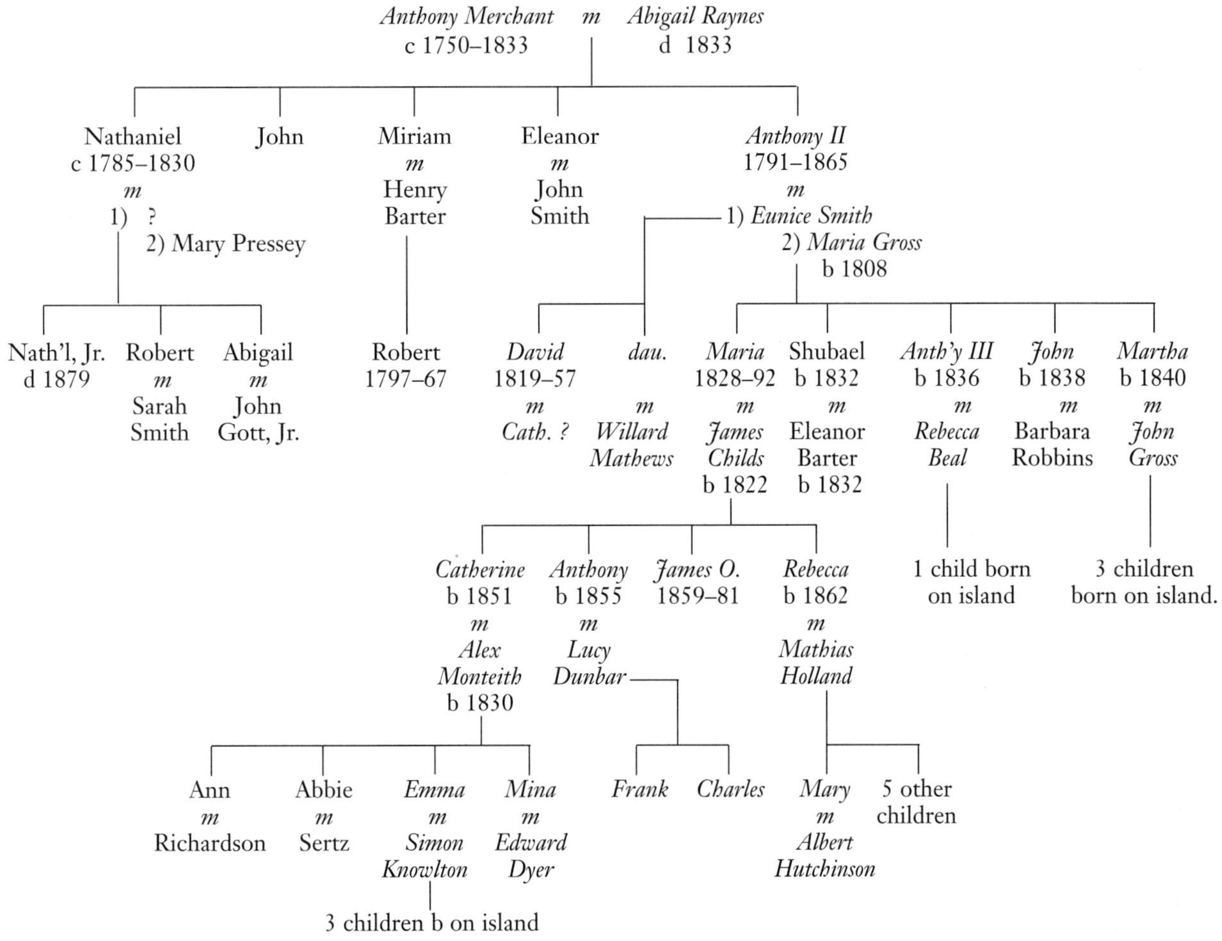

Ram, Hardwood, Ewe, and Harbor

The origins of these names are obvious enough, and they have been attached to the islands for at least a hundred years. No "history" of any significance is associated with them since they were never inhabited. They were normally used for sheepgrazing by the residents of Merchant Island, but they were not always owned by the latter. Ewe was deeded by the State of Maine to a Deer Isle resident in 1876 (Hancock 393/113); Hardwood was one of the islands acquired by David Thurlow of Crotch Island in the first half of the nineteenth century (Hancock 109/4411, an 1856 deed to his daughter-in-law). But the deeds are silent with regard to history, as are other records. The State of Maine owns Ram Island today; the others belong to cottagers on Merchant Island and Isle au Haut.

Bills and Nathan

Bills Island is named after William Barter, as Pell, or Pell's, is named after his father (or brother) Peletiah, all early settlers on Isle au Haut. Peletiah probably lived on his island, but Bills was too small to sustain a settler and suitable only for sheepgrazing; it is probable that it was grazed continuously from post-Revolutionary times until the last ram was removed in 1965. Other fauna on the island included voles, which abounded until recently but are now declining in number due to some ecological shift. The dwelling on this island was built by the present owner in the 1960s and is used as an occasional summer residence.

Some confusion reigned in the title to Bills in the latter decades of the nineteenth century, a confusion often found in island title search. In 1876 the State of Maine, finding Bills had never been properly deeded, sold it, along with half a dozen other small islands, to Edward A. Pierce of Boston—"Bill's Island, a third of a mile northwest of Pills" (a slip of the pen that might justifiably have bothered Peletiah); Pierce sold the island in 1898 to Abbie C. Cater of Cambridge, Massachusetts (Knox Lands 5/624 and 5/804). In 1879, the town of Isle au Haut, concerned more, it would appear, with taxes than with clear title, sold the island for $1.94 in tax default to John Barter; his heirs in 1894 conveyed to Ruth A. Sturdivant, a summer resident on Isle au Haut (Knox Lands 2/455 and 2/588). I do not know which sequence of title finally proved valid, but assume the present owner's lawyers figured it out.

Nathan Island, no larger than Bills, and used similarly over the years, has also taken the given name of an early owner—more likely than not Nathaniel Merchant (1785–1830), who was brought up on neighboring Merchant Island. Merchants were in possession of the island in the mid-nineteenth century, for Maria Merchant Childs in 1866 inherited "Nathan's Island" from her father Anthony Merchant, Jr. (Knox Lands 2/208). In 1883, the island never having been properly conveyed by either Massachusetts or Maine, the latter sold it to James Childs, Maria's son or husband, for $6 (Knox Lands 5/444). In 1902 Isle au Haut tax records show the estate of Albert B. Otis in ownership of the ten-acre island, valued at $25.

Beyond these few details, I find no history of the two islands worth noting. Bills Island, to the great satisfaction of the present owner, has managed to keep its possessive "s," where Nathan, like most islands similarly named, has lost its.

Pell

This island was first called *Sheep Island*, like many others, but became known as *Pell's* from an early date after Peletiah Barter, its initial owner and only probable resident. Peletiah Barter, born in 1772 in the Muscongus Bay region, was one of the first settlers on Isle au Haut. He had several of the original lots there, and as early as 1802 had title—or at least laid claim—to Sheep Island as well; a note in Lathrop Lewis's survey of Great "Isle of Holt" in 1803 indicates that Sheep Island was surveyed for Peletiah Barter the year before (Hancock Plan Book II: 29). He was not, however, the only claimant, for in 1804 Anthony Merchant, at the same time he petitioned for title to Merchant Island on the basis of improvements he had made there, asked for title to Sheep Island on the same grounds; Merchant's request was denied.

What year Peletiah Barter moved onto his island (if he did) and how long he remained there are uncertain. Since he owned what must have been considered even then a prime lot on Isle au Haut—the hundred-acre lot on the Thorofare just south of Point Lookout—it seems unlikely that he would have abandoned this choice site for a mere twenty-acre island during the prime years of his life. Yet he does appear to have lived there at one time. Later deeds refer to Sheep Island as "formerly occupied by Peletiah Barter" (e.g., Hancock 3/442). And there are the ancient cellar hole and well still visible to signify, if not

Peletiah's, at least someone's year-round residence.

In the absence of census data for Pell Island or of an authority clever enough to determine the date of its cellar hole, let me speculate as follows on Peletiah's residence: he remained on Isle au Haut until his children were grown (he had ten, according to Hosmer, 187), and perhaps until after the death of his wife—say, until the 1820s or 1830s; he was then in his fifties or sixties and, being still in good health, removed to his island, which he undoubtedly knew well from having kept sheep there. He probably already had a well and rudimentary shelter on it. A few years later, as his health failed him, he gave up his island and returned to Isle au Haut. We find in 1847 a deed not uncommon for that era: Peletiah's conveyance of Pell to "the inhabitants of Deer Isle" in return for the town's care of him during his "age and infirmity" (Hancock 81/371). The fact that special provision was made for the removal of that year's crop of hay by Anthony Merchant suggests Peletiah had already quit the island. This is, to be sure, hypothesis; but if Peletiah's residence on the island had been many years longer than I suggest, it would have attracted more attention. No maps I have seen show residence on Pell, and references to Peletiah's living there do not exist in any profusion.[69]

After Peletiah Barter's death in about 1852, title reverted to a succession of local owners: Lucretia, Margaret, and William S. Turner; Mary A. Lewis. None of them lived there. Isle au Haut tax records for 1902 show the twenty-five-acre island owned by Ezra Turner III and valued at $50—indicating modest usage. Pell was used for sheep pasturage and, to judge from photographs at the turn the century which show the island virtually treeless, the sheep fed well. During the twentieth century Pell has been owned by benevolent rusticators who have allowed the island to revert to its natural state.

[69] It is also possible—if I do not muddy the waters too much—that our Peletiah was a son or nephew of the original Peletiah, for there were clearly two in the region.

Burnt (off Isle au Haut)

This island was given its name in Revolutionary times, presumably in consequence of a then-recent burning-over from natural or other causes, and it has never been changed. Early title to the island involved several families well known in the area, notably Merchants and Barters. Anthony Merchant, in his successful petition to the Commonwealth of Massachusetts in 1804 for title to Merchants Island where he was living, also asked for the right to buy Burnt Island "for A reasonable price," on the basis of improvements he claimed to have effected there; his request was apparently granted (Noyes, Family histories: Merchant). In 1808 a deed showed the conveyance of forty acres on Burnt Island from Anthony Merchant to Robert Barter of Isle au Haut; the fee was $150, and ownership of the island was said to be shared at the time with James Barter (Knox Lands 2/142; the deed was recorded only in 1848). Then there came a conveyance in 1810 from John Merchant, son of Anthony, to John Smith of Vinalhaven, who had married one of Anthony's daughters; Smith conveyed it in 1814 to Henry Barter, who married another Merchant daughter, Miriam (Knox Lands 2/21 and 1/367). Henry Barter felt quite justifiably that his title was not perfectly secure, in view of the numerous conveyances of portions of Burnt Island that I omit here, so in 1816 he took the precaution of squaring his claim with the Commonwealth of Massachusetts for a fee of $54.59 (Knox Lands 2/29).

Henry and Miriam Barter moved onto Burnt Island sometime after 1816, built a farmhouse that stood through the twentieth century, and lived out their lives there. They appear to have had a young family with them, possibly the family of their son Robert: according to Deer Isle records, a school operated on Burnt Island in 1842 (Clayton Gross, *Island Ad-Vantages*, May 14, 1976). Henry must have died shortly before 1850, for there is another flurry of conveyances about this time. The last deed I have seen on which his name appears is dated 1846; it is a conveyance to Noah Barter, whose relationship to Henry is unclear to me. It was Robert Barter who apparently inherited principal interest in the island, including the farm; since he had himself been living on Wreck Island for some years by this time, he sold his interest to James Turner of Isle au Haut in 1849 (Hancock 126/479).

James Turner owned Burnt Island for the next thirty-odd years. He appears in the federal census for 1850 through 1880, with his wife Ann and households as follows: three males and five females (1850), five males and six females (1860), three males and two females (1870), and three males and one female (1880).[70] It is not certain, however, that the family *lived* on the island, though the farm was in use. The Walling map of Hancock County in 1860, for instance, does not show James Turner on Burnt Island; D. Kent (of whom I know nothing) is the only resident shown at that date. Dr. Noyes, Deer Isle genealogist, notes several settlers at unspecified dates: William Coombs, whose daughter is said to have been born there (Family histories: Coombs); and (from Bester Robbins) a William Benson and Timothy Hutchinson sometime after mid-century.

There is some ambiguity, then, about residence on Burnt Island in the last half of the nineteenth century: How many families lived on the island at any one time? Did they also have homes on Isle au Haut, perhaps their principal homes? Claims of residence, I believe, should be treated with caution. The indisputable facts are that James Turner owned and farmed the island successfully for more than thirty years. In addition to being a successful farmer, James Turner was also a prosperous trader ("huckster" was the unflattering designation given him in the 1870 census). The 1862 tax record for Isle au Haut does not show him especially affluent (see page 357), but the 1882 record does: he owned one of the most expensive homesteads in the plantation and paid the highest resident tax, by a wide margin (see page 359). The agricultural census of 1880 itemizes his produce on Burnt Island: five acres under tillage, twenty in meadowland, one hundred and fifty acres unimproved, fifteen tons of hay harvested annually, and a flock of one

[70] There was another James Turner on Isle au Haut, two years senior to this one and normally listed as James Turner I: he was a sea captain, and his wife was Matilda (or Martha). The two are often confused in public records.

This photograph shows the west half of Burnt Island off the north end of Isle au Haut, about 1900; the original Barter homestead, which still stands, is visible at the left end of the island with a barn behind it. Pell Island is in the near background, to the left; McGlathery is in the distant background, center, and Spruce Island to its right (just visible). The Burnt Island Thorofare, once the passage for the Rockland-Bar Harbor ferry, lies between Burnt Island and Birch Point in the foreground. (Courtesy of Charles B. Lakin.)

hundred and fifty sheep (see page 472). This was significant husbandry.

The Colby atlas of 1881 shows, in addition to the Turner farm on Burnt Island, an iron mine on the south shore near the stone wharf (in reality, it was located just south of the westernmost tip of the island). It could not have operated for long, to judge from the meager evidence of it today.

The Turners quit the island during the 1880s and sold to Patrick Welch, a non-resident, from whom title passed in 1890 to Charles C. Beaman, one of the founders of the summer colony at Point Lookout on Isle au Haut. The farmhouse was still in sturdy enough condition for residence, and after some repairs by yet another Turner—Clarence—Mr. Beaman persuaded Captain H. Yatts Cain, then living on the east side of Isle au Haut, to move onto Burnt Island as resident caretaker. The Cains were intimately connected with Burnt Island for the next fifty years. Alice Cain Crowell, later a resident on Kimball Island, was born there in 1897. Her mother died there in 1900, and after her death the four Cain children were sent to Sedgwick for their schooling while Captain Cain remained on the island. He fished and farmed, in addition to his light caretaking duties, and sold produce at Point Lookout. Alice Cain returned to the island with her husband, Captain Jack Crowell, in the 1920s and lived there intermittently during his polar voyages (see page 364) until World War II. As friend and confidante of Mary Beaman Holmes, who succeeded her brother William Beaman as owner of the island, Alice Crowell took part in organizing many of its celebrated festivities, including the Holmes's golden wedding anniversary in 1847: hundreds of guests were ferried for the occasion from Point Lookout, Stonington, and elsewhere to the stone

Yatts Cain family and homestead on Burnt Island (Isle au Haut), 1895. Left to right: *Captain Yatts, Helen, Charles (in high chair), Arthur on Geneva Turner Cain's knee; the farmhouse still stands.*
(Courtesy of Revere Memorial Library, Isle au Haut.)

landing on the southwest shore (now abandoned); an all-Negro band, meanwhile, was the focus of the entertainment. It was doubtless the most formidable celebration Burnt Island had ever known.

Finally, if plumbing may be said to deserve an historical note, it is of interest that the "modern" bath fixtures in both the old farmhouse and the log cabin constructed by the Holmes on the north shore of the island came from Oliver Wendell Holmes's house, which was being dismantled in Boston in the 1930s; Mary Beaman's husband was a descendant. The island and its buildings were passed on to Mary Beaman Holmes's descendants, who made it their summer home through the twentieth century.

Fog

The earliest name given to this island was *Webb's*, presumably after Seth Webb or one of his descendants, though I have discovered no record that any Webb ever held title to the island or lived there. It is so named on Rufus Putnam's survey of the "Isle of Holt Division" in 1785 (Hancock Plan Book II: 23) and appears thus in a deed from the Commonwealth of Massachusetts to Asa Turner in 1818, the sale price given as $53.03 (Knox Lands 2/20). Thereafter, in recorded deeds through most of the nineteenth century, it is called *Fogg Island*, and the spelling is so consistently the same that but for the careless orthography of those days, one naturally wonders whether the island might have been named after some earlier settler of that name, of whom there were several in Blue Hill Bay, rather than for the mists that frequently enshroud the area. But I know of no Fogg who lived there.

There were, however, early settlers. The earliest was probably Thomas Cutter, who is shown in the federal census of 1800, aged over forty-five and possibly with spouse (the census-taker's listing is obscure). Cutter is noted, without his given name, by George Hosmer (*Sketch of Deer Isle*, 179) as the first settler of the island. He is said to have drowned attempting to land cattle on the island from his gundelo; lost with him were a Mr. Sheldon, his wife, three children, and a "colored man named Hall."[71] The next settler, according to Hosmer, was John Crockett; he, too, was drowned off the island, within sight of his family, while sailing to Isle au Haut. His wife, Rebecca Carter of Brooklin, was subsequently supported by the town of Deer Isle (according to correspondence between Deer Isle and Sedgwick, dated March, 1829, and cited by Dr. Noyes, Family histories: Crockett and Carter).

This is the sum of our knowledge of residence in the first half of the century. The island continued to be owned by Turners: Asa conveyed to James II for $125 in 1836 (Hancock 133/42, recorded only in 1868). The Turners apparently used the island for grazing and perhaps timber, but did not live there; at least the Isle au Haut tax bill to James Turner II for the island in 1873 mentions no buildings.

Dr. Noyes's informant David Robbins names two residents on Fog Island, sometime after mid-century: one "Scotch" Robinson (unclear whether the sobriquet is after the nationality or the malt), who married an aunt of David Robbins; the other, David Eaton, a bachelor who died eventually at Duck Harbor. I find no confirmation of Robinson's residence, but David Eaton may be confused with David *Easton*, an eighty-year-old fisherman listed in the 1880 census in the household of DeForest Bennett. The latter is listed specifically as on "Cutter's or Fog Island": a twenty-eight-year-old farmer, with wife Gloria and a household of six. Bennett is listed in the 1882 tax list as paying the poll tax, but I know nothing more of his activities. One further residence is reliably reported in the 1870s, presumably before Bennett's: that of Peleg Thomas, a Rockland fisherman, who spent two years on Fog Island (after three on Merchant) with his wife Hannah and four young children.[72]

[71] One of Dr. Noyes's informants, David Robbins (not the most reliable), makes Sheldon the first settler, not Cutter; he also notes the drowning off the island.

[72] The source here is Mrs. Matthew Holland in a 1917 interview with Dr. Noyes; Mrs. Holland was brought up on Merchant Island and went to school with the Thomas children.

There are, thus, reports of up to half a dozen settlers or households on Fog Island in the nineteenth century, and it is probable that there were as many again, especially during the three or four decades in mid-century when we have no reports of residence. Why were there not more settlers, and why, when they came, was their residence so brief? One reason surely was the drownings, assuming they have been correctly reported. Such tragedies discourage settlement, needless to say. But equally important as a reason for meager residence on the island, is the probable cause of the drownings in the first place—at least for Thomas Cutter's: the island is awkwardly positioned for landings. The incoming seas over Popplestone Ledge are barely broken before they surge into the only manageable "harbor" on the east side of the island; outside this cove the strong tidal eddies are hazardous in foul weather and dangerous even in normal conditions. None of the inhabited islands in the area—York, Burnt, Kimball, Merchant, McGlathery—had handicaps comparable to Fog's.

In 1876 James Turner II, who had owned the island for forty years, mortgaged to two Bangor men, apparently paid up the mortgage, and then in 1879 conveyed for $400 to Henry C. Sproul of Eden on Mount Desert (Knox Lands 2/308 and Hancock 170/118). Sproul, who owned property on Isle au Haut and on neighboring islands, may have had grand designs for Fog Island—a resort (to complement the inn he and Edward DesIsle built on the east side of Isle au Haut), a farm (like the one he started on Merchant Island), even quarrying (for in 1886 he mortgaged to Job Goss, the Deer Isle contractor)—but nothing came of his plans. Buildings, including a barn, are mentioned in deeds of this era, but no significant activity is reported. In 1896 Sproul sold to Albert Small of Isle au Haut, and Small is charged for the island in tax records for the next decade or so.

Sheepgrazing, as far as I have been able to discover, has been the only significant activity on Fog Island in the twentieth century. The Smalls were running sheep on the island in the early 1900s (according to Harvard Ingraham, a descendant of the Conleys on York Island, who used to help shear the sheep on Fog Island before World War I). And sheep owned by Bruce Eaton of Stonington were still on the island in the 1990s, according to a later owner. The center of the island is still open, with several springs and dry wells showing, along with the corral for shearing, but spruce are slowly crowding in.

York

This is an island with layers of history stretching back to Revolutionary times. The name *York* is given to the island on surveys completed by Rufus Putnam in 1785 (Hancock Plan Book II: 23), which means that Captain Benjamin York of White Island in Eggemoggin Reach—also called York Island at one time—had already acquired title. "Claimed title" might be more appropriate, for the State of Maine, according to a detailed report on island ownership in 1914, never acknowledged that York Island was properly conveyed by either Maine or Massachusetts (see Maine, Forestry Commission, *Report*, 1914).

There is no good evidence that Benjamin York lived on his island (though Dr. Benjamin L. Noyes makes the hypothesis—Family histories: York). Another early settler clearly did: Moses Staples, according to Rufus Putnam's island census of 1785, was living on the island, having arrived the same year (see Appendix 1).[73] He evidently did not stay long. In 1793, according to Swans Island historian Dr. Small (pages 75–79), Moses Staples moved from Deer Isle to Swans and remained there the rest of his life; he died in 1846 at the age of ninety-three.

Another reported settler, again a transient, was Abner Coffin Lunt, forebear of the Lunts of Long Island (Frenchboro). He was woodsman, farmer, and coaster and lived in many places

[73] Putnam also shows Moses Staples on Deer Isle, where he had been living since 1764; Putnam may have intended to show Staples's residence on York Island as seasonal rather than year-round.

during his short life: Scarborough, the Fox Islands, and Pretty Marsh, where he died. In 1791 he is said to have spent the winter on York Island with his son Amos; they reportedly built a log cabin, chopped wood, hunted and trapped, and used their small fishing schooner for transportation (T. B. Lunt, *Lunt Family*, 129).

Neither Moses Staples nor Abner Lunt laid claim to the island, so far as is known. Benjamin York, who did, sold it in 1798 to James Cooper, Jr. of Vinalhaven for $240 (Hancock 20/469). According to an 1877 account of early settlers on Isle au Haut by W. G. Turner, a lifelong resident on the east side of the island, James Cooper, Jr. lived on York and "it went by the name of *Cooper's Island* for a long time." There is no need to doubt the latter statement, but I am doubtful about Cooper's *permanent* residence there, since there is much evidence to suggest that the Coopers—James the father, James the son, and many others—lived more or less continuously in the Indian Point sector of North Haven from the 1780s on; it is more likely that James Cooper, Jr., like Moses Staples before him, used the island seasonally for fishing and perhaps for pasturage. In 1822 James, still said to be of Vinalhaven—that is, North Island—sold the island to George Kimball of Isle au Haut (Knox Lands 2/36), and in 1824 Kimball sold to Joseph Knowlton. The price in the latter conveyance—$700—suggests that improvements had been made by this date (Knox Lands 4/526).

A period of some twenty-five years follows when title to York Island passed back and forth between the Knowltons, Joseph and Robert, and Henry Wilson, during which time both Wilson and Robert Knowlton are believed to have lived there periodically. I will pass over a sequential treatment of the recorded deeds and attempt to reconstruct residence on the island from other sources. Henry Wilson, who had one of the original lots on the east side of Isle au Haut, is described by Dr. Noyes as a trader who operated from York Island and lived there at the head of the harbor, that is, on the site of what later was the Conley house, which Noyes indeed describes as a remodeling of the original Wilson homestead. Robert Knowlton (Noyes makes no mention of Joseph) was the eldest son of an early settler on Isle au Haut who drowned, leaving Robert to take charge of the family. The Knowltons settled first at Reunion Farm on the east side of Isle au Haut; in the mid-1830s, to simplify the care of his flock of three hundred or more sheep, Robert swapped his farm for Henry Wilson's island and moved into the latter's homestead there (Noyes, Family histories: Knowlton). The mortgage deed that appears to cover this transaction is dated 1835 and refers to "all the buildings and improvements" on the island, which is further evidence that York was inhabited at this time—at least seasonally (Knox Lands 5/35). The Knowltons lived on York Island for about six years and, according to Robert's daughter Lourania Knowlton Stinson (as reported by Dr. Noyes), two children were born while they were there: she herself was one, and the other was Ezra, who died in infancy and was buried beside his grandfather on Isle au Haut. The Knowltons removed to Webb Cove on Deer Isle in the early 1840s; their fortunes, which were by no means strained on York Island, apparently were further improved by a legacy from a wealthy relative in Boston. Robert died on Deer Isle in 1877 at the age of eighty-three.

York Island, as far as I am aware, had no regular habitation from the 1840s to the 1870s. This may explain the curious absence of any buildings shown there on the 1860 Hancock County map: some of the Knowlton buildings may already have burned or been taken down, and the rest left in such poor repair that they were overlooked by surveyors.

There is a further clue respecting residence on York Island—that is, seasonal versus year-round residence: the normal habit along the coast was for islands after a few years to take the name of current settlers. Had Knowltons, Wilsons, or any others lived on the island year-round, this would have been reflected in the name. Apart from the short-lived name *Cooper's Island* (noted above), York Island was never called anything else.

In 1847 York Island had been acquired by a newly arrived Irish settler in the region, Patrick Conley; he bought from Henry Wilson, who had either held title from his earliest association with the island in 1825 or foreclosed on Knowlton mortgages (Hancock 120/382). The island remained in the Conley family for a century and was inhabited by Conleys for more than half of that time. Since a fair amount is known about their residence on York Island from descendants—in particular, the late Augusta (Gussie) Conley Ingraham and her son Harvard—I dwell in some detail on the Conley era, both for its own inherent interest and as an indication of what life on islands in the late nineteenth century was like.

Patrick Conley arrived from Nova Scotia and settled on the east side of Isle au Haut in the late 1840s or early 1850s.[74] He married Helen Turner, a neighbor, and they had eight children. Patrick was primarily a farmer. He accumulated a large flock of sheep and used York, as well as other outlying islands, for their pasturage. He himself never lived there, but after his death in the mid-1870s his sons built the two-and-a-half-story frame house above the harbor that became the center of York Island's economic and social life and remained a landmark for more than forty years.

The Conleys appear in census schedules as follows (age is at first appearance; spouses are in parentheses; Fa means farmer, Fi means fisherman; males in household are to left of slash, females to right).

Householder	**1870**	**1880**	**1900**	**1910**
Patrick Conley, 55 (Helen), Fa	6/4[75]	6/5[76]		
Davis F. Conley, 45, Fi			1/0	1/0
James T. Conley, 43 (Edwina), Fi				2/3[77]

Conleys also appear in Isle au Haut tax schedules: in 1862 Patrick appears with modest holdings, before the family moved to York Island; in 1882 Helen Conley has the most expensive homestead in the plantation, the usual oxen and livestock, and her tax is the second highest of Isle au Haut residents (see pages 356 and 358).

[74] He may have come with a brother, William, who appears in the 1860 census schedule on Kimball Island.

[75] The family was living at Reunion Farm on the east side of Isle au Haut in 1870.

[76] Helen Conley, Patrick's widow, is head of the York Island household in 1880.

[77] There is another household on York Island in the 1910 schedule: a fisherman, Peter Jacobson, and his wife Mary. I know nothing about this couple.

Richs Cove on east side of Isle au Haut, with York Island in background, 1890s. (Courtesy of Revere Memorial Library, Isle au Haut.)

As early as 1879, Isle au Haut town records show three pupils in a school on York Island (all Conleys, one imagines), and in 1880 Lizzie Conley, who had recently returned from Castine Normal School, is listed as the teacher. Although several of Patrick and Helen's children lived on the island at various times after they reached maturity, James was the only married Conley to settle there. His wife was Edwina Page of Belfast, whose family moved to the east side of Isle au Haut when she was sixteen.[78] James and Winnie lived with Helen Conley until after the birth of their second child, then built their own home on the harbor shore. This house was still standing in the 1990s. When the oldest of their four children reached high school age, Winnie moved to Camden for the school year. James remained on the island and the family was reunited during the summer months and school vacations. But York Island was more their home than Camden, to judge from a census of 1910 that lists James, Edwina, and one child, Walter, as still residents on the island, along with Davis (Chatto and Turner, *Register*). Augusta Conley Ingraham was on the island in 1906 when her first child, Harvard, was born (apparently the last born on York), though she is shown in the 1910 census, together with her siblings Raymond and Gertrude, as having left home. Some years later, in the 1920s, James and Winnie wintered regularly in Florida, returning to the island each spring for the fishing season. James was more fisherman than farmer, fishing most of his life from a peapod; he also kept weirs. But even more than fisherman or weirman, James was responsible for the wharves and storehouses that flourished in the 1890s and for a time thereafter. He died in Camden in 1939, after being taken from the island by the Coast Guard, too late to arrest the severe case of pneumonia he had contracted. Winnie died, also in Camden, in 1947.

Davis Conley was the island's most steadfast resident. A bachelor all his life, he is described as calm, even phlegmatic, where James was excitable. He was predominantly a fisherman and an excellent sailor, hauling his traps for many years from a Friendship sloop. He lived with Helen in the big house and after her death in 1896 stayed on there,

[78] According to a child of this pair (Augusta, or Gussie, who first heard the story in her cradle), it was a case of love at first sight, James being hopelessly smitten as he assisted in the unloading of the Pages' effects at the landing near Richs Cove.

Fishing fleet in York Island harbor, 1890s; the large dwelling at left is Helen Conley's. (Courtesy of Revere Memorial Library, Isle au Haut.)

frequently joined by his sister Lizzie, who was also unmarried. Davis was active in plantation affairs—that is, on Isle au Haut—and served for several years as selectman. He was a gregarious sort and sometimes showed up at meetings wearing a Prince Albert and a derby hat. "Quite a character!" Richard S. Bowditch writes of him in his memoirs (Revere Memorial Library). One January night in the late 1920s, when Davis was living alone on the island, the kitchen stove apparently overheated and the house was burned to the ground before help could arrive. Davis was dazed but unhurt. He continued for a time to live in one of the other buildings on the island, but later moved to Richs Cove on Isle au Haut; he was apparently the last year-round resident on York Island until modern times. Davis was drowned in the 1930s while fishing from a peapod somewhere out beyond the Turnip Patch (fishing grounds south of the island)—no one knew where; his peapod was recovered near Matinicus.

I would like to return now to York Island Harbor in the last years of the nineteenth century, an era of great activity in the fishing industry there. Deer Islanders, compelled by those unwritten laws of territoriality that only fishermen themselves understand to fish the waters east of York Island, often used the harbor there as their base. Before the time of gasoline engines, the round trip by sail to the fishing grounds from Green's Landing or Southeast Harbor on Deer Isle consumed the better part of a day, and the excellent harbor at York accordingly became of great importance to the Deer Islanders. During any weeknight of the summer season, as many as two dozen fishing vessels might be found there; on weekends the Deer Islanders normally returned home. A smack from Rockland usually spent the week at York buying fish as they were brought in.

The Conleys, needless to say, played their part in catering to the needs of this transient community of fishermen. James added a store to his house on the shore, and Winnie kept accounts. Four cabins were built along the inside of the harbor to rent to fishermen who wished to live ashore, and additional boarders may have been accommodated in Helen's house or at James and Winnie's; an item in the files at the Revere Memorial Library indicates that J. T. Conley could accommodate up to twelve guests at $7 a

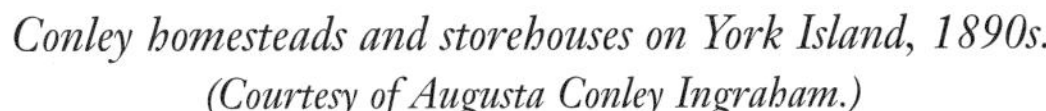

Conley homesteads and storehouses on York Island, 1890s.
(Courtesy of Augusta Conley Ingraham.)

week. My impression is that most of the boarders at the Conleys were summer vacationers or, in season, duck hunters whom the Conley boys would row out to Great Spoon Island. A large wooden pier was built along the west side of the harbor, with fish-drying sheds and several warehouses for bait and other supplies. How much the Deer Islanders were indebted to the Conleys for these various services is suggested in Helen Conley's obituary notice in the *Ellsworth American* of February 27, 1896: a special steamer, it was said, was hired expressly to carry Deer Island mourners from Green's Landing (Stonington) to the funeral service on York.

With the coming of the first "make-and-break" gas engines early in the 1900s, the need of a seaward base for the Deer Isle fleet lessened, and activity at York's harbor gradually declined. The smack from Rockland, or its motorized successor, continued to come to York Island periodically as late as the 1930s, for Gussie's son Harvard Ingraham, who was born in 1906, used to come out on it when he worked seasonally on the island; by this time, however, the heyday of the harbor was long passed.

James Conley, having acquired sole title to York Island during his lifetime by buying out his siblings' interests, left it to his two sons, who sold it after World War II to a Boston doctor; the doctor and then his heirs ran sheep on the island until the early 1980s when they sold to a young couple from Stonington with three children. This family built a home on the east side of the harbor and lived there seasonally, some years through December. He was a lobsterman and fished from the island; they also raised sheep (thirty-five to forty at last count). Several of the old buildings still stand at the head of the harbor, including a much reworked version of James Conley's homestead. A new barn has risen on the foundation of the old; a new wharf rests on the crib of the original landing. Life on York Island has not stood still.

Conleys of York Island

Note: Prepared with the help of Augusta Conley Ingraham and her son Harvard.

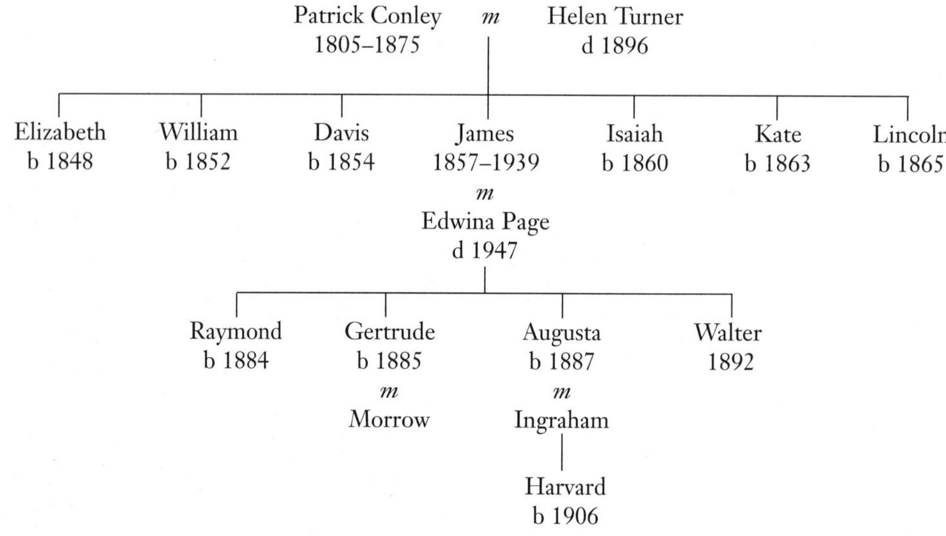

Great and Little Spoon

The Spoon Islands is the name given this seaward pair in the Isle au Haut Division of 1785 (Hancock Plan Book II: 23). The larger of the pair was deeded before 1824 to John Rich, who settled on the northeast end of Isle au Haut; Rich sold to Sewall Watson of Castine in 1829, calling it Large Spoon Island (Hancock 62/433). Watson apparently sold to David Thurlow of Crotch Island, for either David or his son David conveyed two acres to the United States government for a lighthouse. Margaret Hundley, a descendant, dates this sale by David Thurlow at 1838 (from family records); an 1876 conveyance from Henry Brookman to Henry C. Sproul, land traders from Bucksport, refers to the sale by David Thurlow at an unspecified date (Knox Lands 2/314). Nothing came of the light station. The 1876 conveyance included Great Spoon—less the government's two acres—along with Eastern Ear and numerous lots on Isle au Haut. I do not have a full record of subsequent conveyances, but another Bucksport man, O. P. Cunningham, defaulted on taxes for his half of Great Spoon in 1901, and it was seized by the Plantation of Isle au Haut (Knox Lands 3/412). The owner in the last decades of the twentieth century acquired the island in 1965 from a New Hampshire man, who had bought it sight unseen and was discouraged when he went out to look it over. (This owner, incidentally, has heard a curious local name for the island—*Fill Boat*—but has no idea of its origin.)

Little (or Western) Spoon, meanwhile, was

Looking northwest from Great Spoon Island (near foreground) to York Island and north half of Isle au Haut, May 1972; Merchant is the longish island beyond Isle au Haut, southwest corner of Deer Isle to right, Camden Hills in distance over North Haven; most of the mid-Penobscot Islands are visible in this unusual aerial perspective. (Photo by Robert Hylander.)

originally owned by Daniel Gilbert, an early settler on the east side of Isle au Haut, who sold to Patrick Conley in 1839—that is, eight years before Conley acquired York Island. The high price he paid for this small island, $100, suggests that the fishing grounds must have been very valuable off Great Spoon, for Conley surely would not have paid this price for pasturage, if indeed he had sheep at the time; in later years the Conleys used Great Spoon as well as Little for pasturing their sheep, and descendants are under the impression (a false one) that the family owned both. Grazing has continued on these islands until recent years.

Eastern Ear and Western Ear

These austere islands off the two southern tips of Isle au Haut have been used principally for the fishing privilege and have normally been owned or leased by Isle au Haut fishermen. Eastern Ear, *Island B* in the Isle au Haut Division, is shown on an updated map of the division in 1824 as "deeded to D. Gilbert" (Hancock Plan Book II: 29). This would be Daniel Gilbert, born in 1785, who settled on a lot on the eastern shore of Isle au Haut opposite York Island and remained there until about 1850 (Hosmer, *Sketch of Deer Isle*, 194). Gilbert sold to Henry Brookman of Bucksport, who owned numerous island properties in the Matinicus group, and Brookman in 1869 sold to Henry C. Sproul, also of Bucksport (Knox Lands 2/249); the island continued to be leased to local fishermen from Head Harbor. Ivan Calderwood (*Days of Uncle Dave's Fish-house*, 232) tells a legend of Eastern Ear that I pass along without vouching for its authenticity. A fisherman, lost in his dory from a Portland trawler off Isle au Haut when the weather suddenly thickened one October day, attempted to reach Head Harbor, but failed; he came ashore on Eastern Ear where he was later found, his clothes torn off him by the seas and his only identifying mark the letters "W. C." tattooed on one arm. He was buried there, but his body was later claimed by relatives and removed.

Western Ear, called *Head Island* on the earliest surveys, was first conveyed from the State of Maine to Ebenezer Leland of Duck Harbor for $5 in 1824 (Knox Lands 2/65). Record of this deed, however, was apparently not discovered by state officials when reviewing ownership in 1874, preliminary to an auction of coastal islands. Western Ear, it was found, was first claimed by Benajmin Merithew, who made improvements on it; he conveyed it to Ebenezer Leland, who conveyed to his son-in-law John Harvey, who deeded it to his son James, who sold to Job Goss of Crotch Island, who returned it to James Harvey, who willed it to his widow. All of these claimants, except Goss, were residents of the south and southwestern shores of Isle au Haut. John Harvey, a brother of George Harvey of Russ Island, lived for many years at Duck Harbor; his son James is said to have lived for a time on the Ear itself, before he drowned en route to Green's Landing. The State of Maine acknowledged the claim of Emily Hamilton Harvey, James's widow, and formally deeded Western Ear to her for $8.60—reflecting an increase of $2.60 in the value of the island over fifty years (Maine Archives, "1874 Island Sales"). It still belonged to Harvey descendants in the 1990s. The skeleton of a fish shack, many generations removed from Benjamin Merithew's "improvement," still stands facing the half-tide channel used by lobstermen.

Saddleback Ledge

Island N is the designation of this island in the "Isle of Holt" Division of 1785, and it is marked "sold" (Hancock Plan Book II: 23). The buyer is not named, and unless the "sold" was added at a later date, it is difficult to imagine who would wish to possess this almost unapproachable rock. (This was long before the seaward islands and ledges were acquired for fishing rights.) The sale appears not to have materialized, for in 1837 Massachusetts and Maine jointly deeded Saddleback Ledge to the United States government for a light station; the price was $10 (Knox Lands 5/83). The tower was erected in 1839 on an appropriation of $10,000 (raised from a $5,000 estimate the year before). This made Saddleback Light one of the most expensive in Maine.[79] The inspectors were, in any case, pleased with the work: a Civil Engineer singled out Saddleback Light in 1842 as "the only establishment on the coast of Maine that possesses any claim whatsoever to superiority over its fellows. It is the only such structure in New England erected by an 'architect and engineer'" (National Archives: Saddleback file).

The first keeper was probably Watson Hopkins; we know that his daughter Margaret was born there in 1844 (Winslow, *Fish Scales and Stone Chips*, 249). In 1852, when a party of Castine yachtsmen visited the island, the keeper was Mr. Burgess[80]; this was presumably Samuel Burgess, who moved the following year to Matinicus Rock and was the father of the legendary Abby Burgess (see page 60).

[79] Matinicus Rock Light in 1827, for instance, cost $4,000; Negro Island Light off Camden cost $5,000 in 1834.

[80] *Wilson Museum Bulletin*, Castine, Winter 1974–75, including a diary of the cruise.

Saddleback Ledge Light, off Isle au Haut, showing rig for plucking passengers off arriving vessels and swinging them ashore, date unknown—but this light was manned from the 1830s to the 1960s.
(Courtesy of Deer Isle Historical Society.)

The Saddleback Ledge station was surely one of the most hazardous and lonely on the Atlantic coast. The island is barely large enough to hold the tower and equipment necessary to keep the light operating; there is no soil of any type on the ledge. In the great storms, when the island was awash, the keeper and his family were obliged to retreat to the tower. A keeper in 1927 (W. W. Walls) reported that after a storm he picked up 124 dead seabirds, blown into the tower with such force that they fractured the light. Landing on the island was always a chore, since there was no wharf and the sea plunged to great depth on all sides. In 1885 a "landing derrick" was installed: a boom that was operated from the island and swung out over the water to pluck the newest arrival from the waiting tender, or deposit on deck some happy departee. Still, despite its hazards, I believe there never was loss of life from accidents on Saddleback Ledge.

In the twentieth century the family keepers gave way to crews of three or four males working in shifts; the length and frequency of their letters in the Lighthouse Column of the *Maine Coast Fisherman* in the 1940s are testimony to the tedium of their assignment. But if they grew lonely, there was the comfort of seeing seven other lights from the Saddleback station. Count 'em, next time you are out there after dark: Monhegan, Matinicus, Two Bush, Eagle, Mark, Goose Rock, and Isle au Haut; were it not for Eastern Ear off Isle au Haut, you could probably see Mount Desert Rock as well.

Saddleback Light, after being manned for a century and a quarter, was automated in the 1960s.

Keepers of Saddleback Light, 1871–1912

Note: The following partial list of keepers and assistant keepers at the Saddleback Light Station from 1871 to 1912 is drawn from files at the National Archives.

Keeper	Dates	Keeper	Dates
James H. Orcutt	1871–86	Henry C. Neal	1902–07
George W. Blodgett	1886–98	Jerome C. Brown	1907–09
Fred J. Rich	1898–1902	Verney L. King	1910–12[81]

Assistant Keeper

1871–86: A total of eight assistant keepers served during these years, all but two for less than two years:

Charles A. Gott	1876–81	Thomas H. Orcutt	1883–86

1887–98: A dozen assistant keepers served during these years, including:

Roscoe Lopaus	Will C. Tapley
Levi L. Farnham	Charles E. B. Stanley
Herbert C. Richardson	Fred W. Marong, Jr.
William H. Thompson	Charles W. Thurston

1902–12: The following assistant keepers served during this decade:

Name	Dates	Name	Dates
Charles A. Burke	1902–05	James V. Calderwood	1908 (1 mo.)
Marmal R. Newman	1905, 1908	Willie W. Corbett	1908–10
Thomas L. Godfrey	1903 (3 months)	Leo Allen	1910–12
Edward E. Dyer	1906 (2 months)	Fred T. Robinson	1912
Raymond D. Randall	1906–07		

[81] Served as assistant keeper, 1903–09.

Islands of the Eastern Shore

Sears Island to Naskeag Harbor

The islands treated in this division span six townships, and so have little in common, except for the cluster near Castine. Castine was the earliest European community in the Penobscot Bay region and settlers were on the islands in Castine, or Pentagoët, Harbor before written records existed to help us identify them. Castine takes its name from Baron de Castin, a French settler of the late seventeenth century.

The name of the river, or estuary, that empties into Castine Harbor, the Bagaduce, formerly Majabigwaduce, has a more obscure origin. Fanny Eckstorm (*Indian Place-names*, 193) traces it to Micmac for "big tideway river"; she ridicules all other explanations, including Williamson's suggestion (I: 71) that it is named after a French major who once lived in the area. Whether she is right or wrong, the various spellings given to the river by early cartographers and mariners confound any amateur in Indian place-names: e.g., *Majebeguadeaux*, *Mecha Baguadooz*, and, within a page and a half of one voyager's journal in 1776, these three variations: *Margarbagadooze*, *Margerbagadooz*, and *Majorbagadeuz*.[1]

Eggemoggin Reach similarly had many strange spellings: *Algomongin*, *Algamolgen*, *Edgemaroggan*, and so forth. Fanny Eckstorm (page 204) believes the word means "fish weir place." Naskeag, said to mean "extremity" in local Indian dialect, had European settlers at the end of the seventeenth century and was one of the most frequented harbors in the region before the Revolution; its multiple spellings include *Nusket*, *Neskege*, *Naskig*, *Nascheague*, and for many years in eighteenth-century charting, *Nesky*.

The islands are dealt with clockwise around the eastern periphery of Penobscot Bay, beginning with Sears Island and ending with Mahoney in Jericho Bay.

[1] Joseph Holt's journal of a Penobscot Bay voyage, *New England Historical and Genealogical Register*, X: 30, 1856.

Sears

Fannie Eckstorm insists with such vigor (*Indian Place-names*, 67) that the Indian name for this island was *Wassumkeag*, for "bright sandy beach," that it requires some courage to oppose her. Searsport historians, however, do. The late William H. Pendleton, for instance, a former president of the Searsport Historical Society, acknowledged the meaning of the Indian name but questioned its particularity; that is, *Wassumkeag* meant any "bright sandy beach," not necessarily the one on the east side of this island. (From correspondence with author in 1982; William Pendleton also questions whether this was the *Awassawamkick* or *Hazel Nut Island* where, according to Fannie Eckstorm again, an early French settler, Monsieur Gaulin, lived.[2])

Captain John Smith, meanwhile, on a rough map he made of the mouth of the Penobscot River in 1616, called both this island and the

[2] The names come from a report in the papers of Samuel Penhallow, chronicler of the first Indian war (1676), who was sent to see "monser gaulin" in 1703 about an indignity to a son-in-law of Sieur de Castin at Naskeag; *New England Historical and Genealogical Register*, 34: 90. Searsport historians do not question Penhallow's mission; they merely doubt that Hazel Nut Island was the island in question.

larger island up the river (*Orphan*, now Verona) *Gunnell's Islands* (Map 1616 Smith). We know that Smith anglicized all "savage" names in the region, so the latter designation—which is never found again—may have been after a member of his expedition. The only other names I find associated with the island in charting before the 1760s appear on a map drawn in 1754 (Johnson): here two names that convey nothing to me are shown on the east and west sides of the island, respectively, one evidently designating Stockton Harbor and the other Mack Point: *Giles Harbor* and *Goose Faro*.

If all these early names are eliminated for one reason or another, our island remains nameless until the eve of the American Revolution when the name *Brigadier* is authoritatively attached to it on the British Admiralty chart "Atlantic Neptune" (1776). Which brigadier it is named for is in question: Brigadier Samuel Waldo, owner of the Muscongus Patent which included the island; or Brigadier Jedediah Preble, first commander of neighboring Fort Pownall who owned extensive lands adjoining the fort. Samuel Waldo, Jr. received from his father's estate numerous islands, among them "Preble Island in Giles Harbor, 861 acres"—which seems clearly to be our island, though Waldo is not known to have lived there.[3]

The erection of Fort Pownall at the mouth of the Penobscot River in 1759 and the Treaty of Paris four years later, which ended the French and Indian War, opened the inner bay to settlers. It was not many years before they reached Brigadier Island. The "Atlantic Neptune" shows no settlers, but it is likely that one or two families were there by the mid-1770s. Alice V. Ellis, historian of Stockton Springs, writes (*Story of Stockton Springs*, 23) that an early settler in the area, Samuel Griffin of New London, Connecticut, arrived in 1775 and "the first winter he lived for a while with the family of Job Pendleton on Brigadier Island." It is likely that she confuses the Pendletons: the only known Job Pendleton in this era settled in 1769 on what is now named Job Island off the southern end of Islesborough, and to my knowledge he never lived elsewhere (Farrow, *History of Islesborough*, 239); Peleg Pendleton, however, an uncle of Job, is believed to have built a house on the mainland facing Brigadier Island in about 1775. At approximately the same time, according to the island's principal historian, Joel W. Eastman,[4] James Nichols built a home on the south end of the island. Nichols, then, would be the first known settler, on the eve of the Revolutionary War.

The war disrupted the normal development of Brigadier Island. Fort Pownall on the adjoining peninsula was razed in 1775 to keep it from falling into the hands of the British; in 1779 the British occupied Castine across the bay, and the American expedition sent to recover the town suffered disaster. One of the fleeing American vessels, the brig DEFENSE, sought refuge in Stockton Harbor, but was pursued there by a British frigate and sunk (Map 1779 Penobscot Expedition). The English remained in the area for several years after the war, awaiting settlement of the eastern boundary—that is, whether the St. Croix River or the Penobscot—but by the mid-1780s earlier settlers were returning and new ones arriving. Six families are believed to have been residing in 1790 on Brigadier Island, by then a part of Frankfurt Plantation, incorporated in 1789. They were those of Nathan and William Griffin, William and Jonathan Staples, Alexander Young, and William Pendleton (Eastman, 19).

Henry Knox, some years before he retired as Secretary of War in 1794, had acquired the Waldo Patent through his wife, a granddaughter of Samuel Waldo; much of the early history of Brigadier Island revolves around his personal interest in it. In 1792 he commissioned a French mineralogist to prepare a report on his Maine lands, including Brigadier Island, on which the Frenchman reported seven families in residence; in 1794 or early 1795 Knox himself came onto the island for the first time. He reportedly paid the squatters six shillings each for their labor and gave them a year to leave.[5]

[3] For this detective work on the island's name I am indebted to the late William H. Pendleton and his colleague Robert Brooks, who discovered the partial distribution of Samuel Waldo's estate in the Massachusetts Archives.

[4] *A History of Sears Island*, 1976 (see Bibliography for full listing). This notice draws from Eastman's well-researched booklet.

[5] The exact number of settlers and who they were is uncertain: Eastman puts the number at seven, the six listed above, from the 1790 census, plus Benjamin Carver; Dr. Benjamin Lake Noyes, citing a 1794 "deed," notes six residents—Thomas Pendleton, William and Nathan Griffin, and William, Jonathan, and Alexander Staples (the conveyance explicitly notes Benjamin Carver is not a resident), and says that the quitclaim bounty was ten shillings to each (Noyes, Family histories: Staples).

Correspondence between Henry Knox and his agents at the "grazing farm" he created there suggests the husbandry of the era.[6] A letter from Knox in 1794 to William Griffin asks the latter to serve as caretaker, with instructions that the island be kept brush free and in good order, that the residents be restrained from cutting more than one cord of wood apiece, that Griffin buy sheep for Knox and care for them, and that he keep intruders off the island. Reports in 1796, relayed from John Gleason (Knox's principal supervisor in Thomaston), note various activities and personalities on Brigadier Island: an estimated thirty-five thousand cords of standing timber were available on the island, half spruce, half hardwood; a dock was proposed west of the half-tide bar; the wreck of a vessel off the island appeared to have a sound hull but the four cannons in her forecastle were destroyed (this was presumably from the ill-fated American expedition against Castine in 1779); a Mr. Lathrop had cut eighty tons of hay and fifty-three cords of wood for the Boston market; Lathrop—evidently a tenant, or possibly the farm manager—had made 595 pounds of cheese and 179 pounds of butter (of which he had consumed, respectively, 205 and 49 pounds). Knox's correspondence in 1797 with John Rynier, an agent living off the island, outlined his ambitious plans for his island farm: one hundred head of cattle within four or five years, two to three hundred sheep, extensive crops of corn, oats, barley, and rye, initial expenses to be defrayed by the fishery (Eastman, 24). The farm, needless to say, never achieved this level of productivity.

From 1799 to 1802 the farm manager on Brigadier Island was John Witherspoon, nephew of the president of Princeton University and presumably a Knox family friend. His reports indicate the gradual decline of the enterprise. In December 1800 he reported that high winds had damaged much of the standing timber, torn away banks along the shore, blown down two buildings at the south end of the island, and ripped the roofs off several barns. Should he stay on the island any longer, Witherspoon asked? if so, he needed help. The following August he wrote Knox more cheerfully that the livestock were doing well. He wanted to know about next winter's wood: an estimated hundred cords could be cut. How much did General Knox himself want? Should the rest go to Boston (that is, for sale)? In October 1801 Witherspoon corrected a mistaken report to Knox that he was taking down one of the barns: he was simply repairing it. What was the rumor, he asked in return, that Knox will "let the island the next year"? He hoped, if this were so, that he could continue as caretaker.

A year later, Knox's far-flung ventures in Maine had put him heavily in debt, and Brigadier Island was advertised for sale. Some of the farm equipment, including twenty-seven sheep and hay, netted $304.40 at a sale (according to an item in the Knox Papers).[7] The island itself was valued (by Knox's appraiser) at $28,870, but of course no buyer came forward at this figure. Title passed to a creditor in 1804 and from him, two years later, to the Massachusetts traders Thorndike, Sears & Prescott. It was David Sears, apparently as beguiled by Brigadier Island as Henry Knox had been, who bought out his two partners in 1813, three years before he died. The island remained in the Sears family for more than a century and in due course took the family name, as the town itself did when it was incorporated in 1845.

David Sears, Jr., inheriting his father's extensive properties both in the Waldo Patent and elsewhere, never lived on the island, but, as his father had, he maintained and expanded Knox's farm. A series of managers ran it—William Ritchie in mid-century, for example, with his wife, ten children, and three paid hands. Five children are shown in an island school in 1846, eight in 1850, with Mr. Ritchie as school agent (Searsport town records). According to the agricultural census of 1850, there were one hundred and fifty acres of improved land on Sears Island, four oxen, seventeen cows, eight of them milking, fifty-six sheep, and assorted crops—something less than Henry Knox had envisaged, but a very respectable farm for that era nonetheless. Tax figures for 1867 show compara-

[6] The correspondence is in the Knox Papers at the Massachusetts Historical Society, especially letters dated August 29 and 30, 1794; October 21, 1796; December 20, 1800; August 30, 1801; October 28, 1801; November 16, 1802; and January 6, 1806.

[7] John Witherspoon—who bought a ram at the sale—was still on Brigadier Island in 1802, but he acquired Butter Island about this time and spent the rest of his life there (see page 244).

ble livestock and a real estate valuation, including two dwellings, of $12,670—only three other residents of Searsport had higher valuations in 1867 (principally for vessels owned).

David Sears III *did* live on the island—at least he summered there. His residence, built on the southern tip in 1853, appears on the 1859 topographical map of Waldo County. The family lived in a certain style, one gathers from an account of an 1871 cruise in the region that refers to a stopover at Brigadier Island "where Mr. Sears had sent his yacht" to greet the cruise party (letter at Northeast Harbor library). A map surveyed in the 1870s shows a road down the center of the island linking the two clusters of farm and residence buildings, various other roads branching off to the shore, and half a dozen weirs at the southeast tip (Map 1882 CGS 311). These were presumably salmon weirs, salmon having been netted, speared, and weired from the island during their annual run since the time of earliest settlement.

David Sears II and III died within a few years of each other in the 1870s, and the island passed briefly—for eleven days, to be precise—out of the family's hands, but it was reacquired by David Sears IV and his brother Henry. David IV continued to summer there and to maintain the farm, Eastman tells us; indeed, the farm expanded during the 1870s, to judge from the agricultural census of 1880: one hundred and forty acres of tilled land, six hundred acres of pasture and orchard, fourteen milking cows, seventy-five sheep, and an overall valuation of $17,650. Thereafter, however, the Sears's interest in the island appears to have waned. The farm was leased during the 1880s and 1890s to Levi A. Dow, a cattle breeder, who evidently kept a magnificent herd of longhorns, but it was a herd he brought with him, not native to the island. In 1893 the Sears summer home burned, and this ended the family's residence on the island. A dozen years later, the Bangor Investment Company, a subsidiary of the Bangor & Aroostook Railroad, bought Sears Island from David Sears IV for $55,000 as part of a proposed rail and ocean terminal extending from Cape Jellison to Searsport. Franklin W. Cram was the architect of the grand plan, and it projected for Sears Island a recreational and resort area. Pending materialization of this project, the farm buildings were kept intact and leased to Charles Cayting, who hired local farmhands to run the still large establishment. Fire struck the island again in 1917, destroying most of the buildings at the farm; although some were rebuilt by the Bangor Investment Company, at Cayting's request, this marked the end of significant farming

Painting of farm buildings on Sears Island as they appeared about 1916; the painting is by Gertrude Sylvester Gordan, who spent several years on the island in that era. (Photographed by Little Letterpress Co., Searsport.)

on the island. Cayting himself became bankrupt in 1922.[8] A succession of leases during the next ten years brought other transient occupants to Sears Island, most of them more interested in pulpwood—or possibly rumrunning—than in farming. In 1934 the farm buildings, having fallen into disrepair through neglect and vandalism, were razed to reduce the fire hazard. Since then the island has gradually reverted to its natural state.

If the demise of the famous farm on Brigadier/Sears Island is moderately depressing, a project for the island in the twentieth century has been positively blood-curdling for conservationists: a vast oil and cargo terminal that would dwarf Franklin Cram's scheme of the 1890s. How would Henry Knox and David Sears feel about this enterprise? Better not ask: they were, after all, among the formidable developers of their respective eras.

[8] An article by Gertrude P. Gordon, daughter of a farm manager in 1916–17, is in *Maine Life*, September 1973; it describes the farm at the time of the 1917 fire.

GROUP I: Islands at Castine

Nautilus

This island had several names before Nautilus. One, according to Castine's historian George A. Wheeler (page 40), was *Bank's Island*, after a pre-Revolutionary settler in Castine named Aaron Banks. Another was *Cross Island*, because a Jesuit priest is said to have been killed and buried there as early as 1654 (Doudiet, *Majabibwaduce*, 102). This is the name used in some accounts of the Battle of Castine in 1779, but other accounts of the siege give the island its present name, after one of the three British war sloops initially assigned to defend the town.[9] (The naming of an *American* island after a *British* war vessel during the Revolutionary War, it should be said, could only have occurred in Castine where loyalist sentiment was strong.)

Nautilus Island, then uninhabited, played a minor part in the events of 1779. It had been the site of a small British battery after Castine was seized in June. When the American forces arrived six weeks later to raise the siege, the island was quickly taken and its battery enlarged to harass the British, still entrenched across the Bagaduce; Paul Revere, artillery officer for the American force, was in charge of strengthening the battery, the ramparts of which are still discernible.[10]

There is only fragmentary evidence about residence on the island before the middle of the nineteenth century. A post-Revolutionary surveyor (John Peters), for instance, reported "a house and family and considerable improved land" on the eastern end of the island (notes by Surveyor Peters, no date, transcribed by Ellenore Doudiet at the Wilson Museum in Castine). By the 1830s buildings—still standing at the end of the twentieth century—were said to have been constructed for fish curing operations; the flakes were set up on the meadow above the cove facing Castine (Doudiet, 102). I have not discovered the names of these early settlers or employees on Nautilus Island. Doubtless they are in census schedules for Castine—and after 1817 for Brooksville[11] —but not distinguished from the

[9] In London recently I looked up the subsequent career of the NAUTILUS at the Public Records Office. In June 1780 it was judged to be no longer in serviceable condition and so was scuttled by its then master, Thomas Farnham, in Halifax—less than a year after the famous battle (letters from Thomas Farnham).

[10] The Battle of Castine itself, which was a failed effort by American naval vessels and privateers, hastily assembled in Boston and ports eastward, to eject the British from the Castine peninsula, ended in the scuttling of most of the American fleet up the Penobscot River. It has been considered the greatest American naval disaster before Pearl Harbor (e.g., *Harvard Magazine*, July-August, 1979, p. 26). Two of the best first-hand accounts by participants are: General Solomon Lovell (the American troop commander), in *Weymouth Historical Society*, 1, 1881; and John Calef (a local Loyalist), *Siege of Penobscot*, New York: William Abbott, 1910 (reprinting of a 1781 account).

[11] When Brooksville was incorporated in 1817, unbarred islands remained with Castine (e.g., Holbrook); barred islands, like Nautilus, were assigned to the township to which they were barred—in this case, Brooksville. It made no difference that ties between Nautilus and Castine were always closer than those between Nautilus and Brooksville.

Waterfront at Castine, looking toward Brooksville, 1880s; the steamer in background is the FRANK JONES. *(Courtesy of Deer Isle Historical Society.)*

West end of Nautilus Island from the eastern arm, c. 1890, showing the Williams cottage, pier, and the GREAT EASTERN, *H. G. Williams's private steamer. Many of the buildings date from the fish-curing business on the island earlier in the century. (Courtesy of Ellenore Doudiet.)*

residents of the mainland. The *existence* of a community of some sort on Nautilus Island can be taken for granted in the first half of the nineteenth century: Castine in this era was the busiest coastal port east of Wiscasset; it fitted out and sent forth to the Banks fisheries up to five hundred fishing vessels a year. It is not imaginable that a spacious and gracious island across the harbor could have remained unappreciated and unused.

By the late 1830s activity on the island can be traced in deeds. In 1839 Andrew Gray, a farmer on the peninsula to which Nautilus was barred and who claimed the island, sold it for $625 to William Witherle and John H. Jarvis, Castine business partners (Hancock 66/255). The fee was a considerable one for the era and suggests a certain level of development on Nautilus. William Witherle was the more active of the partners and, in the 1850s bought out the Jarvis interest (Hancock 104/213).[12] The new firm was operated as Witherle & Co. until the 1870s. Curing fish continued to be the principal activity on the island. William Witherle owned a fleet of schooners which he provisioned at his stores in Castine proper and which unloaded their catch on Nautilus; after drying, the fish were stored in

[12] The sale excluded a five-acre lot on the westerly point of the island that had been sold to the United States government for a light station (Hancock 104/548); this station was eventually established at Dices Head across the mouth of the harbor.

Aerial photo of Castine Harbor, May 1975: Nautilus Island at center right, Holbrook beyond to right, in front of Cape Rosier. Many of the mid-Penobscot Bay islands are visible at the top of the photo—from Pickering at the left to Colt Head on the right. (Photo by Robert Hylander.)

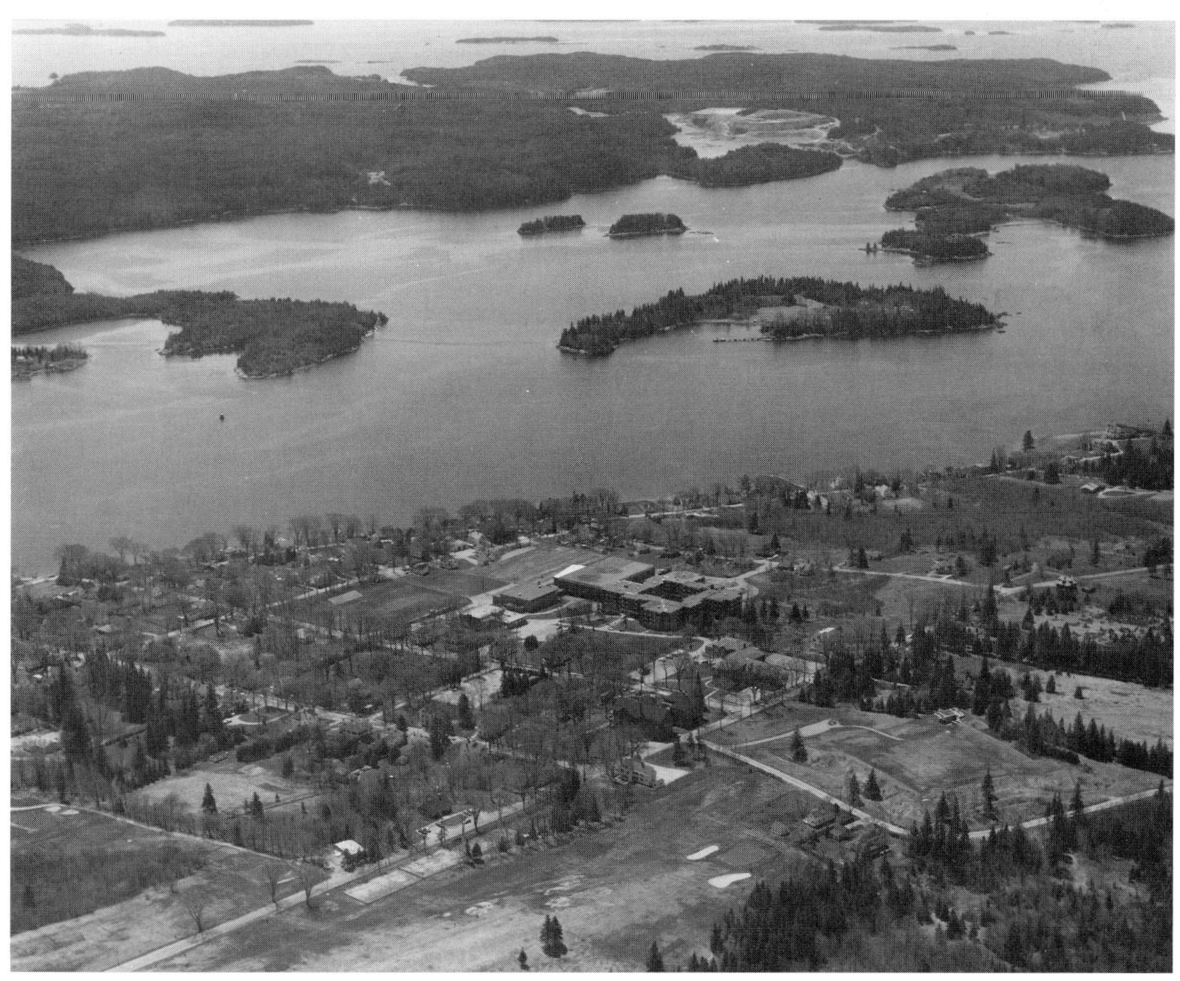

sheds along the cove. A dwelling was built for an overseer and his family. An early overseer for Witherle was Benjamin Coombs of Castine, who in due course opened his own fish curing establishment in Castine itself, facing Nautilus Island. A cousin, Jesse Coombs, succeeded him; he appears on the island on the Walling map of Hancock County in 1860 ("J. Cooms") as well as in the 1870 federal census for Brooksville: aged sixty-five, fish-curer, with wife Dessie, and a domestic, Abby Howard. Another superintendent of the fish works—possibly an assistant to Coombs—was Rufus Ames, whose children were visited periodically by a Castine youngster who has left the fragmentary record of the Witherle enterprise summarized above.[13]

Brooksville tax records show a gradual decline in the valuation of the island from the 1850s to the 1880s: $1,600 and $1,700 in the 1850s (Witherle and Jarvis), $1,200 in 1868 (Witherle alone),[14] $800 in 1874 and 1882 (William and George Witherle, respectively). Livestock were shown on the island only in 1868: one horse and one cow.

In 1872 Witherle & Co. put the island up for sale, advertising it as "an excellent situation for Farming or Fishing or a very fine location for a Summer Residence." In addition to the farmhouse, there was a barn, storehouse, and a wharf; the stock consisted of a horse and two cows.[15] Ten years later the island was sold to Henry C. Williams of Brooklyn, New York, who built a summer residence there in 1883.[16] The Williams family conveyed Nautilus Island to J. Howard Wilson in 1906 (Hancock 438/438). Mr. Wilson, who had summered for some years in Castine, remodeled the Williams "cottage" which served his family as a summer residence through World War II.[17] Since 1948 the dwelling has been the year-round residence of Mr. Wilson's daughter, Ellenore Doudiet, curator of the Wilson Museum on the facing shore of Castine.

I close with mention of Noah Brooks's tale, "The Waif of Nautilus Island," first published in *Scribner's* in 1872 (4: 65), though I do not fit the characters in his tale to any known residents of the island: From the wreck of an "East Injiman" on Man o' War reef (unidentified) a spar washes ashore onto Nautilus Island with a dead man and a living child, aged about two, who calls herself Mamie. The elderly couple living on the island, Miah and Thankful Morey, take Mamie into their family and raise her, along with an orphaned nephew, Obed. Many years later the mystery of Mamie's identity is solved when from a plank washed ashore with her bearing the last three letters of the vessel's name, USA, it is discovered that she was a passenger on the ARETHUSA, lost on a voyage from Calcutta to Boston. She is reclaimed by an uncle, lives for a time in the city, but in due course returns to Nautilus to marry Obed, to whom she was promised. All does not end happily: Mamie later drowned, Noah Brooks tells us, while crossing the bar against an incoming winter tide.

[13] The visitor was Fannie M. Hibbert, born in 1850, who left her informal account in 1917 (copy at the Wilson Museum). The particular visit she reports was in 1862.

[14] The island is named *Noodles* in this tax return, a name that attached to the island for some years—I do not know why.

[15] *Castine Gazette*, June 1872, reproduced in *Wilson Museum Bulletin*, II: 1.

[16] The 1886 valuation of the island was $2,000, up $1,200 from four years before; a few sheep had been added to the horse and cow.

[17] Brooksville Grays returned to Nautilus Island in the 1920s as resident caretakers for the Wilsons: first Truman, then his son Herbert. Elaine Gray (now Austin, daughter of Herbert) was born on the island in 1928.

Mill

The tidal mill that gave this island its most enduring name existed so long ago that even the spillway to channel the tidewater is barely discernible. The mill had ceased to operate by 1800. Other names for the island are the surnames, and sometimes given names, of residents either on the island itself or on the Brooksville peninsula to which it is barred: *Nina White's Island*, *Jarve's* or *Jarvis Gray's Island*, *Ina Gray's Island*. The Grays (or Greys, the spelling was interchangeable) were moderately prosperous farmers on their peninsula. Abner Gray, for instance, had an eighty-acre farm in 1868, with oxen, cows, and eight sheep, and he kept a horse and carriage; his valuation was $906, which placed him in the top bracket of Brooksville taxpayers.

Although Grays were associated with all four of the islands barred to their peninsula (Nautilus, Mill, Hospital, and Rogers) and claimed each of them at one time or another, title was often held by outsiders. Mill Island, for instance (identified only as "an island near Andrew—or Abner—Gray's"), was owned by a non-resident named John Snowman, according to tax records from the 1850s to the early 1880s; its value remained constant at $50. In 1882 William Jarvis Gray bought the island, built a home there, and settled in with his family for nearly a quarter of a century. He left the island, with its single dwelling, to a bachelor son Maurice, who in turn left it to descendants who still use the island in season. A Gray owner in the 1970s assured me that the island had been in the family since the 1820s and that there was an informal understanding that things would stay that way, with a further understanding that there would be no commercial development. At last report the Grays were seeking to have the name of the island formally changed from Mill to Grays.

With respect to "commercial development," it was a near thing for the Grays a hundred years ago. But for an economic recession in the 1890s, Mill Island might have become the hub of an elegant resort planned for Gray's Point by developers. A blueprint of the project in the possession of the current owners shows a road layout, a dozen or more commodious sites for inns and summer homes, and a pier for excursion steamers. The scheme, happily for the Grays, came to naught.

Hospital

The name of this island[18] is said to come from a quarantine station there. I have discovered no records to verify the existence of such a facility, yet do not doubt some such usage. Castine was a very busy port in the first half of the nineteenth century and would have had to maintain, if not precisely a "quarantine station," at least a sector of the harbor where stricken ships could anchor. The name *Hospital* was well fixed by mid-century, as evidenced by Fitz Hugh Lane's well-known painting of 1852, "Castine from Hospital Island." George A. Wheeler, in his 1875 history of Castine (page 71), calls it *Hospital* or *Noodle Island.* [19]

The record of habitation on Hospital Island is meager, and perhaps there was never year-round residence to warrant the census-taker's notice. Frequent use of the island, however, must be taken for granted in so busy a port. Persons taxed for the island in Brooksville records are: William F. Woodward, $150–200 in 1852–54; R. H. Bridgman, $50 in 1868 for "Woodard's I." The Walling map of Hancock County in 1860 shows a dwelling on the island, but the name of the family in residence is indecipherable—probably Woodward. The Grays of Grays Point, however, were never far off when title was at stake, so it is not surprising that Abner and Stanley Gray sold to Dr. Willard C. Collins of Bucksport in 1882 for $200 (Hancock 184/535).[20] The island, owned by Dr. Collins, was assessed at $50 in 1886.

The low valuation of Hospital Island after the Woodwards suggests that the dwelling and perhaps other facilities burned. The cellar hole still visible on the island is a sizable one; there was a dug well (still in use, according to the present owners), a stone pier on the east shore, and there were apple trees. There is, in short, evidence of a modest husbandry in mid-century which had faded by the 1880s. The only other local use of the island I know of was early in the 1900s when Horatio Crie of Criehaven, or Ragged Island (who was later to become Commissioner of Sea

[18] Hospital Island is shown improperly on recent editions of the Coast and Geodetic Survey (No. 13309): the name on the chart denotes Rogers Island; Hospital Island proper is west of Rogers, separated on the chart by a two-foot depth.

[19] I believe Wheeler errs in the latter name: in Brooksville tax records of the 1860s, *Noodles* is an alternate for Nautilus Island. I have also seen Nautilus spelled *Notless* in deeds (e.g., Hancock 123/565), a rendering of the name that could readily become *Noodles*.

[20] Despite such conveyances, a Maine Forestry Commission report as late as 1914 stated that the island had never been properly deeded by either Maine or Massachusetts (Maine: Forestry Commission *Report*, 1914, p. 160).

and Shore Fisheries), kept his gear there when weir-fishing in the vicinity.

In the 1930s the island was acquired as a summer property by Owen and Ethel Staples, who built a cottage at the north end between the old pier and an ancient Indian shell heap. In due course title passed to relatives, who plan to use the island as their predecessors did.

Islands in Castine Harbor off Brooksville shore: the photo is taken from Mill Island, with Hospital Island in the mid-distance and Rogers Island in background. (Courtesy of Maine Historic Preservation Commission.)

Castine Harbor in winter, 1904, schooners frozen solid in rare Bagaduce ice.
(Courtesy of Maine Historic Preservation Commission.)

Rogers (or Moores)

This island, east of Hospital, is not named on contemporary charts (or—rather it is *mis*-named "Hospital I." on CGS 13309). Indeed, I find only one map on which it does appear: in the 1881 Colby atlas of Hancock County, which calls it *Great Island*. Great Island appears on some deeds, also *Big Island*, and more often than not *Moores Island*, after Daniel Moore. Daniel farmed it during much of the last half of the nineteenth century. He acquired it in 1855 from Timothy and Lewis O. Fernald, paying $800 to each, a considerable escalation in the value of the island in the five years since it had been conveyed from Andrew Gray to Timothy Fernald for $300 (Hancock 93/534 and 100/202-3).[21] A road from the bar to the "highway," on Gray's Point, is mentioned in the 1855 conveyance, suggesting that the island had already been inhabited when Daniel Moore bought it. The following valuations on "Fernell's Island" are found in Brooksville tax records, chargeable to Daniel Moore: 1868, $200; 1874, $100; 1886, $75. These are modest valuations indeed for an island of this size and cause one to question Moore's enterprise.

A deep well, nearly 30 feet, at water's edge on the south side of the island, on what was called Big Island Cove, was reportedly used by schooners to replenish their casks before voyages. This well, still in use today, probably predates Daniel Moore's residence. The foundations of the Moore homestead are still visible in the center of the island, though the house itself, according to the present caretaker, Kenneth Howard, was moved many years ago to Castine. A house is

[21] Timothy Fernald is shown in the 1850 census as a sailor, aged fifty-five, with a family of nine and $1,600 real estate valuation—but it is not indicated whether he was living on his island.

shown on the island on Walling's map of Hancock County in 1860.

George D. Moore, a descendant of Daniel, sold Big, or Moores, Island to Mary E. Warren in 1907 (Hancock 445/116), and she sold it to Frank F. Read, a summer resident in Castine, soon thereafter. The father of a recent owner acquired the island in 1910, and the name currently in use comes from this family. Local residents used the island periodically into the 1920s, and even had small camps there, but since 1930 the Rogers family has itself been in residence—first in a cottage built that year and, after this building was destroyed by lightning, in the present cottage constructed in 1970.

Holbrook

It will surprise no student of the history of Castine that this commodious island at the entrance to the Bagaduce had early habitation. *How* early—leaving aside Indian occupation—we cannot say for certain, but the "Atlantic Neptune," which was surveyed before the Revolution, shows settlers on the island at that time: two homesteads in one edition, three in another, all at the south end facing the shore of what is now Harborside. There is no indication who these early settlers were. The island is unnamed on these British Admiralty charts, but another English map of the area, drawn by a British officer during the Battle of Castine in 1779, shows the island as *Bakeman's* (Map 1779 Penobscot Expedition). The Bakemans, a Dutch family already established at this time on Cape Rosier, owned the island, and one or more of them may have lived there. The island was also called *Smart's Island,* apparently after John Bakeman's brother-in-law who, according to Ellenore Doudiet, owned part or all of the island at one time; it is not known whether he lived there. In 1783 John Bakeman sold Smart's or Bakeman's Island for £150 to Jesse Holbrook, described as a mariner (Hancock 2/99). Jesse Holbrook, we know, settled on his island and lived there until his death in 1791: his gravestone, which still stands, explicitly states that he died there. Jonathan Holbrook, probably Jesse's son and heir, sold the island in 1801 to Elisha Dyer, a wealthy investor in Castine; the fee was $750, which suggests significant improvements by that date (Hancock 8/193).

Residence on Holbrook Island is obscure during the early decades of the nineteenth century—and, indeed, it is possible there was no regular habitation. In 1820 John Witherspoon of Butter Island acquired a mortgage deed on the island from the heirs of John Perkins (Hancock 47/454), but we know that Witherspoon spent his entire adult life on Butter. Title returned to Robert Perkins, John's son, in 1823, and the latter apparently sold to Benjamin Hook of Castine. In 1832 Benjamin Hook is shown in Castine tax records as owner of "Holbrook's Island," valued at $600; he also owned a "house and garden" in town, valued at $600, as well as $1,200 in neat stock—a significantly high valuation. Some confusion arises between the identities of Benjamin Hook, Sr. and Jr.: in 1834, Benjamin, Jr., who is listed the year before with only a modest home in town (valued at $100), is shown as owner of Holbrook Island; in 1839 he is shown with the island (then valued at $800), the house in town ($1,200), and a horse and carriage ($330); and in 1841 he is still shown with the two properties—the town house and the island—with slightly lower valuation. By 1850, however, Benjamin, *Sr.* owned the island, valued at $600 with cattle at $95 and sheep at $80; he had no town residence.

It would be easy to imagine that Benjamin, Jr. simply became Benjamin, Sr. when his father died, and moved his residence to the island—but we know the ages of the two Benjamins from census and family records. Benjamin, Sr. was born in 1783, son of Josiah, and died only in 1862; Benjamin, Jr. was born in about 1810. He is shown in the 1840 federal census for Castine, in his forties (should be thirties), with a household of eight. Benjamin, Sr., whom I do not find in the 1840 census, is in the 1850 census, the last household listed in Castine proper, which I assume to be on Holbrook Island. The household is worth listing in full, for it includes several surnames which figure in the island's history:

Benjamin Hook,[22] 63, farmer
Abraham Moor, 45, farmer
Henry J. Neyman, 20, farmer
Harriet Neyman, 18
Lucinda Murray, 18
Maria Smith, 16
Lucinda Holland, 63
Julia Holland, 6
A. C. Brown, 23, shoemaker
John Pettingill, 48, laborer
Robert Bowden, 41, mariner

In 1860, Benajmin Hook, Jr. and Sr., are in the same household: Benjamin, Sr. is seventy-five, Benjamin, Jr. is fifty-one, "book-keeper." It is not clear from the census listing where the household is located—that is, whether on the island or in town—but, according to a local physician, Benjamin, Sr. is known to have died on the island in 1862 (Journal of Dr. S. L. Stevens, at the Wilson Museum in Castine).[23]

Who, then, comprised Benjamin Hook's extended entourage on Holbrook Island in 1850? Abraham Moor (or Moore) appears in deeds affecting the island as early as the 1830s. In 1834, for instance, giving his address as "Pickering Island," he was deeded by Benjamin Hook for $25 the following properties: a lot in Castine, an undivided half of Holbrook Island, as well as Pickering Island itself and two small adjacent islands (Hancock 58/460). At that price the transaction was a quitclaim—or a joke—but why? I have found no explanation of this conveyance, but twenty years later Abraham Moore came into legitimate possession of the island: In 1853 Benjamin was obliged to surrender title to Holbrook Island to Joseph Redman of Brooksville on order from the Supe-

[22] The surname is spelled with and without an "e" in tax and census records.

[23] I am indebted to Ellenore Doudiet for calling this journal to my attention.

Ferry from North Castine to Brooksville, before there were passable roads around the upper Bagaduce.
(Courtesy of Maine Historic Preservation Commission.)

rior Judicial Court—presumably for a bad debt; Redman conveyed to Frederick A. Hook (a son of Benjamin, Sr.), and Frederick in 1856 conveyed for $171 to Abraham Moore, together with the mortgage and note (Hancock 100/171 and 102/225). Abraham Moore is listed in Castine tax records as the owner of Holbrook Island through the 1860s, with valuations on the island of $600 (or less), livestock between $60 and $90, and $100 for fifty sheep. He was still in Benjamin Hook's household in the 1860 census.[24]

[24] A recent owner of Holbrook Island, Anita Harris, recounted many colorful tales of Abraham Moore: Crestfallen over his expulsion from Yale just before his graduation, he came first to Pickering Island, then to Holbrook, to live out the remainder of his blasted life; he wore a beard that reached to his waist, donned seven shirts in the autumn which he kept on until spring, and whiled away the winter evenings scraping at his fiddle and inlaying canes—a quite explicit portrait of an 1830s dropout.

Castine Harbor from South Brooksville, looking northwest across Smith Cove, 1885. (Courtesy of Maine HistoricPreservation Commision.)

Castine from Nautilus Island, c. 1890; the shed on the shore was built in mid-century by Witherle & Co. (Courtesy of Maine Historic Preservation Commission.)

The Neymans (next in the Benjamin Hook household in the 1850 census) present a different problem. According to Anita Harris, a life-long resident of Holbrook Island (whose report has currency in local circles), the Neymans, born on Holbrook Island, were the natural children of Benjamin Hook and his inamorata, a Mrs. Ryder née Cilly. There were as many as half a dozen children born of the union, at least three of whom died of diphtheria. The name "Neyman," Anita Harris argued, was chosen to hide their identity (pig Latin, she said, for "nameless"). The mother appears not to have been on the island in 1850 or 1860, but a "Mrs. Neyman" is said to have died of tuberculosis on the island in 1863, fourteen months after Benjamin Hook's death (Dr. Stevens's journal). Henry J. Neyman, meanwhile, was deeded the island in 1858 by Benjamin Hook, subject to the mortgage to Joseph Redman noted above and another to Charles J. Abbott (Hancock 107/397, recorded in 1863). If there was a cloud on Benjamin Hook's title, Henry J. Neyman removed it, for it was from him that Edward K. Harris of Boston bought the island in 1893—to inaugurate a new era in the island's history (Hancock 269/109).

Henry J. Neyman is shown as "of California" in the 1858 deed, and he was indeed in California at that date, according to Anita Harris, having joined the Gold Rush earlier in the decade. He apparently returned, for he is noted as living on Holbrook Island in an 1885 mortgage deed (Hancock 203/245). Anita Harris has stated that he married a wealthy Brooklyn widow and eventually left the area. Lucinda Neyman, the only other surviving child of Benjamin Hook and Mrs. Ryder, lived much of her life on the island.[25] She was educated at the Bucksport Seminary. Anita Harris, who remembered the elderly spinster from childhood, described her as a "resourceful and lovable character." Lucinda spent her last years at a nursing home in Bangor and is buried on Holbrook Island (1827–1909).

The surname Holland—Lucinda, sixty-three, and Julia, six, are in Benjamin Hook's household in the 1850 census—is a familiar one on Holbrook Island: the 1840 census shows a Mary Holland, in her fifties, head of a household on the island—one male, two females. I have not identified these Hollands, nor the other members of the 1850 household. Two *surnames* reappear in Benjamin Hook's household in 1860: Amanda *Smith*, forty-eight, domestic, and Charles *Brown*, ten.

This is a patchy record of residence for so important an island. All that we can be certain of is that Hooks were intimately associated with Holbrook Island for half a century and they or their retainers lived there for much of this period. Locally the island was known as *Hook's Island.* The island's valuations remained constant at $600 through the mid-1960s, then dropped by 1870 to $360. Farming appears to have given way in the 1870s and 1880s to pulping operations conducted by Will Hook, a grandson of Benjamin, Sr. and a Castine merchant; maps printed in the early 1880s show numerous structures at the southwest tip of the island, possibly buildings to house the lumbermen.[26]

When Edward K. Harris bought from the Neymans in 1893, most of the earlier buildings were in disrepair and had to be torn down. The Harrises built their own barns, wharf, roads, caretaker's cottage and home, and farmed the island. They and their descendants were in more or less continuous residence on Holbrook until Anita Harris's death in 1985. Her will stipulated that her house be taken down and that the island be given to the State of Maine as a "wildlife and natural area." The Holbrook Island Sanctuary includes, in addition to the island, a large tract of land on the Brooksville shore.

[25] She may indeed be the Lucinda *Murray* in the 1850 census, misnamed by the census-taker; the difference in Lucinda Murray's age and Lucinda Neyman's was only a few years—not an unusual error in census-taking.

[26] A final note on the Hooks: Jeanette Eustace Hooke, legal widow of Benjamin, was shown in the 1870 census, aged eighty, living in the household of her son Frederick A. Hooke.

Group 2: Eggemoggin Reach and Naskeag

Harbor (South Brooksville)

The protected harbor formed by this island leads to a presumption that it was visited by mariners long before there was settlement at South Brooksville. Fogbound or overtaken by darkness en route up Eggemoggin Reach to Castine,[27] early navigators must often have sought temporary shelter behind Harbor Island, and once at anchor, the sailors must have roamed over the island for distraction. We can merely imagine these first visits by passing voyagers, for there is no record or evidence of them.

We are equally unsure of the earliest settlement on Harbor Island, but it can be taken for granted that the active use of it dates from the earliest settlement at South Brooksville in the eighteenth century. Surely the island was cut over for cordwood, as all islands were in Revolutionary or post-Revolutionary times, and it is probable that cattle, sheep, or hogs were pastured on Harbor Island early in the nineteenth century. This is still hypothesis, be it said, for I have not yet discovered a clear record of habitation on Harbor Island before the 1870s.

In 1871 Robert Condon sold the island to George N. Howard for $225, reserving for himself the right to take fifty cords of "merchantable wood" from it during the next two years (Hancock 138/534). Both Condon and Howard were shown as of Brooksville, and this suggests that neither of them was then living on the island, which was part of Castine.[28] George Howard, or one of his family, apparently settled there during the 1870s, for the Colby map of Hancock County in 1881 shows "G. H. (N?) Howard" living in a homestead at the head of the northeast cove of what was called *Buck's Island*.[29] Another map of the same era shows this homestead as well as another building near the south shore, and the center of the island partially cleared (Map 1882 CGS 309). A recent owner confirms that the homestead, or "cottage," was occupied year-round by a Howard family in the last years of the nineteenth century.

There is, then, reason to believe that Harbor Island was occupied by Howards for some twenty-five to thirty years. The absence of stone walls and of a significant cellar hole at the site of the dwelling indicates that they were not farmers, and indeed Harbor Island would have provided very meager farming compared to the mainland. What occupation the male Howards followed I do not know. A young resident on the shore opposite the island in the 1880s recalls George Howard, the father, a son named George, and two daughters.[30] Their home was apparently unpainted and their existence marginal. The house remained standing into this century, but it was not again occupied after the Howards died or removed. Title to the island passed between various members of the families of Jeremiah Jones, Melvin Chatto, and others, evidently for sheep raising and possibly as investment. The only other commercial venture on the island—at a somewhat later date—was a two-year experiment in raising foxes, an experiment that failed.

In 1927 two summer residents at South Brooksville, Franklin T. Kurt and Charles E. Gibson, bought the island to prevent its being cut over for pulp and thereby becoming a scenic blight. Since Mr. Kurt and Mr. Gibson were the first non-local owners of Harbor Island, the prospect of a higher tax return raised the long-

[27] I once debated with a maritime scholar whether, in sailing "up"or "down" Eggemoggin Reach, one was on a northwesterly or southeasterly course. Living at the Naskeag end of the Reach and facing daily "down" it as I composed these volumes, it naturally seemed that "down" was northwesterly. But mellowing over the years and minding that one does indeed go *down* to the sea in ships and *up* into the interior, I now think my maritime friend has the best of the argument: to go *down* Eggemoggin Reach, one goes southeasterly.

[28] When Brooksville was incorporated in 1817, principally out of the earlier township of Castine, it was agreed that islands barred to the mainland would belong to the township to which they were barred while all others would remain part of Castine; Harbor Island was one of several in the latter category.

[29] The harbor had been known as Buck or Buck's Harbor for many years—after Jonathan Buck, an early settler in Bucksport—but the island was normally called Harbor Island. (Though locally called "Buck's Harbor," the official name of the harbor at South Brooksville is *Buck Harbor*, to distinguish it from *Bucks Harbor* proper in Machias Bay).

[30] Deposition of Mrs. George Chatto, August 1, 1958, in connection with a title hearing on Harbor Island (Courtesy of Herbert T. Silsby II.)

dormant question of which township should properly have jursidiction over the island: Castine, on the basis of its ancient claim to all unbarred islands in the original township; Sedgwick, on the grounds that its dividing line with Castine, before the incorporation of Brooksville, bisected Buck Harbor and implicitly the island as well; or Brooksville, since the island was patently within its confines. The public hearing on the issue produced many learned legal arguments for the three claimants—until the owners indicated it was immaterial to them which township gained jurisdiction so long as that town provided suitable education for any children living on the island. The claims were abruptly withdrawn and Harbor Island remained in limbo, untaxed, until Mr. Kurt's son, having acquired it and wishing to build a summer cottage there, petitioned the State Legislature for remedy. A bill was passed in 1957 assigning Harbor Island to Brooksville, and the ancient dilemma was resolved.

The Kurts had bought out the Gibson interest in the 1930s, and at the end of the twentieth century Kurt descendants still owned the island and used it for summer residence. They rely on the spring-fed "lake" at the head of the northeast cove for their fresh water—much as the Howards did a century ago, and perhaps passing mariners a century and more before that.

Chatto

This island was called *Smith's Island* before the Civil War, presumably after one of the Smiths in Brooklin, who were as numerous then as now. Michael Foram, or Foream or Forham—the spelling of the name changes in the deed—sold to George W. Chatto in 1863, and the latter gave his name to the island. George was born on Long Island in Blue Hill Bay in 1836; he fought with the Union Army in the Civil War and was captured, but exchanged after two years in prison; thereafter he spent twenty-three years in Brooklin in a house at the head of the street leading to the town landing—the island was included with this property. He was a sea captain, among other things, and sailed both fishing and coastal vessels. The family used the island for firewood, grazing sheep, and berrying, but apparently put up no buildings.[31]

George Chatto left Brooklin in 1886 and sold his house and island soon thereafter to a New Yorker who planned to build a summer home there; the idea was abandoned after the death of the latter's wife. George R. Allen of Brooklin owned the island in 1895, when it was valued at $400—and thereafter I lose sight of ownership for a quarter of a century.

In the 1920s William Sholes of Washington, D. C., a cottager at The Haven on Center Harbor, bought Chatto Island at a tax sale. Sholes subsequently sold to another summer resident at Center Harbor, whose descendants still owned this much-used island, with appropriate easements, at the end of the twentieth century.

Chatto forms one of the most protected anchorages in Eggemoggin Reach. One early chart shows an Indian "fort" on the harbor (Map 1721 Coasting Pilot)—though I have heard nothing of any relics. In the latter half of the nineteenth century, the harbor was used by the fishing fleet that fed the McFarland Bros. fishworks; today it is shared by the Center Harbor Yacht Club, the Brooklin Boat Yard, and anyone else able to drop a mooring.

[31] I am indebted to a descendant of George Chatto, Mrs. Harriet A. Lowell, for a copy of the 1863 deed and details about her grandfather.

Little (east of Torreys)

This small island, unnamed on charts, might be omitted from this inventory were it not for the fact that from where I sit it frames my view of Eggemoggin Reach and the Deer Isle Bridge. Slight history attaches to the island. It was owned in the nineteenth century by Babsons and Tainters, who farmed the facing shore. In 1884 the town of Brooklin gave to owner Samuel Tainter permission to build a weir northwesterly from the island. In 1890 Babsons and Tainters sold to a Dr. Francis H. Williams, retaining their weir rights. He camped periodically on the island, which in 1895 tax records was valued at $25. Dr. Williams left the island to a son and daughter in 1938, and two years later they sold to Alan C. Bemis. The protected harbor inside Little Island was for many years the anchorage for one of the best-known and fastest wooden yachts in the bay, Bemis's Herreshoff yawl CIRRUS.

Babson, Little Babson, and the Torreys

These three islands—or four, depending on whether the barred Torreys are counted separately or together—lie protected from open seas inside Eggemoggin Reach, and, to judge from their middens, were much favored by the Tarratine Indians. The legend running between the two clusters of islands and into the northern shore of the Reach, as it appears on British Admiralty charts, reads "Dry at low Spring tide." This is not quite so, but there are more than a few contemporary mariners in the area who, searching for their moorings in fog on a September ebb, would agree the point is well taken.

In the first survey of islands in Hancock County, prepared in 1785, Western Torrey is called *Torreys* and the other three—from west to east—are *Islands C, D, and E*; the first two are shown as having already been sold to Jonathan Tourley (surely Jonathan Torrey) who, according to Hosmer (*Sketch of Deer Isle*, 46), had been settled on the Reach side of Deer Isle since 1763; and Island D is marked as "sold to York" (Hancock Plan Book II: 6). This would be Benjamin York, then residing on nearby White Island. Although the Hancock Plan does not show it, Benjamin also owned the fourth island—then called *George's Island*—having bought it in 1784 from George Goodin of Naskeag, who had owned it, according to his deed, since 1776 (Lincoln 17/91). George's Island is decribed as "twenty acres of woodland"—and if I dwell on this, it is because, becoming part owner of this island myself 170 odd years later just after a logging operation, I have often wondered how many times the island was cut over in the intervening years: twice in this century that I know of, once at least in the last before it was called *Sheep Island*, and probably on other occasions of which there is no record: on the average, say, once every fifty to seventy-five years.

The Torrey islands kept their post-Revolutionary name without interruption that I know of. The Babsons took their name eventually from a family in Naskeag that at one time owned much of the shore opposite the two islands, and the islands as well. Through the nineteenth century and into the twentieth, all four islands were used by a succession of local owners alternately for grazing sheep and cutting cordwood. There is no evidence that any of these islands was ever inhabited, though Babson[32] and Eastern Torrey have modest sources of fresh water.

In this century, ownership of the four islands has passed to summer cottagers, though only Little Babson has been used for residence. There is a nice story associated with this residence. Some years ago—evidently in a fit of absentmindedness—the owners put their island home up for sale, but when they read their advertisement in the *New Yorker*, promptly took it off the market.

[32] Big Babson evidently kept its name *Sheep* through the nineteenth century: Brooklin tax records listed the owner in 1895 as George Law and noted the thirty-eight-acre island, which was valued at $180, as "formerly John Cousin's homestead." Knowing every inch of this island, I must deny there was ever a homestead on it.

Naskeag Harbor, upper right, and nearby islands, at high tide June 1944. Note the shoals that have beset mariners using this famous anchorage for over three centuries: the bar between the mainland and Harbor Island, the ledge west of the bar, the Triangles between Hog Island and the main. Note also the dramatic changes in vegetation in fifty years: Hog Island, bare in 1944, was heavily wooded by the 1990s, while Babson and White islands, wooded in 1944, were bared by fire and logging in the 1970s—and are now slowly making their comeback. (United States Air Force photo, courtesy of Alan C. Bemis.)

Hog (Naskeag)

Early editions of the "Atlantic Neptune" link this island with its nearest neighbor to the east as the *Harbor Islands* of Naskeag. Later editions give the island its present name, a common one at the time and signifying exactly what it says: an island where hogs were kept—presumably from one of the numerous farms along the opposite shore in Plantation IV (now Brooklin). In the Deer Isle Division surveyed in 1785, it is given as *Island F* and was shown as "sold to John Reed" (Hancock Plan Book II: 6); John Reed was the agent for the Massachusetts Commission charged with the disposal of public lands in Maine. In due course the island was conveyed to one of the Smiths of Naskeag. This family was closely associated with Hog Island during the first half of the nineteenth century. In the federal census of 1810, John Smith was living there with a family of six. In 1820 James Gray is shown as head of a family of six on Hog Island. No residents are shown in the 1830 census, but John Smith is back again in 1840, aged fifty-nine, wife Mercy, with nine in the household (six male, three female).[33] This is the last time Hog Island is shown in the federal census, residents thereafter being counted in the Brooklin tally. The 1850 schedule for Brooklin shows the households of John and Ebenezer Smith, both farmers, aged respectively sixty-seven and thirty-four, with families of four (three males, one female) and six (three males, three females). Ebenezer appears in 1852 tax records for Brooklin with a house and barn, one cow, and six sheep; Abraham—who was in his father's household in 1850 and so presumably still on the island—was shown with two dwellings, barn, four cows, six sheep, sixty-four acres, and a twenty-ton vessel named RAINBOW. It seems likely that Abraham had inherited the bulk of his father's estate.

There is other evidence of Smith residence on Hog Island. An 1844 deed shows conveyance by John Smith "of Hog Island Plantation" (no less!), administrator of the estate of Joshua Smith, also of Hog Island, to Dudley Smith, including all buildings except "one dwelling house west of the barn" (Hancock 76/357). In another deed of this period Dudley and Abraham Smith "of Hog Island," both mariners, acquire a parcel on the Naskeag shore (Hancock 86/197). Dr. Noyes, Deer Isle genealogist, notes the birth of two Smith girls on Hog Island in the 1840s—Lucy and Hannah, children of William and Lucy Smith (Noyes, Family histories: Staples).[34] Two clearly defined cellar holes are still visible at the northern end of the island—one just south of the larger cove on the northwest shore, the other several hundred yards to the east. Their construction indicates that they were built in the first half of the nineteenth century. Stone walls are not found on the island in profusion, but it is probable that these early settlers were principally farmers.

The absence of any buildings on Hog Island in the Hancock County map of 1860 suggests that the farms may have burned or been removed. Moreover, in mortgage and other deeds relating to the island in the 1850s and 1860s there is no mention of homesteads; merely, on occasion, of "machinery and fixtures" (e.g., Hancock 127/227, 1866). The Smiths, in any case, were no longer recorded on the island after Abraham Smith sold his portion to Daniel Cain of Blue Hill in 1853 (Hancock 98/37). The island, after numerous subdivisions, mortgages, and even a title contest between out-of-state parties in an Ellsworth court, passed to the Atlantic Fish Oil and Guano Company located on Long Island, New York.

Lewis A. Edwards, a New York businessman, was the owner of the fish oil company, and his object in acquiring Hog Island, needless to say, was to establish a "pogy" factory there. It was built in 1870 (Murray, *Centennial Celebration, Brooklin*, 23). The operation was presumably a small one at that time, or only just begun, for the Industrial Census of that year, which lists three other pogy factories in Brooklin, makes no mention of the Hog Island facility. It was located on the northwest bend of the island, opposite The Triangles (three hoary spring-tide ledges in mid-channel, nemesis of many mariners); the granite foundations of the pogy works are still visible on the shore. How many workers the factory employed is unknown. Some of them presumably rowed the short distance across from Naskeag Harbor, but there was also a boardinghouse on the island; it is shown on an 1882 chart, near or on the site of the most easterly of the two farms (Map 1882 CGS 309). A census for 1880 shows seventeen residents on Hog Island (*Maine Register*, 1901, p. 187). The principal product of the factory, according to a descendant of Lewis Edwards (Richard Bliss of Chester, Vermont, to whom I am indebted for the foregoing information) was fertilizer rather than fish oil. The menhaden left the area abruptly at the end of the 1870s, about the

[33] According to Smith descendants, John and Mercy Reed Smith had thirteen children, of whom at least six were living with them on the island in 1840: Albert, twenty-three; Joshua, twenty-one; Dudley, fourteen; Abraham, twelve; Mercy, seventeen; and Isabella, fifteen.

[34] These should be Lucinda and Sarah (born 1840 and 1844), children of Ebenezer and Hannah.

time of Lewis Edwards's death, and the pogy factory equipment was sold to the Eastern Marble Company, a quarrying corporation active in the Penobscot Bay region. But if quarrying was planned on Hog Island, no significant motions were ever started. According to Brooklin tax records in 1895, "Edwards & Co." still owned Hog Island, assessed at $200.

A single building is shown on Hog Island in maps surveyed early in the twentieth century—whether the factory itself or the boardinghouse it is difficult to determine (Maps 1904-06 Castine quad)—but it is not likely there was regular habitation on the island at this late date. Title to Hog at about this time passed to the Bowdens of Brooklin, who had served as agents and later caretakers for the Edwards company; they reportedly acquired the island by paying its defaulted taxes. Henry Smith, a farmer on the opposite shore and a descendant of the earlier Smiths of Hog Island, kept sheep there in the 1930s and still had weir rights off the island when the Bowdens sold in 1941 to E. B. White, who had recently moved to Brooklin. Mr. White also kept sheep for a time, which explains why aerial photographs and topographical maps through World War II show the island comparatively free of growth. By the late twentieth century it was totally overgrown and in sectors very nearly impenetrable. In 1954 E. B. White sold the island—"to simplify life," he said (this was another of the Christmas stocking islands: a gift from one fond spouse to another on Christmas morning). By the 1990s, however, a family member of the late E. B. White had bought the island back.

Harbor Island (Naskeag)

There were two Harbor Islands at Naskeag in early days: the present one, and Hog described above. The harbor itself, as noted, was a well-known anchorage from the seventeenth century, a convenient haven for mariners who wished to avoid the unmarked passages around Brûle-côte (now Swans) Island. Moreover, there were farms at Naskeag where depleted larders could be replenished. A 1688 census ordered by Governor Andros of the Bay Colony found both English and French settlers at Naskeag (see page 10), and it is likely that habitation was more or less continuous from that time on, despite the Indian wars. A voyager in 1770 found a dozen families at Naskeag, with two hundred acres of cleared land (Owen, "Narrative of American Voyages," 234).

It may be taken for granted, then, that this island knew many transients. But who were its earliest settlers? There is, of course, no separate census for Harbor Island, whose residents were normally counted with the rest of the settlers in Plantation IV, later Sedgwick, and later still (1849) Port Watson, then Brooklin. William Williamson (I: 75) notes that Harbor Island was inhabited in the 1820s, but he does not mention by whom or by how many. The 1830 federal census schedule for Plantation IV lists Edward Carter, in his twenties, with a sizable household (three males, six females), and this may be the first of the Carters to occupy the island. In 1833 the land agent for Maine, for $42.75, conveyed to Isaac Carter, Jr. title to Harbor Island, in accordance with an agreement reached nine years before (Knox Lands 5/170). Whether or not Isaac Carter lived on the island is uncertain. He appears in both the 1840 and 1850 census schedules for Brooklin (aged, respectively, sixty and seventy, with four, then two, in his household), but he had conveyed the island as early as 1838 to his son John Black Carter. The Walling map of Hancock County in 1860 shows the residence of E. Carter on Harbor Island, opposite the bar; the Colby atlas of the county in 1881 shows two residences—those of J. B. Carter at the above location and E. Carter at the west end of the island. These residents would be John Black and Edward Carter, both sons of Isaac, between whom the island was divided in 1871. I do not find Edward in the 1880 census schedule, but John B. Carter is there, sixty-five, with his wife Lucinda, fifty-eight; he died a few years later. An 1882 chart shows no buildings at the west end, but three facing the harbor—one opposite the bar, as above, and two, possibly house and barn, somewhat to the east; there was also fencing, and most of the island was cleared (Map 1882 CGS 309). Family photos of this era confirm that the island was bare. In 1883 Edward Carter sold part of his share of the island to Daniel A. Hanson, husband of J. B. and Lucinda Carter's daughter Minnie; this lot was a strip across the center of the island from the north to the south shore. The balance of Edward Carter's share was conveyed to other heirs of J. B. and Lucinda.[35]

Lucinda Carter, sharp-tongued widow of J. B. Carter, was said by local residents to be the dominant personality on Harbor Island in the last decade of the nineteenth century. She lived with her son Ward and his family; they appear in the 1880 census as Ward Carter, twenty-three, his wife May, twenty-four, and three minor children, a son and two daughters. The son, Jasper, died in the 1890s, and the daughters eventually grew to maturity on the island.

It was during this era that an accident occurred at the Harbor Island bar that has been much embellished (and distorted) in the retelling. I believe the following account, told me in the 1970s by a local resident in her nineties (who remembered the night of the accident) and verified by Brooklin vital statistics, is accurate as to basic detail—minus inuendo.[36] A Mexican dancer-actress-author named Beulah Sadonia l'Oro, whose father was Aztec and mother "an American lady," had been vacationing on Harbor Island for several seasons in a cabin overlooking the harbor. She had staying with her at the time of the episode in question a female ward named Madine Foster, thirteen years old. Dr. Leroy Carter of Boston, another son of Lucinda, was visiting the island in August 1895 and took Beulah in a rented gig to a gathering in Blue Hill. They left Madine Foster with friends on the Naskeag road and picked her up after dark on their return. The wind was already high, and the young girl wished to spend the night with her friends, but the doctor and Beulah decided otherwise. What exactly happened on the fifty-yard passage from the shore to the island, no one knows, but the skiff overturned and all three were drowned. Beulah's grave, marked by a single uncut stone with no surname, is in the Brooklin cemetery.

Lucinda Carter died before 1900, and her surviving son remained on the island—I do not know for how long. The western end was farmed until about World War I, and sheep continued to graze there for some years after that. Carter and Hanson descendants continued to own the island through the twentieth century and to summer there.

[35] I am indebted to a Hanson descendant, Arnold C. Hanson, for details of the Harbor Island ownership.

[36] The local resident was Edith Cousins Livermore, who was brought up a few miles from the scene; June Eaton, former Brooklin Town Clerk, searched the vital records.

Carters and Hansons of Harbor Island (Naskeag)

Note: Arnold C. Hanson, a descendant, has provided the detail for this genealogical tree.

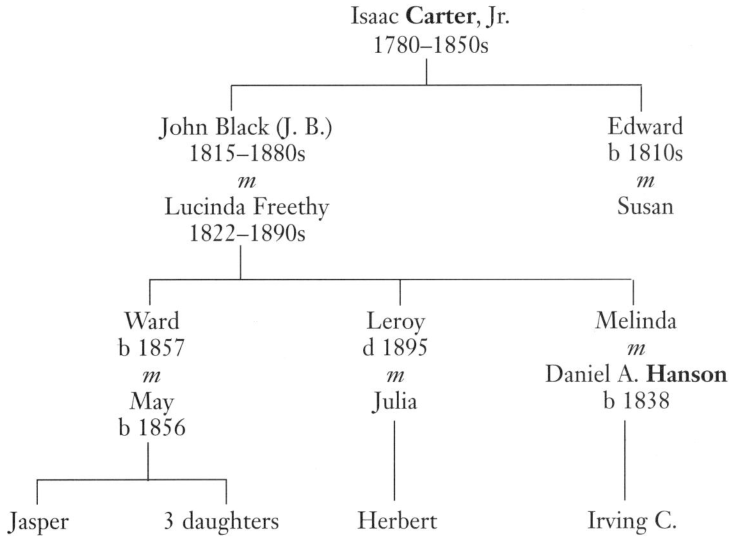

Smutty Nose and Mahoney

Rutherford (*Dictionary of Maine Place Names*, 85) says Smutty Nose is descriptive of a "dark rock on a lighter background," but I incline to the view that it was named by some fisherman out of Naskeag in a whimsical mood. A pre-Revolutionary mariner is almost lyrical in his description: "a remarkable white, rocky, tufted island without the southern head [i.e., of Naskeag Harbor], and pretty bold too" (Owen, 734). The tiny island, needless to say, has no use other than as a navigational marker and for the fishing privilege.

Mahoney appears as *Matthews Island* on one sheet of Colby's atlas of 1881 and as *Mahona* on another, but these are probably both misprints. The island, which was evidently never conveyed properly before 1874, was sold that year by the State of Maine to George W. Black of Brooklin as Mahoney and was charged to him in 1895 tax records ($25). The island was probably wooded at the time. It was undoubtedly pulped more than once over the years, but in recent times the "stripping" has been done by nesting seabirds and crows. The stench from the island is strong enough today to keep fastidious mariners upwind. I have never discovered the identity of Mahoney—if, indeed, he existed.

Swans Island

Swans

Which early navigator gave the name *Brûle-côte* to this island is unknown. Legend, not surprisingly, points to Champlain, who named *Monts-déserts* and *Isle Haulte* during his 1604–05 expeditions; but neither his charts nor his log mention *Brûle-côte*. We must therefore assume that some later French explorer christened this island, for it was known by this name to mariners a century or more before the American Revolution and gradually anglicized by British cartographers to *Burnt Coat* (e.g., Maps 1754 Johnson and 1776 Atlantic Neptune). Burnt Coat is still the name of the island's principal harbor in the southwest sector.

Colonel James Swan and First Settlement

The island had no settlement (at least no recorded settlement) before the Revolution, as other large islands in the region had—for example, Mount Desert Island (1762), the Fox Islands (1762), Deer Isle (1763). Perhaps one settler was in the vicinity *during* the Revolution—a disillusioned veteran of the Quebec campaign of 1776 named Thomas Kench who, according to one account, moved onto Harbor Island in Burnt Coat Harbor in 1777 (Small, *History of Swans Island*, 59). Settlers on Burnt Coat Island proper arrived only with the purchase of the island by Colonel James Swan in 1785. An unspecified number of "Colonel Swan's people" was reported at Burnt Coat Harbor in December 1785 (see Rufus Putnam's census, Appendix 1).

James Swan was an engaging and ambitious Scotsman who embraced the Colonists' cause, took part in the Revolutionary War, and after the war acquired vast lands in Kentucky, Virginia, and on the coast of Maine. He was barely thirty when he purchased Burnt Coat Island and twenty-four surrounding islands from the Commonwealth of Massachusetts for £1,920. He promptly built a lumbermill and a gristmill in the "mill pond" flowing into Burnt Coat Harbor and advertised for settlers: he would give a deed for one hundred acres, after seven years, to any settler who came with his family, built a home, and farmed his land; he promised ten acres to any fisherman who settled on the island. For a decade or so the community at Burnt Coat Harbor flourished: settlers came from Deer Isle and Mount Desert; there was great profit in the magnificent virgin timber still on the island; and the fisheries were abundant. A steady flow of coasters came to Burnt Coat Harbor to haul away the lumber and other produce and to bring fresh supplies. Colonel Swan built a home on the east side of the harbor in the flat-roof Colonial style, in imitation of his friend General Knox's mansion Montpelier at Thomaston; Swan's agent, Joseph Prince of Beverly, Massachusetts, settled on Harbor Island.

As a business venture, Colonel Swan's enterprise did not succeed. Although he had powerful friends, such as Knox and Lafayette, his fiscal ambitions outran his discretion, and he accumulated huge debts in the United States and abroad. He never settled for long on his island (it took his name in the 1790s); he lived partly in Boston, with an elegant summer home in Dorchester (he was an early "rusticator"), and partly in France. A questionable debt in Paris in 1808 put him in debtors' prison there, where he remained for over twenty years—not because he was unable to settle the debt (many of his friends were prepared to do that) but because he would not acknowledge it. In a word, he remained in prison *on principle* and when, with the accession of Louis Philippe, he was finally released in 1830 at the age of seventy-six, he died before he could return home.

James Swan's travails did not, of course, interrupt the settlement of his island domain. Settlers came and occupied what lands they found free. Joseph Prince was empowered to convey title, but there is no record that he made any conclusive sales before he quit the area himself about 1800. In 1812 Swan, from his Paris prison, mortgaged to Michael O'Maley, a Baltimore merchant, the greatest part of his archipelago. Thereafter settlers had to deal with O'Maley or his attorney Rufus Allyn (and briefly, in the 1820s, Daniel Webster); there are, indeed, references in early town reports to the abatement to certain townsmen of the "omely tax." The impression I gain from the complex mortgages and "strawman"

Colonel James Swan, first proprietor of Burnt Coat Island and the smaller surrounding islands; he spent much of his life in a Paris prison for indebtedness.
(Painting by Gilbert Stuart. Swan Collection. Bequest of Elizabeth Howard Bartol. Courtesy of Museum of Fine Arts, Boston.)

transactions concocted in connection with the liquidation of Colonel Swan's domain is that the settlers themselves bore little financial burden.[1]

Early Settlers

I have not discovered a 1790 census schedule for Burnt Coat Island, and there may not have been one; schedules from 1800 on, however, are complete (see table on pages 420–23 for residents from 1800 to 1850). Here are brief identifications of the earliest settlers drawn from census data and from sketches by Swans Island historian Dr. H. W. Small (pages 59–159):

Joseph Prince has been noted as Colonel Swan's agent; he is shown in the 1800 census as having come from Boston. His sizeable household included six daughters under ten—also a Negro slave.

Milliken is not noted by Dr. Small; census schedules show him from Trenton—which suggests he may have been named Thomas, son of Benjamin Milliken, a founder of Ellsworth.

John Rich, Jr. settled on the east side of the island in 1794, but removed within three years to the east side of Isle au Haut.

William Davis also arrived in 1794 and removed in 1797 to Long Island (Frenchboro), where he left many descendants.

Moses Staples, Sr. came from Deer Isle in about 1790, when he was granted a hundred acres from Swan's agent; he was a shipwright, the second "permanent" settler on Swans Island. He built first on the west side of Burnt Coat Harbor and later moved to the east shore. He left many descendants.

John Finney, an Irishman who deserted from the British army during the Revolutionary War, came first to Deer Isle, where he married a daughter of Moses Staples, then removed to Swans Island before 1800.

Isaac Coombs is not noted by Dr. Small; he is shown as having come from Vinalhaven.

David Smith, known as "King David," is counted the first "permanent" settler on Swans Island, actually on Harbor Island; he came in 1791 to work in Swan's mills and eventually moved to Swan's homestead on the harbor.

Joseph Banks is not noted by Dr. Small, and I have no information about him; the surname suggests he came from Castine.

William Wells, also not noted by Dr. Small, is shown in the 1810 census on Pond Island, and may have been there in 1800.

Other settlers before 1800, noted by Dr. Small but not in the 1800 census schedule, included the following:

Thomas Kench, as mentioned earlier, was truly the first settler—arriving in 1777 after deserting from the Continental Army following the Quebec campaign; he lived on Harbor Island and removed to Brooksville in 1796.

Joseph Toothaker came to Swans Island in 1792 and settled on the northwest peninsula above the carrying place; he was found dead of gunshot wounds on Harbor Island a few years later—whether due to accident or foul play is uncertain. He left no family. The bay southwest of Swans Island is named after him (though spelled differently).

Joshua Grindle came from Sedgwick in 1794 and returned there in 1800.

Alexander Nutter was a coasting sea captain from Gloucester who came in 1796 and left for Mount Desert Island and the eastward a few years later.

There was a restlessness among the early settlers of Swans Island: of the fourteen householders identified above who resided on the island before 1800, only three remained (barely twenty percent). This reflects a far greater turnover than one finds on comparable islands in the region and, indeed, higher than one might expect on Swans Island given the unusual stability of its residents after 1800. Why? I doubt if there was a single compelling reason for early removal, but there are possible explanations. For one, the inability of Colonel Swan or his agents to make good on their promises of clear title—whether through carelessness or overlapping mortgages—may have discouraged settlers from putting down firm roots. Second, many early arrivals were lumbermen, normally a transient element in any community; farming, which by contrast promotes continuity, was slow to emerge on Swans Island. Meanwhile,

[1] The transactions affecting specific islands in the archipelago are discussed in the island notices that follow this entry. A summary appears in *Bangor Historical Magazine*, III: 21/499.

the tardy settlement of this island, some decades later than others in the region, may mean that the pioneering adjustments that any new community must undergo occurred on Swans Island at a time when they were more apparent than elsewhere—that is, reflected in census data and public records. In other words, the earliest Swans Islanders may have been no more restless than their counterparts on other islands, but we know more about them because they came later.

Swans Island remained for three or more decades an unorganized territory, taxed (if at all) by the State of Maine. Four distinct sub-communities emerged in those years, three of which survive: Swans Island proper, on the peninsula making the west side of Burnt Coat Harbor, locally known as Old Harbor; Minturn[2] on the opposite shore of the harbor; and Atlantic on Mackerel Cove on the north side of the island. The fourth sector was the northeast shore, which had no good anchorages but the best farmland. In 1834 Swans Island was organized as a plantation, including all the islands in Colonel Swan's original purchase except Marshall, which remained unorganized, and the

[2] I have not discovered the origin of this name; the names of sectors did not necessarily emerge in the early nineteenth century.

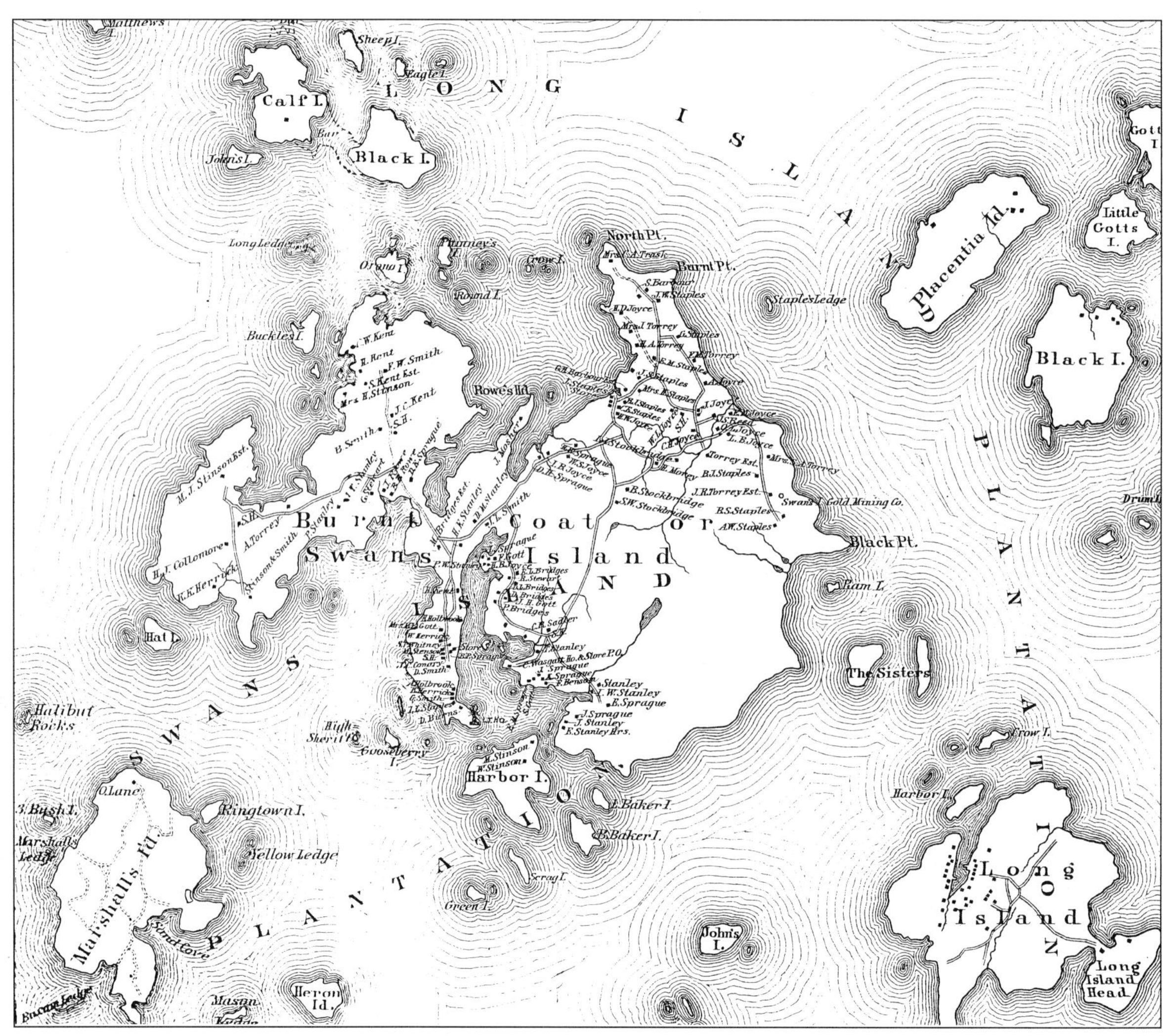

Plan of Swans Island Division, 1881, from the Colby Atlas of the State of Maine, *showing roads and names of residents on Swans Island proper, Harbor Island, and Marshall Island; only housesites are shown on other inhabited islands.*

Lobster pound and dwellings at Mackerel Cove on Swans Island, c. 1900.
(Courtesy of Swans Island Historical Society.)

Village of Swans Island, looking from the Minturn side of Burnt Coat Harbor, c. 1900. (Original slide by George R. Neal, printed by W. H. Ballard.)

Placentia group.[3] For sixty years the plantation performed the municipal tasks for which it was designed: organization of schools (there were at one time six districts), improvement of roads, care of the indigent, and the levy of taxes to cover costs.[4] In 1896 the plantation became a full-fledged township.

Occupations of Swans Islanders

Fishing, rather than logging or farming, proved to be the bread-and-butter occupation of Swans Islanders in the nineteenth century. It was carried on principally from Old Harbor. The early fishing here, as elsewhere along the coast, was for cod, normally from small boats in local waters. By mid-century, stimulated by the surge in the cod fisheries as well as by generous government bounties, Swans Islanders were ready for the Grand Banks: in 1853 the first schooner from Old Harbor was on the Banks, followed by others in succeeding years. The islanders had begun to diversify even before the decline of Grand Banks fishing following the repeal of federal bounties in 1866: mackerel fishing, for instance, engaged a considerable number of Swans Island fishermen before the Civil War, and the expertise they developed in the use of gill nets earned them a wide reputation in fishing communities from the Bay of Fundy to the Gulf of the St. Lawrence. In the 1870s they fished

[3] Great and Little Gott islands were not included in the Swan purchase and remained attached to Mount Desert Island (now to the township of Bernard); Placentia and Eastern Black islands, though part of Swan's purchase, were also attached to Mount Desert until the organization of Frenchboro in 1810 (see page 446). Pond, Western Black, and Calf (Opechee) were also part of Frenchboro until 1901, when the latter two were returned to Swans Island.

[4] The plantation tax records have disappeared, but a record of plantation meetings is preserved in Dr. Small's *History of Swans Island* (1898). This volume, together with a study by a Guggenheim Fellow who spent a year on the island in the 1950s (Perry D. Westbrook, *Biography of an Island*), provide the most detailed published data on the island's history.

Village of Swans Island looking across Burnt Coat Harbor, c. 1900.
(Courtesy of Swans Island Historical Society.)

locally for menhaden, and two "pogy factories" operated for a few years in Old Harbor before the menhaden quit the area, never to return in commercially significant numbers.

By 1880, according to a comprehensive Congressional report on the American fisheries, twenty-one large vessels sailed from Swans Island in the mackerel and cod fisheries, employing 186 men.[5] This was a fleet comparable in size to those of much larger communities along the coast: e.g., Deer Isle, Vinalhaven, Boothbay, and even Portland (Goode, *Fishing Industries of the United States*, 39).

In 1886 the large annual schools of mackerel left the coast, and Swans Islanders, like other Maine fishermen, turned to different fisheries. The herring industry was then in high gear, both for the canneries and for bait. But it was lobster fishing that seized most islanders. This meant different life habits, different lifestyles. No longer the lengthy expeditions—sometimes up to five months—to the Grand Banks or Labrador. Rather, daily trips into local waters, normally alone. A tax record of 1895 (the oldest I have discovered for Swans Island) shows that of two hundred and thirty taxpayers on the island, sixty-two owned their own boats, the average value of which was about $250. The days of the corporately owned $10,000-and-up Bankers and mackerel schooners had passed. Lobstering has been the principal source of revenue for islanders in the twentieth century. If the catch has not matched that of some other fishing communities in Penobscot Bay, the Swans Islanders themselves have lost nothing in inventiveness over the years: in the mid-1980s the forty-odd lobstermen still active on Swans Island, in an effort to turn back the sad trend of declining fisheries, became the first community of fishermen in Maine to implement the state's new trap limit program (*Island Journal*, IV: 19).

Fishing, while the dominant occupation on Swans Island for two centuries, has not been the only preoccupation of the islanders. Farming has been a complement to fishing, and there were few households in the nineteenth century that did not have some livestock and keep a garden. The table at the end of this entry reflects the significance of farming on Swans Island. In 1850 farmers made up about forty percent of the wage-earners on the island; as late as 1880 farmers still constituted more than fifteen percent of the wage-earners (see the table on island occupations, page 278).

Other occupations included quarrying, which was introduced at Minturn in the last decade of the nineteenth century but ended by the first decade of the twentieth. Imported Swedish quarrymen (two hundred of them) did the quarrying, but few remained; no islanders appear to have taken up the trade. All that remains of the brief enterprise are the scars on the hillside behind Minturn. There was also occasional boatbuilding, as there is apt to be wherever men of the sea gather: in 1856, for instance, a ninety-five-ton schooner was launched for the Grand Banks fishery (O'Leary, *Maine Sea Fisheries*, 618). And there were stores to be kept, often in connection with one of the three post offices that were created to serve the island's needs. A tax record in 1895 lists no fewer than seven stores—and it will be instructive to note them here with their owners and valuations.

Storekeepers & Facilities	Valuation	Stock-in-Trade
A. K. Taylor, house, store, 2 horses and carriage	$300	$600
J. H. West, wharf, store, stable, boardinghouse	500	–
Isaac Stinson,[6] house and store	500	300
Benjamin Staples, house and store	1,200	1,300
Sylvester Morse, house and store	1,200	2,000
Durille Joyce, house and store	1,600	2,300
Edmond Bridges	–	700

Summer Tourism and the Island

Swans Island escaped the heavy impact of late nineteenth century summer tourism, which profoundly altered life on many comparable islands in the region: North Haven, Islesboro, Isle au Haut, and of course Mount Desert, close by on the northeast horizon. Some rusticators came, of course. There were boardinghouses and a "hotel" at Atlantic (the Ponceana), which together accommodated up to several hundred vacationers in a season. There was even a development effort at

[5] Federal census figures in 1880 show the number of fishermen on Swans Island to be 144; assuming the figures to be accurate, the Swans Island captains must have taken on crew from other communities.

[6] Isaac Stinson was postmaster at this time at Swans Island (Old Harbor); Durille Joyce (below) was postmistress in Atlantic, 1884–1897 (Small, 236).

Irish Point called Idlewyld, which failed. Instead, after the inn and boardinghouses closed, the most determined of the vacationers built cottages—about thirty of them in due course, mostly on the old farmlands on the northeast shore. In the 1950s the value of the cottagers' holdings amounted to one-sixth of the total town assessment; on Isle au Haut, by contrast, the cottagers' share of the total tax bill was about two-thirds in the same era.[7]

Why, then, did a significant summer community fail to take root on Swans as on sister islands, since Swans surely lacked nothing in exotic panorama, variety of natural settings, and other qualities rusticators sought? One reason was clearly the length of the pocketbooks Swans Island's vacationers brought with them compared to those of vacationers elsewhere: as often as not, the visitor would be not some rising industrialist eager to show off his yacht and his scrubbed children, but an impecunious college professor who grew and sold a modest crop of berries or flowers to supplement his income. There was neither the will nor the wherewithal to create anything resembling a "summer colony." Another consideration may have been the inconvenience of ferry schedules, upon which any summer community must rely. Before 1895 there was, in truth, no regular service to and from Swans Island beyond the mailboat that came erratically from Tremont on Mount Desert Island (mail had previously come once a week from Brooklin). In 1895 daily service from Rockland was organized and lasted until 1941, when the ferry was commandeered for war service. Though the cottagers would have preferred service from Mount Desert Island, the Rockland service was satisfactory during those years—except that there was always uneasiness as to whether it would continue. After World War II the mail connection was at first with Stonington,

[7] Westbrook, 142; Perry Westbrook devotes an informative chapter in his volume to cottagers on Swans Island.

Quarry Pond at Minturn on Swans Island, looking out Burnt Coat Harbor to the southwest.
(Courtesy of Swans Island Historical Society.)

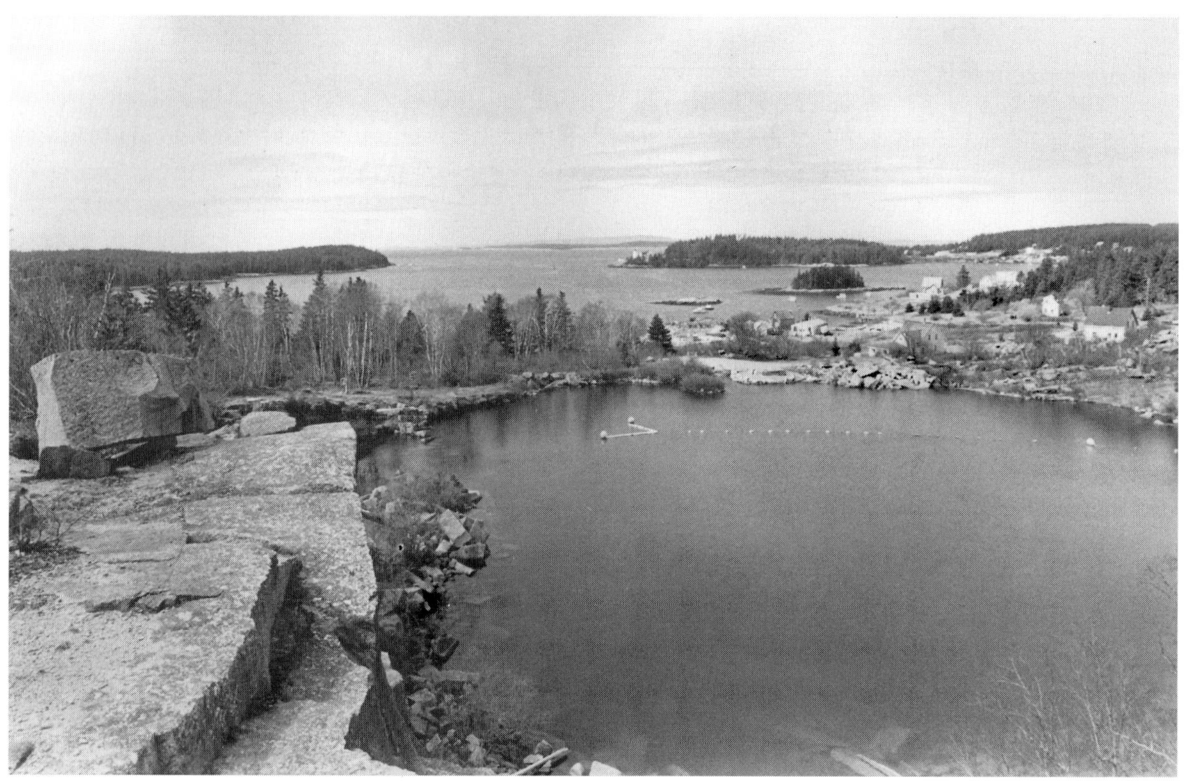

which was unsatisfactory for both cottagers and islanders (the islanders were never reconciled to the loss of the daily Rockland connection in 1941). Eventually, Maine State ferry service was established from Bass Harbor—at first to Minturn, later to Atlantic—but the long years of uncertainty surely discouraged prospective cottagers.[8]

Religion on Swans Island

And, finally, we turn to organized religion on Swans Island.[9] The early settlers were Congregationalists, but neither they nor Colonel Swan (as he had engaged himself to do when he acquired Burnt Coat Island from Massachusetts) built a church. Services were held in settlers' homes: Sunday sermons and mid-week prayers. It was not until 1814 that the first minister, a Baptist, came onto the island. As was to happen repeatedly in the years to come, the arrival of a clergyman stimulated a lively, but brief, response: a Baptist Society was formed, and dozens of islanders were "converted." On numerous occasions through the nineteenth century the same thing occurred—the arrival of a fresh disciple and more conversions. In 1883 the Baptists built their church at Atlantic.

A Methodist Society, meanwhile, had been organized in 1834 in response to another of the periodic revivals that touched the island population. A Methodist church was built in the community of Swans Island in 1888. In Minturn the Advent Church went through a parallel cycle; its chapel was built in 1893. Each of the three sectors of the island, then, had its church—as it had its school, its store, and even its post office—yet it would be difficult to show that these churches had a unifying effect on either the three separate districts or on the island as a whole.

Why? It would be trifling with the impulses that motivate Swans Islanders to suggest precise and cogent reasons why they were attracted to or became indifferent to a given religious denomination, or indeed to any religious identity. It might be said (cautiously) that the Puritanism from which the religion of the early settlers sprang was too austere for their daily lives. They lived in a setting of austerity: in a northern latitude, well out to sea, in the path of fierce tempests. They needed no more austerity for the good of their souls. The

[8] The last word on summer development on Swans Island has probably not been written: though large sections of the island have been bought by conservationists, new efforts by realtors in the 1990s indicated that the never-overpopulated island might see new construction.

[9] Both Dr. Small and Perry Westbrook discuss religion on Swans Island, and I rely on them for details of the several churches and movements that flourished.

Homesteads at Atlantic on Swans Island, near present ferry landing; note boardwalks—presumably for the comfort of early rusticators. (Courtesy of Swans Island Historical Society, photo donated by Roberta Joyce.)

door was thus open for the revivalist sects to work their magic where they could—say, where susceptabilities were heightened by family or communal tragedies. Baptists, Methodists, and Adventists, it should be remembered, were revivalists in the nineteenth century; it was their mission to rekindle the embers of a waning faith. It is in the nature of revivals that the crescendoes they induce are inevitably followed by valleys of indifference, even despondency. The cycles of religious fervor and drought on Swans Island, then, should come as no surprise.

But are the cycles inherent to life on this island—or peripheral to it? The latter, I believe. Swans Islanders, by the nature of their geography and history, are more moved by practical considerations like the number of fish in the ocean and the price of lobsters than they are by questions of redemption and salvation. They are more or less immune to evangelism, at least to any permanent impact it might have on their lives. This, I believe, is why religion played a marginal role in the life of the island.

The smaller islands in this division are taken up in a generally clockwise sequence from Burnt Coat Harbor, beginning with Harbor Island and its satellites and ending with John Island off Frenchboro.

Residence on Swans Island, 1800–1850

Note: The following residents of Swans Island from 1800 to 1850 appear in the federal census. Age is shown at date of first appearance. Males are to left of slash, females to right. Spouses and occupations, where shown, are taken from the 1850 schedule: Fa, farmer; Fi, fisherman; S, sailor or mariner; C, carpenter or shipwright. The dollar figure beside some householders represents their 1839 tax (the highest figure that year was $8.31).[10]

Name	1800	1810	1820	1830	1840	1850
Prince, Joseph, Esq., -45	3/9					
Milliken, (illegible), -45	4/1					
Rich, John, Jr., -45	1/3					
Davis, William, -45	3/1					
Staples, Moses, -26[11]	1/1	4/1	4/1	2/1	1/1	
Finney, John, -45 $1.81	1/1	1/4	3/4	-	1/0	
Coombes, John, -45	1/3					
Smith, David, -45	3/3	5/4	5/5	7/5	2/3[12]	
Banks, Joseph, -45	1/4					
Wells, William, -45	3/4					
Joice [Joyce], James, 45+		4/4	4/1	1/0		
Peters, Morris, -45		2/3	3/5			
Staples, Moses, Jr., 30 (Betsy), C $5.39		2/4	4/5	4/5	4/2	2/3
Staples, John, 45+		4/4				
Weed, Jeremiah, -45		3/3				
Babbage, Courtney[13], -45			3/5			
Conra [Conary], Israel, 27 (Martha)			2/1	5/3	-	3/1
Cook, John, 45+			1/1	1/1		
Name	**1800**	**1810**	**1820**	**1830**	**1840**	**1850**

[10] The 1839 tax spread reflects the relative wealth of Swans Islanders in that era.

[11] Unless this is Moses Staples, Jr., the age is in error: Moses Staples, Sr. was born in the 1750s and would have been in his forties in 1800. He died in 1845 (Hosmer, 45).

[12] Betsy Smith is head of household in 1840.

[13] This Courtney Babbage was probably related to the Courtney Babbidge, Jr. of Babbidge Island (see page176). Though they were close to each other in age, there is no evidence to suggest that they were the same person.

Name	1800	1810	1820	1830	1840	1850
Finney, John, 45+			5/4	4/5		
Gott, John, 45+ $2.24			7/3	5/2	2/2	
Kent, Samuel, -45 $ .19			6/4	5/3	1/3	
Linnen, Bryant, 45+			6/2			
Merchant, Anthony, -45			3/2	1/1[14]		
Robertson, David, 45+			8/5			
Smith, Benjamin, 26 (Margaret), Fa $5.08			3/2	6/3	5/3	3/2
Smith, David, Jr., 28 (Lucy), Fa $2.82			1/3	3/5	3/6	4/5
Stinson, Benjamin, 34 (Sarah), Fa $8.31			4/2	5/5	5/6	3/3
Staples, Joshua, -45			5/4			
Staples, Abel, 46 (Rebecca), Fa $3.54			5/3	-	4/3	3/1
Staples, Mark, -45			3/3			
Stinson, David, -45			2/1			
Stanley, William, 45+			4/3			
Torrey, Levi, 32 (Olive), Fa $2.03			4/1	4/5	5/5	3/2
Torrey, Asa, -45			3/2			
Vernember?, Gilbert, 45+			2/1			
Kempton, Zacheus, 30s				2/3		
Kempton, Samuel, 40s				1/2		
Haley, William, 30s				7/2		
Fife, William, 26 (Sarah), trader $2.49				1/0	3/3	3/3
Gott, Samuel, 27 (Mary), S $ .48				1/4	3/6	5/5
Nutter, William, 20s				5/2		
Sprague, William, 40s $ .45				5/2	3/2[15]	
Billings, Enoch, 40s $2.39				4/3	5/3	
Pray?, James, 30s				4/3		
Cushing, Stewart, 30s				3/5		
Robinson, William, 40s				5/3		
Smith, Asa, 28 (Abigail), S $ .10				2/2	3/5	7/5
Kent, Benjamin, 20s				2/2	2/0	
Albry?, Will, 40s				4/5		
Joyce, Ebenezer, 31 (Catherine), C $2.98				4/3	5/5	5/5
Staples, Ebenezer, 40s				4/6		
Staples, Bryant, 20s				3/2		
Finney, Moses, 20s				1/3		
Staples, Alexander, 30s				2/4		
Joyce, William, 28 (Mary), Fa $3.17				5/1	5/3	6/4
Babbage, Alfred, 20s				4/2		
Carpenter, Richard, 30s				4/4		
Name	**1800**	**1810**	**1820**	**1830**	**1840**	**1850**

[14] Abigail Merchant is head of household in 1830.
[15] Rebecca Sprague is head of household in 1840.

Name	1800	1810	1820	1830	1840	1850
Stockbridge, John, 34 (Ruth), Fa				8/2	8/3	4/2
Babbage, Joseph, 34 (May), Fa $1.90					4/3	4/2
Billings, Johnson, 25 (Eliza), Fi $2.39					2/4	2/4
Colamy, Thomas, 32 (Mary), Fi $ .50					2/5	3/5
Gott, John, Jr., 39 (Abigail), Fa $1.76					2/4	2/4
Gott, Joseph, 29 (Eunice), Fa $2.71					3/3	5/2
Gott, Edward, 26 (Susan), Fa $1.97					2/2	3/6
Hardy, Silas, Esq., 30s $ .25					3/2	
Joyce, James II, 41 (Jane), Fa $2.89					6/7	6/4
Lane, Abel, 40s $4.61					2/3	
Lane, Hannah, 40s					2/2	
Morey, Elias, 51 (Jane), Fa $3.17					4/2	1/3
Smith, John, 39 (Lydia), S $3.61					1/4	2/4
Saddler, Moses, 28, Fa $ .44					2/1	3/1
Saddler, Thomas, 34 (Hannah), Fa $1.09					4/3	4/6
Saddler, Joshua, 30s $1.13					5/2	
Staples, Augustus, 28 (Susanah), Fa					2/4	3/4
Staples, Benjamin, 40 (Lucy), Fa $2.24					6/2	4/2
Staples, Asa E., 20s $ .89					1/1	
Sprague, James, Jr., 22, Fi $1.66					4/1	5/1
Stinson, Benjamin F., 28 (Hannah), trader $3.20					2/2	3/3
Stinson, John, 20 (Lucy), Fi $ .79					2/2	3/4
Stanley, William II, 49 (Ruth), Fi $4.56					5/4	2/3
Stanley, Edmond, 26 (Betsy), S $ .28					1/2	4/3
Stewart, Otis, 20s					1/1	
Trask, Joshua, 23 (Mary), Fa $3.47					4/2	4/3
Torrey, Levi, Jr., 24 (Joan), S					1/1	4/3
Torrey, Joseph R., 26 $ .85					1/1	2/3
Conway, Moses, 31 (Mary), S						1/3
Smith, James, 34 (Mary) S						3/3
Kent, Samuel II, 46 (Mary), Fa						5/2
Smith, William, 30 (Prudence)						1/2
Stinson, David II, 29 (Henrietta), Fa						2/1
Herrick, Kimball, 48 (Abigail), Fa						2/2
Gott, Ambrose, 26 (Sarah), Fi						2/4
Stewart, George, 21 (Elizabeth), S						4/1
Rowe, James, 36 (Cordelia), Fa						1/2
Robinson, Samuel, 40 (Alvira), S						3/3
Beal, Alfred, 21 (Lydia), S						1/1
Annis, William, 46 (Betsy), S						1/6
Monroe, Alexander, 26 (Sarah), S						3/3
Kent, Hiram, 26 (Nancy), S						2/2
Name	**1800**	**1810**	**1820**	**1830**	**1840**	**1850**

Name	1800	1810	1820	1830	1840	1850
Bridges, Daniel, 28 (Clarissa), Fi						2/2
Stanley, Peter, 28 (Sarah), Fi						1/2
Stanley, Olziah?, 24 (Sophia), Fi						2/1
Bridges, Moses, 58 (Emely), Fa						5/4
Stanley, Joseph, 33 (Abigail), Fi						3/2
Sprague, James, 60 (Rebecah?), Fa						2/3
Sprague, John, 30 (Martha), Fa						2/1
Sprague, David, 26 (Phebe), S						2/1
Conway, David, 45 (Susan), S						4/4
Ross, Thomas, 33 (Dianah), S						2/3
Benson, Mary, 57						2/3
Kieth (Smith?), Isaac, 21 (Menetta), S						2/1
Kinsman, Abraham, 71 (Ruth), Fa						2/1
Joyce, Isiah, 28 (Olive), S					1/4	
Stockbridge, Benjamin, 33 (Sarah), S						3/2
Morey, Hezekiah, 28 (Nora), S						1/3
Morey, Otis, 26 (Elizabeth), C						1/1
Reed, Jacob, 47 (Sally), blacksmith						5/6
Joyce, William, Jr., 24 (Mary), Fi						1/2
Staples, Seaman, 26 (Stephanie), C						2/2
Joyce, Asa, 28 (Isabella), S						3/2
Staples, John, 30 (Mariah), S						2/5
Barber, Solomon, 35 (Harriet), S						3/2
Chandler, George, 26 (Rebecca), Fi						1/2
Joyce, Roderick, 25 (Catherine), Fa						4/1

	1800	1810	1820	1830	1840	1850
Totals						
No. of Households	10	8	26	38	47	75
No. of Persons	51	56	173	243	276	423

Agricultural Valuations, Swans Island, 1850 and 1980

Note: Valuations for Swans Island farmers in the federal agricultural censuses of 1850 and 1880 are listed below (only those over $250 for 1850 and over $900 for 1880). The numbered columns represent the following (livestock count is erratic in 1850):

Column 1	"Improved"/ "unimproved" acres (1850) Acres explicitly in tillage/other uses (1880)
Column 2	Total value of farm ($)
Column 3	Tons of hay harvested
Column 4	Number of cows (all ages)
Column 5	Number of sheep
Column 6	Value of livestock ($)
Column 7	Bushels of potatoes harvested (1880 only)

Name	1 Acre	2 Val	3 Hay	4 Cow	5 Shp	6 Live	7 Pot
1850 (48 farmers total)[16]							
Stinson, John	60/130	272			30	-	
Smith, John	35/166	461				111	
Bridges, Moses	12/50	285				90	
Gott, Joseph	25/115	275			67	75	
Morey, Elias	40/68	250				95	
Reed, Joseph	15/59	526				45	
Staples, Benjamin	60/75	287				115	
Staples, Abel	30/114	331				76	
1880 (46 farmers listed)[17]							
Stinson, Michael (Harbor I.)	6/44	900	6	3	35	280	0
Herrick, William	1/18	1,000	2	2	23	135	90
Sprague, David	2/176	900	14	6	30	350	90
Staples, Joseph W.	2/55	1,200	12	4	0	150	190
Barbour, Solomon	1/177	1,500	12	4	1	140	150
Gott, Ambrose	1/90	900	6	1	0	20	10
Bridges, Parker	3/77	900	16	6	2	290	100
Smith, David	1/42	1,000	4	3	57	280	25
Morse, Sylvester (tenant)	7/216	1,500	18	7	50	490	600
Carrey, Hezekiah	3/0	900	10	8	6	280	140
Joyce, Levi	5/61	1,300	12	6	10	256	150
Jaynes, James	2/81	1,400	16	6	16	242	150
	1 Acre	**2 Val**	**3 Hay**	**4 Cow**	**5 Shp**	**6 Live**	**7 Pot**
Totals (for the 46 farmers listed in 1880):	57 tilled	29,000	305	145	495	7,439	3,520

[16] Of the forty-eight farmers shown in the agricultural census, fifteen had a yoke of oxen.

[17] I count thirty-seven farmers on Swans Island in the regular census schedule for 1880 (see page 278, above); the discrepancy doubtless arises from counting error.

Harbor

This island, which protects one of the best and earliest-known harbors on the coast of Maine, has been known by its present name from the time of the first white settlement in the area—sometimes with slight modification such as *Burnt Coat Harbor Island* or simply *Old Harbor Island*. It is believed to have been used for many centuries by Indians, as the deep middens bear witness.

The first settler, according to Swans Island historian Dr. H. W. Small (page 58), was Thomas Kench, who allegedly deserted from the Continental Army after Benedict Arnold's campaign against Quebec in 1775 and came to this island. He lived alone—indeed, he was for some years the only known settler in the entire Swans Island area—and, perhaps, because of his desertion discouraged visitors. He built a cabin near the shore, had a cow and a few sheep, and, according to legend, planted an oyster bed in the harbor. He quit the island only in 1796, by Small's account, after the arrival of the David Smith family, which apparently violated his sense of privacy. Walter A. Snow, Brooksville genealogist and historian, gives a somewhat different account of Kench's residence: he settled on Harbor Island only in 1782, after his honorable discharge from a unit under the command of James Swan (*Brooksville*, page 44). Unless this was a coincidence, one imagines it was Swan who persuaded Kench to settle among the islands he was about to purchase. Thomas Kench evidently remained only a few years, for Snow places him in Brooksville before 1790.

David Smith, a Revolutionary War veteran from New Hampshire, had settled initially on Deer Isle, but came to Swans Island in 1791 in response to Colonel Swan's advertisement for employment in his gristmills. He lived on Harbor Island for only a few years before buying property on Swans Island proper—but long enough for his second wife to give birth to one of his twenty-four children, the first recorded birth in the Swans Island area (Small, 25, 63). Another early settler on Harbor Island, perhaps preceding the Smiths, was Swan's agent, Joseph Prince, who is listed in the first United States census of 1790, living with his family of six on one of the "small islands" in Hancock County not belonging to any town—a category that embraced Harbor Island more readily than Swans Island proper. Small (pages 23, 143) also notes that Joseph Prince, who came from Beverly, Massachusetts, as Swan's "confidential agent," built a home on Harbor Island and remained there until about 1800.

In the absence of separate census schedules for the period 1800 to 1840, when the residents of Harbor Island are indistinguishable from those on Swans Island, let me simply review Dr. Small's findings with respect to residence on Harbor Island, which he calls "an attractive location for the earliest settlers" (pages 132, 143–45). A Dr. Thurston and a Mr. Bunker, neither further identified, are said to have lived on the island at an early date and to have established a store there. James T. Sprague of Union brought his family to the island in 1820, but stayed only a few years before removing to Marshall Island. The next residents were Zachariah and Seth Kempton from Hampden, Maine, who came in 1821, according to Small, and remained for about four years; they kept a store, cured fish, and provisioned vessels that stopped in Burnt Coat Harbor, an active port in the early decades of the nineteenth century.[18] The Kemptons sold to Silas Hardy, who also traded on the island for some years before moving to Swans Island proper to establish the first significant store there. A deed of 1839 shows Silas Hardy conveying all of Harbor Island for $850 to Hardy and Oliver Lane (Knox Lands 5/334); to judge from Silas Hardy's plantation tax that year (25 cents), the island had considerably less value than the purchase price.

We may turn now to federal census data, which are more explicit for Harbor Island from 1840 on—not, of course, covering *all* residents but at least the households found by the census-taker on his decennial visits. With Dr. Small's help it is possible to piece together island relationships.

In 1840, Hannah Lane is shown as head of

[18] Small may be a few years off on his dates here: a Hancock County deed notes the conveyance of the island from Michael O'Maley, another of Swan's agents, to Seth and Zachariah Kempton, "gentlemen" of Hampden, only in 1828—for a fee of $750 (Hancock 5/14).

Residence on Harbor Island, 1840—1880

Note: Age is at first appearance in schedules. Spouses are in parentheses. Occupations are shown as follows: Fa, farmer; Fi, fisherman; S, sailor; M, master mariner. Males are to left of slash, females to right.

Householder	1840	1850	1860	1870	1880
Lane, Hannah, 40s	2/2				
Stinson, William, 33 (Elizabeth), Fa		2/2	4/3	3/0[19]	3/2[20]
Lane, Hardy, 20s (Livonia)		6/5			
Stinson, Michael, 26 (Naomi), S/M			1/2	5/2	
Hardy, Seth, 27 (Sarah)), S				2/1	
Gray, Fred B., 30 (Elizabeth), Fi					1/4
Stanley, John S., 24 (Elwilde)					1/1

[19] Household included sons Oliver and John Stinson, twenty-two and eighteen, both fishermen.
[20] Household included son Hardy L. Stinson, thirty-four, a fisherman; and a housekeeper.

the only family residing on the island, with two young males in her household, plus a female over thirty. Hannah, who was forty-eight at the time, is the widow of Oliver Lane, Sr., and the two young males are her sons Hardy and Oliver who, as we have seen, had just acquired the island; the fourth person could be their sister Elizabeth, who married William Stinson (Small, 145). The 1850 census shows two families on Harbor Island: that of William Stinson, with whom Hannah is now living, and that of Hardy Lane, who married Livonia Stinson, William's sister; Oliver, Small tells us, had by this time sold his share in the island to William Stinson, prior to moving to Marshall Island—and, to tie things up all around, he (Oliver) married another of William's sisters, Keturah (Small, 117). In 1860 William Stinson, now a widower, is still on the island; his younger brother Michael is also there in a separate household. The agricultural census of 1860 shows William with seventy acres of improved land, four cows, two oxen, and thirty sheep. In 1870 there are three families on Harbor Island: William Stinson's all-male household (he was now a widower); Michael's growing entourage; and the family of Seth Hardy, son of the 1830s trader, Silas Hardy. In 1880 William Stinson is still in residence—he was the longest recorded inhabitant of the island—and there were two additional households, both transient.

Michael Stinson, who became a master mariner, had removed to Swans Island by 1880. William remained until his death in 1890, and his heirs, together with Captain Michael, according to Dr. Small (page 119), still owned Harbor Island in 1898 when Small's history was published. The earliest tax records on the islands surrounding Swans Island, in 1897, show Michael Stinson owning a quarter of Harbor Island, with a dwelling and forty-five sheep, the total valued at $1,235.

The residents of Harbor Island lived in the northeast sector, near the harbor, and the foundations of their homes may still be located. The Hancock County map of 1860 shows William Stinson living in the saddle, where a summer cottage built after World War II stands today, and Michael's home is shown near the northeast tip. Twenty years later William's residence is shown as a cluster of three buildings, Michael's—or Michael's *former* residence—as two (Map 1883 CGS 3). Remains of other structures are also discernible today along the north shore where there was a landing. Three dug wells still exist on the island in the vicinity of these dwellings. A small burial ground was located near William Stinson's farm, and Stinsons are undoubtedly there, including William's wife Elizabeth; the few stones left are illegible, according to the present owner.

I have not consulted census schedules for Harbor Island after 1880, and the memories of Swans Islanders whom I consulted in the 1970s extended very imperfectly back to the end of the nineteenth century. Carlton Joyce recalled two Hardy fishermen living on the island when he was young: Arthur and John, sons of Seth Hardy in the 1870 census. Joyce told the story of John Hardy coming across to the store at Minturn one wintry day and of how, being asked perfunctorily if things were well on Harbor Island, he replied laconically: "Well enough. Arthur died last night." There were surely others who lived and died on Harbor Island in the quarter century after William Stinson, but I have not discovered who they were.

In 1915 the island was bought from Alvah L. and Margaret A. Stinson by Alexander Forbes, a Boston yachtsman and devotee of the Maine coast. After using the island as a summer residence for his family for almost fifty years, he deeded it in 1962 to the Harbor Island Trust, which operates in the interests of a few families involved in the corporation. Sheep have continued to graze the island, but the once open fields and pastures are gradually reverting to woodlands—a boon, no doubt, to the more than a hundred species of birds that pause here in their annual migration.

Baker Islands, Scrag, and Green

These four islands seaward of Harbor Island were never settled as far as is known; indeed, only Big or Outer Baker of the four has certain fresh water and might have been capable of sustaining a family. Title to the two westerly of the four was held for many years by local fishermen for the privilege. In 1897, according to Swans Island tax records, Inner or Little Baker was owned by David Smith (valued at $25), Big or Outer Baker by Augusta Herrick ($100), Scrag by the heirs of William Stinson ($10), and part of Green by William Herrick (no value). These were all local Swans Islanders. A century later (1990s), Scrag, together with Harbor Island itself, is held by the Harbor Island Trust set up by Alexander Forbes; the Baker Islands[21] are held by his descendants; and Green is held by cottagers on Swans Island.

[21] The origin of the name Baker is not known—the islands are lettered *A* and *B* in the Burnt Coat Division of 1785 (Hancock Plan Book II: 7)—but the designation Baker Islands appears on maps from the 1870s.

Heron

This was *Little Marshall's Island* on the first post-Revolutionary surveys (Hancock Plan Book II: 9), but appears as *Heron* on maps printed in the nineteenth century. The origin of the name is presumably from a blue heron rookery that was once there. The island was apparently wooded in early years but was kept clear by grazing. In the nineteenth century it was used principally for the fishing privilege: local fishermen shared the island in 1897, according to Swans Island tax records—Edgar H. and David Smith, Parker Bridges, Michael Stinson, and the heirs of William Stinson. The total valuation was $200. In 1968 Heron was deeded to the National Park Service (Acadia). Today, like many of the outer islands, it is a nesting ground for eider duck and other species.

Since Heron lies close to a major passage from the open sea to more protected coastal waters (Toothacher Bay), it has been the site of numerous mishaps. The schooner D. B. WEBB, for example, returning to Deer Isle in June 1885 with three hundred barrels of mackerel, was a total loss off Heron Island, though the crew was saved (Captain Gray's Chronology, *Island Ad-Vantages*, February 20, 1976).

Marshall

This was the third largest island in Colonel Swan's dominion, after Swans itself and Outer Long Island, yet to my knowledge there were never more than a few families living year-round on Marshall at the same time in the nineteenth century, and usually no more than one. This was doubtless due to poor anchorages, compared to the numerous protected harbors around Swans Island—although there is some protection from prevailing southerlies inside Ringtown Island on the northeast shore. William D. Williamson, writing in the 1820s (I: 76), remarked on the bold and rocky shores "against which vessels have not infrequently been driven and sometimes wrecked." Anyone who has contemplated the southern and westerly aspects of Marshall Island will not be surprised.

It is listed as *Bear* or *Marshall's Island* on "Atlantic Neptune" maps in the Revolutionary era. Bears must have been common enough on this island in the eighteenth century, but the identity of Marshall is obscure. Dr. Noyes, Deer Isle's genealogist, states that this was a Joshua Marshall (Noyes, Family histories: Smith); there were indeed Marshalls on Deer Isle in the Revolutionary era, but George Hosmer, Deer Isle historian, indicates no connection between any of them and the island in question, and Dr. Small, Swans Island historian, takes no notice of any Marshall at all on or around Swans Island. It is not likely that Joshua, whoever he may have been, ever resided on Marshall Island.

Nor is it certain that another early settler associated in name with Marshall Island ever lived there: Samuel Emerson was given sixty acres on Marshall in 1798 by Swan's agent Joseph Prince, the deed to be delivered after seven years, to permit settlement and some "improvements" (Hancock 5/481). I am unable to identify this Samuel Emerson.

Nineteenth-Century Settlers

There were certainly settlers, in any case, by the 1820s. Williamson writes that the island, despite its forbidding shores, has "rich loamy soil, is mostly cleared and is the residence of a few families." Two householders, we learn from the 1820 census, were John (it should be Jeptha) Benson and James Sprague. The Spragues came originally from Union, pausing for a short stay on Harbor Island (Burnt Coat Harbor) before moving to Marshall; but they remained only a few years, according to Small (page 132), before settling permanently on Swans. I introduce here a residence table for Marshall Island in the nineteenth century in order to identify the settlers more easily (spouses, if known, are in parentheses; dollar amounts after some householders represent the census-taker's highest estimate of real estate and personal valuation between 1850 and 1880).

Residence on Marshall Island, 1820–1880

Householder	**1820**	**1830**	**1840**	**1850**	**1860**	**1870**	**1880**
Benson, John [Jeptha]	1/0	5/5					
Sprague, James	5/1						
Smith, Joseph		2/3					
Herrick, Kimball, 40s			3/5				
Lane, Oliver, 28, Fa $5,125				3/2	4/2		
Holmes, Lewis, 50 (Louise), Fa $3,550						1/2	
Obear, Wesley, 38 (Catherine), sailor						1/1	
Orne, Amos D., 38 (Delphina), farmer							3/2

Jeptha Benson's residence on Marshall Island was of longer duration than James Sprague's—and the alleged reason for his coming is of some interest. Both Hosmer (page 171) and Small (page 138) note that Benson, who was a soldier in both the Revolutionary War and the War of 1812, went on to the island in about 1814 and remained there for some twenty years. Neither of these historians note anything untoward in his coming. Dr. Noyes, however, gives us a lurid account of Benson—one that stretches credulity (Noyes, Family histories: Benson). Born in 1763, Jeptha is said to have abandoned one family in Hebron, Maine, before he appeared in the area—that is, on Little Deer Isle—in about 1800. There he courted simultaneously two young ladies, Phebe Eaton and Martha Howard, each of whom in 1814 gave birth to a child sired by Jeptha. It was this dilemma, according to Noyes, that prompted his abrupt departure from Little Deer Isle and removal to the comparative security of Marshall Island which was then deserted. So far the tale is plausible, but Dr. Noyes goes on to state that after Jeptha established residence on Marshall Island, togther with a Swans Island widow and her three children, the bastard son of Phebe Eaton was deposited on his island doorstep for maintenance; whereupon he abandoned the unwanted child on a half-tide ledge. The macabre legend has a happy ending: the child was discovered by a kindly Deer Isle fisherman (Amos Thurston) and reared by him before going on to a successful career as a master mariner in Camden, still bearing the name Rufus Benson.

The legend aside, Jeptha apparently farmed the island successfully. The log cabin he built for himself initially was replaced by a frame homestead within a few years. The fields were cleared, and the "rich loamy soil" produced profitable crops. The widow Mary Ross, a daughter of Thomas Kench, the original settler of nearby Harbor Island, bore Jeptha six more children, although they were not formally married until 1831 (W. A. Snow, *Brooksville Pioneers*, II: 168). The 1830 census shows the Benson menage in its prime: Jeptha, Widow Ross, four sons and four daughters (or daughters-in-law). Another settler on the island in 1830 was Joseph Smith, probably a Smith from Swans Island. All of Jeptha and Mary's children, in due course, quit the island—two were said to have drowned off its shores—and in 1835 Jeptha himself, never having had good title to Marshall, was dispossessed by Rufus Allyn, Swan's agent. He spent his last years in Brooksville.

Ownership of the island became rather complex after 1835 and was not always related to residence. Moses Bridges, for some years a resident of Western Calf (now Opechee) Island and an owner of other of Colonel Swan's interests, apparently acquired title to Marshall Island from Swan's agents in 1839 (Small, 156), though he did not immediately settle there; he is listed as still living on Calf Island in the 1840 census. The only family on Marshall in 1840 is that of Kimball Herrick, another person who figures in the numerous deeds disposing of Swan's islands in the Opechee group. Kimball Herrick, a native of Brooklin, had lived previously on Western Calf; he spent three years on Marshall before settling permanently on Swans Island with his wife, Abigail Babson, and their three daughters (Small, 123). Moses Bridges, meanwhile, having spent several years on Marshall Island (not, however, during a census-taker's visit), sold it to Silas Hardy in 1847—or, rather, he "swapped" it with Hardy, a trader and storekeeper at Burnt Coat Harbor, for a desirable piece of property in the latter area called "The Point," the site of Colonel Swan's original mills on Swans Island. It is doubtful that Marshall Island was Bridges's to sell or swap: mortgage deeds in the Hancock County registry for this period show a bewildering profusion of interests extending to land speculators as far away as Roxbury, Massachusetts.[22]

Oliver Lane, Silas Hardy's son-in-law, was able to disentangle title and by the mid-1850s owned the entire island, except for an interest in mining and mineral rights still held by a Roxbury investor (Hancock 38/446); these rights were never exercised, so far as is known. Oliver Lane was already resident on the island at this time; he is listed in the 1850 census with a family of four plus one "laborer," Silas Banks. He is still there in the 1860 census and is shown with two hundred acres of improved land (unlikely), a few cows, four

[22] Moses Bridges may have been repaid in kind: "The Point" proved also to have been under mortgage, and he himself was dispossessed when the mortgage was foreclosed.

oxen, and two hundred sheep. His farm on Long Point, the northeast corner of Marshall, is shown on the Hancock County Map of 1860. Small (page 146) says that Oliver Lane resided on the island until 1874, that is, a quarter of a century, all told. He is not, however, listed in the 1870 census, when two other families are shown: Lewis Holmes, a farmer, with wife and child, and approximately the same cultivated land and livestock shown a decade earlier for Oliver Lane; and Wesley Obear, a mariner with his eighteen-year-old wife. The 1880 census shows only one family, that of Amos D. Orne, a farmer. According to the 1880 agricultural census, Orne had eight acres of tilled land, including an acre and a half in barley and two and a half in potatoes; one hundred sixty acres of meadow; nine hundred acres unimproved; twenty acres in hay; and two hundred sheep. This was more substantial husbandry than that claimed by any island farmer in Hancock County in 1880 except James W. Blaisdell of Butter Island; Orne, moreover, was a tenant farmer, not the owner (see Appendix 3, page 476). The absence of a community on Marshall Island in the nineteenth century did not prevent the few who settled there from enjoying relative prosperity.

The Ringtown Community

The busiest era on Marshall Island appears to have come in the early years of the twentieth century, before World War I. Oliver Lane, who had left the island in the 1860s but continued to own it, died intestate in 1902 (followed within a few months by his wife Elizabeth), and his five children inherited Marshall Island. Three of the four sons—Hardy, John, and George—remained active on the island for some years, though their regular residence was in Rockport. During the summer months they farmed the island, sailing home to Rockport on weekends with half a dozen freshly slaughtered lambs from their large flock and returning with the next week's supplies. The two sons of a logger on the island named Merithew took part in the weekly sheep drive.[23]

[23] One of the sons, Dennis Merithew, recounted the details of the Lane brothers' activities as well as of the logging community on Marshall Island to Clayton Gross of Stonington; Clayton Gross's piece summarizing Merithew's recollections appeared in the *Island Ad-Vantages*, November 5, 1976. The Merithews lived on the island from 1908 to 1914.

Meanwhile, the Lanes leased the island to loggers who were responsible for creating the Ringtown settlement there. In 1902, for instance, timber rights were leased for eight years to a Manchester, New Hampshire company (Hancock 433/166). Ringtown was located on the northeast shore of the island, east of Ringtown Island, after which the community was named. As many as one hundred and fifty persons, according to Merithew, were at times centered in this community—loggers, teamsters, millmen, and their families.[24] Horses from stables in Ringtown were used for hauling logs. There were numerous logging roads crisscrossing the island, and there was for a time a narrow-gauge railway that crossed the island to a steam mill, located on the western shore opposite Two Bush Island. Work at the mill, according to Merithew, was paid at $9 for a sixty-hour week.

The Merithews lived in a frame homestead about midway down the island, but most dwellings were more humble and temporary. There were also two boardinghouses, one of them accommodating up to forty-five loggers. A school was maintained on the island with up to fifteen pupils; classes were normally held wherever the teacher boarded. Three or four babies, Dennis Merithew recalled, were born on the island while he was there. Merithew also remembered the names of some of the residents: the Edwin Eatons, for instance (whose children—three girls and a boy—were in the school) lived at the Lanes' farm on Long Point; two of the teachers were Joyce Fifield of Deer Isle and Phoebe Kent of Swans Island; Jim Sullivan was night watchman; the Frank Richards family lived at Ringtown; the steam mill was owned by Mr. Doane. Most of the loggers and millmen were French Canadian and came from some distance; the only name Merithew recalled in this group was Laplante (three children in this family). The mail carrier from Swans Island was Nelson Carter—and making a landing at Ringtown, Merithew remembered, was not easy.[25]

[24] The figure 150 may seem high, given the total of fourteen on Marshall Island shown in the *Maine Register* for 1910, but many at Ringtown were transient or seasonal workers and would not be counted in normal census tallies.

[25] The 1910 federal census lists additional residents on Marshall Island, but unfortunately, the only name legible in the listing I consulted was Ira Whitmore, with wife Eunice and a household of five (two males and three females).

The Ringtown community has disappeared, with few traces: the debris of a few camps, twisted bedsprings, empty gasoline drums, broken crockery, the burned-out cab of an ancient truck deep in an alder grove. Fires inevitably followed the loggers, some so stubborn that for days at a time local lobstermen were unable to pull their traps downwind. In one of these fires the old farm on Long Point burned, to judge from the charred beams in the waterlogged cellar.

Given this devastation that affected most of Marshall Island—excepting Sand Cove on the southeast shore where half a dozen summer camps have preserved an air of quiet gentility—it is not surprising that the island has had a turbulent and querulous twentieth century. Developers have attempted to create a resort on the island, accessible by flights to the airstrip they built there; Acadia National Park has eyed Marshall Island as a possible recreational area for its patrons; local lobstermen have protested any new activity for fear it would harm their catch; and environmentalists have been appalled by all prospects. I happily leave coverage of these contingencies to a new generation of historians.

Ringtown

This is *Island W* in the post-Revolutionary surveys completed under Rufus Putnam's supervision (Hancock Plan Book II: 9), and I have never discovered the origins of its present name.[26] *Ringtown* appears on maps in the last half of the nineteenth century. The island was apparently assumed to go with Marshall Island in conveyances of the latter during the nineteenth century, but in 1892 was deeded separately by the State of Maine to Oliver Lane for $5 (Hancock 280/231). Since Oliver Lane still owned Marshall at this date, the conveyance was a housekeeping operation to tidy up the Forestry Commission's files. Oliver Lane left the island to his heirs, whose descendants in due course sold to vacationers from New Hampshire. Ringtown Island never had habitation, nor indeed any particular use isolated from activity on Marshall. It did, however, lend its name to the bustling logging community on Marshall Island early in the twentieth century (see above).

[26] The only person I have heard of in the vicinity with the name, or nickname, "Ringtown" was the eldest son of Elijah Robbins: Ringtown Bill, after his residence near the William Ring farm on Deer Isle. I know of no special association between Ringtown Bill and this island; he appears to have been killed in a brawl in 1905 (Noyes, Family histories: Robbins).

Hat

Hat Island is without natural water and therefore was never inhabited, although its noble profile and good soil cover must have tempted early settlers. I find reference in Noyes (Family histories: Eaton) to the death on Hat Island in the 1870s of a Swans Islander named Gross, but there is no indication that he was living or even squatting there at the time. The island has been cut over several times since the eighteenth century, used for grazing sheep, and in this century owned primarily for fishing rights. It now belongs to a family that vacations in the region. To my knowledge the island has never had another name.

Buckle

This is *Island P* in the Burnt Coat Division of 1785 (Hancock Plan Book II: 7). and I have no idea where the name *Buckle* came from. It appears on deeds from at least 1850 forward (e.g., Hancock 116/11). Since there were no early settlers in the region named Buckle, or anything resembling Buckle, the reference must be to the object—perhaps to a small island barred to a larger one, as the buckle to a shoe. (There is another Buckle Island in Deer Island Thorofare, similarly barred to Spruce Island.)

Dr. Small (page 152) states that Abram Holbrook of Deer Isle came to Swans Island in 1836 and sometime thereafter settled for "a number of years" on Buckle Island before returning to Deer Isle. Hosmer (*Sketch of Deer Isle,* 193) notes Abram Holbrook living on Deer Isle in the 1880s, but makes no reference to his earlier sojourn on Swans or Buckle. Abram, who had eight children, according to Dr. Small, must have been a fisherman rather than a farmer, for it is difficult to imagine Buckle Island sustaining a farm that could feed a family of ten. There is no evidence that the island was ever farmed: no deep cellar, which any farmhouse would have had; no stone walls or rock piles from cleared land. Buckle Island, on the other hand, was close to excellent and much-frequented fishing grounds, and this was doubtless what brought Abram Holbrook there. But fishing was made hazardous by the abnormally strong mid-tide currents running through Casco Passage and York Narrows; frequent drownings were reported off Buckle Island in the mid-nineteenth century (e.g., Small, pages 68, 199, 202). It may have been such accidents that eventually sent Abram and his family back to Deer Isle. The owner of "Buckles Island" in 1897, according to Swans Island tax reports, was a non-resident named Reuben Stewart (valuation $150).

The only other resident of Buckle Island I know of was a twentieth-century hermit from Ellsworth named Ralph Dawes, who was neither farmer nor fisherman, properly speaking, but simply squatted on the island for some fifteen years before World War II. According to Carlton Joyce, he came first with a crippled brother who eventually died. Ralph Dawes's "home," a miniscule five-by-eight-foot shack, was at the southeast end of the island, and his shallow well is still evident. He survived, a recent owner judged from the debris in his kitchen "midden," on whiskey and Absorbine Jr. In his last years, before Dawes quit the island, his neighbors across the cove and then the island's owners, the Carl Lawsons, took care that he did not starve.

These, to my knowledge, were the only regular residents of Buckle Island—excluding, of course, the pair of osprey that seasonally nested on the northeast tip, familiar to generations of passing mariners until a winter storm blew out their nest in the mid-1970s.

Johns (off Opechee)

It may seem extraordinary that this small island, totally surrounded by reefs and without even the semblance of a harbor, was once inhabited, but this appears to be the case. The 1830 census lists David Carter, in his fifties, his wife of the same age, and four teenage children; the 1840 census shows Shadrick (or Shadrach) Herrick, in his thirties, wife, and two children. I do not identify this David Carter, but Shadrick Herrick was a son of Ebenezer, who owned both Eastern and Western Calf (Black and Opechee) in the 1830s, and a brother of Kimball Herrick, who lived for a time on Western Calf (Opechee) and in 1840 was on Marshall Island. The house site of these settlers is obscure today, no more than an indistinct pile of rocks; there may never have been a cellar. Neither of these residents ever owned the island, according to records at the Hancock County Registry of Deeds.

It must have been the society of neighbors on Western Calf that brought the Carters and Herricks to Johns Island, for the arable soil there is too meager to have supported subsistence farming, and the surrounding waters, as noted, too shoal for launching boats except at high tide. It is the only island known to the late Ralph Benson around which it is possible both to walk and to navigate by rowboat at low water—meaning that the channel between Johns and Opechee, if one is clever enough to find it, is narrow enough to leap across.

The origin of the island's name is unknown to me, but it appears in deeds dating from the 1830s and, as far as I am aware, was never called anything else. The ownership record has too many gaps to be of much use to us, but two early deeds are of passing interest. One, in 1847, shows the award of the island to Nathaniel Sawyer of Sedgwick in consequence of a debtor's suit brought against Samuel Kent of Swans Island who then owned Johns; Kent was ordered to jail (Hancock 81/520). If Samuel Kent ever went to jail, he soon came out and repossessed his island, for he is shown as selling it in 1857, "together with all the privileges of the shore," to John W. Stillman of Camden; the sale price was $50 (Hancock 104/331). The Kents, however, were tenacious: Swans Island tax records of 1897 show another Kent—Martha P., presumably a descendant of Samuel—in possession of the island, although there is no record of when or how she acquired it from John Stillman. Colson Robbins owned Johns during most of the period he lived on Opechee (see next entry) and used it for pasturing sheep. Thereafter it passed to the fish-packing companies that owned most of the islands in the Opechee group from about 1920 to the 1960s, at which time it was acquired by cottagers.

Opechee

This is called *Charles Island* in early charting, but I have discovered no clue as to who Charles was. An alternate name, *Western Calf*, is shown on Rufus Putnam's survey of the Burnt Coat Division in 1786 (Hancock Plan Book II: 10); the island was included in the package sale of the Burnt Coat group that year to Colonel Swan. When Eastern Calf on Casco Passage came to be called Black Island early in the nineteenth century, Western Calf became simply *Calf Island*, and that name persisted in charting into the early twentieth century; it is still used by local lobstermen. The official name today is associated with the Robbins family who lived on the island from 1900 to World War I. The schoolteacher for the Robbins children, Mary Ann Carroll, was unhappy with so prosaic a name as Calf, and in casting about for a substitute hit upon—or one of her pupils hit upon—the name *Opechee*, from Longfellow's poem "Hiawatha":

> ... Forth into the forest straightway
> All alone walked Hiawatha
> Proudly, with his bow and arrows;
> And the birds sang round him, o'er him,
> "Do not shoot us, Hiawatha!"
> Sang the robin, the Opechee,
> Sang the blue-bird, the Owaissa,
> "Do not shoot us, Hiawatha!"

And so, with the concurrence of federal chartmakers, the Indian name for robin, as Longfellow taught us, became the official name for the island of the Robbins family.

The Robbinses, however, came there near the end of a long line of settlers. For some thirty-five years after James Swan acquired the island in 1786, title passed from one attorney or agent to another in the complex unraveling of his island empire and the settlement of his debts; there is no indication that any of these titleholders ever lived on or visited Opechee. Maine historian William D. Williamson (I: 75) noted that it was of "good soil and inhabited"; he presumably meant after 1820, for no inhabitants are shown in the federal census of that year.

A chart of residence and ownership from the 1820s to the 1920s will enhance our understanding of who was associated with Calf Island and when; the data are gathered from deeds, census figures, and materials loaned by a recent owner.

Opechee Island Residents and Owners, 1822–1920

Note: Residence is at left, ownership at right. Age is as given in decennial census (shown by a "C"—e.g., 1830C). Spouses, if known, are in parentheses. The "size" column shows the size of household, males to left of slash, females to right. In the ownership column, the symbol > means "conveyed to."

Householder	**size**	**date**	**Ownership**
Peter Powers		1822	Michael O'Maley > P. Powers
Kimball Herrick, 20s (Abby)	1/2	1830C	
Moses Bridges, 30s (Emily)	4/5		
		1831	Powers > Eben. Herrick(1/2)
		1836	Powers > Eben. Herrick (1/2)
		1839	Herrick > Thomas Ross (1/2)
Moses Bridges, 40s (Emily)	4/7	1840C	
Stillman Bridges, 20s (Carol)	1/2		
John Ross, 20s (Betsy)	1/3		
		1842	Herrick > Nat'l Allen (1/2)
		1845	Allen > Benjamin Cole, Jr.
Benjamin Cole, Jr., 44	4/3	1850C	
Benjamin Cole, Jr., 54	4/3	1860C	
		1863	Cole > William Thompson
Henry Burns, 66 (Comfort)	7/2	1870C	
Henry Burns, 78 (Comfort)	5/2	1880C	
		1886	William Thompson heirs > Willis Watson
Colson Robbins, 41 (Lizzie)	5/3	1900C	Watson > Colson Robbins
Colson Robbins, 51 (Lizzie)	3/3	1910C	
George C. Robbins, 24 (illeg.)	3/2		
Chester Robbins, 29 (Phebe)	2/1		
Watson Walls, 57 (Rose)	1/2		
		1918	Robbins > West Coast Fish Co.
Carl Lawson family		1920	

The earliest resident whom we can identify with assurance is Peter Powers, who bought Calf Island for $750 from Swan's agent Michael O'Maley in 1822 and is noted explicitly in the deed as living on the island at the time (Hancock 43/521). Peter Powers was probably related to Prescott Powers, who is noted in both the 1820 and 1830 census schedules as resident on Pond Island (see page 440). Peter Powers apparently quit Calf Island before the end of the decade, for he is not listed in the 1830 census; he removed first to Blue Hill, where he is shown in Jonathan Fisher's "Diaries" (see Bibliography), and later to Brooklin. Ebenezer Herrick, to whom Powers sold the island in two parcels, for $500 each, did not live there, but two deeds refer to other residents (Hancock 73/462 and 73/466): in 1831 Moses Bridges and Kimball Herrick, Ebenezer's son, were living on the island.[27] Both are shown with their families in the 1830 census; in 1836 only Moses Bridges is mentioned in the conveyance, Kimball Herrick having removed by this time to Marshall Island (see page 428). Moses Bridges is still on Calf Island in 1840, according to the federal census, along with his son Stillman's family and John Ross. The latter's brother Thomas at this time held a half interest in the island which he had acquired from Ebenezer Herrick. John Ross was married to Elizabeth Bridges, daughter of Moses, and according to Small the couple "lived some years" on Calf

[27] Moses Bridges was probably a brother-in-law of Ebenezer Herrick, whose wife was Priscilla Bridges (Small, 123).

Island before removing to Swans. John Ross was drowned in Eggemoggin Reach in about 1846 (Small, 139, 156, 198).[28]

According to Blue Hill genealogist Elizabeth Wescott, there was another Herrick family on Calf Island in this era, that of Tenney Herrick, who married a sister of Nathaniel Allen of Pond Island; their daughter Mary Ann was said to be "of Calf Island" at the time of her marriage to Captain Warren Wells, grandson of the "William Walls" shown in the 1810 census of Pond Island.

Bridgeses and Herricks, then, were linked in the ownership of and residence on the islands north and west of Swans during the second quarter of the last century: Marshall, Johns, and both Eastern and Western Calf. In what sectors of Western Calf they settled is uncertain, for subsequent habitation has obliterated evidence of their cellar foundations.

In 1845 Nathaniel Allen of Pond Island, having acquired title to all of Calf Island, sold it to Benjamin Cole, Jr. for $1,200, and the deed indi-

[28] John Ross had very early roots in the area: he was a grandson of Thomas Kench of Harbor Island, the earliest settler on Swans Island, and a stepson of Jeptha Benson of Marshall Island.

Opechee Group, northwest of Swans Island, at low tide May 1944: Pond Island at top, with exposed bar to Thrumcap; Opechee, with the Colson farm site in the lower field; Black Island, lower right with traces of recent logging. (United States Air Force photo, courtesy of Alan C. Bemis.)

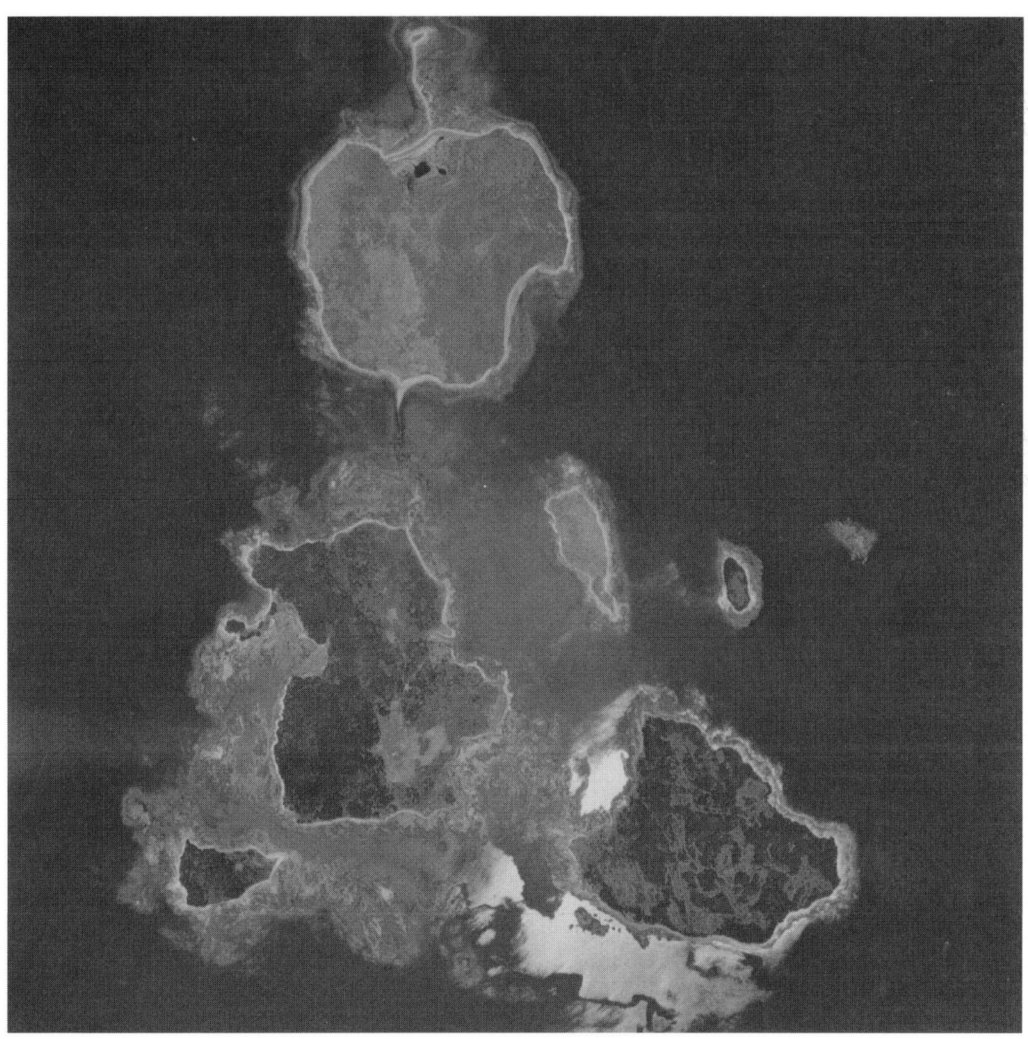

cates that the Cole family was already settled there (Hancock 106/81); Benjamin Cole, according to Elizabeth Wescott, was a brother-in-law of Nathaniel Allen. The Coles remained for almost two decades, perhaps the longest residence on Calf Island. The farm, which shows on the Hancock County map of 1860, was on the southeast end, facing Black Island. According to the agricultural census of 1850, Benjamin Cole had sixty acres of improved land, a dozen cows, a pair of oxen and forty-eight sheep; his real estate valuation was $1,500, and his personal valuation $1,000.

In 1863 Benjamin Cole sold Calf Island, along with Sheep and Eagle, to William Thompson of Trenton for $1,500; the deed indicates that Cole had already quit the island and was living in Brooksville (Hancock 123/113). William Thompson was an absentee owner but evidently had a tenant on the island: Henry Burns and his adult family are listed in both the 1870 and 1880 census schedules (in the plantation of Frenchboro, to which Calf Island belonged). They presumably lived in the old Cole farm, the only bulding shown in most maps of this era (e.g., Maps 1881 Colby, Hancock, and 1883 CGS 3); one chart, however, shows at least four structures, two at the Cole site, one on the east nub facing Black Island, and another on the small cove north of the nub (Map 1885 CGS 307). According to the agricultural census of 1880, Henry Burns had five acres of tilled land and thirty acres in meadow; he took in fifteen tons of hay and owned fifty-four sheep, a respectable operation for a farmer in his late seventies, and not inferior to that of other island farmers in this era (see Appendix 3). I do not know when the Burns family quit the island, but given Henry's age, it was probably not long after 1880. The farm had apparently burned, been razed, or fallen in by 1900 when the Robbinses moved onto the island; at least members of that family interviewed in the 1970s had no recollection of a building. Colson Robbins's plow, meanwhile, finished off what was left of a cellar hole, so that today evidence of the Cole-Burns farm site is no more to be discovered than evidence of the Powers, Herrick, and Bridges homesteads some decades earlier; possibly they were all in the same spot. All the Robbinses found on the island, apart from cleared fields, were the remains of a sawmill on the south side of the cove on the western shore, probably an enterprise started by Dr. Willis Watson of Bass Harbor when he owned most of the islands in the Opechee group during the 1880s and 1890s and kept a dairy farm on Pond.

Colson Robbins, a sea captain earlier in his life, was Dr. Watson's resident farmer on Pond Island from 1895 to 1900. As early as 1898 he bought weir rights on Calf Island from his

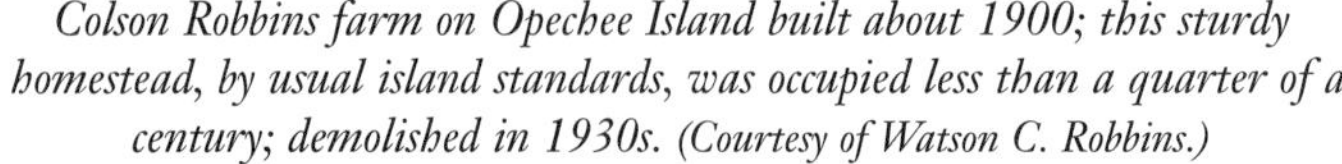

Colson Robbins farm on Opechee Island built about 1900; this sturdy homestead, by usual island standards, was occupied less than a quarter of a century; demolished in 1930s. (Courtesy of Watson C. Robbins.)

employer and in 1900 bought the island outright, along with Sheep and Eagle; he had already acquired Black Island and subsequently bought Johns, so he owned all the islands in the group except Pond itself. The family, which included half a dozen children (Chester, Lettie, George, Vola, Lem, and Jay) lived first in fish camps on the small cove on the eastern shore called Gundelo Cove. Colson soon built a two-and-a-half story frame house and barn in the center of the island and moved the bulk of his family there, leaving the buildings at Gundelo Cove to his married sons. At the peak of the Robbinses' residence on the island, the cluster of buildings at the cove included the homes of Chester's and George's families, more barns and sheds, a boathouse, and the school for two generations of Robbins children.

It was at this school that Mary Ann Carroll, a teacher on many Maine islands in her eventful life, presided for some years. Her letters shed interesting light on the life of Opechee Island. In one dated September 22, 1903, for example, after

Sketch of Opechee Island c. 1910 by Jay Robbins, at the age of twelve. The Colson Robbins farm is lower center, at the intersection of several "roads." (Courtesy of Mrs. Jay Robbins.)

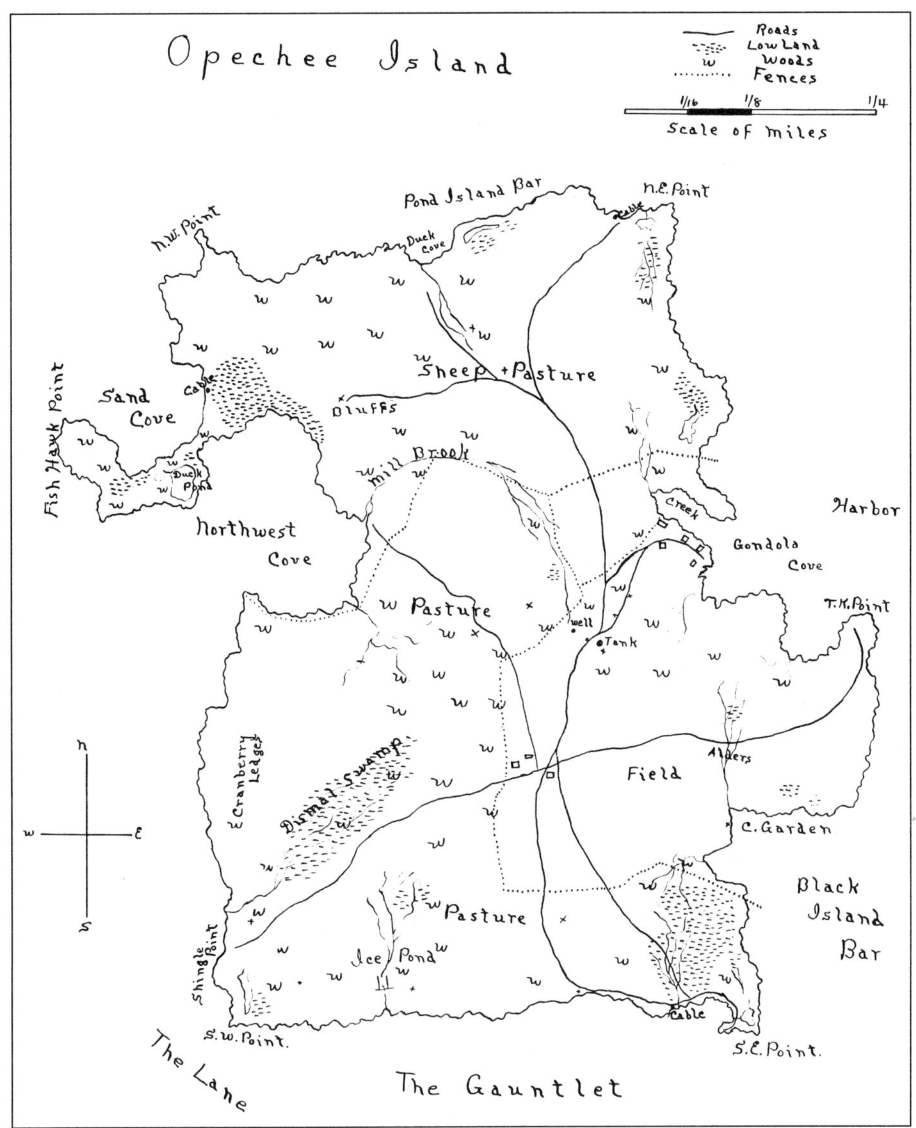

returning from a vacation in Boston, she expressed concern over rumors that the new owner of Pond Island, Fountain Rodick of Bar Harbor, was already selling lots to summer "rusticators" (the rumors were unfounded); she was grateful that Colson Robbins had done well with his weirs that summer; and she noted with approval Chester's impending marriage to the daughter of Watson and Rose Walls—another family living on Opechee. In a letter at the end of the same year (December 29), on returning from another absence, she remarked on the extreme isolation of the island in winter, when they often had to wait many days for weather moderate enough for Colson and his sons to row across the bay to Mackerel Cove for mail and supplies, or to Bass Harbor to drop off or pick up any members of the family leaving for or returning from the mainland. On February 29, 1904 she wrote that "the ice has torn up Mr. Robbins' weirs and killed more than half his sheep on Pond Island," for while he could walk to several of the other islands where he had sheep, the ice was too treacherous across the bar to reach Pond (Carroll letters).

The Robbinses were primarily weirmen, but they farmed as well. They ploughed most of the arable land on the island with two pairs of oxen and filled the barns with hay and other produce. They cut ice from a shallow pond at the south end of the island. Colson's flock of sheep, pastured on the surrounding islands, averaged more than one hundred. As weirmen, the Robbinses were part of a growing community of fishermen who came each summer to the vicinity to tend weirs. The latter lived in makeshift cabins on nearby islands and used Gundelo Cove as their home port; on summer evenings this "harbor," which bared at low tide, would be crowded with many types of craft—dories and sailboats in the first days, later "make and break" launches, like Chester Robbins's EUREKA, with its twin exhaust pipes projecting upward like a miniature steamer. The site where the weirmen tarred their nets is still visible on the northeast shore.

By 1915, according to Robbins descendants, thirty-three people were living on Opechee Island, and even if this number included some transients, it was still the largest population the island had known in all its history. The half dozen households on the island were connected by telephone after the Swans Island Telephone Company completed its off-island system in 1909 (*Ellsworth American*, June 23, 1909); the line ran across Opechee before dropping into Jericho Bay and across to Naskeag Harbor, and Colson Robbins shrewdly tied into this line, using extra equipment to build an intra-island system of his own. Pieces of this abandoned line may still be seen in a cove on the western shore. A full accounting of the Robbinses' rich life on Opechee Island would take more space than is available here.

One naturally wonders why Colson Robbins ever ended so pleasing an existence, to which his descendants look back with such affection. There were, of course, reasons—reasons not very different from those that caused most island families to remove, generally many years before the Robbinses did. One was schooling: as Chester's and George's children reached high school age, it was necessary for them to leave the island for further education, and the parents went with them. Another reason was the decline of weiring profits; it was said that the chum from a sardine factory in Naskeag Harbor spoiled the weir fishing, but whether or not this was the case, the catches became more and more erratic by World War I. Perhaps the most curious reason of all, which tells something of Colson Robbins's character, is one offered by his son, Lem: Colson, when approached by a fish-packing company that wished to buy his islands, agreed to sell them—for $100,000, a figure he believed high enough to scare off any bidders; it proved not to be, and when this sum was offered to him, according to Lem, Colson honored his rash agreement. This sale was completed in 1918, and the last of the family quit the island at about that time.

Residents were on the island for a few more years. Elmer Bridges of Brooklin was caretaker for Colson Robbins for a year or so, living in the George Robbins homestead with his family. Cassie Hamlin (later Cassie Hamlin Gross, of Stonington) taught school on the island in the fall of 1918 and reported she had seven or eight pupils, including two from Pond Island; the school at that date was supported by Swans Island.[29] The last year-round tenancy, by the Carl Lawson family, was from about 1920 to 1923. Father and son were both weirmen, tending weirs for the West Coast Fisheries Company, the new owner. Carl Lawson, Sr. lived in the Colson Robbins farm, his son Carl in one of the houses on Gundelo Cove, where his wife gave birth to two of their children. The island telephone system was still operating, according to Mrs. Carl Lawson, Jr., but off-island service had been discontinued. The fields and meadows, meanwhile, became quickly overgrown, since farming and grazing had ceased.

With the departure of the Lawsons, Opechee became an abandoned island, except for incidental visits by weirmen, clammers, occasional lobstermen, and picnickers in season. Some of the Robbins family returned periodically and camped in Colson's house, but this building deteriorated rapidly and, I believe, collapsed before World War II. Various fish-packing companies owned the island until it was acquired in 1969, along with other islands in the archipelago, by a cottager fron Mount Desert Island. Two decades later ownership passed to cottagers in Brooklin, who have used Opechee in connection with their ecological enterprise, the Maine Enviromental Research Institute (MERI).

[29] Jurisdiction over Opechee Island has shifted over the years. Some census schedules in the nineteenth century list Opechee with other Hancock County islands (that is, in no township); other schedules show it under Long Island (Frenchboro). Owners persistently indicate a link to Swans Island, yet tax records before 1900 do not confirm the association.

Pond (off Swans Island)

This island was used by Indians for many seasons before the first white men set foot on it. The kitchen middens on the southwest shore are said to be nine feet deep in places, which makes them among the deepest known in the region. Trained archaeologists were happily able to probe the shell heaps systematically and found many artifacts before the middens were disrupted in recent years by amateur curio seekers.

Pond is called *Pound Island* on British Admiralty charts of the Revolutionary era—evidently a misspelling (though the Pond Island opposite Cape Rosier is correctly spelled in the same series). Both had freshwater ponds in early days, though they became tidal many years ago when seas broke through the outer wall. Lamp Island, off the northern tip of Pond, was originally called *Thrumcap*—as many islands of similar shape and size were in Revolutionary times—after the woolen skullcaps worn by Colonial sailors. It was a landmark to earlier mariners, as an English traveler makes clear in his description of it during a voyage through the area in 1770: "a small tufted island, which lies to the northward of the range of islands that extends from Burntcot [i.e., Casco] passage" (Owen, "Narrative of American Voyages," 733).

Pond Island was part of Colonel Swan's dominion in 1786 and remained within his control, or the control of his agents, until 1835. A chronological table shows both ownership of and residence on the island from the post-Revolutionary era to World War I, as I have been able to re-create it; the ownership detail comes principally from the records of a recent owner, and the residence from census data and other evidence.

Residents and Owners of Pond Island, 1786–1914

Note: Residence is on the left; age of householder is as shown in the federal census (noted by "C"—e.g., 1810C). Size of household is given (males left of slash, females to right). The symbol > in the ownership column means "conveyed to."

Householder	**Size**	**Date**	**Ownership**
		1786	Massachusetts > James Swan
William Wills (or Wells)	11	1810C	
		1817	Michael O'Maley, Swan's agent, acquires title
Prescott Powers, 50s	4/4	1820C	
Prescott Powers, 60s	7/8	1830C	
Thomas Connly		17/12[30]	
Nathaniel Allen, 40s	6/5	1840C	O'Maley > Nathaniel Allen
Nathaniel Allen, 50s	6/4	1850C	
- Madison Babson, 35			
Nathaniel Allen, 62, farmer	3/2	1860C	
- Adelbert Gott, 17, laborer			
- Alphonse Cousins, 14			
		1863	Allen > William Thompson
Residents unknown		1870	
Naham Young, 29 (Lydia)	3/1	1880C	
- John F. Cousins, 17			
		1886	Thompson heirs > Willis Watson
Benson family (tenant farmers)	1890		
Colson Robbins (tenant farmer) [31]	1895		
		1900	Watson > Fountain Rodick
		1914	Rodick > A. C. Farnsworth

[30] I have no explanation for the high number of residents in 1830; possibly they were farm workers in connection with the harvest.

[31] Colson Robbins served as tenant farmer for Willis Watson until 1900 when he removed to Calf Island (see above).

Pond Island was inhabited in 1810, according to the federal census, by the family of William Wills (alternately spelled Wells or Walls). According to Blue Hill genealogist Elizabeth Wescott, a Herrick forebear of hers said to be "of Calf (that is, Opechee) Island" married Captain Warren Wells; this was a grandson of William. I know nothing of the arrangements William Wells made with Colonel Swan's agents for tenancy. The next settler, Prescott Powers, was a son of the Congregational minister on Deer Isle, Reverend Peter Powers, and spent some fifteen years or more on Pond Island before removing with his family to Blue Hill in 1832 (Hosmer, *Historical Sketch of Deer Isle*, 133); he, too, was probably a tenant farmer, since there is no record of his ever having owned the island.

One imagines that the Wells and Powers families lived on the crest of the island, as subsequent residents did. However, the late Ralph Benson—who was born on Pond and knew it as well as anyone living in recent years—recalled an ancient cellar hole in the northwest sector of the island, closer to the pond, and this could have been the housesite of these first known European settlers.

In 1835 Nathaniel Allen, Jr. acquired title to Pond Island from Michael O'Maley, Colonel Swan's agent, and moved onto the island either before or immediately after his purchase; deeds from the mid-1830s refer to Nathaniel Allen "of Pond Island" (e.g., Hancock 81/24, concerning a conveyance of a half interest in Calf, or Opechee, Island). The Allens remained on Pond Island, as the census shows, for at least a quarter century. Madison Babson, shown in the 1850 census as a member of Nathaniel Allen's household, married Nathaniel's daughter Julia in about 1854, after the death of his first wife in 1850; they removed to Surry a few years later (Elizabeth Wescott correspondence). The Allen farm is shown on the Hancock County map of 1860, standing near the center of the island at the same location where later farms stood; indeed, some of the buildings may have been the same. I have discovered little more about the Allens and their boarders than I have about their predecessors on Pond Island. The Nathaniel Allen in the 1860 census appears to have been well off: he is shown with a real estate valuation of $2,500 and a personal valuation of $750. He had one hundred and thirty acres of improved land, twelve cows, two oxen, and sixty sheep. By any standard of island husbandry for the era, this represented prosperity,

The 1870 census does not list Pond Island separately (it had been part of Long Island Plantation since the 1840s), but the farm was probably worked by Henry Burns, who is believed to have been living as a tenant on Opechee Island. Of Naham (or Nathan) Young in the 1880 census I know only that he had four acres of tilled land, fifty in meadows, took in thirty-five tons of hay, and kept fifty-two sheep; this is from the 1880 agricultural census (Appendix 3). A chart surveyed early in the 1880s shows six buildings clustered in the center of the island (Map 1883 CGS 3) and about two-thirds of the island cleared.[32]

In 1886 Pond Island was sold by the heirs of William Thompson of Trenton, an absentee owner, to Dr. Willis Watson of Bass Harbor. He too was an absentee owner, but for some years he made an effort to run a dairy farm on the island, using families from the area as tenant farmers. One of these—I believe not the first—was the Benson family of Bernard, who were in residence from about 1890 to 1895; Ralph Benson was born on Pond Island in 1893. There were, in addition to the farmhouse, two large barns during this era, as a well as a milking shed and other outbuildings. The Bensons were followed by Colson Robbins, who remained until 1900 when he bought Calf Island from Dr. Watson and moved his family there. The Robbins were the last year-round residents on Pond Island. Colson continued to pasture sheep there, but full-scale farming ended with the Robbinses' removal, and the buildings fell into disrepair.

In 1900 Pond Island was sold to a wealthy young resident of Bar Harbor named Fountain Rodick, and he spent several seasons on the island tending a weir. He built himself a cabin with an elegant fireplace on the bar facing Opechee, was visited occasionally by friends, including a yachting brother, and lived what I picture as a hermit-like existence in considerable luxury. According to Ralph Benson, he had two fine catches of herring, but out of compassion refused to sell them, and they eventually perished; no herring, it is reported, ever returned to that cove.

Fountain Rodick sold Pond Island in 1914 to A. C. Farnsworth of Brooklin, owner of a fish-packing company there, and the island was owned by Mr. Farnsworth and his heirs for the next thirty-five years. During the early years of the Farnsworth ownership, weir fishing was extensive in the area, and a number of weirmen lived seasonally—and sometimes longer—on the island. William Allen of Brooklin, for example, lived there in 1918, and his children went to school on Opechee Island (Eulalie Bridges interview). Pond was used recreationally during the 1930s, especially by residents of Brooklin and Naskeag acquainted with the Farnsworths. The Watson buildings disappeared one by one, some razed and the timbers floated across to Naskeag Harbor for further use there, others burned by fires that swept periodically over the unoccupied island, whether by design or otherwise. Little remains today of the original farming complex astride Pond Island, beyond the well-laid cellars and stone walls.

The last venture on Pond Island worth recording was the effort of an owner in the 1950s, Ranson P. Kelley of Boothbay, to establish a sportsman's club there. He stocked the island with game birds and posted it, but the habits of local residents long used to having free use of the island would not be altered by a few signs, and the game birds disappeared as quickly as they were introduced. Mr. Kelley eventually despaired of his

[32] There is a local legend about a Cousins who lived on Pond Island, possibly neither of those in the residence table, since the one in the legend is called Fred. On the evening of his marriage to a Swans Island girl, Fred Cousins and his bride started back to Pond in a dense fog and were never seen again. The theory evolved that the steamer MOUNT DESERT, which called at Mackerel Cove in those days, unknowingly ran down Fred's dory in the fog. Since then the ghost of the steamer, "Old Monty," periodically appears in this area to those with lively imaginations—on foggy nights at about nine o'clock, accompanied by muffled cries (see Lufkin diaries).

project and sold Pond in 1962 to a cottager from Mount Desert Island, who was content to allow the island to revert to its natural state.

Pond Island has surely had tragedies off its shores, too numerous to review. The most bizarre I have heard of was in 1959 when two Islesford fishermen were discovered frozen in their gasless vessel on the northeast shore of the island; they had been driven fifteen miles by a March gale from the vicinity of Baker Island, where they were last seen three days before, across Bass Harbor Bar and Blue Hill Bay.

Sheep and Eagle

These are *Islands U* and *V* in the Burnt Coat Division of 1785, and title has normally resided with the owners of Calf (Opechee) Island. Settlers on Opechee in the nineteenth century used Sheep Island for grazing—it has been treeless for as far back as there is any record—and Eagle for occasional fuel and possibly for wayward rams. After World War I, when farming ended on Opechee, fish companies owned the islands and used them for weirs and clamming. The sheep have long since been removed and the weirs are gone, leaving the islands to revert to their natural cycle of growth and decay. Sheep Island sustains a growing population of nesting eider in season and a smaller colony of petrels.

Black (off Opechee)

The name given this island on the "Atlantic Neptune" is *Grass Island*, which indicates it was predominantly meadowland in that era. Rufus Putnam, on his Hancock County survey of 1785, called it "*Eastern Calf* or *Grass*," and by the 1820s it was called *Black Island*, the official name it has had ever since. Williamson, in his description of this area in the 1820s, noted that "Little Black Island" was inhabited (I: 75), but I believe he is in error. At least, there is no record of settlement, then or later, in census data, deeds, or local history.

It is indeed curious why so large and conveniently located an island was *not* inhabited. There is fresh water on Black Island, the soil is fertile, and while there is no harbor, the anchorages off the shores are no worse than off many islands in the vicinity that were settled. One reason may be that nearly all the owners of Black Island during the century following its sale from the James Swan estate in the 1820s—Moses Bridges, Kimball Herrick, Nathaniel Allen, Willis Watson, and Colson Robbins—either lived or maintained farms on Pond or Calf islands and preferred to use Black Island as supplementary to their farming operations rather than for tenant residence; it is known, for example, that several of these farmers regularly pastured sheep on Black Island. Another reason it was never settled may have been that it was used by Indians during the summer months and so took on the character of a special preserve for them. I have no certain evidence that Indians came regularly through the *nineteenth* century, but there is some presumption of it in the abundant reports of their summer visits early in the twentieth century. Carlton Joyce of Swans Island remembers as a boy waiting impatiently for the Indians' arrival on Black Island each spring, for he had a friend (Lolo) among them. Lem Robbins, who spent his youth on Pond and Opechee islands, recalls the regular summer visits of Indian Jo, who camped on the southwest shore of Black Island near a spring. These were Tarratine Indians, I believe, and came from the Penobscot River. They came after ash, sweetgrass for their basket weaving, and also for seal oil and skins.

If there was no year-round settlement on Black Island, there was incidental habitation, in addition to the Indians. During the weiring era, for instance, weirmen often camped on the island, and Colson Robbins built a rough cabin on the shore facing Opechee, which he rented out; one such cabin, his son Lem recalls, was built from the deck planks of a wreck off the island around 1900. Another itinerant resident on Black Island was Elmer Bridges, who was caretaker for some years on Opechee after Colson Robbins left. One can imagine incidental habitation such as this stretching back to the earliest residence on Pond and Opechee—but if Black Island ever had more sustained settlement, it has eluded me. In 1994 this island was placed by the current owner under a "forever wild" conservation easement.

Orono

"Blue-eyed" Orono was sachem of the Tarratines in the latter half of the eighteenth century, and since he sided with the Colonists against the British in the Revolutionary War, it was altogether fitting that an island should be named after him. Why this particular one, is unknown; nor was his name attached immediately to it, for it appears as *Island N* in the Burnt Coat Division surveyed in 1785 (Hancock Plan Book II: 7). Both names are used in an 1850 conveyance from Charles S. Abbot to Jacob S. Reed (Hancock 116/11).

It is a matter of some chagrin that the history of a quarry island like this, which nourished several dozen residents as recently as the early 1900s, should be so quickly obliterated. Perhaps this is because the island knew only quarrying—and that, briefly. There were never, to my knowledge, settlers on Orono. Undoubtedly sheep were kept there after it was cleared, but no farms, no stone walls, no wells were there. Jacob S. Reed was a gristmill operator from Brooklin who moved his mill and his family to Swans Island in 1845 (Small, 150); it is not known what object he had in buying Orono, along with Buckle, Phinney, and Round, unless, indeed, to pasture sheep. The island passed to his heirs and from them in 1889 for $400 to Garrett Coughlin, a quarry operator from Vinalhaven (Hancock 235/6). Coughlin sold in 1894 to J. Dunlop Smith of Barre, Vermont, for $25,000, a fee that, if correctly recorded, must have made farmers and fishermen on neighboring islands incredulous (Hancock 281/437). The reason was, of course, granite, and it may be assumed that quarrying operations began soon after 1894; J. Dunlop Smith was associated with the Empire Granite Company of Barre. In 1897 the town valuation on the island and its "furnishings" was $3,060 (Swans Island records).

The title record is clear enough—at least to this point—but the quarrying operation itself is obscure. A stone wharf was constructed on the southwest shore of the island not far from the quarries, and schooners loaded the stone here; the wharf still stands, only slightly abused by winter storms. Some thirty or forty quarrymen were said to have been employed—seasonally, I assume—and three or four dwellings were built on the island to house them, including a story-and-a-half boardinghouse on the eastern side. The late Carlton Joyce, who provided the foregoing information, remembered the Orono whistle each morning summoning the quarrymen to work.

The operation lasted no more than ten or a dozen years, if that long, and had surprisingly little impact on the area. It is curious, for instance, that younger members of the Robbins family who were living at the time on Opechee Island within sight of Orono had no recollection of the quarrying operation when I interviewed them sixty years later. The owners apparently fell into dispute among themselves, perhaps over the enormous price they had paid for the island at a time when the quarrying industry was moving from Maine to Barre, not the other way around; the dispute was settled in a court action in 1909 between J. Dunlop Smith and a co-owner, Edgar Bronk (Hancock 466/112). A successor corporation, Garner and Company of New York, sold the island in 1910; title eventually passed to cottagers on Swans Island. The island was not subsequently occupied, except seasonally by fishermen and clammers who lived in the abandoned dwellings as long as they stood; none remain today.

Phinney and Round

These two islands in Mackerel Cove (formerly *Randle Bay*) on the north side of Swans Island were respectively *Islands K* and *I* in the Burnt Coat Division of 1785 (Hancock Plan Book II: 7). Neither was ever settled, being without fresh water supply and too small to sustain a family in year-round residence. The original spelling of Phinney was *Finney*, after an early-nineteenth-century Irish settler, John Finney, who deserted from British military service at St. Croix and found his way first to Deer Isle, then Swans Island; he married the eldest daughter of Moses Staples (Small, 107). John Finney probably used the seven-acre island for pasturage. Edmund F. Bridges is shown as owner in the 1890s—the value of the island was $100—and in the mid-twentieth century the island was acquired by a cottager from Mount Desert Island. This owner, a Boston attorney and yachtsman, persuaded Swans Islanders in a 1954 plantation meeting to change the name to "Asa's Island," on the understanding that he, Asa, would make an appropriate contribution to the school fund (Westbrook, *Biography of an Island*, 223). There the matter rests. The Swans Islanders have done their part: the name "Asa's or Phinney Island" appears dutifully on tax lists. But the name on coastal charts is *Phinney Island*, and if I have any understanding of these matters, it will remain that way.

Round Island, south of Phinney, is not named on current Coast and Geodetic Surveys, although it was on earlier issues (e.g., Map 1885 CGS 307). It was never regularly occupied even in season, according to local residents, until the summer cottage now standing there was moved from Bass Harbor in the 1950s. The title search prepared for the current owners traces title back to 1850 and shows possession by several well-known traders in island property in the region—Charles Abbott, Jacob Read, A. S. Littlefield, and others—but gives no clue as to what special use was made of Round Island, if any. It was undoubtedly cut over several times for pulp, used intermittently for pasturage, and, as always, held for the fishing privilege.

One of the two islands—I am not certain which—proved the saving of Colson Robbins of Opechee early in the twentieth century, when he was caught by ice floes while returning from the village of Atlantic with the family mail late one wintry afternoon; he made his way to the nearest island and lit a huge bonfire of driftwood, a signal to his anxious family on Opechee that he was safe. When the tide changed at midnight, breaking up the ice jam, he rowed safely home under a full moon (recounted by Lem Robbins, Colson's son).

Sister Islands

These twins are named the *Seal Islands* on some editions of the "Atlantic Neptune," and this name reappears in the Burnt Coat Division surveyed in 1785 (Hancock Plan Book II: 9) and on a coastal chart as late as the 1850s (Map 1854 Eggmoggin Reach). Maps from the 1860s on show the islands by their present name (e.g., Map 1860 Hancock County, Walling). Tax records on Swans Island show the islands owned locally through the nineteenth century. I do not know the origin of the name *Sister Islands*, but the late owner of the western Sister has suggested (with a fine masculine flourish) that it comes from the naturally feminine nature of islands in general and the sensuality of the rocks on the northwest corner of his.

Neither island has a cellar hole to indicate prolonged habitation, but the western Sister had a fish shack at the northwest tip as early as the 1880s (Map 1883 CGS 103). A more recent camp is at the same site today, and since 1964 a small summer cottage has been on the west side of the eastern Sister. Deer have been on this island periodically: not long ago, sailing past the Sisters toward the eastern entry to Burnt Coat Harbor in thick fog, we saw a buck cross our bow swimming, as we thought, straight out to sea—until I checked our bearings and discovered he was on a true course to the tip of the eastern Sister.

Harbor and Crow (off Frenchboro)

These two islands, one of them protecting the entrance to Lunts Harbor at Frenchboro, have been frequented for three or more centuries by mariners who used this anchorage. Neither charts nor local report, however, indicate prolonged settlement on either island; a non-local owner and sometime inhabitant of Harbor Island today may indeed claim longest residence. The islands are lettered *D* and *E* in the survey of the Burnt Coat Division in 1785, at the time of James Swan's purchase (Hancock Plan Book II: 7). I have not traced the title record of the islands, but it will come as no surprise that Lunts of Frenchboro were in possession in the 1870s and probably for as many years before as since (Maine Archives: "1874 Island Sales").

Long Island (Frenchboro)

Long Island,[33] though its location and outline are suggested on maps dating from the seventeenth century, is not named on charts until the early eighteenth century (e.g., Map 1721 Coasting Pilot: *Long Isle*). There was no recorded settlement before the Revolution and, indeed, not in all likelihood until the 1790s, although mariners for two centuries surely knew the harbor.

Early Settlers

According to Swans Island historian Dr. Small (page 75), William Davis, who came to Swans in 1794, went onto Long Island three years later, together with John Rich; Rich soon left for Isle au Haut, but Davis is believed to have remained and was apparently the earliest settler. He was the forebear of the many Davises who have lived on the island.

For reasons that are unclear, census-takers appear to have overlooked Long Island in early schedules. Residents are not shown until 1820 when three householders are listed: William Pomroy (or Pomeroy), Thomas Pomroy, and Asa Smith—see census table at the end of this entry. Asa Smith, according to Vivian Lunt (page 8), was a son of David Smith of Swans Island; William Pomroy, she says, came onto the island in 1818 or 1820 when the other two were already there. I have discovered nothing about the origin of these Pomroys, neither of whom is shown as householder in the 1830 census. William Williamson's assertion (I: 76) that there were fifteen or twenty families in residence on Long Island in the 1820s (his history purports to cover the years before 1820, the date of Maine's statehood, but was published only in 1832) is surely in error: even in 1830 there were only six households on Long Island, according to the federal census.

Lunts, to judge from the 1830 census, arrived on Long Island during the preceding decade, and there was never a time thereafter when the island did not have half a dozen or more Lunt households. Indeed, the island was known during much of the nineteenth century as *Lunt's Long Island.* I include below an abbreviated tree of the first three generations of Lunts known to have settled on Long Island. Amos and Abner were the sons of a peripatetic Revolutionary War veteran who came from Scarborough and settled eventually in Pretty Marsh (Mount Desert) after living on both Fox islands and briefly on York Island off Isle au Haut (T. B. Lunt, *Lunt Family* 70). The two brothers, married for some years when they arrived on Long Island, evidently overlapped with the Pomroys, for two of Amos's sons, Israel B. and Amos, Jr., married daughters of William Pomroy. Amos and Abner both lived into the 1850s and were the senior residents on the island at mid-century, but it was evidently Israel B. who provided the initiative for and gave structure to the island's economy. According to Vivian Lunt, he built a store on the harbor, fitted out vessels for the fisheries, and engaged in coastal trade; he was also instrumental in the organization of an island school in 1843 and

[33] The history of Long Island is covered in some detail by Vivian Lunt in the third edition of her *Long Island Plantation: a History of Frenchboro* (1976). The present notice does not attempt the full coverage she provides.

of a Baptist Church the same year. Israel and Amos, Jr. had twenty-three children between them born on Long Island, and a number of them, of course, remained: the 1850 census shows no fewer than thirteen Lunt households of a total of twenty-seven; in 1893, the number of male Lunts eligible for the militia was sixteen of a total pool of twenty-seven (Frenchboro town records).

The second-largest family on Long Island were the Riches of Richs Head, where William and Charity Gott Rich settled in the 1820s (Vivian Lunt, 9). The Riches, like the Lunts, had large families, many of whom married and settled on Long Island. They remained on the Head through most of the nineteenth century, and for a time had their own school there. Nineteenth-century maps do not show more than three or four house sites on the Head at any one time, but Vivian Lunt has identified eight distinct cellar holes, all of them on the north shore facing Richs Cove. These homesteads were abandoned by 1900 as the Riches and other settlers on the Head drew in to Lunts Harbor, a more secure anchorage.

The population on Long Island grew steadily through the nineteenth century and peaked at 197 in 1910. The distribution shifted somewhat. The Hancock County map of 1860, for instance, showed three dwellings on the Head and about two dozen flanking the harbor, together with the church and parsonage; charts surveyed in the 1870s showed four buildings at the Head, five in the interior, and nearly three dozen around the harbor (Map 1883 CGS 3). The occupations hardly changed: there were a few farmers—two appear in the agricultural census of 1880 (Nancy P. Lunt, Israel's widow, and William Rich on Long Island Head)—but the overwhelming majority were fishermen or mariners. The twenty-seven young men eligible for the militia in 1887 and the same number in 1893 were *all* identified as fishermen.[34]

Long Island Plantation

Long Island Plantation was organized in 1840, including Great and Little Duck, Black, and Placentia islands to the north and west; Harbor and Crow, hard by; and for reasons unknown, Pond, Calf (Opechee), and western Black at the opposite extremity of the Swans Island Division.[35] In 1847 a township named *Islandport* was incorporated, but the act of incorporation was repealed the next year and a plantation substituted. The name *Frenchboro*, according to Vivian Lunt, comes from a lawyer named E. Webster French who promised to secure the island a post office if a part of it was named for him; the post office, established about 1859, was accordingly called Frenchboro in his honor.[36] A combined schoolhouse and church was built in 1843, Vivian Lunt tells us, out of funds raised locally by Israel Lunt; this was the year a Baptist congregation was organized on Long Island under the ministry of C. P. St. Clair. Startling claims were made for this ministry in a report dated 1845:

> They [the Long Islanders] were notorious for their profanity, general wickedness, and intemperance; and when the work of God commenced, opposition to it was strong among them. But a stronger than they was there [sic], and most of the twenty-three families now resident on the Island are praying families. How changed the scene! Piety, peace, order and harmony now reign, where once sin, infidelity and polluting habits degraded society (Millet, *History of the Baptists in Maine*, 364).[37]

Amen!

A few excerpts from Frenchboro town meetings (records survive from the 1880s) reflect the quality of life on the island.

1886 *Voted:* to divide the school year into three sessions: two of eight weeks, starting the first Monday in September and March; and one of three months, starting the first Monday in December. Mistresses would teach the shorter sessions, a master the longer.

1888 *Voted:* that anyone found taking the young out of birds' nests shall be fined $5.

[34] A farmer, a draftsman, and seven quarrymen also appear on the 1893 list, but they were resident on other islands (Black and Pond) belonging to Long Island Plantation, or Frenchboro.

[35] All but Black, Pond, Harbor, and Crow were eventually set off to other plantations or townships.

[36] There appears to be some question about the date of the post office: according to an authority on the matter—the late Paul Hanneman of Brewer—the Frenchboro post office was established only in 1892. I have not resolved this discrepancy.

[37] I am indebted to Elizabeth Wescott of Bucksport for calling this passage to my attention.

Northeast side of harbor at Frenchboro, 1880s or earlier: house at left rear was homestead of Israel B. Lunt, and large warehouse on shore was his also; the latter still stands. (Courtesy of Vivian Lunt.)

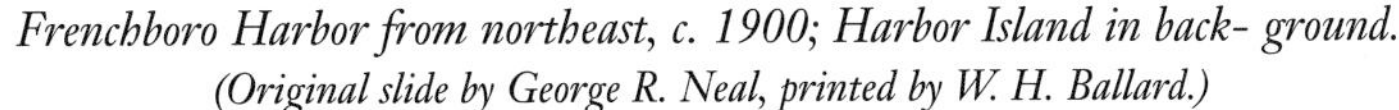

Frenchboro Harbor from northeast, c. 1900; Harbor Island in back- ground. (Original slide by George R. Neal, printed by W. H. Ballard.)

1888 *Voted:* that any female from fifteen years old to seventy years found or heard to be quarreling, Brawling or Molesting any person on the Public Road or byepaths or fields shall be arrested by the Constable and taken before the Trial Justice and fined $5 and costs.
Note: An evil day for women's rights, with no explanation of what prompted the action; it may, of course, have been a joke. The males of Frenchboro, in any event, atoned for the affront by passing a resolution on women's suffrage in 1919: 14 to 9.

1888 *Voted:* that no lobster traps be hauled on Sunday; the fine was $15.
Note: This action was some years before the State of Maine banned lobster fishing on Sunday.

1889 A peddler's license ($3) was issued to Sylvester Morse of Swans Island to peddle on Long Island.

1894 *Voted:* that no traps be in water between August 1 and October 1; the fine was $10.
Note: The object was evidently to protect lobsters during the shedding period. Some Canadian communities still have such a closed season (e.g., Grand Manan: July to November), but I believe the State of Maine never enacted such a law.

1896 The 34 ballots cast in the Presidential election were as follows: Republicans, 24; Democrats, 9; Peoples' Party, 1.
Note: Participation in primary elections was less active: in 1898, for instance, only seven Republicans and four Democrats voted.

School, Church, and Character on Long Island

Schoolteachers on Long Island were, for half a century, educated islanders who served in rotation without pay. In 1888 Alexander MacDonald, then a Bowdoin sophomore, was hired for a few months both to teach and to provide religious instruction. He evidently had slight hopes in the latter regard, to judge from his early reactions to the Long Island community: "My first impression...was anything but desirable. There seemed to be a spirit of jealousy and enmity between the people that would eat up all the good that could be accomplished" (Vivian Lunt, 37). His arrival, however, marked the beginning of both a religious revival on the island and more serious schooling. A Congregational Church was organized by Alexander MacDonald in 1889—the earlier Baptist Church having apparently been moribund for some years after C. P. St. Clair's claims of initial successes—and a new church building was erected in 1890. The school was also transferred to the new building, until in 1907 enrollment (sixty pupils) exceeded facilities and a new schoolhouse was built near the head of the harbor; this building is still in use. The MacDonalds—Alexander and his brother Angus—passed on to other work (Alexander founded the Maine Sea Coast Mission in 1905), but Frenchboro continued to retain qualified teachers in the school, most of whom also served as ministers. The longest tenure, by Gladys Muir, was from 1932 to 1956.

Long Islanders, like the residents of many outlying fishing communities, gained a reputation for being inhospitable to outsiders. Visitors once found them so. In 1852, for example, three Castine gentlemen (including the painter Fitz Hugh Lane) stopped for a night off the island and received a cool reception: they found most of the buildings deserted, including "Squire Lunt's," no dug wells, and a generally "dismal" atmosphere. "The specimen of native seen," one of the yachtsmen wrote in his diary, "had a very ancient and Fish like appearance."[38] Another yachtsman, forty years later, likened the islanders more to beasts of burden than to fish: Long Island, this visitor wrote, was "conspicuous above all the Maine islands for the semi-civilized character of its fishermen. It is said that for the want of animals they harness themselves to the plough" (Drake, *Nooks and Corners of the New England Coast*, 288).

These harsh and facetious judgments, needless to say, tell us more of the prejudices of nineteenth-century yachtsmen than of the qualities of the Long Islanders. Indeed, whose ancestors among us would not stand condemned of being "semi-civilized" for sometimes putting a shoulder to the plough?

Other economic activity on the island, in addition to fishing and limited farming, included lumbering. An early sawmill was on the island, according to Vivian Lunt (page 149); it was appar-

[38] Diary of William Howe Witherle, printed in *Wilson Museum Bulletin* of Castine, Vol. II, No. 2, 1974–75.

ently idle for many years after the first need for sawn lumber was met, then revived in the 1870s and operated to the end of the century. In the twentieth century the Head and Deep Cove sectors were cut over in the 1920s and a considerable portion of the northwest shore, some three thousand cords, in 1939. There was also some boat-building in the harbor, the island women made rugs, and many families kept sheep.

Struggle to Keep Frenchboro Alive

The greatest test of the ingenuity of Long Islanders came in the latter half of the twentieth century as they sought to keep the community alive. Would it survive, or would it become another of the many year-round island communities in the twentieth century to founder: Criehaven, Hurricane, Dix, and Eagle islands, or neighboring Great Gott, Black, and Bartlett islands, and the other Long Island in Blue Hill Bay?

World War II brought serious dislocation to Long Island, as to isolated island communities everywhere. Young men went off to various services (fifteen from Frenchboro) and some families removed; by 1945 the school population had fallen to thirteen, the lowest count in a century. The community rallied. Servicemen returned, many of them building new homes with GI loans. The price of lobsters, which had escalated during the war, remained mercifully high and revitalized the fisheries. Ferry service from McKinley (now Bass Harbor) on Mount Desert Island was established in 1950—the first regular service the island had had, excluding a local mailboat three times a week to Swans Island; when the McKinley service was discontinued ten years later for lack of profits, the Long Islanders successfully petitioned the State legislature to restore it.[39] In 1956 an electric cable was laid from Swans Island that provided Frenchboro with normal service, consigning to the dustbin the noisy backyard generators. In the 1970s, thanks to the ingenuity of a visiting Bangor schoolteacher and telephone buff (Jeff Webber),

[39] The ferry by the 1990s ran twice weekly, on successive days—to allow housewives to do their shopping by car on Mount Desert Island or in Ellsworth, under obligation to spend the night ashore. This modern shopping pattern inevitably cut down on the number of island stores, which dropped from three or four to one.

Frenchboro foster children sliding on ice, 1970s. (Courtesy of Vivian Lunt.)

Frenchboro was provided first with an intra-island dial system, then via microwave off-island service to the Ellsworth switchboard. Long Island was becoming truly modernized.

Still, there were recurrent crises, though the island population remained more or less steady at about fifty. One such crisis occurred in 1964 when, because of postwar birth-rate fluctuations, the number of school pupils fell to two—that is, below the state's limit for an approved school district. This would mean loss of the state's subsidy for the island school, amounting to about half of the school budget. The islanders promptly petitioned the State Division of Child Welfare for foster children of school age to be placed in island homes. State officials began—with reservations, it should be said—to identify eligible foster parents. In due course the foster children came: a total of fifteen in six island families over the next few years. Was the program a success? There were difficult adjustments, to be sure, both for the children and the parents. But the school was saved through state subsidies until the student population stabilized.[40]

Another effort to stabilize Frenchboro's always precarious population has been the homesteading movement begun in the 1980s. Frenchboro, unlike many coastal islands in Maine, was not available for real estate development because most of the island was owned since the 1960s by David and Margaret Rockefeller for conservation purposes. Islanders wished to be sure that the little open land left would go to year-round settlers, not vacationers, and so created the Frenchboro Future Development Corporation for this purpose. The Maine State Housing Authority, on application, made a grant to the Corporation for ten dwellings, later scaled back to seven. Hundreds of applications were received and processed as the three-bedroom homes were under construction; the first homesteaders arrived in 1988.

Has the program succeeded? The last word is not in, of course, but with a dozen families having come and gone, a few preliminary conclusions are possible. The most serious problem and the reason for most departures was lack of jobs: serving as sternman to an established lobsterman could tide a homesteader over the first months, but it was not a permanent occupation—and there were few other prospects. There were social difficulties as well. The native islanders, most of them interrelated, are a closely knit community; without meaning to be exclusive, they inevitably create a barrier that is difficult for outsiders to penetrate. The islanders, one departing homesteader wrote in 1993, "are so accustomed to their way of life... that they had no concept of the changes we had to make to try to fit in" (*Island Journal*, XII: 29).

For those who come to Frenchboro for short visits, there is not this problem of integration. The island's homecoming day is on August 12, the anniversary of the signing of the Atlantic Charter by Roosevelt and Churchill in 1940[41]: some three hundred or more former residents come out on a special ferry from Bass Harbor to enjoy a midday church "supper" of lobsters. At other times, in season, visitors come by private boat (there will not infrequently be as many as two dozen visiting vessels at anchor in the outer harbor) or on day tours from Mount Desert Island. The museum and several shops are open daily to greet these visitors, and a take-out restaurant on the harbor serves meals all day long. If there was a perceived deficiency in the islanders' hospitality to outsiders in the nineteenth century, they have more than compensated in the twentieth.

[40] The one-room schoolhouse covers grades one through eight; graduating students go on to high school on Mount Desert Island.

[41] The charter was signed off Placentia Island, *Newfoundland*, but the rendezvous was off Placentia Island, *Maine*—neighbor to our Long Island (Frenchboro).

Residents of Long Island (Frenchboro), 1820–1880

Note: The following are shown on Long Island (Frenchboro) in federal census schedules. Age, if shown, is at first appearance. Spouses, if known, are in parentheses. Males in a household are to left of slash, females to right.

Householder	1820	1830	1840	1850	1860	1870	1880
Pomeroy, Thomas	3/10						
Pomeroy, William	1/3						
Smith, Asa	4/2						
Lunt, Israel B., 34 (Nancy)		1/0	4/7	5/9	5/8		
Lunt, Abner, 49 (Jane)		10/4	7/2	4/2			
Lunt, Amos C., 38 (Pricilla)		4/4	5/3	5/1			
Rice, Thomas, 52 (Mary)		4/6	2/2	2/1			
Rich, William, 50s		4/1	1/1				
Lunt, Amos C., Jr, 32 (Elizabeth)		3/1	-	5/5	4/6	2/3[42]	
Rice, Jacob, 26 (Dorcus)			3/1	3/3	1/2	3/2[43]	
Rich, Gilbert, 24 (Caroline/Mary)			2/3	3/3	2/3	1/4	1/2
Rich, John, 50s			3/2				
Davis, Ezra, 26 (Rebecca)			4/6	5/1	5/3		
Lunt, George, 50s			5/1				
Lunt, Russell Bartholomew, 26 (Asenath)			3/5	6/3	6/2	4/1	3/1
Lunt, Jacob, 33 (Sally)			6/1	6/2			
Tinker, Jonathan			1/2				
Allen, Samuel			3/4				
McCready, William			1/4				
Lunt, George C., 26 (Miriam)				3/2	3/1	2/2	5/2[44]
Walls, John, 24				3/1			
Twist, George, 30 (Mary)				2/3			
Rich, William II, 31 (Eleanor)				3/5	4/5	3/2	2/3
Davis, William, 28 (Polly)				3/4	1/1		
Davis, Joseph, 34 (Betsy)				4/2	6/3		
Lunt, Andrew, 29 (Lovina)				3/4			
Pomroy, Francis, 38 (Jarushia)				3/2			
Lunt, Joshua, 21 (Rebecca)				2/1	3/1		
Lunt, Richard, 36 (Abigail)				2/2	2/1	2/1	2/1
Davis, James L., 34 (Abigail)				1/1	1/2	2/2	4/2
Davis, Rebecca, 67				0/2			
Rich, John , Jr., 30 (Jane)				2/3	-	2/4	
Lunt, Polly, 25				1/3			
Householder	**1820**	**1830**	**1840**	**1850**	**1860**	**1870**	**1880**

[42] Elizabeth is head of household in 1870.
[43] Dorcus is head of household in 1870.
[44] This household included George B. Lunt, sixty-nine, as well as George C. Lunt II, forty (Harriet).

Householder	1820	1830	1840	1850	1860	1870	1880
Lunt, William D., 27 (Elizabeth/ Mary)				2/1	4/1	5/1	4/1
Lunt, Joseph D., 28 (Rehobeth)				3/2	3/2	-	1/4
Pomroy, Moses, 28 (Caroline)				2/2			
Lunt, Hezekiah, 27 (Lydia)					2/1		
Lunt, Joseph W. II, 32 (Alice)					2/4	4/2	7/4
Lunt, Israel II, 34 (Dorcus)					2/4	-	1/1
Vauties, Francis, 22 (Mary)					2/1		
Lunt, Abner II, 50					4/1		
Murphy, Henry, 32 (Nancy)					1/4	2/4	2/2
Dawes, Jonathan, 60 (Charlotte)					1/1	2/1	
Dawes, George, 28					5/3		
Butler, George, 46 (Lois)					4/1	3/1	
Davis, Mary, 46					2/4		
Rice, Abraham, 23 (Melissa)					1/3	3/3	5/4
Rice, Thomas II, 80 (Mary)					1/2		
Barbour, David, 50 (Oliva)					3/2		
Lunt, Augustus, 25 (Susan)						1/2	
Davis, Mary, 50						0/5	2/4
Joyce, Reuben, 31 (Mary)						4/2	4/2
Walls, Lafayette, 24 (Caroline)						1/1	
Davis, William, 53 (Mary T.)[45]						2/5	2/3
Cousins, Joseph, 67						1/2	
Rich, George, 32 (Lucy)						1/1	4/2
Teel, William J., 35 (Rhoda, 1880)						2/0	1/1
Davis, William, 32 (Emmaline)						3/4	
Davis, Levi, 28 (Sarah)						1/2	3/5
Davis, Edgar, 30 (Etta)						3/1	
Lunt, Benjamin S, 26 (Ann)						2/2	
Burns, Henry, 66 (Comfort)						7/2[46]	
Morris, Abram, 58 (Susan)						2/1	
Wilson, Byron, 25 (Victoria)						1/0	4/4
Ross, Robert, 55 (Mary)						1/1	4/2
Lunt, Augustus, 28 (Elizabeth) [47]						1/1	
Davis, Betsy, 51							1/5
Merithew, Caroline, 20							1/1
Leary, Sam, 34							2/3
Pinkham, Hortense, 36							3/2
Rich, Samuel, 32 (Abby)							1/3
Lunt, Bertrand, 31 (Iona?)							2/3
Householder	**1820**	**1830**	**1840**	**1850**	**1860**	**1870**	**1880**

[45] This William Davis may have appeared above—in 1850 and 1860.
[46] Henry Burns in 1870 may have been on Calf (Opechee) Island, which was then part of Long Island Plantation.
[47] There were evidently two Augustus Lunts on the island: this one and another married to Susan (above).

Swans Island

Householder	1820	1830	1840	1850	1860	1870	1880
Davis, Rebecca II, 60							1/1
Dunham, Stephen, 66 (Betsy)							1/1
Osier, Thomas, 29 (Almenia)							1/3
Gray, Charles, 40 (Flora)							1/3
Lunt, Hannah, 38							1/2
Murphy, John T., 29							2/2
Marshall, George, 30							1/2
Totals:							
No. of Households	3	6	16	29	28	32	33
No. of Persons	19	42	114	155	153	138	157
Householder	**1820**	**1830**	**1840**	**1850**	**1860**	**1870**	**1880**

Lunts of Long Island (Frenchboro): The First Three Generations[48]

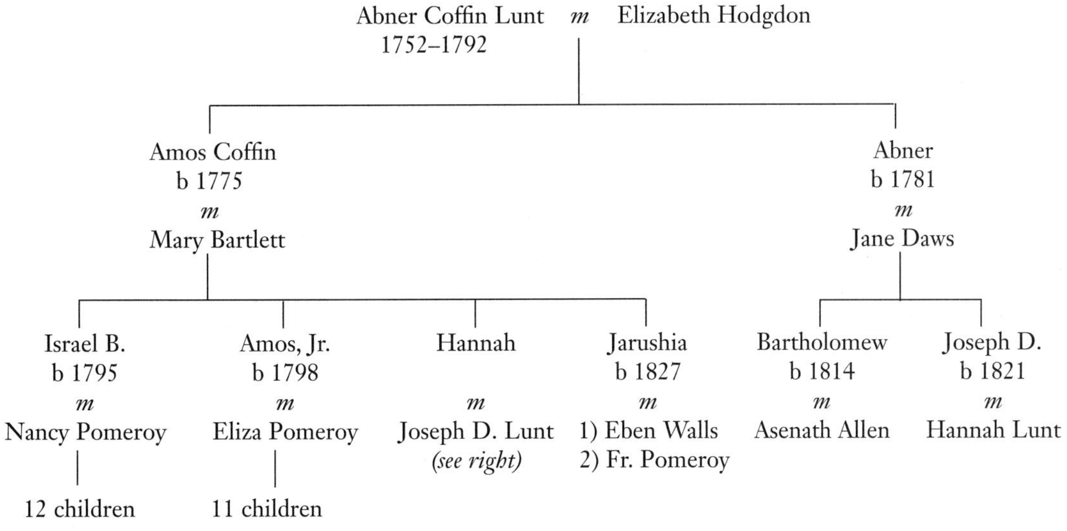

[48] Compiled from Thomas S. Lunt, *The Lunt Family*, Salem: Salem Press Co., 1913.

John (off Frenchboro)

Whoever John was, after whom this island is named, he could not have been a settler on either Burnt Coat or Long Island (that is, Swans or Frenchboro)—for the name appears on charts before there were settlers in the area (Map 1776 Atlantic Neptune). He was a mariner, perhaps, or a passing fisherman. In 1897, according to Swans Island records, *Outer Johns Island* was shared by two local fishermen, each assessed $63: John H. Gott and Isaiah Stanley. Apart from this small wisdom, I have nothing to relate about John Island.

Bibliography and Sources

Section I: Books and articles (listed by author); local newspapers and selected periodicals; federal, state, county, and town records; and personal papers (listed by author).

Section II: Maps, atlases, charts, and surveys.

Section III: Interviewees and corresondents (consulted in the 1970s for the original edition of this volume). These entries are as they were in the original edition—except that I have indicated an informant's passing where I am aware of it.

Section I: Books, articles, etc.

Allen, Mildred Sellers. *Deer Isle's History*. Rockland: Courier–Gazette Press, 1934. (A pamphlet, based on Deer Isle records—but not attempting to rival George Hosmer's more detailed volume.)

Allis, Frederick, Jr. "William Bingham's Maine Lands, 1790–1820," Colonial Society of Massachusetts, *Publications*, Vols. 36 and 37, 1954. (An important collection of records and materials on the extensive Bingham holdings on the Maine coast.)

Ames, J. E. "Leadbetter Records," 1917. (A privately printed genealogy of the Leadbetter family, including members of this family who settled in the Fox Islands.)

"Andros Tracts," Publications of the Prince Society, Boston: T. R. Marvin & Co., 1868, three vols. (Includes an account of Governor Andros's 1768 expedition to Pentagoët, along with other materials relating to his life and trial.)

Bangor Historical Magazine, 1885–1894. (The nine volumes of this critical source of Eastern Maine history were republished in 1993 by Picton Press in Camden; there are three volumes in the new edition, along with an all-name index, and the pagination is continuous. Articles consulted in the present study are referenced both under the original volume and page and under the new continuous pagination: thus, III: 206/684 means page 206 of the original Volume III or page 684 of the new three-volume edition.)

Beacom, Seward E. *White Schoolhouses on an Island: A History of the Schools of North Haven, Maine, 1790 to 1958*. Rockport, ME: Archimedes Press, 1980. (A publication of the North Haven Historical Society.)

Bishop, W. H. "Fish and Men in the Maine Islands," *Harpers New Monthly Magazine*, 1880 (reprinted by Lillian Berliawsky Books, Camden, ME).

Blanchard, Fessenden S. *Ghost Towns of New England*. New York: Dodd, Mead & Co., 1960. (Chapter Eight covers Hurricane Island.)

Beveridge, Norwood P. *The North Island: Early Times to Yesterday*. North Haven, ME, 1976; revised, 1989. (The only general history of North Haven, assembled for the local Bicentennial Committee; the volume is copiously illustrated and presents an excellent record of early settlement, but does not pretend to give a full account of the island's history.)

Blunt, Edmund M. *The American Coasting Pilot, Containing Directions for the Principal Capes and Headlands on the Coasts of North and South America*. New York: Edmund and George W. Blunt, various editions. (The first edition of this famous navigational handbook appeared in 1796 and was updated every few years during the nineteenth century; the best known sea passages are described and many of the islands named.)

Bourque, Bruce J. "Aboriginal Settlement and Subsistence on the Maine Coast," *Man in the Northeast*, No. 6, 1973. (A piece exploring seasonal Indian movement to the coast, by the chief archaeologist of the Maine State Museum.)

————. "Report on an Archeological Survey of Bear, Little Spruce Head and Compass Islands, Penobscot Bay, Maine." Mimeographed, 1975. (A report prepared for the owners of these islands, privately circulated.)

————. "Fishing in the Gulf of Maine: A 5,000 Year History," a chapter in G. Lawless, ed., *The Gulf of Maine*. Brunswick: Blackberry Press, 1977. (An anthropological study of the resourcefulness of

Indian fishermen along the coast of Maine before the arrival of the first Europeans.)

Brooklin, Town of. Town Records. (Tax records from the mid-nineteenth century show husbandry on local islands—e.g., Hog and Harbor.)

Brooks, Noah. "The Waif of Nautilus Island," *Scribners*, 4: 65 (1872); reprinted in Brooks, *Tales of the Maine Coast.* (A fanciful tale of Nautilus Island in Castine Harbor.)

Brooksville, Town of. Town Records. (Tax records from the 1840s show valuations on Nautilus and other islands in Castine Harbor.)

Burrage, Henry S. *The Beginnings of Colonial Maine, 1602–1658.* Portland: Marks Printing House, 1914. (A detailed history of the era by the State Historian, printed for the State of Maine.)

Calderwood, Ivan E. *Days of Uncle Dave's Fish-house.* Rockland: Courier-Gazette, Inc., 1969. (The best-known volume of Ivan Calderwood's tales of Vinalhaven, based on conversations with local fishermen—more colorful than historical.)

Calef, John. *Siege of Penobscot.* New York: William Abbatt, 1910. (Reprint of a 1781 account of the Battle of Castine in 1779 by a local Loyalist.)

Carroll, Mary Ann. Letters, 1903–04. (These scattered letters, preserved from the many written to family and friends by the island school teacher on Opechee and other islands around Mount Desert Island, give useful insights into island life at the turn of the century; some are in the possession of the Robert Smallidge family of Northeast Harbor.)

Carter, Robert. *Carter's Coast of New England.* Somersworth, N H: New England Publishing Co., 1969. (Reprint of an account of an 1858 charter cruise from Providence to Bar Harbor.)

Castine, Town of. Town Records. (Tax records for Castine through the nineteenth century are very complete, but they cover only one island in our inventory: Holbrook, the only island with husbandry enough to tax.)

Chadbourne, Ava H. *Maine Place Names and the Peopling of Its Towns.* Portland and Freeport, ME: Bond Wheelwright Co., 1955. (In 1970 several county reprints of the original volume were issued, with illustrations but no new material.)

Chanler, William Astor, Jr. *And Did Those Feet in Ancient Time: A Seven Hundred Acre Island Reminiscence.* Rockport, ME: Outerbridge Books, 1984. (A personal memoir of early twentieth-century life on this once thriving island, by a life-long seasonal resident.)

Chase, Virginia. "Sanctuary," *Down East* magazine, 4: 26 (1957). (Account of the summer retreat for the "convalescent insane" on Widow Island in the early 1900s; by the daughter of the founder of the facility.)

Chatto and Turner. *Register of the Towns of Sedgwick, Brooklin, Deer Isle, Stonington and Isle au Haut.* Auburn, ME: Lawton Register Co., 1910. (Important genealogical resource for these communities.)

Church, Ella Rodman. "A Visit to Dix Island," *Southern Magazine* (Baltimore, MD), 16: 615 (1875). (Account of a day's visit to the famous quarry island by a group of southern vacationers.)

Colby, C. William. "Spruce Head Island: The Jewel in the Crown." (Personal notebook of a Sprucehead Island historian and lobsterman, including several hundred pages of historical, genealogical, and other information about this island; collected between the 1970s and 1990s.)

Condon, Vesta. "An Island Store One Hundred Years Ago," *Bulletin*, Society for the Preservation of New England Antiquities, XXXII (1941) 2: 52. (A description of the Condon store on Wheaton Island in Matinicus Harbor in the 1840s, drawing on store records in the possession of a Condon descendant.)

Cook, Joel. *An Eastern Tour at Home.* Philadelphia: David McKay, 1899. (Account of a trip downeast, including a segment on Islesboro.)

Cooper, J(ohn) F(erdinand). "North Haven–Little Thoroughfare in the Old Days," c. 1920. (A four-page typescript of detailed recollections by a resident of the Little Fox Island Thorofare sector in the 1870s; includes details of residents and homesteads on the nearby islands. A copy of the typescript is at the North Haven Historical Society.)

Courier-Gazette. Published under this and similar titles in Rockland for more than a century. (Nineteenth-century files of this journal include significant material on islands of the western Penobscot Bay.)

Crotch Island Quarterly. See Gross, Clayton.

Dakin, Moses. *Monterey, or the Mountain City.* Boston: Mead's Press, 1847.
(An appendix gives a brief description of several islands in the Islesborough area in the 1840s.)

Dale, T. Nelson. *Commercial Granite of New England.* Washington, DC: Government Printing Office. 1927. (Prepared for the Department of the Interior—U. S. Geological Survey Bulletin 738; covers the largest quarries in the Penobscot Bay region.)

Deer Isle, Town of. Town Records. (Records for the township of Deer Isle that survived a town hall fire in the 1970s date back to the 1790s; they cover all the smaller islands around Deer Isle and as far south as Isle au Haut, until the latter's incorporation with its neighbors in 1874.)

"Documentary History of the State of Maine." See Maine Historical Society.

Doudiet, Ellenore W. *Majabigwaduce: Castine, Penobscot, Brooksville.* Castine: Castine Scientific Society, 1978. (Profusely illustrated record of the Bagaduce region by the director of the Wilson Museum in Castine and a lifelong resident of Nautilus Island.)

Down East magazine. Published monthly in Camden, since the 1960s. (A popular journal with excellent photographs and extensive coverage of contemporary developments on the coast and the islands.)

Drake, Samuel Adams. *Nooks and Corners of the New England Coast.* New York: Harper and Bros., 1875. (Account of a voyage in the 1870s; a chapter covers Penobscot Bay.)

Drinkwater, Norman, Jr. "The Stone Age of Dix Island," *Down East* magazine, September 1963, pp. 43–47.

Eastman, Joel W. *A History of Sears Island, Searsport, Maine.* Searsport Historical Society, 1976. (A meticulous study of this strategically located island from pre-Revolutionary times to the modern era; prepared for the owner, Central Maine Power Company.)

Eaton, Cyrus L. *Annals of Warren.* Hallowell: Masters & Livermore, 1877; reprinted in 1975. (A formidable history of the St. George and eastern Muscongus Bay region.)

————. *History of Thomaston, Rockland and South Thomaston.* Hallowell: Masters, Smith & Co., 1865; reprinted in 1972. (The best early history of the communities on the southwest shore of Penobscot Bay, including the offshore islands.)

Eckstorm, Fannie Hardy. *Indian Place-names of the Penobscot Valley and Coast.* Orono: University of Maine Press, 1941. (Authorative study of Indian origins of names in the Penobscot Bay region.)

Ellis, Alice V. *The Story of Stockton Springs, Maine.* Belfast, 1955; prepared under the aegis of the Historical Committee of Stockton Springs. (Includes data on settlement of Brigadier, now Sears, Island.)

Ellsworth American. Weekly newspaper published in Ellsworth, ME. (Back files of this journal, now over a century old, include rich material on coastal history.

Enk, John C. *A Family Island in Penobscot Bay: the Story of Eagle Island.* Rockland: Courier-Gazette, Inc., 1953. (A painstaking study of the Quinns of Eagle Island through four generations, based—as the author explains—"largely on the recollections of Capain Erland L. Quinn.")

Farrow, John Pendleton. *History of Islesborough, Maine.* Bangor: Thos. W. Burr, 1893; reprinted in 1965 by the Camden Herald Publishing Co. for the Islesboro Historical Society. (Full-length history of Islesborough and surrounding islands, including extensive genealogical data.)

Fish, Reverend E. S. "History of Brooklin." Bangor: Burr & Robinson, 1876. (Centennial address marking the anniversary of the American Revolution and reviewing the history of Brooklin.)

Fisher, Reverend Jonathan. "Diaries." (These diaries, written in a personal code, were kept by the first minister in Blue Hill during his long pastorate from the 1790s to 1835; a decoded transcript is at the Blue Hill Public Library.)

Goode, George Brown. "Fishery Industries of the United States." United States, 47th Congress, first session (1881–82), *Miscellaneous Documents*, Vol. 7, Sect. II. (A comprehensive review of the American fisheries in 1880, region by region; the sections dealing with our area are pp. 35–57.)

Grindle, Roger L. *Tombstones and Paving Blocks: The History of the Maine Granite Industry*. Rockland: Courier-Gazette, Inc., 1977. (Well-documented and suitably illustrated record of quarrying in Maine, with particular attention to union organization.)

Gross, Clayton. *Island Chronicles: An Account of Days Past in Deer Isle and Stonington.* Stonington, ME: Penobscot Bay Press, 1977. (A collection of articles by the principal contemporary historian of Deer Isle, selected from his column "Day Before Yesterday" in *Island Ad-Vantages.*)

————. "Yesterday—the History of Crotch Island," *Crotch Island Quarterly*, Spring 1974, pp. 28–55. (Prepared for the environmentalist group that acquired the island in 1970; this issue of the journal was the only one to appear.)

Hancock County. Registry of Deeds. (Deeds are identified as follows: volume—or book—left of slash, page to right. Thus *Hancock 36/891* means page 891 of volume 36. All deeds recorded in Hancock County since 1789, and some earlier deeds, are included in these volumes in Ellsworth.)

Hatch, Louis C. *Maine: A History.* Somersworth, N H: New Hampshire Publishing Co., 1974. (Reprint of the three-volume edition of 1919; one of the best histories of the state written in the twentieth century.)

History of Islesboro, Maine, 1893–1983. Portland: Seavey Printers, 1984, printed for the Islesboro Historical Society. (Prepared by a committee of the Historical Society as a sequel to Farrow's *History of Islesborough*—see above. The volume consists of articles by local residents on topics such as schools, transportation, local businesses, the summer colony, etc.)

Hosmer, George L. *An Historical Sketch of Deer Isle, Maine; with Notices of Its Settlers and Early Inhabitants.* Boston: Stanley & Usher, 1886, and Fort Hill Press, 1905; reprinted by Courier-Gazette, Inc., 1976. (The definitive early history of Deer Isle through 1882, compiled more from conversations with elder inhabitants than published records, but considered nonetheless authoritative; the most extensive segment of the volume includes "notices" of early settlers and their descendants.)

Howard, R. H., and Henry E. Crocker. *A History of New England.* Boston: Crocker & Co., 1880, two volumes. (Maine is covered in Vol II, with a county-by-county description and history.)

Hutchinson, Vernal. *When Revolution Came: the Story of Old Deer Isle in the Province of Maine During the War for American Independence.*Ellsworth, ME: *Ellsworth American*, 1972.

————. *A Yankee Town in the Civil War.* Stonington, CT: Stonington Publishing Co., 1957; reprinted by Bond Wheelwright Co., Freeport, ME, 1967. (Despite some inaccuracies, these two volumes provide documented accounts of Deer Isle during the American Revolution and the Civil War.)

Island Ad-Vantages. Published weekly in Stonington on Deer Isle. (This publication has included extensive coverage of island history and lore.)

Island Journal and *Island News.* Publications of the Island Institute in Rockland—respectively annual and bi-monthly. (Both publications provide a rich source of Maine island research and commentary; indispensable for students of Penobscot Bay islands.)

Isle au Haut, Plantation of. Plantation Records. (Most early records of Isle au Haut, held on Deer Isle, were destroyed in a fire there in the 1970s; records since incorporation in 1874—tax, school, and town reports—are in the Revere Memorial Library on the island.)

Islesboro, Town of. Town Records. (Town reports and tax records exist from the 1790s, though the latter have no significant data on surrounding islands before the 1860s; the Islesboro Historical Society has full census schedules of the township from 1790.)

Jackson, Malcolm Putnam. "Earliest Settled Lots in South Thomaston, Maine," 1971; privately printed. (See Map 1971 Jackson.)

Knox County. Registry of Deeds. (The regular Knox County deeds are listed as described under Hancock County, above. A separate section covering lands formerly part of the Muscongus Patent and owned by General Knox is also located at the Registry in Rockland—denoted as *Knox Lands* in the present volume.)

Lincoln County. Registry of Deeds. (Some very early deeds, before the establishment of Hancock County in 1789, are recorded in Wiscasset, but the number of island properties conveyed is negligible; they are listed as described under Hancock County, above.)

Long, Charles A. E. *Matinicus Isle: Its Story and Its People.* Lewiston: Lewiston Journal Printshop, 1926. (A meticulous history of this long-settled island, with careful documentaion; covers some of the surrounding islands, including Criehaven.)

Long Island, Plantation of. Plantation Records. (Though Long Island—or Frenchboro—Plantation was organized in 1840, tax records exist only from 1867; all records are kept at the fire station.)

Lovell, General Solomon. "Journal." Weymouth Historical Society publication, No. 1, pp. 93–106 (1881). (Account of the Penobscot campaign of 1779, by the American general in charge of the assault.)

Lufkin, Captain Henry L. "Diaries." (The original diaries of this Deer Isle mariner, covering the years 1847–54, are in the Deer Isle Historical Society; excerpts were published serially in *Island Ad-Vantages* during 1970 and 1971.)

Lunt, Thomas B. *The Lunt Family.* Salem: Salem Press Co., 1913. (Privately printed genealogical study of the Lunt family, including many Lunts who settled on Long Island, Frenchboro.)

Lunt, Vivian. *Long Island Plantation: History of Frenchboro, Maine.* 1976. (This privately printed edition of Vivian Lunt's history of the fishing community off Swans Island is more than an update of earlier versions; it includes new data from church and plantation records. Vivian Lunt has been the moving force for half a century in the island's historical society and in its civic life.)

———. *Frenchboro: Long Island Plantation, The First Hundred Years.* Ellsworth, ME: Downeast Graphics & Printing Inc., 1980; reprinted 1993. (Vintage photographs of this offshore island plantation.)

Lyons, O. P. (editor). *A Brief Historical Sketch of the Town of Vinalhaven, from its earliest known settlement.* Rockland, ME: Free Press Office, 1889. (A short but useful survey of Vinalhaven and surrounding islands, prepared for the centennial of the township; a second edition, with essentially the same material, was published in 1900 under the new editor's name: Albra Josephine Vinal.)

Maine, State of. Archives. In addition to complete federal census schedules for Maine communities and copies of many town records in the Archives, the following items were of particular use in this volume:

Plan Book 8. Coastal Islands from St. Croix to Penobcsot Rivers, as surveyed by Rufus Putnam and others, 1784–1786. (These plans, which name—or letter—and give acreage of all islands in our area except Islesborough and the western shore, are reproduced in county plan books; habitation is not shown as a rule.) List of Islands on Maine Coast assigned by Massachusetts to 1838.

(Hand-written list of islands conveyed by the Commonwealth of Massachusetts both before and after the division of coastal islands between the two states in the 1820s.)

"Records of Island Sales, 1786–1874." (This list is made up principally of islands sold at auction in 1874; the reference used in this volume is *Maine Archives, "1874 Island Sales."*)

Maine, State of. Bureau of Industrial and Labor Statistics. *Report*, published annually, 1887 to 1910. (Includes information on union activity, both among lobstermen and quarry workers.)

Maine, State of. Bureau of Taxation. Valuations and tax records. (Includes tax data on unorganized islands in Penobscot Bay, from the late 1800s.)

Maine, State of. Forestry Commission, *Report*, published annually (as a rule) from 1880s; see in particular the report for 1914, pp. 99–165.(The Forestry Commission was charged with responsibility for Maine public lands, including islands; the Commissioner's report accordingly gave attention to the disposition of the islands, especially those which had never been deeded properly by Maine or Massachusetts.)

Maine Historical Society. *Collections* or *Collections and Proceedings*. Portland, ME: various publishing houses, irregular. (The numbering of the several series and volumes is bewildering, but the materials in these collections are of primary importance to students of Maine history. Especially noteworthy are the Baxter Manuscripts, contained in Volumes IV–XXIV of *Collections*, Series 2, entitled "Documentary History of the State of Maine"; the "Documentary History" is identified as such in the present volume, with appropriate volume and page indicated. Other items—articles, letters, manuscripts, etc.—are referenced by author, then volume and page.)

Maine State Register or *Yearbook*. Published annually or biennially from the 1830s. (By the late 1800s this publication not only identified town officials but discussed local commercial and business activity—e.g., manufacturing, canning, local hotels and boardinghouses.)

Massachusetts, Commonwealth of. Archives. (Items found in the Massachusetts Archives are identified by date or by volume and page of the archival collection; an appropriate description of the item is given in the text.)

Matinicus, Plantation of. Plantation Records. (Tax records exist from the early 1800s, though without significant detail until the 1860s; school records, including Criehaven, are complete from the 1860s; all early records on Matinicus are kept in the old schoolhouse.)

Millet, Reverend Joshua. *History of the Baptists in Maine.* Portland: Charles Day & Co., 1845. (A record of early Baptist churches in Maine, including several island parishes.)

Morison, Samuel Eliot. *Samuel de Champlain: Father of New France.* Boston: Little, Brown & Co., 1972. (Includes a detailed treatment of Champlain's 1604–05 expedition in the Penobscot Bay region.)

———. *European Discovery of America: The Northern Voyages.* Boston: Little, Brown & Co., 1971. (Definitive history of early explorations of the

North American coast, including the Penobscot Bay region.)

Murray, George M. (editor). *Centennial Celebration, Brooklin, Maine*, privately printed, 1949. (Prepared for the Brooklin Centennial Commission to mark the 100th anniversary of the separation of Brooklin from Sedgwick; includes miscellaneous materials and interviews.)

North Haven, Town of. Town records. (School and tax records as well as town reports have been kept since separation from Vinalhaven in 1846, but records before the 1880s shed little light on the husbandry of inhabited islands of Little Thorofare.)

Northeast Archives of Folklore and Oral History (NEAFOH). Tapes and selected transcripts of oral interviews with senior citizens in Maine— including a few dozen familiar with island history; located at Anthropology Department, University of Maine at Orono.)

Noyes, Dr. Benjamin Lake. Papers, documents, notes, etc. The voluminous research of this inquisitive Stonington doctor in the last decade of the nineteenth century and the early decades of the twentieth has been assembled in some two dozen volumes at the Deer Isle Historical Society. The items of particular relevance to the present study were as follows:

General History of the Families of Deer Isle (identified in this study as *Noyes, Family histories: surname.)*
Eastern Penobscot Bay Islands: Early Settlers, based on interviews with Bester Robbins and Hiram Morey, c. 1915 (identified as *Noyes, Robbins interview*; the islands described are principally in Deer Island Thorofare.)
History of Devil Island (identified as *Noyes, "Devil Island."*)

O'Leary, Wayne M. "The Maine Sea Fisheries, 1839–90: The Rise and Fall of a Native Industry," 1981. (A convincing analysis of the Maine—especially Penobscot Bay—fisheries in the nineteenth-century by a doctoral student at the University of Maine; copious statistical data underscore his argument. Essential reading for any serious student of the Maine coast.)

Owen, Captain William. "Narrative of American Voyages and Travels, 1766–1771." New York Public Library *Bulletin*, XXXV (1931), pp. 71–98, 139–62, 263–300, 659–85, 705–55. (Captain Owen was an English mariner who had been given a grant to Campobello Island and in 1770 made a leisurely voyage down the coast to inspect his domain.)

Pendleton, Everett Hall. *Brian Pendleton and His Descendants, 1599–1910.* Privately printed, 1910. (Genealogical research on the Pendleton family, covering the branch that settled Islesborough and neighboring islands; a copy is at the Islesboro Library.)

Pratt, Charles. *Here on the Island, Being an Account of a Way of Life Several Miles off the Maine Coast.* New York: Harper & Row, 1974. (Profusely illustrated appreciation of Isle au Haut in the twentieth century by a summer resident.)

Prince, Hezekiah. *Remarks of my Life p^r Me.* Thomaston: Thomaston Historical Society, 1979. (Memoirs and other records of Hezekiah Prince, a late-eighteenth-century magistrate in the Thomaston area.)

Provost, Honorius (prêtre). "Thomas Lefebvre et le Fief Kouesanouskek," n.d. Typescript of a paper prepared at the Seminaire de Québec, translated by Shirley P. Barrett. (This item, written by an archivist-priest in Quebec, discusses the activities of an early French trader who was granted a seignory on the St. George peninsula and operated a trading post there in the first decade of the eighteenth century; I am indebted to Malcolm Jackson and Edward Coffin of Owls Head for calling this paper to my attention.)

Putnam, Rufus. "Report of Settlers from Eastport to Penobscot Bay," 1785. (This is the report of the official surveyor of islands downeast in behalf of Lincoln County. Putnam lists all island settlers and the length of their residence—including those on Deer Isle and the Fox Islands. The original is in the Maine Archives, reproduced in the present volume as Appendix 1.)

Rhodes, Janet. *Beach Island: a Light History of Penobscot Bay to 1800 and Then of Her Center Island.* Rockland, ME: Coastwise Press, 1992. (An affectionate account of this long-settled island by a part owner and seasonal resident; she divides her efforts about equally between early settlement and summer residence in the twentieth century.)

Richardson, Eleanor Motley. *Hurricane Island: The Town that Disappeared.* Rockland, ME: Island Institute, 1989. (Painstaking account of this once prosperous quarry island, with many old photographs and the testimony of early twentieth century residents.)

———. *North Haven Summers: An Oral History.* Westford, MA: Courier Companies, 1992; privately printed for author. (An account of the summer colony on North Haven by a descendant of early cottagers.)

Robinson, Reuel. *History of Camden and Rockport, Maine.* Camden: Camden Publishing Co., 1907. (Includes an excellent account of the Waldo Patent and subsequent property dispositions in the region.)

Rosier, James. *A True Relation of the Most Prosperous Voyage Made this Present Year 1605, by Captain George Waymouth, in the Discovery of the Land of Virginia....* London: Impensis Geor. Bishop, 1605. (First edition of Rosier's much disputed narration. In recent research I have used an 1858 edition that belonged to George Prince and includes his argument that the river Waymouth explored was the St. George, not as previously supposed the Penobscot, or even the Kennebec; Prince's copy also includes his annotations thirty years later (1888) on his own 1858 argument as well as on Rosier's narration itself. This copy is at Baker Library, Dartmouth College.)

Rowe, William Hutchinson. *The Maritime History of Maine: Three Centuries of Shipbuilding and Seafaring.* Freeport, ME: Bond Wheelwright Co., 1948. (A standard study of the subject, with emphasis on the Casco Bay region.)

Rutherford, Philip R. *A Dictionary of Maine Place Names.* Freeport, ME: Bond Wheelwright Co., 1970. (A county-by-county inventory of the origins of Maine place names, including those of most islands.)

St. George, Town of. Town Records. (The town office in Tenants Harbor has a nearly complete set of all records from incorporation in 1803.)

Scott, Captain Walter. Articles published in *Island Ad-Vantages* of Stonington, 1950s–60s. (These random pieces by the son of the resident caretaker of Pickering Island at the end of the nineteenth century give significant—if repetitious—coverage of mid-Penobscot Bay islands; the articles are on file at the Deer Isle Historical Society.)

Searsport, Town of. Town Records. (Some school and tax records from the mid-nineteenth century covering Sears Island are at the Penobscot Marine Museum.)

Simpson, Dorothy. *The Maine Islands: In Story and Legend.* Philadelphia: J. B. Lippincott Co., 1960. (A survey of the major islands along the Maine coast, including several in Penobscot Bay; the author is a native of Ragged Island, or Criehaven.)

Small, Dr. H. W. *A History of Swan's Island, Maine.* Ellsworth: Hancock County Publishing Co., 1898; reprinted in 1975 by Gelvert Associates of Quakertown, Pa. (The principal early history of Swans Island, with coverage of residence on neighboring islands.)

Smalley, Albert J. *St. George.* Tenants Harbor: The Pierson Press, 1976. (History of the township of St. George, including islands off the southwestern shore of Penobscot Bay; the author was a retired Coast Guard commander, native to the region. See also Map 1970 Smalley.)

Smith, Captain John. *A Description of New England: or the Observations and Discoveries of Captain John Smith (Admirall of that Country) in the North of America in the year of our Lord 1614....* London: Humphrey Lownes, 1616. (Account of John Smith's voyage to the Muscongus-Penobscot Bay region in 1614; some copies, including one at the British Library, include the map he drew during the expedition. See Map 1614 Smith for full description.)

Snow, Walter A. "Genealogical History of the Pioneers of Brooksville, Maine," six volumes, 1966–67. (Typescript at the Brooksville Historical Society.)

———. *Brooksville, Maine: A Town in the Revolution.* Ellsworth, ME: Downeast Graphics, 1976. (The two items above, prepared by the foremost genealogist in Brooksville, include biographies of the earliest settlers in the township, several of whom lived for a time on islands in the region.)

Sterling, Robert T. *Lighthouses of the Maine Coast.* Brattleboro, VT: Stephen Daye Press, 1935. (A standard work on the subject.)

Stonington, Town of. Town Reords. (Tax and other records from the town's incorporation in 1897 are at the town office; see page 282 for an 1896 listing of owners and valuations of islands in Deer Island Thorofare.)

Sullivan, James. *The History of the District of Maine.* Boston: Thomas and E. T. Andrews, 1795. (An early history of Maine, before statehood, by a one-time governor. The volume has been criticized by some historians for its inaccuracies.)

Swans Island, Town of. Town Records. (Plantation and town reports date from incorporation in 1834, but significant tax data relating to the surrounding islands date only from the 1890s.)

Turner, W. G. "The First Settlement of Isle au Haut," 1877. (Recollections of a settler born on the island early in the 1800s; at the Revere Memorial Library on Isle au Haut.)

Vinal, Albra Josephine. See Lyons, O. P., above.

Vinalhaven, Town of. Town Records. (Scattered tax records exist from the 1790s, but significant indication of island husbandry dates only from the last decades of the nineteenth century.)

Vinalhaven Neighbor, 1937–1939. (A periodical published briefly in Vinalhaven, containing some historical materials; copies at the Vinalhaven Historical Society.)

Waldo, County of. Registry of Deeds. (The deeds are listed as described under Hancock County, above.)

Wasson, George S. *Sailing Days on the Penobscot: The Story of the River and the Bay in the Old Days*. New York: W. W. Norton & Co., 1932; second edition, 1949. (Valuable descriptions of the Penobscot Bay area—including an excellent chapter on Isle au Haut—by a novelist turned historian; the "Old Days" are mainly the 1870s and 1880s.)

Westbrook, Perry D. *Biography of an Island*. New York: Thomas Yozeloff, 1958. (A meticulous account of everyday life on Swans Island, mostly contemporary but with glimpses of the past, by a Guggenheim Fellow who spent a year on the island.)

Wheeler, George A. *History of Castine, Penobscot and Brooksville, Maine; including the Ancient Settlement of Pentagoët*. Bangor, ME: Burr & Richardson, 1875. (The best-known early history of the Castine region; very little detail on local islands.)

Williamson, William D. *The History of the State of Maine, from its first Discovery, A.D. 1602, to the Separation, A.D. 1820, Inclusive*. Hallowell, ME: Glazier, Masters & Co., 1832, two volumes; reprinted by Bond Wheelwright Co. of Freeport, ME, 1974. (Still considered a landmark history of Maine in the Colonial and post-Colonial period; islands in Penobscot Bay are described in Vol. I, pp. 62–76.)

Winslow, Sidney L. *Fish Scales and Stone Chips*. Portland, ME: Machigonne Press, 1952. (Recollections of fishing and quarrying on Vinalhaven and neighboring islands.)

Witherspoon, Hazel May, and William Carrol Hill (compilers). "John Witherspoon and Descendants." *New England Historical and Genealogical Register*, January 1945, pp. 29–34. (A careful account of the Witherspoons of Butter Island, based on family records.)

Section II: Maps, Atlases, Charts, and Surveys

Several hundred maps have been consulted for this research in the Massachusetts Archives, the Maine Historical Society, the British Library, the Public Records Office in Kew Gardens, London, and elsewhere. The following items, of relevance to the current volume, are listed below. For some maps, especially the earlier ones, I show where I consulted them, though copies exist in other collections. Titles in quotes are as they appear on a given map or chart; if an item has no title, I have provided one—without quotes. Maps are listed chronologically, by date of publication. The first three items are map catalogs or reference works.

Catalogue of the Manuscript Maps, Charts, and Plans and of the Topographical Drawings in the British Museum. London, 1861 ("New England Listings" in Volume III include items on coastal Maine.)

The Land of Norumbega: Maine in the Age of Exploration and Settlement. Portland: Maine Humanities Council, 1989. (Catalog for an exhibition of maps relating to discovery and early settlements in Maine. The exhibit, held at the Portland Museum of Art, included European maps from the sixteenth to the eighteenth centuries.)

"Reference List of Manuscripts relating to the History of Maine." Orono: University Press, 1939. (Maps are listed in Part II, with an introduction by Fannie Eckstorm.)

Map 1607. Champlain, Samuel de. "Description des costs, pts, rades, Iles de la Nouvelle France faict selon son vray meridien...observés par le Sr de Champlain," 1607. (A map drawn by the French explorer, based on his findings along the Maine coast in 1604 and 1605. The general shape of the bays and location of the rivers are more or less correctly shown—as far as our area is concerned—but the islands are haphazardly indicated. Place-names in the Penobscot Bay region are: *Isle Haute; Ile des Monts Déserts; Orsenes isles*, the Matinicus group; *Isles perdües*, Islesborough; *Pentegoët*, Castine; and *Norumbegue*, vicinity of Bangor. The first two names survive.)

Map 1614. Smith, John. Map of New England Coast, 1614. (This map first appeared in Captain Smith's account of his 1614 expedition—see Section 1 of Bibliography for listing. The detailing of Penobscot Bay, though primitive, is recognizable; Smith sought to anglicize the "barbarous" Indian and French names he discovered in the region and won the approval of Prince Charles, later Charles I, for the changes. None of Smith's place-names, probably after members of his entourage, have survived. Two homesteads, however, are shown: one at *Aberdeen*, the present Castine, and another at *Dubarte*, near modern Camden; this is the earliest suggestion of European "settlement" in the Penobscot Bay region, six years before the MAYFLOWER and, indeed, a century and a half before habitation in the area took on any permanence.)

Map 1691. "A New Mapp of New England from Cape Cod to Sables," surveyed by Thos. Pound, no date shown. (The date given in the British Library listing is 1691. Various clusters of islands in Penobscot Bay are named *Fox Islands*, including Deer Isle; several outer islands are named—e.g., *Green*, *I. Holt*, *Nomans Land*, *Mentinick*, and *Mentinicus Rock*. *Owls Head* is shown as an island, presumably Monroe. Anchorages are shown on the south side of *Long Island*, or Islesboro, and at Naskeag—which is unnamed.)

Map 1700. "A New Chart of ye Coast of New found Land, New Scotland and New England...," at the British Library. (This small-scale chart of the North American coast from the Straits of Belle Isle to Cape Cod is interesting because of its evidence of far denser settlement in Newfoundland and Nova Scotia than in Maine; for instance, there are sixty to seventy place-names indicating settlement on the south and east coasts of Newfoundland, but only six or seven from New Brunswick to Casco Bay.)

Map 1700? Coastline of New England, from Connecticut to Penobscot Bay, at the Public Record Office in Kew Gardens, no certain date. (A very small-scale map with numbered identifications written in margin. A few place-names appear in Penobscot Bay: *Muzle Ridge*, *Owles Head*, *Megundagind hills* near Camden, and *Mr. Castaing* at the "old Fr. town"—that is, Castine.)

Map 1703. "Carte du Canada ou de la Nouvelle France, et les Decouvertes qui y ont étés faites; par Guillaume des'Isle de l'Academie Royale des Sciences." (This unique map records French claims of vast territories in the Ohio and Mississippi valleys and northward to the Arctic. French Acadia stretches southwestward along the New England coast as far as the Kennebec River; the English colonies are confined to a narrow band along the Atlantic littoral. Most important settlements in Nouvelle France are named, and the location of Indian tribes is shown.)

Map 1721. Southhack, Cyprian. "New England Coasting Pilot from Sandy Hook to Cape Canso (Nova Scotia)," 1721, first edition. (This famous chart of the New England coast, companion of all navigators in the eighteenth century, appeared in various formats and editions. The scale is too small for significant detailing, but the general contours are accurate and settlement is indicated. In the Penobscot Bay area, in addition to various Indian encampments, the following are shown: *La farver House*, southwest shore of the bay; four houses belonging to *Monsieur Casteen* across the Bagaduce from modern Castine; and *French inhab.* on Deer Isle, which is unnamed. Some of the islands named on earlier charts are named here, and there is one addition in our area: *Long Island*—that is, Frenchboro. It is of interest that the Penobscot Bay region is the most sparsely settled of the entire New England coast: half a dozen French settlers are shown in the Passamaquoddy-Machias area, and English settlements are numerous west of Pemaquid, while Nova Scotia is heavily settled. The legend written beside Penobscot Bay seeks to attract new settlers and—if we ignore the primitive punctuation—suggests why there are still so few: "Very great and a fine River with several branches in it. Inlets in ye Bay many Islands much Ship timber here. Navigable for Ships and small vessels, if peace with the Indians it will be a place of great trade for Fish Lumber, building of Ships, etc. Woodland.")

Map 1754. "Plan of Coast from Casco to Penobscot Bays, Dedicated to His Excellency William Shirley, Governor of Massachusetts Bay Colony." Surveyed by Joseph Heath and printed in Boston by Thomas Johnston. (The most accurate profile of the Maine coast to this date. The islands named on earlier charts are named again, with several additions: e.g., *Wooden Ball* for Matinicus Rock; *Ragged Arse* for Criehaven; and *Seal Islands* for the cluster east of *Mintinikus*. Confusion still reigns in mid-bay: *Great Fox Island* is shown for both Vinalhaven and North Haven; Deer Isle is *Fox Island*; and the islands scattered between are called the *Fox Isles*. *Burnt Coat Island* is named, I believe, for the first time. Naskeag Harbor is misspelled *Point Neskey*, a name that survived on local maps for some decades.)

Map 1755. Mitchell, John. Map of Maine, first published in London; reissued until about 1780. (This map, sometimes called the "Jay Map" because it was used extensively by the first chief justice, is similar to the preceding map, though of smaller scale; it was probably drawn from the same surveys.)

Map 1763. "A Survey for Six Townships on the East Side of the River Penobscot in the Territory of Sagadahock in New England." (The six townships were between the Penobscot and Mount Desert, or Union, rivers; boundaries are shown but no habitation. The Sagadahock territory referred in this era to all the land between the Kennebec and St. Croix rivers.)

Map 1764. "A Plan of the Bay and River of Penobscot and the Islands lying therein commonly called the Fox Islands,...surveyed by order of Governor Francis Bernard." (This map, located in the Public Record Office, is the most accurate to date of the Penobscot Bay region. Though habitation is not shown, the shape of the islands is meticulous for the era; not more than half a dozen of any significance are omitted. A portion of this map is reproduced on page 4.)

Map 1765? Maine Coast from Kennebec River to St. Croix, with shipping "tracts" in Penobscot Bay. (This map, also in the Public Record Office in Kew Gardens, is crudely drawn, compared to the preceding item, but is of interest because of the indication of early settlement: e.g., three homesteads on the west side of Deer Isle; four at Pulpit Harbor on North Haven; three along Fox Island Thorofare; three at Matinicus; five on Metinic; and fifteen around the shores of Islesboro. This tally did not, of course, reflect total settlement in the region as late as 1765, but suggests the areas where populations were expanding.)

Map 1765. Jones, John and Barnabas Mason (surveyors). "A Plan of the Islands Eastward laying from Penobscot Bay and the Granted Townships, with their Distances and Bearings from Each other and the Continent…agreeable to a Resolve of the Great and General Court for the Province of Massachusetts Bay…." (This early roll of maps, in twelve segments from the Fox Islands to Mount Desert, gives the outline of many islands and names the larger ones, but does not show habitation. The original is in the Massachusetts Archives; a wall-size reproduction of the Mount Desert sector is in the Northeast Harbor Library.)

Map 1772. "A Plan of the Sea Coast from Cape Elizabeth on the West Side of Casco Bay to St. John's River in the Bay of Fundy…Surveyed Agreeably to the Orders and Instructions of the Right Honorable the Lords Commissioners for Trade and Plantations to Samuel Holland, Esq., Surveyor General of the Lands for the Northern District of North America, by his Deputy Ensign George Sproule of His Majesty's 59th Regiment," original at the British Library. (This map has been reproduced in various segments and is frequently confused with the "Atlantic Neptune," the next item. Both show the same meticulous detailing of the coast characteristic of Samuel Holland's work; the map has been called the "Sproule Map," since most of the surveys were apparently prepared by Holland's deputy. This map differs from the "Neptune" in its unmistakably earlier date of publication and in the fact that it was not prepared explicitly for the British Admiralty.) *Note: A segment of this tinted map was reproduced on the cover of Volume IV of this series.*

Map 1776. Des Barres, J. F. W. "Charts of the Coasts and Harbours of New England, composed and engraved by Joseph Frederick Wallet Des Barres, Esq., in Consequence of an Application of the Right Lord Viscount Howe, Commander in Chief of His Majesty's Ships in North America—from the Surveys taken by Samuel Holland, Esq." London: 1776, first publication; reissued until 1784. (This comprehensive album, known as the "Atlantic Neptune," was prepared from surveys dating back to 1764 when the charts were ordered by the Admiralty. The series covering the Penobscot Bay region is undoubtedly the most important early map for settlement in the region: the current names of the islands are shown, as well as the location of homesteads—often very precisely. Each printing varies from its predecessor as new data were added—but having consulted different editions, whose date of publication is often missing, I make no effort to distinguish between one edition and another. Copies of the "Atlantic Neptune" may be found in the Massachusetts Archives, at the Maine Historical Society, and at many university libraries.)

Map 1779. "Penobscot River and Bay, with the Operations of the English Fleet under Sir George Collyer, against the Division of Massachusetts troops operating against Fort Castine." (Manuscript map, in ink and watercolor, representing the disposition of vessels and fortifications in the famous naval engagement at Castine in 1779; reproduced in *Maine: the Sesquicentennial of Statehood*, Washington, DC: Library of Congress, 1970, pp. 20–21.)

Map 1782. "Northeastern Fisheries." Drawn under the supervision of F. Harden Allen. (Shows the principal offshore fisheries for Maine fishermen, from the Gulf of Maine to the Grand Banks; a copy of the map is at the Monhegan Island Museum. A sketch of this map by Jon Luoma was included in Volume III of this series.)

Map 1785. Putnam, Rufus (surveyor), Plans of the Islands of Hancock County. (Rufus Putnam was chief surveyor for Lincoln County, charged by the Massachusetts Commission for "unappropriated lands" to survey the coastal islands between the Penobscot and St. Croix rivers; habitation is not shown in his surveys proper, but the islands are named or numbered, often with indication as to their sale or disposition in the 1780s. The originals are in the Maine State Archives, and copies made in the 1880s are in the Hancock Registry of Deeds, Plan Book II.)

Map 1785. Maps and Plans of Knox County. (These plans, reproduced from surveys in the Massachusetts Archives, cover the islands in what is now Knox County and may be found in the Registry of Deeds in Rockland. The most important plan for this study, surveyed in 1785 by Jonathon Stone and John Mathews under the supervision of Rufus Putnam, is the "Fox Island Division of Islands." As in the Hancock County plans, habitation is not shown, but the major islands are named or lettered.)

Map 1786. Vinal, John. "A Plan of Vinalhaven." (This map, with a few additional notations, is identical to the "Fox Island Division" in the previous entry. It is in the Massachusetts Archives, Map No. 1343.)

Map 1786. Penobscot Bay Islands. (This early survey includes a few islands south of Long Island, Islesborough, showing only their shape and approximate acreage.)

Map 1795. Warren, Samuel (surveyor). "Long Island (Islesborough)." (A map of Islesborough six years after incorporation; no habitation is shown, but the nearby islands are named. Map No. 1331 in Massachusetts Archives.)

Map 1815. Greenleaf, Moses. "An Improved Map of Maine." (An early attempt to map the entire province; meager coverage of the coast.)

Map 1837. Porter, Captain Seward. "Chart of the Coast of Maine." (Based largely on the "Atlantic Neptune" and reflecting little advance in charting since the Revolutionary era.)

Map 1854. United States. Coast and Geodetic Survey. "Eggemoggin Reach." (An early coastal survey, with more attention to depths than topography.)

Map 1857. Hopkins, C. H. (surveyor). "A Topographical Map of Lincoln County, Maine," Philadelphia: Lee & Marsh, 1857. (One of the earliest of the detailed topographical maps of Maine counties, showing island names and some habitation; despite inaccuracies, the most useful map of the region, including western Penobscot Bay, since the "Atlantic Neptune.")

Map 1859. Kelsey, D., and D. H. Davidson (surveyors). "Map of Waldo County, Maine, " Portland: J. Chace & Co. (Shows approximate site locations and names of residents throughout the county, including those on Islesborough, the Fox Islands, and many of the smaller islands.)

Map 1860. Walling, H. F. (surveyor). "Topographical Map of Hancock County," New York: Lee & Marsh. (Like the two preceding items, this map shows homesites and names of settlers throughout the county, including Deer Isle, Isle au Haut, and Swans Island.)

Map 1863. United States. Coast and Geodetic Survey. "Rockland Harbor." (Part of a series of coastal charts; includes detail on Monroe and Sheep islands as well as Owls Head.)

Map 1864. United States. Coast and Geodetic Survey. "St. George's River and Muscle Ridge Channel, Maine." (Excellent detailing of coast, but little topography of islands and mainland.)

Map 1873. United States. Coast and Geodetic Survey, No. 105. "From Penobscot Bay to Kennebec River Entrance." (Includes the southwest shore of Penobscot Bay, showing the coastal islands below Whitehead Island in some detail; topography was done between 1856 and 1869.)

Map 1874. United States. Coast and Geodetic Survey. "Approaches to Dix Island, Maine." (Reprint of a segment of a larger coastal survey, with considerable detail on island habitation and quarrying in the Muscle Ridge Islands, based on topographical studies from 1868 to 1871; the reprint was prepared in 1970 by the Lobster Lane Book Shop at Spruce Head.)

Map 1880. United States. Coast and Geodetic Survey, Coast Chart 4. "Penobscot Bay." (Surveyed between 1863 and 1875, this chart includes remarkable topography of all islands in the bay: house sites, schools, cemeteries, cleared fields, fencing, road systems, etc.)

Map 1881. Colby, George N. (compiler). *Atlas of Hancock County, Maine.* Ellsworth, ME: S. F. Colby & Co., 1881. (A collection of detailed town maps, showing homesites and most residents; comparable to the 1860 Walling map of the county, updated. A new edition of this collection, entitled *Old Maps of Hancock County, Maine in 1881*, was published in Fryeburg in 1990 by Saco River Printing.)

Map 1882. United States. Coast and Geodetic Survey, No. 309. "East Penobscot Bay." (First issue of this detailed chart of Deer Isle and Isle au Haut area, according to surveys undertaken between 1867 and 1875; the topography, which includes vegetation, is more accurate than in the Colby atlas.)

Map 1883. United States. Coast and Geodetic Survey, Coast Chart 3. "Mt. Desert, Frenchman and Blue Hill Bays and Approaches, Maine." (This chart includes some islands in the easternmost sector of our region—e.g., in the Swans Island Division.)

Maps 1904–06. United States, Department of the Interior. Geological surveys, by township. (The earliest of the geological surveys—called "quads" or "folios"—covering our area were published between 1904 and 1906, based on surveys completed during the immediately preceding years.)

Map 1970. Smalley, Albert J. "St. George, Maine." Privately printed. (A map showing the earliest recorded conveyances of land—including islands—in what is now the township of St. George; compiled by an ardent student of the region.)

Map 1971. Jackson, Malcolm Putnam. "Earliest Settled Lots in South Thomaston, Maine." Privately printed. (A parallel study to the preceding item, by the founder of the Muscle Ridge Museum.)

Section III: Interviewees and correspondents

Barton, Harold (1895–1975)
Resided in Camden; brought up on Job Island before World War I, son of a tenant farmer there.

Benson, Ralph G. (1893–1975)
Lobsterman at Bass Harbor; born on Pond Island (off Opechee) where father was caretaker; spent summers in boyhood on Placentia and Black islands; fished for many years in the Great Gott area.

Beverage, Samuel
Lifelong resident of North Haven, descended from numerous early settlers; meticulous amateur historian of North Haven and the offshore islands.

Bosse, Louis (b. 1900)
Owls Head resident; formerly lived on and later owned Great Pond Island; familiar with the Muscle Ridge Islands, especially in first decades of this century. (Deceased)

Bridges, Eulalie (Mrs. Elmer) (b. 1887)
North Brooklin resident; lived on Opechee Island, 1918, when her husband was caretaker. (Deceased)

Burton, Albert (b. 1889)
Retired lobsterman and one-time stonecutter, resident of Sprucehead; began quarry work on Clark Island, 1910. (Deceased)

Calderwood, Elsie (b. 1890)
Resident of Vinalhaven; lived formerly at Crocketts Cove and as a child often visited Kimballs on Leadbetter Island. (Deceased)

Carman, Dorothy (Mrs. Malcolm)
Lifelong resident of Deer Isle, descended from several early settlers; ardent amateur historian of Deer Isle and outlying islands; genealogist and secretary of the Deer Isle Historical Society. (Deceased)

Cline, Ralph (1893–1976)
Lobsterman at Sprucehead, descended from Rackliffs, Elwells, and Makers in area; particularly familiar with the offshore islands in the Whitehead group.

Crowell, Alice Cain (Mrs. Jack; b. 1897)
Resident of Rockport and Kimball Island. Born on Burnt Island off Isle au Haut and grew up there; lived several years on Burnt in 1920s with husband Jack Crowell; after World War II, they lived on Kimball Island eight or ten months each year. (Deceased)

Doudiet, Ellenore (Mrs. Norman W.)
Island resident in Castine Harbor and Director of the Wilson Museum; familiar with islands in the area, especially Nautilus.

Duffy, Harry (b. 1906)
Blue Hill resident; brought up on Long Island, where forebears lived for seventy years or more.

Dyer, Frank (1896–1976)
Lobsterman; lived on many islands throughout Penobscot Bay; born on High Island (off Dix), lived with father Samuel on Wooden Ball, Crotch (Hurricane), and others; grandfather was Elijah Dyer of Minot and Warren islands off Islesboro.

Elwell, Herbert (b. 1900?)
Lobsterman and buyer at Sprucehead; lived seven years on Hewett Island tending weirs as young man; amateur genealogist of Elwell, Maker, and Gregory families of Sprucehead area. (Deceased)

Gross, Louise Holt (1900–80)
Daughter of Allen Carter Holt, keeper of Mark Island Light off Stonington, 1913–19; Louise and her brother lived on the island during these years.

Hanneman, Paul
Resident of Brewer, Maine; authority on post offices in Maine—and miscellaneous other lore. (Deceased)

Hardie, Wolcott (1915–76)
Brought up on Bear Island (off Great Spruce Head Island) where his father James was caretaker, 1913–40; he succeeded his father, and his son succeeds him.

Hundley, Margaret
Stonington resident; descended from several early settlers on Deer Isle, including Captain David Thurlow of Crotch Island; amateur historian of islands in Deer Island Thorofare.

Hurd, Harlan (b. 1891)
Lobsterman from Ash Point; fished and lived seasonally in the Muscle Ridge Islands for fifty years. (Deceased)

Ingraham, Augusta Conley (1887–1977) and her son Harvard C. (b. 1910)
Daughter and grandson of James Conley of York Island off Isle au Haut. Augusta was born there, remained to 1900; she and her son remained in close touch with the island until 1930s. (Both deceased)

Joyce, G. Carlton (b. 1890)
Lifelong resident of Swans Island; familiar with history of outlying islands. (Deceased)

Littlefield, Fred B. (b. 1890)
A former logger, related to a number of families in Sedgwick and Brooksville, and familiar with life on islands off Cape Rosier around World War I. (Deceased)

Livermore, Edith Cousins (b. 1885)
Born on Naskeag Point in Brooklin, and lived on Naskeag Harbor; recalled the Carter family on Harbor Island in the 1890s. (Deceased)

Means, Winifred Cole (b. 1895?)
North Brooklin resident; brought up on Long Island in Blue Hill Bay. (Deceased)

Morton, Joseph (1889–1981)
Lifelong Vinalhaven resident; lived on Greens Island where father was storekeeper early in the twentieth century. (Deceased)

Nice, Letha (Mrs. John B.) (b. 1890?) and son Millard (b. 1911)
Bass Harbor residents; Letha was married on Black Island (off Great Gott) in 1910 and lived there until 1920; Millard is descended from six generations of settlers on the island and still fishes off its shores. (She is deceased; Mollard moved South.)

Orcutt, Clara (b. 1884)
Stonington resident; stepdaughter of Fred Carver of Hog Island (off Cape Rosier); lived there and on Eagle Island from 1800s to about World War I. (Deceased)

Post, Luella S. (Mrs. David C.) (b. 1901?)
Resident of Owls Head; daughter of Woodbury Snow (see below) and descendant of Thorndikes of Metinic Island; spent many seasons there, both as a child and with her own family in 1930s.

Quinn, Erland (b. 1901)
Resident of Camden; born and brought up on Eagle Island, the fifth generation of Quinns who settled there; familiar with the history of all islands in mid-Penobscot Bay. (Deceased)

Rackliff, Bernard
Lobsterman living in Makerville sector of Sprucehead; amateur historian of area and genealogist of Rackliff, Elwell, Gregory, and related families.

Robbins, Dennis (b. 1910)
Stonington resident; descendant of Hezekiah and David Robbins, who lived on a number of the islands in Deer Island Thorofare in the nineteenth century; his wife, a descendant of the Merchants of Merchant Island, is knowledegable about late-nineteenth-century residents there.

Robbins, L. S. (b. 1890)
Ellsworth resident; brought up on Pond and Opechee islands, where his father was caretaker (on Pond) and farmer (on Opechee) from 1895 to 1915. (Deceased)

Rossiter, Willis (b. 1903)
Lifelong resident on Gilkeys Harbor, Islesboro; familiar with history of all islands in area—especially Warren, Seven Hundred Acre, and Minot. (Deceased)

Ryan, Alie
South Brooksville resident; collector of steamboat lore in Penobscot Bay-Blue Hill Bay region. (Deceased)

Simmons, Gordan C. (b. 1915)
Summer lobsterman in the Muscle Ridge Islands; has spent most seasons since childhood on an island there, which he now owns.

Smalley, Commander Albert J. (b. 1900)
Retired Coast Guardsman and lifelong resident of St. George; historian of early settlement, including the offshore islands. See Section I for his published studies. (Deceased)

Snow, Wilbert (b. 1884)
Writer and professor emeritus at Wesleyan University (Connecticut); born on Whitehead Island, descended from Nortons of Whitehead and Norton islands. (Deceased)

Snow, Woodbury (b. 1880)
Retired fisherman in Rockland; lived and fished for many years on Metinic, where his grandsons still lobster. (Deceased)

Sullivan, Steven (b. 1955)
Coast Guardsman training at New London—surely the youngest informant in this listing; native of Camden and student of genealogical ties in the Muscle Ridges.

Thompson, Leslie (b. 1895)
Retired fisherman, resident of Sunshine on Deer Isle; familiar especially with the Marshall Island fisheries. (Deceased)

Webster, Kenneth (b. 1915?)
Resident in Vinalhaven; owned and kept sheep for many years on islands southwest of Vinalhaven (Carvers, Otter, Narrows, etc.).

Weed, Abbie Shepherd (b. 1895)
Resident of Little Deer Isle; daughter of caretaker on Butter Island during "Dirigo" era (early 1900s)

and worked there in her teens; later cared for children of caretaker on Great Spruce Head Island. (Deceased)

Wescott, Elizabeth
Resident of Blue Hill; genealogist of many Blue Hill Bay families, including several that settled on the islands and from whom she herself is descended (Tinkers, Daws, etc.).

Wilson, Leslie (b. 1900?) and wife Olive Rhodes (b. 1900?)
Residents in Rockland; both spent early years on Ragged Island (Criehaven). He was a fisherman and storekeeper; she was a descendant of both Cries and Halls of Matinicus. (Both deceased)

Witham, Edwin (b. 1910)
Fish merchant in Rockland, long familiar with fishing industry among the outer islands—especially Large Green and Metinic. (Deceased)

Young, Clayton (b. 1910)
Lifelong resident of Matinicus and storekeeper there for many years; familiar with the recent history of all islands in the area.

Young, Clifford (b. 1894)
Also a lifelong resident of Matinicus, a descendant of early settlers; the last Matinican to farm there seriously. (Deceased)

Appendices

Appendix 1: *Rufus Putnam's List of Island Inhabitants from Passamaquoddy to Vinalhaven, 1785*

Reproduced on the pages that follow are the relevant pages of Rufus Putnam's report as he wrote them—since little would be gained and much lost by my attempting to interpret his orthography or modernize his spelling. The title page (which is covered with his tallies) reads: "Gen. Putnam's Report. A description in the county of Lincoln with an estimate of Lands surveyed there in 1785 of Townships between Scoodic & Cobscook rivers and between Cobscook & Passamaquoddy Bays." The initial report, submitted on December 16, 1785, is five pages in length: the first three pages describe land in Plantations VII–XII east of Indian River, which is well out of our region—I omit these pages. Pages 4 and 5, which are reproduced, list all the island inhabitants from the Machias region to Blue Hill Bay; although these residents are also out of the region covered in this volume, their listing here gives readers a sense of the sparse habitation on the eastern coast. On March 18, 1786 the census tallies for Deer Isle, Isle au Haut, and the Fox Islands—including their outlying islands—were completed by Rufus Putnam's colleagues: Jonathan Stone, Samuel Titcomb, John Mathews, and Mr. Peters. I also reproduce these as Rufus Putnam transcribed them; the page numbering (pp. 113 and 114) suggests that these two sheets are part of a larger report, which I have not seen.

A few aids may be useful in following the census: nearly all the islands in our region have the same name today as they had then—the exceptions being Hopkins (now Alley), Robertsons (now Tinker), Little Placentia (now Great Gott), Sheep (now Sheephead), Little Isle au Haut (now Kimball), and White (now Merchant); the word appearing frequently as 'pofestion" is "possession" (in old orthography); John is sometimes—but not always—rendered as "Jn°."

{4} A List of Inhabitants found on the Islands or having improvements on them —

Hog Island — in Machias bay — this Island has been partly clear'd and claim'd by the Reverend James Lyon —

Knights's Island in Machias bay, this Island has had a House built and Saltworks erected on it by the same Mr. Lyon, but are both gone to Decay —

Larreb's — Islands in Machias bay, these Islands have been improv'd ten or twelve years, by Stephen Jones Esqr. & Company, who have a Hous and family living on the largest of them.

Beal's — Island in Misspeckey Reach — Manwaring Beal has liv'd on this Island ten Years, has a very considerable improvement at the Northern end, there is a piece of Salt Marsh the Southern end, but the remainder of the Island is of very little value —

Drescos Island near the Mouth of Indian River, has some improvements made on it and is claim'd by Elihu Norton —

Knox or Nichols's Island in Narrowsguagus bay — has a house & considerable improvement at the Southern end, is an old settlement claim'd by Capt. Nichols, who has a tenant on it.

Stave. Island in Frenchman's Bay, this Island has a House and considerable improvement made on the Northerly part of it by Col. Nathan Jones, who has a Tenant on it, but how long since it was first begun is uncertain —

Bartlets — Island, Between Mount Desert & long Island in blue-hill bay, Mr. Christopher Bartlet, has been settled here eighteen years, & has a very considerable Improvement on the Northerly part —

Hopkins's Island in Mount Desert Bay, William Hopkins has a

House and considerable improvements on this Island for several years —

Long Island in Blue Hill Bay — James Carter, has had a considerable improvement on the Westerly side of this Island for several Years but has no house there at present —

Robertsons — Island — John Robertson, has lived on this Island Twenty years — — — — — — — — — — —

East Cranberry Island — Widow Margaret Stanley on a settlement of Eighteen years standing — — — — — — —

West Cranberry Island — Sands Stanley on a Settlement of Eighteen years, Aaron Bunker Nine Years, Jonathan Rich on a settlement Eighteen years, — Andrew Herrick has had an improvement of Eighteen years standing, but is vacant at present —

Little Placentia Island, Daniel Gott has been settled here fifteen Years,

South Duck Island — Aaron Bunker has made some improvements here, but has no house or Family on it — —

These are all the Inhabitants and Improvements on the Islands Eastward of Jericho Bay, at the time of Survey, Except Major Swans People at Burnt Coat Harbour,

N.13 — Deer Island, Isle of Holt, & Fox Island divisions of Islands, (the field work of Capt. Stone four weeks, and of Mr. Titcomb, Mr. Peters and Mr. Mathews, each six weeks) are not yet protracted, when those plans are completed a list of settlers on them will be added — — — — pr.

Boston December 16th 1785

Rufus Putnam

The Honble. Saml. Philips Junr. Esqr.
and others Committe —

List of Inhabitants on Deer Island Planed P. 118

	Names	Time when Settled		Names	Time when Settled
1	Nathan Dow	1765	41	Thomas Robbins	1775
2	Nathan Dow Junr.	do	42	William Bavige	1766
			43	John Sones	1782
3	Theophilus Eaton	1767	44	Joseph Whitmore	1765
4	Levi Carmon	do	45	William Whitmore	1775
5	Francis Haskel	1770	46	Wm Richards	1765
6	Abijah Haskel	1770	47	William Greenlow	1763
7	Jonathan Haskel	do	48	Thomas Stevenson Junr.	1765
8	Ezekiel Marshel	1765	49	Joseph Colbe	do
9	Ephraim Marshel	do	50	Joseph Tyler	do
10	Mark Haskel	do	51	Belcher Tyler	do
11	Ignations Haskel	1770	52	George Freize	1764
12	Thomas Haskel	1767	53	John Freize	do
13	Johona Haskel	1762	54	Nathaniel Robins	1765
14	Ezra Howard	1765	55	Stephen Bavige	1773
15	Ambrows Coulby	do	56	Countnes Bavige	do
16	Nethaniel Bray	1766	57	John Freize Junr.	1765
17	Peter Haskel	do	58	Thomas Stevenson Esqr.	do
18	Benjn Cole	1767	59	John Campell	1763
19	Benjn Cole Junr.	do		~~Hamilton~~	~~1764~~
20	Ezekiel Morey	do	60	Wm Foster	1763
			61	Charles Greenlow	do
21	John Hooper	do	62	David Torrey	do
22	Lot Curtis	1774	63	Jonathan Torrey	do
23	Chase Preese	1765	64	Moses Staple	1764
24	John Preese	do	65	Joshona Staple	do
25	John Preese Junr.	do	66	Robert Lin	1765
			67	Thomas Thompson	do
26	James Saunders	1773	68	John Gleason	1763
	~~Timothy Saunders~~	~~do~~			

27	Jonathan	Eaton	1765
28	Elijah	Dunham	1766
29	Joseph	Dunham	do
30	Elijah	Dunham Junr	do
31	Samuel	Trunday	1765
32	John	Reins	1765
33	William	Reins	do
34	Johnson	Reins	do
35	Thomas	Smalle	do
36	Widow	Reins	do
37	Job	Smalle	1764
38	Charles	Cillers	1768
39	Joseph	Cillers	do
40	Joseph	Crocket	do

69	Peter	Hardy	1763
	~~Benjn Wood~~		~~1768~~
	~~Eliakim Eaton~~		~~1763~~
			do
70	Jeremiah	Eaton	~~do~~
	~~William~~	~~Eaton~~	
71	John	Howard	1767
72	Francis	Haskil	1768
73	Nathan	Haskil	1782
74	John	Dow	1765
75	Cornelius	Brimhall	1777
76	Rinecous	Carman	1765
77	John	Glayson	1763
78	Mikel	Lunt	1783
79	Robertson	Crocket	1783 - 83
80	Benjn	Ray	1784
81	John	Martin	1784
82	Hezekiah	Lain	1784
83	Thomas	Hamelton	1784
84	Thomas	Conaway	1785
85		Bointon	1785
86	Revd Peter	Powers	1785 Total 90

Page	Names	Time when settled
114	Sheep Island by South west Harbour of Deer Island. on a possession	
	Timothy Saunders	14 years
112	Little Deer Island P. 112	
	Benjn Weed	1768
	Eliakem Eaton	1763
110	Pikerings Island P. 110	
	Saml Pikering	10 years
109	Eagle Island Page 109	
	Allen Calf	1778
109	Great Sprucehead Island page 109	
	Wm Blasstow	

Names	Time settled
Gibson Perney	19 years
Mark Eames	16 do
Jn Perney	20
Nathn Worcester	20
David Worcester	20
Anthony Dyer	19
George Tate on a possession of	20
Joseph Dyer	14
Benjn Dyer	10
Austen Eames	20
Wm Dyer	20
Joseph Waterman	20
do one other bought	20
Charles Stuert	20
on purchased possession	20
Samuel Thomas	20
Samuel Thomas Jr	20

Names	
John Calderwood	{ 1
Jno Calderwood Junr	2
Jonathan Foster old settlem	
Anthony Comes	16 years
Ennese Leadbetter Junr	7
Joel Philbrooks	possessed by Joel Philbrook 21
Job Philbrooks	
Jno Smith	
John Crane	14
James Jewell	17
Isaac Aney	20
Israel Carver	16
James Douglass	
Issacher Lane	20
Widow Mary Comes	
Thomas Brown	21
Reuben Brown part of his fathers possession	

Butter Island page 108	
Ralph Annis —	1770
Benjn Annis —	d^o
Stave Island P 111	
Wm Eaton —	1763
Isle of Holt p 106	
James Barton —	1783
Nathaniel Sheldon —	1783
John Baxter —	1785
Reuben Nobel —	1785
John Holman on an old possestion —	
Little Isle of Holt P 106	
Seth Webb on a possestion of —	18 year
Youth Island P 106	
Moses Staples —	1785
White Island P 106 Anthony Marchent —	1770
Iron Island Division Page — 104	
Ebenezer Crabtree on right of possestion & 2 other possestion —	19 year

Benjn Hunt —	10 —
Joseph Worcester	20 —
Thomas Beverage	15 —
Stephen Carver	17 —
Jno Robben	13 —
Archabald McMuller	14 —
James Cooper —	20 —
Thomas Cooper	20 —
Wm Cooper —	20 —
James Cooper Junr	20 —
Benjn Robbens right of possestions	20 —
John Berverick right of Possestion	20 —
James Heard —	15 —
James Dunum right of Possestion	15 —
Benjn Carr —	20 —
Jno Baxter Carr —	20 —
Eliphalet Carr —	20 —
Wm Bervick —	13 —
Abner Hunt right of possestion	20 —
James Whaleing	20 —
Widow Winslow an old Settelment	
John Burges Junr	20
Ezekiel Burges	20
Saml Young	20
Norton —	20
Doged —	20
(right of Possestion)	

Thadeleus Carver	20 —
James Stenson	16 —
Jeremiah Philbrook	12 —
Prince Leedbetter	12 —
Wm Vinal Esqr old Settelment —	
Jno Hamelton on Small Island —	16 —
Joseph Green on Green Island	16 —
Thomas Green	4 —
Isaac Crocket on Crockets Island	20 —
Jno Burges on a Small Island —	2 year
Wm Penney on an old Settelment —	
James Jewell Junr	young Men
Jno Leedbetter	young Men
Saml Calderwood	young Men
James Calderwood	young Men

Boston March 18th 1786

Rufus Putnam

Appendix 2: *Comparison of Island Fisheries, Penobscot Bay, 1880*

Note: This table attempts to compare the fishing industry in 1880 on six large Penobscot Bay islands. Statistical data are taken from Goode, Fishing Industries of the United States *(except for federal census data: population totals under the islands and the number of fishermen in the second line as shown in the census schedules).*[1] *Where there is a slash, the figure to the left refers to fishermen on seagoing vessels (over five tons); to right, on offshore boats and dories.*

	Deer Isle 3,068	**Vinalhav'n** 2,855	**No. Haven** 755	**Swans I.** 604	**Isle Haut** 274	**Matinicus** 247
No. of fishermen	199/140	99/90[2]	145/90	186/74	40	40
No. of fishermen (census)	324	201	112	?	52	48
Seagoing vessels before 1880	1850: 35	1850s: 90	1850s: 40	1825: 25	1820s: 6	
No. of vessels (all types)	42	20	20	21	3	11
Tonnage of vessels	915.35T	392.55T	636.09T	885T		245.51
Value of vessels	$18,910	$15,550	$22,625	$30,000	$10,250	
Other (can=canneries; PG= pogy factories; sm=smokehouses)	3 can	2 can	1 can	2 PG; 3 sm	1 can	1 sm[3]

[1] Discrepancies in the number of fishermen may reflect crews hired in other ports.

[2] A total of one hundred and eighty shorefishermen were active on Vinalhaven and North Haven togther; I have divided them evenly.

[3] There were seven smokehouses on Matinicus in 1840.

Appendix 3: *Agricultural Activity on Smaller Islands of Penobscot Bay, 1880*

Note: This table shows the federal census-taker's estimate of agricultural activity on the smaller islands in Penobscot Bay in 1880, according to the following key:

Till	Acres under tillage	**Hay**	Tons of hay harvested
Med	Acres in meadow	**She**	Number of sheep
Uni	Unimproved acres		

Island, Farmer	Till	Med	Uni	Hay	She
BEACH					
James Staples and son	4	25	130	16	40
BEAR (off Great Spruce Head)					
Jonathan M. Eaton	3	10	55	7	8
John B. Eaton	2	40	120	8	100
BURNT (off Isle au Haut)					
James Turner II	5	20	150	15	150
BUTTER					
James W. Blaisdell	10	50	225	70	190
EAGLE					
John L. Quinn	3	5	23	12	28
Louisa Quinn	3	55	12	31	
Orena G. Quinn	3	15	100	10	50
James Quinn	3	55	10	50	
GREAT SPRUCE HEAD					
Ambrose Walton	2	30	14	0	
HARBOR (Swans)					
William Stinson	3	121	20	65	
HEWETT					
James Brannen	8	60	20	6	-
HOG (off Cape Rosier)					
Fred Carver	2	10	58	28	3
KIMBALL (off Isle au Haut)					
Benjamin and Simon Smith	6	50	275	15	150
MARSHALL					
Amos D. Orne	8	160	900	20	200
MCGLATHERY					
Peter Eaton farm	3	10	55	5	6
MERCHANT					
Alex Monteith	5	20	150	15	50
OPEECHEE					
Henry Burns	5	30	185	15	54

Island, Farmer	Till	Med	Uni	Hay	She
PICKERING Amos Foote Dow	6	65	325	25	38
POND (off Swans Island) Nahum B. Young	4	50	200	35	52
RAGGED (Criehaven) Robert Crie	10	220	35	12	-
WARREN ("Dyer's Island") Elijah Dyer	20	55	25	11	20

Appendix 4A: *Penobscot Bay Islands in Hancock County, State Taxes and Valuations, 1887–1912*

Note: The islands listed below, with owners, were taxed or valued as follows in the years shown, according to records in Augusta; blanks mean figures were not shown.

Island (Acres)	Owners (By tax year)	1887 Tax	1896 Tax	1912 Valuation	1921 Valuation
Butter	A. T. Eels	$5.50		$2,600	
(260)	R. Witherspoon	6.75			
	Harriman bros.		$5.85		
	Mrs. R.S. Ithell				5,200
Eagle	Quinns	8.25	11.25	5,000	
(300)	J. Gilbert Hill, etc. [1]				
Beach	John Staples	1.38			
(75)	C. A. Snedeker		1.44	600	1,000
Bradbury	John Staples	1.93			
(150)	J. M. Vogel		3.20	1,200	1,200
Hog	C. H. Cooper	1.93			
(75)	F. A. Carver		1.58	1,500	
Pond	C. H. Cooper	.82			
(22)	F. A. Carver		1.08	200	
Western	Ephraim Redman	.49			
(27)	F. A. Carver		.91	200	
Little Spruce Hd	J. G. Lambert	.82			
(40)	C. W. Fuller		.91	250	
Pickering	S. B. Collins	7.15	6.95	3,300	
(300)	E. O. Ladd				5,000
Great Spruce Hd	J. G. Lambert	2.75			
(240)	Kathryn Buel			875	
Bear	J. G. Lambert [2]				
(40)	Caroline Fuller			160	160
Mark/Resolution (30)	Preston Pleyer			300	300
Scott Is. (8)	Edwin Blaster				300
Birch (10)	H. W. Park				500
Marshall	Oliver Lane	11.00		3,000	
	H. D. Lane		15.17		4,215
Harbor (Swans)	M. Stinson	4.12			
	J. M. Hardy		9.30		

[1] There were many owners of Eagle Island in 1921; valuations were not listed.
[2] Bear Island was counted with Great Spruce Head through the 1890s.

Appendix 4B: *Penobscot Bay Islands in Knox County, State Taxes and Valuations, 1921*

Island (Acres)	Owner	1921 Valuation
Andrews (100)	Thomas Dwyer	$1,500
Andrews Neck (100)	A. F. Rackliff	1,200
Bar, off Grafton (5)	E. V. Shea	250
Birch (8)	Mabel Jennings	500
Camp (1)	S. M. Bird	25
Crow (4)	Alden G. Shea	100
Dix (60)	Thomas Dwyer	1,200
Fisherman (5)	Alvin Hurd	125
Flag, w. buildings (4)	Alden G. Shea	200
Grafton (54)	E. V. Shea	750
Hewetts (100)	McLoon heirs	1,000
High (40)	Consol. High I. Granite Co.	1,000
Hurricane	Hurricane I. Quarries Co.	10,000
Inner Pond (2)	Olive Rackliff	50
Lasells (148)	Grace Cilley Tibbetts	1,480
Little Bermuda (1)	Grace Cilley Tibbetts	25
Otter (15)	Thomas Dwyer	375
Pleasant (80)	Jordan estate	1,000
Saddle (47)	Grace Cilley Tibbetts	500
Sheep (100)	Grace Cilley Tibbetts	1,000

Index

Note to Readers: *This Index includes, in addition to place-names and general categories of interest to readers, the names of all islanders and many others mentioned or listed in the text and tables. Those with the same surname presumed to be in a given family (e.g., living on the same island) are listed alphabetically under that surname. Wives, where identified, are named in parentheses after their husbands, with their maiden names if known; the married names of females in a family, if known, are also shown in parentheses—with a cross reference to the husband's family if relevant. If two or more members of a family are mentioned together in the text or appear in the same table, the page reference is entered under the family; references for individual family members are used only when they appear alone. Page references for significant notice of a family are in italics. Also italicized are page references for the principal notice of all islands in this volume.*

L

M

Q

R

S

T

Y

Z